THE HISTORY OF SCIENCE IN WESTERN CIVILIZATION

Volume III
Modern Science, 1700-1900

L. Pearce Williams
Henry John Steffens

University Press
of America™

Q
125
·W7913
vol.3

Library of Congress Catalog Card Number: 77-18484

Preface to Volume III

Any one volume attempt to deal with the development of science in the modern world must be incomplete. The reason is quite simple: the volume of scientific writings for the 18th and 19th centuries is enormous. Moreover, these two centuries witnessed the "lateral" expansion of science into areas hitherto untouched by the scientific spirit. New sciences -- biochemistry, entomology, paristology -- to mention only a few were created. To print representative samples of every science, and to illustrate the main ideas in each, would take far more space than is available to us. We have, therefore, decided upon the high spots in the development of modern science, and have presented them as we see them. This means a concentration on the physcial sciences for, until the 19th century, the life sciences lagged far behind. Even in the physical sciences, however, we have had to be more selective than we would have liked. There is hardly a mention, for example, of the birth and growth of astrophysics after the law of Kirchhoff and Bunsen made possible the physical and chemical analyses of the stars. We fervently hope that what we have provided, in both our narrative and in our document selections, will give the reader some sense of the depth of thought on fundamental scientific issues in the 18th and 19th centuries.

There is, of course, an obvious qualification necessary to our title for this volume, Modern Science. The whole 20th century has been left out. We have provided only the briefest of outlines of three developments in the 20th century in our Epilogue. The reason for this is again simple: there is another scientific revolution that begins in 1900 with Planck's enunciation of the quantum of action and in 1905 with Einstein's Special Theory of Relativity. The face of the history of modern science changes dramatically. It would be impossible to do justice to both the "old" modern science and the 'new' modern science in one volume. A fourth volume is necessary. In that work, the modern revolutions in the physical and the biological sciences can be delineated and described with some hope of arriving at broad understanding.

We would like, at this time, to thank both Patricia Guilford and Roberta Ludgate who typed the manuscript for this work. They sacrificed untold hours of their time to meet the deadlines for publication. We are deeply grateful to them.

Ithaca, New York
October, 31, 1977

L. Pearce Williams
Henry John Steffens

THIS BOOK IS GRATEFULLY DEDICATED TO

HENRY GUERLAC

TABLE OF CONTENTS

CHAPTER ONE -- THE ENLIGHTENMENT

I. Narrative

The century from the publication of Newton's *Principia* in
1687 to the outbreak of the French Revolution in 1789 is unique
in the intellectual history of Western man. Science, which had
been for centuries a matter of concern to only a small group of
intellectuals, was suddenly moved to the very center of European
culture. It was science which was now looked to for all sorts of
wondrous things from the cure of disease to the healing of sick
societies and reason, as exemplified by science, was deified.
The discovery of science as *the* new intellectual tool, par excellence, rivalled in importance the discovery of new lands or new
peoples for the educated aristocracy of the 18th century. This
deification of science and reason was part of a complicated attack on the political, social and economic institutions of the
day that we may only note in passing. Yet, it is worth noting
for it was in the name of science and reason that the political
revolutions of the end of the century were fought. The Enlightenment sought to substitute reason and science for traditions and
prejudices inherited from the "Dark Ages." Nature, it had been
shown, was reasonable; should human societies not emulate Nature?
The all-pervasiveness of the worship of a rational Nature may be
dramatically illustrated by a brief examination of the American
Declaration of Independence in which the credo of the Enlightenment is summed up. The influence of science is clear; the
political world reflects the physical world. Just as God had
endowed matter with mass, shape and motion, so had He endowed men
with natural rights. Just as matter followed natural laws to
create natural harmony, so too could men achieve social harmony
if they would but heed their own natures.

In Congress, July 4, 1776.
A DECLARATION
By the Representatives of the
United States of America,
In General Congress Assembled.

When in the Course of human Events, it becomes necessary for
one People to dissolve the Political Bands which have connected
them with another, and to assume among the Powers of the Earth,
the separate and equal Station to which the Laws of Nature and of
Nature's God entitle them, a decent Respect to the Opinions of
Mankind requires that they should declare the causes which impel
them to the Separation.
We hold these Truths to be self-evident, that all Men are
created equal, that they are endowed by their Creator with certain unalienable Rights, that among these are Life, Liberty, and
the Pursuit of Happiness--That to secure these Rights, Governments are instituted among Men, deriving their just Powers from

the Consent of the Governed, that whenever any Form of Government becomes destructive of these Ends, it is the Right of the People to alter or to abolish it, and to institute new Government, laying its Foundation on such Principles, and organizing its Powers in such Form, as to them shall seem most likely to effect their Safety and Happiness. Prudence, indeed, will dictate that Governments long established should not be changed for light and transient Causes; and accordingly all Experience hath shewn, that Mankind are more disposed to suffer, while Evils are sufferable, than to right themselves by abolishing the Forms to which they are accustomed. But when a long Train of Abuses and Usuprations, pursuing invariably the same Object, evinces a Design to reduce them under absolute Despotism, it is their Right, it is their Duty, to throw off such Government, and to provide new Guards for their future Security. Such has been the patient Sufferance of these Colonies; and such is now the Necessity which constrains them to alter their former Systems of Government.

Having thus briefly noted the effects of science upon the world of the 18th century, we must turn our attention to the actual course of science during the Enlightenment. We can distinguish a number of facets. There is, first of all, the problem of science and philosophy. As we have seen, the Scientific Revolution did not occur in a philosophical vacuum. There were epistemological and ontological issues at stake that were as important as the specific physical problems dealt with. These philosophical issues tended to follow national or cultural lines. At the beginning of the Enlightenment, there were clearly distinguishable differences between the ways in which the French, the Germans and the English looked at the world of science and the world of nature. Only slowly did the Newtonian world-picture come to dominate scientific thinking and even when it did, it did so with English, French and German accents still marking off the separate traditions. We shall, therefore, first look at the ways in which science developed within the three great cultural traditions (French, German and English) in the 18th century, with special emphasis upon the relations between science, philosophy and scientific institutions. We shall then offer an extended illustration of the way in which one science--chemistry--was revolutionized in the 18th century by the peculiar philosophical problems and solutions that occupied the French savants of the period. In this fashion, both the substance and the tone of science in the Enlightenment may be grasped in short compass.

    A.   French Science during the *Siècle des lumières* (The Century of Lights)

France inherited two important scientific traditions from the 17th century. Cartesianism had accustomed the French to think in deductive geometrical terms, relying on "clear and distinct ideas" and "la logique française" to tie the ideas together into coherent theories. Science, in this tradition, was theoretical, depending ultimately upon God's beneficence in granting (French) men the basic ideas upon which to build a system of the world. The second tradition was intensely practical. Louis XIV and his great Minister, Colbert, early recognized that the new science could be put to work for the state. This was certainly in the front of Colbert's mind when he urged the foundation of the *Académie Royale des Sciences* in 1666. The Academy was to work for the French state, just as did all other corporations and institutions. Louis used his new scientific body to draw up a map of France for administrative purposes and there was clearly every intention to put science and scientists to work for the benefit of the Sun King. The two traditions met in the profession of the civil and the military engineer. Mathematics was a deductive science based upon clear and distinct mathematical ideas; the design of fortresses and the building of roads and bridges were intensely practical activities that required the use of mathematics. The provision of engineers for the service of the state became a matter of some urgency to the state, and France created a system of schools unmatched anywhere else for their formation of mathematically sophisticated engineers. The physics the engineers learned in these schools at the beginning of the 18th century was Cartesian but the principles they applied to the solution of practical problems drew heavily upon the tradition created by Galileo in his *Discourses on Two New Sciences*.

Beyond the professional engineer, Cartesianism was spread among the literate public by popularizers. Perhaps the most famous and most influential of these was Bernard de Fontenelle (1657-1757) who became Secretary of the Academy of Sciences in 1699. He remained Secretary for almost 40 years and in his charming and fascinating essays spread the gospel of Descartes. His enthusiasm was contagious and Cartesian science held sway in France until the 1740's.

Francois Marie Arouet, who later added de Voltaire to his name (1694-1778) was responsible for the introduction of Newtonian ideas into France. Voltaire first came to appreciate the differences between the philosophical and scientific atmospheres of England and France when he took an extended visit to England in 1726 and 1727. He was greatly impressed by his first exposure to the works of Bacon, Locke, and Newton, and to the English system of representative government. He was both moved and impressed by the state funeral accorded Sir Isaac Newton upon his death in 1727 and by the fact that Newton was buried in Westminster Abbey with hero's honors. He returned to France a convinced Anglophile and set out to enlighten his countrymen on their neighbors across the channel. In his *Philosophical Letters on the English* (1733), he gave expression to his Anglomania. In letter Fourteen, (See Documents), he compared Newton and Descartes with interesting consequences.

Upon his return to France from England, Voltaire threw himself into a frenzy of scientific activity. Together with his mistress, the Marquise du Chatelet (1706-1749) who was an accomplished mathematician, Voltaire carefully studied Newtonian science at a laboratory set up in the Marquise's chateau. The result of this partnership was the first French translation of the *Principia* by the Marquise and Voltaire's *Elements of the Philosophy of Newton*, published in 1738. It was now possible for any interested Frenchmen with the necessary scientific and mathematical qualifications to read and understand Newton. To do so, of course, meant immediately to call the Cartesian system of the world into doubt.

Coincident with Voltaire's enthusiasm for Newton were two French government-sponsored expeditions which had a profound effect on the Cartesian-Newtonian problem. A major controversy occurred at the French Academy of Science in the 1730's, ostensibly over the question of accurate longitude determination. This was a question of obvious practical import in this age of extended overseas voyages, but it also involved a direct confrontation between Cartesian and Newtonian physics. The Cartesians maintained the earth was shaped like an egg; the Newtonians that it was shaped like an oblate spheroid, flattened at the poles and bulging at the equator. Each side had extensive theoretical arguments to support its conclusion, arguments based upon assumptions which reached the heart of both traditions. Louis XV was persuaded to authorize two scientific expeditions, one to Lapland and the other to Peru, to measure the lengths of the degree of longitude of those places and to end the controversy once and for all. The Peru expedition left in 1735 and the one to Lapland in 1736.

Attesting to the rigor of science expeditions in those days, the returns were finally submitted in 1744. Newton was found to be correct. The degree of longitude was discovered to be shorter in Peru than in Lapland, some 110,600 meters to 111,900 meters (in modern measure), and the earth appeared to be bulged out at the equator. These expeditions served to provide Newtonian physics with great respectability, but, more importantly, it produced two confirmed and skillful French Newtonians. Pierre Louis Moreau de Maupertuis (1695-1759), the leader of the Lapland expedition and the young mathematician Alexis Clairaut (1715-1765), a member of the expedition, were impressed with Newton's works. Clairaut was particularly appreciative of the power of the mathematics used by Newton.

This was the start of the very successful French Newtonian tradition in theoretical mechanics and astronomy. It was a major change in orientation in French science. The last half of the 18th century saw the French combination of the mechanical and astronomical aspects of Newton's *Principia* with continental developments in mathematics, to the benefit of both subjects. Jean-le-Rond D'Alembert (1717-1783), Joseph Louis Lagrange (1736-1813) and Pierre Simon Laplace (1749-1827) are the great figures in this very successful combination.

D'Alembert was at the peak of his mathematical productivity between 1743 and 1754. In 1743 he published his *Treatise on Dynamics*, which contains a powerful new interpretation of Newton's third law of motion--the action-reaction law. He presented the 'D'Alembert principle' in this work, which stated that the internal forces of inertia, those forces which resisted acceleration, must be equal and opposite to the forces which produce the acceleration. The appropriate use of this broader interpretation of the third law enabled D'Alembert to devise the differential equations of motion for any rigid system. D'Alembert pursued his new insight with the help of the calculus. In 1744 he applied his principle to fluids in the *Treatise on Equilibrium and the Motion of Fluids* and in 1745 he attempted to apply it in a *General Theory of Winds*. Physical astronomy also received D'Alembert's mathematical attention, resulting in his three-volume *System of the World*, published in 1754.

The two great figures in the formulation of the complete Newtonian world picture were Lagrange and Laplace. Lagrange was the greatest mathematician of the 18th century. His work stressed the greatest possible generality of methods and the use of clear, symmetrical notation. He was interested in theory and was satisfied to let his students attend to any possible applications. Lagrange considered mechanics to be just a branch of mathematics. His great work, *Analytical Mechanics*, published in Paris in 1788, represented the high point in the study of mechanics. Sir William Rowan Hamilton, the brilliant mathematician of the 19th century, called Lagrange's *Mécanique analytique* a mathematical poem. Lagrange wrote a truly prodigious number of papers and publications covering almost every area of pure mathematics. In addition to mechanics, he developed the calculus of variations, established the theory of differential equations and provided many new solutions and theorems in the theory of numbers.

A great part of Laplace's success in astronomy came from his application of Lagrange's powerful mathematical techniques to problems of astronomy. Laplace was a fine mathematician in his own right, but he became interested in unresolved astronomical problems and was determined to "offer a complete solution of the great mechanical problem presented by the solar system, and make theory coincide so closely with observation that empirical equations should no longer find a place in astronomical tables." Laplace had already been fascinated by irregularities in the orbits of Jupiter and Saturn. He now devoted himself to the whole of the solar system and published a general summary of his thoughts, including a history of astronomy, entitled *Exposition of the System of the World* in 1796. This popular work was followed by a detailed analytical treatment of the solar system in 5 volumes, the *Celestial Mechanics*, published between 1799 and 1825.

   This is the great work of synthesis of Newtonian astronomy. Laplace included all major developments in astronomy during the 18th century in his work, as well as an historical treatment of the subject (in the fifth volume published in 1825). The first two volumes appeared in 1799, containing methods for determining planetary motions and the motion of the tides. These methods were applied to obtain accurate astronomical tables and correct orbits of the planets in the third and fourth volumes published in 1802 and 1805. In general, the most important aspect of the work was the translation of the study of astronomy from one based on the geometry used in the *Principia*, to one founded on the more complete form of the differential calculus. The *Mécanique céleste* combines the extensive work of Newtonian theory with the sophistication of continental mathematics.

   The success of Laplace's work had a profound effect on the Newtonian world picture. The solar system emerged from Laplace's treatment as a perfectly self-regulating system. All the apparent irregularities, such as those observed in the planets Saturn and Jupiter and the motion of the moon were shown to be self-correcting needing no periodic divine intervention as Newton had suggested. The changes in the velocities of Saturn and Jupiter were shown to be the result of their mutual gravitational interactions. The moon's observed irregularities were analyzed and revealed to be self-correcting over a very long time period.

   The solar system, in fact the whole universe, seemed to be a perfectly operating machine. It appeared to be totally described in terms of Newtonian laws and thereby completely determined. Laplace put this interpretation of the world into dramatic form in 1812 with his notion of a Divine Calculator: "a Divine Calculator who, knowing the velocities and positions of all the particles in the world at a particular instant, could calculate all that had happened in the past and all that would happen in the future." In sharp contrast to the conception of the universe which Sir Isaac Newton believed in, there seemed to be no need for God's intervention in the world described by the *Mécanique céleste*. The famous exchange between Laplace and Napoleon illustrates the removal of God's actions from the determined Newtonian universe. Napoleon had been informed that Laplace's work contained no mention of God. Upon presentation of a copy of the *Mécanique céleste*, Napoleon remarked, "M. Laplace, they tell me you have written this large book on the system of the universe, and have never even mentioned its Creator." Laplace answered that he had no need for that hypothesis!

   The consequences of the Laplacian world-view are worth noting. In this universe, there was no room for God, or for miracles or for anything but stark materialism and absolute determinism. Ultimate particles zipped through space. Their paths could be described by partial differential equations. This was reality and this was all. It was this world that many accepted as the Newtonian universe at the end of the eighteenth century.

The stark mathematics of Laplace's vision appealed to a very limited number of educated people. There was another Newtonian tradition that had a far wider following. The English philosopher, John Locke (1632-1704), had provided a philosophical foundation for the new science in the years immediately following the publication of the *Principia*. Locke, like Newton, emphasized experience and experiment. His work focused attention upon the psychology of sensations and the relations between words and things. Locke's French followers eagerly continued his explorations in this area and prepared the way for the linguistic reformation in chemistry that was such an important aspect of the Chemical Revolution.

The combination of the works developed by the disciples of Newton and those of Locke produced what is usually called the tradition of empiricism. It is from empiricism that the Enlightenment drew support for most of its political and social theories. Locke in his *An Essay Concerning the Human Understanding*, first published in 1690, elaborated upon the idea that all our ideas are records of sensations. He compared the mind at birth to a blank tablet, gradually written upon as we develop our sensations. All our knowledge is acquired by means of the senses, and is remembered, ordered and organized in the mind. Therefore, there are two types of idea, ideas of sensation and ideas of reflection. By means of reflection, the mind organizes the simple ideas of sensation into more complex ideas.

The extension of this line of reasoning into areas of political and social thought produced the concept of man dependent upon his experiences and upon his environment. The path to the progress of society depended upon a program of education and upon an improvement of living conditions. Education could direct men toward better experiences. Few doubted in the 18th century that an application of science and technology could produce a rapid and salutory change in living conditions. The combination of enthusiasm for education and for science and technology as a means of assuring progress should be recognized as the classical western liberal theme. This theme has been heard continuously in western society since the late 17th century, but never so clearly as in the age of the Enlightenment.

Locke's sensationalist psychology confronted the Cartesian tradition at many of the same points that Newtonian science opposed Cartesian science. Both Locke and Newton denied the applicability of *a priori*, innate ideas. The Cartesians placed great emphasis upon rational constructions of the mind. They believed that these rational constructs could be related to the physical world. Descartes felt secure in this belief because he believed that God was not malicious and therefore would not allow disparity between conceptions formulated in the mind and the physical world. Both Newton and Locke argued that knowledge derived from introspection could not be simply related to the outside world. External reference points were necessary. Without these external reference points, namely those provided by the

sensations, we could not understand the outside world. Nor could
we reach an objective understanding or description of how the
mind works, which creates this understanding of the outside
world.

Both Newton and Locke worked to exclude innate ideas, both
in principle and as a matter of method. Locke did not seriously
question the existence of the external, physical world, as later
philosophers were to do, because he believed there must be something which was responsible for our ideas of sensation. This
was the same assumption which the Newtonians made, in fact which
most working scientists make. The emphasis was placed upon
description, not at all upon the explanation of the nature of
things. The deemphasis of explanation led, paradoxically, to
the assumption of several implicit explanations which were incorporated without serious questioning into the corpus of Newtonian
science. It was these assumed explanations, such as the corpuscular nature of light and the fluid nature of heat, electricity
and magnetism, which were to lead the followers of the empirical
path of Newtonian science into grave difficulties during the 19th
century.

The orientation of the 18th century toward science, progress
and empiricism was certainly a major aspect of enlightenment
thought. But there are other intellectual traditions during this
same period which are frequently neglected, although they are
probably of equal importance in the full course of western intellectual development. The strong reaction against Newtonian
science and sensationalist psychology must be considered in an
account of the Enlightenment.

There was a tradition in France which emphasized the study
of natural history; the study of plants and animals and man in
their natural states. This study should be conducted with emo-
tion, subjectively, and with a feeling of wonder for the mysteries of the natural world. In the latter half of the 18th century,
there were a growing number of men who were dissatisfied with
the boundless confidence placed upon man's rationality and the
emphasis upon mathematical science and dispassionate abstract
theorizing.

This orientation away from mathematical science is identifi-
able with the Romantic movement at the end of the century. The
Romantic movement began, in large part, as a moral revolt against
Newtonian physics. It is an extremely difficult movement to
characterize when dealing with the histories of politics,
philosophy or the arts. But in the history of science, the
Romantic movement does take on some general, but still meaningful, characteristics. The moral revolt against physics took the
form of an attempt to defend qualitative, non-mathematical science: science which draws the scientist into it as an involved
observer. For the Romantic, science should involve subjectivity
and an individual, intuitive response to nature observed. The
study of natural history was ideally suited to this Romantic
disposition. The Romantics rejected the mathematical, materialistic world of Newtonian physics, with its eternal, self-
regulating motions of matter in the void. They sought a world
which was growing and changing, very much like an organism grows

and develops in a wonderful and not fully understood way. In short, the Romantic sought a deeper intuitive experience of nature than the advocates of the mathematical Newtonian universe could, or deemed proper, to provide.

In France, Jean Jacques Rousseau (1712-1778) was the most influential advocate of the Romantic approach to science. Rousseau insisted on moving away from the mechanistic world view so prevalent in France, toward a more organismic view. He was deeply interested in botany and in natural history because he believed that these were subjects in which the investigator could immerse himself and obtain an understanding of the totality of nature. Rousseau and the group of followers he inspired began and continued a criticism of the practice of science at the Academy of Science and sometimes of the Academy itself.

This anti-quantitative, anti-mechanistic orientation took a violent turn during the French Revolution. The main reaction was against mathematical physics in particular, with claims that it was arrogant and even undemocratic. These claims were anti-intellectual in tone and therefore different in intent from Rousseau's position. But they revealed the depth of feeling against Newtonian science. Above all, the arrogance of mathematics (or perhaps only of mathematicians) was disliked and the study of natural history, of botany and zoology was favored during the Revolution, in fact, briefly encouraged.

The French Revolution and the reign of Napoleon caused some rather dramatic changes in the course of French physical science, quite apart from the concerns of the Romantics. The French physical sciences continued to emphasize theoretical mechanics and astronomy, to the relative neglect of enthusiasm for experimentation. The French seemed willing to believe that Laplace's Divine Calculator was actually just a very good French mathematical physicist. Lagrange had contributed to this confidence by his statement "Science is science when expressed mathematically." Mathematics and theoretical physical science continued to be the most highly revered forms of science in France. But, despite this continued prestige, actual scientific output in the physical sciences declined sharply in France after the defeat of Napoleon. This decline appears in large part to be the result of Napoleon's insistence upon extreme practicality of the sciences. Young men with mathematical talents were drafted into the Napoleonic armies and so many must have hidden their abilities and sought other outlets for their intellectual energies than science.

B. German science during the *Aufklärung*

The scientific scene in Germany differed markedly from that in France during the Enlightenment. Whereas France had risen to heights under Louis XIV, Germany had spent most of the 17th century recovering from the devastation of the Thirty Years' War. The Treaty of Westphalia in 1648 had guaranteed the future weakness of Germany by dividing it into hundreds of petty states, none strong enough to create unity or to threaten France. Such diversity was an almost fatal political attribute, but it had some

advantages in the cultural and intellectual sphere. Where Louis
XIV strove to impose a unity of institutions, thoughts and
religion upon his people, the Germans fairly reveled in their
differences and in their individuality. Each petty court was the
center of intellectual and social life and sometimes stimulated
the creation of genius. Johann Wolfgang von Goethe (1749-1832)
thrived at the small court of Weimar and made of Weimar a center
of German intellectual life. Frederick the Great of Prussia tried
to emulate the Sun King by creating a scientific center in the
Prussian Academy of Sciences. The University of Göttingen became
a center of mathematical studies when mathematics was despised at
most academic centers. Thus, the political division of Germany
stimulated rather than repressed the growth of an indigenous
German culture. The great scientific achievements of Germany in
the 19th century were firmly rooted in the foundations of German
thought in the *Aufklärung*, as the Germans called their enlightenment.

We may notice immediately one special character of German
thought in the 18th century. Far more than in England or in
France, the Germans were dedicated to their Christian heritage.
In France, the acceptance of Newtonian science and Lockean
philosophy tended to the creation of atheism or deism and led to
the (at the time) shocking statement by Laplace that he did not
need God in his cosmos. In England, the same influences led to
libertine ideas and a radical Christianity that was sometimes
indistinguishable from materialism. In Germany, however, extreme
care was taken to preserve the faith from the incursions of
materialistic and atheistic ideas. From the beginning of the
Aufklärung, with the writings of Gottfried Wilhlem Leibniz (1646-
1716) to its end with Immanuel Kant (1724-1804), German philosophers were intent upon conserving the possibility of the preservation of Christianity. The result was that German science differed
markedly from its French or English versions. Nature could not
simply be analyzed and mathematized; it had also to be seen as a
whole as God's creation and this requirement gave a peculiar
flavor to German *Naturwissenschaft*.

Another peculiarity of Germany was its educational system.
Because there was no unified German state and because every prin-
cipality felt its own particular pride, the development of university education in Germany followed a unique path. There were no
single great university centers, like Paris in France, or Oxford
and Cambridge in England. Rather, there were many universities
scattered through the German lands. What this meant was that it
was impossible to impose a philosophical or scientific orthodoxy
upon the students. And, since German students made it a practice
to wander from university to university, they were naturally exposed to different points of view and different ways of looking at
their studies. The result was an invigorating intellectual experience that permitted German savants greater freedom in their
speculations and their learned productions than were to be found
elsewhere. Finally, the German universities served an ideal that
also affected the character of German science. The university did
not exist, as in England, to turn out "gentlemen" or, as in
France, to form functionaries of the state. The ideal of the

German university was *Wissenschaft*--a wide knowledge of the world
and of man. It was not enough to know a great deal about a very
little; the German scholar was expected to have a broad vision of
the whole of reality. Philosophy, therefore, played an essential
part in German education and the German scientists of the 18th
and 19th centuries were firmly grounded in the philosophical
foundations of the sciences. This emphasis upon breadth of
vision reinforced the concept of science that emerged from the
study of Nature within a theological context. We may illustrate
these tendencies by using Goethe as an example.

Goethe gives us a good sense of how far removed the Germans
were from the French Newtonian approach to science. Goethe reported in a letter in 1770 that the French treatise on a mechanical, deterministic universe, Baron de Holbach's *System of Nature*,
had produced little enthusiasm in Germany, despite its great
acclaim in France. The work was totally outside the German
interest in nature. "Not one of us had read the book through,"
wrote Goethe,

> for we found ourselves deceived in the expectations with
> which we had opened it. A system of nature was announced,
> and therefore we hoped to learn really something of
> nature,--our idol. . . . But how hollow and empty did
> we feel in this melancholy, atheistical half-night, in
> which the earth vanished with all its images, the heaven
> with all its stars. There was to be matter in motion
> from all eternity, and by this motion, right, left, and
> in every direction, without anything further, it was to
> produce the infinite phenomena of existence. . . .

Goethe was the leader of the anti-Newtonian movement in Germany. His approach to nature was essentially poetic. Goethe
began his study of science where Rousseeau had begun, with the
study of plants. He turned first to the classification scheme of
Carl Linnaeus (1707-1778) in an attempt to learn about plants.
The Linnean scheme of classification consisted of counting the
number of stamens and pistils of plants. It was a classification
by numbers, very useful to most botanists of the period because
it brought some order into the chaos of the great number of newly
discovered plant families and species. But it was repulsive to
Goethe, because he found nothing in the scheme but nomenclature.
There was no place for imagination, and above all for the appreciation of the beauty of different flowers and plants. The Linnean scheme could be applied equally well whether the plant was
dead or alive. For Goethe, the Linnean system of studying botany
had little to do with the study of nature

Goethe rejected artificial classification and adopted a
system of natural classification, dependent upon a study of the
whole life cycle of the plant. Each plant must be considered as
a growing, living thing in nature. Plants should be studied from
the seed, throughout the growth cycle, until natural death. This
was a very different approach to botany. It involved the observer
in a very subjective, intuitive way, allowing him the full range
of sense impressions in his study of a plant. It led to an appreciation of the plant as a living entity, and perhaps, a deeper
understanding of plant life. It contrasted sharply with the

orderliness and rigid formality of the artificial classification schemes.

Goethe's major work in botany was his *Metamorphosis of Plants*. He suggested that all plants are really variations of an archetypal plant, the *Urpflanz*. "All have a similar form," he wrote, "yet none is the same as the other. So this chorus of growth shows a mysterious law." This mysterious law was the "inner necessity and truth" governing the development and organization of plants and of all living things.

The search for the archetypal forms of plants and the organizing principles of nature was extended by Goethe first to botany, then to zoology and finally to the physical sciences. The organizing principles and the basic forces of nature became the central concern of his scientific work. For Goethe and his growing following in Germany, nature could not be interpreted solely in terms of matter and motion; in terms of determined mechanisms. Nature was permeated with non-material forces which must be considered as well. Newtonian science was neither complete, nor did it provide an understanding of nature.

Goethe's most vehement attack upon Newtonian science took the form of his denial of Newton's theory of colors. In his *Farbenlehre* (Lessons about Colors), completed in 1810, he claimed that Newton had tortured nature with his experiments. Newton was charged with having distorted the nature of colors, both by his experiments and by his use of mathematics. The fundamental differences in approach between Goethe and Newton are perhaps best illustrated by this controversy. Goethe insisted upon involving the observer in the phenomena observed. Goethe's and Newton's investigations of color phenomena were completely different. Newton wrote at the beginning of his Opticks: "My design in this Book is not to explain the Properties of Light by Hypotheses, but to propose and prove them by Reason and Experiments." In the *Farbenlehre*, Goethe wrote: "one must first get at colors as physical phenomena, from the point of view of Nature, if one would gain control over them for the purposes of Art." Newton spoke of reason and experiment while Goethe spoke of nature and art.

Goethe believed that Newton had destroyed any chance of understanding colors by his careful, closely linked systematic series of experiments designed to analyse the components of white light, the colors. Newton forced the colors to appear from white light by means of prisms, knife blades, hairs, soap bubbles, etc., describing the resulting spectra of colors exactly and calling the processes which produced them refraction, inflection and reflection.

For Goethe, colors had no exactly describable, innate properties which Newton's colored rays seemed to possess. Color perception was an optical act, dependent upon the observer and his perceptions. In a complicated way, Goethe believed that light and darkness combined to produce colors, with the eye of the observer an essential part of the whole process. His concern was with the psychology and physiology of color perception, not with the analysis of colors. To call Goethe's criticism simply wrong is to miss his point, then as now. His direct criticisms of

Newton's experiments were very wide of their mark, but he was attempting to criticize the sterility of the Newtonian approach to nature. Newtonian science excluded the observer by attempting to make use of exact experimental techniques and mathematics. This exclusion was unacceptable to Goethe because it was not natural; man was part of nature and should not be removed from it. On this level, Goethe's criticism was profound. The same problems were to be raised again in the early 20th century, but they were taken more seriously on their second appearance.

Goethe, it might be objected, was really not a scientist even though he did dabble in science. His objections to the Newtonian world-view are interesting but they did not necessarily reflect the opinions of the "real" scientists in Germany in the 18th century. There is some cogency to this argument but it can be shown that there were "real" scientists who felt uneasy with the results of Newtonian physics. Such a one was Leonhard Euler (1707-1783).

Leonhard Euler was a member of the "Swiss Renaissance" of the late 17th and 18th century that provided a number of distinguished mathematicians and physicists to the scientific world. At the center of this burst of creative activity was the Bernouilli family whose members were creative and brilliant mathematicians. It was the Bernouillis who seized upon the calculus, especially in its Leibnizian form, and turned it into a major instrument of physical research. Euler was a disciple of the Bernouillis and fully realized his early mathematical promise. In his physics, however, he soon became unhappy with the bases of Newtonian physics. The law of universal attraction appeared to imply attractive action at a distance and this Euler, along with other distinguished physicists such as Christian Huyghens, found incomprehensible. One of the oldest dicta of physical philosophy in the West was that bodies could not act where they were not and the doctrine of universal gravitation obviously seemed to contradict this. Euler, therefore, felt it necessary to fill all space with a subtile ether and to use this ether to explain various physical phenomena. Among these was that of light. Euler picked up the pulse-wave theory of Huyghens and gave it full mathematical treatment.

Euler was one of the most prolific scientists who ever lived. His collected works, now being prepared in a modern edition, will run to well over 100 volumes. Some, indeed most, were highly technical and required considerable mathematical skill to be understood. But Euler was also a child of the Enlightenment. He wanted to reach the general public, and did so with one of the classics of the 18th century. His *Letters to a German Princess*, published in three volumes (1768-1772) was the last great exposition of the Cartesian system. Action at a distance was ignored and the old mechanisms of Cartesian impact physics were applied to the phenomena of light, electricity and magnetism. Euler did not win the battle in the 18th century. The Newtonians did triumph then. But Euler kept alive the idea of an ether to which physicists might wish to appeal to explain mysterious actions. In the 19th century the ether was, once again, to come center stage.

C. English Science in the Age of Reason.

English scientific activity in the 18th century represents a contrast to both French and German science. Not surprisingly, the works of Sir Isaac Newton shaped the orientation of English science. Unlike the French, the English chose to emphasize the empirical approach to science, using Newton's *Opticks* as the model and example. The English were remarkably good experimenters, but they were also noticeably poor mathematicians. They remained steadfast in their use of geometry and, with a very few exceptions, paid little attention to the calculus. The great developments in continental mathematics and the successful application of the new, more powerful, mathematics to theoretical physics and astronomy remained unappreciated by the English well into the 19th century. Newton's *Principia* remained unchanged and only partially understood in England, despite several popularized accounts of it.

A small group of men were responsible for the acceptance of Newton's *Principia* in the late 1690's. Edmund Halley (1656-1742) was particularly interested in Newton's work on cometary orbits and used the *Principia* to good advantage in the calculations of the paths and return periods of comets. David Gregory, an astronomer in Edinburgh, and William Whiston, Newton's successor at Cambridge, both taught Newton's works before the end of the 17th century. Finally Colin Maclaurin (1698-1746), probably the most skillful English Newtonian and a mathematician at Edinburgh, popularized Newton's work and contributed to the theory of the calculus. But, besides the work of these men, there was little theoretical mechanics and astronomy to speak of in England until almost mid-19th century.

English science was largely a science of amateurs; men of independent means who pursued questions that interested them, teaching themselves and conducting experiments with equipment they made themselves. These men were enthusiastic and often adept experimenters, usually devoid of mathematical skills. The English Universities were of little help. They stressed an education in the classics, with little emphasis upon natural philosophy and no awareness of continental mathematics.

By the beginning of the 19th century the English amateur scientist was aided by two new developments: a growing number of privately published science magazines and several established private scientific societies, quite often outside the influence of the rather dormant Royal Society of London.

The new science magazines and pamphlets provided the means for the dissemination of all types of scientific papers, articles and notes; not only those which had the official sanction of the Royal Society, or as in France, the Paris Academy of Science. The English amateur scientist could subscribe to several different magazines and thereby become aware of new work by his fellow amateurs, usually in chemistry, meteorology, agriculture, or, after 1800 and the discovery of the Voltaic pile by Alessandro Volta (1745-1827), the exciting new field of current electricity. These magazines published papers which were largely non-mathematical, produced by men of similar interests and abilities and above all, offered the English experimenter the possibility of seeing his own work in print.

The Royal Society of London was at a low point in prestige at the end of the 18th century. Its place was filled by several small, local scientific societies which sprang up in England, most frequently in those areas in the throes of the Industrial Revolution. They were attended by local manufacturers and businessmen and by middle-class science enthusiasts in general. The most famous of these societies were the Lunar Society of Birmingham and the Manchester Literary and Philosophical Society. The Lunar Society met once a month on the evening of the full moon, so that the members could easily find their way home again. The societies attracted men of ability, with James Watt and Erasmus Darwin attending the Lunar Society and later John Dalton and James Prescott Joule joining the Manchester Society. This strong emphasis upon self-education and individual experimentation and the lack of mathematical skill continued to characterize English science until almost mid-19th century. English developments in mathematics and the English universities do not seriously affect science until the 1840's.

The English excelled in the field of astronomy during the 18th century. They were fine observational astronomers who rapidly accepted the theoretical framework of Newton's *Principia*. The 18th century came to grips with the vastly expanded universe conceived during the 17th century. Men such as Thomas Digges and Giodano Bruno had modified the Copernican universe to introduce the notion of stars scattered randomly through an infinite space. It took a serious mental adjustment during the 17th century to accommodate such a universe. Blaise Pascal (1623-62), the French mathematician, philosopher and religious figure, was deeply worried by the direction of the discoveries in astronomy and wrote: "I am deeply frightened by the eternal silence of these infinite spaces." It was this vast universe which Sir Isaac Newton considered in his *Principia* with the laws of universal gravitation which controlled the motions of the planets, the moon and even the comets.

Astronomy until about 1750 was really the study of the solar system. Primary attention was devoted to the motions of the five visible planets, the moon, the sun, and the comets which entered the solar system. The stars were observed, of course, but as objects in the "starry background." About 1750, there was a change in the development of astronomy toward a concentration upon the stars. The Milky Way had already been noticed and described by Galileo as a band of countless stars. In 1750, the English astronomer Thomas Wright (1711-86) suggested that the Milky Way was a disc-like system of stars, with the solar system included in this same system, somewhere near the center. The Milky Way was observed because it was seen in the plane of this disc. Observation out of the plane of the disc of the stellar system offered fewer stars to see. Wright also was interested in the patches in the sky called nebulae, which appeared faint and cloud-like. He suggested that these, perhaps, were star systems similar to the Milky Way, but at a very great distance away.

Suddenly, the stars had become the chief new interest in astronomy. William Herschel (1738-1822) devoted his long and productive life to the study of this new sidereal astronomy. He was a great astronomer primarily because he was a patient, careful observer and because he built his own reflecting telescopes. He wanted to study the nebulae, and, if possible, see the separate parts which composed these cloud-like structures. But, as he constructed larger and better telescopes in order to produce better resolution, he discovered to his surprise that more and more nebulae appeared. His larger telescopes produced better resolution, but they also increased in light gathering power. His new, larger telescopes could resolve the old nebulae to a much greater degree, but in the process many more appeared which could not be resolved.

Herschel confirmed Wright's concept that the solar system was part of a galaxy of stars, the Milky Way, which was shaped roughly like a disc. But he believed that some nebulae, such as the one observed in Orion, were gaseous in nature and were within our own galaxy. Other nebulae seemed to be outside of the Milky Way, and perhaps were even comparable in size to our galaxy.

In the process of his very careful mapping of the heavens over the years, Herschel began to draw conclusions about the construction of the heavens and the relationships between the stars. In 1803, he argued that certain double stars, which were always observed together, were actually physically connected to each other by their mutual gravitation. These stars actually revolved around a common center of gravity, behaving as they should according to the law of gravitational attraction. The Newtonian world view was extended to include not just the solar system, but the stars, and by implication the galaxy and the universe.

It was in experimental science that the English excelled during the Age of Reason. The reason was not hard to find. In his Queries, appended to the *Opticks*, Newton has suggested a whole new theory of matter and left it to his followers to discover the hard facts that would confirm or refute it. The result was the creation of a Newtonian world-view that, by the end of the century, was both comprehensive and seductive.

The problem of the ultimate nature of ponderable matter was essentially a chemical one and is best left for discussion under the Chemical Revolution. We may, however, at this point, mention one aspect that well illustrates the Newtonian legacy. In Query 31, Newton had suggested that matter in the gaseous state was the result of a repulsive force associated with the particles of the various gases. Such an idea was difficult for even devoted Newtonians to swallow for universal attraction appeared to be the only force with which ponderable matter acted. Stephen Hales (1677-1761) performed a series of classic experiments on "airs" that proved, to his satisfaction at least, that matter was endowed with a true repulsive force when it existed as a gas. In his *Vegetable Statics* (1727) Hales described his experiments. The work was one that later influenced Lavoisier.

For the 17th century, the question of the nature of heat had apparently been solved. It was, as Francis Bacon "proved," the intestine motion of the particles of which bodies were composed.

In the 18th century, that view was successfully challenged by Joseph Black (1728-1799). He discovered both latent and specific heats and found it difficult to account for these in terms of molecular motions. Instead, he suggested and others assumed, that heat was a substance that had no weight, but that was endowed with repulsive powers by which the particles of heat repelled one another. The particles of heat (later dubbed caloric) could be forced into combination with ordinary, ponderable matter and thus disappear from view. This "disappearing" caloric was the matter of latent heat. Notice here that caloric had all the properties, except weight, of ordinary matter and fit nicely into the Newtonian scheme of things.

Electricity and magnetism had fascinated Newton, but he was unable to crack their mysteries. This was left for his successors. The solution to the problem of magnetism had to wait until the 19th century, but electricity seemed to yield to the questing mind of Benjamin Franklin in the 1740's. Franklin, at that time, has to be classified as an Englishman for the American Revolution had not yet occurred to even his mind. Franklin's work (See Readings) illustrates well just how much could be done with genius and a few simple pieces of apparatus. From his experiments, Franklin concluded that electricity was composed of particles that were endowed with attractive and repulsive forces, just like the particles of ordinary matter. Again, the Newtonian framework proved capable of containing new scientific advance.

In spite of these novelties, English science was not as vigorous as it might have been. The torch had passed from English to French hands and the most dramatic scientific progress was to be made across the channel from Newton's home. Science at the beginning of the 19th century was definitely Newtonian , but it had a French accent.

II. Eighteenth Century Science, Readings

  A. French Science.

1. *In letter XIV of his Letters on the English, Voltaire described
the difference between the Newtonian and the Cartesian world view.*

     A Frenchman arriving in London finds quite a change, in
philosophy as in all else. Behind him he left the world full;
here he finds it empty. In Paris one sees the universe composed
of vortices of subtile matter; in London one sees nothing of the
sort. With us, it's the pressure of the moon that causes the
rising of the tide; with the English, it's the sea gravitating
toward the moon; so that when you think the moon ought to give us
a high tide, these gentlemen think it ought to be low; none of
which unfortunately can be verified, for in order to know the
truth of it we should have had to examine the moon and the tides
at the first moment of creation.
     You will also notice that the sun, which in France has no-
thing to do with the business, over here contributes his twenty-
five per cent or so. According to your Cartesians, everything is
done by means of an impulse that is practically incomprehensible;
according to Mr. Newton it is by a kind of attraction, the reason
for which is no better known. In Paris you picture the earth as
shaped like a melon; in London it is flattened on both sides.
Light, for a Cartesian, exists in the air; for a Newtonian it
comes here from the sun in six and a half minutes. All the operations of your chemistry are owing to acids, alkalis, and subtile
matter; in England, the concept of attraction dominates even in
this.
     The very essence of things is totally different. You agree
neither on the definition of soul nor on that of matter. Descartes assures us that soul is the same thing as thought, and
Locke pretty well demonstrates the contrary.
     Descartes declares, again, that matter is nothing but exten-
sion; to that, Newton adds solidity. Here are some tremendous
contrarieties.

          Non nostrum inter vos tantas componere lites.*

     This famous Newton, this destroyer of the Cartesian system,
died in March of last year, 1727. In life he was honored by his
countrymen, and he was buried like a king who had benefited his
subjects.
     The eulogy on Mr. Newton that was delivered by M. de
Fontenelle before the Académie des Sciences has been read with
eagerness, and has been translated into English. In England
people looked forward to the opinion of M. de Fontenelle, expec-
ting a solemn declaration of the superiority of English philosophy, but when they found him comparing Descartes to Newton, the
whole Royal Society of London was aroused. Far from acquiescing
in such a judgment, they found a good deal of fault with the discourse. Several even (and those by no means the most philosophical) were shocked at the comparison for the sole reason that
Descartes was a Frenchman.
     It must be confessed that these two great men were remark-

---

* "It is not for me to settle such high debate as that between
you."--Virgil, *Eclogues*, III, 108.

ably unlike in their way of life, in their fortune, and in their philosophy.

Descartes was born with a lively and strong imagination which made of him a man as extraordinary in his private life as in his thinking. That imagination could not be concealed even in his philosophical works, where at every moment one is struck by ingenious and sparkling comparisons. Nature had almost made him a poet, and as a matter of fact he did compose for the Queen of Sweden an entertainment in verse which, for the honor of his memory, has not been printed.

He tried the profession of arms for a while, and afterward, having become a philosopher altogether, thought it not unworthy of himself to have a love affair. He had by his mistress a daughter named Francine, who died young, and whose loss he deeply mourned. And so he experiences all that belongs to the human lot.

For a long time he believed that in order to philosophize freely he would have to escape from society, and especially from his native country. He was right; the men of his time knew too little to help him clarify his ideas, and were in fact capable of little more than doing him harm.

He left France because he followed after truth, which was persecuted there in those days by the miserable philosophy of scholasticism; but he found no more rationality in the universities of Holland, to which he retired. For while the sole propositions of his philosophy that were true were condemned in France, he was also persecuted by the pretended philosophers of Holland, who understood him no better, and who, having a nearer view of his glory, hated him personally even more. He was obliged to leave Utrecht. He had to undergo the accusation of atheism, the last resource of calumniators; he who had employed all his intellectual sagacity in a search for new proofs of the existence of a God was suspected of believing in none.

Such a deal of persecution presumes very great merit and a brilliant reputation; both were his. Reason even began to gleam a little in the world, piercing through the darkness of scholasticism and theprejudices of popular superstition. At last his name became so famous that there was some effort to attract him to France with the promise of rewards. A pension of a thousand *écus* was offered him. He came back with that expectation, paid the expenses of the patent (which was sold in those days), failed to receive the pension, and returned to philosophize in his North Holland solitude at the same time as the great Galileo, at the age of eighty, groaned in the prisons of the Inquisition for having proved the motion of the earth. In the end he died in Stockholm, prematurely, of a bad regimen, in the presence of a number of learned men, his enemies, and in the hands of a physician who loathed him.

The career of Sir Isaac Newton was altogether different. He lived for eighty-five years, always tranquil and happy, and held in honor in his own country. It was his great good fortune to have been born not only in a free country but in a time when, the irrelevancies of scholasticism being banished, reason alone was cultivated; and the world must needs be his pupil, not his enemy.

One curious difference between him and Descartes is that in
the course of so long a life he was free from both passion and
weakness. He never had intimacies with a woman; this was confirmed to me by the doctor and the surgeon in whose arms he died.
One may admire Newton for it, but one should not blame Descartes.

According to public opinion in England, of these two philosophers the first was a dreamer and the other a sage.

Few people in London read Descartes, whose works, in effect,
have lost their utility; hardly any read Newton either, for it
takes considerable knowledge to understand him. Nevertheless,
everybody talks about them, granting nothing to the Frenchman and
everything to the Englishman. Some folk believe that if we are
no longer satisfied with the abhorrence of vacuums, if we know
that air has weight, if we use telescopes, we owe it all to
Newton. Over here he is the Hercules of fable, to whom the ignorant attributed all the deeds of the other heroes.

In a criticism made in London of M. Fontenelle's discourse,
somebody went so far as to say that Descartes was not a great
geometrician. Those who talk in this way may reproach themselves
for beating their nurse. Descartes made as great progress, from
the point at which he found geometry to the point to which he
carried it, as Newton did after him. He was the first who found
the way to give the algebraic equations of curves. His geometry,
which thanks to him has by now become a commonplace, was in his
time so profound that no professor dared undertake to explain it,
and no one in Holland understood it but Schooten, and no one in
France but Fermat.

He carried the same spirit of geometry and inventiveness
over into dioptrics, which in his hands became a new art entirely;
and if here or there he made a mistake, it is clear that a man
who discovers new lands cannot suddenly know all there is to know
about them. Those who come after him and make those lands bear
fruit at least owe their discovery to him. I will not deny that
all the other works of M. Descartes swarm with errors.

Geometry was a guide that, in a way, he himself had created
and that would have conducted him safely through physics; he
abandoned that guide in the end, however, and gave himself up to
the systematizing spirit. From then on, his philosophy was no
more than an ingenious romance, at best seeming probable to the
ignorant. He erred on the nature of the soul, on the proofs of
the existence of God, on the subject of matter, on the laws of
motion, on the nature of light. He admitted innate ideas, he
invented new elements, he created a world, he made man according
to his own fashion--in fact, it is rightly said that man according to Descartes is Descartes' man, far removed from man as he
actually is.

He carried his errors in metaphysics so far as to assert
that two and two make four only because God has willed it so. But
it is not too much to say that he was admirable even in his aberrations. When he was wrong at least he was systematically wrong,
and with logical coherence. He got rid of the absurd chimeras
with which we had infatuated our youth for two thousand years.
He taught the men of his time how to reason, and how to fight him
with his own weapons. If he has not paid in sterling, it is cer-

tainly something to have decried the counterfeit.

I do not think one can truly compare his philosophy in any way with that of Newton: the first is an experimental sketch, the second a finished masterpiece. But he who has set us on the road to truth is perhaps as worthy as he who since then has gone on to the end of it.

Descartes gave sight to the blind; they saw the faults of antiquity and their own as well. The course he opened to us has since become boundless. The little book of Rohaut offered us for a while a complete system of physics; today, the collected works of all the academies of Europe do not amount even to the beginnings of a system. On going deep down into that abyss, we found it infinite.

2. *The leading mathematical physicist of the Enlightenment in France was Jean Le Rond d'Alembert (1717-1783). He served with Denis Diderot (1713-1784) as editor of the great* Encyclopédie *that is the major landmark of the French* siècle des lumières. *D'Alembert wrote many of the articles on mechanics for the* Encyclopédie. *The selections that follow are translations of the articles on Dynamics, Oscillation, and Living Force.* *

DYNAMICS (*Encyclopedic order. Understanding. Reason, Philosophy or Science. Science of Nature; Mixed Mathematics, Mechanics, Dynamics.*) signifies the *science of powers* or *motive causes*, that is, of the forces that put bodies into motion.

This word is formed from the Greek word δύναμις, power, which comes from the verb δύναμαι, I can.

Mr. Leibnitz was the first to make use of this term to designate the most transcendant part of mechanics which treats of the movement of bodies, insofar as it is caused by motive forces acting continually and actually. The general principle of *Dynamics*, taken in this sense, is that the product of the accelerative or retardive force by the time is equal to the element of speed; the reason given for this is that the speed increases or decreases at each instant in virtue of the sum of the small repeated impulses that the motive force gives to the body during this instant; on which see the article *Accelerative* and the article *Cause*.

The word, dynamics, has come into common usage in recent years among geometers to mean, particularly, the science of the motion of bodies that act upon one another, in what manner soever, either by pushing one another or in pulling one another by means of some other body interposed between them and to which they are attached, by a thread, a rigid lever, a plane, etc.

According to this definition, the problems in which one determines the laws of the percussion of bodies are problems of dynamics, See *Percussion*.

There are other problems which involve the determination of the motion of several bodies, attached to one another by some flexible or rigid body, and which thereby alter their motions mutually. The first of this kind to have been solved is known today under the name of the *problem of centers of oscillation*.

In this problem, what is sought is the determination of the motion of a number of weights attached to the same rod of a pendulum. In order to see what the difficulty is, it should be realized first that if each of these weights was alone attached to the rod it would, in the first moment of its motion, describe a small arc whose length would be the same, no matter at what place on the rod it was attached, for the rod, having been displaced from the vertical position, the action of weight on the body is the same no matter where it is placed and ought to produce

Encyclopédie ou Dictionnaire raisonne des sciences, des arts et des métiers, par une société de gens de lettres. 32 vols., Paris, 1751-1780. Arts. Dynamique (1755), Oscillation (1765) and Forces vives (1757). Translated by L. Pearce Williams.

the same effect at the first moment. This is why each of the
weights that is attached to the rod tends to describe a small
line that is equal for all the weights. But since the rod is
supposed rigid, it is impossible that these weights can all describe equal lines at the same moment. Those that are closer to
the center of suspension will obviously traverse a smaller space
and those that are farther away will travel farther. It follows
necessarily, therefore, from the rigidity of the rod that the
speed with which each body tends to move will differ and that,
instead of being equal for all, it will increase in those lower
down and decrease in those higher up. But what will be the law
by which they increase and decrease? This is the problem; the
solution can be found in the article, OSCILLATION. [Note: The
volume in which Oscillation appeared was published in 1765, ten
years after the volume from which this article is taken. See it
following this article.]

Mr. Huyghens and many others after him resolved this problem
by different methods. Since this time, and especially in the
last twenty years, Geometers have applied themselves to many
questions of this kind. The memoirs of the academy of Petersburg
contain a number of these problems treated by Messrs. John and
Daniel Bernoulli, father and son, and by Mr. Euler, all of whom
are celebrated names today. Messrs. Clairaut, de Montigny and
d'Arcy have also published solutions to problems of *Dynamics* in
the memoirs of the Academy of Sciences. The first of these three
geometers provided methods which facilitate the solution of a
great number of questions pertaining to this science in the
memoirs of the Academy for 1742. I published a *Treatise on
Dynamics* in 1743 in which I gave a general principle for the
resolution of all problems of this kind. Here is what I wrote in
the preface:

> Since this part of mechanics is no less difficult than
> interesting, and since the problems that belong to it make
> up a very large class, the greatest geometers have applied
> themselves to it in the last few years but, up to now,
> they have resolved only a very few of the problems of this
> kind, and of these, only particular cases. The greater
> part of the solutions that they have given us, moreover,
> have been based on principles that no one has yet demon-
> strated in a general way. Such, for example, is the prin-
> ciple of the *conservation of living forces* (*See conserva-
> tion of living forces* under the word Force). I have,
> therefore, believed it necessary to treat this subject
> extensively and show how all the problems of *Dynamics* can
> be treated successfully by a very simple and direct method,
> consisting solely of the combination of the principles of
> equilibrium and of compound motion. The principle is
> illustrated in a small number of selected problems, some
> of which are already well known, and others of which are
> entirely new. Still others have been poorly solved, even
> by the better geometers.

Here, in a few words, is my principle for the resolution of
these kinds of problems. Let us imagine that there is impressed

on a number of bodies, motions that they cannot conserve because of their mutual interactions and that they are forced to alter and change into others. It is certain that the motion that each body has at first can be considered as composed of two other arbitrary motions (*see* DECOMPOSITION and COMPOSITION *of motion*), and that one can take for one of these compound motions that which each body ought to have as a result of the action of the other bodies. Now, if each body, instead of the motion that was originally impressed upon it, had received this motion, it follows that each of these bodies would have conserved this motion without change, since by our assumption, it is the motion that each of the bodies would have taken by itself. Thus, the other part of the compound motion ought to be such that it does not disturb anything in the first of the compound motions, that is to say, that this second motion ought to be such for each body that if it, alone, had been imposed without any other motion, the system would have remained at rest.

From this it follows that to follow the motion of many bodies which act upon one another, it is necessary to decompose the motion that each body has received, and from which it tends to move itself, into two other motions in which one is destroyed and the other of which is such and so directed that the action of the surrounding bodies can neither alter nor change it. Applications of this principle which illustrate its use and its convenience will be found in the *articles* OSCILLATION, PERCUSSION and others.

From this principle, it is easy to see that all the laws of the motion of bodies can be reduced to the laws of equilibrium. In order to resolve a problem whatsoever in *Dynamics*, one needs only, first of all, to decompose the motion of each body into two, of which one being supposed known, the other must necessarily be also. Now one of these motions ought to be such that bodies that have it do not destroy it. For example, if they are attached to a rigid rod or a pendulum, this rod should suffer neither fracture nor extension. Furthermore, the bodies concerned should remain at the same distance from one another. The second motion ought to be such that if it alone were impressed, the rod, or more generally, the system, would remain in equilibrium. This condition of the rigidity of the rod and the condition of equilibrium will always yield all the equations necessary to find, for each body, the direction and the magnitude of one of the compound motions and, thereby, the direction and the value of the other.

I believe that I can state that there is no *dynamical* problem that cannot be solved easily and like child's play by means of this principle, or at least that cannot be easily reduced to an equation. This latter, after all, is all that can be expected of *Dynamics* since the resolution or the integration of the equation afterwards is a matter of pure analysis. Conviction of what I have here advanced will come from reading the different problems in my treatise on *Dynamics*. I have chosen the most difficult ones that I could and I think that I have resolved them as simply and as directly as the questions permit. Since the publication of my treatise on *Dynamics*, in 1743, I have frequently had the occasion to apply the principle to such various matters as the problem of the motion of fluids in containers of different shapes (*see my*

treatise on the equilibrium and motion of fluids, 1744), the
oscillations of a fluid that covers a spherical surface (*see my
researches on winds, 1746*), the theory of the precession of the
equinoxes and of the mutation of the axis of the Earth in 1749,
the resistance of fluids in 1752, and to other problems of this
kind. I have always found this principle to be extremely easy
and fecund. I dare to say that I speak of it without bias, as I
would of the discovery of someone else, and that I could produce
authentic and weighty testimonials on its behalf. It seems to me
that this principle, in effect, reduces all the problems of the
motion of bodies to the consideration of the simplest case, equilibrium. *See* EQUILIBRIUM. It is not based on any bad or obscure
metaphysics; it only considers in problems of motion what is
really there, that is, the space traversed and the time spent in
traversing it. It makes no use of actions or of forces nor, in a
word, of any of those secondary principles which can be good in
themselves and sometimes useful to shorten or facilitate solutions, but which can never serve as basic principles since they
are founded upon metaphysical ideas which are never clear.

OSCILLATION, s.f. *term in Mechanics*, which means the same as
vibration; that is to say, the motion of a pendulum in descending
and in rising or, to put it another way, its descent and following
rise taken together.
     The *axis of oscillation* is a straight line parallel to the
horizon which passes, or which is supposed to pass, through the
center or fixed point around which the pendulum oscillates, and
which is perpendicular to the plane in which it oscillates. See
AXIS.
     If a simple pendulum is suspended between two half cycloids
the diameters of whose generating circles are equal to half the
length of the pendulum string, all the oscillations of this pendulum, large and small, will be isochronic, that is, accomplished
in equal times. See CYCLOID and ISOCRONE.
     The time of a complete *oscillation* in an arc or any cycloid
is to the time of perpendicular descent along the diameter of the
generating circle as the circumference of the circle is to the
diameter.
     If two pendula describe similar arcs, the times of their
oscillations will be to each other as the ratio of half their
lengths.
     The number of isochronic *oscillations* made by two pendula in
the same time are to each other inversely as the time of each
oscillation taken separately.
     The laws governing the motion and oscillations of a simple
pendulum (one composed of a single, small weight, A, that can be
regarded as a point, and a rod or string, CA (Fig. 36, Mechan.)
are given at some length in the *article*, PENDULE. The weight or
mass of such a pendulum can be considered as vanishing.
     It is much more difficult to determine the laws of a compound
pendulum, that is, the *oscillations* of a rod BA (fig. 22) that
may be regarded as without weight or mass, and that is loaded
with many weights, D, F, H, B. It is obvious that this rod will
not oscillate in the same way as one attached to only one weight,

such as B, for example. For, let us suppose that there is only
one weight, B, then this weight will tend to describe the small
line, BN, at the first instant: now, if there are other weights
at H, F, D, these weights will tend to de-
scribe the lines HM, FL, DK equal to BN in   [D'Alembert provides no dia-
the same instant so that the portion DB of   gram. The reader may wish
the rod ought to be in KN and, consequently, to provide his own.]
AD will be in AK. Now this cannot happen un-
less the rod ADB is broken at D. Since the
rod was assumed to be rigid, it is impossible
that the weights B, H, F, D can describe the
lines BN, HM, FL, DK, etc., but it is necessary that these weights describe the lines BC,
HI, FG, DE which are such that the rod ADB
always preserves itself, without bending, as
a straight line AEC. It is possible to conceive a simple pendulum of a certain length,
which oscillates in the same time that the
compound pendulum ADB does. Thus the difficulty is reduced to finding the length of
this simple pendulum and to find the length
of this simple pendulum is the same as what
the Geometers call *to find the center of
oscillation*.

    The celebrated Mr. Huyghens was the first to resolve this
problem in his excellent work, *De horologio oscillatorio*. But
the method that he used to resolve it, although good and exact,
contained some difficulties.

    The whole doctrine of this great geometer on the center of
oscillation is based on the following hypothesis: that the common
center of gravity of many bodies ought to rise to the same height
from which it fell, whether the bodies be united or separate from
one another in rising, provided that they each begin to rise with
the speed acquired in falling. See, CENTER OF GRAVITY.

    This hypothesis has been denied by a few authors and regarded
by others as very doubtful. Even those who agree with it cannot
help but admit that it would be foolhardy to admit it without
proof in a science in which everything should be demonstrated.

    Since their time, this principle has been demonstrated by
many geometers and it turns out to be nothing else than the famous
principle otherwise known as the *conservation of living forces*,
which geometers have since used with so much success in the solution of problems of dynamics. See DYNAMICS AND LIVING FORCES.

    However, since Mr. Huyghens' principle appeared uncertain
and indirect to many geometers, M. Jacques Bernoulli, professor
of mathematics at Basel who died in 1705, sought a solution to
the problem that it involved. He found one that was simple
enough, drawn from the law of the lever, and published it in the
memoirs of the Academy of Sciences of Paris in 1703. After his
death, his brother John Bernoulli published another solution to
the same problem in the memoirs of the same academy in 1714 that
was even easier and simpler. We should not neglect to mention
that, about the same time, Mr. Taylor, the celebrated English
geometer, found a solution much like that of Mr. Bernoulli and

presented it in his book entitled, *Methodus incrementorum*. This led to a dispute between the two geometers in which each accused the other of plagiarism. The various documents in this dispute are published in the acts of Leipzig of 1716 and in the works of Mr. Bernoulli, published at Lausanne in-4°, at Lausanne in 1743. Leaving this aside, here is the precis of the theory of Mr. Bernoulli. It consists, in general, in finding first what the gravity of a simple pendulum of the same length as a compound pendulum should be so that the two pendula have the same period of *oscillation*. For this condition to be fulfilled, the *moment* of the two pendula must be the same. Then, Mr. Bernoulli substitutes for this simple pendulum of known length and of a given weight, another simple pendulum moved solely by natural gravity, and he then easily finds, by a simple proportion, the length of this new pendulum required to give vibrations of the same period as the other.

Although Mr. Bernoulli's solution is simple enough, it can even be made more simple, just by using his own principle, as I demonstrated in my treatise on dynamics, Bk. II, chap. iii, probl. 1. There I also gave another extremely simple method for resolving this problem. Here is an idea of this method.

It is obvious that the bodies B, H, F, D, being unable to describe the lines BN, HM, FL, DK, describe the lines BC, HI, FG, DE, which are to each other as the distances AB, AH, AF, AD to the point of suspension A. From this it follows that the whole difficulty is reduced to finding one of these lines like BC. Now, instead of supposing that the bodies B, H, F, D, tend to move with the speeds BN, HM, FL, DK, one can suppose that they tend to move with speeds BC − CN, HI − IM, FG + GL, DE + EK, which amounts to the same thing. Now, of these speeds, there exists really only BC, HI, FG, DE, then it follows that if the bodies B, H, F, D, moved only with the speeds −CN, −IM, GL, EK, then the rod AB would remain at rest. See DYNAMICS. Thus, from the law of the lever, one will have −B × CN × AB − H × IM × AH + F × GL × AF + D × EK × AD = 0. In this equation there is only one unknown since if we suppose that BC is given, then all the other quantities follow. Thus from this equation we can evaluate BC and, by the ratio of BC to EN one can find the ratio of the speed of the compound pendulum to that of a simple pendulum of length BA. From this it follows that one can easily find the length of the simple pendulum that is isochronous with the compound pendulum by looking for a pendulum whose length is to AC as BN is to BC. See on this my treatise on dynamics, Bk. II, Chap. iii, probl. 1. You will find there other interesting remarks on the problem involved here.

[Again, there is no diagram in the text. The reader may use this space for one.]

The *center of oscillation* of a pendulum is, thus, properly speaking, following what we have just said here, a certain point in this pendulum, extended if necessary, which oscillates as if this point alone and isolated were suspended at the distance at which it is from the point of suspension.

Or, alternatively, it is a point such that if one supposes that all the gravity of the compound pendulum were gathered there, these different *oscillations* would occur in the same time as before.

Thus the distance from this point to the point of suspension is equal, as we have just said, to the length of the simple pendulum whose *oscillations* would be isochronous with that of the suspended body. See CENTER.

FORCE VIVE, or FORCE OF BODIES IN MOTION. This is a term imagined by Leibnitz to distinguish the *force* of a body actually in motion from the force of a body that just tends to move without moving. This latter requires an explanation at some length.

Let us suppose, says Leibnitz, a heavy body lying on a horizontal plane. This body makes an effort to descend but this effort is always blocked by the resistance of the plane so that it is reduced to a simple tendency to move. Mr. Leibnitz calls this *force* and others of the same nature, *dead forces*.

Now let us imagine, adds the same philosopher, a heavy body that is thrown up from below and which, in rising, is constantly slowed by the effect of its weight until its *force* is completely lost. This will happen when it has risen to the highest point to which it can go. It is obvious that the *force* of this body is destroyed by degrees and consumes itself in its passage. Mr. Leibnitz calls this latter *force*, *living force*, to distinguish it from the first which is born and dies at the same instant. In general, he calls *living force* the *force* of a body which moves in a motion that is continually retarded and slowed by obstacles until the motion is destroyed after having been successively diminished by insensible degrees. Mr. Leibnitz agrees with common opinion that the dead *force* is equal to the product of the mass and the *virtual* velocity, that is to say the velocity with which the body tends to move. Thus in order that two bodies that strike one another or are drawn directly to one another can come to equilibrium, it is necessary that the product of the mass and the *virtual* velocity be the same for one and the other. Now, in this case, the *force* of each of these two bodies is a dead *force* since it is stopped suddenly and entirely by contrary *force*. Therefore, in this case, the product of the mass by the velocity ought to represent the *force*. But Mr. Leibnitz argues that the *living force* ought to be measured in another way and that it is as the product of the mass and the square of the velocity. A body which has a certain *force* when it moves with a given velocity will, then, have a *force* four times as great if it moves with twice this velocity, nine times as great if it moves with triple the velocity, etc. Therefore, if the velocities are successively 1, 2, 3, 4 etc., the *force* will be as 1, 4, 9, 16, etc., or as the squares of the numbers 1, 2, 3, 4: whereas if this body were not really in motion but only tended to move with the velocities 1, 2, 3, 4, etc., the force then being only a dead *force*, would be as 1, 2, 3, 4, etc.

In the system of those opposed to the doctrine of *living*

forces, the force of the body in motion is always proportional to what is called the *quantity of motion*, that is, to the product of the mass of the body and the velocity instead of the product of the quantity of motion and the velocity as in the other system.

To reduce this question to its simplest terms, it is necessary to know if the *force* of a body with a certain velocity becomes double or quadruple when the velocity is doubled. All students of Mechanics up to Mr. Leibnitz believed that it was simply doubled. This great philosopher was the first to maintain that it was quadruple and he proved it in the following fashion. The *force* of a body can only be measured by its effects and by the obstacles that it can overcome. Now if a heavy body be thrown upwards with a certain velocity so that it rises to a height of fifteen feet, it ought, according to everyone, rise to 60 feet if it be thrown with a velocity double the first, see ACCELERATION. In this case, it has, then, four times the effect and overcomes four times the resistance. Its *force*, therefore, is four times the first. Jean Bernoulli added a large number of other proofs to this one of Leibnitz in his *Discourse on the laws of the Communication of Motion*, published in 1726 and joined to the general collection of his works. He showed that a body that compressed a spring with a certain velocity could compress equally four springs similar to the first when its velocity was doubled, nine springs with triple the velocity etc. Mr. Bernoulli strengthened this argument in favor of *living forces* by other very curious and interesting observations which we will have occasion to notice below in the article on the CONSERVATION OF LIVING FORCES. At this time, a kind of schism between scientists on the measure of *forces* occurred.

The main response that has been made to the objections of the partisans of *living forces* (See the *Memoirs of the academy* of *1728*) consists in reducing decelerated motion to uniform motion and maintaining that in this case the *force* is proportional simply to the velocity. It is argued that a body which traverses fifteen feet upwards will traverse sixty feet if its velocity is doubled but that it will travel these sixty feet in a time that is double that of the first motion. If its motion were uniform, it would traverse twice 120 feet in the same time, see ACCELERATION. Now in the case where it travels fifteen feet in uniformly decelerated motion, it would travel thirty feet in the same time and sixty feet in twice the time with uniform motion. The effects are, therefore, as 120 to 60 or 2 to 1 and consequently the *force* in the first case is only double the other, not four times it. Thus, some conclude, a heavy body traverses four times the space with a double velocity, but it does it in twice the time and that is equivalent to a double force, not a quadruple one. The space must be divided by the time, it is argued, in order to arrive at the effect to which the *force* is proportional and not simply make the *force* proportional to the space traversed. The defenders of *living forces* respond to this by saying that the nature of a greater *force* is that it lasts for a longer time and that, therefore, it is not surprising that a heavy body which traverses four times as much space does so in double the time. The real effect of the *force* is to make the body traverse four times as much space.

The amount of time involved is irrelevant because the amount of time involved is the result of the greater or lesser magnitude of the force. It is, therefore, not true to say, as their adversaries do, that the *force* in a given situation is that much smaller, all other things being equal, as the time is greater. Rather, it is infinitely more natural to believe that it is that much greater as it takes more time to be consumed.

For the rest, it is well to remark that in order to suppose the *force* proportional to the square of the velocity, it is not necessary, as the partisans of *living forces* say, that this *force* consume itself really and actually in acting; it suffices to imagine that it can be consumed and annihilated, little by little by infinitely small degrees. In a body moved uniformly, the *force* is no less proportional to the square of the velocity, according to these philosophers, even though this *force* remains always the same, because if this *force* acted against resistance which lessened it by degrees, its effect would then be as the square of the velocity.

We refer our readers to what has been written for and against *living forces* in the *Memoirs of the Academy, 1728*, in those of Petersburg, Vol. I, and in other works. But instead of treating everything that has been said on the question, it will perhaps not be useless to present here in succinct form the principles that can serve to resolve it.

When one speaks of the *force* of moving bodies, either one does not have a precise idea of the word used, or one can only understand by it the property that bodies have of moving, overcoming resistances that they meet or resisting other bodies. It is not, therefore, by the space that a body traverses uniformly nor by the time that it takes to traverse it, nor, finally, by the simple, sole and abstract consideration of its mass and its velocity that one ought to estimate its *force*. It is only by the obstacles that a body meets and by the resistance offered by these obstacles that force can be measured. The greater an obstacle that a body can overcome or which it can resist, the greater one can say is its *force*, provided that, without wishing to represent by this word some hypothetical thing that resides in the body, one only uses it as a short method of expressing a fact. It is like saying that a body has twice as much velocity as another instead of saying that it traverses twice as much space in the same time, without supposing that this word, *velocity*, represents something inherent in the body.

This being understood, it is clear that one can oppose three kinds of obstacles to bodies: absolutely invincible obstacles that immediately destroy its motion, whatever it may be; obstacles that have just sufficient resistance to stop the body and which do so in an instant, this being the case of equilibrium; and finally, obstacles that destroy its motion little by little, this being the case with retarded motion. Since invincible obstacles destroy equally all kinds of motion, they cannot be used to estimate *force*. Only in equilibrium and retarded motion can this be done. Now everyone agrees that there is equilibrium between two bodies when the products of their masses by their virtual velocities, that is, by the velocities with which they tend to move, are equal one to the other. Thus, in equilibrium, the product of the mass by the velocity, or what amounts to the same thing, the quantity of motion can represent *force*. Everyone also agrees that in regarded motion, the number of obstacles conquered is as the square of the velocity so that a body that has compressed a spring, for example, with a certain velocity will be able to compress four springs with double the velocity, not two, and nine with triple the velocity, etc. From this fact, the partisans of *living forces* conclude that the *force* of the bodies that are actually in motion is, in general, as the product of the mass by the square of the velocity. Now what confusion must there be if the measure of *forces* is different in equilibrium and in retarded motion? After all, if one wishes to reason with clear ideas, one ought to understand by the word *force* only the effect produced in overcoming or resisting an obstacle. It must, however, be admitted that the opinion of those who regard *force* as the product of the mass and the velocity is applicable not only in the case of equilibrium but also in that of retarded motion if, in this latter case, one measures the *force*, not by the absolute quantity of obstacles, but by the sum of the resistances of these obstacles. This sum of resistances is proportional to the quantity of motion since, according to the general view, the quantity of motion that the body loses at each instant is proportional to the product of the resistance by the infinitely small duration of the instant, and that the sum of these products is obviously the total resistance. The whole difficulty reduces, therefore, to finding out if one ought to measure the *force* by the absolute quantity of the obstacles or by the sum of their resistances. It seems to me more natural to measure the *force* by this latter method for an obstacle is an obstacle only insofar as it resists, and the obstacle, speaking precisely, is the sum of the resistances. Moreover, in estimating the *force* in this manner, one has the advantage of having a common measure for both equilibrium and retarded motion. Nevertheless, since we only have a distinct and precise idea of the word *force* in restricting this word to the expression of an effect, I believe that one ought to leave everyone his own master in choosing how he will decide on the above. The whole question is really only a metaphysical one that is futile and that will involve us in a dispute over words that is no longer worthy of occupying Philosophers.

3.   *Professor Hankins of the University of Washington is an*
authority on 18th century mechanics and particularly on the work
of d'Alembert. In this article* he lays out the basic issues be-
hind the attempt in the 18th century to distinguish between various
kinds of "force" in mechanics and to provide a rational mechanics
free of metaphysical obfuscations.

    The history of science contains many famous quarrels and
polemics, some dealing with fundamental problems and others arising from personality conflicts and squabbles over priority. All
fields of science have had their share of controversy, but one
would expect to find less of it in those "exact" sciences, such
as mechanics, that are highly mathematical and also subject to
experimental demonstration. This has not been the case, of
course. The concepts used in mechanics are abstract and not at
all obvious. The whole history of mechanics has been a series of
attempts to clarify these concepts and to demonstrate their validity, and arguments between opposing schools of thought have been
frequent and often acrimonious. Of all these quarrels, the most
famous was the *vis viva* controversy which began with Leibniz'
publication of his "Brief Demonstration of a Notable Error of
Descartes" in 1686 and ended at some undetermined date in the
eighteenth or possibly even the nineteenth century. Like many
such controversies it was never actually resolved. The enthusiasm of the combatants subsided either from fatigue, or more likely

*From ISIS, *56* (1965), pp. 281-97.

from the realization that they had been talking past each other for over fifty years and were in disagreement over basic suppositions about the nature of force and matter.

Of course we can explain the controversy very easily today. The concept of the "force of a body in motion" which taxed the scientific minds of the seventeenth and eighteenth centuries is ambiguous; it can refer either to the momentum or to the energy of a moving body and both of these quantities are conserved. Leibniz was searching for some active principle that was conserved and kept the universe from "running down" and slowly coming to a halt. This he found in the *vis viva* of matter which he measured by the product of the mass and the square of the velocity. Descartes, on the other hand, had insisted that the "quantity of motion," the product of mass and the simple speed, was the quantity which was conserved. Thus Leibniz came close to stating the law of conservation of energy in mechanics while Descartes came close to stating the law of conservation of momentum. It was very soon pointed out by Huygens and others that momentum is conserved only when it is considered as a vector quantity, and with this one correction the conservation of momentum was accepted by both sides in the dispute. *Vis viva* was a different matter, however. In certain ideal situations such as in perfectly elastic collisions, *vis viva* is definitely conserved, but it is not clear whether *vis viva* is only a convenient mathematical expression useful for certain kinds of problems or a fundamental physical concept of great significance.

There were actually two different points at issue in the controversy. The first had to do with the effects produced by a moving body when it is stopped by a collision or by gravity; the other was the problem of conservation. What is the correct measure of the "force of a body in motion"; and does the total amount of *vis viva* in the universe awlays remain the same? These questions were the subject matter of the controversy and the best scientific minds of the eighteenth century treated them with only limited success.

In the first years of the controversy. Leibniz found his foes among the Cartesians, but with the publication of the Leibniz-Clarke correspondence in 1717 the controversy was revived and the Newtonians joined the Cartesians in combating *vis viva*. Several prominent Continental scientists went over to the side of *vis viva* in the 1720's and this brought interest in the problem to a higher pitch. Most significant among these were Jean Bernoulli and William 'sGravesande, both of whom apparently "deserted" to the opposition. The bitterest polemic appeared in 1728 and was the work of Samuel Clarke, who accused his opponents of attempting to besmirch the name of the great Sir Isaac Newton.

During the 1740's the controversy died down and caused little excitement after the middle of the century. Usually credit is given to Jean d'Alembert for having resolved the controversy in his *Traité de dynamique* published in 1743, but d'Alembert's discussion hardly provides an obvious solution to the problem. Although he dismissed the argument as a mere "dispute of words too undignified to occupy the philosophers any longer," his explanation of this indignity is confused and obscure. Also d'Alembert

was not the first to call the *vis viva* controversy a "dispute of
words." Both 'sGravesande and Roger Boscovich said the same
thing; and their explanations were more valuable than d'Alembert's
although they received less attention.

Modern historians have realized that the *vis viva* controversy
was much more than a dispute of words. It is hard to understand
how men of such talent as Leibniz, Newton, and Jean Bernoulli
could have argued for fifty years over semantics alone. There
were important philosophical problems involved, especially the
meaning of the word "force," a particularly elusive concept, and
the nature of matter. The historian is also called upon to explain why conservation of energy did not gain acceptance until
150 years after it had been stated as a general law by Leibniz.
In attempting to shed some light on these questions I have chosen
to discuss the work of d'Alembert, 'sGravesande, and Boscovich
and have attempted to discover the obstacles to their understanding of the problems involved.

*   *   *

In his *Traité de dynamique*, d'Alembert stated that the force
of colliding bodies should be measured proportional to the simple
velocity when they are in "equilibrium"--that is, when their momenta are equal in magnitude and opposite in direction--since it
seemed intuitively clear to him that the two bodies have the same
"force of motion" in this case. If the collision were inelastic,
each body in motion would completely destroy the motion of the
other. On the other hand "everyone agrees that in retarded motion, the number of obstacles overcome is as the square of the
velocity." This statement seems strange to us. It is particularly difficult to understand what d'Alembert meant by "the number of obstacles to overcome." The phrase is somewhat clarified
if one looks back through the history of the *vis viva* controversy.
As an example of the number of obstacles overcome, d'Alembert
suggested the number of similar springs that might be closed by
an object in motion colliding with them one after the other or
all at once. This probably refers to Bernoulli's thought experiments in his *Discours sur les loix de la communication du mouve-
ment* (1724) where Bernoulli showed that the number of springs
compressed by a moving ball is proportional to the square of its
velocity. Nevertheless, we must admit that "the number of obstacles overcome" is a very ambiguous measure of "forces" and does
not carry the explanation beyond that already given by Bernoulli.

D'Alembert did claim that the "force of motion" could only
be measured by the effect produced by the moving body and that
several different effects can be measured. As a result the "force
of motion" must be an ambiguous term. But d'Alembert qualified
his conclusion by showing a marked preference for momentum over
vis viva. In retarded motion the "total resistance" to the moving
body is best measured by the sum of the resisting forces multiplied by the infinitesimal intervals of time that they are applied
to the moving body. The "sum of the resistances" is proportional
to the change in momentum ($\int F\ dt = \int m\ dv$). D'Alembert believed
this was a better measure than the "number of obstacles overcome"
since it is the "sum of the resistances" and not the number of

obstacles that stops the moving body.

Two fundamental ideas in d'Alembert's philosophy of mechanics caused him to declare the *vis viva* controversy a dispute of words and, at the same time, to prefer the concept of momentum to that of *vis viva*. In the first place, d'Alembert rejected the concept of force altogether in his mechanics. He claimed that the only mechanical phenomena observed in the world are matter and its motion. Forces are the "obscure and metaphysical" inventions of philosophers:

> All we see distinctly in the movement of a body is that it crosses a certain space and that it employs a certain time to cross it. It is from this idea alone that one should draw all the principles of mechanics when one wishes to demonstrate them in a distinct and precise manner; thus it is not surprising that I have kept away from *motive causes* to consider only the motions they produce . . . we have no precise and distinct idea of the word force unless we restrict this term to express an effect . . . the question of the measure of forces is entirely useless in mechanics and even without any real object.

Therefore the "force of a body in motion" had no meaning for d'Alembert. By "force" we refer only to the effect that a body produces when it collides with some other object, and this effect depends on the object struck as well as the moving object. If different "effects" are measured, one is bound to get different expressions for the causes producing those effects, and to this extent the controversy over the force of motion is a semantic quibble. But d'Alembert did not explain satisfactorily why different measures are obtained in different circumstances, and his statement that both methods are valid because both give the correct answer is certainly not a complete solution to the problem.

D'Alembert also preferred momentum to *vis viva* because in his general system of mechanics momentum is conserved while *vis viva* is not. He believed that the elements of matter consist of small, hard, Newtonian particles. Whenever perfectly "hard" particles collide there must be an instantaneous change in velocity. Moreover "hard" particles do not rebound because they have no "springiness"; all relative motion between them ceases immediately upon collision. Momentum is conserved in all cases, of course, but not *vis viva* since energy is lost in the case of inelastic impact. Only in those problems where "hard" particles change their velocities gradually in a continuous fashion will the conservation of *vis viva* hold and so d'Alembert limits its use to this particular case. It is a valuable mathematical device for solving a special class of problems, but it cannot be a fundamental and general law of mechanics.

In the development of his mechanics d'Alembert consistently followed his belief that the laws of dynamics can be derived from purely geometrical considerations of impenetrable extension. Since he denied the existence of forces, he could only explain problems in statics by the equilibrium between "virtual momenta." Two bodies are in equilibrium when the products of their masses and "virtual velocities" are equal in magnitude and opposite in direction. Therefore d'Alembert tried to use the dynamic concept of momentum in treating equilibrium conditions of simple machines, and a confusion between energy and momentum was the inevitable result. He was guilty of this very elementary error in his article "Perpétuel" for the *Encyclopédie*. The multiplication of force in a machine cannot produce perpetual motion because "Whatever is gained in power [puissance] is lost in time; so that the quantity of movement [that is, the momentum] remains always the same . . . thus the virtual quantities of movement of these two bodies will be the same and consequently there should be nothing surprising in their equilibrium." This is a ghastly error. One might hope that d'Alembert wrote his article in a hurry and that he actually knew better than to make such an elementary slip, but since he never wrote a treatise on simple machines, it is difficult to find other statements to compare with this one. Several of his close associates did write such treatises, however, and they committed the same error with regularity.

The Abbé Charles Bossut went to great lengths to describe what he meant by a moving force. It is measured by the product of the mass and the velocity of the moving body.

> Now we have a fixed and determined moving force [momentum] which can be used to overcome a certain resistance, or what amounts to the same thing, to elevate a certain load [fardeau]. The quantity of movement will always be the same whatever means are employed to transmit it to the load being treated. Vainly we multiply the levers and wheels of our machine. . . . If they increase the exertion [fardeau] they diminish its velocity in the same ratio; if, on the contrary, they increase the velocity, it is at the expense of the mass.

Notice the indiscriminate use of weight and mass. Bossut confused power (Fv) and momentum (mv) at a place where he was striving for precision and clarity in his textbook. No inadvertence this time--he just did not understand the difference between work and momentum.

Another of d'Alembert's friends at the Academy, Étienne Bezout, an expert on applied mechanics and author of a textbook for the French military academies, involved himself in even greater absurdities. Bezout attempted to work out a complete theory of machines which would allow comparison of the "work" done by different agents, for example, a man turning a crank and a horse walking on a treadmill. According to Bezout the effort of a man supporting a weight is "equal to the quantity of movement which results from the mass of the body multiplied by the velocity that the weight gives it in an instant; it is clear, however, that if this man were capable of only this effort, the equilibrium would last only an instant; because at the second instant the weight renews the action destroyed in the first instant." At each instant momentum is "absorbed" by the weight and this momentum must be provided by the man supporting it. Thus the effort of the man is measured by the "virtual momentum" transferred to the weight. This turns out to be what we now call impulse, or $\int F\,dt = \int d(mv)$; the effort is equal to the force multiplied by the time during which that force is exerted. In the following section Bezout applies this measure to simple machines. He loses himself in a maze of measurements and calculations which obscure the fact that according to his measure of effort, the worker is accomplishing just as much by leaning on the handle of his machine as when he turns it to lift a heavy weight! He measures the input of the machine by impulse ($F\,dt$) rather than by work ($F\,dx$), which leads him to many absurd conclusions. Far from removing the clouds of confusion from the *vis viva* controversy, d'Alembert's rational mechanics led many of his successors astray. He made a genuine contribution when he pointed out that it was futile to argue about the force of a moving body without considering the effects that it could produce, but his assumption of perfectly hard particles composing matter and his rejection of forces led to even further confusion.

But if d'Alembert was unable to resolve the *vis viva* controversy, we may ask what was required in the way of explanation that he did not provide. One might first ask for correct equations relating impulse to momentum and work to kinetic energy; but these expressions were available very early and recognized by the disputants in the controversy as valid laws of motion. The expression $F\,dx = mv\,dv$ was familiar to Varignon, Hermann, Euler, Bernoulli and d'Alembert. The expression $F\,dt = m\,dv$ was even more common. Why, then, was there a controversy? The only answer can be that the mathematical expressions by themselves were not sufficient to remove the existing confusions.

Another possible approach was the direct measurement of the effects of collision to discover how the changes of motion are actually produced. 'sGravesande performed the most extensive experiments on collision and his results influenced many commentators on the controversy, including d'Alembert. His favorite demonstration was to let heavy balls or cylinders fall on a soft material such as clay or wax and then compare the depressions produced. If they were identical, it could be assumed that the falling objects had struck the clay surface with the same "force." Similar experiments had been performed earlier by Mariotte and Poleni; but 'sGravesande took a more active part in the controversy than either of them. In 1720 he published his enormously successful *Mathematical Elements of Natural Philosophy*. After praising this excellent exposition of Newton's philosophy, the English mathematicians were dismayed to see 'sGravesande turn to defend Leibniz' theory of *vis viva* in an article entitled "Essai d'une nouvelle théorie sur le choc des corps," which appeared in 1722 in the *Journal littéraire de la Haye*, a journal that 'sGravesande had founded in 1713. In his *Mathematical Elements* of 1720, 'sGravesande had described how the "actions of powers" to overcome obstacles are to be measured. "When both the spaces run through and the intensities are different, the actions of the powers are to one another in a ratio compounded of the intensities and the spaces gone through." He immediately applied this law to simple machines, but did not use it in his experiments on collision. Although 'sGravesande had not yet accepted Leibniz' measure of the force of motion, he had stated categorically by 1720 that the "actions of powers" are to be measured by the products of the impressed forces and the *distances* traversed.

The crucial experiment which caused 'sGravesande to change his mind and join the supporters of *vis viva* was essentially the same as that performed by Poleni. He let bodies of different mass but of the same shape fall on clay. The imprints were found to be the same when the heights of fall were in inverse proportion to the masses. By Galileo's law of free fall, the heights of fall were in proportion to the squares of the velocities. Therefore the imprints in the clay were identical when the balls striking the clay had the same *vis viva*. If we can believe 'sGravesande's biographer, Jean Allamand, who described this experiment, 'sGravesande said, "Ah, c'est moi qui me suis trompé," and immediately began a series of experiments to clarify his new position.

'sGravesande realized earlier than d'Alembert that the term, "force of motion" was ambiguous since the only real measures of this "force" are the effects that it can produce. In a collision, however, there are measurable effects and the "force of motion" should have real meaning.

> As regards the term "force," I will try to expose the ambiguity of this word, as well as in the word "movement"; it will be seen that there is more misunderstanding than real difference among those who argue about the measure of force and . . . [then] I will pass on to the problem of impact where it will be seen that what was before only a *dispute of words* [italics mine] now becomes a dispute about real things.

In 1722, 'sGravesande described one very interesting experiment that put him on the track of the correct explanation. When two inelastic spheres moving in opposite directions collide, all motion will be destroyed in the impact if their masses are inversely proportional to their velocities. Since the momenta of the spheres are equal in magnitude and opposite in sign, they add up to zero and the conservation of momentum holds. But if the "forces of motion" of the two spheres are measured not by the momentum, but by the mass times the square of the velocity, one has to admit that they collide with different "forces." The ball with the smaller mass and greater velocity has a larger *vis viva;* and yet this case seems to be an obvious example of equal "forces" destroying each other. The "effect" observed is clearly proportional to the momentum and not to the *vis viva* of the colliding balls. But 'sGravesande was able to demonstrate that the "forces" are indeed different by allowing two similar copper balls of unequal masses to strike a fixed clay ball. The apparatus was arranged so that the balls struck the clay with the same momentum in each case; but the lighter ball with the higher velocity made a much deeper impression in the clay. By a series of similar experiments, he showed that two different effects can be measured in an inelastic collision--the changes in the velocities of the bodies and the compressions of the colliding bodies--and that one of these effects is proportional to the simple velocity, while the other is proportional to the square of the velocity. Therefore

he distinguished between the "force" and the "inertia" of objects
in collision: ". . . in order for two unequal bodies to remain
at rest after a collision, their forces must necessarily be unequal. This experiment can be explained by assuming that 'force'
and 'inertia' are different from each other; and this experiment
clearly shows the distinction." "Force" should be measured by
the compressions of the colliding bodies and "inertia" should be
measured by the changes in their velocities. 'sGravesande was
unwilling to discard either measure of the "force of motion" and
said that the law of equality between action and reaction holds
for *two* actions and *two* reactions. Mme. du Châtelet described
this experiment and 'sGravesande's analysis very fully in her
Institutions de physique, since it allowed her to defend what
appeared to be the weakest point in the theory of *vis viva*.

Another puzzling theoretical problem that was used to argue
against *vis viva* concerned accelerated motions. If an object is
accelerated uniformly by a constant force, equal amounts of momentum are produced in successive equal intervals of time. But the
same is not true for the *vis viva*. If the "force of motion" is
measured by the product of the mass and the square of the velocity, the amount of "force" required to produce any increase in
velocity depends on the initial velocity of the moving body. For
example, a body gains more *vis viva* in being accelerated from 10
to 15 feet/second than in being accelerated from 5 to 10 feet/
second, even though the applied force and the time of acceleration is the same in both cases. This result appears paradoxical
at first and it provided one of the major criticisms of the *vis
viva* theory. Newton insisted that this result alone invalidated
the theory of *vis viva*. He argued that since the "force of motion" of a falling body is produced by its weight, increasing
amounts of "force" can be produced in successive intervals only
if the weight increases proportionately, which is absurd.

In attempting to explain the paradox, 'sGravesande analyzed
the loss of "force" in inelastic collisions. In this case more
vis viva is lost in the first moments of deceleration than in the
later moments, even though the decelerating force remains uniform.
'sGravesande's explanation was written in answer to criticisms by
the Swiss mathematician Calandrin. In 1733 an extract from
Poleni's *Epistolae mathematicae* was published in the *Journal his-
torique de la république des lettres*. Poleni had dropped balls
onto tallow to compare impacts and had shown that the "force of
motion" is proportional to the square of the velocity—essentially
the same experiment that 'sGravesande had performed. In the same
volume Calandrin published an anonymous article countering Poleni's interpretation. He analyzed the problem in the following
way. If a cylinder strikes a clay surface, the resistance of the
clay will always be the same because the same area is in contact
with the cylinder at all times. Since the resistance is constant,
equal amounts of "force" should be consumed in equal units of
time. Therefore "the times during which two forces act on tena-
cious material until these forces are destroyed will always be
proportional to these forces." Thus Calandrin insisted that the
"force" lost was proportional to the change in momentum.

'sGravesande replied to Calandrin's article with some mis-

givings. He had been subjected to a scathing attack by Samuel
Clarke five years before, and he was hesitant to involve himself
in any similar polemics. However, he felt called upon to point
out where he differed from Calandrin's analysis of the nature of
forces in a collision. He agreed that if a cylinder strikes a
clay surface, the resistance of the clay should be uniform (which
is incorrect, but this does not affect the argument); but he
denied that equal amounts of "force" are consumed in equal times.
The cylinder is moving faster when it first strikes the clay and
consequently it pushes more clay out of the way during the first
instant than during any later instant. If the resistance of the
clay is likened to a series of strings that are broken by a moving
object, more strings are broken per unit of time while the object
is moving more slowly. "It can be seen that in order to compare
the efforts of two pressures in equal times, it is necessary to
take into account both the pressure and the speed of the points
or surfaces being struck; and it is only by multiplying the intensity of this speed that one is able to determine the effort." In
modern terminology, the "intensity of the pressure" is the force
and the "effort of the pressure" is the power, or the work done
per unit of time. In other words, to get the effect of the "force
of motion," it is not enough to consider the force alone. It is
also necessary to multiply it by the velocity with which the object moves, since the faster it moves, the more obstacles it will
encounter if the resisting medium is uniform. 'sGravesande continues:

> When a cylinder enters into a soft body and loses its
> force, the tenacity of the parts of that body remains the
> same; and since the same surface is acting, it is always
> the same number of parts which resist, and the intensity
> of the pression is always the same, but the speed of the
> surface which presses and is pressed changes at every in-
> stant; as a result the efforts which destroy the force of
> bodies in the equal moments which follow are unequal, and
> proportional to the speeds. Thus they are proportional
> to the distances covered in equal times. Now the sum of
> all the efforts being equal to all the force lost, it
> follows that this force is proportional to the sum of all
> the little spaces covered, that is, which is proportional
> to the square of the velocity.

'sGravesande is saying that the "force of motion" is the "intensity of the pressure" multiplied by the increment of time and by
the velocity, or $pv\ dt$; but $v\ dt = dx$ (the increment of distance
covered in the time dt), so $\int pv\ dt = \int p\ dx = kv^2$. Since 'sGravesande believed that collisions are never instantaneous, but take
place in a continuous manner by gradual deformation of the colliding bodies, he could compare the "effort" of an object in
collision to the "effort" in a simple machine. In a simple machine, a small weight may counterbalance a much heavier weight if
the small weight moves proportionately faster when the machine is
set in motion. In collisions and in simple machines, the velocities of the moving objects during the actions are all-important.
   In the article by Calandrin and in 'sGravesande's reply, the

point of confusion was clearly exposed. 'sGravesande admitted
that when the "tenacity" is constant the decrease in velocity is
proportional to the time. But the "efforts" exerted by the resisting medium are different during different time intervals of
equal duration. However, 'sGravesande was not dogmatic about his
theory. He realized that those who measured the force of motion
in another way were measuring a different thing and he concluded
his article by saying again that the word "force" is ambiguous:
"Let someone give another sense to the word 'force'; let him say
that this other sense is more natural. I do not oppose that; all
I wish to insist on is that what I call force ought to be measured
by the product of the mass and the square of the velocity. By
regarding force in another way, one can admit another measure."

The work of 'sGravesande was largely experimental, but other
scientists attempted to untangle the conflicting points of view
in a more theoretical manner. One of the most interesting studies
of *vis viva* was by the Jesuit scientist Roger Boscovich. Boscovich also claimed that the *vis viva* controversy was a "dispute of
words," and he demonstrated the difference between the effects of
momentum and *vis viva* using a geometrical diagram. His argument
was similar to that given by 'sGravesande. When the force decelerating a moving object is plotted against the time, the area between the curve and the time axis represents the change in momentum produced. But when the force is plotted against distance,
the area represents the change in *vis viva*. Although Boscovich's
geometrical treatment of the problem was significant, his theory
of matter was far more important. The equivocal concept of "force
of motion" was becoming more apparent through the works of d'Alembert, 'sGravesande, and Boscovich himself, but the law of conservation of *vis viva* was still a subject of dispute.

If *vis viva* is always conserved, there can be no perfectly
hard bodies in the universe and all changes in velocity must take
place continuously. Until an acceptable theory of matter excluding the collision of hard particles was available, the conservation of *vis viva* could not become a general theory of mechanics.
The first really satisfactory model permitting the conservation
of *vis viva* was the system of mass points which Boscovich elaborated at great length in his *Philosophiae naturalis theoria*
(1758). It permitted the conservation of *vis viva* in all cases;
yet Boscovich was himself a strong opponent of *vis viva*. He
firmly opposed the idea of any innate force in matter. For him
all forces were "dead" in the Leibnizian sense:

> Indeed it will be sufficiently evident, both from what
> has already been proved as well as from what is to follow,
> that there is nowhere any sign of such living forces, nor
> is this necessary. For all the phenomena of Nature depend
> upon motions and equilibrium, and thus from dead forces
> and the velocities induced by the action of such forces.
> For this reason, in the dissertation *De viribus vivis*,
> which was what led me to this theory thirteen years ago,
> I asserted that there are no living forces in Nature. . . .

Boscovich would have had theological as well as physical reasons
for denying the existence of an active force in matter since such

an interpretation smacks of Spinozism. But in addition to denying
that *vis viva* was an active agent in matter, he also rejected it
as a valid measure of the "force of motion." Although he had
shown in the *De viribus vivis* that the force of motion can be
measured proportional to either the velocity or the square of the
velocity, depending on whether the "pressure" is integrated over
the time or over the distance of application, Boscovich believed
that momentum was the "real" measure of force and that the use of
vis viva was valid only as a method for computation.

The conservation of momentum was clearly understood and accepted by Boscovich: "The quantity of motion in the Universe is
maintained always the same, so long as it is computed in some
given direction in such a way that motion in the opposite direction is considered negative, and the sum of the contrary motions
is subtracted from the sum of the direct motions." This was the
only conservation principle that Boscovich would accept. Leibniz
had felt the necessity for some conservation principle that would
prevent the world from "running down" like a watch in need of an
occasional winding. Conservation of momentum could no longer
satisfy this need when expressed as a vector quantity because
hard bodies in collision can lose all their motion although the
total momentum *does* not change. In writing the *Theoria*, Boscovich
was apparently unconcerned about the possibility of the universe
"running down," and he made no attempt to prove that motion in
his system would never be totally lost. However, he did treat
the closely allied problem of the composition and resolution of
forces. He believed he had caught the defenders of Leibniz in an
error and wrote a rather confused section of the *Theoria* where he
tried to prove that no "force of motion" is contained in a moving
body or transferred to another body by impact. The only forces
are those mutually acting "dead forces" that arise when bodies
collide. Nothing is passed from one body to the next and no
active force or *vis viva* exists in a moving object. He could not
deny that the quantity mv^2 is conserved in elastic collisions,
but he did deny that this quantity represented any real thing.

All Boscovich's demonstrations in the *Theoria* against *vis
viva* involve the collision of gross bodies, and he made no reference to his new theory of matter in these arguments. But when
he turned to the exposition of his theory he unconsciously provided a plausible explanation for the conservation of *vis viva*,
while he vigorously argued at the same time against its existence.
One of the most obvious criticisms of Leibniz' law of the conservation of *vis viva* is the frequency with which it seems to be
violated. *Vis viva* is destroyed in inelastic collisions, but
Leibniz had enough faith in his theory to postulate that the
motion was retained in the parts of the body.

> 'Tis true, their wholes lose [some force] with respect to
> their total motion; but their parts receive it, being
> shaken [internally] by the force of the concourse. And
> therefore loss of force is only in appearance. The forces
> are not destroyed, but scattered among the parts. The
> bodies do not lose their forces; but the case here is the
> same as when men change great money into small.

Since Leibniz did not believe in action at a distance, he assumed that bodies in collision actually make contact; and to avoid the consequences of assuming perfectly hard particles he postulated an "infinitely fluid" matter containing no smallest parts. Boscovich, on the other hand, was led to his system by Leibniz' law of continuity which forbade any discontinuity in the velocity of a body in motion. Therefore, he denied any actual contact between the parts of matter and, as a result, he was able to simplify the meaning of "force." In Boscovich's theory, impact, pressure, gravity, friction, chemical action, light--all were explained by the motion of point masses moving in a force field. Action at a distance was the only force acting in his system.

According to Boscovich all matter is composed of nonextended mass "points." These points exert forces on each other which vary with the distance between them. At very short distances there is a strong force of repulsion which increases to infinity as the points are brought closer together, preventing them from coming into contact. As the distance is increased, the force alternates between repulsion and attraction and finally follows the inverse square law of gravitational attraction for large separations. Boscovich illustrated his theory by his famous curve (Fig. 1). At certain distances where the force changes from repulsion to attraction the mass points will be in stable equilibrium. Boscovich called these distances "points of cohesion" (marked C on the diagram) and he used them to explain cohesion and the structure of matter.

Such a theory provides a perfect explanation of how the motion of bodies in collision can be "absorbed by the little parts." If every body is composed of point masses, when the points are displaced--perhaps by a collision--from their "points of cohesion," they will be subject to a restoring force and will "oscillate about the limit point of cohesion which they had passed through; and this they will do first on this side and then on that, over and over again unless they are disturbed by forces due to other points outside them." In a simple case, Boscovich realized that some external force is necessary to bring an end to the oscillations. In inelastic collisions, he believed that the particles are displaced until they are at new points of cohesion and in this way energy would be stored since the motion would be regained if the particles were to return to their original positions.

In Boscovich's famous curve, the ordinate represents force and the abscissa represents distance (see Fig. 1). If a particle is displaced from a point of cohesion, its change in velocity can easily be determined since the area bound by the curve and the axis is proportional to the square of the velocity. Boscovich stated this fact and derived it using calculus. Between any two limits A and B, the area bound by the curve and the axis taken with regard to sign equals $\int_A p \, dx = \frac{1}{2}mv_B^2 - mv_A^2$. Not only did Boscovich derive this expression for the conservation of potential and kinetic energy; his theory also illustrates it admirably. In any relative motion of two mass points, the points may lose kinetic energy, but when they return to their original positions, this kinetic energy is restored.

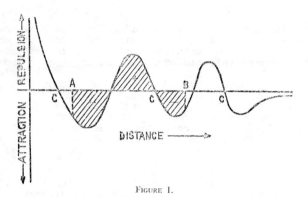

FIGURE 1.

Boscovich even described how potential energy is released in a chemical reaction:

> By a slight motion due to external points approaching close enough to [the material] to be capable of impressing a non-uniform motion on the points of the particles . . . all the points in an extremely short time will cross the limit and then they will fly off from one another with a huge repulsive force and a high velocity. This kind of thing is seen to take place in the sudden explosion of gunpowder, which . . . on contact with the smallest spark goes off almost at once, and with a great repulsive force drives out the ball from the cannon.

It is surprising that Boscovich did not realize how well suited his theory was to explain the conservation of *vis viva*. Although the term *vis viva* originally referred only to the "force" of a moving body, it was well understood that *vis viva* could be "stored" in a compressed spring or in a weight elevated against gravity. Boscovich's own mathematical derivation shows that in his system *vis viva* is always conserved although it is frequently "stored" in the form of potential energy. There is no way in his system that energy can be lost in friction or in the collision of inelastic bodies since the points of matter never come in contact. Possibly he did realize this, but felt that the acceptance of Leibniz' mechanics would require the acceptance of his philosophy of active matter as well. In any case, Boscovich used the square of the velocity as a method for computation, but did not propose any more general conservation law for this quantity.

It was in the explanation of gross phenomena that Boscovich was hampered by his refusal to accept the conservation of *vis viva*. He was hard pressed to explain why mechanical oscillations or chemical reactions ever cease. These are obvious signs of "activity" which disappear slowly and for no apparent reason. Boscovich believed the complex structure of matter could explain this phenomenon. He suggested that his points might be joined together into clusters to form grosser particles similar to the particles postulated by Newton. Using these particles he attempted a Gassendist explanation of the decrease of activity. Particles may be made of points arranged in such an order that the particles thus formed have "hooks."

> In such a way atoms might be formed like spirals . . . by means of atoms of this nature an explanation could be given of a very large number of phenomena, such as the connection of masses by means of hooks inserted into hooks or coils; and in this way also an explanation could be given of the reason why, in the case of two particles of which one has approached the other with a very great velocity, there arises a fresh connection of great strength, that is, one so strong that there is no rebound of the particles from one another.

Such an explanation is merely dodging the question. In Boscovich's theory these spiral atoms are compounds of mass points which have no hooks and the problem always reduces ultimately to one of forces acting at a distance.

His second explanation of decaying oscillations appeared in a description of elastic collisions. After elastic spheres collide, each sphere will return to its original form, then go beyond it, and finally oscillate. Boscovich attempted to explain why this oscillation will die down:

> A tremor or oscillation will be produced, which will be gradually diminished and ultimately be destroyed, partly by the action of external bodies, just as the motion of a pendulum is stopped by the resistance of the air, and partly by the action of less elastic particles which are interspersed, which can gradually break down the oscillation by their friction, and also by contrary motions and a relapse by which they will change their own distribution somewhat.

But these explanations are no better than the hooks and spirals. Certainly friction is impossible between points which never come in contact, and if the oscillation is prevented by particles which "change their positions somewhat," the sphere is no longer elastic.

In his last attempt to explain the loss of motion, Boscovich dealt with fermentation. In chemical reactions the points are set in violent motion "and oscillate backwards and forwards; and in this backward and forward motion being perturbed and rapid, we have a sufficiently clear notion of what fermentation is." To explain the gradual reduction of this violent motion, Boscovich resorted to the same explanations given above and added some new ones.

> The fermentation diminishes gradually, and at length ceases; . . . The irregularity of the particles, from which bodies are formed, and the inequality of the forces, especially contribute to the diminution and final stoppage of the motion. Thus when certain particles, or the whole of them enter cavities in larger particles, or when they insert their hooks into the hooks or openings

of others, these cannot be disentangled, and certain re-
lapses and compressions of the particles happen in a mass
irregularly agitated, which diminish the motion and practically destroy it altogether; and due to this the motion
even in soft bodies can be stopped after loss of shape.
Also the roughness of the particles alone may do much
toward diminishing and finally stopping the motion; just
as the motion in a rough body is stopped by friction.
Impact with external bodies has a great effect, e.g. the
air stops a pendulum. Much may be due to the emission of
particles in all directions, as in evaporation; or when a
body freezes, many igneous particles fly off by the action of the particles of the mass, impress a motion in
the opposite direction on those as they move; and while
those that had increased the oscillation, one after the
other fly off, those that are left are such as were
diminishing these oscillations by internal and external
actions.

Boscovich's reference to the loss of igneous particles is a partial acceptance of the conservation of "activity." As the most
"active" particles leave the reaction the ones remaining have
less activity on the average and the reaction dies down. Unfortunately Boscovich did not pursue this line of reasoning any further and he failed completely to recognize that *vis viva* is never
lost in his system.

In all these explanations, Boscovich made the mistake of
dealing with the particles of matter as if they were gross bodies,
subject to friction, impact, etc. Only his last suggestion concerning the loss of the most active particles is compatible with
his theory. If he had stayed in the realm of points and forces,
he might have been forced to the position of Leibniz and the conservation of energy. We must remember that in Boscovich's system
there is only potential and kinetic energy. He explains light,
heat, electricity, chemical reaction, and mechanical motion all
in terms of forces and points. The question of "transforming"
one kind of energy into another does not arise. The points and
forces reduce all forms of energy or "activity" to one, just as
they reduce all kinds of force to one. We can suppose that if
Boscovich had been on the other side of the *vis viva* controversy,
he would have followed the lead of Leibniz and the dictates of
his own system which point directly to the conservation of energy.

*   *   *

The *vis viva* controversy was clearly more than a case of
misunderstanding. Although the scientists of the eighteenth century were frequently arguing past each other, there were several
important points of disagreement. The most important of these
was the nature of matter. Once perfectly hard inelastic particles
are admitted into physics, the conservation of *vis viva* becomes
impossible, and momentum is the only quantity conserved in collisions. Also the concept of force was sufficiently obscure that
d'Alembert rejected it from his mechanics altogether. Clearly
d'Alembert was not the one to clear up the confusion over *vis*

viva. The experiments of 'sGravesande revealed two different measurable "effects" in inelastic collisions. The changes in motion observed are proportional to the momenta of the colliding bodies, but the flattening of the spheres or the imprints which they make in soft objects are proportional to their *vis viva.* Two different effects are observed and two different things are being measured. The conservation of *vis viva* could be demonstrated theoretically only for idealized mechanical problems of perfectly elastic collisions or pendulums experiencing no friction. Nor was any satisfactory model available for the conservation of energy until Boscovich invented his famous system; and even then, Boscovich did not recognize the significance of *vis viva* in his theory. The law of conservation of energy had to wait until physicists of the nineteenth century discovered energy equivalents in a variety of phenomena and finally established the law on experimental evidence.

4. *Not everyone in the Enlightenment could accept Newtonian physics for the idea of universal attraction smacked too much of occult qualities. Leonhard Euler (1707-1783) was a Swiss mathematician and physicist who clung to the Cartesian system. In his* Letters to a German Princess *he spelled out his ideas in simple and popular form. The work found a large audience, thus guaranteeing the continued influence of Cartesian ideas on the development of science in the 19th century.*

Letter XVII.

Of Light, and the Systems of Descartes and Newton.

Having spoken of the rays of the sun, which are the focus of all the heat and light that we enjoy, you will undoubtedly ask, What are these rays? This is, beyond question, one of the most important inquiries in physics, as from it an infinite number of phenomena is derived. Every thing that respects light, and that renders objects visible, is closely connected with this inquiry. The ancient philosophers seem to have taken little interest in the solution of it. They contented themselves with saying that the sun is endowed with the quality of shining, of giving heat and light. But is it not worth while to inquire, Wherein does this quality consist? Do certain portions, inconceivably small, of the sun himself, or of his substance, come down to us? Or, is the transmission similar to the sound of a bell, which the ear receives? though no part of the substance of the bell be separated from it--as I observed in explaining the propagation and perception of sound.

Descartes, the first of modern philosophers, maintained this last opinion; and having filled the whole universe with a subtile matter composed of small globules, which he calls the second element, he supposes that the sun is in a state of continual agitation, which he transmits to these globules, and pretends that they again comunicate their motion in an instant to every part of the universe. But since it has been discovered that the rays of the sun do not reach us instantaneously, and that they take eight minutes to fly through that immense distance, the opinion of *Descartes*, which laboured besides under other difficulties, has been given up.

The great *Newton* afterward embraced the former system, and maintained that the luminous rays are really separated from the body of the sun, and the particles of light thence emitted with that inconceivable velocity which brings them down to us in about eight minutes. This opinion, which is that of most modern philosophers, particularly the English, is called *the system of emanation*--it being imagined that rays emanate from the sun and other luminous bodies, as water emanates or springs from a foun-

---

Letters of Euler on Different Subjects in Natural Philosophy addressed to a German Princess, ed. by David Brewster (2 vols., New York, 1833). Vol. I: pp. 77-89; vol. II: pp. 82-3; 85-93; 212-221; vol. I: pp. 191-3; 229-232; 294-8.

tain.

This opinion appears at first sight very bold, and irreconcilable to reason. For were the sun emitting continually, and in all directions, such floods of luminous matter, with a velocity so prodigious, he must speedily be exhausted; or at least some alteration must, after the lapse of so many ages, be perceptible. This, however, is contradicted by observation. It cannot be a matter of doubt, that a foundtain which should emit streams of water in all directions would be exhausted in proportion to the velocity of the emission; much more the sun, whose rays are emitted with a velocity so inconceivable. Let the particles of which rays of light are formed be supposed as subtile as you please, nothing will be gained; the system will ever remain equally untenable. It cannot be affirmed that this emanation is not made in all directions; for wherever you are placed, the whole sun is visible, which proves incontestably that rays from every point of the sun are emitted towards the spot which you occupy. The case is very different from that of a fountain, which should emit streams of water in all directions. For one point in the fountain could furnish only one stream directed to a particular spot; but every point of the sun's surface must emit an infinite number, diffusing themselves in all directions. This circumstance alone infinitely increases the expenditure of luminous matter, which the sun would have to make.

Another difficulty, and which appears equally insuperable, is, that the sun is not the only body which emits rays, but that all the stars have the same quality: and as everywhere the rays of the sun must be crossing the rays of the stars, their collision must be violent in the extreme. How must their direction be changed by such collision! This collision must take place with respect to all luminous bodies visible at the same time. Each, however, appears distinctly, without suffering the slightest derangements from any other—a certain proof that many rays may pass through the same point without disturbing each other, which seems irreconcilable to the system of emanation. Let two fountains be set a playing upon each other and you will immediately perceive their different streams disturbed and confounded: it must of consequence be concluded, that the motion of the rays of light is very essentially different from that of a *jet d'eau* and in general from all substances forcibly emitted.

Considering afterward transparent bodies through which rays are freely transmitted in all directions, the supporters of this system are under the necessity of affirming, that these bodies contain pores, disposed in straight lines, which issue from every point of the surface, and proceed in all directions; it being inconceivable how there could be any line through which a ray of the sun might be transmitted with such amazing velocity, and even without the slightest collision. Here then are bodies wonderfully porous, which have the appearance nevertheless of being extremely solid.

Finally, in order to enjoy vision, the rays must enter into the eye, and penetrate its substance with the same velocity. All these difficulties taken together will, I doubt not, sufficiently convince you that the system of emanation has in no respect a foundation in nature; and you will certainly be astonished that it could have been conceived by so great a man, and embraced by so many enlightened philosophers. But it is long since Cicero remarked, that nothing so absurd can be imagined as to find no supporter among philosophers. For my own part, I am too little a philosopher to adopt the opinion in question.

7th June, 1760.

Letter XVIII.

Difficulties attending the System of Emanation.

However strange the doctrine of the celebrated *Newton* may appear, that rays proceed from the sun by a continual emanation, it has, however, been so generally received, that it requires an effort of courage to call it in question. What has chiefly contributed to this is, no doubt, the high reputation of the great English philosopher, who first discovered the true laws of the motions of the heavenly bodies; and it was this very discovery which led him to the system of emanation.

Descartes, in order to support his theory, was under the necessity of filling the whole space of the heavens with a subtile matter, through which all the celestial bodies move at perfect liberty. But it is well known, that if a body moves in air it must meet with a certain degree of resistance; from which *Newton* concluded, that however subtile the matter of the heavens may be supposed, the planets must encounter some resistance in their motions. But, said he, this motion is not subject to any resistance: the immense space of the heavens, therefore, contains no matter. A perfect vacuum, then, universally prevails. This is one of the leading doctrines of the Newtonian philosophy, that the immensity of the universe contains no matter in the spaces not occupied by the heavenly bodies. This being laid down, there is between the sun and us, or at least from the sun down to the atmosphere of the earth, an absolute vacuum. In truth, the farther we ascend, the more subtile we find the air to be; from whence it would apparently follow, that at length the air would be entirely lost. If the space between the sun and the earth be an absolute vacuum, it is impossible that the rays should reach us in the way of communication, as the sound of a bell is transmitted by means of the air. For if the air intervening between the bell and our ear were to be annihilated, we should absolutely hear nothing, let the bell be struck ever so violently.

Having established, then, a perfect vacuum between the heavenly bodies there remains no other opinion to be adopted but that of emanation; which obliged *Newton* to maintain, that the sun and all other luminous bodies emit rays which are always particles, infinitely small, of their mass, darted from them with incredible force. It must be such to a very high degree, in order to impress on rays of light that inconceivable velocity with which they come from the sun to us in the space of eight minutes. But let us see whether this theory be consistent with *Newton's* leading doctrine, which requires an absolute vacuum in the heavens, that the planets may encounter no manner of resistance to their motions. You must conclude, on a moment's reflection, that the space in which the heavenly bodies revolve, instead of remaining a vacuum, must be filled with the rays, not only of the sun, but likewise of all the other stars which are continually passing through it from every quarter, and in all directions, with incredible rapidity. The heavenly bodies which traverse these spaces, instead of encountering a vacuum, will meet with the matter of luminous rays in a terrible agitation, which must disturb these bodies in their motions much more than if it were in a state of rest.

Thus *Newton*, apprehensive lest a subtile matter, such as *Descartes* imagined, should disturb the motions of the planets, had recourse to a very strange expedient, and quite contradictory to his own intention, as, on his hypothesis, the planets must be exposed to a derangement infinitely more considerable. I have already submitted to you several other insuperable objections to the system of emanation; and we have now seen that the principal, and indeed the only reason which could induce *Newton* to adopt it, is so self-contradictory as wholly to overturn it. All these considerations united, leave us no room to hesitate about the rejection of this strange system of the emanation of light, however respectable the authority of the philosopher who invented it.

Newton was without doubt one of the greatest geniuses that ever existed. His profound knowledge, and his acute penetration into the most hidden mysteries of nature, will be a just object of admiration to the present and to every future age. But the errors of this great man should serve to admonish us of the weakness of the human understanding, which, after having soared to the greatest possible heights, is in danger of plunging into manifest contradiction.

If we are liable to weaknesses and inconsistencies so humiliating, in our researches into the phenomena of this visible world, which lies open to the examination of our senses, how wretched must we have been had God left us to ourselves with respect to things invisible, and which concern our eternal salvation! On this important article a revelation was absolutely necessary to us; and we ought to avail ourselves of it with the most profound veneration. When it presents to us things which may appear inconceivable, we have but to reflect on the imperfection of human understanding, which is so apt to be misled, even as to sensible objects. Whenever I hear a pretended freethinker inveighing against the truths of religion, and even sneering at it with the most arrogant self-sufficiency, I say to myself, Poor weak mortal, how inexpressibly more noble and sublime are the subjects which you treat so lightly than those respecting which the great *Newton* was so grossly mistaken! I could wish your highness to keep this reflection ever in remembrance; occasions for making it occur but too frequently.

10th June, 1760.

Letter XIX.

A different System respecting the Nature of Rays and of Light, proposed.

You have seen that the system of the emanation of the rays of light labours under insuperable difficulties, and that the doctrine of a vacuum for the heavenly bodies to range in is equally untenable, as the rays of light would completely fill it. Two things, then, must be admitted: first, the space through which the heavenly bodies move is filled with a subtile matter; secondly, rays are not an actual emanation from the sun and other luminour bodies, in virtue of which part of their substance is violently emitted from them, according to the doctrine of *Newton*.

That subtile matter which fills the whole space in which the heavenly bodies revolve is called *ether*. Of its extreme subtilty no doubt can be entertained. In order to form an idea of it, we have only to attend to the nature of air, which, though extremely subtile, even on the surface of the earth, becomes more and more so as we ascend; and entirely ceases, if I may use the expression, when it comes to be lost in the ether. The ether, then, is likewise a fluid as the air is, but incomparably finer and more subtile, as we are assured that the heavenly bodies revolve freely through it, without meeting any perceptible resistance. It is also, without doubt, possessed of elasticity, by means of which it has a tendency to expand itself in all directions, and to penetrate into spaces where there would otherwise be a vacuum; so that if by some accident the ether were forced out of any space, the surrounding fluid would instantly rush in and fill it again.

In virtue of this elasticity, the ether is to be found not only in the regions which are above our atmosphere, but it penetrates the atmosphere universally, insinuates itself by the pores of all bodies, and passes irresistibly through them. Were you, by the help of the air-pump, to exhaust the air from a receiver, you must not imagine that you have produced an absolute vacuum; for the ether, forcing itself through the pores of the receiver, completely fills it in an instant. Having filled a glass tube of the proper length with mercury, and immerged it, when inverted, in the cistern, in order to make a barometer, it might be supposed that the part of the tube which is higher than the mercury is a vacuum, because the air is completely excluded, as it cannot penetrate the pores of glass; but this vacuum, which is apparent only, is undoubtedly supplied by the ether, insinuating itself without the smallest difficulty.

It is by this subtilty and elasticity of ether that I shall by-and-by explain to you the remarkable phenomena of electricity. It is even highly probably that ether has an elasticity much superior to that of air, and that many of the phenomena of nature are produced by means of it. For my own part, I have no doubt that the compression of the air in gunpowder is the effect of the elastic power of ether. And as we know by experiment that the air in it is condensed almost 1000 times more than common air, and that in this state its elasticity is likewise 1000 times greater, the elasticity of the ether must in this case be so too,

and consequently 1000 times greater than that of common air. We
shall then have a just idea of ether, in considering it as a
fluid in many respects similar to air, with this difference, that
ether is incomparably more subtile, and more elastic.

Having seen then that the air, by these very qualities, is
in a proper state for receiving the agitations or shakings of
sonorous bodies, and to diffuse them in all directions, as we
find in the propagation of sound, it is very natural to suppose
that ether may in the same circumstances likewise receive agitations in the same manner, and transmit them to the greatest distances. As the vibrations of the air produce *sound*, what will be
the effect of those of ether? You will undoubtedly guess at once
light. It appears in truth abundantly certain, that light is
with respect to ether, what sound is with respect to air; and
that the rays of light are nothing else but the shakings or vibrations transmitted by the ether, as sound consists in the
shakings or vibrations transmitted by the air.

The sun, then, loses nothing of his substance in this case,
any more than a bell in vibrating; and, in adopting this system,
there is no reason to apprehend that the mass of this orb should
ever suffer any diminution. What I have said of the sun must
also be extended to all luminous bodies, such as fire, a wax
taper, a candle, &c.

It will undoubtedly be objected, that these terrestrial
luminaries evidently waste, and that unless they are continually
fed and kept up, they will be speedily extinguished; that consequently the sun must in time be wasted away, and that the parallel of a bell is not accurate. But it is to be considered, that
these fires, besides their light, throw out smoke, and a great
deal of exhalation, which must be carefully distinguished from
the rays of light. Now the smoke and exhalation evidently occasion a considerable diminution, which must not be imputed to the
rays of light; for were it possible to separate them from the
smoke and other exhalations, the luminous quality alone would
occasion no expenditure. Mercury may, by means of art, be rendered luminous, as you have probably seen, and that without any
diminution of its substance, which proves that light alone produces no waste of luminous bodies. Thus, though the sun illuminates the whole world by his rays, he loses nothing of his own
substance, his light being only the effect of a certain agitation, or violent concussion of his minute particles, communicated
to the adjoining ether, and thence transmitted in all directions
by means of this fluid to the remotest distances, as a bell when
struck communicates its own agitation to the circumambient air.
The more we consider this parallel between sonorous and luminous
bodies, the more we shall find it conformable to nature, and
justifiable by experience; whereas the more we attempt to reconcile the phenomena of nature to the system of emanation, the more
difficulties we encounter.

14th June, 1760.

Letter XX.

Of the Propagation of Light.

The propagation of light in the ether is produced in a manner similar to that of sound in the air; and just as the vibrations occasioned in the particles of air constitute sound, in
like manner the vibration of the particles of ether constitutes
light or luminous rays; so that *light is nothing else but an
agitation or concussion of the particles of ether*, which is
everywhere to be found, on account of its extreme subtilty, in
virtue of which it penetrates all bodies.

These bodies, however, modify the rays of light in many
different ways, by transmitting or stopping the propagation of
the concussions. Of this I shall treat at large in the sequel.
I confine myself at present to the propagation of rays in the
ether itself, which fills the immense space in which the heavenly
bodies revolve. There the propagation takes place in perfect
liberty. The first thing which here presents itself to the mind
is the prodigious velocity of the rays of light, which is about
900,000 times more rapid than that of sound, though this last
travels no less than 1100 feet in a second.

This amazing velocity would be sufficient of itself to overturn the system of emanation; but in that which I am attempting
to establish, it is a natural consequence, from the principles
laid down, as I hope to demonstrate. They are the same with
those on which is founded the propagation of sound in the air;
and this depends at once on its density and elasticity. It is
evident, that if the density of air were diminished, sound would
be accelerated; and if the elasticity of the air were increased,
the same thing would happen. If the density of the air diminished, and its elasticity increased at once, we should have a
twofold reason for the increase of the velocity of sound. Let us
conceive, then, the density of the air diminished, and its elasticity increased, till its density and elasticity became equal
to those of ether, and we should then no longer be surprised that
the velocity of sound had become many thousands of times greater
than it actually is. For you will be pleased to remember, that
according to the first ideas we formed of ether, this fluid must
be inconceivably rarer and more elastic than air. Now both of
these qualities equally contribute to accelerate the velocity of
vibrations. From this explanation, the prodigious velocity of
light is so far from presenting any thing irreconcilable to
reason, that it rather perfectly harmonizes with the principles
laid down; and the parallel between light and sound is in this
respect so firmly established, that we may confidently maintain,
that if air should become as subtile and as elastic as ether, the
velocity of sound would become as rapid as that of light.

The subtilty of ether, then, and its great elasticity, are
the reason which we assign for the prodigious velocity of the
motion of light; and so long as the ether preserves this same
degree of subtilty and elasticity, this velocity must continue
the same. Now it cannot be doubted that the ether has, through
the whole universe, the same subtilty and the same elasticity.

For were the ether less elastic in one place than in another, it would force itself into it till the equilibrium was perfectly restored. The light of the stars, therefore, moves with as great velocity as that of the sun; and as the stars are at a much greater distance from us than the sun, a much greater quantity of time is requisite to transmit their rays to us. However great the distance of the sun may appear, whose rays, nevertheless, reach the surface of our globe in eight minutes, the fixed star nearest to us is at least 400,000 times more distant than the sun; a ray of light issuing from that star will employ then 400,000 times eight minutes in travelling to us, that is 53,333 hours, or 2,222 days, or six years nearly.

It is then upwards of six years since the rays of light issued from that fixed star, the least remote, and probably the most brilliant, in order to render it visible to us; and these rays have employed a period so considerable to fly through the space which separates us from that star. Were God just now to create a new fixed star at the same distance, it could not become visible to us till more than six years had elapsed, as its rays require that length of time to travel this distance. Had one been created at the beginning of the world a thousand times more distant than that which I have mentioned, it could not yet be visible to us, however brilliant, as 6000 years are not yet elapsed since the creation. The first preacher of the court of Brunswick, Mr. Jerusalem, has happily introduced this thought in one of his sermons. The passage runs thus:--

"Raise your thoughts from the earth which you inhabit, to all the bodies of the vast universe, which are so far above you; launch into the immensity of space which intervenes between the most remote which your eyes are able to discover, and those whose light, from the moment of creation till now, has not as yet, perhaps, come down to us. The immensity of the kingdom of God justifies this representation." (*Sermon on the Heavens, and Eternal Beatitude.*)

I flatter myself that these reflections will excite a desire of further instruction respecting the system of light, from which is derived the theory of colours and of vision.

17th June, 1760.

Letter XXIV.

The true Principle of Nature on which are founded all the Phenomena of Electricity.

The summary I have exhibited of the principal phenomena of electricity has no doubt excited a curiosity to know what occult powers of nature are capable of producing effects so surprising.

The greatest part of natural philosophers acknowledge their ignorance in this respect. They appear to be so dazzled by the endless variety of phenomena which every day present themselves, and by the singularly marvellous circumstances which accompany these phenomena, that they are discouraged from attempting an investigation of the true cause of them. They readily admit the existence of a subtile matter, which is the primary agent in the production of the phenomena, and which they denominate the electric fluid; but they are so embarrassed about determining its nature and properties; that this important branch of physics is rendered only more perplexed by their researches.

There is no room to doubt that we must look for the source of all the phenomena of electricity only in a certain fluid and subtile matter; but we have no need to go to the regions of imagination in quest of it. That subtile matter denominated *ether*, whose reality I have already endeavoured to demonstrate, is sufficient very naturally to explain all the surprising effects which electricity presents. I hope I shall be able to set this in so clear a light, that you shall be able to account for every electrical phenomenon, however strange an appearance it may assume.

The great requisite is to have a thorough knowledge of the nature of ether. The air which we breathe rises only to a certain height above the surface of the earth; the higher you ascend the more subtile it becomes, and at last it entirely ceases. We must not affirm that beyond the region of the air there is a perfect vacuum which occupies the immense space in which the heavenly bodies revolve. The rays of light, which are diffused in all directions from these heavenly bodies, sufficiently demonstrate that those vast spaces are filled with a subtile matter. . . .

Letter XXV.

Continuation. Different Nature of Bodies relatively to Electricity.

Ether being a subtile matter and similar to air, but many thousand times more rare and more elastic, it cannot be at rest, unless its elasticity, or the force with which it tends to expand, be the same everywhere.

As soon as the ether in one place shall be more elastic than in another, which is the case when it is more compressed there, it will expand itself into the parts adjacent, compressing what it finds there till the whole is reduced to the same degree of elasticity. It is then in equilibrio, the equilibrium being nothing else but the state of rest, when the powers which have a tendency to disturb it counterbalance each other.

When, therefore, the ether is not in equilibrio the same thing must take place as in air, when its equilibrium is disturbed; it must expand itself from the place where its elasticity is greater towards that where it is less; but, considering its greater elasticity and subtilty, this motion must be much more rapid than that of air. The want of equilibrium in the air produces wind, or the motion of that fluid from one place to another. There must therefore be produced a species of wind, but incomparably more subtile than that of air, when the equilibrium of ether is disturbed, by which this last fluid will pass from places where it was more compressed and more elastic to those where it was less so.

This being laid down, I with confidence affirm that all the

phenomena of electricity are a natural consequence of want of equilibrium in ether, so that wherever the equilibrium of the ether is disturbed the phenomena of electricity must take place; consequently, electricity is nothing else but a derangement of the equilibrium of the ether.

In order to unfold all the effects of electricity, we must attend to the manner in which ether is blended and enveloped with all the bodies which surround us. Ether, in these lower regions, is to be found only in the small interstices which the particles of the air and of other bodies leave unoccupied. Nothing can be more natural than that the ether, from its extreme subtility and elasticity, should insinuate itself into the smallest pores of bodies which are impervious to air, and even into those of the air itself. You will recollect that all bodies, however solid they may appear, are full of pores; and many experiments incontestably demonstrate that these interstices occupy much more space than the solid parts; finally, the less ponderous a body is, the more it must be filled with these pores, which contain ether only. It is clear, therefore, that though the ether be thus diffused through the smallest pores of bodies, it must however be found in very great abundance in the vicinity of the earth.

You will easily comprehend that the difference of these pores must be very great, both as to magnitude and figure, according to the different nature of the bodies, as their diversity probably depends on the diversity of their pores. There must be, therefore, undoubtedly, pores more close, and which have less communication with others; so that the ether which they contain is likewise more confined, and cannot disengage itself but with great difficulty, though its elasticity may be much greater than that of the ether which is lodged in the adjoining pores. There must be, on the contrary, pores abundantly open, and of easy communication with the adjacent pores; in this case it is evident that the ether lodged in them can with less difficulty disengage itself than in the preceding; and if it is more or less elastic in these than in the others, it will soon recover its equilibrium.

In order to distinguish these two classes of pores, I shall denominate the first *close*, and the others *open*. Most bodies must contain pores of an intermediate species, which it will be sufficient to distinguish by the terms *more* or *less close*, and *more* or *less open*.

This being laid down, I remark, first, that if all bodies had pores perfectly close, it would be impossible to change the elasticity of the air contained in them; and even though the ether in some of these pores should have acquired, from whatever cause, a higher degree of elasticity than the others, it would always remain in that state, and never recover its equilibrium, from a total want of communication. In this case no change could take place in bodies; all would remain in the same state as if the ether were in equilibrio, and no phenomenon of electricity could be produced.

This would likewise be the case if the pores of all bodies were perfectly open; for then, though the ether might be more or less elastic in some pores than in others, the equilibrium would

be instantly restored, from the entire freedom of communication--
and that so rapidly that we should not be in a condition to remark the slightest change. For the same reason it would be
impossible to disturb the equilibrium of the ether contained in
such pores; as often as the equilibrium might be disturbed, it
would be as instantaneously restored, and no sign of electricity
would be discoverable.

The pores of all bodies being neither perfectly close nor
perfectly open, it will always be possible to disturb the equilibrium of the ether which they contain: and when this happens,
from whatever cause, the equilibrium cannot fail to re-establish
itself; but this re-establishment will require some time, and
this produces certain phenomena; and you will presently see, much
to your satisfaction, that they are precisely the same which
electrical experiments have discovered. It will then appear that
the principles on which I am going to establish the theory of
electricity are extremely simple, and at the same time absolutely
incontrovertible.

27th June, 1761.

Letter XXVI.

On the same Subject.

I hope I have now surmounted the most formidable difficulties which present themselves in the theory of electricity. You
have only to preserve the idea of ether which I have been explaining; and which is, that extremely subtile and elastic matter diffused, not only through all the void spaces of the universe, but through the minutest pores of all bodies in which it
is sometimes more and sometimes less engaged, according as they
are more or less close. This consideration conducts us to two
principal species of bodies, of which the one has pores more
close, and the other pores more open.

Should it happen, therefore, that the ether contained in
the pores of bodies has not throughout the same degree of elasticity, and that it is more or less compressed in some than in
others, it will make an effort to recover its equilibrium; and
it is precisely from this that the phenomena of electricity take
their rise, which, of consequence, will be varied in proportion
as the pores in which the ether is lodged are various, and grant
it a communication more or less free with the others.

This difference in the pores of bodies perfectly corresponds
to that which the first phenomena of electricity have made us to
remark in them, by which some easily become electrical by communication, or the proximity of an electrical body, whereas others
scarcely undergo any change. Hence you will immediately infer
that bodies which receive electricity so easily by communication
alone are those whose pores are open; and that the others, which
are almost insensible to electricity, must have theirs close,
either entirely or to a very great degree.

It is, then, by the phenomena of electricity themselves that
we are enabled to conclude what are the bodies whose pores are
close or open. Respecting which permit me to suggest the follow-

ing elucidations.

First, the air which we breathe has its pores almost entirely close; so that the ether which it contains cannot disengage itself but with difficulty, and must find equal difficulty in attempting to penetrate into it. Thus, though the ether diffused through the air is not in equilibrio with that which is contained in other bodies where it is more or less compressed, the re-establishment of its equilibrium is not to be produced without extreme difficulty; this is to be understood of dry air, humidity being of a different nature, as I shall presently remark.

Further, we must rank in this class of bodies with close pores, *glass*, *pitch*, *resinous bodies*, *sealing-wax*, *sulphur*, and particularly *silk*. These substances have their pores so very close that it is with extreme difficulty the ether can either escape from or penetrate into them.

The other class, that of bodies whose pores are open, contains, first, water and other liquors, whose nature is totally different from that of air. For this reason, when air becomes humid it totally changes its nature with respect to electricity, and the ether can enter or escape without almost any difficulty. To this class of bodies with open pores likewise must be referred those of animals, and all metals.

Other bodies, such as wood, several sorts of stones and earths, occupy an intermediate state between the two principal species which I have just mentioned; and the ether is capable of entering or escaping with more or less facility, according to the nature of each species.

After these elucidations on the different nature of bodies with respect to the ether which they contain, you will see with much satisfaction how all the phenomena of electricity, which have been considered as so many prodigies, flow very naturally from them.

All depends, then, on the state of the ether diffused or dispersed through the pores of all bodies, in as far as it has not throughout the same degree of elasticity, or as it is more or less compressed in some than in others: for the ether not being then in equilibrio will make an effort to recover it. It will endeavour to disengage itself as far as the openness of the pores will permit from places where it is too much compressed, to expand itself and enter into pores where there is less compression, till it is throughout reduced to the same degree of compression and elasticity, and is, of consequence, in equilibrio.

Let it be remarked, that when the ether passes from a body where it was too much compressed into another where it is less so, it meets with great obstacles in the air which separates the two bodies on account of the pores of this fluid, which are almost entirely close. It however passes through the air as a liquid and extremely subtile matter, provided its force is not inferior, or the interval between the bodies too great. Now, this passage of the ether being very much impeded, and almost entirely prevented by the pores of the air, the same thing will happen to it as to air forced with velocity through small apertures--a hissing sound is heard--which proves that this fluid is then put into an agitation which produces such a sound.

It is, therefore, extremely natural that the ether, forced to penetrate through the pores of the air, should likewise receive a species of agitation. You will please to recollect, that as agitation of the air produces sound, a similar agitation of ether produces light. As often, then, as ether escapes from one body to enter into another, its passage through the air must be accompanied with light; which appears sometimes under the form of a spark, sometimes under that of a flash of lightning, according as its quantity is more or less considerable.

Letter XXVII.

Of Positive and Negative Electricity. Explanation of the Phenomenon of Attraction.

You will easily comprehend, from what I have above advanced, that a body must become electrical whenever the ether contained in its pores becomes more or less elastic than that which is lodged in adjacent bodies. This takes place when a greater quantity of ether is introduced into the pores of such body, or when part of the ether which it contained is forced out. In the former case, the ether becomes more compressed, and consequently more elastic; in the other, it becomes rarer, and loses its elasticity. In both cases it is no longer in equilibrio with that which is external; and the efforts which it makes to recover its equilibrium produce all the phenomena of electricity.

You see, then, that a body may become electric in two different ways, according as the ether contained in its pores becomes more or less elastic than that which is external; hence result two species of electricity: the one, by which the ether is rendered more elastic, or more compressed, is denominated *increased* or *positive electricity*; the other, in which the ether is less elastic, or more rarefied, is denominated *diminished* or *negative electricity*. The phenomena of both are nearly the same; a slight difference only is observable, which I shall mention.

Bodies are not naturally electrical--as the elasticity of the ether has a tendency to maintain it in equilibrio, it must always require a violent operation to disturb this equilibrium, and to render bodies electrical; and such operations must act on bodies with close pores, that the equilibrium, once deranged, may not be instantly restored. We accordingly find that glass, amber, sealing-wax, or sulphur are the bodies employed to excite electricity.

The easiest operation and for some time past, the most universally known, is to rub a stick of sealing-wax with a piece of woolen cloth, in order to communicate to that wax the power of attracting small slips of paper and of other light bodies. Amber, by means of friction, produces the same phenomena; and as the ancients gave to this body the name of *electrum*, the power excited by friction obtained, and preserves, the name of *electricity*--natural philosophers of the remotest ages having remarked that this substance acquired by friction the faculty of attracting light bodies.

This effect undoubtedly arises from the derangement of the

equilibrium of the ether by means of friction. I must begin,
therefore, with explaining this well-known experiment. Amber and
sealing-wax have their pores abundantly close, and those of wool
are abundantly open; during the friction, the pores of both the
one and the other compress themselves, and the ether which is
contained in them is reduced to a higher degree of elasticity.
According as the pores of the wool are susceptible of a compression greater or less than those of amber or sealing-sax, it must
happen that a portion of ether shall pass from the wool into the
amber, or, reciprocally, from the amber into the wool. In the
former case, the amber becomes *positively* electric, and in the
other *negatively*--and its pores being close, it will remain in
this state for some time; whereas the wool, though it has undergone a similar change, will presently recover its natural state.

From the experiments which electric sealing-wax furnishes,
we conclude that its electricity is *negative*, and that a part of
its ether has passed during the friction into the wool. Hence
you perceive how a stick of sealing-wax is, by friction on
woollen cloth, deprived of part of the ether which it contained,
and must thereby become electric. Let us now see what effects
must result from this, and how far they correspond with observation and experience.

Fig. 39.

Let A B, Fig. 39, be a stick of sealing-
wax, from which, by friction, part of the ether
contained in its pores has been forced out;
that which remains, being less compressed, will
therefore have less force to expand itself, or,
in other words, will have less elasticity than
that contained in other bodies in the circumambient air: but as the pores of air are still
closer than those of sealing-wax, this prevents
the ether contained in the air from passing
into the sealing-wax, to restore the equilibrium: at least this will not take place till
after a considerable interval of time.

Let a small and very light body C, whose
pores are open, be now presented to the stick
of sealing-wax, the ether contained in them,
finding a free passage, because it has more
force to expand itself than is opposed to it by
ether shut up in the stick at c, will suddenly
escape, will force a passage for itself through
the air, provided the distance is not too
great, and will enter into the sealing-wax.
This passage, however, will not be effected
without very considerable difficulty, as the
pores of the sealing-wax have only a very small
aperture, and consequently it will not be
accompanied with a vehemence capable of putting the ether in a
motion of agitation, to excite a sensible light. A faint glim-
mering only will be perceptible in the dark, if the electricity
is sufficiently strong.

But another phenomenon will be observable which is no less
surprising--the small body C will spring towards the sealing-wax

as if attracted by it. To explain the cause of this, you have
only to consider that the small body C, in its natural state, is
equally pressed on all sides by the air which surrounds it; but
as in its present state the ether makes its escape and passes
through the air in the direction C c, it is evident that this
last fluid will not press so violently on the small body on this
side as on any other, and that the pressure communicated to it
towards c will be more powerful than in any other direction,
impelling it towards the sealing-wax as if attracted by it.

Thus are explained, in a manner perfectly intelligible, the
attractions observable in the phenomena of electricity. In this
experiment, the electricity is too feeble to produce more surprising effects. I shall have the honour of presenting you with
a more ample detail in the following Letters.

4th July, 1761.

Letter LXI.

. . . Every magnet exhibits phenomena altogether similar.
You have only to place one on a table covered with filings of
steel, and you will see the filings arrange themselves round the
loadstone A B, nearly as represented in Fig. 113, in which every
particle of the filings may be considered as a small magnetic

Fig. 113.

needle, indicating at every point round the loadstone the magnetic direction. This experiment leads us to inquire into the cause
of all these phenomena.

The arrangement assumed by the steel filings leaves no room
to doubt that it is a subtile and invisible matter which runs
through the particles of the steel, and disposes them in the
direction which we here observe. It is equally clear that this
subtile matter pervades the loadstone itself, entering at one of
the poles, and going out at the other, so as to form, by its continual motion round the loadstone, a vortex which reconducts the
subtile matter from one pole to the other; and this motion is,
without doubt, extremely rapid.

The nature of the loadstone consists, then, in a continual
vortex, which distinguishes it from all other bodies; and the
earth itself, in the quality of a loadstone, must be surrounded
with a similar vortex, acting everywhere on magnetic needles, and
making continual efforts to dispose them according to its own
direction, which is the same I formerly denominated the magnetic
direction: this subtile matter is continually issuing at one of

the magnetic poles of the earth, and after having performed a
circuit round to the other pole, it there enters, and pervades
the globe through and through to the opposite pole, where it
again escapes.

We are not yet enabled to determine by which of the two
magnetic poles of the earth it enters or issues; the phenomena
depending on this have such a perfect resemblance, that they are
indistinguishable. It is undoubtedly, likewise, this general
vortex of the globe which supplies the subtile matter of every
particular loadstone to magnetic iron or steel, and which keep
up the particular vortices that surround them.

Previous to a thorough investigation of the nature of this
subtile matter, and its motion, it must be remarked, that its action is confined to loadstone, iron, and steel; all other bodies
are absolutely indifferent to it: the relation which it bears
to those must therefore be by no means the same which it bears to
others. We are warranted to maintain, from manifold experiments,
that this subtile matter freely pervades all other bodies, and
even in all directions, for when a loadstone acts upon a needle,
the action is perfectly the same whether another body interposes
or not, provided the interposing body is not iron, and its action
is the same on the filings of iron. This subtile matter, therefore, must pervade all bodies, iron excepted, as freely as it
does air, and even pure ether; for these experiments succeed
equally well in a receiver exhausted by the air-pump. This
matter is consequently different from ether, and even much more
subtile. And, on account of the general vortex of the earth, it
may be affirmed that the globe is completely surrounded by it,
and freely pervaded, as all other bodies are, excepting the loadstone and iron; for this reason iron and steel may be denominated
magnetic bodies, to distinguish them from others.

But if this magnetic matter passes freely through all non-
magnetic bodies, what relation can it have to those which are
such? We have just observed, that the magnetic vortex enters at
one of the poles of every loadstone, and goes out at the other;
whence it may be concluded that it freely pervades loadstones
likewise, which would not distinguish them from other bodies.
But as the magnetic matter passes through the loadstone only from
pole to pole, this is a circumstance very different from what
takes place in others. Here, then, we have the distinctive
character. Non-magnetic bodies are freely pervaded by the magnetic matter in all directions: loadstones are pervaded by it in
one direction only; one of the poles being adapted to its admission, the other to its escape. But iron and steel, when rendered
magnetic, fulfil this last condition; when they are not, it may
be affirmed that they do not grant a free transmission to the
magnetic matter in any direction.

This may appear strange, as iron has open pores, which transmit the ether, though it is not so subtile as the magnetic matter. But we must carefully distinguish a simple passage, from
one in which the magnetic matter may pervade the body, with all
its rapidity, without encountering any obstacle.

31 October, 1761.

Letter LXII.

*Nature of the Magnetic Matter, and of its rapid
Current. Magnetic Canals.*

I am very far from pretending to explain perfectly the phenomena of magnetism; it presents difficulties which I did not find
in those of electricity. The cause of it undoubtedly is, that
electricity consists in too great or too small a degree of compression of a subtile fluid which occupies the pores of bodies,
without supposing that subtile fluid, which is the ether, to be
in actual motion: but magnetism cannot be explained unless we
suppose a vortex in rapid agitation, which penetrates magnetic
bodies.

The matter which constitutes these vortices is likewise much
more subtile than ether, and freely pervades the pores of loadstones, which are impervious even to ether. Now, this magnetic
matter is diffused through and mixed with the ether, as the ether
is with gross air; or, just as ether occupies and fills up the
pores of air, it may be affirmed that the magnetic matter occupies and fills the pores of ether.

I conceive, then, that the loadstone and iron have pores so
small that the ether in a body cannot force its way into them,
and that the magnetic matter alone can penetrate them: and which,
on being admitted, separates itself from the ether by what may be
called a kind of filtration. In the pores of the loadstone alone,
therefore, is the magnetic matter to be found in perfect purity:
everywhere else it is blended with ether, as this last is with
the air.

You can easily imagine a series of fluids, one always more
subtile than another, and which are perfectly blended together.
Nature furnishes imstances of this. Water, we know, contains in
its pores particles of air, which are frequently seen discharging
themselves in the form of small bubbles: air again, it is
equally certain, contains in its pores a fluid incomparably more
subtile--namely, ether--and which on many occasions is separated
from it, as in electricity. And now we see a still further progression, and that ether contains a matter much more subtile than
itself--the magnetic matter--which may perhaps contain, in its
turn, others still more subtile, at least this is not impossible.

Having considered the nature of this magnetic matter, let us
see how the phenomena are produced. I consider a loadstone, then;
and say, first, that besides a great many pores filled with ether,
like all other bodies, it contains some still much more narrow,
into which the magnetic matter alone can find admission. Secondly, these pores are disposed in such a manner as to have a communication with each other, and constitute tubes or canals,
through which the magnetic matter passes from the one extremity
to the other. Finally, this matter can be trasnmitted through
these tubes only in one direction, without the possibility of
returning in an opposite direction. This most essential circumstance requires a more particular elucidation.

First, then, I remark, that the veins and lymphatic vessels
in the bodies of animals are tubes of a similar construction,

Fig. 114.

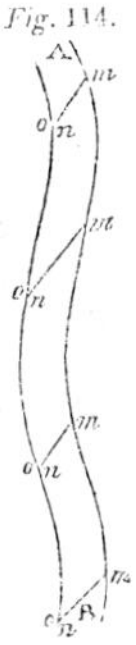

Fig. 115.

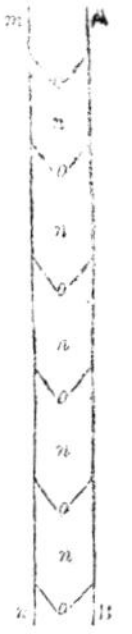

containing valves, represented in Fig. 114, by the strokes m n, which, by raising themselves, grant a free passage to the blood when it flows from A to B, and to prevent its reflux from B to A. For if the blood attempted to flow from B to A, it would press down the moveable extremity of the valve m on the side of the vein o, and totally obstruct the passage. Valves are thus employed in acqueducts, to prevent the influx of the water. I do not consider myself, then, as supposing anything contrary to nature, when I say that the canals in loadstones, which admit the magnetic matter only, are of the same construction.

Fig. 115, represents this magnetic canal, according to my idea of it. I conceive it furnished inwardly with bristles directed from A towards B, which present no opposition to the magnetic matter in its passage from A to B, for in this case they open of themselves at n, to let the matter pass at o; but they would immediately obstruct the channel were it to attempt a retrograde course from B to A. The nature of magnetic canals consists, then, in granting admission to the magnetic matter only at A, to flow towards B, without the possibility of returning in the opposite direction from B towards A.

This construction enables us to explain how the magnetic matter enters into these tubes, and flies through them with the greatest rapidity, even when the whole ether is in a state of perfect rest, which is the most surprising; for how can a motion so rapid be produced? This will appear perfectly clear to you, if you will please to recollect that ether is a matter extremely elastic; accordingly, the magnetic matter, which is scattered about, will be pressed by it on every side. Let us suppose the magnetic canal A B still quite empty, and that a particle of magnetic matter m presents itself at the entrance A; and this particle pressed on every side at the opening of the canal, into which the ether cannot force admission, it will there be pressed forward with prodigious force, and enter into the canal with equal rapidity: another particle of magnetic matter will immediately present itself, and be driven forward with

the same force; and in like manner all the following particles.
There will thence result a continual flux of magnetic matter,
which, meeting with no obstruction in this canal, will escape
from it at B with the same rapidity that it enters at A.

My idea then is, that every loadstone contains a great
multitude of these canals, which I denominate magnetic; and it
very naturally follows, that the magnetic matter dispersed in the
ether must enter into them at one extremity, and escape at the
other, with great impetuosity; that is, we shall have a perpetual
current of magnetic matter through the canals of the loadstone:
and thus I hope I have surmounted the greatest difficulties which
can occur in the theory of magnetism.

3d November, 1761.

Letter LXIII.

Magnetic Vortex.   Action of Magnets upon each other.

You have now seen in what the distinctive character of the
loadstone consists; and that each contains several canals, of
which I have attempted to give a description.

Fig. 116 represents a loadstone A B, with three magnetic
canals a b, through which the magnetic matter will flow with the

Fig. 116.

utmost rapidity, entering at the extremities marked a, and escaping at those marked b: it will escape indeed with the same
rapidity; but immediately meeting with the ether blended with the
grosser air, great obstructions will oppose the continuation of
its motion in the same direction; and not only will the motion be
retarded, but its direction diverted towards the sides c c. The
same thing will take place at the entrance, towards the extremities a a a; on account of the rapidity with which the particles
of magnetic matter force their way into them, the circulation
will quickly overtake those which are still towards the sides
e e, and these in their turn will be replaced by those which,
escaping from the extremities b b b, have been already diverted
towards c c; so that the same magnetic matter which issues from
the extremities b b b quickly returns towards those marked a a a,
performing the circuit b c d e a; and this circulation round the
loadstone is what we call the *magnetic vortex.*

It must not be imagined, however, that it is always the same
magnetic matter which forms these vortices: a considerable part
of it will escape, no doubt, as well towards B as towards the
sides, in performing the circuit; but as a compensation, fresh

magnetic matter will enter by the extremities a a a, so that the
matter which constitutes the vortex is succedaneous and very variable: a magnetic vortex, surrounding the loadstone, will, however, always be kept up, and produce the phenomena formerly observed in filings of steel scattered round the loadstone.

You will please further to attend to this circumstance, that
the motion of the magnetic matter in the vortex is incomparably
slower out of the loadstone than in the magnetic tubes, where it
is separated from the ether, after having been forced into them
by all the elastic power of this last fluid; and that on escaping
it mixes again with the ether, and thereby loses great part of
its motion, so that its velocity in travelling to the extremities
a a a is incomparably less than in the magnetic canals a b,
though still very great with respect to us. You will easily
comprehend, then, that the extremities of the magnetic canals, by
which the matter enters into the loadstone and escapes from it,
are what we call its poles; and that the magnetic poles of a
loadstone are by no means mathematical points, the whole space in
which the extremities of the magnetic canals terminate being one
magnetic pole, as in the loadstone represented by Fig. 113, where
the whole surfaces A and B are the two poles.

Now, though these poles are distinguished by the terms *north*
and *south*, yet we cannot affirm with certainty whether it is by
the north or south pole that the magnetic matter enters into
loadstones. You will see, in the sequel, that all the phenomena
produced by the admission and escape have such a perfect resemblance that it appears impossible to determine the question by
experiments. It is therefore a matter of indifference whether we
suppose that the magnetic matter enters or escapes by the north
pole or by the south.

Be this as it may, I shall mark with the letter A the pole by
which the magnetic matter enters, and with B that by which it
escapes, without pretending thereby to indicate which is north or
south. I proceed to the consideration of these vortices, in
order to form a judgment how two loadstones act upon each other.

Let us suppose that the two loadstones A B and a b, fig.
117, are presented to each other by the poles of the same name A,
a, and their vortices will be in a state of total opposition.

Fig. 117.

The magnetic matter which is at C will enter at A and a, and
these two vortices attempting mutually to destroy each other, the
matter which proceeds by E to enter at A will meet at D that of
the other loadstone returning by e to enter at a: from this must
result a collision of the two vortices, in which the one will

repel the other; and this effect will extend to the loadstones themselves, which, thus situated, undergo mutual repulsion. The same thing would take place if the two loadstones presented to each other the other poles B and b: for this reason the poles of the same name are denominated *hostile*, because they actually repel each other.

But if the loadstones present to each other the poles of a different name, an opposite effect will ensue, and you will perceive that they have a mutual attraction.

In Fig. 118, where the two loadstones present to each other the poles B and a, the magnetic matter which issues from the pole B, finding immediately free admission into the other loadstone by

Fig. 118.

its pole a, will not be diverted towards the sides in order to return and re-enter at A, but will pass directly by C into the other loadstone, and escape from it at b, and will perform the circuit by the sides d d, to re-enter, not by the pole a, but by the pole A, of the other loadstone, completing the circuit by e f. Thus the vortices of these two loadstones will unite, as if there were but one; and this vortex, being compressed on all sides by the ether, will impel the two loadstones towards each other, so that they will exhibit a mutual attraction.

This is the reason why the poles of different names are denominated *friendly*, and those of the same name *hostile*, the principal phenomenon in magnetism, in as much as the poles of different names attract, and those of the same name repel each other.

7th November, 1761.

Letter LIV.

Different Sentiments of Philosophers respecting Universal Gravitation. The Attractionists.

It is established, then, by reasons which cannot be controverted, that a universal gravitation pervades all the heavenly bodies, by which they are attracted towards each other; and that this power is greater in proportion to their proximity.

This fact is incontestable; but it has been made a question, whether we ought to give it the name of *impulsion* or *attraction*. The name undoubtedly is a matter of indifference, as the effect is the same. The astronomer, accordingly, attentive only to the effect of this power, gives himself little trouble to determine whether the heavenly bodies are impelled towards each other, or whether they mutually attract one another; and the person who examines the phenomena only is unconcerned whether the earth attracts bodies. or whether they are impelled towards it by some invisible cause.

But in attempting to dive into the mysteries of nature, it is of importance to know if the heavenly bodies act upon each other by impulsion, or by attraction; if a certain subtile invisible matter impels them towards each other; or if they are endowed with a secret or occult quality, by which they are mutually attracted. On this question philosophers are divided. Some are of opinion, that this phenomenon is analogous to an impulsion; others maintain, with *Newton*, and the English in general, that it consists in attraction.

It must be observed, that the terms *attract* and *draw* are not perfectly synonymous; that accordingly it is not to be supposed there is an intermediate body between the sun and the earth.

The English, and those who have adopted the same opinion, explain it in this matter: They maintain, that the quality of mutual attraction is proper to all bodies; that it is as natural to them as magnitude; and that it is a satisfying solution of the question, that the Creator willed this mutual attraction of bodies. Had there been but two bodies in the universe, however remote from each other, they would have had from the first a tendency towards each other, by means of which they would have in time approached and united. Hence it follows, that the greater a body is, the more considerable is the attraction which it exerts upon others; for as this quality is essential to matter, the more of it any body contains, the greater is its attractive force.

As the sun, therefore, considerably surpasses all the planets in magnitude, its attractive force must be much greater than theirs. They likewise remark, that the mass of Jupiter being much greater than that of the earth, the attractive force which he exercises over his satellites is much more powerful than that with which the earth acts upon the moon.

According to this system, the gravity of bodies on the earth is the result of all the attractions exercised upon them by the particles of our globe; and if it contained more matter than it actually does, its attraction would become more powerful, and the gravity of bodies would be increased. But if, on the contrary, the mass of the earth should happen by some accident to be diminished, its attractive force too would be diminished, as well as the gravity of bodies at its surface.

It has been objected to these philosophers, that, on their hypothesis, any two bodies whatever at rest, for instance, on a table, must attract each other, and consequently approach. They admit the consequence; but they insist, that in this case the attraction would be too small to produce any sensible effect; for if the whole mass of the earth, by its attractive force, produces in every body only that effect which we perceive in the weight of a body, a mass many millions of times smaller than the earth will produce an effect as many times smaller.

It must readily be admitted, that if the weight of a body became many millions of times less, the effect of gravity upon it must be reduced to almost nothing: attraction, therefore, cannot be perceptible, except in bodies of very great magnitude. The partisans of the system of gravitation, therefore, are not vulnerable on this side; and they produce in support of their opinion an experiment made in Peru by the French academicians, in which they perceived the effect of a slight attraction of a prodigious mountain on adjacent bodies. In adopting, therefore, the system of attraction, we need be under no apprehension of its leading us to false consequences; and it has hitherto been always confirmed by the new facts which have been discovered.

7th September, 1760.

Letter LXVIII.

More particular Account of the Dispute respecting Universal Gravitation.

Having given you a general but exact idea of the powers which produce the principal phenomena of the universe, and on which are founded the motions of all the heavenly bodies, it is of importance to consider with more attention those powers which are the principal points of the system of attraction.

It is supposed in this system, that all bodies mutually attract each other in the ratio of their mass, and relatively to their distance, in conformity to a law already explained. The satisfactory manner in which most of the phenomena in nature are accounted for proves that this supposition is founded in truth; and that the attraction which different bodies exercise upon each other may be considered as a most undoubted fact. It now remains that we inquire into the cause of these attractive powers; but this research belongs rather to the province of metaphysics than of mathematics. I dare not therefore flatter myself with the prospect of absolute success in the prosecution of it.

As it is certain that any two bodies whatever are attracted to each other, the question is, What is the cause of this attraction? On this point philosophers are divided. The English maintain that attraction is a property essential to all the bodies in nature, and that these bodies, hurried along by an irresistible propensity, tend mutually to approach, as if they were impelled by feeling.

Other philosophers consider this opinion as absurd, and contrary to the principles of a rational philosophy. They do not deny the fact: they even admit that powers exist which are the causes of the reciprocal tendency of bodies towards each other: but they maintain, that they are foreign to the bodies; that they belong to the ether, or the subtile matter which surrounds them, and that bodies may be put in motion by the ether, just as we see that a body plunged into a fluid receives several impressions from it. Thus, according to the first, the cause of the attraction resides in the bodies themselves, and is essential to their nature; and according to the last, it is out of the bodies, and in the fluid which surrounds them. In this case, the term attraction would be improper; and we must rather say that bodies are impelled towards each other. But as the effect is the same whether two bodies are reciprocally impelled or attracted, the word attraction need not give offence, provided it is not pretended by that term to determine the nature itself of the cause.

To avoid all confusion which might result from this mode of expression, it ought rather to be said that bodies move as if they mutually attracted each other. This would not decide whether the powers which act on bodies reside in the bodies themselves or out of them; and this manner of speaking might thus suit both parties. Let us confine ourselves to the bodies which we meet with on the surface of the earth.

Every one readily admits, that all these would fall downwards, unless they were supported. Now, the question turns on the real cause of this fall. Some say that it is the earth which attracts these bodies, by an inherent power natural to it; others, that it is the ether, or some other subtile or invisible matter, which impels the body downwards: so that the effect is, nevertheless, the same in both cases. This last opinion is most satisfactory to those who are fond of clear principles in philosophy, as they do not see how two bodies at a distance can act upon each other, if there be nothing between them. The others have recourse to the divine Omnipotence, and maintain that God has endowed all bodies with a power of mutual attraction.

Though it be dangerous to venture on a dispute concerning the limits of Divine power, it is nevertheless certain that if attraction were an immediate work of that power, without being founded in the nature of bodies, this would be the same thing as saying that God immediately impels bodies towards each other, and this would amount to a perpetual miracle.

Let us suppose that before the creation of the world God had created only two bodies, at a distance from each other; that nothing absolutely existed out of them, and that they were in a state of rest; would it be possible for the one to approach the other, or that they should have a propensity to approach? How could the one feel the other at a distance? Whence could arise the desire of approaching? These are perplexing questions. But if you suppose that the intermediate space is filled with a subtile matter, we can comprehend at once that this matter may act upon the bodies, by impelling them: the effect would be the same as if they possessed a power of mutual attraction.

Now, as we know that the whole space which separates the heavenly bodies is filled with a subtile matter, called *ether*, it seems more reasonable to ascribe the mutual attraction of bodies to an action which the ether exercises upon them, though its manner of acting may be unknown to us, rather than to have recourse to an unintelligible property.

Ancient philosophers satisfied themselves with explaining the phenomena of nature from qualities which they called *occult*, saying, for example, that opium causes sleep, from an occult quality, which disposes it to procure sleep. This was saying just nothing, or rather was an attempt to conceal ignorance. We ought, therefore, likewise to consider attraction as an occult quality, in as far as it is given for a property essential to bodies. But as the idea of all occult qualities is now banished from philosophy, attraction ought not to be considered in this sense.

18th October, 1760.

Letter LXXXIX.

Of the Question respecting the best World possible; and of the Origin of Evil.

You know well, that it has been made a question, Whether this world be the best possible? It cannot be doubted, that the world perfectly corresponds to the plan which God proposed to himself when he created it.

As to bodies and material productions, their arrangement and structure are such, that certainly they could not have been better. Please to recollect the wonderful structure of the eye, and you will see the necessity of admitting that the conformation of all its parts is perfectly adapted to fulfil the end in view, that of representing distinctly exterior objects. How much address is necessary to keep up the eye in that state, during the course of a whole life? The juices which compose it must be preserved from corruption; it was necessary to make provision that they should be constantly renewed and maintained in a suitable state.

A structure equally marvellous is observable in all the other parts of our bodies, in those of all animals, and even of the vilest insects. And the structure of these last is so much the more admirable, on account of their smallness, that it should perfectly satisfy all the wants which are peculiar to each species. Let us examine only the sense of seeing in these insects, by which they distinguish objects so minute, and so near, as to escape our eyes, and this examination alone will fill us with astonishment.

We discover the same perfection in plants; every thing in them concurs to their formation, to their growth, and to the production of their flowers, of their fruits, or of their seeds. What a prodigy, to behold a plant, a tree, spring from a small grain cast into the earth, by the help of the nutritious juices with which the soil supplies it! The productions found in the bowels of the earth are no less wonderful: every part of nature is capable of exhausting our utmost powers of research, without permitting it to penetrate all the wonders of its construction. Nay, we are utterly lost, while we reflect how every substance-- earth, water, air, and fire--concur in the production of all organized bodies; and finally, how the arrangement of all the heavenly bodies is so admirably contrived as perfectly to fulfil all these particular destinations.

After having reflected in this manner, it will be difficult for you to believe that there should have been men who maintained, that the universe was the effect of mere chance, without any design. But there always have been, and there still are, persons of this description; those, however, who have a solid knowledge of nature, and whom fear of the justice of God does not prevent from acknowledging Him, are convinced, with us, that there is a Supreme Being who created the whole universe, and, from the remarks which I have just been suggesting to you respecting bodies, every thing has been created in the highest perfection.

As to spirits, the wickedness of man seems to be an infringement of this perfection, as it is but too capable of introducing the greatest evils into the world; and these evils have, at all times, appeared incompatible with the sovereign goodness of God. This is the weapon usually employed by infidels against religion, and the existence of God. If God, say they, was the author of the world, He must also be the author of the evil which it contains, and of the crimes committed in it.

This question, respecting the origin of evil--the difficulty of explaining how it can consist with the sovereign goodness of God, has always greatly perplexed philosophers and divines. Some have endeavoured to give a solution, but it has satisfied only themselves. Others have gone so far as to maintain that God was, in fact, the author of moral evil, and of crimes; always protesting, at the same time, that this opinion ought to bring no imputations on the goodness and holiness of God. Others, finally, consider this question as a mystery which we cannot comprehend; and these last, undoubtedly, have embraced the preferable sentiment.

God is supremely good and holy; He is the author of the world, and that world swarms with crimes and calamities. These are three truths which it is apparently difficult to reconcile; but, in my opinion, a great part of the difficulty vanishes as soon as we have formed a just idea of spirit, and of the liberty so essential to it that God himself cannot divest it of this quality.

God having created spirits, and the souls of men, I remark, first, that spirits are beings infinitely more excellent than bodies; and, secondly, that, at the moment of creation, spirits were all good: for time is requisite to the formation of evil inclinations: there is, therefore, no difficulty in affirming that God created spirits. But it being the essence of spirits to be free, and liberty not being capable of subsisting without a power of sinning has nothing inconsistent with divine perfection, because a spirit could not be created destitute of that power.

God has, besides, done every thing to prevent crimes, by prescribing to spirits precepts, the observance of which must always render them good and happy. There is no other method of treating spirits, which cannot be subject to any constraint; and if some of them have abused their liberty, and transgressed these commandments, they are responsible for it, and worthy of punishment, without any impeachment of the Deity.

There remains only one objection more to be considered-- namely, that it would have been better not to create such spirits, as God foresaw they must sink into criminality. But this far surpasses human understanding; for we know not whether the plan of the world could subsist without them. We know, on the contrary, by experience, that the wickedness of some men frequently contributes to the correction and amendment of others, and thereby conducts them to happiness. This consideration alone is sufficient to justify the existence of evil spirits. And as God has all power over the consequences of human wickedness, every one may rest assured, that in conforming to the commandments of God, all events which come to pass, however calamitous they may appear to him, are always under the direction of Providence, and finally terminate in his true happiness.

This providence of God, which extends to every individual in particular, thus furnishes the most satisfactory solution of the question respecting the permission and the origin of evil. This likewise is the foundation of all religion, the alone "object of which is to promote the salvation of mankind."

30th December, 1760.

B. German Science

Johann Wolfgang von Goethe was the intellectual leader of Germany at the end of the 18th century. He was fascinated by science, for he thought to find in nature the principles of order and beauty that inspired his poetry and other writings. The Newtonian world was too austere and bare for him. Nature could not be just the motion of sub-sensible particles in Euclidean space for that would mean that the rich world of the senses was mere illusion. His rejection of Newtonian physics was nowhere more vividly displayed than in his work on colors.

It may naturally be asked whether, in proposing to treat of colours, light itself should not first engage our attention: to this we briefly and frankly answer that since so much has already been said on the subject of light, it can hardly be desirable to multiply repetitions by again going over the same ground.

Indeed, strictly speaking, it is useless to attempt to express the nature of a thing abstractedly. Effects we can perceive, and a complete history of those effects would, in fact, sufficiently define the nature of the thing itself. We should try in vain to describe a man's character, but let his acts be collected and an idea of the character will be presented to us.

The colours are acts of light; its active and passive modifications: thus considered we may expect from them some explanation respecting light itself. Colours and light, it is true, stand in the most intimate relation to each other, but we should think of both as belonging to nature as a whole, for it is nature as a whole which manifests itself by their means in an especial manner to the sense of sight.

The completeness of nature displays itself to another sense in a similar way. Let the eye be closed, let the sense of hearing be excited, and from the lightest breath to the wildest din, from the simplest sound to the highest harmony, from the most vehement and impassioned cry to the gentlest word of reason, still it is Nature that speaks and manifests her presence, her power, her pervading life and the vastness of her relations; so that a blind man to whom the infinite visible is denied, can still comprehend an infinite vitality by means of another organ.

And thus as we descend the scale of being, Nature speaks to other senses--to known, misunderstood, and unknown senses: so speaks she with herself and to us in a thousand modes. To the attentive observer she is nowhere dead nor silent; she has even a secret agent in inflexible matter, in a metal, the smallest portions of which tell us what is passing in the entire mass. However manifold, complicated, and unintelligible this language may often seem to us, yet its elements remain ever the same. With light poise and counterpoise, Nature oscillates within her prescribed limits, yet thus arise all the varieties and conditions of the phenomena which are presented to us in space and time.

---

* Goethe's *Theory of Colours*, translated from the German with Notes by Charles Eastlake. (London: John Murray, 1840) Pp. xxxvii-xlix; 283-289; 293-303.

Infinitely various are the means by which we become acquainted with these general movements and tendencies: now as a simple repulsion and attraction, now as an upsparkling and vanishing light, as undulation in the air, as commotion in matter, as oxydation and deoxydation; but always, uniting or separating, the great purpose is found to be to excite and promote existence in some form or other.

The observers of nature finding, however, that this poise and counterpoise are respectively unequal in effect, have endeavoured to represent such a relation in terms. They have everywhere remarked and spoken of a greater and lesser principle, an action and resistance, a doing and suffering, an advancing and retiring, a violent and moderating power; and thus a symbolical language has arisen, which, from its close analogy, may be employed as equivalent to a direct and appropriate terminology.

To apply these designations, this language of Nature to the subject we have undertaken; to enrich and amplify this language by means of the theory of colours and the variety of their phenomena, and thus facilitate the communication of higher theoretical views, was the principal aim of the present treatise.

The work itself is divided into three parts. The first contains the outline of a theory of colours. In this, the innumerable cases which present themselves to the observer are collected under certain leading phenomena, according to an arrangement which will be explained in the Introduction; and here it may be remarked, that although we have adhered throughout to experiment, and throughout considered it as our basis, yet the theoretical views which led to the arrangement alluded to, could not but be stated. It is sometimes unreasonably required by persons who do not even themselves attend to such a condition, that experimental information should be submitted without any connecting theory to the reader or scholar, who is himself to form his conclusions as he may list. Surely the mere inspection of a subject can profit us but little. Every act of seeing leads to consideration, consideration to reflection, reflection to combination, and thus it may be said that in every attentive look on nature we already theorise. But in order to guard against the possible abuse of this abstract view, in order that the practical deductions we look to should be really useful, we should theorise without forgetting that we are so doing, we should thorise with mental self-possession, and, to use a bold word, with irony.

In the second part we examine the Newtonian theory; a theory which by its ascendancy and consideration has hitherto impeded a free inquiry into the phenomena of colours. We combat that hypothesis, for although it is no longer found available, it still retains a traditional authority in the world. Its real relations to its subject will require to be plainly pointed out; the old errors must be cleared away, if the theory of colours is not still to remain in the rear of so many other better investigated departments of natural science. Since, however, this second part of our work may appear somewhat dry as regards its matter, and perhaps too vehement and excited in its manner, we may here be permitted to introduce a sort of allegory in a lighter style, as a prelude to that graver portion, and as some excuse for the earnestness alluded to.

We compare the Newtonian theory of colours to an old castle, which was at first constructed by its architect with youthful precipitation; it was, however, gradually enlarged and equipped by him according to the exigencies of time and circumstances, and moreover was still further fortified and secured in consequence of feuds and hostile demonstrations.

The same system was pursued by his successors and heirs: their increased wants within, the harassing vigilance of their opponents without, and various accidents compelled them in some places to build near, in others in connexion with the fabric, and thus to extend the original plan.

It became necessary to connect all these incongruous parts and additions by the strangest galleries, halls and passages. All damages, whether inflicted by the hand of the enemy or the power of time, were quickly made good. As occasion required, they deepened the moats, raised the walls, and took care there should be no lack of towers, battlements, and embrasures. This care and these exertions gave rise to a prejudice in favour of the great importance of the fortress, and still upheld that prejudice, although the arts of building and fortification were by this time very much advanced, and people had learnt to construct much better dwellings and defences in other cases. But the old castle was chiefly held in honour because it had never been taken, because it had repulsed so many assaults, had baffled so many hostile operations, and had always preserved its virgin renown. This renown, this influence lasts even how: it occurs to no one that the old castle is become uninhabitable. Its great duration, its costly construction, are still constantly spoken of. Pilgrims wend their way to it; hasty sketches of it are shown in all schools, and it is thus recommended to the reverence of susceptible youth. Meanwhile, the building itself is already abandoned; its only inmates are a few invalids, who in simple seriousness imagine that they are prepared for war.

Thus there is no question here respecting a tedious siege or a doubtful war; so far from it we find this eighth wonder of the world already nodding to its fall as a deserted piece of antiquity, and begin at once, without further ceremony, to dismantle it from gable and roof downwards; that the sun may at last shine into the old nest of rats and owls, and exhibit to the eye of the wondering traveller that labyrinthine, incongruous style of building, with its scanty, make-shift contrivances, the result of accident and emergency, its intentional artifice and clumsy repairs. Such an inspection will, however, only be possible when wall after wall, arch after arch, is demolished, the rubbish being at once cleared away as well as it can be.

To effect this, and to level the site where it is possible to do so, to arrange the materials thus acquired, so that they can be hereafter again employed for a new building, is the arduous duty we have undertaken in this Second Part. Should we succeed, by a cheerful application of all possible ability and dexterity, in razing this Bastille, and in gaining a free space, it is thus by no means intended at once to cover the site again and to encumber it with a new structure; we propose rather to make use of this area for the purpose of passing in review a pleasing and varied series of illustrative figures.

The third part is thus devoted to the historical account of early inquirers and investigators. As we before expressed the opinion that the history of an individual displays his character, so it may here be well affirmed that the history of science is science itself. We cannot clearly be aware of what we possess till we have the means of knowing what others possessed before us. We cannot really and honestly rejoice in the advantages of our own time if we know not how to appreciate the advantages of former periods. But it was impossible to write, or even to prepare the way for a history of the theory of colours while the Newtonian theory existed; for no aristocratic presumption has ever looked down on those who were not of its order, with such intolerable arrogance as that betrayed by the Newtonian school in deciding on all that had been done in earlier times and all that was done around it. With disgust and indignation we find Priestley, in his History of Optics, like many before and after him, dating the success of all researches into the world of colours from the epoch of a decomposed ray of light, or what pretended to be so; looking down with a supercilious air on the ancient and less modern inquirers, who, after all, had proceeded quietly in the right road, and who have transmitted to us observations and thoughts in detail which we can neither arrange better nor conceive more justly.

We have a right to expect from one who proposes to give the history of any science, that he inform us how the phenomena of which it treats were gradually known, and what was imagined, conjectured, assumed, or thought respecting them. To state all this in due connexion is by no means an easy task; need we say that to write a history at all is always a hazardous affair; with the most honest intention there is always a danger of being dishonest; for in such an undertaking, a writer tacitly announces at the outset that he means to place some things in light, others in shade. The author has, nevertheless, long derived pleasure from the prosecution of his task: but as it is the intention only that presents itself to the mind as a whole, while the execution is generally accomplished portion by portion, he is compelled to admit that instead of a history he furnishes only materials for one. These materials consist in translations, extracts, original and borrowed comments, hints, and notes; a collection, in short, which, if not answering all that is required, has at least the merit of having been made with earnestness and interest. Lastly, such materials,--not altogether untouched it is true, but still not exhausted,--may be more satisfactory to the reflecting reader in the state in which they are, as he can easily combine them according to his own justment.

This third part, containing the history of the science, does not, however, thus conclude the subject: a fourth supplementary portion is added. This contains a recapitulation or revision; with a view to which, chiefly, the paragraphs are headed numerically. In the execution of a work of this kind some things may be forgotten, some are of necessity omitted, so as not to distract the attention, some can only be arrived at as corollaries,

and others may require to be exemplified and verified: on all
these accounts, postscripts, additions and corrections are indispensable. This part contains, besides, some detached essays;
for example, that on the atmospheric colours; for as these are
introduced in the theory itself without any classification, they
are here presented to the mind's eye at one view. Again, if
this essay invites the reader to consult Nature herself, another
is intended to recommend the artificial aids of science by cir-
cumstantially describing the apparatus which will in future be
necessary to assist researches into the theory of colours.

In conclusion, it only remains to speak of the plates which
are added at the end of the work; and here we confess we are
reminded of that incompleteness and imperfection which the
present undertaking has, in common with all others of its class;
for as a good play can be in fact only half transmitted to writing, a great part of its effect depending on the scene, the
personal qualities of the actor, the powers of his voice, the
peculiarities of his gestures, and even the spirit and favourable
humour of the spectators; so it is, in a still greater degree,
with a book which treats of the appearances of nature. To be
enjoyed, to be turned to account, Nature herself must be present
to the reader, either really, or by the help of a lively imagination. Indeed, the author should in such cases communicate his
observations orally, exhibiting the phenomena he describes--as a
text, in the first instance,--partly as they appear to us un-
sought, partly as they may be presented by contrivance to serve
in particular illustration. Explanation and description could
not then fail to produce a lively impression.

The plates which generally accompany works like the present
are thus a most inadequate substitute for all this; a physical
phenomenon exhibiting its effects on all sides is not to be
arrested in lines nor denoted by a section. No one ever dreams
of explaining chemical experiments with figures; yet it is customary in physical researches nearly allied to these, because
the object is thus found to be in some degree answered. In many
cases, however, such diagrams represent mere notions; they are
symbolical resources, hieroglyphic modes of communication, which
by degrees assume the place of the phenomena and of Nature herself, and thus rather hinder than promote true knowledge. In the
present instance we could not dispense with plates, but we have
endeavoured so to construct them that they may be confidently
referred to for the explanation of the didactic and polemical
portions. Some of these may even be considered as forming part
of the apparatus before mentioned.

We now therefore refer the reader to the work itself; first,
only repeating a request which many an author has already made in
vain, and which the modern German reader, especially, so seldom
grants:--

> Si quid novisti rectius istis
> Candidus imperti; si non, his utere mecum.

Relation to Other Pursuits--
Relation to Philosophy.

The investigator of nature cannot be required to be a
philosopher, but it is expected that he should so far have attained the habit of philosophizing, as to distinguish himself
essentially from the world, in order to associate himself with
it again in a higher sense. He should form to himself a method
in accordance with observation, but he should take heed not to
reduce observation to mere notion, to substitute words for this
notion, and to use and deal with these words as if they were
things. He should be acquainted with the labours of philosophers,
in order to follow up the phenomena which have been the subject
of his observation, into the philosophic region.

It cannot be required that the philosopher should be a
naturalist, and yet his co-operation in physical researches is as
necessary as it is desirable. He needs not an acquaintance with
details for this, but only a clear view of those conclusions
where insulated facts meet.

. . . The worst that can happen to physical science as well
as to many other kinds of knowledge is, that men should treat a
secondary phenomenon as a primordial one, and (since it is impossible to derive the original fact from the secondary state), seek
to explain what is in reality the cause by an effect made to
usurp its place. Hence arises an endless confusion, a mere verbiage, a constant endeavour to seek and to find subterfuges whenever truth presents itself and threatens to be overpowering.

While the observer, the investigator of nature, is thus
dissatisfied in finding that the appearances he sees still contradict a received theory, the philosopher can calmly continue to
operate in his abstract department on a false result, for no
result is so false but that it can be made to appear valid, as
form without substance, by some means or other.

If, on the other hand, the investigator of nature can attain
to the knowledge of that which we have called a primordial phenomenon, he is safe; and the philosopher with him. The investigat-
or of nature is safe, since he is persuaded that he has here
arrived at the limits of his science, that he finds himself at
the height of experimental research; a height whence he can look
back upon the details of observation in all its steps, and forwards into, if he cannot enter, the regions of theory. The
philosopher is safe, for he receives from the experimentalist an
ultimate fact, which, in his hands, now becomes an elementary one.
He now justly pays little attention to appearances which are
understood to be secondary, whether he already finds them scientifically arranged, or whether they present themselves to his
casual observation scattered and confused. Should he even be
inclined to go over this experimental ground himself, and not be
averse to examination in detail, he does this conveniently, instead of lingering too long in the consideration of secondary
and intermediate circumstances, or hastily passing them over
without becoming accurately acquainted with them.

To place the doctrine of colours nearer, in this sense,

within the philosopher's reach, was the author's wish; and although the execution of his purpose, from various causes, does not correspond with his intention, he will still keep this object in view in an intended recapitulation, as well as in the polemical and historical portions of his work; for he will have to return to the consideration of this point hereafter, on an occasion where it will be necessary to speak with less reserve.

Relation to Mathematics.

It may be expected that the investigator of nature, who proposes to treat the science of natural philosophy in its entire range, should be a mathematician. In the middle ages, mathematics was the chief organ by means of which men hoped to master the secrets of nature, and even now, geometry in certain departments of physics, is justly considered of first importance.

The author can boast of no attainments of this kind, and on this account confines himself to departments of science which are independent of geometry; departments which in modern times have been opened up far and wide.

It will be universally allowed that mathematics, one of the noblest auxiliaries which can be employed by man, has, in one point of view, been of the greatest use to the physical sciences; but that, by a false application of its methods, it has, in many respects, been prejudicial to them, is also not to be denied; we find it here and there reluctantly admitted.

The theory of colours, in particular, has suffered much, and its progress has been incalculably retarded by having been mixed up with optics generally, a science which cannot dispense with mathematics; whereas the theory of colours, in strictness, may be investigated quite independently of optics.

But besides this there was an additional evil. A great mathematician was possessed with an entirely false notion on the physical origin of colours; yet, owing to his great authority as a geometer, the mistakes which he committed as an experimentalist long became sanctioned in the eyes of a world ever fettered in prejudices.

The author of the present inquiry has endeavoured throughout to keep the theory of colours distinct from the mathematics, although there are evidently certain points where the assistance of geometry would be desirable. Had not the unprejudiced mathematicians, with whom he has had, or still has, the good fortune to be acquainted, been prevented by other occupations from making common cause with him, his work would not have wanted some merit in this respect. But this very want may be in the end advantageous, since it may now become the object of the enlightened mathematician to ascertain where the doctrine of colours is in need of his aid, and how he can contribute the means at his command with a view to the complete elucidation of this branch of physics.

In general it were to be wished that the Germans, who render such good service to science, while they adopt all that is good from other nations, could by degrees accustom themselves to work in concert. We live, it must be confessed, in an age, the habits of which are directly opposed to such a wish. Every one seeks,

not only to be original in his views, but to be independent of
the labours of others, or at least to persuade himself that he is
so, even in the course of his life and occupation. It is very
often remarked that men who undoubtedly have accomplished much,
quote themselves only, their own writings, journals, and compen-
diums; whereas it would be far more advantageous for the individual, and for the world, if many were devoted to a common pursuit.
The conduct of our neighbours the French is, in this respect,
worthy of imitation; we have a pleasing instance in Cuvier's
preface to his "Tableau Elémentaire de l'Histoire Naturelle des
Animaux."

He who has observed science and its progress with an unprejudiced eye, might even ask whether it is desirable that so many
occupations and aims, though allied to each other, should be
united in one person, and whether it would not be more suitable
for the limited powers of the human mind to distinguish, for
example, the investigator and inventor, from him who employs and
applies the result of experiment? Astronomers, who devote themselves to the observation of the heavens and the discovery or
enumeration of stars, have in modern times formed, to a certain
extent, a distinct class from those who calculate the orbits,
consider the universe in its connexion, and more accurately
define its laws. The history of the doctrine of colours will
often lead us back to these considerations.

*   *   *   *   *

Relation to General Physics.

The state in which general physics now is, appears, again,
particularly favourable to our labours; for natural philosophy,
owing to indefatigable and variously directed research, has gradually attained such eminence, that it appears not impossible to
refer a boundless empiricism to one centre.

Without referring to subjects which are too far removed from
our own province, we observe that the formulæ under which the
elementary appearances of nature are expressed, altogether tend
in this direction; and it is easy to see that through this correspondence of expression, a correspondence in meaning will
necessarily be soon arrived at.

True observers of nature, however they may differ in opinion
in other respects, will agree that all which presents itself as
appearance, all that we meet with as phenomenon, must either indicate an original division which is capable of union, or an
original unity which admits of division, and that the phenomenon
will present itself accordingly. To divide the united, to unite
the divided, is the life of nature; this is the eternal systole
and diastole, the eternal collapsion and expansion, the inspiration and expiration of the world in which we live and move.

It is hardly necessary to observe that what we here express
as number and restrict to dualism is to be understood in a higher
sense; the appearance of a third, a fourth order of facts progressively developing themselves is to be similarly understood;
but actual observation should, above all, be the basis of all

these expressions.

Iron is known to us as a peculiar substance, different from other substances: in its ordinary state we look upon it as a mere material remarkable only on account of its fitness for various uses and applications. How little, however, is necessary to do away with the comparative insignificancy of this substance. A two-fold power is called forth, which, while it tends again to a state of union, and, as it were, seeks itself, acquires a kind of magical relation with its like, and propagates this double property, which is in fact but a principle of reunion, throughout all bodies of the same kind. We here first observe the mere substance, iron; we see the division that takes place in it propagate itself and disappear, and again easily become re-excited. This, according to our mode of thinking, is a primordial phenomenon in immediate relation with its idea, and which acknowledges nothing earthly beyond it.

Electricity is again peculiarly characterised. As a mere quality we are unacquainted with it; for us it is a nothing, a zero, a mere point, which, however, dwells in all apparent existences, and at the same time is the point of origin whence, on the slightest stimulus, a double appearance presents itself, an appearance which only manifests itself to vanish. The conditions under which this manifestation is excited are infinitely varied, according to the nature of particular bodies. From the rudest mechanical friction of very different substances with one another, to the mere contiguity of two entirely similar bodies, the phenomenon is present and stirring, nay, striking and powerful, and so decided and specific, that when we employ the terms or formulae polarity, plus and minus, for north and south, for glass and resin, we do so justifiably and in conformity with nature.

This phenomenon, although it especially affects the surface, is yet by no means superficial. It influences the tendency or determination of material qualities, and connects itself in immediate co-operation with the important double phenomenon which takes place so universally in chemistry,--oxydation, and de-oxydation.

To introduce and include the appearances of colour in this series, this circle of phenomena was the object of our labours. What we have not succeeded in others will accomplish. We found a primordial vast contrast between light and darkness, which may be more generally expressed by light and its absence. We looked for the intermediate state, and sought by means of it to compose the visible world of light, shade, and colour. In the prosecution of this we employed various terms applicable to the development of the phenomena, terms which we adopted from the theories of magnetism, of electricity, and of chemistry. It was necessary, however, to extend this terminology, since we found ourselves in an abstract region, and had to express more complicated relations.

If electricity and galvanism, in their general character, are distinguished as superior to the more limited exhibition of magnetic phenomena, it may be said that colour, although coming under similar laws, is still superior; for since it addresses itself to the noble sense of vision, its perfections are more generally displayed. Compare the varied effects which result from

the augmentation of yellow and blue to red, from the combination
of these two higher extremes to pure red, and the union of the
two inferior extremes to green. What a far more varied scheme is
apparent here than that in which magnetism and electricity are
comprehended. These last phenomena may be said to be inferior
again on another account; for though they penetrate and give life
to the universe, they cannot address themselves to man in a higher sense in order to his employing them æsthetically. The general, simple, physical law must first be elevated and diversified
itself in order to be available for elevated uses.

   If the reader, in this spirit, recalls what has been stated
by us throughout, generally and in detail, with regard to colour,
he will himself pursue and unfold what has been here only lightly
hinted at. He will augur well for science, technical processes,
and art, if it should prove possible to rescue the attractive
subject of the doctrine of colours from the atomic restriction
and isolation in which it has been banished, in order to restore
it to the general dynamic flow of life and action which the present age loves to recognise in nature. These considerations will
press upon us more strongly when, in the historical portion, we
shall have to speak of many an enterprising and intelligent man
who failed to possess his contemporaries with his convictions.

Relation to the Theory of Music.

   Before we proceed to the moral associations of colour, and
the æsthetic influences arising from them, we have here to say a
few words on its relation to melody. That a certain relation
exists between the two, has been always felt; this is proved by
the frequent comparisons we meet with, sometimes as passing
allusions, sometimes as circumstantial parallels. The error
which writers have fallen into in trying to establish this analogy we would thus define:
Colour and sound do not admit of being directly compared
together in any way, but both are referable to a higher formula,
both are derivable, although each for itself, from this higher
law. They are like two rivers which have their source in one and
the same mountain, but subsequently pursue their way under totally different regions, so that throughout the whole course of both
no two points can be compared. Both are general, elementary effects acting according to the general law of separation and tendency to union, of undulation and oscillation, yet acting thus in
wholly different provinces, in different modes, on different
elementary mediums, for different senses.
   Could some investigator rightly adopt the method in which
we have connected the doctrine of colours with natural philosophy
generally, and happily supply what has escaped or been missed by
us, the theory of sound, we are persuaded, might be perfectly
connected with general physics: at present it stands, as it
were, isolated within the circle of science.
   It is true it would be an undertaking of the greatest difficulty to do away with the positive character which we are now
accustomed to attribute to music--a character resulting from the
achievements of practical skill, from accidental, mathematical,

æsthetical influences--and to substitute for all this a merely physical inquiry tending to resolve the science into its first elements. Yet considering the point at which science and art are now arrived, considering the many excellent preparatory investigations that have been made relative to this subject, we may perhaps still see it accomplished.

Concluding Observations on Terminology.

We never sufficiently reflect that a language, strictly speaking, can only be symbolical and figurative, that it can never express things directly, but only, as it were, reflectedly. This is especially the case in speaking of qualities which are only imperfectly presented to observation, which might rather be called powers than objects, and which are ever in movement throughout nature. They are not to be arrested, and yet we find it necessary to describe them; hence we look for all kinds of formulæ in order, figuratively at least, to define them.

Metaphysical formulæ have breadth as well as depth, but on this very account they require a corresponding import; the danger here is vagueness. Mathematical expressions may in many cases be very conveniently and happily employed, but there is always an inflexibility in them, and we presently feel their inadequacy; for even in elementary cases we are very soon conscious of an incommensurable idea; they are, besides, only intelligible to those who are especially conversant in the sciences to which such formulæ are appropriated. The terms of the science of mechanics are more addressed to the ordinary mind, but they are ordinary in other senses, and always have something unpolished; they destroy the inward life to offer from without an insufficient substitute for it. The formulæ of the corpuscular theories are nearly allied to the last; through them the mutable becomes rigid, description and expression uncouth: while, again, moral terms, which undoubtedly can express nicer relations, have the effect of mere symbols in the end, and are in danger of being lost in a play of wit.

If, however, a writer could use all these modes of description and expression with perfect command, and thus give forth the result of his observations on the phenomena of nature in a diversified language; if he could preserve himself from predilections, still embodying a lively meaning in as animated an expression, we might look for much instruction communicated in the most agreeable of forms.

Yet, how difficult it is to avoid substituting the sign for the thing; how difficult to keep the essential quality still living before us, and not to kill it with the word. With all this, we are exposed in modern times to a still greater danger by adopting expressions and terminologies from all branches of knowledge and science to embody our views of simple nature. Astronomy, cosmology, geology, natural history, nay religion and mysticism, are called in in aid; and how often do we not find a general idea and an elementary state rather hidden and obscured than elucidated and brought nearer to us by the employment of terms, the application of which is strictly specific and secondary. We

are quite aware of the necessity which led to the introduction
and general adoption of such a language, we also know that it has
become in a certain sense indispensable; but it is only a moderate, unpretending recourse to it, with an internal conviction of
its fitness, that can recommend it.

After all, the most desirable principle would be that writers should borrow the expressions employed to describe the details of a given province of investigation from the province
itself; treating the simplest phenomenon as an elementary formula, and deriving and developing the more complicated designations from this.

The necessity and suitableness of such a conventional language where the elementary sign expresses itself, has been duly
appreciated by extending, for instance, the application of the
term polarity, which is borrowed from the magnet to electricity,
&c. The *plus* and *minus* which may be substituted for this, have
found as suitable an application to many phenomena; even the
musician, probably without troubling himself about these other
departments, has been naturally led to express the leading
difference in the modes of melody by *major* and *minor*.

For ourselves we have long wished to introduce the term
polarity into the doctrine of colours; with what right and in
what sense, the present work may show. Perhaps we may hereafter
find room to connect the elementary phenomena together according
to our mode, by a similar use of symbolical terms, terms which
must at all times convey the directly corresponding idea; we
shall thus render more explicit what has been here only alluded
to generally, and perhaps too vaguely expressed.

C. English Science

1. *The great triumph of Newtonian science had been the solution of the problem of the motion of the planets within our own
solar system. Newton's principle of universal attraction had, in
fact, been proven true here. But, was gravitation really universal? Could scientists really consider gravitation to be a universal
property of all matter, just on the basis of observations of the
few planets within the ken of earthlings? It was not a burning
question of the time, but it was unsettling. Before the Newtonian
system could be considered the true one, it was necessary to discover exactly how good it was. This was done by Sir William
Herschel, a musician turned astronomer, who built and maintained
the best reflecting telescope of the day. With incredible patience,
Herschel scanned the heavens and recorded his observations. The
result of this work was all that he could have wished. He was
able to show that the principle of universal gravitation was, in
fact, universal for it applied to double star systems far removed
from the earth. Newton, in fact, had been right. Herschel reported his findings to the world in a paper in the* Philosophical
Transactions *of 1803.*

We have already shewn the possibility that two stars, what-soever be their relative magnitudes, may revolve, either in cir-cles or ellipses, round their common centre of gravity; and that, among the multitude of the stars of the heavens, there should be many sufficiently near each other to occasion this mutual revolu-tion, must also appear highly probable. But neither of these considerations can be admitted in proof of the actual existence of such binary combinations. I shall therefore now proceed to give an account of a series of observations on double stars, comprehending a period of about 25 years, which, if I am not mis-taken, will go to prove, that many of them are not merely double in appearance, but must be allowed to be real binary combinations of two stars, intimately held together by the bond of mutual attraction.

It will be necessary to enter into a certain theory, by which these observations ought to be examined, that we may find to what cause we should attribute such changes in the position, or distance, of double stars, as will be reported; and, in order to make the required principles very clear, I shall give them in a few short and numbered sentences, that they may be referred to hereafter.

In Fig. 1, let us call the place of the sun, which may also be taken for that of the observer, O. In the centre of an orbit or plane N F S P is α Geminorum; and, if any other star is to be examined, we have only to exchange the letter α for that by which such double star is known. This letter is always understood to represent the largest of the two stars which make up the double star; and a general expression for its smaller companion will be x. N, F, S, P, represent the positions of the different parts of the heavens, with respect to α, north, following, south, and pre-ceding; and the small letters n, f, s, p, stand for the same directions with respect to O. x α P, is the angle of position of the two stars x and α, with the parallel F P.

As the motion of an observer affects the relative situation of objects, we have three bodies to consider, in our investiga-tion of the cause of the changes which will be pointed out; the sun, the large star, and the small star, or, as we have shortly called them, O, α, x. This admits of three cases: a motion of one of the three bodies; another, of two; and a third, of all the three bodies together. We shall now point out the consequences that will arise in each of the cases.

Single Motions.

No. 1. Motion of x. When α and O are at rest, the motion of x may be assumed, so as perfectly to explain any change of the distance of the two stars, and of their angle of position.

---

* Sir William Herschel, "Account of the Changes that have happened, during the last Twenty-five Years, in the relative Situation of Double-Stars; with an Investigation of the Cause to which they are owing," *Philosophical Transactions* (1803), pp. 340-8; 350-61.

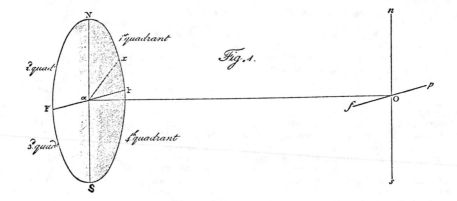

Fig. 1.

No. 2. Motion of ∝. When x and O are at rest, and ∝ has a motion, either towards P, N, F, or S, then the effect of it, whatever may be the angle P ∝ O, will be had by entering the following Table, with the direction of the given motion.

Motion.	Distance.	Angle.	Quadrants.
∝P	− +	+ −	1st and 4th 2 --- 3
∝F	+ −	− +	1 --- 4 2 --- 3
∝N	− +	− +	1 --- 2 3 --- 4
∝S	+ −	+ −	1 --- 2 3 --- 4

No. 3. Motion of O. 1st case. When ∝ and x are at rest, the angle P ∝ O is 90 degrees, a proper motion of O, towards either p, f, n, or s, which will be extremely small when compared with the distance of O from ∝, can have no effect on the apparent distance, or angle of position, of the two stars; and therefore no other motion, composed of the directions we have mentioned, will induce a change in the comparative situation of ∝ and x.

2d case. When the plane PNFS is oblique to the ray ∝O, and the angle P ∝ O more than 90 degrees, the effect of the motion of O will be had by the following Table.

Motion.	Distance.	Angle.	Quadrants.
Op	+	−	1st and 2d 3 --- 4
Of	−	+	1 --- 2 2 --- 4
On	+ −	+ −	1 --- 3 2 --- 4
Os	− +	− +	1 --- 3 2 --- 4

3d case. When the angle P ∝ O is less than 90 degrees, the following Table must be used.

Motion.	Distance.	Angle.	Quadrants.
Op	−	+	1st and 2d 3 --- 4
Of	+	−	1 --- 2 3 --- 4
On	− +	− +	1 --- 3 2 --- 4
Os	+ −	+ −	1 --- 3 2 --- 4

Double Motions.

No. 4.   If we admit different motions in two of our three bodies, and if the ratio of the velocities, the directions of the motions, and the ratio of the distances of the bodies be given quantities, a supposition in which we admit their concurrence, may explain the phenomena of a double star, but can never be probable.

Motions of the three Bodies.

No. 5.   If we admit different motions in every one of the three bodies, O, α, x, and if the velocities and directions of the motions, as well as the relative distances of the three bodies are determined, an hypothesis which admits the existence of such motions and situations, may resolve the phenomena of a double star, but cannot have any pretension to probability.

*   *   *   *   *

α Geminorum.

From my earliest observations on the distance of the two stars which make up the double star in the head of Castor, given in the first of my catalogues of double stars, we find, that about 23 years and a half ago, they were nearly two diameters of the large star asunder.   These observations have been regularly continued, from the year 1778 to the present time, and no altera-tion in the distance has been perceived: the stars are now still nearly 2 diameters of the large one asunder.

It will be necessary to enter a little into the practicabil-ity of ascertaining distances by a method of estimation apparently so little capable of precision.   From a number of observations and experiments I have made on the subject, it is certain that the apparent diameter of a star, in a reflecting telescope, de-pends chiefly upon the four following circumstances: the aperture of the mirror with respect to its focal length; the distinctness of the mirror; the magnifying power; and the state of the atmo-

sphere at the time of observation. By a contraction of the aperture, we can increase the apparent diameter of a star, so as to
make it resemble a small planetary disk. If distinctness should
be wanting, it is evident that the image of objects will not be
sharp and well defined, and that they will consequently appear
larger than they ought. The effect of magnifying power is, to
occasion a relative increase of the vacancy between two stars
that are very near each other; but the ratio of the increase of
the distance is not proportional to that of the power, and sooner
or later comes to a maximum. The state of the atmosphere is perhaps the most material of the four conditions, as we have it not
in our power to alter it. The effects of moisture, damp air, and
haziness, (which have been related in a paper where the causes
that often prevent the proper action of mirrors were discussed,)
show the reason why the apparent distance of a double star should
be affected by a change in the atmosphere. The alteration in the
diameter of Arcturus, extending from the first to the last of the
ten images of that star, in the plate accompanying the abovemen-
tioned paper, shows a sufficient cause for an increase of the
distance of two stars, by a contraction of their apparent disks.
A skilful observer, however, will soon know what state of the air
is most proper for estimations of this kind. I have occasionally
seen the two stars of Castor, from 1½ to 2 and 2½ diameters
asunder; but, in a regular settled temperature and clear air,
their distance was always the same. The other three causes which
affect these estimations, are at our own disposal.

*   *   *

Whatever may be the difficulties, or uncertainties, attending
the method of determining the distance of two close stars by an
estimation of the apparent diameter, it must however be confessed,
that we have no other way of obtaining the same end with so much
precision. Our present instance of $\propto$ Geminorum, will show the
degree of accuracy of which such estimations are capable, and at
the same time prove, that the purpose for which I shall use the
estimated interval between the two stars will be sufficiently
answered. By an observation of the 10th of May, 1781, we have
the diameter of the largest of the two stars to that of the
smallest as 6 to 5; and, according to several measures I have
taken with the micrometer, we may admit their distance, diameters
included, to be five seconds. Then, as the vacancy between the
two stars is nearly, but not quite, 2 diameters of the large one,
I shall value it as 1⅞. From this we calculate, that the diameter of the large star, under the circumstances of our estimation,
is nearly 1",35: so that an error of one quarter of such a diameter, which is the most we can admit, will not exceed 0",34. Nor
is it of much consequence, if the measure of 5" should not be
extremely correct; as a small mistake in that quantity will not
materially affect the error of estimation by the diameter, which,
from what has been said, if the measure was faulty to a second,
would not amount to more than one-fifteenth part of it.
Having thus ascertained that no perceptible change in the
distance of the stars has taken place, we are now to examine the

angle of position. In the year 1779, it was 32° 47' north preceding; and, by a mean of the three last measures I have taken,
it is now only 10° 53'. In the space of about 23 years and a
half, therefore, the angle of position has manifestly undergone a
diminution, of no less than 21° 54'; and, that this change has
been brought on by a regular and gradual decrease of the angle,
will be seen when the rest of the measures come to be examined.

*   *   *

I shall now enter into an examination of the cause of the
change in the angle of position of the small star near Castor.
A revolving star, it is evident, would explain in a most
satisfactory manner, a continual change in the angle of position,
without an alteration of the distance. But this, being a circumstance of which we have no precedent, ought not to be admitted
without the fullest evidence. It will therefore be right to
examine, whether the related phenomena cannot be satisfactorily
explained by the proper motions of the stars, or of the sun.

Single Motions.

(a) The three bodies we have to consider, are O, α, and x;
and, supposing them to be placed as they were observed to be in
the year 1779; the angle x α P, in Fig. 1, will be 32° 47' north
preceding. We are at liberty to let the angle P α O be what will
best answer the purpose. Then, in order to examine the various
hypotheses that may be formed, according to the arrangement of
the principles we have given, we shall begin with No. 1; and, as
this admits that all phenomena may be resolved by a proper motion
of x, let us suppose this star to be placed any where far beyond
α, but so as to have been seen, in the year 1779, where the angle
of position, 32° 47' north preceding, and the observed distance,
near 2 diameters of the large star, required it. With a proper
velocity, let it be in motion towards the place where it may now
be seen at the same distance from Castor, but under an angle of
position only 10° 53' north preceding. It may then be admitted,
that a small decrease of the distance which would happen at the
time when the angle of position was 21° 50', could not have been
perceived; so that the gradual change in the observed angle of
position, as well as the equality of the distance of the two
stars, will be sufficiently accounted for. But the admission of
this hypothesis requires, that α Geminorum and the solar system
should be at rest; and, by the observations of astronomers, which
I shall soon have occasion to mention, neither of these conditions can be conceded.

(b) If, according to No. 2, we admit the motion of α, we
shall certainly be more consistent with the observations which
astronomers have made on the proper motion of this star; and, as
a motion of the solar system, which I shall have occasion to mention hereafter, has not been rigidly proved, it may, for the sake
of argument, be set aside; nor has a proper motion of the star x
been any where ascertained. The retrograde annual proper motion
of Castor, in right ascension, according to Dr. Maskelyne, is

0",105. This, in about 23½ years, during which time I have taken notice of the angle of position and distance of the small star, will amount to a change of nearly 2",47. Then, if we enter the short Table I have given in No. 2, with the motion ∝P, we find, that in the first quadrant, where the small star is placed, the distance between the two stars will be diminished, and the angle of position increased. But since it appears, by my observations, that the distance of the stars is not less now than it was in 1780; and that, instead of an increase in the angle of position, it has actually undergone a diminution of nearly 22 degrees; it follows, that the motion of ∝ Geminorum in right ascension, will not explain the observed alterations in the situation of this double star. If, according to Mr. De la Lande's account, we should also consider the annual proper motion of ∝ in declination, which is given 0",12 towards the north, we shall find, by entering our Table with the motion ∝N, amounting to 2"82, that the distance of the two stars will be still more diminished; but that, on the contrary, the angle of position will be much lessened; and, by combining the two motions together, the apparent disks of the two stars should now be a little more than one-tenth of a second from each other, and the angle of position 35 degrees south preceding. But, since neither of these effects have taken place, the hypothesis cannot be admitted.

(c) That the sun has a proper motion in space, I have shown with a very high degree of evidence, in a paper which was read at the Royal Society about twenty years ago. The same opinion was before, but only from theoretical principles, hinted at by Mr. De la Lande, and also by the late Dr. Wilson, of Glasgow; and has, since the publication of my paper, been taken up by several astronomers, who agree that such a motion exists. In consequence of this, let us now, according to No. 3, assign to the sun a motion in space, of a certain velocity and direction. Admitting therefore ∝ and x to be at rest, let the angle P ∝ O be 90 degrees; then, by the 1st case of No. 3, we find that none of the observed changes of the angles of position will admit of an explanation. There is moreover an evident concession of the point in question, in the very supposition of the above angle of 90 degrees; for, if x be at the same distance as ∝ from the sun, and no more than 5" from that star, its real distance, compared to that of the sun from the star, will be known; and, since that must be less than the 40 thousandth part of our distance from Castor, these two stars must necessarily be within the reach of each other's attraction, and form a binary system.

(d) Let us now take the advantage held out by the 2d case of No. 2, which allows us to place x far behind ∝; in which situation, the angle P ∝ O will be more than 90 degrees. The star x being less than ∝, renders this hypothesis the more plausible. Now, as a motion of Castor, be it real or apparent, has actually been ascertained, we cannot set it aside; the real motion of O, therefore, in order to account for the apparent one of ∝, must be of equal velocity, and in a contrary direction; that is, when decomposed, 0",105 towards f, and 0",12, towards s. The effect of the sun's moving from O towards f, according to the 1st Table in No. 3, is, that the distance between the two stars will be

diminished, and the angle of position increased. But these are
both contrary to the observations I have given. The motion of O
in declination towards s, according to the same Table, will still
diminish the angle of position. Then, since a motion in right
ascension increases the angle, while that in declination diminishes it, the small star may be placed at such a distance that
the difference in the parallax, arising from the solar motion,
shall bring the angle of position, in 23½ years, from 32° 47' to
10° 53'; which will explain the observed change of that angle.
The distance of the star x, for this purpose, must be above 2⅓
times as much as that of ∝ from us. But, after having in this
manner accounted for the alteration of the angle of position, we
are, in the next place, to examine the-effect which such a difference of parallax must produce in the apparent distance of the
two stars from each other. By a graphical method, which is quite
sufficient for our purpose, it appears, that the union of the two
motions in right ascension and declination, must have brought the
two stars so near, as to be only about half a diameter of the
large star from each other; or, to express the same in measures,
the centres of the stars must now be 1",8 nearer than they were
23½ years ago. But this my observations cannot allow; for we
have already shown, that any change of more than 3 or 4-tenths of
a second must have been perceived.

If, on the other hand, we place the star x at such a distance that the solar parallax may only bring it about 4-tenths of
a second nearer to ∝, which is a quantity we may suppose to have
escaped our notice in estimating the apparent distance of the two
stars, then will the angle of position be above 20 degrees too
large. This shows, that no distance, beyond Castor, at which we
can place the star, will explain the given observations.

(e) The last remaining trial we have to examine, is to suppose x to be nearer than ∝; the angle P ∝ O, will then be less
than 90 degrees; and the effect of a motion of O towards f, by
the 2d Table in No. 3, will be an increase of the distance of the
two stars, and a diminution of their angle of position. But the
motion Os, which is also to be considered, will add to the increase of the distance, and counteract the diminution of the
angle. It is therefore to be examined, whether such an increase
of distance as we can allow to have escaped observation, will
explain the change which we know to have happened in the angle,
during the last 23½ years. By the same method of compounding
the two motions as before, it immediately appears, that we cannot
place the small star more than about 1-tenth of the distance O∝ on
this side of Castor, without occasioning such an increase of the
apparent distance of the two stars as cannot possibly be admitted;
and that, even then, the angle of position, instead of being less,
will be a few degrees larger, at the end of 23½ years, than it
was at the beginning. This hypothesis, therefore, like all the
foregoing ones, must also be given up, as inconsistent with my
observations.

It is moreover evident, that the observations of astronomers
on the proper motion of the stars in general, will not permit us
to assume the solar motion at pleasure, merely for the sake of
accounting for the changes which have happened in the appearances

of a double star. The proper motion of Castor, therefore, cannot
be intirely ascribed to a contrary motion of the sun. For we can
assign no reason why the proper motion of this star alone, in
preference, for instance, to that of Arcturus, of Sirius, and of
many others, should be supposed to arise from a motion of the
solar system. Now, if they are all equally intitled to partake
of this motion, we can only admit it in such a direction, and of
such a velocity, as will satisfy the mean direction and velocity
of the general proper motions of the stars; and place all deviations to the account of a real proper motion in each star separately.

Double Motion.

(f) In order to explain the phenomena of our double star,
according to No. 4, by the motion of two bodies, for instance α
and x, it will be required that they both should move in given
directions; that the velocities of their motions should be in a
given ratio to each other; and that this ratio should be compounded with the ratio of their distances from O; a supposition
which must certainly be highly improbable. To show this with
sufficient evidence, let us admit that, according to the best
authorities, the annual proper motion of Castor is--0",105 in
right ascension, and 0",12 in declination towards the north.
Then, as the small star, without changing its distance, has moved
through an angle of 21° 54', the only difference in the two motions of these stars, will be expressed by the extent of the
chord of that angle. To produce the required effect, it is therefore necessary that the motion of α, which is given, should regulate that of the small star, whose relative place at the end of
23½ years is also given. Then, as α moves in an angle of 53° 31'
north preceding, and with a velocity which, being expressed by
the space it would describe in 23½ years, will be 3",51, it is
required that x shall move in an angle of 29° 25', likewise north
preceding, and with a velocity of 3",02. The ratio of the velocities, therefore, and the directions of the motions, are equally
given. But this will not be sufficient for the purpose: their
distance from O must also be taken into consideration. It has
been shown, that the two stars cannot be at an equal distance
from us, without an evident connection; it will therefore be
necessary for those who will not allow this connection, to place
one of them nearer to us than the other. But, as the motions
which have been assumed, when seen from different distances, will
subtend lines whose apparent magnitudes will be in the inverse
ratio of the assumed distances, it is evident that this ratio, if
the motions are given, must also be a given one; or that, if the
distances be assumed, the ratio of the motions must be compounded
with the ratio of the distances. How then can it be expected
that such precise conditions should be made good, by a concurrence
of circumstances owing to mere chance? Indeed, if we were inclined to pass by the difficulties we have considered, there is
still a point left which cannot be set aside. The motion of the
solar system, although its precise direction and velocity may
still be unknown, can hardly admit of a doubt; we have therefore

a third motion to add to the former two, which consequently will bring the case under the statement contained in our 7th number, and will be considered hereafter.

(g) If we should intend to change our ground, and place the two motions in O and x, it will then be conceded, that the motion of ∝ is only an apparent one, which owes its existence to the real motion of the sun. By this, the effect of the solar parallax on any star at the same distance will be given; and it cannot be difficult to assume a motion in x, which shall, with the effect of this given parallax, produce the apparent motion, in the direction of a chord from the first to the last angle of position pointed out by my observations; taking care, however, not to place the stars ∝ and x at the same distance from us; and using the inverse ratio of the solar parallax as a multiple in the assigned motion. For instance, let the sun have a motion of the velocity expressed as before by 3",51, and in a direction which makes an angle of 53° 31' south following with the parallel of ∝ Geminorum; and let the small star x have a real motion in an angle of 18° 40' south preceding from the parallel of its situation, and with a real velocity which, were it at the distance of ∝, would carry it through 1",89. Then, if the distance of the small star be to that of the large one as 3 to 2, the effect of the solar parallax upon it will be ⅔ of its effect upon ∝; that is, while ∝, which is at rest, appears to move over a space of 3",51, in an angle of 53° 31' north preceding, the parallactic change of place in x will be 2",34 in the same direction. This, though only an apparent motion, will be compounded with the real motion we have assigned to it, but which, at the distance of ∝, will only appear as 1",26; and the joint effect of both will bring the star from the place in which it was seen 23½ years ago, to that where now we find it situated. ∝, in the same time, will appear to have had an annual proper motion of--0",105 in right ascension, and 0",12 in declination towards the north; and thus all phenomena will be explained.

From this statement, we may draw a consequence of considerable importance. If we succeed, in this manner, in accounting for the changes observed in the relative situation of the two stars of a double star, we shall fail in proving them to form a binary system; but, in lieu of it, we shall gain two other points, of equal value to astronomers. For, as ∝ Geminorum, according to the foregoing hypothesis, is a star that has no real motion, its apparent motion will give us the velocity and direction of the motion of the solar system; and, this being obtained, we shall also have the relative parallax of every star, not having a proper motion, which is affected by the solar motion. Astronomical observations on the proper motion of many different stars, however, will not allow us to account for the motion of ∝ Geminorum in the manner which the foregoing instance requires; the hypothesis, therefore, of its being at rest, must be rejected.

(h) If we place our two motions in O and ∝, we shall be led to the same conclusion as in the last hypothesis. The known proper motion of ∝, and the situations of the small star in 1779 and 1803, given by my observations, will ascertain the apparent motion of x, now supposed to be at rest. Then, since the change

in the place of x must be intirely owing to the effect of parallax, it will consequently give us, in the same manner as before,
the quantity and direction of the motion of the solar system, and
the relative distances of all such stars as are affected by it.
But, here again, the solar motion required for the purpose is
such as cannot be admitted; and the hypothesis is not maintain-
able.

Motion of the three Bodies.

(*i*) There is now but one case more to consider, which is,
according to No. 5, to assign real motions to all our three
bodies; and this may be done as follows. Suppose the sun to move
towards λ Herculis, with the annual velocity 1.
Let the apparent motion of ∝ Geminorum be as it is stated in
the astronomical tables before mentioned; but suppose it to arise
from a composition of its real motion with the effect of the systematic parallax, as we may call that apparent change of place of
stars which is owing to the motion of the solar system. Let the
real motion of x, aided by the effect of the same parallax, be
the cause of the changes in the angle of position which my observations have given. We may admit the largest of the two stars of
our double star to be of the second magnitude; and, as we are not
to place x too near ∝, we may suppose its distance from O to be
to that of ∝ from the same as 3 to 2. In this case, O will move
from the parallel of ∝, in an angle of 60° 37' north following,
with an apparent annual velocity of ,4536. The motion of ∝ in
right ascension, may be intirely ascribed to solar parallax; but
its change of declination, cannot be accounted for in the same
manner. Let us therefore admit that the solar velocity, in the
direction we have calculated, will produce an apparent retrograde
motion in ∝, which, in 23½ years, will amount to 2",085 in right
ascension. But the same parallax will also occasion a change in
declination, towards the south preceding, of 3",701; and, as this
will not agree with the observed motion of ∝, we must account for
it by a proper motion of this star directly towards the north.
The real annual velocity required for this purpose, must be
1,3925.
The apparent motion of x, by parallax, at the distance we
have placed this star, will be 2",832 towards the south preceding;
and, by assigning to it an annual proper motion of the velocity
1,3354, in the direction of 73° 10' north preceding its own
parallel, the effect of the solar parallax and this proper motion
together, will have caused the small star, in appearance, to revolve round ∝, so as to have produced all the changes in the
angle of position which my observations have given; and, at the
same time, ∝ will have been seen to move from its former place,
at the annual rate of 0",105 in right ascension, and 0",12 in
declination towards the north.
In this manner, we may certainly account for the phenomena
of the changes which have taken place with the two stars of ∝
Geminorum. But the complicated requisites of the motions which
have been exposed to our view, must surely compel every one who
considers them to acknowledge, that such a combination of circum-

stances involves the highest degree of improbability in the accom-
plishment of its conditions. On the other hand, when a most simple and satisfactory explanation of the same phenomena may be had
by the effects of mutual attraction, which will support the moving
bodies in a permanent system of revolution round a common centre
of gravity, while at the same time they follow the direction of a
proper motion which this centre may have in space, it will hardly
be possible to entertain a doubt to which hypothesis we ought to
give the preference.

2. *The American colonies were not especially conducive to original scientific work. There were few instruments, no laboratories,
and little public interest. Benjamin Franklin (1706-1790) is so
interesting precisely because he did important scientific work in
such a barren setting. In a series of letters to the Englishman,
Peter Collinson, Franklin narrated his experiments and ideas on
the nature of electricity.**

To Peter Collinson:

Sir   Philada. July 28. 1747
        The necessary Trouble of copying long Letters which perhaps,
when they come to your Hands, may contain nothing new or worth
your Reading, so quick is the Progress made with you in Electricity, half discourages me from writing anymore on that Subject.
Yet I can not forbear adding a few Observations on Mr. Muschen-
broek's wonder Bottle. vizt.
        1 The Non-electric, contained in the Bottle, differs, when
electrised from a Non-electric electrised out of the Bottle in
this; That the Electrical Fire of the latter is accumulated *on
it's Surface*, and forms an Electrical Atmosphere round it, of
considerable Extent; but the Electrical Fire is crouded *into the
Substance* of the former; the Glass confining it.
        2 At the same Time that the Wire and Top of the Bottle &c.
is electrised *positively* or *plus*, the Bottom of the Bottle is
electrised *negatively* or *minus* in exact Proportion. i.e. Whatever
Quantity of Electrical Fire is thrown in at the Top, an equal
Quantity goes out of the Bottom. To understand this, Suppose the
common Quantity of Electricity in each Part of the Bottle, before
the Operation begins, is equal to 20, and at every Stroke of the
Tube, suppose a Quantity equal to 1 is thrown in; then after the
first Stroke, the Quantity contained in the Wire and upper Part
of the Bottle will be 21, in the Bottom 19. After the second, the
upper Part will have 22, the lower 18, and so on, till after 20
Strokes, the upper Part will have a Quantity of Electrical Fire
equal to 40, the lower none: and then the Operation ends; for no
more can be thrown into the upper Part, when no more can be driven
out of the lower Part. If you attempt to throw more in, it is
spued back thro' the Wire, or flies out in loud Cracks *thro' the
Sides of the Bottle.*
        3 The Equilibrium can not be restored in the Bottle by
inward Communication, or Contact of the Parts; but it must be done
by a Communication form'd *without* the Bottle, between the Top and
Bottom, by some Non-electric touching both at the same Time.   In
which Case, if the Contact be large especially, it is restored
with a Violence and Quickness inexpressible; or touching each
alternately,   in which Case the Equilibrium is restored by
Degrees.
        4 As no more Electrical Fire can be thrown into the Top of
the Bottle, when all is driven out of the Bottom. So in a Bottle

*Leonard W. Labaree, et l., eds., *The Papers of Benjamin Frank-
lin*, vol. 3, New Haven, 1961, pp. 156-62, 352-65.

not yet electrised, none can be thrown into the Top, when none *can* get out of the Bottom; which happens either when the Bottom is too thick, or when the Bottle is placed on an Electric-per-se. Again, when the Bottle is electrised, but little of the Electrical Fire can be *drawn out* from the Top, by touching the Wire, unless an equal Quantity can at the same Time *get in* at the Bottom. Thus place an Electris'd Bottle on clean Glass or dry Wax, and you will not, by touching the Wire, get out the Fire from the Top. Place it on a Non-electric, and touch the Wire, you will get it out in a short Time; but soonest, when you form a direct Communication, as above.

So wonderfully are these two States of Electricity, the *plus* and *minus* combined and ballanced in this miraculous Bottle! situated and related to each other in a Manner that I can by no Means comprehend! If it were possible that a Bottle should in one Part contain a Quantity of Air strongly comprest, and in another Part a perfect Vacuum; We know the Equilibrium would be instantly restored *within*. But here we have a Bottle, containing at the same Time a *Plenum* of Electrical Fire and a *Vacuum* of the same Fire; and yet the Equilibrium can not be restored between them but by a Communication without! Tho' the Plenum presses violently to expand, and the hungry Vacuum seems to attract as violently in Order to be filled. . . .

Experiments confirming the above

Exper. I. Place an electrised Vial on Wax. A small Cork Ball suspended by a dry Silk Thread held in your Hand, and brought  near to the Wire, will first be attracted and then repell'd. When in this State of Repellency, sink your Hand, that the Ball may be brought towards the Bottom of the bottle, it will there be instantly and strongly attracted, 'till it has parted with it's Fire. If the Bottle had an Electrical Atmosphere as well as the Wire, an Electrified Cork would be repell'd from one as well as from the other.

Exper. II. From a bent Wire sticking in the Table, let a small Linen Thread hang down within half an Inch of the Electrised Vial. Touch the Wire of the Vial repeatedly with your Finger; and at every touch you will see the Thread instantly attracted by the Bottle. This is best done with a Vinegar Cruet, or some such belly'd Bottle. As soon as you draw any Fire out from the upper Part, by touching the Wire, the lower Part of the Bottle *draws* an equal Quantity *in* by the Thread.

 Exper. III. Fix a Wire in the Lead, with which the Bottom of the Bottle is armed, so as that bending upwards, it's Ring End may be level with the Top, or Ring End of the Wire in the Cork, and at 3 or 4 Inches Distance. Then electrise the Bottle, and place it on Wax. If a Cork suspended by a Silk Thread hang between these two Wires, it will play incessantly from

one to the other, 'till the Bottle is no longer electrised. That
is, it fetches and carries Fire from the Top to the Bottom of the
Bottle till the Equilibrium is restored. . . .

Exper. V. Let a Ring of thin Lead or Paper
surround the Bottle, even at some Distance from
or above the Bottom: From that Ring let a Wire
proceed up till it touch the Wire of the Cork.
A Bottle, so fixt, can not by any Means be electrised; the Equilibrium is never destroyed. For
while the Communication between the upper and
lower Parts of the Bottle is continu'd by the
outside Wire what is driven out at Bottom is
constantly supplied from the Top. Hence a Bottle can not be
electrised that is foul or moist on the Outside.

Sir   Philada. Apl. 29. 1749
        I now send you some Further Experiments and Observations in
Electricity made in Philadelphia 1748. viz.
        §1. There will be the same Explosion and Shock if the elec-
trified Phial is held in one Hand by the Hook, and the Coating
touched by the other; as when held by the Coating and touched at
the Hook.
        §2. To take the charged Phial safely by the Hook, and not at
the same Time diminish it's Force, it must first be set down on
an Electric per se.
        §3. The Phial will be electrified as strongly, if held by
the Hook, and the Coating apply'd to the Globe, or Tube, as when
held by the Coating and the Hook apply'd.
        §4. But the Direction of the Electrical Fire being different
in Charging, will also be different in the Explosion. The Bottle
charged thro' the Hook will be discharged thro' the Hook. The
Bottle charged thro' the Coating, will be discharged thro' the
Coating and not otherwise: For the Fire must come out the same Way
it went in.
        §5. To prove this; Take two Bottles that were equally
charg'd thro' the Hooks, one in each Hand; bring their Hooks near
each other, and no Spark or Shock will follow; because each Hook
is disposed to give Fire, and neither to receive it. Set one of
the Bottles down on Glass, take it up by the Hook, and apply it's
Coating to the Hook of the other; then there will be an Explosion
and Shock, and both Bottles will be discharged.
        §6. Vary the Experiment, by Charging two Vials equally, one
thro' Hook, the other thro' the Coating: Hold that by the Coating
which was charged thro' the Hook; and that by the Hook which was
charged thro' the Coating. Apply the Hook of the first to the
Coating of the other and there will be no Shock or Spark. Set
that down on Glass, which you held by the Hook, take it up by the
Coating, and bring the two Hooks together; a Spark and Shock will
follow, and both Phials be discharged.
        In this Experiment the Bottles are totally discharged, or the
Equilibrium within them restored. The *Abounding* of Fire in one of
the Hooks (or rather in the internal Surface of one Bottle) being
exactly equal to the *Wanting* of the other: and therefore, as each
Bottle has in itself the *Abounding* as well as the *Wanting*, the

Wanting and Abounding must be equal in each Bottle. See §§8, 9, 10, 11. But if a Man holds in his Hands two Bottles, one fully electrified, the other not at all; and brings their Hooks together; he has but half a Shock, and the Bottles will both remain half electrified; the one being half discharged and the other half charged.

7. Farther, Place two Vials equally charged on a Table at 5 or 6 Inches Distance; Let a Cork Ball, suspended by a Silk Thread, hang between them. If the Vials were both charg'd thro' their Hooks, the Cork, when it has been attracted and repell'd by the one, will not be attracted but equally repell'd by the other. But if the Vials were charged, the one thro the Hook and the other thro' the Coating, the Ball when it is repell'd from one Hook will be as strongly attracted by the other, and play vigorously between them, till both Vials are nearly discharg'd.

8. When we use the Terms of *Charging* and *Discharging* the Phial, 'tis in Compliance with Custom, and for want of others more suitable: since We are of Opinion, that there is really no more electrical Fire in the Phial, after what is called it's *Charging* than before; nor less after it's *Discharging*; (excepting only the small Spark that might be given to and taken from the Non-electric Matter, if separated from the Bottle, which Spark may not be equal to a 500th. Part of what is called the Explosion) For, if on the Explosion, the Electrical Fire came out of the Bottle by one Part, and did not enter in again by another; then, if a Man standing on Wax and holding the Bottle in one Hand, takes the Spark by touching the Wire Hook with the other, the Bottle being thereby *discharg'd*, the Man would be *charg'd*; or, whatever Fire was lost by one, would be found in the other; since there is no Way for it's Escape. But the Contrary is true.

9. Besides, the Vial will not suffer what is called a *Charging*, unless as much Fire can go out of it one Way as is thrown in by another. A Phial can not be charged, standing on Wax, or Glass, or hanging on the prime Conductor, unless a Communication be form'd between it's Coating and the Floor.

10. But suspend two or more Phials on the prime Conductor, one hanging to the Tail of the other, and a Wire from the last to the Floor: an equal Number of Turns of the Wheel shall charge them all equally; and every one as much as one alone would have been. What is driven out at the Tail of the first, serving to charge the second; what is driven out of the second charging the third, and so on. By this Means, a great Number of Bottles might be charged with the same Labour, and equally high with one alone, were it not that every Bottle receives new Fire and loses it's old with some Reluctance, or rather gives some small Resistance to the Charging, which in a Number of Bottles becomes more equal to the Charging Power, and so repels the Fire back again on the Globe, sooner than a single Bottle would do.

11. When a Bottle is charg'd in the common Way, it's inside and outside Surfaces stand ready, the one to give Fire by the Hook, the other to receive it by the Coating: The one is full and ready to throw out, the other empty and extreamly hungry: yet as the first will not *give out*, unless the other can at the same Instant *receive in*; so neither will the latter *receive in*, unless

the first can at the same Instant *give out*. When both can be done at once, 'tis done with inconceivable Quickness and Violence.

12. So a strait Spring (tho' the Comparison does not agree in every Particular) when forcibly bent, must, to restore itself contract that Side, which in the bending was extended, and extend that which was contracted; if either of these two Operations be hindered, the other can not be done. But the Spring is not said to be *charged* with Elasticity when bent, and *discharg'd* when unbent; it's Quantity of Elasticity is always the same.

13. Glass, in like Manner, has, within it's Substance always the same Quantity of Electrical Fire; and that, a very great Quantity in Proportion to the Mass of Glass, as shall be shewn hereafter.

14. This Quantity, proportioned to the Glass, it strongly and obstinately retains, and will neither have more nor less; tho it will suffer a Change to be made in it's Parts and Situation; that is, We may take away Part of it from one of the Sides, provided we throw an equal Quantity into the other.

15. Yet when the Situation of the Electrical Fire is thus altered in the Glass, when some has been taken from one Side, and some added to the other; it will not be at Rest or in its natural State, till 'tis restored to it's original Equality. And this Restitution can not be made thro the Substance of the Glass, but must be done by a Non-electric Communication formed without, from Surface to Surface.

16. Thus the whole Force of the Bottle and Power of giving a Shock, is in the Glass itself; the Non-electrics in Contact with the two Surfaces serving only to give and receive to and from the several Parts of the Glass; that is, to give on one Side, and take away from the other.

17. This was discovered here in the following Manner. Purposing to analize the electrified Bottle, in Order to find where it's Strength lay; we placed it on Glass, and drew out the Cork and Wire, which, for that Purpose, had been loosly put in. Then taking the Bottle in one Hand, and bringing a Finger of the other near its Mouth, a strong Spark came from the Water, and the Shock was as violent as if the Wire had remained in it; which shew'd that the Force did not lie in the Wire. Then to find if it resided in the Water, being crowded into and condensed in it, as confined by the Glass; which had been our former Opinion; we electrified the Bottle again, and placing it on Glass, drew out the Wire and Cork as before, then taking up the Bottle, we decanted all its Water into an empty Bottle, which likewise stood on Glass; and taking up that other Bottle, we expected, if the Force resided in the Water, to find a Shock from it; but there was none. We judged then, that it must either be lost in Decanting, or remain in the first Bottle. The latter we found to be true: For that Bottle on Trial gave the Shock, tho' filled up as it stood with fresh unelectrify'd Water from a Tea Pot. To find then whether Glass had this Property merely as Glass, or whether the Form contributed any Thing to it; we took a Pane of Sash Glass, and laying it on the Hand, placed a Plate of thin Lead on it's upper Surface; then electrified that Plate, and bringing a Finger to it, there was a Spark and Shock. We then took two Plates of Lead of equal

Dimensions, but less than the Glass by two Inches every Way, and
electrified the Glass between them, by electrifying the uppermost
Lead; then separated the Glass from the Lead; in doing which, what
little Fire might be in the Lead was taken out; and the Glass
being touched in the electrified Part with a Finger, afforded
only very small pricking Sparks, but a great Number of them might
be taken from different Places. Then dextrously placing it again
between the Plates of Lead, and completing the Circle between the
two Surfaces, a violent Shock ensu'd. Which demonstrated the
Power to reside in the Glass as *Glass*; and that the Non-electrics
in Contact served only like the Armature of the Loadstone, to
unite the Forces of the several Parts, and bring them at once to
any Point desired. It being a Property of a Nonelectric, that
the whole Body instantly receives or gives what Electrical Fire
is given to or taken from any one of its Parts.

    18. Upon this We made what we call'd an *Electrical Battery*,
consisting of eleven Panes of large Sash Glass, arm'd with thin
leaden Plates, pasted on each Side, placed vertically, and supported at two Inches Distance on Silk Cords; with Hooks of thick
Leaden Wire one from each Side standing upright, distant from
each other; and convenient Communications of Wire and Chain from
the giving Side of one Pane to the receiving Side of the other;
that so the whole might be charg'd together, and with the same
Labour as one single Pane; and another Contrivance to bring the
giving Sides, after charging in Contact with one long Wire, and
the Receivers with another; which two long Wires would give the
Force of all the Plates of Glass at once thro' the Body of any
Animal forming the Circle with them. The Plates may also be
discharg'd separately, or any Number together that is required.
But this Machine is not much used, as not perfectly answering our
Intention with Regard to the Ease of Charging, for the Reasons
given §10. We made also, of large Glass Panes, *Magical Pictures*,
and self moving animated Wheels, presently to be described. . . .

    20. The Magical Picture is made thus. Having a large Mezzo-
tinto with a Frame and Glass (Suppose of the King, God preserve
him) Take out the Print, and cut a Pannel out of it, near two
Inches all round distant from the Frame; if the Cut is thro' the
Picture, tis not the Worse. With thin Paste or Gum Water, fix
the Border, that is cut off, on the inside of the Glass, pressing
it smoothe and close; then fill up the Vacancy by Gilding the
Glass well with Leaf Gold or Brass; gild likewise the inner Edge
of the Back of the Frame all round except the Top Part, and form
a Communication between that Gilding and the Gilding behind the
Glass: then put in the Board, and that side is finished. Turn up
the Glass, and gild the foreside exactly over the Back Gilding;
and when this is dry, cover it by pasting on the Pannel of the
Picture that had been cut out, observing to bring the corresponding Parts of the Border and Picture together; by which the Picture
will appear of a Piece as at first, only Part is behind the Glass
and Part before. Hold the Picture horizontally by the Top, and
place a little moveable gilt Crown on the Kings Head. If now the
Picture be moderately electrified, and another Person take hold
of the Frame with one Hand, so that his Fingers touch it's inside
Gilding, and with the other Hand endeavour to take off the Crown,

he will receive a terrible Blow and fail in the Attempt. If the
Picture were highly charg'd, the Consequence might perhaps be as
fatal as that of High Treason: For when the Spark is taken thro'
a Quire of Paper laid on the Picture, by Means of a Wire Communication, it makes a fair Hole thro' every Sheet; that is thro' 48
Leaves (tho' a Quire of Paper is thought good Armour against the
Push of a Sword, or even against a Pistol Bullet) and the Crack
is exceeding loud. The Operator, who, to prevent its falling,
holds the Picture by the upper End, where the inside of the Frame
is not gilt, feels Nothing of the Shock, and may touch the Crown
without Danger, which he pretends is a Test of his Loyalty. If a
Ring of Persons take a Shock among them the Experiment is called
the *Conspiracy*.

21. On the Principle in §7. That the Hooks of Bottles,
differently charged, will attract and repel differently, is made
an electrical Wheel, that turns with considerable Strength. A
small upright Shaft of Wood passes at right Angles thro' a thin
round Board of about a Foot Diameter, and turns on a sharp Point
of Iron, fixt in the lower End, while a strong Wire in the upper
End, passing thro' a small Hole in a thin Brass Plate, keeps the
Shaft truly vertical. About 30 Radii of equal Length made of Sash
Glass, cut in narrow Strips, issue Horizontally from the Circumference of the Board; the Ends most distant from the Center being
about 4 Inches apart. On the End of every one, a Brass Thimble
is fixt. If now the Wire of a Bottle, electrified in the Common
Way, be brought near the Circumference of this Wheel, it will
attract the nearest Thimble, and so put the Wheel in Motion: That
Thimble, in passing by, receives a Spark, and thereby being electrified is repell'd and so driven forwards, while a second, being
attracted, approaches the Wire, receives a Spark and is driven
after the first; and so on till the Wheel has gone once round,
when the Thimbles, before Electrified, approaching the Wire,
instead of being attracted, as they were at first, are repell'd;
and the Motion presently ceases. But if another Bottle, which
had been charg'd thro' the Coating be placed near the same Wheel,
it's Wire will attract the Thimbles repell'd by the first, and
thereby doubles the Force that carries the Wheel round; and not
only, taking out the Fire that had been communicated to the Thimbles by the first Bottle, but even robbing them of their natural
Quantity, instead of being repell'd when they come again towards
the first Bottle, they are more strongly attracted: so that the
Wheel mends its Pace till it goes with great Rapidity, 12 or 15
Rounds in a Minute; and with such Strength, as that the Weight of
100 Spanish Dollars, with which we once loaded it, did not seem
in the least to retard it's Motion. This is called an *Electrical
Jack*; and if a large Fowl were spitted on the upright Shaft, it
would be carried round before a Fire with a Motion fit for
Roasting.

22. But this Wheel, like those driven by Wind, Water or
Weights, moves by a foreign Force, viz. that of the Bottles. The
Selfmoving Wheel, tho constructed on the same Principles, appears
more surprizing. 'Tis made of a thin round Plate of Window Glass,
17 Inches Diameter, well gilt on both Sides, all but two Inches
next the Edge. Two small Hemispheres of Wood are then fixt with

Cement to the Middle of the upper and under Sides, centrally opposite, and in each of them a thick strong Wire 8 or 10 Inches long,
which together make the Axis of the Wheel. It turns horizontally
on a Point at the lower End of it's Axis which rests on a Bit of
Brass, cemented within a Glass Salt-Seller. The upper End of it's
Axis passes thro' a Hole in a thin Brass Plate, cemented to a long
strong Piece of Glass, which keeps it 6 or 8 Inches Distant from
any Non-electric, and has a small Ball of Wax or Metal on its Top
to keep in the Fire. In a Circle on the Table, which supports
the Wheel, are fixt 12 small Pillars of Glass, at about 4 Inches
Distance, with a Thimble on the Top of each. On the Edge of the
Wheel is a small leaden Bullet, communicating by a Wire with the
Gilding of the upper Surface of the Wheel: and about 6 Inches from
it, is another Bullet, communicating in like Manner with the under
Surface. When the Wheel is to be charg'd by the upper Surface, a
Communication must be made from the under Surface to the Table.
When it is well chargd it begins to move; the Bullet nearest to a
Pillar, moving towards the Thimble on that Pillar; and passing by,
electrifies it, and then pushes itself from it: The succeeding
Bullet, which communicates with the other Surface of the Glass,
more strongly attracting that Thimble, on Account of it's being
before electrified by the other Bullet: and thus the Wheel in-
creases it's Motion, till it comes to such a Height, as that the
Resistance of the Air regulates it. It will go half an Hour, and
make, one Minute with another, 20 Turns in a Minute; which is 600
Turns in the whole: The Bullet of the upper Surface giving in each
Turn 12 Sparks to the Thimbles, which makes 7200 Sparks, and the
Bullet of the under Surface receiving as many from the Thimbles:
these Bullets moving in the Time, near 2500 Feet. The Thimbles
are well fixt, and in so exact a Circle, that the Bullets may pass
within a very small Distance of each of them. If instead of 2
Bullets, you put 8, 4 communicating with the upper Surface, and
four with the under Surface, placed alternately; which 8, at about
6 Inches Distance completes the Circumference; the Force and
Swiftness will be greatly increased; the Wheel making 50 Turns in
a Minute; but then it will not go so long. These Wheels may perhaps be apply'd to the Ringing of Chimes and Moving Orreries. . . .

26. 'Tis amazing to observe in how small a Portion of Glass
a great Electrical Force may lie. A thin Glass Bubble about an
Inch Diameter, weighing only six Grains, being half filled with
Water, partly gilt on the outside, and furnished with a Wire Hook,
gives when electrified, as great a Shock as a Man is willing to
bear. As the Glass is thickest near the Orifice, I suppose the
lower half, which being gilt, was electrified, and gave the Shock,
did not exceed two grains; for it appeared, when broke, much
thinner than the upper half. If one of these thin Bottles be
electrified by the Coating, and the Spark taken out thro the
Gilding, it will break the Glass inwards, at the same Time that
it breaks the Gilding outwards.

27. And allowing, for the Reasons before given §§8, 9, 10,
that there is no more Electrical Fire in a Bottle after Charging
than before, how great must the Quantity be in this small Portion
of Glass! It seems as if it were of its very Substance and
Essence. Perhaps if that due Quantity of Electrical Fire, so

obstinately retain'd by Glass, could be separated from it, it would no longer be Glass, it might loose it's Transparency, or its Fragility, or Elasticity. Experiments may possibly be invented hereafter to discover this. . . .

  29. There is one Experiment more, which surprizes us, and is hitherto not satisfactorily accounted for. It is this. Place an Iron Shot on a Glass Stand, and let a damp Cork Ball, suspended by a Silk Thread hang in Contact with the Shot. Take a Bottle in each Hand, one that is electrified thro' the Hook, the other thro' the Coating. Apply the *giving* Wire to the Shot, which will electrify it positively, and the Cork shall be repell'd. Then apply the *requiring* Wire, which will take out the Spark given by the other, when the Cork will return to the Shot. Apply the same again, and take out another Spark, so will the Shot be electrified negatively, and the Cork in that Case shall be repell'd equally·as before. Then apply the giving Wire, and give to the Shot the Spark it wanted, so will the Cork return: Give it another, which will be an Addition to it's natural Quantity, so will the Cork be repell'd again; And so may the Experiment be repeated, as long as there is any Charge remaining in the Bottles; Which shews that Bodies, having less than the common Quantity of Electricity, repel each other, as well as those that have more.

  Chagrin'd a little that We have hitherto been able to discover Nothing in this Way of Use to Mankind, and the hot Weather coming on, when Electrical Experiments are not so agreable; 'tis proposed to put an End to them for this Season somewhat humorously in a Party of Pleasure on the Banks of SchuylKill, (where Spirits are at the same Time to be fired by a Spark sent from Side to Side thro' the River). A Turky is to be killed for our Dinners by the Electrical Shock; and roasted by the electrical Jack, before a Fire kindled by the Electrified Bottle; when the Healths of all the famous Electricians in England, France and Germany, are to be drank in Electrified Bumpers, under the Discharge of Guns from the Electrical Battery.

To Peter Collinson Esqr. F.R.S. London

III.   The Chemical Revolution

The first question to ask about the history of chemistry is why the so-called Chemical Revolution occurred in the late 18th century while the "Scientific Revolution" in physics and astronomy was well on the way to completion almost one century earlier? Chemistry as a science had its origins in the 17th century, but it has an unusual relationship to the developments of astronomy and physics. The great methodological and theoretical conceptions devised in these fields during the Scientific Revolution were largely inapplicable, and in some instances were actually detrimental to chemistry. One of the major achievements in physics during this period was the systematic attempt to eliminate the secondary qualities of bodies from scientific consideration. Primary qualities should be considered exclusively, and should be treated mathematically. Galileo, in his polemical essay *The Assayer* (1623) drew attention to the importance of this distinction between what we now call primary and secondary qualities, as well as to the use of mathematics. (vol. II, p. 245　.)   In this work Galileo writes as one of the first philosophers of science, indicating an emphasis which should occur in science, with which Descartes and Newton later concurred. On the question of qualities of bodies, Galileo wrote:

> Now I say that whenever I conceive any material or corporeal substance, I immediately feel the need to think of

it as bounded, and as having this or that shape; as being
large or small in relation to other things, and in some
specific place at any given time; as being in motion or
at rest; as touching or not touching some other body; and
as being one in number, or few, or many. From these conditions I cannot separate such a substance by any stretch
of my imagination. But that it must be white or red,
bitter or sweet, noisy or silent, and of sweet or foul
odor, my mind does not feel compelled to bring in as
necessary accompaniments. Without the senses as our
guides, reason or imagination unaided would probably
never arrive at qualities like these. Hence I think that
tastes, odors, colors, and so on are no more than mere
names so far as the object in which we place them is concerned, and that they reside only in the consciousness.
Hence if the living creature were removed, all these qualities would be wiped away and annihilated. But since we
have imposed upon them special names, distinct from those
of the other and real qualities mentioned previously, we
wish to believe that they really exist as actually different from those.

Making the distinction between those qualities which were
essential to bodies and those qualities which were of secondary
importance offered a clear opportunity for two major lines of intellectual concern. Under the guidance of Descartes and Newton,
science chose to focus attention upon primary qualities such as
extension, mobility, and impenetrability, finding them to be
readily susceptible to mathematical treatment. For John Locke
and the empiricists, the secondary qualities and our means of perceiving them provided the area of intense interest. Natural
philosophy and philosophy separate at this juncture, following
increasingly divergent paths and addressing different interests.
One of the most important, although infrequently emphasized, results of the Scientific Revolution is this start of separation
between two major areas of intellectual concern.

Chemistry, until the most recent times, was based upon a concern for secondary qualities. Mathematically described relationships between primary qualities were fine for physics and astronomy, but not for chemistry and especially not for the chemistry
of the 17th century. The practicing chemist could not do chemistry by rejecting secondary qualities. The colors of various
metals, the difference in smell and consistency between water and
acids did make an important difference and one which the chemist
could not ignore. The essential primary qualities of matter, of
such concern to the new physics, did not help chemistry at all.

The conception of matter, devised and confidently asserted
within the framework of the mechanical philosophy by the end of
the 17th century, also failed to interest and aid chemistry. Both
Newton and Descartes placed gross matter in a mechanical setting.
They both believed that there was one basic matter in the universe. This concept of matter and motion was of little use to the
practicing chemist. There was an attempt to incorporate chemistry
into the mechanical philosophy, as we shall see, but for most

chemists there seemed clearly to be many more than a single substance in the universe.

Chemistry could not even make use of the two most powerful intellectual tools developed during the Scientific Revolution to aid in doing science: mathematics and the method of abstraction. Sophistications of geometrical method, the developments in algebra and of analytical geometry and finally the invention of the calculus were of no use to chemistry. The technique of abstracting a specific physical problem from a complex group of phenomena, idealizing the situation so that mathematics would be applicable and then finding a solution to the less complex case in terms of mathematically expressed laws was not applicable in chemistry. Because of the absence of chemical theory, problems either could not be isolated because the larger context was not appreciated, or else the problems which were isolated lent themselves to experiments which yielded results with no meaningful interpretation. Perhaps the best example of this was the oft repeated potted tree experiment, performed by Van Helmont and Robert Boyle to name but two. After careful attempts at weighing soil, pot, water and tree, the conclusion reached after many years was that water must be responsible for the growth and increase in weight of the tree. This meticulously obtained result was meaningless by itself and unintelligible in the contemporary theoretical context of chemistry. How, after all, did water turn into wood?

For the practicing chemist, there were (and still are) three basic and interrelated questions which must be answered together to provide a meaningful theoretical context for chemistry: (1) What is the definition of matter which will work for the chemist; what is the basic substance or substances in chemical reactions? (2) What is the origin of the chemical qualities: acidity, color, metallic properties, and the like? (3) What is the source of chemical activity; why do some reactions take place and others fail under all conditions? These three questions must be satisfied if a useable theoretical framework is to be developed.

Our concern with the basis for chemical theory assumes, of course, that the men doing chemistry in the 17th century were interested in devising a chemical theory. It is clear from our point of view that chemical theory was an essential part in the formation of chemistry as a science. But there were many factors operating in the 17th century which blocked the development of the science of chemistry along theoretical lines. The main blocks to chemical theory were the very successful empirical approaches to practical chemical problems and the continuance of the occult traditions and techniques of alchemy.

Since the Middle Ages, there had been an increasingly successful and well developed tradition of applied chemistry in the fields of metallurgy, ceramic glazing and dyeing, distillation of alcohols and medicine. Chemical knowledge in these areas increased by trial and error. Those techniques and chemicals which were effective were adopted into the craft tradition. Those which did not work were discarded without hesitation and without the need to wonder about theories or proper reasons for rejection. Stained glass windows and bell casting are but two of the highly

developed medieval crafts employing a wide range of practical
chemical knowledge. During the Renaissance, the range of chemical
knowledge was extended to include the manufacture of gun powder
from saltpeter and the more successful extraction of various
metals from their ores. The development of the techniques of ex-
tracting silver from lower grade ores by using mercury increased
silver production from German mines but, more importantly for
European civilization, they made possible the Spanish exploitation of the silver mines of Peru.

Throughout this successful, practical chemical tradition we
notice the glaring absence of chemical theory. New minerals and
ores were discovered and worked with, the construction and use of
furnaces was greatly improved and techniques were sufficiently
developed to meet the demands of fairly complex problems such as
silver extraction. The same situation obtained for the use of
chemicals in medicine. The pharmaceutical tradition is probably
the oldest and most continuous tradition of knowledge in western
civilization. Recipes for the production of medicaments which
worked were passed on in an unbroken chain. Chemicals were included in this tradition, at least as early as the ancient Egyp-
tians. The Ebers Papyrus, dated about the 16th century B.C.,
makes mention of salt, alum, sodium carbonate, copper compounds
and various minerals, to be used for specific ailments. This
long tradition was added to during the Renaissance; the most
familiar addition being Glauber's salt, still in use today as a
laxative and diurent. Those chemicals which worked were used,
with no recourse, nor the possibility of recourse, to chemical
theory.

At first glance, it would seem that alchemy should have provided the source for an abundance of chemical theories. But
alchemy invested its creativity in occult incantations, cryptic
descriptions of technique and the search for the way to the transmutation of metals. The whole theoretical structure of alchemy
had nothing to do with observable chemical reactions. Even if
transmutation seemed plausible, a continuous tradition of attempted conversions from base metals to silver and gold had produced
little to support enthusiasm for this concept on the part of men
outside of the mysteries of alchemy. Even the techniques employed
by the alchemists were of no special value when contrasted to
those of metallurgists and apothecaries. Alchemical techniques
were linked to incantations and were often not as good as those
subjected to the constant test of practical result.

So while physics and astronomy were developing rather complete theoretical frameworks during the Scientific Revolution,
the practical, working chemist got along nicely without a theoretical frame of reference. To say the least, there seemed to be
no compelling urge to establish chemical theory during the Scientific Revolution. Yet there were several serious attempts to
formulate comprehensive chemical theories at this time. The historical independence of the practical chemist from either theory
or alchemy accounts for the strange situation in the 18th century
when several well formulated, but contradictory, chemical theories
existed side by side without serious conflict until the end of
the 18th century. The history of chemistry offers us an interesting case study in the relationship between theory and practice.

The Middle Ages and early Renaissance inherited a relatively simple theoretical scheme of chemistry from the Greeks. It was an Aristotelian system composed of the four Elements, Air, Earth, Fire and Water, and the four Qualities, Hot, Cold, Wet, Dry. This system could provide straightforward answers to our three basic chemical questions. The basic substances in chemical reactions were the four Elements. Their chemical qualities were derivable directly from the four Qualities and the explanation for chemical reactions consisted of the Strife of the Opposites. To this explanatory structure was appended the medical scheme of the four bodily Humours. Health was the balance and ill health the imbalance of blood, phlegm, yellow bile and black bile. This loose, explanatory scheme for both chemistry and medicine remained current until the 18th century. But under the stimulus of the widespread attack on Aristotelian philosophy, and with the steady accumulation of more information on chemicals and chemical techniques, new systems of chemistry were proposed.

The Copernicus of chemistry was Theophrastus Bombast von Hohenheim who by calling himself the peer of the great Roman medical writer, Celsus, has gone into history as Paracelsus (1493-1541). Paracelsus, unlike Copernicus, was a conscious revolutionary dedicated to the total reform of medicine and given to such public revolutionary acts as burning the works of Galen to reveal his contempt for his great predecessor. The key to medicine--indeed, the key to everything--was alchemy, but it was to be a reformed alchemy which Paracelsus was to use. Paracelsus did not base his "reform" of alchemy on reason or even on experience in the ordinary sense of the word. Paracelsian alchemy was filled with magic, not reason, and the experience to which he appealed was mystical, not common observation. Yet, students of his works insist that there is a hard core of meaningful chemical doctrine under the various layers of mystical and often meaningless nonsense. His doctrine, which did serve to stimulate further chemical advances, if only by opposing him, was based upon a few central ideas. For Paracelsus, all processes are ultimately chemical. Those in the outer world are regulated by two "spirits," an *archaeus* and *vulcanus*. To define these two active powers, it would be well to turn to Paracelsus himself:

> This is the way that nature proceeds with us in God's creatures, and follows from what I have said before, nothing is fully made, that is, nothing is made in the form of ultimate matter. Instead all things are made as prime matter and subsequently the *vulcanus* goes over it and makes it into ultimate matter through the art of alchemy. The *archaeus*, the inner *vulcanus*, proceeds in the same way, for he knows how to circulate and prepare according to the pieces and the distribution, as the art itself [alchemy] does with sublimation, distillation, reverberation, etc. For all these arts are in men just as they are in the outer alchemy, which is the figure of them. Thus the *vulcanus* and the *archaeus* separate each other. This is alchemy, which brings to its end that which has not come to its end, which extracts lead from

its ore and works it up to lead, that is the task of alchemy. Thus there are alchemists of the metals, and likewise alchemists who treat minerals, who make antimony
from antimony, sulphur from sulphur, vitriol from vitriol,
and salt into salt. Learn thus to recognize what alchemy
is, that is alone is that which prepares the impure
through fire and makes it pure.*

All this is not very helpful, except as the expression of a
general aim. To make it more specific, Paracelsus developed a
theory of three principles which he rather confusedly added to
the Aristotelian doctrine of earth, air, fire and water. Salt
represented solidity and relative chemical inertness, Sulphur was
the principle of inflammability, and Mercury represented fluidity,
heaviness and metallicity. As the foregoing passage indicates,
Paracelsus was particularly concerned with metals and the chemical processes he mentions that make chemical sense are usually
those associated with the chemistry of metals.

In spite of the fact that there is no original chemical discovery that can be ascribed to him, he did serve to attract attention to chemistry. His disciples did attempt to follow out the
implications of his "theory" and there was an active Paracelsan
school in the seventeenth century. Paracelsus and his followers
did introduce chemistry or chemicals into medicine (sometimes with
fatal results) but even this was not totally new. The Paracelsans
did offer a new chemical perspective and their scheme was more
closely related to actual chemical experience. It served to provide some greater organization for chemicals and to group known
substances together into groups with similar properties. The
three principles of Sulfur, Salt and Mercury could be used to
account for the chemical qualities as well as the reason for chemical reaction. Sulfur, because of its inflammability, stimulated
chemical reaction. Salt, carrying the quality of fusibility,
fixed chemical reactions and tended to stop them. Mercury provided heaviness and metallic properties.

Paracelsus had many followers who continued and modified his
attack on the traditional chemistry and medicine. His foremost
disciple and most important of the new iatrochemists was Johann
Baptista van Helmont (ca. 1580-1648).

Van Helmont, like his master, wrote large, confused, almost
unintelligible treatises. His work on digestion followed directly
from Paracelsus' views. The master had suggested that the stomach
contained an *archeus* which, like a practicing alchemist, undertook the digestion of ingested food. For Van Helmont, digestion
took place by the action of a series of "ferments." Such fermentations also took place outside the body as when grapes fermented
to form wine and wine turned to vinegar. Although such fermentations were considered by Van Helmont to be quite different from
ordinary chemical processes, the "ferment" was at least subject
to study as the *archeus* was not. One of the byproducts of the

*From Paracelsus, *Labyrinth of Errant Physicians*, as quoted in
Marie Boas, *The Scientific Renaissance, 1450-1630*, London, 1962,
pp. 177-78.

study of fermentation was Van Helmont's recognition of one of the
products--what he called chaos or gas which bubbled off in some
violent reactions. Van Helmont could not know it, but gases were
to play a central role in the chemical revolution of the eighteenth century.

Perhaps the most important function that Paracelsus, Van
Helmont and the Paracelsans served was as the point of attack for
the greatest chemist of the seventeenth century, Robert Boyle
(1627-91). Basically, Robert Boyle was not a chemist at all. He
was, rather, a devoted proponent of the mechanical philosophy who
used chemistry to build up empirical evidence for his view of the
world.

"I hoped," he wrote in *Certain Physiological Essays* in 1661,
"I might at least do no unseasonable piece of service to the corpuscular philosophers, by illustrating some of their notions with
sensible experiments, and manifesting, that the things by me
treated of may be at least plausibly explicated without having
recourse to inexplicable forms, real qualities, the four peripa-
tetick elements, or so much as the three chymical principles."*

As Hall points out, Boyle set out to construct a coherent
theory of matter that would replace the metaphysical fancies of
the Aristotelians and the Paracelsans. The task he set himself,
then, was to explain how natural phenomena can be accounted for by
matter and motion. The first requirement was to clean out the
Augean stable of alchemy by ridding chemistry of meaningless
verbiage. That is the real purpose of Boyle's most famous work,
The Skeptical Chemist published in 1661. The Aristotelian and
Paracelsan forms and qualities were shown to be as elusive as
shadows. They could not easily be associated with anything concrete, even ideas, and Boyle suggested that they be discarded.
In their place, he would place the simple, clear and distinct concepts of corpuscles associated together into "minute masses or
clusters," which agglomerations persisted in chemical changes.
The next task was to accumulate evidence to support the view that
gross matter was composed of stable clusters of particles and
that change was merely the result of compositions and decompositions of these clusters. The titles of his works accurately reflect his scientific career. In 1666, he published *The Origins
of Forms and Qualities according to the Corpuscular Philosophy.
Some Thoughts about the Excellency and Grounds of the Mechanical
Hypothesis* appeared in 1674. The next year, a treatise on *Experiments, Notes &c about the Mechanical Origin or Production of
divers particular Qualities: Among which is inserted a Discourse
of the Imperfection of the Chymists' Doctrine of Qualities* followed. Finally we may mention *An Essay of the Great Effects of
even Languid and unheeded Motion* (1685) and *Of the Reconcileable-
ness of specific Medicines to the corpuscular Philosophy* (1685).
These titles reflect his concerns; they do not enumerate his discoveries. Most famous is Boyle's Law which he did not discover.
He did, however, experiment on the relationship between pressure
and volume in a column of air and the law ($pv = k$) was associated

---

*Quoted in A. Rupert Hall, *From Galileo to Newton, 1630-1720*,
London, 1963, p. 224.

with his name. He was one of the first to work with the newly
discovered air pump and his interest in air left a permanent and
happy influence on British chemistry. He was the real founder of
analytical chemistry and recognized the importance of pure reagents. He introduced the use of color indicators as tests for
acidity and alkalinity. His analytical finesse permitted him to
provide proof of the fundamental theorem of his own mechanical
philosophy--namely, that chemical substances (or corpuscular clusters, as Boyle envisioned them) persisted even though they changed
their chemical guise. What the chemist did was merely rearrange
the clusters. And since it was a basic part of the mechanical
philosophy that qualities were the result of corpuscular arrangement, it was to be expected that bodies with new qualities would
result. The fact that the original reagents could be recovered,
seemed to Boyle to be experimental proof of the truth of his corpuscular conjectures.

It was the sheer mass of Boyle's careful experiments and
sound common sense with which Boyle interpreted them that was impressive. The combination certainly impressed Isaac Newton, who
gave a great deal of thought to corpuscular interpretations and
the mechanical philosophy in chemistry as well as physics and
optics. Newton was very interested in chemical questions and
spent a great deal of time working in his chemical laboratory.
His most widely read work on chemistry was the now famous Querie
31, added to the end of his *Optics*. (See volume II of this
work, p. 276.) From the works of Boyle and Newton there derived
what may be termed a corpuscularian or Newtonian theory of chemistry, designed with two purposes: to explain chemical phenomena
within the framework of explanation offered by the mechanical
philosophy. Chemistry should be explained in terms of small,
hard, massy bodies and their motions and attractions with respect
to one another, just as all of physics, and optics could be explained. To this end, matter was composed of sub-visible, small
billiard-ball like particles which clumped together in various
geometrical shapes to form the different types of observable substances. The chemical qualities were derived from the shapes
which were assumed to form the various substances. Acids, for
example, are built of sharp, pointed units, capable of wedging
into and breaking off metal particles. Gold, on the other hand,
was composed of a very solid geometrical arrangement and therefore
was very stable and inactive. The source of chemical reactions
was also readily explained, but in conjunction with the Newtonian
concept of heat as a form of vibrating motion of the particles of
matter. Chemical activity could be ascribed either to universal
attraction, occurring between all bodies, or to a combination of
attraction with the vibrating motion due to heat. In this scheme,
it was easy to see why some reactions, which did not take place
at low temperatures, did occur at high temperatures because of
the increased agitation. It was easy to visualize particles of
matter hitting and bouncing off one another, changing their geometrical arrangement because of all this activity and therefore
reacting to become different substances.

In addition to an explanatory scheme, Newtonian chemistry
provided a very important clue which was recognized fully only by

Lavoisier at the end of the 18th century. If chemical substances were really distinguishable by the arrangements of their particles of matter, then if you started out a chemical process with three pounds of chemicals, you should still have three pounds of substances when it was all over. In other words, the notion of the conservation of matter is implicit in the Newtonian approach to chemistry. But the conservation of mass was not a meaningful concept to chemists in Newton's day, as it would be to Lavoisier, because of two factors: the phlogiston theory and the almost total ignorance about gases and their place in chemical reactions. In general terms, chemistry in the 18th century consists of appraising and eventually rejecting the phlogiston theory and in discovering the third state of matter, the gases.

The phlogiston theory was widely used after 1730 to explain a large number of chemical reactions, particularly those concerned with combustion and the calcination of metals. It was a useful theory and one which was familiar to all chemists in the 18th century. Phlogiston was the "principle of fire" or the "matter of fire." It could be used in a way similar to the way in which oxygen was used after Lavoisier, to explain combustion and calcination. Georg Ernst Stahl (1660-1734) was the most influential proponent of phlogiston chemistry. Phlogiston was accompanied by a new scheme of five chemical principles: air, water, vitreous earth, inflammable earth and metallic earth. Air possessed only physical properties of gaseousness and was not considered to take part in chemical reactions, but the other principles carried with them the chemical qualities of fluidity, fusibility, inflammability and metallic shine.

Phlogiston was used to explain the reactions of combustion and calcination. In the combustion of wood, for example, wood gives off smoke and flame and is reduced to ash; therefore it must have given off "fire-stuff" or phlogiston. Charcoal leaves very little ash when burned, therefore it must be almost pure phlogiston. Sulphur and phosphorus must also be very high in phlogiston. Charcoal was used to extract metals from their ores, therefore ore plus charcoal yields metal. In this reaction the metal absorbed the phlogiston from the charcoal and was separated from the ore. Calcination was also explained in similar terms. Metals, lead for example, when heated until molten left a dross on the surface called a calx. The metal gave up phlogiston in this process, therefore metal minus phlogiston yielded calx. For the first time the major categories of chemical reactions, combustion and calcination, were united by the same explanation; they both involved the giving up of phlogiston.

By mid-18th century there were at least three possible theoretical systems for chemistry: the Aristotelian-Paracelsan system, the Newtonian system and the Stahlian system, of which phlogiston was a major part. Eighteenth-century chemists generally were conversant in all three and picked and chose explanations from these systems as convenience dictated. Most found phlogiston convenient for combustion-calcination reactions, for example, but Englishmen generally preferred the Newtonian-corpuscular context for the rest of their chemistry, while in Germany, Stahl's chemistry remained very popular. The 18th century saw the very rapid increase in chemical information. The most productive chemists of the century tended to direct their efforts toward new information rather than old theory. This was especially true in the new field of gas chemistry.

At the beginning of the 18th century very little was known about the air and nothing was known about what we now call gases. The physical properties of the air had come under investigation earlier by Evangelista Torricelli (1608-47), who began work on the investigation of what we now call barometric pressure, and by Otto von Guericke (1602-86), who dramatically demonstrated the force of atmospheric pressure with his famous "Magdeburg hemispheres" experiment. Many others were interested in the physical properties of the air, but its chemical composition was very difficult to assess.

The air pump provided the means for understanding the chemical nature of the air. Robert Hooke (1635-1703) and Robert Boyle made extensive use of improved air pumps, conducting a wide range of experiments which provided conclusive evidence that air was necessary both for the combustion of a candle and for the life of small animals placed in airtight vessels. Air, or something in the air, was necessary for both life and combustion. Gas chemistry began in England and remained almost entirely empirical. The English "pneumatic chemists" as they were called, piled observation and experiment one upon another, developing important techniques and apparatus as the century progressed.

Of the great many pneumatic chemists of the 18th century, a few must be mentioned. Stephen Hales (1677-1761) was perhaps the most curious because his career consisted of doing huge numbers of seemingly random experiments. He loved to measure pressures, measuring sap pressures in plants and devising a manometer for taking blood pressures of larger mammals. His major work, *Vegetable Statics* (1727), was filled with miscellaneous information, some of which related to experiments leading to the production of "airs." Stephen Hales simply did a great number of experiments leading to the production of many of the common gases. Hales called them all "airs" and was concerned only with the quantities which could be obtained by various methods of production and collection. The *Vegetable Statics* served as a type of recipe book on the production of various airs. It was widely read both in England and on the Continent, serving a useful purpose in the 18th century.

Many could produce "airs," but Joseph Black (1728-99) was the first to appreciate the chemical role of airs in certain chemical reactions. With the realization that airs could be chemically active, pneumatic chemistry moved from the production of airs as a curiosity to the search for their role in chemical reactions. Black had been interested in the differences between mild and caustic alkalis, particularly with respect to their effects on the body. He had received a fine medical education at the University of Glasgow and had studied under a famous professor of medicine, one Dr. Cullen, who was also a lecturer in chemistry with a good chemical laboratory. Black continued to work on the question of the differences between alkalis until he reached an understanding of the problem. The results were published in 1756, in a paper entitled *Experiments upon Magnesia alba, Quicklime, and some other Alcaline Substances*. This short paper was important for reasons rather separate from the subject investigated. Black discovered that an air he called "fixed air" (now called carbon dioxide) took an active part in chemical reactions. Airs must be considered as chemically active. He also discovered that "fixed air" was found in the normal air so that the air must contain fixed air and yet remain different from it. There must be some differences between airs, physical as well as chemical. Finally Black made accurate and consistent use of the chemical balance. He was able to show for the first time that chemical reactions involving "airs" could be accurately followed with a balance and that weight gains and losses could be measured. Before this careful application of measurement, weight changes were quite mysterious, with weight commonly disappearing in the form of smoke and unseen gases. Black's work provided pneumatic chemistry with new accuracy and most importantly, new questions to be asked and investigated.

After the work of Hales and Black, information about gases increased very rapidly. Two Englishmen were again at the front of this work: Henry Cavendish (1731-1810) and Joseph Priestley (1733-1804). Cavendish was responsible for the perfection and description of gas collection techniques over water. His experiments made certain Black's contention that there were airs producible in the laboratory which were distinctly different from regular air. In addition to Black's "fixed air," Cavendish investigated a new, very light air he called "inflammable air," what we now call hydrogen. His paper to the Royal Society of London in 1766, "On Fractius Airs," included his collection techniques and his new findings. It was widely read and served to standardize techniques in pneumatic chemistry.

Joseph Priestley was important to the story because he unwittingly provided the means of overthrowing the phlogiston theory and because his work was known and appropriated by Lavoisier. Priestley was an amateur natural philosopher with serious interests in politics and religion. He was a Unitarian minister and an admirer of the French Revolution, at least in its early years. But he was also a tireless and clever pneumatic chemist. His written works in science are prodigious, covering physics, electricity, magnetism and optics as well as chemistry. His chemical writings are contained primarily in his *Experiments and Observations on Different Kinds of Air*, in three volumes (1774-77), and his *Experiments and Observations relating to Various Branches of Natural Philosophy*, also three volumes (1779-86).

In 1770 Priestley wrote to a friend, "I am now taking up some of Dr. Hale's enquiries concerning air." In the years that followed he studied a long list of airs, making improvements on Cavendish's apparatus and making use of a mercury bath for collection of gases which were soluble in water. He studied nitrous air (nitric oxide), phlogisticated air (nitrogen), nitrous vapour (nitrogen dioxide), acid air (hydrochloric acid, collected over mercury) and many, many others. Along the way he invented soda water or club soda; carbonated water produced by bubbling "fixed air" through water. But most importantly, Priestley was the discoverer of oxygen.

On August 1st, 1774, Priestley obtained oxygen by heating red oxide of mercury with a large convex burning glass. He found that oxygen was practically insoluble in water, but, surprisingly, oxygen made a candle immersed in it burn in a dazzling way. Priestley was completely at a loss to account for the remarkable vigorous flame of the candle. To investigate the properties of this strange new gas further, he conducted two of the standard tests employed by pneumatic chemists; he generated some more of this new air and tested a mouse in the gas and then breathed some himself. Again to his surprise, the mouse placed in a closed container of oxygen lived twice as long as it would have lived in the same volume of ordinary air. He breathed some and exclaimed that "his breast felt peculiarly light and easy for some time afterwards." Led momentarily astray by the sensation, the inventor of soda water speculated upon the possible value of oxygen for treatment at fashionable health spas: "Who can tell," he wrote, "but that in time, this pure air may become a fashionable article in luxury. Hitherto only two mice and myself have had the privilege of breathing it."

Priestley was so surprised at the properties of oxygen because he was a firm believer in the phlogiston theory. His term for oxygen, dephlogisticated air, was natural in terms of this theory. Priestley agreed with Stahl that the burning process gave off phlogiston. A candle was extinguished in a closed vessel after a time because the air became saturated with phlogiston. Ordinary air supported this combustion because it was only partially saturated with phlogiston and could absorb limited amounts more. Since things burn so much more readily in the new air, that air must contain little or no phlogiston, therefore the name dephlogisticated air.

Priestley continued to do many experiments on his new air, deriving it from many different sources. He was convinced, rather ironically, that his discovery was a confirmation of Stahl's phlogiston theory. His two detailed works, *Consideration on the Doctrine of Phlogiston* (1796) and the *Doctrine of Phlogiston Established* (1800) represented the last major supports for the phlogiston theory, against the new chemistry initiated by Lavoisier.

Antoine Laurent Lavoisier (1743-94) changed the direction, methods and content of chemistry by his major works *Méthode de Nomenclature Chimique* (1787) and *Traité Élémentaire de Chimie* (1789). Lavoisier was a conscious innovator. He wanted to change the whole orientation of chemistry and he succeeded. Perhaps the best example of his attitude can be derived from a letter to his admired acquaintance Benjamin Franklin. Lavoisier wrote the letter to accompany two copies of his newly published *Traité Élémentaire de Chimie*, one for Franklin and one for the active American Philosophical Society in Philadelphia. The letter begins with Lavoisier's denunciation of Stahl's phlogiston theory. One of the primary purposes of the *Traité* was the detailed denial of the existence of phlogiston. Lavoisier opposed the unbridled use of speculation and the reliance upon substances with no observable properties. "I have tried," he wrote, ". . . to arrive at the truth by linking up facts; to suppress as much as possible the use of reasoning, which is often an unreliable instrument which deceives us, in order to follow as much as possible the torch of observation and of experiment."

The approach which Lavoisier takes to chemistry was in close agreement with Newton's strictures against "framing hypotheses." Lavoisier was fully aware of Newton's recommended approach to nature. In the letter to Franklin, Lavoisier wrote: "This course [following the torch of observation and experiment], which had not yet been followed in chemistry, led me to dispose my work in an absolutely new arrangement, and chemistry is brought closer than before to experimental physics." "It seems to me," he continued, "that chemistry, presented in this form, has become an infinitely easier study than it was before. The young people, whose heads are not engrossed with some system, seize upon it with avidity. But the older chemists still reject it, and most of them have more trouble grasping and understanding it than those who have not yet studied chemistry." Lavoisier claimed that the French were divided on his chemistry, the English were beginning to accept it and the Germans still adhered firmly to theories and phlogiston. "So you see," Lavoisier concluded with unabashed confidence, "that since your departure from Europe a revolution has occurred in an important area of human knowledge."

Lavoisier was correct in his assessment of the impact of his work. There had been a revolution in chemistry. But Lavoisier's role as leader of this revolution might appear to be a bit unusual. He made no discoveries of new substances nor did he devise any important new pieces of experimental apparatus or new preparation techniques. Lavoisier's letter to Franklin to the contrary notwithstanding, Lavoisier was essentially a theorist, but of a rather special kind. His greatness lay in his ability to assimilate the experimental work of others and to put their results into a new chemical context of his own devising. Lavoisier, unfortunately, seldom gave any recognition to the work of others, but he was able to take their experiments, repeat them himself with his own careful, quantitative procedures, and draw new conclusions based on the same data. He essentially completed the work of Black, Priestley and Cavendish by providing a new interpretation of their experimental results. This was the basis for the Chemical Revolution.

Lavoisier's work may be presented under three main categories: (1) his use of the chemical balance and its implications for the conservation of mass, (2) his use of oxygen and the overthrow of the phlogiston theory, and (3) his use of new chemical nomenclature and his new method of chemistry.

Lavoisier was the first to make constant and accurate use of the chemical balance in all of his experiments. He was not the first to make use of the balance; Joseph Black used the balance to keep track of "fixed air" in his experiments. But Lavoisier was the first to use the balance consistently and with a new confidence. He made explicit the basic assumption implicit in the use of the balance, the indestructibility of matter in chemical reactions and the conservation of matter. Lavoisier wrote in his *Traité*:

for nothing is created in the operations either of art
or of nature, and it can be taken as an axiom that in
every operation an equal quantity of matter exists both
before and after the operation, that the quality and quantity of the principles remain the same and that only
changes and modifications occur. The whole art of making
experiments in chemistry is founded on this principle: we
must always suppose an exact equality of equation between
the principles of the body examined and those of the products of its analysis.

This attitude, and a commitment to it ended once and for all
the alchemical notion of the transmutation of the elements. Specifically, Lavoisier ended the prevalent notion that water could
be transmuted to earth. In 1770 he wrote a paper entitled "On
the nature of water and on the experiments which have been supposed to demonstrate the possibility of its conversion to earth."
The process of distillation of water had frequently produced a
white residue, considered by many who believed in transmutation
to be evidence for the transformation of water to earth. Since
transformations were expected to be possible, it came as no surprise that this should take place. Lavoisier, however, did not
accept this orientation and therefore set out to show that no
transformation had occurred. By very careful weighing of the
water, the flask used and the residue produced, Lavoisier was
able to show beyond doubt that water was not converted into earth;
the residue was material which had dissolved out of the glass
during the long distillation process. The weight of the residue
equalled the weight lost by the distillation flask. Both the
experiment and the conclusion were made possible by Lavoisier's
commitment to the new concept of the conservation of matter.

The rejection of phlogiston was also related to Lavoisier's
firm belief in the indestructibility of matter. The theory of
phlogiston contained many explanations which included the assumption that phlogiston exhibited the property of levity. Adding
the matter of fire or phlogiston frequently resulted in decrease
in weight. It was not unusual to entertain the concept of levity
in chemistry before the systematic use of the balance and careful
accounting for products of reaction such as gases and smoke became common practice. But for Lavoisier's careful techniques,
levity was out of the question. For him, this was a fundamental
error of the phlogiston theory.

Lavoisier had probably rejected the phlogiston theory as
early as 1772, but he had nothing with which to replace that
theory to account for combustion and calcination. His famous
"Sealed Note" of 1772, sent to the Academy of Science, indicated
the direction of his thinking. He wanted to get the credit for
what he believed to be the imminent demise of the phlogiston
theory, but he was not yet sure what form the death blow would
take. The note contained the following:

About eight days ago I discovered that sulphur, in
burning, far from losing weight, on the contrary gains
it; that is to say that from a *livre* of sulphur one can
obtain much more than a *livre* of vitriolic acid, making

allowance for the humidity of the air; it is the same
with phosphorus; this increase of weight arises from a
prodigious quantity of air that is fixed during the combustion and combines with the vapours.

This discovery, which I have established by experiments
that I regard as decisive, has led me to think that what
is observed in the combustion of sulphur and phosphorus
may well take place in the case of all substances that
gain in weight by combustion and calcination: and I am
persuaded that the increase in weight of metallic calces
is due to the same cause. Experiment has completely confirmed my conjectures: I have carried out the reduction
of litharge in closed vessels, with the apparatus of
Hales, and I observed that, just as the calx changed into
metal, a large quantity of air was liberated and that this
air formed a volume a thousand times greater than the
quantity of litharge employed. This discovery appearing
to me one of the most interesting of those that have been
made since the time of Stahl, I felt that I ought to secure my right in it, by depositing this note in the hands
of the Secretary of the Academy, to remain sealed until
the time when I shall make my experiments known. Paris,
November 11, 1772. Lavoisier.*

Since the litharge was reduced by graphite, Lavoisier could
not reverse the reaction to re-obtain the litharge. In 1772 and
1773, Lavoisier became convinced that both combustion and calcination involved the absorption of something from the air. He was
not sure what was absorbed, but he became convinced that rather
than involving the giving up of phlogiston, the processes of combustion and calcination involved the adding on of something present in the air.

In October 1774, Joseph Priestley visited Paris with his
benefactor Lord Shelbourne. Priestley was invited to dinner by
Lavoisier and during the course of the dinner Priestley described
his discovery and production of dephlogisticated air using red
precipitate of mercury and red lead. Priestley reported that
"all the company and Mr. and Mrs Lavoisier as much as any, expressed great surprise." In November, 1774, Lavoisier repeated
Priestley's experiments. His conclusions, based on the same information, were dramatically different. In a paper presented to
the Academy in 1775, changed and finally published in 1778, Lavoisier argued that calcination involved the combination of a metal
with "the more salubrious and purer portion of the air."

Lavoisier did numerous experiments to determine the amount
of "air" absorbed and the total weight changes involved. By careful attention to the balance and meticulous recording of the
amounts of gases evolved and absorbed in each of his experiments,
Lavoisier built up support for his conviction that it was something from the air which was responsible for both combustion and
calcination. At first he called the something "the pure element

*Cited by Douglas McKie, *Antoine Lavoisier: The Father of Modern
Chemistry* (Philadelphia: J. B. Lippincott Company, 1956), pp.
117-18.

of air." But in 1777, the chemist Carl Wilhelm Scheele (1742-86) demonstrated that the air was composed primarily of two parts; an active part and an inactive part in proportions of about ¼ to about ¾. Lavoisier accepted Scheele's work and in 1780 proclaimed air to be ¼ of oxygen and ¾ nitrogen, as he named them.

By 1783 Lavoisier announced the new chemistry and the rejection of the phlogiston theory. Chemistry must reject the use of such imponderables as phlogiston. Calcination and combustion were to be based upon the chemical activity of oxygen in both processes. This was an important innovation to be sure. Lavoisier accompanied the change with appropriate dramatics. He and Mme Lavoisier burned the works of Stahl and other phlogiston chemists in public. But Lavoisier was not quite honest in his claim to fame. In his *Traité de Chemie*, Lavoisier described oxygen as "this air, which Mr. Priestley, Mr. Scheele and I discovered about the same time." Lavoisier has no claim to the discovery of oxygen, but he was the first to recognize oxygen as a chemically active element.

Lavoisier established the concept of the chemical element, "the last point which analysis is capable of reaching." The elements were substances not susceptible to decomposition. In 1789, with the publication of the *Traité*, Lavoisier listed 33 elements such as oxygen, nitrogen, hydrogen, phosphorus, mercury, zinc, sulphur, etc. The list also included light and "calorique," the substance of heat. Both of these elements would be subjected to extensive scrutiny in the 19th century. The names of the chemical elements were as new as the concept of elements itself. The names represented a new chemical nomenclature. Terms such as "dephlogisticated air" and the complex names included in alchemy were changed to more uniform, simpler and more meaningful names. Lavoisier cast away chemical theory based upon incontestable metaphysical concepts. He fixed upon the properties of the elements and chemicals themselves. The known facts about the characteristics of chemical reactions became the basis for the new chemistry.

Lavoisier's new chemistry provided new answers to the three basic questions of chemistry. Chemical matter became the 33 elements. The chemical qualities were inherent in the elements as fundamental characteristics. The elements must be classified according to their characteristics and their names should reflect their properties. Oxygen meant "acid former," hydrogen meant "water former," etc. The properties of the elements must be determined by observation and experiment, eliminating the speculations on "the principles of activity" prevalent in the chemistry of Paracelsus and Stahl.

Lavoisier attempted to devise a scheme of explanation of chemical activity, based upon his emphasis upon observables. Chemical activity was linked to the chemical qualities of the elements themselves. Oxygen, meaning acid former, participated in chemical reactions which produced acid. The acids Lavoisier obtained all contained oxygen. He emphasized what could be observed, the formation of acids with the action of oxygen, and refused to hypothesize on why this occurred. This was the weakest part of Lavoisier's new chemistry, but it was also the least essential. What was essential was the new reliance upon observable properties, primary and secondary qualities included.

The Chemical Revolution was well underway by 1800. The differences in 50 years were striking. By 1800 the notion of the conservation of matter was widely established, aided by the general use of the chemical balance. The balance became and remained the basic chemical instrument. Metaphysical and alchemical aspects of chemistry were struck a fatal blow by the new chemical nomenclature and the acceptance of the elements. The "airs" were changed into gases, both physically distinguishable one from another and considered to be chemically active. But this account of the Chemical Revolution has neglected two major aspects of chemistry about to become important after 1800: the concepts of definite proportions in chemical combinations and the concept of the specific attractions of chemicals. After 1800 the Chemical Revolution moves rapidly beyond Lavoisier's new chemistry into areas he never envisioned. The concept of definite proportions led to the chemical atomic theory and problems of specific attractions produced answers in the new field of electrochemistry.

CHAPTER TWO -- THE NINETEENTH CENTURY -- THE CENTURY OF SYNTHESIS

I. The Background

A. Philosophies of Science

In the nineteenth century, the pace of scientific advance accelerated rapidly. From a hobby of the amateur, science became the main concern of an ever -growing professional class. The word, scientist, was coined in 1841 and expressed the new awareness that science was of increasing importance in Western civilization. New schools were founded to accommodate the ever-growing interest in science and new opportunities opened up for those with scientific training and aptitude. The result was an almost exponential growth of the population of scientists who, in turn, created journals with almost rabbit-like abandon. The number of scientific publications rose in almost a frightening curve, making it impossible for any one man to master even one of the sciences with which the men, say, of the Scientific Revolution had been concerned. Science was forced to become specialized and scientists, consequently, had to narrow their vision. An intense focus burns deeper, but it sacrifices scope and this was the lot of most of the professional scientists by the end of the nineteenth century. Concentrating on trees, they pushed their way through the forest, leaving the contemplation of the woods to the rare natural philosopher to whom the whole of Nature was more important than its parts. Thus a century which opened with a unified world-view in which only the details needed to be worked out, closed with a mass of details and increasing anxiety over whether the sum of the details would be put together in any whole at all.

There is a natural division in the history of nineteenth century science which comes roughly in the decade 1850-60. From 1800 until this decade, it is possible to view the history of the physical sciences as a search for unity among the forces and particles of which Nature was composed. The beginnings of the search lie in the eighteenth century during which the main outlines of what we shall call the Newtonian view were drawn with some precision. It is this view which represents orthodox science at the beginning of the nineteenth century. Orthodox science followed naturally from the *Principia* and the *Opticks*. Query 31 had stated explicitly Newton's belief in material atoms; the *Principia* had revealed how the atomic particles acted upon one another according to the law of universal gravitation. The eighteenth century was to extend this idea of particles associated with forces to the whole of physical nature. Newton had declared for particles of light; Henry Brougham in the 1790's revealed how it was possible to determine the relative sizes of these light particles. The atomizing of heat was accomplished in the generation following Newton. Joseph Black, considering the problem of latent heat, had suggested that this phenomenon could best be accounted for if heat were considered to be mutually-repelling

atoms of a special matter of heat. This matter of heat was christened caloric by Lavoisier. Electricity and magnetism, too, were
reduced to Newtonian dimensions in the eighteenth century. It
was the careful and precise work of Charles Coulomb in the 1780's
that led him to postulate four new atomic species-- + electricity
and - electricity; N. magnetism and S. magnetism. These particles
repelled similar particles and attracted their opposites. And,
what was even nicer, the attractions and repulsions followed a
Newtonian inverse square law. Thus, at the beginning of the
nineteenth century, it was possible to suggest that the universe
was composed of seven "elementary"particles, of which only the
force laws of heat and light were, as yet, undiscovered. $F =
km_1m_2/e^2$ described the forces acting between material atoms, and
between the various particles of electricity and magnetism. All
that had to be changed in the equation was the constant and the
proper substitution made for material mass to indicate quantity
of electricity or of magnetic fluid. Within this framework, it
was possible to bring the full force of analytical mechanics and
mathematics to bear and this approach often bore precious fruit.
The work of Pierre Simon de Laplace, probably the most eminent
physicist of the first quarter of the nineteenth century, is an
eloquent testimony to the fertility of the Newtonian concept of
the world. (See p. 129.)

Not all natural philosophers were completely happy with the
Newtonian world-view. There were those philosophers, for example,
who found Newton's approach philosophically wanting. In his Third
Rule of Reasoning, it will be remembered,* Newton discussed the
way in which it was possible to pass from the world of sensible
phenomena to that of sub-sensible qualities. Those qualities,
like inertia, impenetrability, etc., which are found universally
in all sensible matter may be assumed, said Newton, to be the
qualities of the ultimate atoms of which sensible matter is composed. At first glance, this appears to be a reasonable assumption but it collapses the minute it is exposed to critical examination. At best, it is nothing but an assumption and, by the end
of the eighteenth century, there were those who felt that the
towering structure of Newtonian science ought to rest on a more
solid foundation than this. Primary among such critics was the
German philosopher, Immanuel Kant. Although Kant considered himself to be a good Newtonian, he could not let Newton's assumption
remain unquestioned. In his great philosophical work, *The Critique of Pure Reason* (1st edition, 1781), Kant pointed out that
we cannot even know whether or not atoms themselves exist. It
followed, therefore, that talk of their qualities merely piled
speculation on conjecture. Strictly speaking, if one followed
the *Critique* as a guide, it would be impossible to do more in
science than merely describe Nature and Nature's laws. No explanation involving sub-sensible entities like atoms could be
offered. This point of view, as we shall see, was to become a
popular one and feed into the positivistic view of science in the
nineteenth century.

Kant did not drop the matter after showing that it was impossible, on philosophical grounds, to assume an atomic constitution

*See above, vol. II, p. 285.

of matter. Instead, in a later treatise entitled, *The Metaphysical Foundations of Natural Science* (1786), he suggested a philosophically sound approach to the problem. What, after all, do we really mean by matter (or anything in Nature, for that matter)? A solid is merely a clearly defined space which prevents our fingers from penetrating it. A table, for instance, repels our hands when they rest on its "surface" and surface may be defined as a zone of repulsive force resisting penetration. The "Table" that we see is merely the result of attractive forces holding in the repulsive force within clearly defined boundaries. Thus, in the last (philosophical) analysis reality consists of the two forces of attraction and repulsion. There is no need to assume a solid (whatever that means) substratum for force. The forces themselves suffice.

There are certain consequences that flow from this doctrine of forces. The most important is the idea of the unity of force. Attraction and repulsion are not confined to material objects. These forces occur in thermal, optical, electrical and magnetic phenomena as well. It did not take long for Kant's disciples to suggest that all those physical forces were merely manifestations of the fundamental attractive and repulsive forces under different physical conditions. All observable forces, therefore, were *really* only the appearance of the attractive and repulsive forces in different guises, depending upon the circumstances. A necessary corollary followed: all physical manifestations of force ought to be convertible into one another. Thus, if light, heat, electricity and magnetism were merely the attractive and repulsive forces disguised, as it were, as optical, thermal, electrical and magnetic forces, then it should be possible to transform light, heat, electricity and magnetism into one another. The mode of transformation appeared to follow naturally from the forces themselves. Attraction and repulsion are polar opposites. There must exist a tension between them and transformations occurred when the tensions became too great to be contained by any specific manifestation as electricity or magnetism. Thus + and -, when combined, do not lead to annihilation but to transformation. And, implicit in the circle of transformations is the conservation of the total force.

There was more to this point of view than physics. Kant and those who followed his lead were concerned to preserve the idea of an active God in Western culture. The problem became particularly intense with the coming of the French Revolution. This event, the greatest, political and social upheaval experienced in modern Europe to that time, was widely viewed as the inevitable result of the breakdown of religion. The eighteenth century French philosophers had sapped the religious foundations of the State in the name of Reason. The blood bath of the Terror appeared to be only the natural result of that intellectual subversion. The culprit, to many, was Newtonian science which, in the hands of the French followers of Newton, gradually extended its sway until there was no room for God. Matter was all. Laplace's remark on the "hypothesis" of God symbolized this mode of thought.

For men with a thirst for scientific truth who did have a "need of that hypothesis," the philosophy of Kant seemed to offer an alternative. The unity of force reflected the unity of the divinity; the polarity of forces reflected the polarity of good and evil in the world and the convertibility of forces provided an hierarchical-continuum by which one could rise from the forces of matter to the forces of divinity itself. The duality of matter and spirit was replaced by the unity of force. The watchmaker God of the eighteenth century who presumably wound the universe up at the Beginning and then abandoned it could be shown up as philosophically naive. In His place was to be the God of field theory who, by binding the world together with lines of force gave daily testimony to His presence. Materialism was a false idol. The Temple of Science was to be reopened for the true believer. And those who followed this philosophy of force *were* true believers to whom the unity, convertibility and polarity of force were but the physical manifestations of the source of all force--God himself.

These ideas of polarity, convertibility and conservation of force were enunciated and developed by a small group of German philosophers at the beginning of the nineteenth century. The resulting "science" dubbed *Naturphilosophie* (Nature philosophy) was of a highly speculative kind and, although it contained a large number of highly original and fertile ideas, its failure to keep in touch with reality through experiment led ultimately to its being discredited and violently rejected by the scientific community. It would be a serious mistake, however, to ignore it. The convertibility of forces was accomplished in the first part of the nineteenth century, in large part by scientists who had been touched by *Naturphilosophie*. And, *Naturphilosophie* provided one of the roads that led to the Principle of the Conservation of Energy.

There was still a third philosophical way to truth in the early nineteenth century. It was possible to reject Newtonian atomism and also be hostile to *Naturphilosophie*. In the eighteenth century, the Abbé de Condillac (1714-80) in France had erected a philosophical system on a base that had clear implications for science. All that we can know, said Condillac following John Locke, are sensations. To sensations we give names in the form of words. When the words are well chosen and merely stand for the sensations (and nothing else!) then the correspondence between Nature and Mind is perfect. The regularity to be found in sensations cannot be explained, only described. Thus the task of science is to give names to sensations, classify them so that their natural affinities will be evident, and group those generalizations together. Mathematics, it should be noted, is an excellent language for mathematical definitions are precise and limited in scope and can be made to fit sensations exactly. Again, the implications of this view are worth making explicit. Most important is that it rules out explanation in the Newtonian sense of the word. The Newtonian, when faced with a problem in physics, tended to make an atomic model of it. The selection by Dalton illustrates this well. (See p. 164.) The model then explains the phenomena. For the positivist, this is illegitimate since we cannot sense atoms and their existence is, therefore, wholly conjectural. All that the positivist scientist can do is

describe the flow of phenomena, hopefully tying individual epi-
sodes together in a mathematical law. For the science of the
nineteenth century, this view was to be a restrictive, rather
than a liberating influence. Most of the great generalizations
of the century were drawn from models and the prohibition on
model construction led to the inability of those committed to
positivism to discover new laws or theories. It is surely no
coincidence that French physics declined seriously after the
death of Laplace and that positivism was the dominant philosophy
of science in France.

B. Different Aspects of Physical Reality

What a natural philosopher saw, measured and hypothesized
about in the early nineteenth century often depended upon the
philosophy he espoused. It is no exaggeration to suggest that a
disciple of Newton and a disciple of Kant literally saw two different world. The selections that follow illustrate the ways in
which these schools differed and how each placed emphasis upon
different aspects of physical reality.

1. Pierre Simon, Marquis de Laplace

*The Newtonian tradition in the nineteenth century was upheld
by Pierre Simon de Laplace. His* Mécanique céleste *completed what
Newton had begun in astronomy and his* System of the World* *was a
thorough-going Newtonian treatment of the domain of physics.*

Science is not like literature; the latter has limits that a
man of genius can reach by means of appropriate language. His
work can be read with the same interest in every age and its
charm, instead of diminishing with age, is increased by the vain
efforts of those who strive to equal it. The sciences, on the
contrary, are as limitless as nature and increase to infinity with
the efforts of successive generations. The most perfect work, by
raising them to heights from which they cannot in future fall,
gives birth to new discoveries and thus prepared the way for
works which will overshadow it. Others will present the theories
of the *Principia* in more simple and more general ways, along with
the truths that have flown from it, but it will always remain as
the monument of the profound genius who revealed to us the greatest law of the universe.

This work and the equally original treatise on optics by the
same author, not only contain new discoveries but also are the
best models that can be suggested for the sciences and are examples of the delicate art of making experiments and reasoning
mathematically upon them. There can be seen the most fortunate

---

Oeuvres de Laplace (Paris, 1846), vol. 6, *Exposition du Systeme
du Monde*, Bk. 5, Ch. 5, "On the Discovery of Universal Gravitation," pp. 433 ff.

applications of that method which consists in rising by a series
of inductions from phenomena to causes and descending from these
causes to all the details of phenomena.

General laws are present in all particular cases; but they
are so complicated there by extraneous circumstances that the
greatest talent is often necessary to lay them bare. It is necessary to choose or produce the phenomena most proper to the effect,
vary them by changing the circumstances, and discover what is
common in these different situations. Thus one rises successively
to more and more general relationships until one reaches general
laws that can be verified, either by test or by direct experiment,
when this is possible, or by determining if they are congruent
with all other known phenomena.

This is the surest method which can guide us in the pursuit
of truth. No philosopher was more faithful to this method than
Newton; no one possessed a greater share of that necessary tact
which permits the investigator to discern general principles in
specific objects and which constitutes the true genius in the
sciences; a tact which permitted Newton to recognize the principle of universal gravitation in the fall of a single body. The
English *savants*, his contemporaries, adopted the method of induction from his example and this served as the base for a great
number of excellent works in physics and the calculus. The
philosophers of antiquity, devoted to the opposite method, and
seeing themselves as the source of knowledge, made up general
causes to explain the world. Their method which gave birth only
to vain systems, had no greater success in the hands of Descartes.
In Newton's lifetime, Leibnitz, Malebranche and other philosophers
also employed it with little advantage. Finally the uselessness
of the hypotheses that they dreamed up and the progress of the
sciences which was due to the inductive method, rallied the sound
thinkers to this latter method which the Lord Chancellor Bacon
had established with all the force of reason and eloquence, and
which Newton even more strongly supported by his discoveries.

At the time when they appeared, Descartes had substituted
intelligible ideas of motion, impulse and centrifugal force for
the occult qualities of the peripatetics. His ingenious system
of vortices, based on his "clear" ideas, had been avidly received
by the philosophers who rejected the obscure and petty doctrines
of the Scholastics, and it was they who believed that the occult
qualities which the French philosopher had so rightly proscribed
were being reborn in universal attraction. It was only after
realizing the vagueness of Cartesian explanations that they could
see attraction as Newton had presented it, that is, as a general
fact to which he had arrived by a series of inductions and from
which he had descended to explain celestial motions. This great
man would have undoubtedly merited the reproach of reestablishing
occult qualities if he had been content to attribute the ellipti-
cal motion of the planets and of comets, the inequalities of the
motion of the moon, that of terrestrial degrees and of weight,
the precession of the equinoxes and the tides of the sea to universal attraction without showing the connection of this principle
with the phenomena. Geometers, however, in rectifying and gener-
alizing his demonstrations and having found the most perfect

accord between observations and the results of mathematical calculations, have unanimously adopted his theory of the system of
the world which has become, by their researches, the basis of all
astronomy. This analytical liaison between particular facts and
a general fact is what constitutes a theory. It was in this way,
by rigorously deducing mathematically all the effects of capillary
action from the single principle of a mutual attraction between
the molecules of matter which becomes sensible only at imperceptible distances, that we flatter ourselves to have found the true
theory of this phenomenon. A few philosophers, struck by the
advantages of admitting into science principles whose causes are
unknown have brought into many branches of the natural sciences
the occult qualities and meaningless explanations of the Ancients.
They have seen the Newtonian philosophy as it appeared to the
Cartesians and have hidden their doctrines under it without having
in common with it that which is the most important point, namely
the rigorous accord of the results with phenomena. . . .

*(After lamenting the fact that Newton saw fit to use geometry,
rather than the calculus, in his exposition of his views, Laplace
went on to point out the advantages of the algebraic way or
"analysis" over the geometric way, or "synthesis.")*

. . . Such is the fertility of analysis that it suffices to translate particular facts into this universal language in order to
see a crowd of new and unexpected truths emerge from their expression. No other language is capable of producing the elegance
which comes from the development of a long series of closely connected expressions, all flowing from the same fundamental idea.
Analysis also has the advantage of leading always to more simple
methods; all that is necessary is to apply it in a convenient
manner by utilizing a happy choice of variables and then giving
to the results either a geometrical or a numerical form. . . .

Attraction, the regulator of the movement and of the form of
the celestial bodies, is not the only such force which exists between their molecules: they also obey the attractive forces upon
which the intimate constitution of bodies depends and which are
sensible only at distances imperceptible to our senses. Newton
was the first to give an example of this kind of forces by demonstrating that when light passes from one transparent medium to
another the attraction of the medium refracts it in such a way
that the sine of the angle of refraction and of the angle of incidence are always in the same ratio as experiment had already
shown. This great physicist in his Treatise on Optics also derived from similar forces the theory of cohesion, affinity, the
then-known chemical phenomena and those of capillary action. He
thus laid down the true principles of chemistry whose general
adoption took even longer than that of the principle of gravitation. He only gave an imperfect explanation of capillary phenomena, however, and their complete theory was the work of his
successors.

Is the principle of universal gravitation a primordial law
of nature or is it only a general effect of an unknown cause?
Cannot affinities be reduced to this principle? Newton, more
circumspect than many of his disciples, said nothing on these

questions for which our ignorance of the intimate properties of matter does not permit us to give a satisfying answer. Instead of framing hypotheses about them, let us restrict ourselves to a few reflections on this principle and on the manner in which it has been used by geometers. . . .

Does attraction communicate itself from one body to another in an instant? The time of its transmission, if it were sensible to us, would manifest itself principally by a secular acceleration in the motion of the moon. I had proposed this method for explaining the acceleration that is observed in this motion and I found that in order to fit the observations it would be necessary to attribute a velocity of seven millions times the speed of light to the attractive force. Since the cause of the secular equation of the moon is well known today, it is now possible to say that attraction is transmitted at least fifty million times faster than light. One can, therefore, without fear of sensible error, consider its transmission as instantaneous.

Particles acting upon one another by the instantaneously transmitted forces of universal gravitation and attraction and susceptible to mathematical analysis, made up the raw materials of Laplace's universe. Its totality could be understood in these terms. In a famous passage,* Laplace spelled out the nature of his physical reality.

We must then, see the present state of the universe as the effect of its anterior state, and as the cause of that which is to follow. An intelligence which, for an instant, could know all the forces of nature and the respective positions of the beings that compose it, and which moreover was vast enough to submit these data to analysis, could embrace the motions of the greatest bodies in the universe as well as those of the lightest atom in the same formula. Nothing would be uncertain for it, and the future, like the past, would be present to its eyes.

---

*Laplace, *Essai philosophique sur les probabilités*, 2nd ed. (Paris, 1814), p. 3.

2. Antoine Laurent Lavoisier

The positivist approach was well illustrated by Antoine. Laurent Lavoisier in his Treatise on Chemistry* *which first appeared in 1789.*

Preface
of the
Author

When I began the following Work, my only object was to extend and explain more fully the Memoir which I read at the public meeting of the Academy of Sciences in the month of April 1787, on the necessity of reforming and completing the Nomenclature of Chemistry. While engaged in this employment, I perceived, better than I had ever done before, the justice of the following maxims of the Abbé de Condillac, in his System of Logic, and some other of his works.

> We think only through the medium of words.--Languages are true analytical methods.--Algebra, which is adapted to its purpose in every species of expression, in the most simple, most exact, and best manner possible, is at the same time a language and an analytical method.--The art of reasoning is nothing more than a language well arranged.

Thus, while I thought myself employed only in forming a Nomenclature, and while I proposed to myself nothing more than to improve the chemical language, my work transformed itself by degrees, without my being able to prevent it, into a treatise upon the Elements of Chemistry.

The impossibility of separating the nomenclature of a science from the science itself, is owing to this, that every branch of physical science must consist of three things; the series of facts which are the objects of the science, the ideas which represent these facts, and the words by which these ideas are expressed. Like three impressions of the same seal, the word ought to produce the idea, and the idea to be a picture of the fact. And, as ideas are preserved and communicated by means of words, it necessarily follows that we cannot improve the language of any science without at the same time improving the science itself; neither can we, on the other hand, improve a science, without improving the language or nomenclature which belongs to it. However certain the facts of any science may be, and, however just the ideas we may have formed of these facts, we can only communicate false impressions to others, while we want words by which these may be properly expressed.

To those who will consider it with attention, the first part of this treatise will afford frequent proofs of the truth of the above observations. But as, in the conduct of my work, I have

---

*A. L. Lavoisier, *Elements of Chemistry, translated from the French by Robert Kerr* (Edinburgh, 1790), pp. xiii-xviii, xx-xxi.

been obliged to observe an order of arrangement essentially differing from what has been adopted in any other chemical work yet
published, it is proper that I should explain the motives which
have led me to do so.

It is a maxim universally admitted in geometry, and indeed
in every branch of knowledge, that, in the progress of investigation, we should proceed from known facts to what is unknown. In
early infancy, our ideas spring from our wants; the sensation of
want excites the idea of the object by which it is to be grati-
fied. In this manner, from a series of sensations, observations,
and analyses, a successive train of ideas arises, so linked together, that an attentive observer may trace back to a certain
point the order and connection of the whole sum of human knowledge.

When we begin the study of any science, we are in a situation, respecting that science, similar to that of children; and
the course by which we have to advance is precisely the same which
Nature follows in the formation of their ideas. In a child, the
idea is merely an effect produced by a sensation; and, in the
same manner, in commencing the study of a physical science, we
ought to form no idea but what is a necessary consequence, and
immediate effect, of an experiment or observation. Besides, he
that enters upon the career of science, is in a less advantageous
situation than a child who is acquiring his first ideas. To the
child, Nature gives various means of rectifying any mistakes he
may commit respecting the salutary or hurtful qualities of the
objects which surround him. On every occasion his judgments are
corrected by experience; want and pain are the necessary consequences arising from false judgment; gratification and pleasure
are produced by judging aright. Under such masters, we cannot
fail to become well informed; and we soon learn to reason justly,
when want and pain are the necessary consequences of a contrary
conduct.

In the study and practice of the sciences it is quite different; the false judgments we form neither affect our existence
nor our welfare; and we are not forced by any physical necessity
to correct them. Imagination, on the contrary, which is ever
wandering beyond the bounds of truth, joined to self-love and
that self-confidence we are so apt to indulge, prompt us to draw
conclusions which are not immediately derived from facts; so that
we become in some measure interested in deceiving ourselves.
Hence it is by no means to be wondered, that, in the science of
physics in general, men have often made suppositions, instead of
forming conclusions. These suppositions, handed down from one
age to another, acquire additional weight from the authorities by
which they are supported, till at last they are received, even by
men of genius, as fundamental truths.

The only method of preventing such errors from taking place,
and of correcting them when formed, is to restrain and simplify
our reasoning as much as possible. This depends entirely upon
ourselves, and the neglect of it is the only source of our mistakes. We must trust to nothing but facts: These are presented
to us by Nature, and cannot deceive. We ought, in every instance,
to submit our reasoning to the test of experiment, and never to

search for truth but by the natural road of experiment and observation. Thus mathematicians obtain the solution of a problem by
the mere arrangement of data, and by reducing their reasoning to
such simple steps, to conclusions so very obvious, as never to
lose sight of the evidence which guides them.

*   *   *

The rigorous law from which I have never deviated, of forming
no conclusions which are not fully warranted by experiment, and
of never supplying the absence of facts, has prevented me from
comprehending in this work the branch of chemistry which treats
of affinities, although it is perhaps the best calculated of any
part of chemistry for being reduced into a completely systematic
body. Messrs Geoffroy, Gellert, Bergman, Scheele, De Morveau,
Kirwan, and many others, have collected a number of particular
facts upon this subject, which only wait for a proper arrangement;
but the principal data are still wanting, or, at least, those we
have are either not sufficiently defined, or not sufficiently
proved, to become the foundation upon which to build so very important a branch of chemistry. This science of affinities, or
elective attractions, holds the same place with regard to the
other branches of chemistry, as the higher or transcendental
geometry does with respect to the simpler and elementary part;
and I thought it improper to involve those simple and plain elements, which I flatter myself the greatest part of my readers
will easily understand, in the obscurities and difficulties which
still attend that other very useful and necessary branch of chemical science.

3. Lorenz Oken

Lorenz Oken (1779-1851) was the arch-priest of Naturphilosophie. *Although he was concerned primarily with organic nature,
he did extend his ideas to the universe as a whole.* His speculations seem, at first glance, fantastic and unreal but they
contained some shrewd insights and fertile intuitions which later
workers exploited.*

Part I

Mathesis--of the Whole

———————

Nothing.

31. The highest mathematical idea, or the fundamental principle of all mathematics is the zero = 0.
     The whole science of mathematics depends upon zero. Zero
alone determines the value in mathematics.

———————

*Lorenz Oken, *Elements of Physiophilosophy*, trans. by Alfred Tulk,
(London, 1847), pp. 7-14, 16-18, 21-22, 29-32, 37-47.

32. Zero is in itself nothing. Mathematics is based upon nothing, and, consequently, arises out of nothing.

33. Out of nothing, therefore, it is possible for something to arise, for mathematics, consisting of propositions, is a something in relation to 0. Mathematics itself were nothing if it had none other than its highest principle zero. In order, therefore, that mathematics may become a real science, it must, in addition to its highest principle, subdivide into a number of details, namely, first of all into numbers, and, finally, into propositions. What is tenable in regard to mathematics must be equally so of all the sciences; they must all resemble mathematics. . . .

Numbers are naught else than different forms of the one unchangeable essence, namely, the 0.

If, then, all numbers are only zero in a state of extension, and are consequently identical with it, the question arises, what are the first finitings of zero, or as what does it appear when it is no longer merely ideal or indefinite; in short, what is the first form of the real zero, or of the essence in general?

Essence of Nothing.

41. The ideal zero is absolute unity, or monas; it is not a singularity, such as one individual thing, or as the number 1, but an indivisibility, a numberlessness, in which neither 1 nor 2, neither a line nor a circle can be found; in short, an unity without distinction, a homogeneity, brightness, or translucency, a pure identity.

42. The mathematical monas is *eternal*. It succumbs to no definitions of time and space, is neither finite nor infinite, neither great nor small, neither quiescent nor moved; but it is and it is not all this. That is the conception of eternity.

Mathematics is thus in possession of an eternal principle.

43. Since all the sciences are equivalent to mathematics, nature must also possess an eternal principle.

The principle of nature, or of the universe, must be of one and the same kind with the principle of mathematics. For there cannot be two kinds of monades, nor of eternities, nor of certainties. The highest unity of the universe is thus the Eternal. The Eternal is one and the same with the Zero of mathematics. The Eternal and zero are only denominations differing in accordance with their respective sciences, but which are essentially one.

44. The Eternal is the *nothing* of Nature.

As the whole of mathematics emerges out of zero, so must everything which is a Singular have emerged from the Eternal or nothing of Nature.

The origin of the Singular is nothing else than a manifestation of the Eternal. Thereby unity, brightness, homogeneity are lost, and converted into multiplicity, obscurity, diversity.

Unity posited manifoldly is an expansion without termination, but one that always remains the same.

Realization or manifestation is an expansion of the Eternal.

Forms of Nothing.

45. The first form of the expansion or manifestation of the mathematical monas, or of 0 is + -. The + - is nothing else than the definition of 0. 0 is the reduction of the positive and negative series of numbers, upon which the whole of arithmetic depends. A series of numbers is, however, nothing else than a repetition of a + 1 or a - 1; consequently, the whole of arithmetic reduces itself to + 1 - 1.

What, however, is a + 1, or - 1? Obviously nothing else than a single + or -. The figure is quite superfluous, and only indicates how often + or - has been assumed; instead, therefore, of + 1 we can posit +; instead of - 1 simply -. The series + 1 + 1 + 1 is synonymous with + + +; or instead of 3 we may posit + + +, and so on for every figure ad libitum. The figures are nothing more than shorter signs for the two highest mathematical forms or ideas of numbers. Numbers are nothing different from the ideas of numbers; they are the latter themselves, only several times posited. Essentially numbers do not exist, but only their two ideas. These ideas, however, exist an infinite number of times.

Multiplicity or *real* infinity is, accordingly, nothing special or particular, but only an arbitrary repetition of the Ideal, an incessant positing of the idea. The idea posited is reality, non-posited it is = 0.

46. The first multiplicity is duality, + -. This duality alters nothing in the essence of the monas, for + - is = 0. It is the monas itself only under another form. In multiplication it is thus the form alone that changes.

There are many forms, but not many essences.

47. The first or primary duality is not, however, a double unity, both members of which are of equal rank, but an antagonism, disunion, or *diversity*. Many diversities are *multiplicity*. The Many is thus complex. The first form is not therefore a simple division of zero or the primary unity, but an antagonistic positing of itself, a becoming manifold.

48. Every Finite is in the same manner only the self-definition of the Eternal. The Eternal becomes, accordingly, real, by binary self-division. When the Eternal is manifested, it is either a positive or negative. The whole of arithmetic is nothing else than a ceaseless act of positing and negating, of affirming and denying.

All realization is nothing else than the act of positing and negating. The act of positing and negating of the Eternal is called realization.

49. Positing and negating is, however, an *act* or function. Arithmetic is, therefore, a ceaseless process of acting or performing. Numbers are *acts* of the primary idea, or, properly speaking, stationary points of its function, and hence proceeds a division into the two ideas + and -. If these remain always alone nothing is added to them. They alone produce the whole science of arithmetic, and simply because they are never exhausted by the act of positing themselves repeatedly, but capable after this of again elevating themselves in power. Since + is in

essence nothing else than a simple positing, a mere affirmation, and - a mere suppression of this affirmation, a negation; so is the positive unity = 1 nothing but an affirmation once declared, and the whole series of numbers is a reiterated affirmation. The act of affirmation alone gives the number, and the latter is thus the definite quantity devoid of intrinsic value. Bare affirmation alone without reference to any substance is unity, duality, &c.

Something.

50. Still, however, there must be something, which is posited and negatived. The form must have a substance.

This something is the primary idea, or the very Eternal of mathematics, the zero; for + - is = 0. The + - is naught else than zero affirmed; the - naught else than this + 0 negatived = - 0. Now since an affirmation once declared is = 1, so are unity and zero identical. Zero differs only from finite unity in that it is not affirmed.

51. The - is not simply the want of affirmation, but its explicit abstraction. The + presupposes the 0; the - the + and 0; the 0, however, presupposes neither + nor -. Purely negative quantities are, as is known, a nonentity, because they can only bear reference to positive magnitudes. The - is, indeed, the retroversion of + into 0; yet alone, therefore, it is not perfectly equal to 0. It is a retrovertent, and consequently the second *act*, which presupposes the positive. By the - we know what is not; the - is, however, a nothing in every respect. The - is the *copula* between 0 and +.

52. If the + is the 0 posited, so is it a nothing posited or determined. This position is, however, a number, and therefore a mathematical something. The nothing thus becomes a something, a Finite, a Real, through the simple positing of itself, and the something becomes a nothing by the removal of this self-position. The nothing itself is, however, the mere neglect of its self-position. The something, the + -, has consequently not arisen or emerged out of nothing, or from the latter something associated with another been produced; but it is nothing itself; the whole undivided nothing has become unity. The nothing *once* posited as nothing is = 1. We cannot speak of production or evolution in this case; but of the complete identity and uniformity of the nothing with the something; it is a virgin product or birth.

53. Zero *must* be *endlessly* positing itself, for in every respect it is indefinite or unlimited, eternal. The number of finite singularities must, therefore, pass into the Infinite.

54. The whole of Arithmetic is nothing but the endless repetition of nothing, an endless positing and removing of nothing.

We can become acquainted with nothing but the nothing, for the Original of our knowledge is the 0.

There is no other science than that which treats of nothing.

Every Real, if it were such in itself, could not be known, because the possibilities of its properties would pass into the Infinite. The nothing alone is cognizable, because it has only a single property, namely, that of having none; concerning which knowledge no doubt can be entertained.

A.--*PNEUMATOGENY*.

Primary Act.

55. The + - or in other words, numbers are acts or functions. Zero is, consequently, the primary act. Zero is, therefore, no *absolute* nothing, but an act without substratum. Generally speaking there is, therefore, *no* nothing; the mathematical nothing is itself an *act*, consequently a something. The nothing is only inventive.

56. An act devoid of substratum is a spiritual act. Numbers are, accordingly, not positions and negations of an absolute nothing, but of a spiritual act.

57. The zero is an eternal act; numbers are repetitions of this eternal act, or its halting points, like the steps in progression. With zero the Eternal therefore originates directly, or both are only different expressions for one and the same act, according with the difference of the science wherein they are employed. Mathematics designates its primary act by the name of zero; Philosophy by that of Eternal. It is an error to believe that numbers were absolute nothings; they are acts and consequently realities. While numbers in a mathematical sense are positions and negations of Nothing, in the philosophical they are positions and negations of the Eternal. Everything which is real, posited, finite, has become this out of numbers; or, more strictly speaking, every Real is absolutely nothing else than a number. This must be the sense entertained of numbers in the Pythagorean doctrine, namely, that everything or the whole universe had arisen from numbers. This is not to be taken in merely a quantitative sense, as it has hitherto been erroneously, but in an intrinsic sense, as implying that all things are numbers themselves, or the acts of the Eternal. The essence in numbers is naught else than the Eternal. The Eternal only is or exists, and nothing else is when a number exists. There is, therefore, nothing real but the Eternal itself; for every Real, or everything that is, is only a number and only exists by virtue of a number. Every Singular is nothing for itself, but the Eternal is in it, or rather it is itself only the Eternal, though not the Eternal in itself, but affirmed or negatived. The existence of the Singular is not its own existence, but only that of the Eternal subjected to an arbitrary repetition; for the act of being and affirming are of one kind.

58. The continuance of Being is a continuous positing of the Eternal, or of nothing, a ceaseless process of becoming real in that which is not. There exists nothing but nothing, nothing but the Eternal, and all individual existence is only a fallacious existence. All individual things are monades, nothings, which have, however, become determined.

*   *   *

God.

61. The self-manifestation of the primary act is *self-consciousness*. The eternal self-consciousness is God.

62. The continued act of self-consciousness, or becoming self-conscious repeated, is called *presentation*. God is therefore comprehended in ceaseless presentation. Presentations are single acts of self-consciousness. Single acts, however, are real things. All real things, however, are the world. The world therefore originates with the presentations of the Eternal.

63. The presentations are, however, manifested or attain only reality through *expression*. The world is therefore the language of God; the creation of the world the speaking of God. "God spake, and it was." It is not merely said, God thought and it was. Thought belongs merely to spirit; in so far, however, as it becomes apparent, it is a word, and the sum of all apparent thoughts is speech. This is the created, realized system of thought. The thought is only the idea of the world, but speech is the idea actualized.

64. As thought differs from speaking, so does God from the world. Our world consists in our apparent thoughts, namely, the words. The universe is the *language* of God. So far as the thoughts lie at the foundation of the words, it can be said, that our world were the play of our thoughts, and the actual world that of God's. The word has become world. Worldly things have no more reality for God, than our words or our language for us. We carry a world within us while we think; we posit or create a world without us while we speak. Thus God carries the world within himself while he thinks; he posits the same without himself or creates it, while he speaks. In so far as thought necessarily precedes speech, it may be said, that there would have been no world, if God had not thought. In the same sense it may be also said, that all things are nothing but presentations, thoughts, ideas of God. So soon as God thinks and speaks is there a real thing. To speak and to create are one. All, that we perceive, are words, thoughts of God; we are ourselves nothing else than such words or thoughts of God, consequently his metatypes or images, in as far as we unite in ourselves the whole system of speech. There is therefore no being without self-consciousness. That only which thinks is (for itself); that which does not think is not for itself, but only for some other consciousness. The world differs from God as doth our speech from us. The self-consciousness of God is independent of the world, even as our self-consciousness is independent of our speech.

65. The divine laws are also the laws of the world; this has therefore been created and governed in accordance with eternal and immutable laws.

66. Physio-philosophy is the history of creation; the creation, however, is the language of God. The system of thought, however, lies necessarily at the foundation of the system of speech. Now the science of the laws of thought is called logic; physio-philosophy is therefore a divine doctrine of speech or a divine logic. The laws of speech instruct us in the genesis of language. Physio-philosophy is, therefore, the science of the genesis of the world, or Cosmogony.

Form of God--Triunity

67. As the complete principle of mathematics consists of three ideas, so also does the primary principle of nature, or the Eternal. The primary principle of mathematics is 0; so soon, however, as it is actual, is it + and -; or the primary idea resolves itself in being at once into two ideas, each of which resembles the other in essence, but differs from it in form. Thus it is here one and the same essence under three forms, or three are one. Now that which holds good of mathematical principles, must hold good also of the principles of nature. The primary act is manifested, or operates under three forms, which correspond to the 0, + and -.

These three ideas of the Eternal are all equivalent to each other, are the same primary act, each of them being whole and undivided, but each otherwise posited. The positing primary act is the whole Eternal; the posited is likewise the whole Eternal, and that which is subtractive, retrogressive, combining the two first, is also the whole Eternal. Although all three ideas are equivalent to each other, still the positing idea ranks first, the posited second, and the combining third; not as if they had first arisen successively (this is impossible, for they are co-existent, namely, before all time), nor as if they occupied different positions (for they are everywhere); but only according to their order and value. How one may be three and three one, is thus rendered comprehensive only by mathematics.

*   *   *

Polarity.

76. Time is an action of the primary power; and all things are active only in so far as they are filled or inspired with the idea of time. The whole activity of things, all their forces arise out of the primary act or primary power, are only moments of the same. There are, however, no positive without negative numbers, consequently also no moments of time without suppression of the same. There is, therefore, no single force, but each is the position of + and -. A force consisting of two principles is called *Polarity*. Time is, therefore, the primary polarity, and polarity is manifested at the very instant in which the creation of the world is stirring.

77. Polarity is the first force which appears in the world. If time is eternal, polarity must also be eternal. There is no world, and in general nothing at all without polar force.

78. Every single thing is a duplicity.

79. The law of causality is a law of polarity. Causality is valid only in time, is only a series of numbers. Time itself has no causality. Causality is an act of generation. The sex is rooted in the first movement of the world.

Motion.

80. Polarity may be viewed as a single positing of + -; if, however, this positing repeats itself, *Motion* originates, viz.

when many + - + - are consecutively posited, and thus the principal poles separate from each other, as in an iron bar when magnetizing. Time is a polar positing of the primary act, and an
endless repetition of this positing; through this originate individual things, whose succession is motion.

81. Primary motion is the result of primary polarity. All
motion has originated from duplicity; consequently from the idea
in a dynamic not a mechanical manner. A mechanical motion, which
might be produced ad infinitum by mechanical impulses, is an ab-
surdity. There is nowhere a purely mechanical motion; nothing,
as it is at present in the word, has become so by impulse; an
internal act, a polar tension lies at the bottom of all motion.

*   *   *

115. Space has not been created, but has emerged out of the
Eternal; it is nothing new in the universe, nothing next to God
and present with him, but co-existent with God.

116. Single things must be both in space and in time; or a
real thing first originates, where time and space cross each other
at one point; they cross, however, every where, and therefore
things are everywhere.

117. There is no void or empty space, no time and no place,
were a Finite could not be; for time and space are virtually the
manifesting primary act, the zero that has become thing.

Point.

118. Time has begun with number, space with the point, with
the spatial nothing, with the zero of space. This point necessarily posits itself "ad infinitum;" it extends itself also in
all directions, and necessarily in equal distances. Such an extended point is the *Sphere*.

119. The sphere is nothing peculiar, nothing new in the
thoughts of God, but only the point expanded, while this again is
but a contracted sphere, just as the totality of numbers is an
expanded 0, and this their contracted sphere.

120. Space is spherical, and, indeed, an infinite sphere.
The sphere has been posited with space, and consequently from
eternity; it is also an idea, and that, indeed, the total idea;
for time and space have in it been posited together.

121. For God to become real, he must appear under the form
of the sphere. There is no other form for God. God manifesting
is an infinite sphere.

122. The sphere is, therefore, the most perfect form; for
it is the primary, the divine form. Angular forms are imperfect.
The more spherical a thing is in form, by so much the more perfect
and divine is it. The Inorganic is angular, the Organic spherical.

123. The universe is a globe, and everything, which is a
Total in the universe, is a globe.

Line, Light, Magnetism.

124. While the point expands, it is active; this active expansion is a simple repetition of the point, and this is a *Line*, which in the sphere, however, is a *Radius*. With time originates not merely a series of numbers, but together with it also the line. The line and time are of one kind, repeated positions of the nothing, of the point. It is consequently clear, how that time were a repeated positing of the Eternal itself: for the line is only a repeated self-positing of the point, of the nothing. God fluctuating in his eternity, and the point, are one in kind; but God acting is a line, being or existing a sphere, i.e. the point in the act of being.

125. The line is nothing new in creation, but time itself, when regarded more closely. God creates the line as little as he does time; but this originates unto him, while he moves, while he thinks. It is impossible to think without producing a line. The line is therefore from eternity, is a series of numbers.

126. The essence of the line does not consist in its two extremities being continued with equal significance into the Infinite; but in its *radiality*, i.e. that one extremity turned towards the centre has become central, converging, absolute; but the other turned towards the periphery has become divergent, finite, multiplicity. The primary line is a line produced with two antagonized characters. The central extremity is 0, the peripheral is the bisected zero = $\pm$. This radial line gives us the antetype of a new polarity. The two extremities are not related as + and - towards each other, but as 0 and + -. At the instant, when a line originates in the universe, it is not a line merely, or an indefinite line that originates; but one that is definite at both extremities, polar, indeed, but after a determinate fashion. Nothing, not even a finite thing, exists in an indefinite manner.

127. There is no mathematically straight line in the world: all real lines are polar; they are all rooted in God by one extremity, by the other in finitude. The primary act becomes in its first operation not merely a posited nothing, a numerical series; not merely time, not merely an aoristic line, but a *Linea determinata*; in short, God can step forth into time only as radius. The *Monas determinata* is a *Monas radialis*, or a centroperipheric monas.

128. The essence of the primary antagonism is a centroperipheric antagonism. As centre is related to periphery, so is here one pole related to the other. Polar existence and central or peripheral existence are one. Primary polarity is centroperiphery. The primary line is constantly in a state of polar action, which is called *tension*; for it is always converging and diverging, at once central and peripheric. Every line originates, therefore, only by tension, and is only by it, yea, every line is nothing else than this tension.

129. A line, one extremity whereof strives towards the centre, the other to the periphery, the one to identity, the other to duality, will exhibit itself in the world as a *line of Light*, in the planet as a *Magnetic line*. Magnetism is centro-

peripheric antagonism, a radial line, 0 - - $\pm$, the action of the
line being cleft at one extremity. Magnetism has its root in the
beginning of creation. It is prophesied with time.

Surface, Electricity, Oxydation.

130. The periphery is the boundary of the sphere, and is,
consequently, a superficies or *Surface*. This, therefore, originates also directly with the positing of the Eternal.

131. As the primary line is not a purely polar, but a radial
line, so is the primary surface not a level, but a curved or convex surface.

132. There is *no level* surface in the universe, no pure surfaces any more than pure lines. All surfaces are curved. For
example, those of drops, of the heavenly bodies, of animals. The
surface of a sphere is no *Continuum*; but consists properly of the
divided peripheric and upright extremities of the radii; it is a
$\pm$.

133. The surface of a globe has no centre, no 0, like the
radius; but is an absolute Dualized, a $\pm$ without 0.

134. This mode of operating of the primary act is manifested
as electricity. Electricity is a merely peripheric antagonism,
without centre, thus without union; an eternally Disintegrated
without rest. Electricity is thus also a special form, under
which polarity makes its appearance, and is likewise rooted in
the primary creation. There is, consequently, no thing which
were not magnetic and electric. . . .

139. The surface stands in antagonism to the line, like
periphery and centre; it stands perpendicular upon the radius,
and can never pass parallel to linear action. Electricity ranks
in eternal antagonism to magnetism.

*   *   *

Matter.

159. Points, which strive towards the centre, are compressed, because they would all occupy one and the same spot.
These points, however, are forces, which take up space and therefore exclude other points. A space that excludes another is
Matter. Everything which has been said of gravity holds good in
respect to matter; for matter is only another word for gravity.
A heavy thing is a material thing.

160. To the totality of a thing belongs not merely its
figure nor its tension or motion simply, but also its *gravity*.
This is, however, a whole sphere. Matter is, consequently, a
total position of the primary act, a trinity of ideas.

161. Matter has been imparted with space and time. All
space is material; ay, matter is itself the space and the time,
the form and the motion; for space is nothing special, but only
extended or formed force. It is here also shown that the nothing
does not exist. There is as little nothing in the universe as
there is an 0 in mathematics. So soon as the nothing is, it is
something. The whole universe is material, is nothing but matter;

for it is the primary act eternally repeating itself in the centre. The universe is a rotating globe of matter.

162. But the universe is an acting gravity, a matter, in which the centroperipheric antagonism is active; it is therefore *everywhere matter only, which acts*. There is no activity without matter, but also no matter without activity, both being one; for gravity is itself the activity, and itself the matter. Matter is only limited activity. A matter which does not move is not; it can only subsist through continuous origination, through life. There is no dead matter; it is alive through its being, through the eternal that is in it. Matter has no existence in itself, but it is the Eternal only that exists in it. Everything is God, that is there, and without God there is absolutely nothing.

163. It is an illusion to believe that matter were an actual something subsisting in itself. It is even so with numbers, upon which a reality also is bestowed, when they are still demonstrable nothings. A number is nothing truly than an affirmation several times repeated, a reiterated deposition of what is nothing, what is no number. This deposition happens likewise in the universe, where it is the primary act, that is deposited. Where, however, this is, no other station can occur. This exclusive property is usually called the *Impenetrable*, the *Material*. It cannot be said in what spot matter arises, so secretly and suddenly does it start into existence. It is matter properly at the first manifestation of being, of time and of space; for at the same instant also the line, surface, density and gravity have been given. The line does not exist if it does not *act*; the sphere does not exist if it be not inert, i.e. if its forces do not strive towards the centre, and consequently to connexion. Nothing exists if it is not material. Matter is accordingly co-existent with the presence of God.

164. The Immaterial does not exist; for even the Material which is *not*, is the Immaterial. Everything that is, is material. Now, however, there is nothing that is not; consequently, there is everywhere nothing immaterial. Immateriality is only an inventive principle, by which to get at matter, like the 0 in mathematics, which is nothing in itself, does not even exist, but that still must be posited, in order that numbers may bear a reference to it.

165. God only is immaterial; he is the only permanent immaterial invention, and the axiom is the Formless, Polarless, Timeless. A spirit with form is a contradiction. But the matter also does not exist, because matter is nothing, because it is only a sphere of central actions, which is gravity.

166. The material universe is called nature. There can be only *one* nature, as well according to time as to space and to divine animation. There is only one God, whose operations expressed, or materially posited, are nature. Nature has originated out of nothing like time and space; or with these has nature also been. God has made heaven and earth out of nothing.

167. God has not found matter co-eternal with himself, and, like an architect, arranged this to his fancy; but he has, out of his own eternal omnipotence, by his will simply, evoked the world out of nothing unto existence. He has thought and spoken, and it was. . . .

Æther.

169. The matter, which is the direct position of God, which fills the whole universe, which is the time in a state of tension and motion, the formed space, the heavy primary essence, I call the *Primary matter*, the matter of the world, cosmic matter, *Æther*. The æther is the first realization of God, the eternal position of the same. It is the first matter of creation. Everything has consequently originated out of it. It is the highest, divine element, the divine body, the primary substance = 0 + -.

170. The æther fills out the whole universe, and is, consequently, a sphere, yea, the world's sphere itself; the world is a rotating globe of æther.

171. The sphere of æther, not as yet individualized, I call *chaos*. From the beginning was chaos, and this was æther, and unto the end will chaos become æther. The æther is the apparent nothing, and thus it is the chaos. This was not the latter and not the former, but an existing nothing.

172. The æther is the imponderable matter, because it is gravity and totality itself, because it is the infinite matter.

173. The æther has no life; it is the only mortuum, because it is the heavy 0. In æther, however, reside all the principles of life, all numbers; it is the substratum, the essence of life. There is only one universal substratum in nature. . . .

b. Light, Line. (*Second form of the World. Motion.*)

182. The æther is from eternity, not merely monas, but also dyas; from eternity it stands in a state of tension with itself, when, as the image of the existing primary act, it has emerged out of itself into two poles. This self-egression or self-manifestation of æther, or of substance simply, is the self-egression of the point into the periphery. As dyas, æther exists under the form of polarity, of central and peripheric effort; the æther in a state of tension is a centroperipheric antagonism.

183. The æther is separated from eternity into a central and peripheric substance, and that indeed through its simple position as a globe. The universe is a duplicity in the form of æther; it is both indifferent and different æther, both central and peripheric. The central mass of æther may be called sun, the peripheric planet. Only one sun can originate in a globe of æther, but many planets.

184. Between the central and peripheral mass of the æther, between the sun and planets, there is tension. Through this solar-planetary tension the æther fluctuating between the two becomes polarized.

185. The tension of the æther proceeds from the centre and thus from the sun. Were the sun to be removed, the polarity of the æther would be annulled; it would be again the indifferent chaotic æther, the null and void matter. For the absolute substance to exist it needed not simply itself, but an identical centre and a dissevered periphery. Is there no peripheric mass, no planet, so also is the tension annulled; centre cannot be without periphery, sun not without planet, nor vice versâ. The tension of æther is thus excited by the sun and conditioned by the

planet. The planet is not the principle, but the Redintegrant of the tension of æther by the opposition.

186. At that part of the universe where no periphery stands opposed to centre, no planet to the sun, the æther is not tense, but indifferent, annulled. There can thus only be *columns* of æther, which are rendered tense, namely, those columns of æther which are found between the sun and the planets. Near to the planets the æther is void of action, indifferent, non-apparent. There are consequently as many apparent æther-columns, as there are heavenly bodies, that stand in the process of polarity opposed to each other. These columns move with the planets around the suns. The indifferent æther of the world-space is, therefore, successively rendered tense, as the planets move around suns, and becomes again indifferent behind the planets.

187. But besides this, that columns of tension only exist, and therefore that the æther is nowhere active as a sphere, there is still no spot in the world-space where there would be only indifferent æther, nothing; for the æther consists of many globes of æther. There is thus nowhere an indifferent æther, consequently nowhere an empty space. The idea of the repletion of space is not that of the sphere, but of the columns of tension, which by their crossing in every direction form a sphere only externally.

188. That which is thought of as originally filling space is not the quiescent but only the moved, tensed æther. The former is the void space, the nothing.

189. The tension of æther is an action, which operates according to the line. This linear activity, which makes its exit from the central mass and is excited hence to the peripheral mass, is *Light*, or in short, light is tension of æther.

190. Light is a traction of lines or radial action; consequently an antetype of magnetism. A ray of light is a radius. The ray of light has two extremities different from each other; that turned towards the sun of 0, that which comes in contact with the planets is $\pm$. Light is, therefore, a splitting, rending action.

191. Light is the life of the æther. Hitherto the æther was an inactive nothing, mere substratum for a future. This nothing, when it becomes centroperipheric, seeks to tear the mathematical point into radii and circumferences, *appears*; and this centroperipheric manifestation we call light.

192. The untensed, indifferent æther is, therefore, *darkness*, and this is the essence, the rest of æther. Chaos was thus darkness; the world arose out of darkness when light became. Light has originated out of darkness when the chaos was moved. Were it possible therefore for all light to vanish, the world would again return into its old nothing; for darkness and nothing are one. God has separated the light from the darkness.

193. If light be only a column of æther in a state of tension, light is or exists only between the planet and the sun; near to the planet and behind it is darkness. The primary sphere is a dark sphere, transpierced only by single rays of light. Each star, however, stands in a state of tension with another; thus many thousand rays of light stream forth from each, and fill out

the world-space in all directions. There is therefore no absolute darkness, because there are infinitely numerous rays of light. In the night also there is always as much light present as is necessary to maintain the heavenly bodies in their action. For the world there is no night, but only for the planets. It will be shown that the air maintains its existence simply through the operation of light; were it therefore always dark, were night to endure for ever, the air must soon assume another composition or mixture, and everything that lives in it must fall to ruin. This is shown also by the diseases and crises of the same.

194. Light is from eternity, for the tense æther was from eternity. The dark chaos exists only as inventive. Light is time that has become real, the first manifestation of God; is God himself positing, is the dyadic God. The dyas is not merely radiality but light; or both are one, time and light are one, motion and light are one. When God numbers, when he draws lines, he thus creates light. God becoming self-conscious is light. Light is God illuminating. Darkness has accordingly never existed, although the light is derived from the darkness, like numbers and figures are out of nothing.

195. Light is no matter. There is no substance called light, but the æther is illuminant through its binary division. The sun does not, therefore, stream forth when it illumines the planets, and loses nothing of its magnitude; it is not to be feared that we shall ever lose it. That the sun is an undulating sea of flame, that it is throughout a volcano, that combustions or electrical processes of light, appearing to us as light, occur in its atmosphere; that the velocity of rotation hurls about the light-particles, and that these particles scattered in the world-space are, by an unknown route, or by means of comets, again brought back to the sun, are opinions unworthy the inquirer into nature. The sun gives out nothing but the impulse, not, however, the mechanical, which makes the space of heaven tremble that it may shine; but the purely spiritual, as the nerves rule the muscle. The sun can never be extinguished, never become dark; for it gives out light, not as a fire, but simply by reason of its standing in the midst; its simple position, its enchainment to the planets is light. A fire upon the sun would not be perceived by us; it would not lighten nor warm us, because of its having no relation to us. The central relation of the sun toward us cannot, however, remain unobserved, and this observation is even that of light. . . .

c. Heat, Density. (*Third form of the World. Shape.*)

198. Light is not simply a motion in itself, a mere continuous excitation of polarity in the æther, but it is also the æther itself *set in motion* thereby. All polar actions resolve themselves finally into motion of the polarized masses. The end of electricity, galvanism, magnetism, is motion. It will be, however, shown that all these polar functions are only repetitions of the primary polarity; this must therefore produce what the former did, namely, ætherial motion.

199. Every point of the æther becomes polar, every one

attracts and *repels* the other; whereby motion arises in the inner-most parts of the æther itself. Not a portion of the æther is moved on, but motion originates in the mass of æther itself. The æther-atoms quit each other.

200. The æther is, however, that which is filling space, is space itself, the Expansissimum of the world, the Formless and therefore that which adopts all forms. The formless æther, when it moves itself, must be connected with a phenomenon, that depends upon its expansion and identification, which is polarized by light. This action of the æther does not therefore depend upon the tension of æther, not upon production from differences in the same, but upon dissolution of the tension, therefore upon exten-sion, upon the indifferent representation of space. This action, which is at the same time universal, can only be heat. Moved æther is *Heat*.

201. Heat is the contest of the indifferent æther with light; light alone produces heat. Without light the world were not only dark, but also absolutely cold. Cold in untensed and quiescent æther, death, nothing; dark and cold are one. Heat is therefore the result of light, but equally eternal with it; it is space represented really, as that is real time.

202. Heat is not moved indifferent ether, which is = nothing; but moved and tensed or the *moved light*.

203. Heat penetrates into thickness as an extending func-tion, but does not oscillate between two poles like light. It is only the function of density, and depends upon nothing else, not upon lines or mere surfaces, but upon the living sphere.

204. Heat and light, although characters of *one* substance, yet stand in an antagonism like thickness and line, or as indif-ference and difference. Heat is properly the first perfected position of the primary act, while light is only the act of posit-ing; the latter therefore is +, the former -. Or also, gravity is the absolute position, simply = 0; light is the commencing egression of this position out of itself + -, heat the completion + 0 -, and therefore the position everywhere; it will everywhere deposit, therefore it is motion, repletion of space, expansion. Light is gravity become real, or 0 become real; 0 however, ren-dered real, is + -. Heat is as - at the same time + - and 0, or light and gravity, material light, light that is filling. Both will also assert the antagonism of their genesis through all forms of the world. The heat seeks to destroy the line, which the light endeavours to establish; heat seeks to produce homoge-neity in the Dissimilar, light to effect the reverse. Heat is slow in its motion; with it the mass of æther must continually move, or move whither it will operate; light, however, acts spiri-tually and rapidly, without motion of the mass, but only glides continually with the latter. Heat is not created, it is no spe-cial matter different from æther. There is no *body of heat*.

205. Heat is everywhere where the aether is, and must con-sequently be regarded as a sphere. Heat is not present merely in the columns of æther between the heavenly bodies, but everywhere. Therefore heat does not move itself in the direction of the line, but it extends itself on all sides, as real space.

C. Conclusion

The three examples we have cited of Laplace, Lavoisier and Oken reveal the deep chasms that separated scientific investigators from one another at the beginning of the 19th century. It would be well to make these differences quite explicit, for they tended to follow national lines. The English were empirical and Newtonian; the French, positivistic, and the Germans, Kantian and given to philosophical speculation like Oken. This meant that these groups literally saw different universes in their scientific work .

For the English, and those elsewhere who followed Bacon, Nature was an objective reality "out there" to be dis-covered by close observation and experiment. Thus, for example, the laws governing the weather might be discovered if only enough people everywhere in Europe kept voluminous records of temperature and barometric pressure . It was a vain hope, but in the early 19th century weather recording was practised by aspiring amateur scientists (and some professionals) who felt that, given enough data, a law would appear.

The Newtonian view, however, was not restricted to recording facts about Nature. It was also possible to speculate, within limits, on the causes of phenomena. Here "metaphysical" models were permitted if they fit Newton's Third Rule of Reasoning . John Dalton achieved prodigies with this method.

The world that Lavoisier described was not, strictly speaking, "out there" but in the mind of the beholder. The mind was but a recording device which takes "pictures" of the world. The concern of the positivist is to get the right labels on the pictures. Hence the popularity of classificatory schemes in France during the early years of the century.

The Nature philosopher stood somewhere between the Newtonian and the positivist. There was a real world "out there" but man was in that world and, by virtue of his participation in the Divine Reason, could intuit its laws. What the Nature philosopher sensed, above all, was the unity of the creation. Meteorology, to someone like Alexander von Humboldt, was not a matter of dead facts but of living forces that bound the earth's atmosphere together in a single, beautiful whole.

II. Newtonian Orthodoxy and the Challenge to Orthodoxy

A. The Conversion of Forces

The differences in philosophy of science in the early nineteenth century led to differences in the kinds of science done and the pace of scientific advance by adherents to these philosophers. As we have already indicated, positivism was predominant in France and had a pernicious effect on French physics. This is not to say that positivism necessarily stifled physics; it only closed off such avenues as required the use of sub-sensible theoretical entities such as atoms. One of the great treaties of the nineteenth century was J. B. Fourier's *Analytic Theory of Heat* which was directly in the positivist tradition. It ignored the question of what heat *really* was, and dealt solely with the mathematical laws of heat flow. It is elegant, precise and beautiful and remains a monument to the power of pure analytical, positivist

thought. By and large, however, positivist contributions were
few and far between. In contrast, the Newtonian tradition flourished. George Green in England and Denis Poisson in France worked
out elegant and, in Poisson's case, comprehensive electrical theories based on the assumed existence of two electrical fluids.
And, later in the century, the whole towering edifice of the
kinetic theory of heat was to be erected on "Newtonian" principles.

The most exciting work of the early decades of the nineteenth
century, however, was done by those who followed in the tradition
of *Naturphilosophie*. The reason for this is simple to understand.
Both Newtonianism and Positivism led their adherents to work out
the logical consequences of previously conceived ideas and theories. The advances made here were akin to mopping up operations
after a battle. *Naturphilosophie*, however, led to a whole new
vision of physical reality. It was like the discovery of a new
continent and its adherents eagerly pushed from new discovery to
new discovery. Some, to be sure, got permanently lost in the
forests of their own speculations, but for those who worked their
way with experiments it was an intoxicating experience. The Newtonian world of zipping particles controlled by laws expressed as
partial differential equations faded and was replaced by a universe of forces whose interactions produced the world of physical
reality.

The first physical entity to disappear was the light corpuscle. Newton, it will be remembered, had devised a highly complex optical theory that utilized both corpuscles and ether waves
to explain optical phenomena. By 1800, the ether waves had disappeared, leaving only the corpuscles. Thomas Young (1773-1829)
in England and Augustin Fresnel (1788-1827) in France somewhat
later, attacked the corpuscular theory and substituted a wave
theory for it.

Thomas Young was a boy genius equally at home in ancient
languages or the sciences. He was an avid amateur musician and
student of sound, which led him eventually to his optical theories. After studying medicine in England, he went to Germany to
continue his education. Although he came into contact with
Naturphilosophie, it does not seem to have unduly impressed him
and it would be wrong to trace his ideas on light to German influences. Nevertheless, the denial of material corpuscles of
anything may have helped him to consider alternatives to the corpuscular theory of light.

The aspect of Newton's theory that Young saw as inadequate
was that which dealt with the "fits" of easy transmission and
reflection, and the colors shown by thin plates of glass. Such
interference phenomena (as they would be called now) resembled
the phenomenon of beats in sound in which waves of similar frequencies reinforced and annulled one another. As a musician,
Young was familiar with "beats" and felt that something akin to
the process explained in sound by wave motion would apply to the
"fits." Thus Young proposed to account for optical phenomena by
waves totally analogous to sound. The only difference was that
the wave lengths were incredibly small. In the years 1801-3,
Young published a series of papers laying out his theory. He

tried to make it acceptable to Newtonians by insisting that he was merely completing what Newton had begun and that the true Newtonian theory of light included an important undulatory component (as it did). The result was catastrophic. Young's papers were held up to ridicule by a vicious review in the *Edinburgh Review* that made Young out to be a fool and a knave. Young riposted with a pamphlet defending his views but the pamphlet, as he ruefully admitted, sold few copies. The bad publicity of the affair began to affect Young's medical practice so he abandoned optics and turned his mind instead to the decipherment of Egyptian hieroglyphics where he made significant contributions.

Young's efforts were not lost. His papers were read in France by Francois Arago who found them interesting enough to entertain the idea of a undulatory theory. More importantly, Arago encouraged the work of a young civil engineer, Augustin Fresnel. Fresnel picked up where Young left off and developed the mathematical theory of undulations.

Fresnel began his optical labors more than ten years after Young had abandoned the field. In the intervening years, a discovery had been made which appeared to destroy the undulatory hypothesis once and for all. In 1810, Etienne Malus, while looking through a piece of iceland spar at the light reflected from a window across the way from his study, discovered polarization by reflection. The effect seemed easily explicable by assuming that the corpuscles of light, like tiny magnets, had polar ends which permitted or prevented the transmission of light, depending upon which end arrived at the surface first. A compressional wave such as that suggested by Young and Fresnel had no "ends" and polarization could not be explained.

When Arago reported the discovery of polarization to Young (along with some experiments by Fresnel), Young's interest in optics was revived. His solution of the problem was to be epoch-making and worth citing in his own words.

> I have been reflecting upon the *possibility* of giving an *imperfect* explanation of the affection of light which constitutes polarization, without departing from the genuine doctrine of undulations. It is a principle of this theory that all undulations are simply propagated through homogeneous mediums in concentric spherical surfaces, like the undulations of sound, consisting simply of the direct and retrograde motions of their particles in the direction of the radius, with their concomitant condensations and rarefactions. And yet it is possible to explain in this theory a *transverse vibration*, propagated also in the direction of the radius, and with equal velocity; the motions of the particles bearing a certain constant direction with respect to that radius; and this is polarization.*

---

*F. Arago, *Biographies of Distinguished Scientific Men*, 2nd Ser. (Boston, 1859), 160n. as cited in A. Rupert Hall & Marie Boas Hall, *A Brief History of Science* (New York, 1964), p. 259.

Fresnel immediately seized upon this idea and developed it mathematically with the sureness of one trained at the *Ecole polytechnique*. The mathematical elegance of Fresnel's treatment, together with the ability of the new wave theory to explain some of the most difficult aspects of optics such as interference and polarization gradually drew support from the scientists of the day. Laplace and J.-B. Biot in France fought the theory and drove Fresnel to an early grave but the numbers of disciples grew. By the late 1820's, most natural philosophers who worried about the nature of light were willing, at least, to entertain the theory of transverse waves. The "proof" of the wave theory came much later. Newton had argued that the bending of a ray towards the normal when light passed into a denser medium was the result of the attraction of the denser medium for the light corpuscle. Hence, the light corpuscle was accelerated and should travel through the denser medium faster than through the less dense one. According to the wave theory, light should travel more slowly through the denser medium. In the 1850's, Hippolyte Fizeau (1819-96) and Léon Foucault (1819-68) made direct measurements of the speed of light in air and in water. It traveled slower in water and the wave theory was vindicated. By that time, however, almost everyone who cared believed in a wave theory of light.

The undulatory theory of light revived an entity as old as science itself--the ether. It seemed only logical to assume that a wave must be a wave in *something*. Since the interstellar space was devoid of ordinary matter, it must be filled with the ether, a subtle fluid whose primary quality was its ability to transmit light vibrations. The only difficulty was that substances on the Earth that transmitted transverse vibrations had the consistency of tempered steel. Two generations of mathematical physicists were to be set the task of reconciling the rigidity required of the ether to serve as the medium for the propagation of light with the tenuity which would permit the planets to revolve in their courses around the Sun for millenia without perceptible slowing in their orbits.

The next of the imponderable fluids to be eliminated from physics was electricity. Coulomb's views of two fluids had, by and large, won the day everywhere but in England and America. (See p. 159 .) The discovery of current electricity through the invention of the Voltaic pile in 1800 only served to reinforce the fluid concept. Volta, in his letter announcing his discovery to Sir Joseph Banks, President of the Royal Society, used the term "current" without ever raising the question of whether or not this was the appropriate word. For the two-fluidists, a "current" rapidly came to mean the simultaneous flow of the two electrical fluids in opposite directions through a wire. It was thus that Ampère used the term in his earliest memoirs on electrodynamics.

Almost immediately upon hearing of the invention of the voltaic pile, William Nicholson and Anthony Carlisle in England discovered that the flow of electricity through water was more complicated than the simple passage of one or two imponderable substances through the particles of ponderable matter. The water was decomposed by the electric current! Clearly, electricity had something to do with chemical affinity and the sciences of electricity and chemistry must have intimate and hitherto relatively unsuspected connections. The work of Humphry Davy at the Royal Institution in the early 1800's dramatically confirmed the importance of electricity for chemistry. Using a voltaic battery of tremendous power, Davy decomposed the alkalis, potash and lye, and isolated sodium and potassium. The large energies necessary to achieve this decomposition clearly indicated the fundamental role that electricity played in chemical composition. Just *how* it played this role, however, was somewhat of a mystery. It was possible to conceive a model involving the particles of imponderable electricity riding piggyback on the ponderable particles of matter which bore a close resemblance to the supposed relation of caloric to matter. In another model, the Swedish chemist J. J. Berzelius envisioned the elements to be like hollow balls, containing various amounts of both positive and negative electricity, according to their position on the newly discovered scale of electrochemical decomposition. Oxygen, the most electronegative element, was filled with pure negative electricity. The other elements contained both positive and negative electricity and were, therefore, polar. Chemical affinity was merely the result of the electrical polarity of the atoms. The difficulty lay in explaining both chemical affinity and the phenomena of electrochemistry with a single model. Either the model used was insufficient to cover both fields or the *ad hoc* elements that had to be added to cover all contingencies made the model so complicated that it was difficult to believe in its truth.

There was a seocnd alternative. There were those who refused to believe in the materiality of electricity or any of the other so-called imponderable fluids. Hans Christian Oersted (1777-1851) of Denmark was one such. As a student, he had become an enthusiast of *Naturphilosophie* and had firmly committed himself to the doctrine of forces. The discovery of the chemical importance of electricity was, to Oersted, solid evidence for the truth of *Naturphilosophie*. He could dispense with the clumsy models of his materialist colleagues. Chemical affinity was, for him, merely the chemical manifestation of the electrical force. It represented a *conversion of force*, not a peculiar action of a *species of matter*. Such a conversion ought, according to Oersted, to be merely the first in a chain of similar conversions in which one force could be turned into another under varying circumstances. So, as early as 1806, Oersted began to look for other conversions. In 1813, in a work on the force of chemical affinity, he suggested that electricity ought to be convertible into magnetism under the proper circumstances. Unfortunately, the circumstances Oersted envisioned prevented him from detecting the conversion. He felt that if what he called the electrical conflict--the necessary result of the antithesis between positive and negative electrical forces--could be forcefully confined, the electrical forces would, so to speak, be squeezed into magnetic force. Hence he passed electricity through very fine platinum wires. There was the evolution of heat, but a compass needle brought near the glowing wire was unaffected. In the winter of 1819, during a public lecture in Copenhagen, it occurred to

Oersted to try the experiment with ordinary wire. The compass
needle moved! Oersted had discovered electromagnetism. When he
announced his discovery in 1820, it astonished the scientific
world. After all, as one of Ampère's friends wrote to him, the
electric current had been a commonplace in physical and chemical
laboratories since 1800. Why had no one performed the simple
experiment that Oersted now reported? Ampère's answer is instructive for it shows how theories can often close off whole areas of
research. Ampère replied that no one had looked for a magnetic
effect of an electric current because Coulomb's experiments in
the 1780's had apparently proved *conclusively* that electricity
and magnetism were two entirely different species of matter,
quite independent of one another. Only someone like Oersted who
had rejected the material theory of the imponderables and believed
in the unity of force would undertake to detect a conversion of
one force into another.

Oersted's discovery did not serve to destroy the material
theory of electricity, although it did make it easier to believe
that electricity was a peculiar force of matter rather than a
species of matter. But, as Ampère was to show, a material theory
of electricity could still be used to explain the new observation.
All that was necessary was to assume that (somehow) electricity
in motion produced the magnetic force. With this assumption, and
equipped with elegant mathematical tools, Ampère erected the
science of electrodynamics between the years 1820 and 1826.

In spite of Ampère's success, there were still those who
doubted his fundamental assumptions. Where was the evidence for
the two electrical fluids which were essential for Ampère's theory? Where was the experimental evidence for the currents that
Ampère assumed to circulate around the molecules of ponderable
matter ? Where was the experimental evidence that magnetization
was merely the alignment of these molecules? The most persistent
questioner was Michael Faraday (1791-1867). Faraday had received
his scientific education as Humphry Davy's assistant at the Royal
Institution. With Davy as his mentor, he had been introduced to
the problems of chemical affinity, electrochemical decomposition
and the whole question of the origin and relations of the forces
of nature. It is difficult to discover the origin of Faraday's
ideas on matter and force. Many of his later thoughts closely resembled the fundamental tenets of *Naturphilosophie* but Faraday
did not read German and there were no translations of German
philosophy early in the century from which he could have drawn
the conclusion that forces were convertible into one another because of their essential unity. One channel through which such
ideas may have reached him was the poet and metaphysician Samuel
Taylor Coleridge. Coleridge had visited Germany at the end of
the eighteenth century and become intoxicated with *Naturphilosophie*. Coleridge knew Davy well and the two spent long hours
together discussing problems of metaphysics. It is possible
that, through Davy, Faraday was given some insight into the
world-view of the Nature philosophers.

Quite recently, it has been suggested that there was a native British tradition, deriving from John Locke in the seventeenth century, upon which Faraday drew. Like Kant and the

Nature philosophers in Germany, the makers of this tradition rejected a material substratum for force, insisted upon the fundamental unity of force and at least hinted at the convertibility of forces. Again, what is missing is a direct link between this tradition and Faraday. What we can say with some certainty is that Faraday came early to the view that ultimate reality consisted of forces, not material particles. And, as he remarked in 1845, "I have long held an opinion, almost amounting to conviction . . . that the various forms under which the forces of matter are made manifest have one common origin." This belief had informed his early researches and led him to his most famous discoveries, as well as to his destruction of the fluid theory of electricity.

Faraday's first discovery was that of electromagnetic rotations in 1821. This was, effectively, the conversion of electromagnetism into mechanical force, and followed directly from Oersted's discovery. Faraday recognized that the circle of magnetic force surrounding a current-carrying wire ought to affect a magnetic pole and was able to construct a simple instrument in which one end of a magnet circulated continually around such a wire. Faraday was after bigger game than this, however. If current electricity created magnetism, then surely magnetism should create an electric current. In 1831, Faraday first discovered the induction of one current by another. The apparatus was really a simple transformer in which the current in the primary coil wound round an iron ring induced a current in the secondary coil when the circuit was made or broken. Shortly thereafter, Faraday was able to produce an electric current by plunging a permanent magnet into a coil of wire. A continuous current could be created by rotating a copper wheel between the poles of a permanent magnet and taking leads off the center and periphery of the wheel. The conversion of magnetism into electricity could now be accomplished at will.

This conversion implied little, however, about the ultimate nature of electricity. It was as easily accounted for by Ampère's theory of two electric fluids as it was by the Nature Philosophers' dreams of force conversions. For Faraday the decisive experiments were those he conducted on electrochemistry, in 1832-1833. His primary concern in this train of researches was the rather mundane one of showing that there was only one electricity despite the number of different sources--friction, chemical action, living organisms--from which electricity could be drawn. The most difficult obstacle to overcome was that of producing an unequivocal chemical decomposition from static electricity. In the course of this investigation, Faraday was able to discover a means of measuring the quantities of electricity required to decompose various compounds and was, thereby, led to the enunciation of his two laws of electrolysis. The quantity of an element deposited at an electrode is directly proportional to the quantity of electricity passed through the electrolyte; and, the same quantity of electricity will cause deposition of different elements in the ratio of their chemical equivalents. It had long been known that electricity was related to chemical affinity. Faraday now proved that this relationship was a quantitatively exact one which reflected fundamental chemical forces. Electricity *was* chemical affinity under a different guise.

More importantly, Faraday also was led to challenge the standard electrical theories of action at a distance. When static electricity was discharged into the air through a piece of blotting paper soaked with an electrolyte, chemical decomposition still took place. Where were the "poles" in such a situation which could force the dissociation of chemical molecules? Clearly, all that was necessary was the mere *passage* of electricity and this led Faraday to suggest that electricity could *not* be a material substance. Rather, he insisted that electricity was a force which, in an electrolyte, acted by the buildup and breakdown of intramolecular tensions. The "current" was the vibration created by the rupture and reestablishment of chemical bonds caused by the migration of ions through the solution. This concept permitted Faraday to generalize his views and account for both insulators and ordinary currents through wires. If, as Faraday now believed, electricity was a peculiar force transmitted from one molecule to another, then an insulator could be viewed as a substance in which the electric force could be sustained at a high intensity before the molecular chain broke. In good conductors, very little intermolecular strain could be borne, so the strain built up and broke down rapidly thus sending a "vibration" along the wire. In electrolytes, the strain broke the chain and forced the temporary dissociation of the chemical molecule. Chemical affinity insured the reestablishment of the bond, but the fragments of the broken molecules migrated, stepwise, in opposite directions. Thus Faraday felt he could account for all the phenomena of electricity without having recourse to two or even one material fluid. Instead, there was only force and its interactions with the forces of material particles.

Much the same treatment was given to magnetism, again by Faraday. If electricity were a force and was convertible into magnetism, then it followed (for Faraday, at least) that magnetism, too, was a force and not a fluid. But magnetism was a peculiar force, restricted to iron, nickel and cobalt. This bothered Faraday for electricity appeared to be a universal force and surely whatever it was converted into must also be universal. As part of his program for the conversion of forces into one another, Faraday had for years attempted to detect some effect of electricity on light, but without success. In 1845, substituting the far-more powerful force of an electromagnet for that of a static electric field, Faraday discovered that a powerful magnetic field would affect a ray of light. If a ray of plane polarized light were passed through a substance of high refractive index along a magnetic line of force, the plane of polarization was rotated. The direction of the rotation depended *solely* upon the polarity of the magnetic line of force; the amount of the rotation was a function of the strength of the magnetic field. This effect convinced Faraday of the universality of magnetism and he set out to prove that all bodies were affected by a magnetic field. The result was the discovery of what Faraday christened dia- and para-magnetism. Diamagnetics conducted the magnetic force poorly and so the lines of force diverged when a diamagnetic was placed in a uniform magnetic field; paramagnetics conducted the magnetic force well, so that the lines of force converged upon a paramagnetic body in a uniform magnetic field. The places where the magnetic lines of force clustered together upon entry and exit from a paramagnetic were the "poles" of induced magnets.

Again all was reduced to forces, not fluids. Faraday's theory could now account for both electricity and magnetism in terms of lines of force interacting with one another and with the forces of matter. Even matter, Faraday felt, was nothing but force and the universe could be conceived as a network of forces acting upon one another where they intersected. By 1850, the universe had been dematerialized; force was all.

There remained but one final step to take: that was to make explicit the quantitative aspects of the conversions of force. By the 1840's, most of the conversions had been accomplished. It is worth listing them: electricity into heat (18th century and common knowledge); heat into electricity (Seebeck in 1821); electricity into cold (Peltier in 1834); electricity into magnetism (Oersted in 1820); magnetism into electricity (Faraday in 1831); magnetization of light, as Faraday called it (Faraday in 1845); electricity into mechanical motion (Faraday in 1821); mechanical motion into electricity (Faraday in 1832); chemical affinity into electricity (Volta in 1800); electricity into chemical affinity (Nicholson and Carlisle in 1800); heat into light (from time immemorial); heat into mechanical motion (early steam engines, and especially James Watt in 1770's); mechanical motion into heat (time immemorial--friction).

This list cries out for some common measure. By the 1840's, work from a number of different areas began to converge on this measure. The conversion of force implied the conservation of force as Faraday illustrated in his arguments against the contact theory of electricity. If, he argued, mere contact of dissimilar metals generated electricity, then one could get something for nothing and this, he felt, was impossible. Similarly, the more orthodox physicists insisted that the dance of their material particles was restricted by the conservation of the kinetic energy of the material particles. The development of thermodynamics also served to focus attention on conservation in heat processes. In 1824, a young French engineer Sardi Carnot had published a small treatise on the ideal heat engine. Using a hydrodynamic analogy, Carnot had argued that heat engines worked much like water wheels. Carolic fell through a thermal potential, just as water fell through a gravitational potential to do work. Both water and caloric, it was assumed, were conserved. By the 1840's it seemed clear to more than one investigator that caloric, in fact, was not conserved and this struck deeply at the material theory of heat. It also stimulated the search for that which did remain constant in the conversion processes listed above.

In the 1840's a series of investigators published papers that established the principle of the Conservation of Energy. We can do little more here than list their names, but suffice it to say that J. R. Mayer (1814-78), James Prescott Joule (1818-89), and Hermann Helmholtz (1821-94) who are considered the major

enunciators of the principle of energy conservation came at it
from three entirely different directions. Mayer was led to it by
philosophical considerations, Joule from the engineering tradition of heat engines and Helmholtz deduced it from Newtonian
mechanics. It could also be assumed (as it was) from *Naturphilosophie* and eagerly embraced by mechanistic physiologists (like
Helmholtz) who wished to rid biology of mystical vital forces.
It was *the* basic unifying generalization of nineteenth century
science. It applied as well to physics as to biology, to chemistry as to cell theory and provided the solid foundation upon
which later nineteenth century science was to be founded. As the
first half of the century had witnessed the discovery of the circle of "force" conversions, so the second half was spent largely
in determining the fate of energy. The effort so spent created
the two great physical theories of the century--field theory and
kinetic theory. Each of these, in turn, was to lead to new questions from which twentieth century science was to be born.

B.   The World of Newtonian Physics

1.   Charles Coulomb on Electrical and Magnetic Attraction

*The nature of electricity and magnetism had escaped Newton.
In the 1780's, Charles Coulomb in France performed a series of
delicate and accurate experiments with a torsion balance of his
own invention. The results permitted Coulomb to suggest that
there must be two fluids of electricity and two fluids of magnetism. Furthermore, these fluids were quite distinct; the electrical ones followed one law, the magnetic quite a different law.
Both, however, were Newtonian in the sense that the laws followed
by both were inverse square laws.*

In a memoir published in 1785 Charles Coulomb used a torsion
balance of his own invention to determine the laws of electrical
action. He ran into some difficulties, however, when he tried to
determine the cause of electrical attraction for the torsion balance had a tendency to discharge itself as the electrified poles
came into contact.*

   In the month of June 1785 I presented to the Academy an electrical balance which measured with exactness and in a simple and
direct manner the repulsion of two balls electrified with the same
electricity. It was easy to prove, using this balance, that the
repulsive action of two balls electrified in the same way with
the same electricity and placed at different distances from one
another was very exactly according to the inverse square of their
distances, but when I wanted to work in the same way to determine
the attractive force of two balls charged with opposite electrici-

---

*Société française de physique, ed., *Collection de Mémoires rela-
tifs à la physique*, Tome I, *Mémoires de Coulomb* (Paris, 1884), pp.
4, 6, 8-9, 116, 119, 146, 250-51, 252, 296-96. Translated by
L. Pearce Williams.

ties, I ran into an inconvenience in practice using this balance
for measuring the attraction of the two balls which did not occur
in the experiment measuring the repulsion. The practical difficulty consists in this, that when the two balls approach one
another and attract each other, the force of attraction which increases as we will soon see in the ratio of the inverse square of
the distances, often increases at a greater rate than the force
of the torsion of the thread which varies only as the angle of
torsion so that it was only after having failed many times that I
was able to prevent the balls which attracted one another from
touching each other. . . .

   . . . I was finally able to get an equilibrium at different
distances of the attractive forces of the two electrified balls
and the force of torsion of my micrometer. Afterwards in comparing these different experiments, I concluded from them that the
attractive force of two electrified balls, one electrified with
what one calls *positive* electricity the other with what is called
negative electricity, was as the inverse of the square of the
distances of the center of these two balls, the same ratio already found for the repulsive force.

*At the end of this memoir, Coulomb summed up his researches
to that date.*

Recapitulation of the Points Contained in This Memoir.

   From the researches which precede, it follows:
   1. That the action either repulsive or attractive of two
electrified globes and, consequently, of two electrical molecules,
is as the product of the density of the electrical fluids of the
two electrified molecules and inversely as the square of the distances;
   2. That in a needle of twenty to twenty-five inches of
length, magnetized by the method of the double touch, the magnetic fluid can be supposed to be concentrated ten lines from the
extremities of the needle;
   3. That when a needle is magnetized, no matter in what position it is placed in the horizontal plane relative to its magnetic
meridian it is always brought to this meridian by a constant force
parallel to the meridian and the resultant of which always passed
through the same point of the suspended needle;
   4. That the attractive and repulsive force of the magnetic
fluid is exactly as was the case of the electric fluid: as the
product of the densities of the magnetic fluids and inversely as
the square of the distances of the magnetic molecules.

*So far, Coulomb's researches were much like those of Newton's
on light. He had feigned no hypotheses and, although he had used
the term electrical and magnetic fluids, it was quite clear that
he was merely using them for convenience. In a sixth memoir on
electricity and magnetism published in 1788, Coulomb discussed
the nature of electrical fluids themselves.*

The Two Natures of Electricity.

Whatever may be the true cause of electricity, all the phenomena and all the mathematical formulae drawn from experiment
may be explained by supposing two electrical fluids; the particles
of the same fluid repel one another inversely as the square of
the distance and they attract the particles of the other fluid in
the same ratio, that is, inversely as the square of the distances.
This law has been found by experiment for electrical attractions
and repulsions and is to be found in the first and second memoirs
on electricity (volume of the Academy for 1785); according to this
supposition, the two fluids in conducting bodies always tend to
reunite until there is an equilibrium, that is, until by their
reunion the attractive and repulsive forces cancel one another
out mutually. This is the state in which bodies are found ordinarily; but if, by some operation, one is able to push into an
isolated conducting body a superabundant quantity of one of the
electrical fluids, it will become electrified, that is to say,
that it will repel the electrical particles of the same kind and
will attract electrical particles of another kind from the superabundant fluid with which it is charged. If the electrified conducting body is placed in contact with another isolated conducting
body, it will share with it the surplus electrical fluid in the
proportions indicated in this memoir and those which precede it;
but, if the body is attached to a non-isolated body, it will lose
all its electricity in an instant since it will share it with the
globe of the earth whose dimensions, relative to it, are infinite.
M. Oepinus has supposed in his theory of electricity that
there is only one electrical fluid whose particles repel one
another mutually and are attracted by the particles of bodies
with the same force that they repel one another. But, in order
to explain the state of bodies in their natural situation, as
well as the repulsion of the two kinds of electricity, he is
obliged to suppose that the molecules of bodies repel one another
mutually with the same force that they attract the electrical
molecules, and that these electrical molecules also repel one
another. It is easy to see that the supposition of M. Oepinus
gives the same results, in terms of mathematical calculation, as
does that of two fluids. I prefer that of the two fluids which
has already been proposed by a few physicists, because it seems
to me contradictory to admit at the same time that particles of a
body have an attractive force which acts inversely as the square
of the distances, as is demonstrated by universal gravitation,
and a repulsive force in the same ratio, inversely as the square
of the distances; this latter force would be necessarily infinitely large, relative to the attractive action which gives rise to
weight.
. . . Since these two explanations only have a degree of
probability more or less great in their favor, I want to point
out, in order that the theory may be placed above any systematic
dispute, that in the supposition of two electrical fluids, I have
no other intention than to present with the fewest elements possible the results of calculation and of experiment and not to
indicate the true causes of electricity.

In 1789, Coulomb turned his attention to the theory of magnetism and presented in his seventh memoir a similar scheme to that on the theory of electricity.

Physicists for a long time have attributed the effects of magnetism to a vortex of fluid matter which turns around either artificial or natural magnets entering by one pole and exiting by the other. This fluid acts, they say, on iron and steel because of the configuration of their parts but it does not act on any other bodies. As new phenomena were met with which were inexplicable by a single vortex, people made up others or combined together a number of magnets: these were then given particular movements, as need arose, to explain the phenomena. It was on such hypotheses that the three memoirs on the cause of magnetism which were crowned by the Academy in 1746 were founded.

I believe that I have proven . . . how difficult it is to account for different magnetic phenomena by means of vortices. It is necessary, thus, to see if, by the simple supposition of attractive and repulsive forces these phenomena may be explained more easily. In order to avoid a dispute, I want to announce as I have already done in the different memoirs which precede this one, that any hypothesis of attraction and of repulsion following any law whatsoever should only be regarded as a formula which expresses an experimental result. If this formula can be deduced from the action of the elementary molecules of a body endowed with certain properties, and if one wishes to draw from this elementary prime action all the other phenomena, and finally if the results of theoretical calculation are found exactly in accord with the measurements that come from experiment, then one should not hope to go farther than this until one has found a more general law which includes in the same calculation bodies endowed with different properties which up to now do not appear to us to have any connection between one another.

M. Oepinus appears to be one of the first who has tried to explain magnetic phenomena by means of calculations of attraction and repulsion. He thinks that the cause of magnetism may be attributed to a single fluid which acts on its own parts or particles by a repulsive force and on the particles of steel or of a magnet by an attractive force. This fluid, once put into the pores of a magnet, is displaced only with difficulty. This system has conducted M. Oepinus to the following conclusion: that in order to explain different magnetic phenomena it is necessary to suppose a repulsive force between the solid particles of the magnet. Since M. Oepinus, many physicists have admitted two magnetic fluids; they have supposed that, when a bar of steel is in its natural state, these two fluids saturated one another; that by the operation of magnetism these fluids were separated and carried to the extremities of the bar. According to these authors, the two fluids exert an attractive action on one another but they repel the particles of their own kind; it is easy to notice that these two systems ought to give the same results in theory.

. . . The conformity that we find here between the fundamental experiments and the results of the calculation seem to give a great weight either to the opinion of M. Oepinus or to the system of two fluids as we have presented it. However it must be noticed that there are a few phenomena which seem to be incapable of being included in these hypotheses; there is one which is of the most important.

We have seen . . . that when a magnetized needle is freely suspended, the sum of the boreal forces which push this needle into the magnetic meridian was exactly equal to the sum of the austral forces; this result, founded on experiments that cannot be contradicted, takes place not only for a needle that one has just magnetized but, if after having magnetized it, the needle is cut in different parts, then for each part. The extremity of the boreal part will still be acted upon by boreal and austral forces of exact equality; but, in the preceding hypotheses, this point should be uniquely charged with boreal fluids and that the action of the two magnetic poles of the globe of the earth should unite to transport it towards the boreal pole. Thus the theory is found here to contradict experiment.

I believe that one can reconcile the result of experiment and of calculation by making a few changes in the hypothesis. Here is one which appears to be able to explain all the magnetic phenomena for which precise measurements have been found from experiments. It consists in supposing in the system of M. Oepinus that the magnetic fluid is enclosed in each molecule or integral part of the magnet or of the steel; that the fluid can be transported from one end to the other of this molecule which would thus give two poles to each molecule but that the fluid cannot pass from one molecule to another. Thus for example if a magnetized needle were of a very small diameter, or if each molecule can be regarded as a small magnet whose northern extremity will be united to the southern extremity of the little needle that precedes it, there will then be only two extremities n and s of this needle which will give signs of magnetism because it will only be at these two extremities that one of the poles of the molecules will not be in contact with the contrary poles of another molecule.

If such a needle were cut in two parts after having been magnetized in a, for example, the extremity a of the part na should have the same force that the extremity s of the whole needle had and the extremity a of the part sa equally should have the same strength that the extremity n of the entire needle had before being cut.

This fact is found to be confirmed by experiment; for, if one cuts a very long and very fine needle in two parts after having magnetized it, each part will prove to be magnetized to saturation and even though one magnetizes it again, it will not acquire a greater directive force.

Each part of our needle, in this new system, no matter how it has been magnetized or cut, will, therefore, be aligned in the magnetic meridian by the austral and boreal forces which are themselves equal and this would seem to be one of the main phenomena for which a hypothesis must be adequate.

2.   John Dalton and *A New System of Chemical Philosophy**

The triumph of the Newtonian world-view came with the atomic theory of John Dalton. Although Newton had explicitly committed himself to an atomic theory, it remained a largely metaphysical hypothesis. Dalton (1766-1844), a Quaker schoolmaster, came to the atomic doctrine through his study of meteorology and the problem of mixed gases. His A New System of Chemical Philosophy, *of which Part I appeared in 1808, is almost as much a treatise on caloric as it is on the atomic nature of matter. For the first time, atoms became physically real entities for they could now be weighed.*

When we consider that all elastic fluids are equally expanded by temperature, and that liquids and solids are not so, it should seem that a general law for the affection of elastic fluids for heat, ought to be more easily deducible and more simple than one for liquids, or solids.--There are three suppositions in regard to elastic fluids which merit discussion.
1. *Equal weights of elastic fluids may have the same quantity of heat under like circumstances of temperature and pressure.*
The truth of this supposition is disproved by several facts: oxygen and hydrogen upon their union give out much heat, though they form steam, an elastic fluid of the same weight as the elements composing it. Nitrous gas and oxygen unite under similar circumstances. Carbonic acid is formed by the union of charcoal, a substance of low specific heat, with oxygen; much heat is given out, which must be principally derived from the oxygen; if then the charcoal contain little heat, and the oxygen combining with it be reduced, the carbonic acid must be far inferior in heat to an equal weight of oxygenous gas.
2. *Equal bulks of elastic fluids may have the same quantity of heat with the same pressure and temperature.*
This appears much more plausible; the diminution of volume when a mixture of oxygen and hydrogen is converted into steam, may be occasioned by a proportionate diminution of the absolute heat; the same may be said of a mixture of nitrous gas and oxygen. The minute differences observed by Crawford, may have been inaccuracies occasioned by the complexity of his experiments.--But there are other considerations which render this supposition extremely improbable, if they do not altogether disprove it. Carbonic acid contains its own bulk of oxygen; the heat given out at its formation must therefore be exactly equal to the whole heat previously contained in the charcoal on this supposition; but the heat by the combustion of one pound of charcoal seems, at least, equal to the heat by the combustion of a quantity of hydrogen sufficient to produce one pound of water, and this last is equal to, or more than the heat retained by the water, because steam is nearly twice the density of the elastic mixture from which it is produced; it should therefore follow, that charcoal should be found

---

*John Dalton, *A New System of Chemical Philosophy*, Part I (Manchester, 1808), pp. 68-75, 141-43, 182-83, 187-89, 211-16.

of the same specific heat as water, whereas it is only about ¼ of it. Were this supposition true, the specific heats of elastic fluids of equal weights would be inversely as their specific gravities.--If that of steam of aqueous vapour were represented by 1, oxygen would be .64, hydrogen 8.4, azote .72, and carbonic acid .46.--But the supposition is untenable.

3. *The quantity of heat belonging to the ultimate particles of all elastic fluids, must be the same under the same pressure and temperature.*

It is evident the number of ultimate particles or molecules in a given weight or volume of one gas is not the same as in another: for, if equal measures of azotic and oxygenous gases were mixed, and could be instantly united chemically, they would form nearly two measures of nitrous gas, having the same weight as the two original measures; but the number of ultimate particles could at most be one half of that before the union. No two elastic fluids, probably, therefore, have the same number of particles, either in the same volume or the same weight. Suppose, then, a given volume of any elastic fluid to be constituted of particles, each surrounded with an atmosphere of heat repelling each other through the medium of those atmospheres, and in a state of equilibrium under the pressure of a constant force, such as the earth's atmosphere, also at the temperature of the surrounding bodies; suppose further, that by some sudden change each malecule of air was endued with a stronger affinity for heat; query the change that would take place in consequence of this last supposition? The only answer that can be given, as it appears to me, is this.--The particles will condense their respective atmospheres of heat, by which their mutual repulsion will be diminished, and the external pressure will therefore effect a proportionate condensation in the volume of air: neither an increase nor diminution in the quantity of heat around each molecule, or around the whole, will take place. Hence the truth of the supposition, or as it may now be called, proposition, is demonstrated.

Corol. 1. The specific heats of equal *weights* of any two elastic fluids, are inversely as the weights of their atoms or molecules.

2. The specific heats of equal *bulks* of elastic fluids, are directly as their specific gravities, and inversely as the weights of their atoms.

3. Those elastic fluids that have their atoms the most condensed, have the strongest attraction for heat; the greater attraction is spent in accumulating more heat in a given space or volume, but does not increase the quantity around any single atom.

4. When two elastic atoms unite by chemical affinity to form one elastic atom, one half of their heat is disengaged. When three unite, then two thirds of their heat is disengaged, &c. And in general, when m elastic particles by chemical union become n; the heat given out is to the heat retained as $m - n$ is to n.

One objection to this proposition it may be proper to obviate: it will be said, an increase in the specific attraction of each atom must produce the same effect on the system as an increase of external pressure. Now this last is known to express or give out a quantity of the absolute heat; therefore the former must do the same. This conclusion must be admitted; and it tends to establish the truth of the preceding proposition. The heat expressed by doubling the density of any elastic fluid amounts to about 50°, according to my former experiments; this heat is not so much as one hundreth part of the whole, as will be shewn hereafter, and therefore does not materially affect the specific heat: it seems to be merely the interstitial heat amongst the small globular molecules of air, and scarcely can be said to belong to them, because it is equally found in a vacuum or space devoid of air, as is proved by the increase of temperature upon admitting air into a vacuum.

Before we can apply this doctrine to find the specific heat of elastic fluids, we must first ascertain the relative weights of their ultimate particles. Assuming at present what will be proved hereafter, that if the weight of an atom of hydrogen be 1, that of oxygen will be 7, azote 5, nitrous gas 12, nitrous oxide 17, carbonic acid 19, ammoniacal gas 6, carburetted hydrogen 7, olefiant gas 6, nitric acid 19, carbonic axide 12, sulphuretted hydrogen 16, muriatic acid 22, aqueous vapour 8, ethereal vapour 11, and alcoholic vapour 16; we shall have the specific heats of the several elastic fluids as in the following table. In order to compare them with that of water, we shall further assume the specific heat of water to that of steam as 6 to 7, or as 1 to 1.166.

Table of the specific heats of elastic fluids.

Hydrogen	9.382	Olefiant gas	1.555
Azote	1.866	Nitric acid	.491
Oxygen	1.333	Carbonic oxide	.777
Atmos. air	1.759	Sulph. hydrogen	.583
Nitrous gas	.777	Muriatic acid	.424
Nitrous oxide	.549	Aqueous vapour	1.166
Carbonic acid	.491	Ether. vapour	.848
Ammon. gas	1.555	Alcohol. vapour	.586
Carb. hydrogen	1.333	Water	1.000

Let us now see how far these results will accord with experience. It is remarkable that the heat of common air comes out nearly the same as Crawford found it by experiment; also, hydrogen excels all the rest as he determined; but oxygen is much lower and azote higher. The principles of Crawford's doctrine of animal heat and combustion, however, are not at all affected with the change. Besides the reason already assigned for thinking that azote has been rated too low, we see from the Table, page 62, that ammonia, a compound of hydrogen and azote, has a higher specific heat than water, a similar compound of hydrogen and oxygen.

Upon the whole, there is not any established fact in regard to the specific heats of bodies, whether elastic or liquid, that is repugnant to the above table as far as I know; and it is to be hoped, that some principle analogous to the one here adopted, may soon be extended to solid and liquid bodies in general.

*   *   *

Chap. II

on the

CONSTITUTION OF BODIES

There are three distinctions in the kinds of bodies, or three states, which have more especially claimed the attention of philosophical chemists; namely, those which are marked by the terms *elastic fluids, liquids, and solids*. A very familiar instance is exhibited to us in water, of a body, which, in certain circumstances, is capable of assuming all the three states. In steam we recognise a perfectly elastic fluid, in water, a perfect liquid, and in ice a complete solid. These observations have tacitly led to the conclusion which seems universally adopted, that all bodies of sensible magnitude, whether liquid or solid, are constituted of a vast number of extremely small particles, or atoms of matter bound together by a force of attraction, which is more or less powerful according to circumstances, and which as it endeavours to prevent their separation, is very properly called in that view, *attraction of cohesion;* but as it collects them from a dispersed state (as from steam into water) it is called, *attraction of aggregation,* or more simply, *affinity.* Whatever names it may go by, they still signify one and the same power. It is not my design to call in question this conclusion, which appears completely satisfactory; but to shew that we have hitherto made no use of it, and that the consequence of the neglect, has been a very obscure view of chemical agency, which is daily growing more so in proportion to the new lights attempted to be thrown upon it.

The opinions I more particularly allude to, are those of Berthollet on the Laws of chemical affinity; such as that chemical agency is proportional to the mass, and that in all chemical unions, there exist insensible gradations in the proportions of the constituent principles. The inconsistence of these opinions, both with reason and observation, cannot, I think, fail to strike every one who takes a proper view of the phenomena.

Whether the ultimate particles of a body, such as water, are all alike, that is, of the same figure, weight, &c. is a question of some importance. From what is known, we have no reason to apprehend a diversity in these particulars: if it does exist in water, it must equally exist in the elements constituting water, namely, hydrogen and oxygen. Now it is scarcely possible to conceive how the aggregates of dissimilar particles should be so uniformly the same. If some of the particles of water were heavier than others, if a parcel of the liquid on any occasion were constituted principally of these heavier particles, it must be supposed to affect the specific gravity of the mass, a circumstance not known. Similar observations may be made on other substances. Therefore we may conclude that *the ultimate particles of all homogeneous bodies are perfectly alike in weight, figure, &c.* In other words, every particle of water is like every other particle of water; every particle of hydrogen is like every other particle of hydrogen, &c.

*   *   *

In 1802, Dr. Henry announced a very curious and important discovery, which was afterwards published in the Philosophical Transactions; namely, *that the quantity of any gas absorbed by water is increased in direct proportion to the pressure of the gas on the surface of the water.* Previously to this, I was engaged in an investigation of the quantity of carbonic acid in the atmosphere; it was matter of surprise to me that lime water should so readily manifest the presence of carbonic acid in the air, whilst pure water by exposure for any length of time, gave not the least traces of that acid. I thought that length of time ought to compensate for weakness of affinity. In pursuing the subject I found that the quantity of this acid taken up by water was greater or less in proportion to its greater or less density in the gaseous mixture, incumbent upon the surface, and therefore ceased to be surprised at water absorbing so insensible a portion from the atmosphere. I had not however entertained any suspicion that this law was generally applicable to the gases till Dr. Henry's discovery was announced. Immediately upon this, it struck me as essentially necessary in ascertaining the quantity of any gas which a given volume of water will absorb, that we must be careful the gas is perfectly pure or unmixed with any other gas whatever; otherwise the maximum effect for any given pressure cannot be produced. This thought was suggested to Dr. Henry, and found to be correct; in consequence of which, it became expedient to repeat some of his experiments relating to the quantity of gas absorbed under a given pressure. Upon due consideration of all these phenomena, Dr. Henry became convinced, that there was no system of elastic fluids which gave so simple, easy and intelligible a solution of them, as the one I adopt, namely, that each gas in any mixture exercises a distinct pressure, which continues the same if the other gases are withdrawn. In the 8th Vol. of Nicholson's Journal, may be seen a letter addressed to me, in which Dr. Henry has clearly pointed out his reasons for giving my theory a preference.

*   *   *

I shall now proceed to give my present views on the subject of mixed gases, which are somewhat different from what they were when the theory was announced, in consequence of the fresh lights which succeeding experience has diffused. In prosecuting my enquiries into the nature of elastic fluids, I soon perceived it was necessary, if possible, to ascertain whether the atoms or ultimate particles of the different gases are of the same size or volume in like circumstances of temperature and pressure. By the size or volume of an ultimate particle, I mean in this place, the space it occupies in the state of a pure elastic fluid; in this sense the bulk of the particle signifies the bulk of the supposed impenetrable nucleus, together with that of its surrounding repulsive atmosphere of heat. At the time I formed the theory of mixed gases, I had a confused idea, as many have, I suppose, at this time, that the particles of elastic fluids are all of the same size; that a given volume of oxygenous gas contains just as many particles as the same volume of hydrogenous; or if not, that we had no data from which the question could be solved. But from a train of reasoning, similar to that exhibited at page 71, I became convinced that different gases have *not* their particles of the same size: and that the following may be adopted as a maxim, till some reason appears to the contrary: namely,--

That every species of pure elastic fluid has its particles globular and all of a size; but that no two species agree in the size of their particles, the pressure and temperature being the same.

* * *

ON CHEMICAL SYNTHESIS.

When any body exists in the elastic state, its ultimate particles are separated from each other to a much greater distance than in any other state; each particle occupies the centre of a comparatively large sphere, and supports its dignity by keeping all the rest, which by their gravity, or otherwise are disposed to encroach up it, at a respectful distance. When we attempt to conceive the *number* of particles in an atmosphere, it is somewhat like attempting to conceive the number of stars in the universe; we are confounded with the thought. But if we limit the subject, by taking a given volume of any gas, we seem persuaded that, let the divisions be ever so minute, the number of particles must be finite; just as in a given space of the universe, the number of stars and planets cannot be infinite.

Chemical analysis and synthesis go no farther than to the separation of particles one from another, and to their reunion. No new creation or destruction of matter is within the reach of chemical agency. We might as well attempt to introduce a new planet into the solar system, or to annihilate one already in existence, as to create or destroy a particle of hydrogen. All the changes we can produce, consist in separating particles that are in a state of cohesion or combination, and joining those that were previously at a distance.

In all chemical investigations, it has justly been considered an important object to ascertain the relative *weights* of the simples which constitute a compound. But unfortunately the enquiry has terminated here; whereas from the relative weights in the mass, the relative weights of the ultimate particles or atoms of the bodies which have been inferred, from which their number and weight in various other compounds would appear, in order to assist and to guide future investigations, and to correct their results. Now it is one object of this work, to shew the importance and advantage of ascertaining *the relative weights of the ultimate particles, both of simple and compound bodies, the number of simple elementary particles which constitute one compound particle, and the number of less compound particles which enter into the formation of one more compound particle.*

If there are two bodies, A and B, which are disposed to combine, the following is the order in which the combinations may take place, beginning with the most simple: namely,

```
1 atom of A + 1 atom  of B = 1 atom of C, binary.
1 atom of A + 2 atoms of B = 1 atom of D, ternary.
2 atoms of A + 1 atom  of B = 1 atom of E, ternary.
1 atom of A + 3 atoms of B = 1 atom of F, quaternary.
3 atoms of A + 1 atom  of B = 1 atom of G, quaternary.
                    &c. &c.
```

The following general rules may be adopted as guides in all our investigations respecting chemical synthesis.

1st. When only one combination of two bodies can be obtained, it must be presumed to be a *binary* one, unless some cause appear to the contrary.

2d. When two combinations are observed, they must be presumed to be a *binary* and a *ternary*.

3d. When three combinations are obtained, we may expect one to be a *binary*, and the other two *ternary*.

4th. When four combinations are observed, we should expect one *binary*, two *ternary*, and one *quaternary*, &c.

5th. A *binary* compound should always be specifically heavier than the mere mixture of its two ingredients.

6th. A *ternary* compound should be specifically heavier than the mixture of a binary and a simple, which would, if combined, constitute it; &c.

7th. The above rules and observations equally apply, when two bodies, such as C and D, D and E, &c. are combined.

From the application of these rules, to the chemical facts already well ascertained, we deduce the following conclusions; 1st. That water is a binary compound of hydrogen and oxygen, and the relative weights of the two elementary atoms are as 1:7, nearly; 3d. That ammonia is a binary compound of hydrogen and azote, and the relative weights of the two atoms are as 1:5, nearly; 3d. That nitrous gas is a binary compound of azote and oxygen, the atoms of which weigh 5 and 7 respectively; that nitric acid is a binary or ternary compound according as it is derived, and consists of one atom of azote and two of oxygen, together weighing 19; that nitrous oxide is a compound similar to nitric acid, and consists of one atom of oxygen and two of azote, weighing 17; that nitrous acid is a binary compound of nitric acid and nitrous gas, weighing 31; that oxynitric acid is a binary compound of nitric acid and oxygen, weighing 26; 4th. That carbonic oxide is a binary compound, consisting of one atom of charcoal, and one of oxygen, together weighing nearly 12; that carbonic acid is a ternary compound, (but sometimes binary) consisting of one atom of charcoal, and two of oxygen, weighing 19; &c. &c. In all these cases the weights are expressed in atoms of hydrogen, each of which is denoted by unity.

In the sequel, the facts and experiments from which these conclusions are derived, will be detailed; as well as a great variety of others from which are inferred the constitution and weight of the ultimate particles of the principal acids, the alkalis, the earths, the methods, the metallic oxides and sulphurets, the long train of neutral salts, and in short, all the chemical compounds which have hitherto obtained a tolerably good analysis. Several of the conclusions will be supported by original experiments.

From the novelty as well as importance of the ideas suggested in this chapter, it is deemed expedient to give plates, exhibiting the mode of combination in some of the more simple cases. A specimen of these accompanies this first part. The elements or atoms of such bodies as are conceived at present to be simple, are denoted by a small circle, with some distinctive mark; and the combinations consist in the juxta-position of two or more of these; when three or more particles of elastic fluids are combined together in one, it is to be supposed that the particles of the same kind repel each other, and therefore take their stations accordingly.

END OF PART THE FIRST.

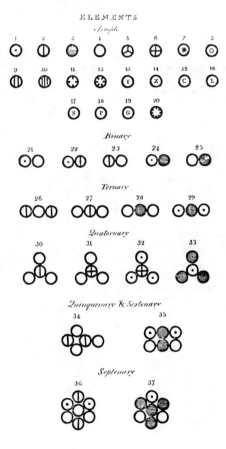

PLATE IV. This plate contains the arbitrary marks or signs chosen to represent the several chemical elements or ultimate particles.

Fig.			Fig.		
1 Hydrog. its rel. weight	-	1	11 Strontites	- - - - - -	46
2 Azote,	- - - - - - - - -	5	12 Barytes	- - - - - - - -	68
3 Carbone or charcoal,	- - -	5	13 Iron	- - - - - - - - -	38
4 Oxygen,	- - - - - - - -	7	14 Zinc	- - - - - - - - -	56
5 Phosphorus,	- - - - - - -	9	15 Copper	- - - - - - - -	56
6 Sulphur,	- - - - - - - - -	13	16 Lead	- - - - - - - - -	95
7 Magnesia,	- - - - - - - -	20	17 Silver	- - - - - - - -	100
8 Lime,	- - - - - - - - - -	23	18 Platina	- - - - - - - -	100
9 Soda,	- - - - - - - - - -	28	19 Gold	- - - - - - - - -	140
10 Potash,	- - - - - - - - -	42	20 Mercury	- - - - - - - -	167

21. An atom of water or steam, composed of 1 of oxygen and 1 of hydrogen, retained in physical contact by a strong affinity, and supposed to be surrounded by a common atmosphere of heat; its relative weight = - - - - - - - 8
22. An atom of ammonia, composed of 1 of azote and 1 of hydrogen - 6
23. An atom of nitrous gas, composed of 1 of azote and 1 of oxygen - 12
24. An atom of olefiant gas, composed of 1 of carbone and 1 of hydrogen - 6
25. An atom of carbonic oxide composed of 1 of carbone and 1 of oxygen - 12
26. An atom of nitrous oxide, 2 azote + 1 oxygen - - - - - - 17
27. An atom of nitric acid, 1 azote + 2 oxygen - - - - - - - 19
28. An atom of carbonic acid, 1 carbone + 2 oxygen - - - - - 19
29. An atom of carburetted hydrogen, 1 carbone + 2 hydrogen - 7
30. An atom of oxynitric acid, 1 azote + 3 oxygen - - - - - - 26
31. An atom of sulphuric acid, 1 sulphur + 3 oxygen - - - - - 34
32. An atom of sulphuretted hydrogen, 1 sulphur + 3 hydrogen 16
33. An atom of alcohol, 3 carbone + 1 hydrogen - - - - - - 16
34. An atom of nitrous acid, 1 nitric acid + 1 nitrous gas - 31
35. An atom of acetous acid, 2 carbone + 2 water - - - - - - 26
36. An atom of nitrate of ammonia, 1 nitric acid + 1 ammonia + 1 water - 33
37. An atom of sugar, 1 alcohol + 1 carbonic acid - - - - - - 35

3. Sir George Mackenzie on Sound

The tendency to materialize all forces was carried to an extreme in the selection that follows.* Yet, this very extreme illustrates the power of the hold that the "Newtonian" view had over people.

Jan. 3. 1820.--Sir George Mackenzie, Bart., read a Paper, entitled, *Speculations on the Nature of Sound.* The facts which he chiefly dwelt upon were, first, That in every experiment, air has intervened between all bodies supposed to have the power of emitting and of conducting sound, and the apparatus of the ear; 2. That sound varies in quality, and that the *quality* is not altered by transmission through different media, although the *intensity* of the sound may be increased or diminished; 3. That the intensity of sound does not depend on the rate of vibration; 4. That different substances have the power of modifying the quality of sound; 5. That there are cases in which sounds interfere with one another; 6. That the same effect, in acquiring any pitch of sound, may be obtained by preserving a spring of the same length, while the volume of air connected with it is altered in dimension, (as in playing on a Jew's harp); or by keeping the volume of air the same, while the dimensions of the spring are altered, (as in the trumpet of an organ). Sir George Mackenzie's opinions, as far as they were stated, are, 1. That sound is a medium *sui generis*; 2. That this medium is emitted by no other substance but air; 3. That it is not conducted through air, but that successive portions of air, when put into a certain condition by impulse, emit it; and that when the impulse reaches the air in connection with the tympanum, the sound emitted by that portion of air alone, is made perceptible to us by the apparatus of the internal ear; and that we learn to judge of the distance of the body that gives the impulse, in a manner analogous to that by which we judge of the distance of objects in perspective; and that our acquaintance with sounds, as they proceed from impulse given by certain means, is derived from an imperceptible induction, similar to that by which a child learns the meaning of words, and forms correct ideas of distance. Lastly, That all means of producing sound, are only means of causing air to emit it.

**Edinburgh Journal of Philosophy*, 2 (1820), p. 374.

4. Joseph Fourier and the *Analytical Theory of Heat**

That certain problems could be handled without recourse to
the notion of an imponderable fluid or of atoms was shown by
Joseph Fourier in his Analytical Theory of Heat. *In this sense,*
he was a member of the unorthodox party, although he would not
have been happy with the philosophical position taken by those
who would substitute forces for particles.

PRELIMINARY DISCOURSE.

Primary causes are unknown to us; but are subject to simple
and constant laws, which may be discovered by observation, the
study of them being the object of natural philosophy.

Heat, like gravity, penetrates every substance of the universe, its rays occupy all parts of space. The object of our
work is to set forth the mathematical laws which this element
obeys. The theory of heat will hereafter form one of the most
important branches of general physics.

The knowledge of rational mechanics, which the most ancient
nations had been able to acquire, has not come down to us, and
the history of this science, if we except the first theorems in
harmony, is not traced up beyond the discoveries of Archimedes.
This great geometer explained the mathematical principles of the
equilibrium of solids and fluids. About eighteen centuries
elapsed before Galileo, the originator of dynamical theories,
discovered the laws of motion of heavy bodies. Within this new
science Newton comprised the whole system of the universe. The
successors of these philosophers have extended these theories,
and given them an admirable perfection: they have taught us that
the most diverse phenomena are subject to a small number of fundamental laws which are reproduced in all the acts of nature.
It is recognised that the same principles regulate all the movements of the stars, their form, the inequalities of their courses,
the equilibrium and the oscillations of the seas, the harmonic
vibrations of air and sonorous bodies, the transmission of light,
capillary actions, the undulations of fluids, in fine the most
complex effects of all the natural forces, and thus has the
thought of Newton been confirmed: *quod tam paucis tam multa*
præstet geometria gloriatur.

But whatever may be the range of mechanical theories, they
do not apply to the effects of heat. These make up a special
order of phenomena, which cannot be explained by the principles
of motion and equilibrium. We have for a long time been in possession of ingenious instruments adapted to measure many of these
effects; valuable observations have been collected; but in this
manner partial results only have become known, and not the mathematical demonstration of the laws which include them all.

I have deduced these laws from prolonged study and attentive

---

*Joseph Fourier, *The Analytical Theory of Heat*, translated, with
notes by Alexander Freeman (N.Y.: Dover, 1955), pp. 1-2, 6-7,
12-13, 450-56.

comparison of the facts known up to this time: all these facts I have observed afresh in the course of several years with the most exact instruments that have hitherto been used.

To found the theory, it was in the first place necessary to distinguish and define with precision the elementary properties which determine the action of heat. I then perceived that all the phenomena which depend on this action resolve themselves into a very small number of general and simple facts; whereby every physical problem of this kind is brought back to an investigation of mathematical analysis. From these general facts I have concluded that to determine numerically the most varied movements of heat, it is sufficient to submit each substance to three fundamental observations. Different bodies in fact do not possess in the same degree the power to *contain* heat, *to receive or transmit it across their surfaces*, nor to *conduct* it through the interior of their masses. These are the three specific qualities which our theory clearly distinguishes and shews how to measure.

*   *   *

The principles of the theory are derived, as are those of rational mechanics, from a very small number of primary facts, the causes of which are not considered by geometers, but which they admit as the results of common observations confirmed by all experiment.

The differential equations of the propagation of heat express the most general conditions, and reduce the physical questions to problems of pure analysis, and this is the proper object of theory. They are not less rigorously established than the general equations of equilibrium and motion. In order to make this comparison more perceptible, we have always preferred demonstrations analogous to those of the theorems which serve as the foundation of statics and dynamics. These equations still exist, but receive a different form, when they express the distribution of luminous heat in transparent bodies, or the movements which the changes of temperature and density occasion in the interior of fluids. The coefficients which they contain are subject to variations whose exact measure is not yet known; but in all the natural problems which it most concerns us to consider, the limits of temperature differ so little that we may omit the variations of these coefficients.

The equations of the movement of heat, like those which express the vibrations of sonorous bodies, or the ultimate oscillations of liquids, belong to one of the most recently discovered branches of analysis, which it is very important to perfect. After having established these differential equations their integrals must be obtained; this process consists in passing from a common expression to a particular solution subject to all the given conditions. This difficult investigation requires a special analysis founded on new theorems, whose object we could not in this place make known. The method which is derived from them leaves nothing vague and indeterminate in the solutions, it leads them up to the final numerical applications, a necessary condition of every investigation, without which we should only arrive at useless transformations.

The same theorems which have made known to us the equations of the movement of heat, apply directly to certain problems of general analysis and dynamics whose solution has for a long time been desired.

Profound study of nature is the most fertile source of mathematical discoveries. Not only has this study, in offering a determinate object to investigation, the advantage of excluding vague questions and calculations without issue; it is besides a sure method of forming analysis itself, and of discovering the elements which it concerns us to know, and which natural science ought always to preserve: these are the fundamental elements which are reproduced in all natural effects.

We see, for example, that the same expression whose abstract properties geometers had considered, and which in this respect belongs to general analysis, represents as well the motion of light in the atmosphere, as it determines the laws of diffusion of heat in solid matter, and enters into all the chief problems of the theory of probability.

The analytical equations, unknown to the ancient geometers, which Descartes was the first to introduce into the study of curves and surfaces, are not restricted to the properties of figures, and to those properties which are the object of rational mechanics; they extend to all general phenomena. There cannot be a language more universal and more simple, more free from errors and from obscurities, that is to say more worthy to express the invariable relations of natural things.

Considered from this point of view, mathematical analysis is as extensive as nature itself; it defines all perceptible relations, measures times, spaces, forces, temperatures; this difficult science is formed slowly, but it preserves every principle which it has once acquired; it grows and strengthens itself incessantly in the midst of the many variations and errors of the human mind.

*　　*　　*

The new theories explained in our work are united for ever to the mathematical sciences, and rest like them on variable foundations; all the elements which they at present possess they will preserve, and will continually acquire greater extent. Instruments will be perfected and experiments multiplied. The analysis which we have formed will be deduced from more general, that is to say, more simple and more fertile methods common to many classes of phenomena. For all substances, solid or liquid, for vapours and permanent gases, determinations will be made of all the specific qualities relating to heat, and of the variations of the coefficients which express them. At different stations on the earth observations will be made, of the temperatures of the ground at different depths, of the intensity of the solar heat and its effects, constant or variable, in the atmosphere, in the ocean and in lakes; and the constant temperature of the heavens proper to the planetary regions will become known. The theory itself will direct all these measures, and assign their precision. No considerable progress can hereafter be made which is not founded on experiments such as these; for mathematical analysis can deduce from general and simple phenomena the expression of the laws of nature; but the special application of these laws to very complex effects demands a long series of exact observations.

* * *

428. Here we shall terminate this section, which is devoted almost entirely to analysis. The integrals which we have obtained are not only general expressions which satisfy the differential equations; they represent in the most distinct manner the natural effect which is the object of the problem. This is the chief condition which we have always had in view, and without which the results of investigation would appear to us to be only useless transformations. When this condition is fulfilled, the integral is, properly speaking, *the equation of the phenomenon;* it expresses clearly the character and progress of it, in the same manner as the finite equation of a line or curved surface makes known all the properties of those forms. To exhibit the solutions, we do not consider one form only of the integral; we seek to obtain directly that which is suitable to the problem. Thus it is that the integral which expresses the movement of heat in a sphere of given radius, is very different from that which expresses the movement in a cylindrical body, or even in a sphere whose radius is supposed infinite. Now each of these integrals has a definite form which cannot be replaced by another. It is necessary to make use of it, if we wish to ascertain the distribution of heat in the body in question. In general, we could not introduce any change in the form of our solutions, without making them lose their essential character, which is the representation of the phenomena.

The different integrals might be derived from each other, since they are co-extensive. But these transformations require long calculations, and almost always suppose that the form of the result is known in advance. We may consider in the first place, bodies whose dimensions are finite, and pass from this problem to that which relates to an unbounded solid. We can then substitute a definite integral for the sum denoted by the symbol Σ. Thus it is that equations (α) and (β), referred to at the beginning of this section, depend upon each other. The first becomes the second, when we suppose the radius R infinite. Reciprocally we may derive from the second equation (β) the solutions relating to bodies of limited dimensions.

In general, we have sought to obtain each result by the shortest way. The chief elements of the method we have followed are these:

1st. We consider at the same time the general condition given by the partial differential equation, and all the special conditions which determine the problem completely, and we proceed to form the analytical expression which satisfies all these conditions.

2nd. We first perceive that this expression contains an infinite number of terms, into which unknown constants enter, or that it is equal to an integral which includes one or more arbitrary functions. In the first instance, that is to say, when the general term is affected by the symbol Σ, we derive from the special conditions a definite transcendental equation, whose roots give the values of an infinite number of constants.

The second instance obtains when the general term becomes an infinitely small quantity; the sum of the series is then changed into a definite integral.

3rd. We can prove by the fundamental theorems of algebra, or even by the physical nature of the problem, that the transcendental equation has all its roots real, in number infinite.

4th. In elementary problems, the general term takes the form of a sine or cosine; the roots of the definite equation are either whole numbers, or real or irrational quantities, each of them included between two definite limits.

In more complex problems, the general term takes the form of a function given implicitly by means of a differential equation integrable or not. However it may be, the roots of the definite equation exist, they are real, infinite in number. This distinction of the parts of which the integral must be composed, is very important, since it shews clearly the form of the solution, and the necessary relation between the coefficients.

5th. It remains only to determine the constants which depend on the initial state; which is done by elimination of the unknowns from an infinite number of equations of the first degree. We multiply the equation which relates to the initial state by a differential factor, and integrate it between defined limits, which are most commonly those of the solid in which the movement is effected.

There are problems in which we have determined the coefficients by successive integrations, as may be seen in the memoir whose object is the temperature of dwellings. In this case we consider the exponential integrals, which belong to the initial state of the infinite solid: it is easy to obtain these integrals. . . .

6th. When the expression sought contains a definite integral, the unknown functions arranged under the symbol of integration are determined, either by the theorems which we have given for the expression of arbitrary functions in definite integrals, or by a more complex process, several examples of which will be found in the Second Part.

These theorems can be extended to any number of variables. They belong in some respects to an inverse method of definite integration; since they serve to determine under the symbols $\int$ and Σ unknown functions which must be such that the result of integration is a given function.

The same principles are applicable to different other problems of geometry, of general physics, or of analysis, whether the equations contain finite or infinitely small differences, or whether they contain both.

The solutions which are obtained by this method are complete, and consist of general integrals. No other integral can be more extensive. The objections which have been made to this subject are devoid of all foundation; it would be superfluous now to discuss them.

7th. We have said that each of these solutions gives *the equation proper to the phenomenon*, since it represents it distinctly throughout the whole extent of its course, and serves to determine with facility all its results numerically.

The functions which are obtained by these solutions are then composed of a multitude of terms, either finite ιr infinitely small: but the form of these expressions is in no degree arbitrary; it is determined by the physical character of the phenomenon. For this reason, when the value of the function is expressed by a series into which exponentials relative to the time enter, it is of necessity that this should be so, since the natural effect whose laws we seek, is really decomposed into distinct parts, corresponding to the different terms of the series. The parts express so many *simple movements* compatible with the special conditions; for each one of these movements, all the temperatures decrease, preserving their primitive ratios. In this composition we ought not to see a result of analysis due to the linear form of the differential equations, but an actual effect which becomes sensible in experiments. It appears also in dynamical problems in which we consider the causes which destroy motion; but it belongs necessarily to all problems of the theory of heat, and determines the nature of the method which we have followed for the solution of them.

8th. The mathematical theory of heat includes: first, the exact definition of all the elements of the analysis; next, the differential equations; lastly, the integrals appropriate to the fundamental problems. The equations can be arrived at in several ways; the same integrals can also be obtained, or other problems solved, by introducing certain changes in the course of the investigation. We consider that these researches do not constitute a method different from our own; but confirm and multiply its results.

9th. It has been objected, to the subject of our analysis, that the transcendental equations which determine the exponents having imaginary roots, it would be necessary to employ the terms which proceed from them, and which would indicate a periodic character in part of the phenomenon; but this objection has no foundation, since the equations in question have in fact all their roots real, and no part of the phenomenon can be periodic.

10th. It has been alleged that in order to solve with certainty problems of this kind, it is necessary to resort in all cases to a certain form of the integral which was denoted as general; and equation (γ) of Art. 398 was propounded under this designation; but this distinction has no foundation, and the use of a single integral would only have the effect, in most cases, of complicating the investigation unnecessarily. It is moreover evident that this integral (γ) is derivable from that which we gave in 1807 to determine the movement of heat in a ring of definite radius R; it is sufficient to give to R an infinite value.

11th. It has been supposed that the method which consists in expressing the integral by a succession of exponential terms, and in determining their coefficients by means of the initial state, does not solve the problem of a prism which loses heat unequally at its two ends; or that, at least, it would be very difficult to verify in this manner the solution derivable from the integral (γ) by long calculations. We shall perceive, by a new examination, that our method applies directly to this problem, and that a single integration even is sufficient.

12th. We have developed in series of sines of multiple arcs functions which appear to contain only even powers of the variable, cos x for example. We have expressed by convergent series or by definite integrals separate parts of different functions, or functions discontinuous between certain limits, for example that which measures the ordinate of a triangle. Our proofs leave no doubt of the exact truth of these equations.

13th. We find in the works of many geometers results and processes of calculation analogous to those which we have employed. These are particular cases of a general method, which had not yet been formed, and which it became necessary to establish in order to ascertain even in the most simple problems the mathematical laws of the distribution of heat. This theory required an analysis appropriate to it, one principal element of which is the analytical expression of *separate functions*, or of *parts of functions*.

By a *separate function*, or *part of a function*, we understand a function $f(x)$ which has values existing when the variable x is included between given limits, and whose value is always nothing, if the variable is not included between those limits. This function measures the ordinate of a line which includes a finite arc of arbitrary form, and coincides with the axis of abscissae in all the rest of its course.

This motion is not opposed to the general principles of analysis; we might even find the first traces of it in the writings of Daniel Bernouilli, of Cauchy, of Lagrange and Euler. It had always been regarded as manifestly impossible to express in a series of sines of multiple arcs, or at least in a trigonometric convergent series, a function which has no existing values unless the values of the variable are included between certain limits, all the other values of the function being nul. But this point of analysis is fully cleared up, and it remains incontestable that separate functions, or parts of functions, are exactly expressed by trigonometric convergent series, or by definite integrals. We have insisted on this consequence from the origin of our researches up to the present time, since we are not concerned here with an abstract and isolated problem, but with a primary consideration intimately connected with the most useful and extensive considerations. Nothing has appeared to us more suitable than geometrical constructions to demonstrate the truth of these new results, and to render intelligible the forms which analysis employs for their expression.

14th. The principles which have served to establish for us the analytical theory of heat, apply directly to the investigation of the movement of waves in fluids, a part of which has been agitated. They aid also the investigation of the vibrations of elastic laminæ, of stretched flexible surfaces, of plane elastic surfaces of very great dimensions, and apply in general to problems which depend upon the theory of elasticity. The property of the solutions which we derive from these principles is to render the numerical applications easy, and to offer distinct and intelligible results, which really determine the object of the problem,

without making that knowledge depend upon integrations or eliminations which cannot be effected. We regard as superfluous every
transformation of the results of analysis which does not satisfy
this primary condition.

5. The Wave Theory of Light

*The first major challenge to Newtonianism was the undulatory
theory of light. In 1827, the* Quarterly Journal of Science, *published by William T. Brande, of the Royal Institution of Great
Britain, commissioned Thomas Young to translate an elementary
account of this theory written by Augustin Fresnel* and appended
to the French translation of Thomas Thomson's textbook on chemistry.*

I. Nature of Light.

The Nature of Light has long been a subject of dispute among
natural philosophers: some of them suppose that it is a material
subject, darted out by luminous bodies; and others, that it consists in the vibrations of an infinitely subtile elastic fluid
diffused through all space, in the same way that sound is known
to be a vibration of the air. The system of undulations, which
was contrived by the genius of Descartes, and which was more ably
completed in its detail by Huygens, has also been adopted by
Euler, and in more modern times by Dr. Thomas Young, to whom the
science of optics is indebted for many important discoveries.
The system of emission, or that of Newton, supported by the great
name of its author, and I might almost say, by that reputation
for infallibility which his immortal Principia had earned for
him, has consequently been more generally adopted. The other
hypothesis was apparently altogether abandoned, when Dr. Young
recalled the attention of philosophers to it by some curious experiments, which afford a striking confirmation of it, and which
appear at the same time to be scarcely reconcilable with the system of emission.
 A variety of new phenomena, observed since that time, have
continued to add to the probability of the truth of the theory of
undulations. Though long neglected, and more difficult to be
followed, in the detail of its applications, than the hypothesis
of emission, it has already enabled us to adapt our calculations
much more correctly to the phenomena; and this is one of the
least equivocal proofs of the truth of any system. When a hypothesis is true, it must lead us to numerical relations between
facts the most different in their appearances: while a false
hypothesis, on the contrary, may represent very accurately the
class of phenomena from which it has been deduced, in the same
way that an empirical formula may represent a limited number of

**A. Fresnel, "Elementary View of the Undulatory Theory of Light,"
Quarterly Journal of Science, 23 (1827), pp. 127-30; 25 (1828),
pp. 198-203; 26 (1828), pp. 168-73, 176-78, 188-91.*

results that have afforded it; but it can never trace the secret
relations which connect these phenomena with others of a totally
different class.

It was in this manner, for example, that Mr. Biot investigated, with as much sagacity as perseverance, the laws of the
beautiful phenomena of colours which Mr. Arago had discovered in
crystallized plates, and found that the tints exhibits by them
followed, with regard to their thicknesses, laws similar to those
of the coloured rings already known; that is to say, that the
thicknesses of two crystallized plates of the same nature, which
exhibited any given tints, were in the same proportion as two
plates of air, which afforded similar tints in the production of
coloured rings. This relation, indicated by analogy, without any
regard to a particular theory, was without doubt very remarkable
and very important; but Dr. Young advanced much further, by means
of the law of interferences, which is an immediate consequence of
the system of undulations. He discovered a much more intimate
relation between these two classes of phenomena; that is, that
the difference of the lengths of the paths of the rays ordinarily
and extraordinarily refracted, in the crystallized plate, is precisely equal to the difference of the paths described by the rays
reflected at the first and second surface of the plate of air
that exhibits the same tint as the crystal: and the phenomena,
instead of a simple analogy, are reduced to the predicament of
identity.

I might add that the laws, so complicated in appearance, of
the phenomena of diffraction, which had escaped all attempts to
detect them with the assistance of experiments, as combined with
the theory of emission, are perfectly consistent, in all their
extent, with the simplest principles of the theory of undulations.
Without doubt observation has assisted also in the discovery of
this relation; but observation alone could never have developed
them; while in this case, as well as in many others, the theory
of undulations might easily have gone before the experiments, and
have predicted beforehand the precise results in their minutest
details.

The example, which has already been mentioned, sufficiently
proves that the choice of a theory is not a matter of indifference
in the investigation of physical phenomena. Its utility is not
confined to the purpose of facilitating the study of facts, by
uniting them into groups more or less numerous, according to the
relation which they bear to each other. Another no less important
end of a good theory must be to contribute to the essential advancement of science, by the discovery of facts, and of relations
between classes of phenomena the most distinct, and in appearance
the most independent of each other. Now it is obvious that if we
set out with an imaginary hypothesis respecting the cause of
light, we shall not reach this end so readily, as if we possessed
the true secret of nature. A theory depending upon a true fundamental hypothesis, however ill it may be suited for the application of mathematical analysis to the mechanical operations which
it involves, will still lead us to intimate relations between
distant facts, which would for ever have remained unknown upon
any other suppositions. Hence, to say nothing of our natural

curiosity to know the truth in all cases, we see how important it is to the progress of optics, and of the kindred science of chemistry, to know whether luminous molecules are actually projected from the sources of light and enter our eyes, or if light is propagated by the undulations of a continuous medium, to the particles of which, the luminous bodies communicate their vibratory motions. And we have no reason to believe that the decision of this question is impossible, because it has long remained unaccomplished: we may even venture to assert that, as far as probability goes, it is already determined; and that, after comparing attentively the application of the two systems to all the facts which have been hitherto discovered, an impartial judge will not hesitate to admit the superiority of the theory of undulations.

In entering into the detail of the facts in question, it will not be advisable to separate them from the theoretical views which have led so immediately to their discovery; and it appears to be equally conducive to the purposes of instruction, and to the advancement of the science, to explain the essential principles and foundations of a theory which has been too long neglected and misunderstood: it will, however, be proper on this occasion to omit many details of calculation, for the sake of conciseness, and having reduced each case to the condition of a mathematical problem, it will be sufficient to take its solution for granted.

The diffraction of light will be considered in the first place, because it relates to the simplest possible case of a shadow cast by an opaque body illuminated by a single radiant point; and this case will be considered somewhat diffusely, as affording the best test of the comparative value of the two theories.

*   *   *

Of coloured Rings.

The coloured rings, exhibited by two glasses pressed together, when one of the surfaces in contact is slightly convex, are explained in a very simple manner by the principle of interferences: they evidently result from the mutual influence of the two systems of undulations reflected at the first and the second surface of the plate of air comprehended between these glasses. But before we enter into the detail of the explanation, it will be necessary to establish a principle with regard to the reflection of light, which will be required for this purpose.

When an agitation is propagated in a medium of uniform elasticity and density, it never returns to the same point; and while it is communicated perpetually to new strata of the medium, it leaves no traces behind, but the strata which it has passed remain in absolute rest; in the same manner as a ball of ivory, which strikes another of equal magnitude, communicates all its motion to this second ball, and remains at rest after the stroke. But the effect is not the same when the second ball is either larger or smaller than the first, for in either case the first ball continues to move after the stroke. When the second ball is greater than the first, the new velocity of the first is in a direction contrary to that of its former motion; and when smaller,

the first ball continues to move in the same direction as before,
so that the new velocities of the first ball, after the stroke,
must be marked by contrary signs in the two cases. This comparison may assist us in understanding the consequence of the arrival
of an undulation at the surface of contact of two elastic mediums
of different densities: the infinitely thin stratum of the first
medium, which is in contact with the second, and which may be compared to the first ball, does not remain at rest after having put
the contiguous stratum of the second medium in motion, on account
of the difference in their masses, and a reflection takes place:
but the new velocity which belongs to the stratum of the first
medium, after the stroke, and which is communicated successively
to the neighbouring strata behind it, must have its sign changed
accordingly as the stratum of the second medium is more or less
dense than that of the first. This important proposition, which
Dr. Young deduced from the considerations which have been here
explained, has also been derived by Mr. Poisson from the formulas
which he has demonstrated by means of a rigorous and refined
analysis. When applied to the reflection of light, it enables us
to infer that, accordingly as an undulation is reflected within
the denser medium or without, the velocity of the particles which
constitutes the undulation is positive or negative respectively;
so that all the corresponding motions must have contrary signs in
the two cases.

We may now return to the phenomenon of the coloured rings,
and we may suppose, to simplify our reasoning, that the reflected
light, which is observed, is perpendicular to the surface, or
very nearly so; and that one of the systems of undulations is
thrown by the illuminating object on the first surface of a plate
of air, which is also the second surface of the upper glass: and
what will be said of this system is applicable to every other.
At the moment when it arrives at the surface of separation of the
glass and the air, it suffers a partial reflection, which diminishes, in some measure, the intensity of the light transmitted to
the air, and excites within the first glass another system of
undulations, of which the intensity is greatly inferior to that
of the transmitted light; so that this light, being very little
weakened by this first reflection, produces, when it arrives at
the second surface of the plate of air, a second system of reflected waves of an intensity nearly equal to that of the waves
which are derived from the first reflection: and hence their
interference produces colours so bright in white light, and dark
and light rings so distinct in homogeneous light. The two surfaces of the plate of air being nearly parallel, in the neighbourhood of the point of contact, where the coloured rings are formed,
the two systems of waves follow the same path: but that which has
been reflected at the second surface, will be found retarded, in
comparison with the other, by an interval equal to twice the
thickness of the plate of air which it was twice crossed. We
must, besides, remark that there is another difference between
them; the first having been reflected within the glass, which is
the denser medium, while the second has been reflected without
the second glass; whence arises, according to the principle already established, an opposition in the direction of the elemen-

tary oscillations. Thus when, from the difference of the paths described, the two systems of undulations ought to agree with each other, and so perform their motions in the same direction, we are to conclude, on the contrary, that they are completely at variance; and, on the other hand, when the difference of the paths would indicate a complete discordance, we must infer that their oscillatory motions agree perfectly with each other. Upon these principles it is easy to determine the position of the dark and bright rings.

In the first place, the point of contact, where the thickness of the plate of air is evanescent, and produces no difference in the length of the paths of the two systems, ought to exhibit a perfect agreement in their oscillations: hence, from the opposition of the signs, the reverse takes place, and they destroy each other; so that the point of contact, when seen by reflection, exhibits a black spot. As we go further from this point, the thickness of the plate becomes greater; and at a certain distance it becomes, for example, equal to half an undulation, which would exhibit a complete discordance; but, from the change of signs, affords a perfect agreement, so as to become the most luminous part of the first bright ring. When the thickness of the plate of air is equal to half the length of an undulation, the difference of the paths described being a whole length, which answers to a perfect agreement, there will again be a perfect discordance, and the part will be the middle of a dark ring. It is easy to see, in general, from the same mode of reasoning, that the blackest points of the dark rings correspond to thicknesses of the plate of air expressed by 0, $\frac{1}{2}d$, $\frac{3}{2}d$, $2d$, $\frac{5}{2}d$, and so forth; and the most brilliant points of the bright rings to thicknesses $\frac{1}{4}d$, $\frac{3}{4}d$, $\frac{5}{4}d$, $\frac{7}{4}d$, $\frac{9}{4}d$, $1\frac{1}{4}d$, and so forth, d being the length of a luminous undulation in air; or, if we take one fourth of this length for our unit, the thicknesses of the plate of air, answering to the maxima and minima of reflected light, will be represented by the following numbers:

Dark rings   0, 2, 4, 6, 8, 10. . . .
Bright rings   1, 3, 5, 7, 9, 11. . . .

It is evident that this unit, or the fourth part of a luminous undulation, is precisely the length of what Newton calls the *fits of the particles of light*: so that if we multiply by 4 the measures of them which he has given, for "the seven" principal kinds of simple rays, we obtain the corresponding lengths of their respective undulations: and we obtain in this manner precisely the same results as when we deduce the lengths of the undulations from the measurement of the fringes produced by two mirrors, or from the diversified phenomena of diffraction. This numerical identity, which was first pointed out by Dr. Young, establishes between the coloured rings and the diffraction of light, an intimate connexion, which, before his time, had escaped the notice of natural philosophers, who had been guided by the system of emanation; this connexion being a natural consequence of the theory of undulation only.

According to the experiment of Mr. Arago, on the displacement of the fringes produced by the interference of two luminous pencils, when one of them has passed through a thin plate of some

refractive substance, we have seen that the luminous undulations
are shortened within the plate, in the proportion that the sine
of refraction of the substance bears to the sine of incidence out
of air. This principle is universally true, and extends to all
refractive substances, whatever their nature may be: for example,
the length of an undulation of light in water, is to its length
in air, as the sine of the angle of incidence of rays passing
obliquely from [water into air], is to the sine of the angle of
refraction. Consequently, if we put some water between the
glasses in contact, which exhibit the coloured rings, the plate
of air being replaced by a plate of water, in which the undulations of light become shorter, in the proportion which has been
stated, the thicknesses of the two plates, which reflect the same
rings, will be to each other in the proportion of the sines of
incidence and refraction, at the passage of light from air into
water. This is precisely the result obtained by Newton from observation, when he compared the diameters of the rings exhibited
in both cases, and deduced from them the respective thicknesses.
This remarkable relation between the phenomena of diffraction,
refraction, and coloured rings, which have no connexion in the
system of emanation, might have been very accurately predicted
from the theory of undulation, since, in this theory, the sines
of the angles of incidence and refraction must necessarily be proportional to the velocities of propagation, or to the lengths of
undulation of the light in the two mediums, as will shortly be
seen in the demonstration of the laws of refraction.

Having explained the formation of the reflected rings by the
interference of the reflections from the first and second surface
of the plate of air, Dr. Young has shown, that the much weaker
rings, which are seen by transmission, result from the interference of the rays directly transmitted with those which have first
been twice reflected within the thin plate; and that they must
naturally be complementary to the reflected rings, as experiment
proves that they are. It is unnecessary to enter into the detail
of their explanation at present; it must only be remembered, that
the great faintness of these rings, when the incidence is perpendicular, depends on the great difference of intensity of the two
portions of light: [and more especially on the effect of the unaltered light, which is inseparable from them, in effacing their
impression on the eye; for there is reason to think their intensity more considerable than Dr. Young at first supposed. Tr.]

*   *   *

Of Double Refraction and Polarisation.

When we throw a luminous pencil on one of the natural faces
of a rhomboid of calcarious spar, it divides itself within the
crystal into two other pencils, which follow different paths, and
then present two images of objects seen through the rhomboid.
This phenomenon has been distinguished by the name of double refraction, with many others of the same kind that are exhibited by
other crystals, especially when they are cut into prisms, in order
to render the separation of the images more sensible.

This bifurcation of the light, however, is not the most remarkable circumstance belonging to double refraction; each of the
pencils, into which the incident rays are divided, is possessed
of some singular properties which make a distinction between its
sides. In order to describe the phenomena in question with precision, it is necessary to employ, and to explain, some particular expressions.

In such crystals, as exhibit the laws of double refraction
in their simplest form, there is always a certain direction,
about which every thing occurs in a similar manner on all sides;
and this direction is called the axis of the crystal. It must
not be considered as a single line; for there may be as many axes
as there may be lines parallel to each other, and yet crystals of
this kind are denominated crystals with a single axis, if, in all
other respects, the optical phenomena are the same in all directions round it: so that the word is merely synonymous with a fixed
direction. It must be supposed that the direction of the axis
depends on the crystalline arrangement of the particles of the
medium, and that it must hold, with respect to the faces, or their
lines of crystallization, a determinate position, which is always
the same for the same crystal, however it may be presented to the
incident rays.

There are some crystals in which the perfect resemblance of
all sides of the axis is not strictly observed, and in which there
are consequently two particular directions more or less inclined
to each, which are possessed of properties resembling those which
belong to a single axis in the simpler form of the phenomenon:
and these are called crystals with two axes; but we shall consider, in the first instance, crystals with one axis only, the optical properties of these being simpler and more easily understood.

A plane drawn through the axis, perpendicularly to the surface of the crystal, is called its principal section. The present
object not requiring an explanation of all the different manners
in which the rays of light are bent by the crystals, but merely
of their mode of propagation in these mediums, and the optical
properties which they acquire in them, we may suppose, for the
sake of simplicity, that the incident rays are always perpendicular to the surfaces of the crystal, and contained in the plane of
its principal section: and when it becomes necessary to study
their progress in different directions with respect to the axis,
we may imagine in each case that the surfaces of their admission
and emersion are made perpendicular to these directions.

This being premised, we may observe, in the carbonate of
lime, which has a very conspicuous double refraction, that one of
the two pencils becomes oblique to the surface when the incident
light is perpendicular; while the other proceeds without being
bent, in the manner of ordinary refraction: and this ray is considered as *ordinarily* refracted, and the former *extraordinarily*:
the pencils are also called respectively *ordinary* and *extraordinary*; and the images, which they form, *ordinary* and *extraordinary*
images. A similar bifurcation takes place under the same circumstances in other doubly refracting crystals, such as rock crystal,
but the separation is so slight that a considerable thickness is
required to render it sensible. It becomes more easily observable,

when the crystal is so cut, that the surface of emersion is inclined to that of admission, which causes the two pencils to emerge at different inclinations, and so become further separated as they proceed. But without entering into the details of experiments, which establish the laws of double refraction, it will be sufficient to explain the principal results to which they have led.

It is remarkable, in the first place, that, when the incident rays are perpendicular to the surface of the crystal, the deviation of the extraordinary pencil always takes place in the plane of the principal section; and in the next place, that this deviation vanishes whenever the pencil is either parallel or perpendicular to the axis.

It has been demonstrated by observation, that when the rays are parallel to the axis they not only follow the same direction, but pass through the crystal with the same velocity; and it is when they are perpendicular to the axis that their velocities differ the most, although they follow the same path. The velocity of the propagation of the ordinary rays is the same in all directions: and for this reason they are subject to the ordinary laws of refraction. The velocity of the extraordinary rays is different according to the angle which they make with the axis, and this velocity is determined, in the system of undulation as well as in that of emanation, from the flexure which they undergo at their admission or emersion in oblique directions, which enables us to find the proportion of the sines of incidence and refraction. The experiments of Huygens, of Dr. Wollaston, and of Malus, on the carbonate of line, and the numerous observations of Mr. Biot, on rock crystal, in which the angular measures of double refraction have been carried to the greatest possible precision, demonstrate that the difference of the squares of the velocities of propagation of the ordinary and extraordinary rays is proportional to the square of the sine of the angle made by the extraordinary ray with the axis, if we compute the velocities according to the doctrine of emanation, as the celebrated author of the Mécanique Céleste has done: and in the theory of undulations, this same ratio is observed in the reciprocals of the squares of the velocities; for the velocities are always reciprocally related in the two systems. This important law, the discovery of which is due to the genius of Huygens, affords us, as its consequences, the facts which have been explained: the two kinds of rays possess the same velocities in the direction of the axis, because in this case the sine vanishes, and the difference of the velocities increases gradually with the sine, as we go further from the axis, until it becomes greatest in the direction perpendicular to it.

This difference of velocity is positive in certain crystals, and negative in others; that is to say, in the one class the ordinary rays advance more rapidly than the extraordinary, and in the other less rapidly. The carbonate of lime, or calcarious spar, affords an example of the first case, and rock crystal of the second.

Such being the general principles of the progress of the ordinary and extraordinary rays, we may now return to the physical properties which they exhibit after their emersion, when they are made to pass through a second crystal, capable, like the first, of dividing the light into two separate pencils. It may here be remarked, that the word *pencil* will be employed for a system of waves separated from another by difference of direction, or simply of velocity, though properly borrowed from the system of emanation, as implying a *bundle* of distinct rays.

We may first consider the state of the ordinary pencil which has been transmitted through a rhomboid of calcarious spar: and which, upon being transmitted through a second rhomboid, produces two new pencils of equal brightness, when the principal section of the second rhomboid forms an angle of 45° with that of the first: in all other positions the two pencils, and the images which they form, are of unequal brightness, and one of them even vanishes entirely when the principal sections are parallel or perpendicular: when they are parallel, the extraordinary image vanishes, and the ordinary image attains its greatest brightness; when perpendicular, the ordinary image disappears, and the extraordinary acquires its maximum of intensity. The extraordinary pencil, on the contrary, transmitted by the first rhomboid, exhibits exactly contrary appearances in passing through the second rhomboid: the ordinary image, that it affords, vanishes when the principal sections are parallel, and becomes brightest when they are perpendicular; and then the extraordinary image vanishes. Thus each pencil is unequally divided, except in the case when the sections make an angle of 45° with each other: but when they are either parallel or perpendicular, each of them will undergo a single refraction only, which is the same with the former when the sections are parallel, but of a contrary nature when they are perpendicular to each other.

It follows from these facts, that the two pencils, produced by the double refraction, have not the same properties in various directions about their axes or lines of motion, since they undergo sometimes ordinary and sometimes extraordinary refraction, accordingly as the principal section of the second crystal is directed parallelly or perpendicularly to another given plane. Supposing, then, that we draw right lines perpendicular to the rays in these planes, and conceive them to be carried by the system of waves in its progress, they will show the direction in which it exhibits opposite optical properties.

The name of polarisation was given by Malus to this singular modification of light, according to a hypothesis which Newton had imagined in order to explain the phenomenon: this great mathematician having supposed that the particles of light have two kinds of poles, or rather faces, enjoying different physical properties: that in ordinary light the similar faces of the different particles of light are turned in every imaginable direction; but that, by the action of the crystal, some of them are turned in the direction of the principal section, and the others in a direction perpendicular to it, and that the kind of refraction, which the particles undergo, depends on the direction in which their faces are turned. It is obvious, that some of the facts may be explained according to this hypothesis. But without particularly discussing it, and showing the difficulties, and even contradictions to which it leads, when closely examined; I shall only

observe, that the differences of the optical properties exhibited
by the two pencils, in directions at right angles to each other,
may also be comprehended by supposing *transverse* motions in the
undulations which would not be the same with respect to different
directions: as they would if the particles of the medium oscil-
lated backwards and forwards in lines perpendicular to the directions of the rays. But it is better to abandon all theoretical
ideas of this kind until we have entered more fully into the
phenomena.

    It is not merely by passing through a crystal, which divides
it into two distinct pencils, that light receives this remarkable
modification; it may also be polarized by simple reflection at the
surface of a transparent body, as Malus first discovered. If we
throw on a plate of glass a pencil of direct light, inclined to
the surface in an angle of about 35°, and then place a rhomboid
of calcarious spar in the way of the reflected ray; we remark,
that the two pencils into which it is divided by the crystal, are
only of equal intensity, when the principal section of the rhomboid makes an angle of 45° with the plane of reflection, and that,
in all other cases, the intensities of the two images are unequal:
this inequality is the more sensible, as the principal section is
further removed from the angle of 45°, and finally, when it coincides with the plane of incidence, or is perpendicular to it, one
of the two images disappears: the extraordinary image in the
former case, and the ordinary in the latter. Thus we see that
the light reflected by glass, at an inclination of 35°, is similarly affected with the ordinary pencil, transmitted by a rhomboid with its principal section in the direction of the plane of
reflection. The reflected pencil is said to be polarised *in the
plane* of reflection; and in the same manner the ordinary pencil
transmitted by a rhomboid is said to be polarised in the plane of
the principal section of the crystal; and we are obliged to say,
on the other hand, that the extraordinary pencil is polarised
perpendicularly to the principal section, because it exhibits in
that direction the same properties which the ordinary pencil
possesses in the plane of the section.

                    *   *   *

    These phenomena are evidently analogous to those which have
been observed in each of the two images produced by a polarised
pencil which passes through a rhomboid of calcarious spar, when
it is turned round the ray. It is also by the same formula that
Malus has represented, in both cases, the variations of intensity
of the images and of the reflected light. If we apply the character i to the angle formed by the primitive plane with that of
reflection, or with the principal plane of the double refraction
to be considered; and if we call the maximum of brightness unity,
the brightness of the image and of the reflected light will both
be expressed by $\cos^2 i$.

    We may examine this formula in the case of a polarised pen-
cil passing through a rhomboid of calcarious spar; and making i
the angle which the plane of polarisation of the ordinary image,
that is, the principal section of the crystal, forms with the
primitive plane, the angle formed with the plane of polarization
of the extraordinary image will be 90° - i; so that since $\cos^2 i$

represents the intensity of the ordinary image, that of the extra-ordinary image will be expressed by $\cos^2(90° - i)$, or by $\sin^2 i$. When $i = 0$, $\sin^2 i = 0$; that is to say, when the principal section coincides with the primitive plane, the extraordinary image vanishes, and all the light passes to the ordinary image, because, in this case, $\cos^2 i = 1$. When $i = 45°$, $\sin^2 i$ and $\cos^2 i$ become equal each to ½; and the two images are of equal intensity: lastly, when $i = 90°$, $\sin^2 i = 1$, and $\cos^2 i = 0$, which implies that the ordinary image vanishes, and all the light passes to the extraordinary image; and the same effects are repeated in the other quadrants. It is obvious that these consequences of the formula agree with the observations. In order that it should be considered as fully demonstrated, it would be necessary that it should be directly verified with intermediate values of i: but it has been subjected, in such cases, to several indirect criterions, which, without being perfectly decisive, very greatly increase the probability of its accuracy; besides that we are encouraged by analogy and by mechanical considerations to conclude that it is rigorously correct.

In examining the fundamental principles of the theory of undulation, we have found that the intensity of the light must be supposed proportional to the living force or energy of each undulation, or simply, for the same medium, to the sum of the squares of the forces of the different points of the undulation, and must consequently be proportional to the square of the common coefficient of these velocities: consequently if $\cos^2 i$ is the intensity of the light of the ordinary image, $\cos i$ is the common coefficient of the velocities of oscillation in this image, and represents their magnitude; and in the same manner, $\sin^2 i$ being the intensity of the light of the extraordinary image, $\sin i$ represents the velocity of the oscillations in the system of undulations which has undergone the extraordinary refraction. We see then that the decomposition of the velocities of oscillation of the primitive polarised pencil, which is resolved into two others at its entrance into the crystal, are proportioned exactly in the same manner as if the oscillatory motions, instead of being in the direction of the rays, were in a transverse direction, and either parallel or perpendicular to the plane of polarisation; for in this case the two velocities conceived to have been united, and to be separated, would be proportional to $\sin i$ and $\cos i$, according to the principle of the composition and resolution of the small motions of a fluid, which must be conformable to the laws of statics. The formula of Malus appears, therefore, to imply, that the oscillatory motions of the ethereal particles are performed in directions perpendicular to the rays: and this hypothesis is rendered still more probable, by other remarkable properties of polarised light which remain to be explained.

Mr. Arago and myself, in studying the interference of polarised rays, discovered that they exert no influence on each other when their planes of polarisation are perpendicular to each other, that is to say, that in this case they produce no fringes, although all the conditions, which are commonly necessary for their appearance, are scrupulously fulfilled. I shall mention the three principal experiments which served to establish this fact;

beginning with that which was made by Mr. Arago. It consists in causing the two pencils, emitted by the same luminous point, and introduced through two parallel slits, to pass through two very thin piles of transparent plates, such as those of mica, or of blown glass, sufficiently inclined to polarise almost completely each of the two pencils, taking care that the two planes, in which they are inclined, should be perpendicular to each other: in this case no fringes are observable, whatever pains we may take to compensate the difference in the paths, by causing the inclination of one of the piles to vary very slowly; although, when the planes of incidence of the piles are no longer perpendicular to each other, we always succeed in this manner in obtaining the fringes; and the same result is obtained with much thicker plates of glass, provided that proper care be taken to form and polish them very correctly; and to vary their inclination very slowly, in order that the fringes may not pass unperceived. In proportion as the planes of the two piles are further removed from parallelism, the fringes are weakened, and they wholly disappear when they are at right angles, provided that the polarisation of the rays have been tolerably perfect. It follows, from this experiment, that the rays of light, polarised in the same plane, interfere with each other in the same manner as rays not modified; but that this influence diminishes as the planes are separated, and disappears when they are at right angles.

*   *   *

When two pencils which interfere are polarised exactly in the same direction, the fringes which they form possess the same character: but when the directions of their polarisation form an acute angle with each other, the fainter fringes, which they now produce, appear to be polarised at once in both directions, since they disappear from the extraordinary image when the principal section of the rhomboid is turned either in the first or the second direction; one of the pencils being excluded in either case, so that the interference can no longer take place, and the light must remain uniform.

Having shown that these phenomena of interference confirm the general hypothesis, it remains to be proved that they are inconsistent with the ingenious theory of *moveable polarisation*, the fundamental principles of which it is necessary to explain.

Mr. Biot supposes, that when a polarised pencil passes through a doubly refracting crystal, of which the principal section is situated obliquely with respect to the primitive plane of polarisation, *the axes of the luminous particles*, which had been situated in this plane, undergo, at their entrance into the crystal, certain oscillations, which carry them alternately to the right and left of the principal section, sometimes arriving at the primitive plane, and sometimes at another plane situated at the same angular distance on the other side, or at the azimuth $2i$, calling the angle formed by the two first planes i. For example, if the principal section makes an angle of 45°, with the primitive plane of polarisation, the axes of the particles vibrate through an arc of 90°, which is now $2i$. Mr. Biot supposes that these oscillations are repeated a very great number of times before the particles attain a *fixed* polarisation, which arranges their axes, so as to make them either parallel or perpendicular to the principal section: and a thickness of some tenths of an inch, or perhaps of some inches, is required, according to this able experimenter, in order that the moveable polarisation should become fixed in the sulfate of lime, at least while the parallelism of the two surfaces prevents the separation of the ordinary and extraordinary pencils, which is always accompanied by the fixed polarisation. But when the faces are parallel, and the thickness of the plate does not exceed the limit, the particles of light which pass through it, instead of being polarised in the principal section, and in the direction perpendicular to it, are polarised either in the primitive plane, or at the azimuth $2i$, accordingly as the last oscillation of their axes was directly towards the first or the second plane, and this whether it was finished or only begun at the time of their emersion; at least, according to Mr. Biot, they are affected by the rhomboid which is employed for analysing the emergent light, as if their last oscillation had been finished. The time occupied by one of these oscillations, or the thickness of the crystal in which each of them is performed, is supposed to be constant for particles of the same nature, but variable in the different kinds of light, in proportion to the length of the "fits" [imagined by Newton.]

Let us now examine the consequences of this, and consider the case of the two halves of a plate of sulfate of lime, about the tenth of an inch in diameter, placed before two mirrors of black glass in the path of the reflected rays. Let us suppose that the mirrors, disposed in such a manner as to produce the fringes, are inclined in an angle of 35° to the rays which proceed from the luminous point, so that they may be completely polarised by reflection before their introduction into the crystallized plates, as in the apparatus already described: and let us suppose that the axes of the two plates are perpendicular to each other, and each make an angle of 45° with the plane of reflection. According to the theory of moveable polarisation, all the emerging rays must be polarised in a direction parallel or perpendicular to this plane, which is that of the primitive polarisation: thus each of the two groups of fringes, which are observed to the right and left, results from the interference of the two pencils polarised both in this plane, or both in the direction perpendicular to it: consequently, if the two groups of fringes could exhibit signs of polarisation, it could only be in one or the other of these orthogonal directions: now the experiment is as opposite as possible to this consequence, since it is precisely when we place the principal section of the rhomboid in one or the other of these directions, that the two images of each group possess the same intensity: and in order that one of them may vanish, it is necessary, on the contrary, that the principal section of the rhomboid should make an angle of 45° with these directions, that is to say, that it should be parallel or perpendicular to the principal sections of the two plates. When it is parallel to the left hand plate, it is the left hand group that disappears from the ordinary image, and the reverse. It is obvious that the direction of the polarisation is the same as in the experiment last related, in which the incident light had not undergone any previous polarisation, before it passed through the crystallized plates.

Thus, whether we employ direct or polarised light, the ordinary and extraordinary pencils into which it is divided in passing through a crystallized plate, are always polarised, the one in the plane of the principal section, and the other in a direction perpendicular to it.

We have hitherto employed plates not less than a twentieth of an inch in thickness, and we have constantly found, in the ordinary and extraordinary rays, the same direction of polarisation as they manifest when they are separated into distinct pencils. It was, however, interesting to ascertain also, by means of interferences, whether the same mode of polarisation was also to be found in much thinner plates, such as those which give colours to polarised light, when it is analysed at its emersion, by means of a rhomboid of calcarious spar: for it is this production of colours that led Mr. Biot to a contrary supposition. For this purpose, I took a plate of sulfate of lime, about one hundredth of an inch in thickness, which exhibited strong colours, and yet was in no danger of having the different groups confounded: and having divided it into two pieces, I placed them in the manner already described. The two groups of fringes, instead of being entirely separated, as they had been when the plates were three or four times as thick, were mixed a little in the intermediate space; but it was easy, nevertheless, to distinguish in each of them the stripes of the three first orders, and to ascertain that the right hand group, for example, was polarized perpendicularly to the axis of the right hand plate; for when the principal section of the rhomboid was turned in this direction, it disappeared entirely from the extraordinary image; and when, instead of the rhomboid, a pile of glass, sufficiently inclined in its direction, was placed before the lens, the left hand group only was discernible, and was in this case perfectly free from the mixture of the colours of the right hand group, exhibiting the usual appearance of a single group. And when the experiment was made with two metallic mirrors, the slight polarisation which they occasion in the reflected rays, being destroyed by a pile of three or four pieces of glass, properly inclined, before their passage through the plates, the same direction of the polarisation is still found for each of the groups of fringes. It is therefore fully proved, that in one of these cases, as well as in the other, the thin plates polarise the ordinary and extraordinary rays in directions parallel and perpendicular to their axes.

6. Michael Faraday and Electricity

The most radical of the challenges to orthodox physics came from Michael Faraday. His discussion of the nature of the electric current and the problem of conduction and insulation* appeared to rule out (at least for him) the possibility of material atoms or imponderable fluids.

§ 19. *Nature of the electric current.*

1617. The word *current* is so expressive in common language, that when applied in the consideration of electrical phenomena we can hardly divest it sufficiently of its meaning, or prevent our minds from being prejudiced by it. . . . I shall use it in its common electrical sense, namely, to express generally a certain condition and relation of electrical forces supposed to be in progression.

1618. A current is produced both by excitement and discharge; and whatsoever the variation of the two general causes may be, the effect remains the same. Thus excitement may occur in many ways, as by friction, chemical action, influence of heat, change of condition, induction, &c.; and discharge has the forms of conduction, electrolyzation, disruptive discharge, and convection; yet the current connected with these actions, when it occurs, appears in all cases to be the same. This constancy in the character of the current, notwithstanding the particular and great variations which may be made in the mode of its occurrence, is exceedingly striking and important; and its investigation and development promise to supply the most open and advantageous road to a true and intimate understanding of the nature of electrical forces.

1619. As yet the phenomena of the current have presented nothing in opposition to the view I have taken of the nature of induction as an action of contiguous particles. I have endeavoured to divest myself of prejudices and to look for contradictions, but I have not perceived any in conductive, electrolytic, convective, or disruptive discharge.

1620. Looking at the current as a *cause*, it exerts very extraordinary and diverse powers, not only in its course and on the bodies in which it exists, but collaterally, as in inductive or magnetic phenomena.

1621. *Electrolytic action.*--One of its direct actions is the exertion of pure chemical force, this being a result which has now been examined to a considerable extent. The effect is found to be *constant* and *definite* for the quantity of electric force discharged . . . ; and beyond that, the *intensity* required is in relation to the intensity of the affinity or forces to be

*M. Faraday, *Experimental Researches in Electricity*, 3 vols. (London, 1839-55), Vol. I, pp. 515-19, 523, 528-35; Vol. II, pp. 284-93.

overcome. . . . The current and its consequences are here proportionate; the one may be employed to represent the other; no part of the effect of either is lost or gained; so that the case is a strict one, and yet it is the very case which most strikingly illustrates the doctrine that induction is an action of contiguous particles. . . .

1622. The process of electrolytic discharge appears to me to be in close analogy, and perhaps in its nature identical with another process of discharge, which at first seems very different from it, I mean *convection*. . . . In the latter case the particles may travel for yards across a chamber; they may produce strong winds in the air, so as to move machinery; and in fluids, as oil of turpentine, may even shake the hand, and carry heavy metallic bodies about; and yet I do not see that the force, either in kind or action, is at all different to that by which a particle of hydrogen leaves one particle of oxygen to go to another, or by which a particle of oxygen travels in the contrary direction.

*　　*　　*

1625. *Heat* is another direct effect of the *current* upon substances in which it occurs, and it becomes a very important question, as to the relation of the electric and heating forces, whether the latter is always definite in amount. There are many cases, even amongst bodies which conduct without change, that at present are irreconcileable with the assumption that it is; but there are also many which indicate that, when proper limitations are applied, the heat produced is definite. Harris has shown this for a given length of current in a metallic wire, using common electricity; and De la Rive has proved the same point for voltaic electricity by his beautiful application of Breguet's thermometer.

1626. When the production of heat is observed in electrolytes under decomposition, the results are still more complicated. But important steps have been taken in the investigation of this branch of the subject by De la Rive and others; and it is more than probable that, when the right limitations are applied, constant and definite results will here also be obtained.

1627. It is a most important part of the character of the current, and essentially connected with its very nature, that it is always the same. The two forces are everywhere in it. There is never one current of force or one fluid only. Any one part of the current may, as respects the presence of the two forces there, be considered as precisely the same with any other part; and the numerous experiments which imply their possible separation, as well as the theoretical expressions which, being used daily, assume it, are, I think in contradiction with facts. . . . It appears to me to be as impossible to assume a current of positive or a current of negative force alone, or of the two at once with any predominance of one over the other, as it is to give an absolute charge to matter. . . .

1628. The establishment of this truth, if, as I think, it
be a truth, or on the other hand the disproof of it, is of the
greatest- consequence. If, as a first principle, we can establish,
that the centres of the two forces, or elements of force, never
can be separated to any sensible distance, or at all events not
further than the space between two contiguous particles . . . ,
or if we can establish the contrary conclusion, how much more
clear is our view of what lies before us, and how much less embarrassed the ground over which we have to pass in attaining to
it, than. if we remain halting between two opinions! And if, with
that feeling, we rigidly test every experiment which bears upon
the point, as far as our prejudices will let us . . . , instead
of permitting them with a theoretical expression to pass too
easily away, are we not much more likely to attain the real truth,
and from that proceed with safety to what is at present unknown?

*   *   *

1642. All these considerations, and many others, help to
confirm the conclusion, drawn over and over again, that the current is an indivisible thing; an axis of power, in every part of
which both electric forces are present in equal amount. . . .

1658. Having arrived at this point in the consideration of
the current and in the endeavour to apply its phenomena as tests
of the truth or fallacy of the theory of induction which I have
ventured to set forth, I am now very much tempted to indulge in a
few speculations respecting its lateral action and its possible
connexion with the transverse condition of the lines of ordinary
induction. . . . I have long sought and still seek for an effect
or condition which shall be to statical electricity what magnetic
force is to current electricity . . . ; for as the lines of discharge are associated with a certain transverse effect, so it
appeared to me impossible but that the lines of tension or of inductive action, which of necessity precede that discharge, should
also have their correspondent transverse condition or effect. . . .
1659. According to the beautiful theory of Ampère, the
transverse force of a current may be represented by its attraction for a similar current and its repulsion of a contrary current. May not then the equivalent transverse force of static
electricity be represented by that lateral tension or repulsion
which the lines of inductive action appear to possess . . . ?
Then again, when current or discharge occurs between two bodies,
previously under inductrical relations to each other, the lines
of inductive force will weaken and fade away, and, as their
lateral repulsive tension diminishes, will contract and ultimately disappear in the line of discharge. May not this be an
effect identical with the attractions of similar currents? *i.e.*
may not the passage of static electricity into current electricity, and that of the lateral tension of the lines of inductive
force into the lateral attraction of lines of similar discharge,
have the same relation and dependences, and run parallel to each
other?

1660. The phenomena of induction amongst currents which I had the good fortune to discover some years ago . . . may perchance here form a connecting link in the series of effects. When a current is first formed, it tends to produce a current in the contrary direction in all the matter around it; and if that matter have conducting properties and be fitly circumstanced, such a current is produced. On the contrary, when the original current is stopped, one in the same direction tends to form all around it, and, in conducting matter properly arranged, will be excited.

1661. Now though we perceive the effects only in that portion of matter which, being in the neighbourhood, has conducting properties, yet hypothetically it is probable, that the non-conducting matter has also its relations to, and is affected by, the disturbing cause, though we have not yet discovered them. Again and again the relation of conductors and non-conductors has been shown to be one not of opposition in kind, but only of degree . . . ; and therefore, for this, as well as for other reasons, it is probable, that what will affect a conductor will affect an insulator also; producing perhaps what may deserve the term of the electrotonic state. . . .

*   *   *

. . . Since the experiments have been made which have persuaded me that the polar forces of electricity, as in induction and electrolytic action . . . , show effects at a distance only by means of the polarized contiguous and intervening particles, I have been led to expect that *all polar forces* act in the same general manner; and the other kinds of phenomena which one can bring to bear upon the subject seem fitted to strengthen that expectation. Thus in crystallizations the effect is transmitted from particle to particle; and in this manner, in acetic acid or freezing water a crystal a few inches or even a couple of feet in length will form in less than a second, but progressively and by a transmission of power from particle to particle. And, as far as I remember, no case of polar action, or partaking of polar action, except the one under discussion, can be found which does not act by contiguous particles. It is apparently of the nature of polar forces that such should be the case, for the one force finds or developes the contrary force near to it, and has, therefore, no occasion to seek for it at a distance.

1666. But leaving these hypothetical notions respecting the nature of the lateral action out of sight, and returning to the direct effects, I think that the phenomena examined and reasoning employed in this and the two preceding papers tend to confirm the view first taken . . . , namely, that ordinary inductive action and the effects dependent upon it are due to an action of the contiguous particles of the dielectric interposed between the charged surfaces or parts which constitute, as it were, the terminations of the effect. The great point of distinction and power (if it have any) in the theory is, the making the dielectric of essential and specific importance, instead of leaving it as it were a mere accidental circumstance or the simple representative of space, having no more influence over the phenomena than the

space occupied by it. I have still certain other results and
views respecting the nature of the electrical forces and excitation, which are connected with the present theory; and, unless
upon further consideration they sink in my estimation, I shall
very shortly put them into form as another series of these electrical researches.

§ 20. *Nature of the electric force or forces.*

1667. The theory of induction set forth and illustrated in
the three preceding series of experimental researches does not
assume anything new as to the nature of the electric force or
forces, but only as to their distribution. The effects may depend upon the association of one electric fluid with the particles
of matter, as in the theory of Franklin, Epinus, Cavendish, and
Mossotti; or they may depend upon the association of two electric
fluids, as in the theory of Dufay and Poisson; or they may not
depend upon anything which can properly be called the electric
fluid, but on vibrations or other affections of the matter in
which they appear. The theory is unaffected by such differences
in the mode of viewing the nature of the forces; and though it
professes to perform the important office of stating *how* the
powers are arranged (at least in inductive phenomena), it does
not, as far as I can yet perceive, supply a single experiment
which can be considered as a distinguishing test of the truth of
any one of these various views.

1668. But, to ascertain how the forces are arranged, to
trace them in their various relations to the particles of matter,
to determine their general laws, and also the specific differences
which occur under these laws, is as important as, if not more so
than, to know whether the forces reside in a fluid or not; and
with the hope of assisting in this research, I shall offer some
further developments, theoretical and experimental, of the conditions under which I suppose the particles of matter are placed
when exhibiting inductive phenomena.

1669. The theory assumes that all the *particles*, whether
of insulating or conducting matter, are as wholes conductors.

1670. That not being polar in their normal state, they can
become so by the influence of neighbouring charged particles, the
polar state being developed at the instant, exactly as in an insulated conducting *mass* consisting of many particles.

1671. That the particles when polarized are in a forced
state, and tend to return to their normal or natural condition.

1672. That being as wholes conductors, they can readily be
charged, either *bodily* or *polarly*.

1673. That particles which being contiguous are also in the
line of inductive action can communicate or transfer their polar
forces one to another *more or less* readily.

1674. That those doing so less readily require the polar
forces to be raised to a higher degree before this transference
or communication takes place.

1675. That the *ready* communication of forces between contiguous particles constitutes *conduction*, and the *difficult* communication *insulation*; conductors and insulators being bodies

whose particles naturally possess the property of communicating their respective forces easily or with difficulty; having these differences just as they have differences of any other natural property.

1676. That ordinary induction is the effect resulting from the action of matter charged with excited or free electricity upon insulating matter, tending to produce in it an equal amount of the contrary state.

1677. That it can do this only by polarizing the particles contiguous to it, which perform the same office to the next, and these again to those beyond; and that thus the action is propagated from the excited body to the next conducting mass, and there renders the contrary force evident in consequence of the effect of communication which supervenes in the conducting mass upon the polarization of the particles of that body. . . .

1678. That therefore induction can only take place through or across insulators; that induction is insulation, it being the necessary consequence of the state of the particles and the mode in which the influence of electrical forces is transferred or transmitted through or across such insulating media.

1679. The particles of an insulating dielectric whilst under induction may be compared to a series of small magnetic needles, or more correctly still to a series of small insulated conductors. If the space round a charged globe were filled with a mixture of an insulating dielectric, as oil of turpentine or air, and small globular conductors, as shot, the latter being at a little distance from each other so as to be insulated, then these would in their condition and action exactly resemble what I consider to be the condition and action of the particles of the insulating dielectric itself. . . . If the globe were charged, these little conductors would all be polar; if the globe were discharged, they would all return to their normal state, to be polarized again upon the recharging of the globe. The state developed by induction through such particles on a mass of conducting matter at a distance would be of the contrary kind, and exactly equal in amount to the force in the inductric globe. There would be a lateral diffusion of force . . . , because each polarized sphere would be in an active or tense relation to all those contiguous to it, just as one magnet can affect two or more magnetic needles near it, and these again a still greater number beyond them. Hence would result the production of curved lines of inductive force if the inducteous body in such a mixed dielectric were an uninsulated metallic ball . . . or other properly shaped mass. Such curved lines are the consequences of the two electric forces arranged as I have assumed them to be: and, that the inductive force can be directed in such curved lines is the strongest proof of the presence of the two powers and the polar condition of the dielectric particles.

1680. I think it is evident, that in the case stated, action at a distance can only result through an action of the contiguous conducting particles. There is no reason why the inductive body should polarize or affect *distant* conductors and leave those *near* it, namely the particles of the dielectric, unaffected: and everything in the form of fact and experiment with conducting masses or particles of a sensible size contradicts such a supposition.

*　　*　　*

A speculation touching Electric Conduction and the Nature of Matter.

To Richard Taylor, Esq.

Dear Sir,　　　　　　　　　　　　Royal Institution, Jan. 25, 1844.

Last Friday I opened the weekly evening-meetings here by a subject of which the above was the title, and had no intention of publishing the matter further, but as it involves the consideration and application of a few of those main elements of natural knowledge, facts, I thought an account of its nature and intention might not be unacceptable to you, and would at the same time serve as the record of my opinion and views, as far as they are at present formed.

The view of the atomic constitution of matter which I think is most prevalent, is that which considers the atom as a something material having a certain volume, upon which those powers were impressed at the creation, which have given it, from that time to the present, the capability of constituting, when many atoms are congregated together into groups, the different substances whose effects and properties we observe. These, though grouped and held together by their powers, do not touch each other, but have intervening space, otherwise pressure or cold could not make a body contract into a smaller bulk, nor heat or tension make it larger; in liquids these atoms or particles are free to move about one another, and in vapours or gases they are also present, but removed very much further apart, though still related to each other by their powers.

The atomic doctrine is greatly used one way or another in this, our day, for the interpretation of phenomena, especially those of crystallography and chemistry, and is not so carefully distinguished from the facts, but that it often appears to him who stands in the position of student, as a statement of the facts themselves, though it is at best but an assumption; of the truth of which we can assert nothing, whatever we may say or think of its probability. The word atom, which can never be used without involving much that is purely hypothetical, is often *intended* to be used to express a simple fact; but good as the intention is, I have not yet found a mind that did habitually separate it from its accompanying temptations; and there can be no doubt that the words definite proportions, equivalents, primes, &c., which did and do express fully all the *facts* of what is usually called the atomic theory in chemistry, were dismissed because they were not expressive enough, and did not say all that was in the mind of him who used the word atom in their stead; they did not express the hypothesis as well as the fact.

But it is always safe and philosophic to distinguish, as much as is in our power, fact from theory; the experience of past ages is sufficient to show us the wisdom of such a course; and

considering the constant tendency of the mind to rest on an assumption, and, when it answers every present purpose, to forget
that it is an assumption, we ought to remember that it, in such
cases, becomes a prejudice, and inevitably interferes, more or
less, with a clear-sighted judgment. I cannot doubt but that he
who, as a wise philosopher, has most power of penetrating the
secrets of nature, and guessing by hypothesis at her mode of
working, will also be most careful, for his own safe progress and
that of others, to distinguish that knowledge which consists of
assumption, by which I mean theory and hypothesis, from that which
is the knowledge of facts and laws; never raising the former to
the dignity or authority of the latter, nor confusing the latter
more than is inevitable with the former.

Light and electricity are two great and searching investigators of the molecular structure of bodies, and it was whilst
considering the probable nature of conduction and insulation in
bodies not decomposable by the electricity to which they were
subject, and the relation of electricity to space contemplated as
void of that which by the atomists is called matter, that considerations something like those which follow were presented to
my mind.

If the view of the constitution of matter already referred
to be assumed to be correct, and I may be allowed to speak of the
particles of matter and of the space between them (in water, or
in the vapour of water for instance) as two different things,
then space must be taken as the only continuous part, for the
particles are considered as separated by space from each other.
Space will permeate all masses of matter in every direction like
a net, except that in place of meshes it will form cells, isolat-
ing each atom from its neighbours, and itself only being continuous.

Then take the case of a piece of shell-lac, a non-conductor,
and it would appear at once from such a view of its atomic constitution that space is an insulator, for if it were a conductor
the shell-lac could not insulate, whatever might be the relation
as to conducting power of its material atoms; the space would be
like a fine metallic web penetrating it in every direction, just
as we may imagine of a heap of siliceous sand having all its
pores filled with water; or as we may consider of a stick of
black wax, which, though it contains an infinity of particles of
conducting charcoal diffused through every part of it, cannot
conduct, because a non-conducting body (a resin) intervenes and
separates them one from another, like the supposed space in the
lac.

Next take the case of a metal, platinum or potassium, constituted, according to the atomic theory, in the same manner.
The metal is a conductor; but how can this be, except space be a
conductor? for it is the only continuous part of the metal, and
the atoms not only do not touch (by the theory), but as we shall
see presently, must be assumed to be a considerably way apart.
space therefore must be a conductor, or else the metals could not
conduct, but would be in the situation of the black sealing-wax
referred to a little while ago.

But if space be a conductor, how then can shell-lac, sulphur, &c. insulate? for space permeates them in every direction. Or if space be an insulator, how can a metal or other similar body conduct?

It would seem, therefore, that in accepting the ordinary atomic theory, space may be proved to be a non-conductor in non-conducting bodies, and a conductor in conducting bodies, but the reasoning ends in this, a subversion of that theory altogether; for if space be an insulator it cannot exist in conducting bodies, and if it be a conductor it cannot exist in insulating bodies. Any ground of reasoning which tends to such conclusions as these must in itself be false.

In connexion with such conclusions we may consider shortly what are the probabilities that present themselves to the mind, if the extension of the atomic theory which chemists have imagined, be applied in conjunction with the conducting powers of metals. If the specific gravity of the metals be divided by the atomic numbers, it gives us the number of atoms, upon the hypothesis, in equal bulks of the metals. In the following table the first column of figures expresses nearly the number of atoms in, and the second column of figures the conducting power of, equal volumes of the metals named.

Atoms.		Conducting power.
1.00	gold	6.00
1.00	silver	4.66
1.12	lead	0.52
1.30	tin	1.00
2.20	platinum	1.04
2.27	zinc	1.80
2.87	copper	6.33
2.90	iron	1.00

So here iron, which contains the greatest number of atoms in a given bulk, is the worst conductor excepting one; gold, which contains the fewest, is nearly the best conductor. Not that these conditions are in inverse proportions, for copper, which contains nearly as many atoms as iron, conducts better still than gold, and with above six times the power of iron. Lead, which contains more atoms than gold, has only about one-twelfth of its conducting power; lead, which is much heavier than tin and much lighter than platina, has only half the conducting power of either of these metals. And all this happens amongst substances which we are bound to consider, at present, as elementary or simple. Whichever way we consider the particles of matter and the space between them, and examine the assumed constitution of matter by this table, the results are full of perplexity.

Now let us take the case of potassium, a compact metallic substance with excellent conducting powers, its oxide or hydrate a non-conductor; it will supply us with some facts having very important bearings on the assumed atomic construction of matter.

When potassium is oxidized an atom of it combines with an atom of oxygen to form an atom of potassa, and an atom of potassa combines with an atom of water, consisting of two atoms of oxgyen and hydrogen, to form an atom of hydrate of potassa, so that an atom of hydrate of potassa contains four elementary atoms. The specific gravity of potassium is 0.865, and its atomic weight 40; the specific gravity of cast hydrate of potassa, in such state of purity as I could obtain it, I found to be nearly 2, its atomic weight 57. From these, which may be taken as facts, the following strange conclusions flow. A piece of potassium contains less potassium than an equal piece of the potash formed by it and oxygen. We may cast into potassium oxygen atom for atom, and then again both oxygen and hydrogen in a twofold number of atoms, and yet, with all these additions, the matter shall become less and less, until it is not two-thirds of its original volume. If a given bulk of potassium contains 45 atoms, the same bulk of hydrate of potassa contains 70 atoms nearly *of the metal potassium*, and besides that, 210 atoms more of oxygen and hydrogen. In dealing with assumptions I must assume a little more for the sake of making any kind of statement; let me therefore assume that in the hydrate of potassa the atoms are all of one size and nearly touching each other, and that in a cubic inch of that substance there are 2800 elementary atoms of potassium, oxygen and hydrogen; take away 2100 atoms of oxygen and hydrogen, and the 700 atoms of potassium remaining will swell into more than a cubic inch and a half, and if we diminish the number until only those containable in a cubic inch remain, we shall have 430, or thereabout. So a space which can contain 2800 atoms, and amongst them 700 of potassium itself, is found to be entirely filled by 430 atoms of potassium as they exist in the ordinary state of that metal. Surely then, under the suppositions of the atomic theory, the atoms of potassium must be very far apart in the metal, *i.e.* there must be much more of space than of matter in that body: yet it is an excellent conductor, and so space must be a conductor; but then what becomes of shell-lac, sulphur, and all the insulators? for space must also by the theory exist in them.

Again, the volume which will contain 430 atoms of potassium, and nothing else, whilst in the state of metal, will, when that potassium is converted into nitre, contain very nearly the same number of atoms of potassium, *i.e.* 416, and also then seven times as many, or 2912 atoms of nitrogen and oxygen besides. In carbonate of potassa the space which will contain only the 430 atoms of potassium as metal, being entirely filled by it, will, after the conversion, contain 256 atoms more of potassium, making 686 atoms of that metal, and, in addition 2744 atoms of oxygen and carbon.

These and similar considerations might be extended through compounds of sodium and other bodies with results equally striking, and indeed still more so, when the relations of one substance, as oxygen or sulphur, with different bodies are brought into comparison.

I am not ignorant that the mind is most powerfully drawn by the phenomena of crystallization, chemistry and physics generally, to the acknowledgement of centres of force. I feel myself constrained, for the present hypothetically, to admit them, and cannot do without them, but I feel great difficulty in the conception of atoms of matter which in solids, fluids and vapours

are supposed to be more or less apart from each other, with intervening space not occupied by atoms, and perceive great contradictions in the conclusions which flow from such a view.

If we must assume at all, as indeed in a branch of knowledge
like the present we can hardly help it, then the safest course
appears to be to assume as little as possible, and in that respect
the atoms of Boscovich appear to me to have a great advantage
over the more usual notion. His atoms, if I understand aright,
are mere centres of forces or powers, not particles of matter, in
which the powers themselves reside. If, in the ordinary view of
atoms, we call the particle of matter away from the powers a, and
the systems of powers or forces in and around it m, then in Boscovich's theory a disappears, or is a mere mathematical point,
whilst in the usual notion it is a little unchangeable, impenetrable piece of matter, and m is an atmosphere of force grouped
around it.

In many of the hypothetical uses made of atoms, as in crystallography, chemistry, magnetism, &c., this difference in the
assumption makes little or no alteration in the results, but in
other cases, as of electric conduction, the nature of light, the
manner in which bodies combine to produce compounds, the effects
of forces, as heat or electricity, upon matter, the difference
will be very great.

Thus, referring back to potassium, in which as a metal the
atoms must, as we have seen, be, according to the usual view,
very far apart from each other, how can we for a moment imagine
that its conducting property belongs to it, any otherwise than as
a consequence of the properties of the space, or as I have called
it above, the m? so also its other properties in regard to light
or magnetism, or solidity, or hardness, or specific gravity, must
belong to it, in consequence of the properties or forces of the
m, not those of the a, which, without the forces, is conceived of
as having no powers. But then surely the m is the *matter* of the
potassium, for where is there the least ground (except in a gratuitous assumption) for imagining a difference in kind between
the nature of that space midway between the centres of two contiguous atoms and any other spot between these centres? a difference in degree, or even in the nature of the power consistent
with the law of continuity, I can admit, but the difference
between a supposed little hard particle and the powers around it
I cannot imagine.

To my mind, therefore, the a or nucleus vanishes, and the
substance consists of the powers or m; and indeed what notion can
we form of the nucleus independent of its powers? all our perception and knowledge of the atom, and even our fancy, is limited to
ideas of its powers: what thought remains on which to hang the
imagination of an a independent of the acknowledged forces? A
mind just entering on the subject may consider it difficult to
think of the powers of matter independent of a separate something
to be called *the matter*, but it is certainly far more difficult,
and indeed impossible, to think of or imagine that *matter* independent of the powers. Now the powers we know and recognize in
every phehomenon of the creation, the abstract matter in none;
why then assume the existence of that of which we are ignorant,

which we cannot conceive, and for which there is no philosophical necessity?

Before concluding these speculations I will refer to a few of the important differences between the assumption of atoms consisting merely of centres of force, like those of Boscovich, and that other assumption of molecules of something specially material, having powers attached in and around them.

With the latter atoms a mass of matter consists of atoms and intervening space, with the former atoms matter is everywhere present, and there is no intervening space unoccupied by it. In gases the atoms touch each other just as truly as in solids. In this respect the atoms of water touch each other whether that substance be in the form of ice, water or steam; no mere intervening space is present. Doubtless the centres of force vary in their distance one from another, but that which is truly the matter of one atom touches the matter of its neighbours.

Hence matter will be *continuous* throughout, and in considering a mass of it we have not to suppose a distinction between its atoms and any intervening space. The powers around the centres give these centres the properties of atoms of matter; and these powers again, when many centres by their conjoint forces are grouped into a mass, give to every part of that mass the properties of matter. In such a view all the contradiction resulting from the consideration of electric insulation and conduction disappears.

The atoms may be conceived of as highly *elastic*, instead of being supposed excessively hard and unalterable in form; the mere compression of a bladder of air between the hands can alter their size a little; and the experiments of Cagniard de la Tour carry on this change in size until the difference in bulk at one time and another may be made several hundred times. Such is also the case when a solid or a fluid body is converted into vapour.

With regard also to the *shape* of the atoms, and, according to the ordinary assumption, its definite and unalterable character, another view must now be taken of it. An atom by itself might be conceived of as spherical, or spheroidal, or where many were touching in all directions, the form might be thought of, as a dodecahedron, for any one would be surrounded by and bear against twelve others, on different sides. But if an atom be conceived to be a centre of power, that which is ordinarily referred to under the term *shape* would now be referred to the disposition and relative intensity of the forces. The power arranged in and around a centre might be uniform in arrangement and intensity in every direction outwards from that centre, and then a section of equal intensity of force through the radii would be a sphere; or the law of decrease of force from the entre outwards might vary in different directions, and then the section of equal intensity might be an oblate or oblong spheroid, or have other forms; or the forces might be disposed so as to make the atom polar; or they might circulate around it equatorially or otherwise, after the manner of imagined magnetic atoms. In fact nothing can be supposed of the disposition of forces in or about a solid nucleus of matter, which cannot be equally conceived with respect to a centre.

In the view of matter now sustained as the lesser assumption, matter and the atoms of matter would be mutually penetrable. As regards the mutual penetrability of matter, one would think that the facts respecting potassium and its compounds, already described, would be enough to prove that point to a mind which accepts a fact for a fact, and is not obstructed in its judgement by preconceived notions. With respect to the mutual penetrability of the atoms, it seems to me to present in many points of view a more beautiful, yet equally probable and philosophic idea of the constitution of bodies than the other hypotheses, especially in the case of chemical combination. If we suppose an atom of oxygen and an atom of potassium about to combine and produce potash, the hypothesis of solid unchangeable impenetrable atoms places these two particles side by side in a position easily, because mechanically, imagined, and not unfrequently represented; but if these two atoms be centres of power they will mutually penetrate to the very centres, thus forming one atom or molecule with powers, either uniformly around it or arranged as the resultant of the powers of the two constituent atoms; and the manner in which two or many centres of force may in this way combine, and afterwards, under the dominion of stronger forces, separate again, may in some degree be illustrated by the beautiful case of the conjunction of two sea waves of different velocities into one, their perfect union for a time, and final separation into the constituent waves, considered, I think, at the meeting of the British Association at Liverpool. It does not of course follow, from this view, that the centres shall always coincide; that will depend upon the relative disposition of the powers of each atom.

The view now stated of the constitution of matter would seem to involve necessarily the conclusion that matter fills all space, or, at least, all space to which gravitation extends (including the sun and its system); for gravitation is a property of matter dependent on a certain force, and it is this force which constitutes the matter. In that view matter is not merely mutually penetrable, but each atom extends, so to say, throughout the whole of the solar system, yet always retaining its own centre of force. This, at first sight, seems to fall in very harmoniously with Mossotti's mathematical investigations and reference of the phenomena of electricity, cohesion, gravitation, &c. to one force in matter; and also again with the old adage, "matter cannot act where it is not." But it is no part of my intention to enter into such considerations as these, or what the bearings of this hypothesis would be on the theory of light and the supposed æther. My desire has been rather to bring certain facts from electrical conduction and chemical combination to bear strongly upon our views regarding the nature of atoms and matter, and so to assist in distinguishing in natural philosophy our real knowledge, *i.e.* the knowledge of facts and laws, for that, which, though it has the form of knowledge, may, from its including so much that is mere assumption, be the very reverse.

I am, my dear Sir, yours, &c.,

Michael Faraday.

III. A "Positivistic" Postscript

Not everyone in the first half of the nineteenth century was as deeply concerned about investigating the nature of ultimate reality as those we have examined. Some scientists, like Laplace, were already convinced that they knew what the world was made of. Others simply took a number of assumptions (usually atomic) for granted and used their intellectual energies to attempt to discover the laws of phenomena--laws which often had little to do with the ultimate nature of the entity under study. The classic case is Fourier's study of heat. Fourier explicitly left aside the question of what heat was. He attacked the problem of how heat, whatever it was, acted. The result was a series of equations which described thermal situations with great accuracy. Such descriptions are not to be despised even though they do not take us any closer to the answer of what the universe consists of. Much of nineteenth century science was of this kind and it was this kind of science, in large part, which gave nineteenth century men the ability to control, as well as describe, Nature. It helps, of course, if one can begin a train of researches from a "correct" assumption on the nature of matter or heat or electricity, but it is not necessary. Sometimes, as we shall see, it is possible to derive a correct law from incorrect premises. A survey of such laws will serve to flesh out our account and make it more historically accurate. To many contemporaries, after all, Fourier's laws were at least as important as Dalton's and Lavoisier's discussion of the nature of caloric.

We may, again, start with the Newtonian tradition since it was the one most generally accepted at the beginning of the nineteenth century. In the 1780's, the mathematical aspect of the Newtonian legacy was carried to new heights by the publication of Louis Lagrange's *Mécanique Analytique* (Analytical Mechanics-- 1788). In this work, Lagrange reduced mechanics to a branch of mathematics by deducing it from axioms. The axioms, needless to say, were based upon Newtonian assumptions about the atomic nature of matter and the action of forces in straight lines, but once they were accepted, the rest of mechanics followed as a logical consequence. Much the same effect was caused by the publication of Pierre Simon de Laplace's masterful *Mécanique céleste* in the closing years of the eighteenth and early years of the nineteenth century. What Laplace did was to apply the results of a hundred years of the development of both mathematics and observational astronomy to some of the problems that Newton had been unable to solve. The most dramatic of these concerned the stability of the solar system. Newton recognized that each planet attracted all other planets and perturbed them in their orbits. So far as he could see, these perturbations should augment with time, necessitating the intervention of God periodically to set the solar system back to its original condition. Laplace showed that the perturbations were periodic, rising to a maximum and then decreasing. The solar system was naturally stable and needed no divine help.

The greatest triumph of Newtonianism in the nineteenth century was the application of perturbation theory to the planet

Uranus. Adams, in England, and Leverrier, in France, almost simultaneously deduced the existence of a new planet which must be the cause of Uranus' strange motions. The English Astronomer Royal refused to listen, so the actual discovery of Neptune in 1846 was left to the French. But, in spite of this triumph, Newtonianism had its pitfalls. The planet Mercury also moves in a curious way that suggested an unknown planetary cause of the perturbations. Leverrier tried the same method on Mercury that had worked so well on Uranus but, to his consternation, could never discover the planet that was affecting Mercury. It was a problem that resisted resolution until Einstein's general theory of relativity was published in 1916.

The laws of action of electricity were also laid bare in the first decades of the nineteenth century. In some cases, the correct results flowed from incorrect assumptions. Denis Poisson (1781-1840), for example, considered electricity to consist of two fluids in which particles of the same fluid repelled one another. When he turned his attention to the distribution of electricity on charged bodies of various shapes, he simply assumed that the pressure of the air kept the particles of electricity on the surface of the charged bodies. A simple experiment could and did reveal this error, but the important point is that it was not an important point to Poisson. His particles of electricity were physical fictions that immediately were reduced to mathematical infinitesimals of charge. These mathematical entities could then be manipulated to yield the correct formulae for charge distribution. Much the same process occurred with the distribution of forces in current electricity. Although Andre-Marie Ampère (1775-1836) was passionately interested in the nature of ultimate reality, his work on electrodynamics lay almost entirely within the mathematical tradition of French physics. A few simple experiments permitted Ampère to understand how the forces of electrical currents were manifested and he was then able to deduce the laws of these actions mathematically. All that he needed to assume were current elements from which forces emanated. His current element, di, like Poisson's charged infinitesimal, was a mathematical entity that could be operated on mathematically. By 1826, Ampère had deduced the basic laws of electrodynamics from a few simple assumptions and experiments. It made no difference for Ampère's theory whether electricity were material, undulatory or etherial although Ampère was a firm supporter of the two-fluid theory.

The 1820's also witnessed the enunciation of the fundamental law of conduction of electricity. Georg Simon Ohm (1787-1854) in Germany was impressed with Fourier's analysis of heat flow and felt that the same analysis could be applied to the flow of electricity. Again, like Fourier, Ohm paid little attention to *what* electricity was but only how it moved from one place to another. In 1827, Ohm published his great work on *The Galvanic Chain treated Mathematically* which sold only a few copies and was generally ignored. Ohm's law began to be recognized as important only in the 1830's and 1840's. It is, of course, the fundamental relationship permitting the construction of electrical measuring devices.

The laws of the generation of electricity from magnetism were enunciated by Faraday in the 1830's. Here the theoretical conception did have some bearing for it was Faraday's insistence upon the reality of the magnetic line of force that permitted him to define his law. The current generated by a moving conductor in a magnetic field depended upon the number of lines of force cut in unit time.

The magnetic line of force was not necessary for all laws of magnetism. Earlier in the century Jean-Baptiste Biot (1774-1862) and Félix Savart (1791-1841) deduced the law of Biot-Savart which describes the magnetic field surrounding a current-carrying wire from a consideration of the distribution of the two magnetic fluids.

The field of thermodynamics is an excellent example of the way in which a science can develop without concerning itself with theoretical entities. We have used Fourier as an example and it would be well to revert to him here. What concerned Fourier was not what heat was--H--but what happened when there was a heat gradient--ΔH. Carnot's memoir on *The Motive Power of Fire*, published in 1824, assumed the reality of caloric but those who followed Carnot soon realized that knowledge of the real nature of heat was not essential. ΔH and ΔT were all that was required and the classical laws of thermodynamics could be written as descriptions of thermal processes. The enunciation of the principle of the Conservation of Energy clarified these relationships and emerged as the first law of thermodynamics. The second law-- that of the increase of entropy--interestingly enough first emerged as the result of the mathematical calculations of Rudolf Clausius (1822-88). The function $\int dQ/T$ where Q is the quantity of heat and T the absolute temperature appeared in his equations and tended always to a maximum. This function he labeled entropy but it took a good deal more labor before a *physical* meaning could be assigned to it. Here is the paradigmatic case of a descriptive law *preceding* a theoretical explanation and emerging quite independently of such explanations.

The principle of the Conservation of Energy provided a common foundation for all these laws. No matter what heat, light, electricity, magnetism or gravitation *really* were, they all obeyed this principle in their actions. Armed with this principle, the laws of action that had been enunciated in the previous decades, and the various philosophical assumptions about fundamental physical reality, the scientists of the second half of the nineteenth century set about the analysis of all physical processes. What was the fate of energy? Could the various transformations of force be used to construct a theoretical edifice that would be both internally self-consistent and comprehend the facts expressed by these laws enunciated in the first half of the nineteenth century? These were to be the questions which motivated the generation of scientists that reached intellectual maturity in the 1850's and 1860's. Their answers were to create two theories of great importance to the future of physics--field theory and kinetic theory.

IV.   Energy Conservation and Its Consequences

In 1957, Thomas S. Kuhn, now Professor of the History of Science at Princeton, read a paper* at a symposium at the University of Wisconsin. It has since become a classic and provides a rich account of the enunciation of the principle of the Conservation of Energy.

Between 1842 and 1847, the hypothesis of energy conservation was publicly announced by four widely scattered European scientists--Mayer, Joule, Colding, and Helmholtz--all but the last working in complete ignorance of the others. The coincidence is conspicuous, yet these four announcements are unique only in combining generality of formulation with concrete quantitative applications. Sadi Carnot, before 1832, Marc Séguin in 1839, Karl Holtzmann in 1845, and G. A. Hirn in 1854, all recorded their independent convictions that heat and work are quantitatively interchangeable, and all computed a value for the conversion coefficient or an equivalent. The convertibility of heat and work is, of course, only a special case of energy conservation, but the generality lacking in this second group of announcements occurs elsewhere in the literature of the period. Between 1837 and 1844, C. F. Mohr, William Grove, Faraday, and Liebig, all described the world of phenomena as manifesting but a single "force," one which could appear in electrical thermal, dynamical, and many other forms, but which could never, in all its transformations, be created or destroyed. That so-called force is the one known to later scientists as energy. History of science offers no more striking instance of the phenomenon known as simultaneous discovery.

*   *   *

. . . Why, in the years 1830 to 1850, did so many of the experiments and concepts required for a full statement of energy conservation lie so close to the surface of scientific consciousness? . . .
The availability of conversion processes resulted principally from the stream of discoveries that flowed from Volta's invention of the battery in 1800. According to the theory of galvanism most prevalent, at least, in France and England, the electric current was itself gained at the expense of forces of chemical affinity, and this conversion proved to be only the first step in a chain. Electric current invariably produced heat and, under appropriate conditions, light as well. Or, by electrolysis, the current could vanquish forces of chemical affinity, bringing the chain of transformations full circle. These were the first fruits of Volta's work; other more striking conversion discoveries followed during

---

*T. S. Kuhn, "Energy Conservation as an Example of Simultaneous Discovery," in *Critical Problems in the History of Science* (Madison: University of Wisconsin Press, 1959), pp. 321, 323-31, 336-41.

the decade and a half after 1820. In that year Oersted demonstrated the magnetic effects of a current; magnetism, in turn,
could produce motion, and motion had long been known to produce
electricity through friction. Another chain of conversions was
closed. Then, in 1822, Seebeck showed that heat applied to a
bimetallic junction would produce a current directly. Twelve
years later Peltier reversed this striking example of conversion,
demonstrating that the current could, on occasions, absorb heat,
producing cold. Induced currents, discovered by Faraday in 1831,
were only another, if particularly striking, member of a class of
phenomena already characteristic of nineteenth-century science.
In the decade after 1827, the progress of photography added yet
another example, and Melloni's identification of light with radiant heat confirmed a long-standing suspicion about the fundamental
connection between two other apparently disparate aspects of nature.

Some conversion processes had, of course, been available
before 1800. Motion had already produced electrostatic charges,
and the resulting attractions and repulsions had produced motion.
Static generators had occasionally engendered chemical reactions,
including dissociations, and chemical reactions produced both
light and heat. Harnessed by the steam engine, heat could produce
motion, and motion, in turn, engendered heat through friction and
percussion. Yet in the eighteenth century these were isolated
phenomena; few seemed of central importance to scientific research; and those few were studied by different groups. Only in
the decade after 1830, when they were increasingly classified
with the many other examples discovered in rapid succession by
nineteenth-century scientists, did they begin to look like conversion processes at all. By that time scientists were proceeding
inevitably in the laboratory from a variety of chemical, thermal,
electrical, magnetic, or dynamical phenomena to phenomena of any
of the other types and to optical phenomena as well. Previously
separate problems were gaining multiple interrelationships, and
that is what Mary Sommerville had in mind when, in 1834, she gave
her famous popularization of science the title, *On the Connexion
of the Physical Sciences.* "The progress of modern science," she
said in her preface, "especially within the last five years, has
been remarkable for a tendency to . . . unite detached branches
[of science, so that today] . . . there exists such a bond of
union, that proficiency cannot be attained in any one branch
without a knowledge of others." Mrs. Sommerville's remark isolates the "new look" that physical science had acquired between
1800 and 1835. That new look, together with the discoveries that
produced it, proved to be a major requisite for the emergence of
energy conservation.

Yet, precisely because it produced a "look" rather than a
single clearly defined laboratory phenomenon, the availability of
conversion processes enters the development of energy conservation
in an immense variety of ways. Faraday and Grove achieved an idea
very close to conservation from a survey of the whole network of
conversion processes taken together. For them conservation was
quite literally a rationalization of the phenomenon Mrs. Sommerville described as the new "connexion." C. F. Mohr, on the other

hand, took the idea of *conservation* from a quite different source, probably metaphysical. But, as we shall see, it is only because he attempted to elucidate and defend this idea in terms of the new conversion processes that Mohr's initial conception came to look like conservation *of energy*. Mayer and Helmholtz present still another approach. They began by applying their concepts of conservation to well-known older phenomena. But until they extended their theories to embrace the new discoveries, they were not developing the same theory as men like Mohr and Grove. Still another group, consisting of Carnot, Séguin, Holtzmann, and Hirn, ignored the new conversion processes entirely. But they would not be discoverers of energy conservation if men like Joule, Helmholtz, and Colding had not shown that the thermal phenomena with which these steam engineers dealt were integral parts of the new network of conversions.

There is, I think, excellent reason for the complexity and variety of these relationships. In an important sense, though one which will demand later qualification, the conservation of energy is nothing less than the theoretical counterpart of the laboratory conversion processes discovered during the first four decades of the nineteenth century. Each laboratory conversion corresponds in the theory to a transformation in the form of energy. That is why, as we shall see, Grove and Faraday could derive conservation from the network of laboratory conversions itself. But the very homomorphism between the theory, energy conservation, and the earlier network of laboratory conversion processes indicates that one did not have to start by grasping the network whole. Liebig and Joule, for example, started from a single conversion process and were led by the "connexion" between the sciences through the entire network. Mohr and Colding started with a metaphysical idea and transformed it by application to the network. In short, just because the new nineteenth-century discoveries formed a network of "connexions" between previously distinct parts of science, they could be grasped either individually or whole in a large variety of ways and still lead to the same ultimate result. That, I think, explains why they could enter the pioneers' research in so many different ways. More important, it explains why the researches of the pioneers, despite the variety of their starting points, ultimately converged to a common outcome. What Mrs. Sommerville had called the new "connexions" between the sciences often proved to be the links that joined disparate approaches and enunciations into a single discovery.

The sequence of Joule's researches clearly illustrates the way in which the network of conversion processes actually marked out the experimental ground of energy conservation and thus provided the essential links between the various pioneers. When Joule first wrote in 1838, his exclusive concern with the design of improved electric motors effectively isolates him from all the other pioneers of energy conservation except Liebig. He was simply working on one of the many new problems born from nineteenth-century discovery. By 1840 his systematic evaluations of motors in terms of work and "duty" establishes a link to the researches of the steam engineers, Carnot, Séguin, Hirn, and Holtzmann. But these "connexions" vanished in 1841 and 1842 when Joule's discouragement with motor design forced him to seek instead a fundamental

improvement in the batteries that drove them. Now he was concerned with new discoveries in chemistry, and he absorbed entirely
Faraday's view of the essential role of chemical processes in galvanism. In addition, his research in these years was concentrated
upon what turned out to have been two of the numerous conversion
processes selected by Grove and Mohr to illustrate their vague
metaphysical hypothesis. The "connexions" with the work of other
pioneers are steadily increasing in number.

In 1843, prompted by the discovery of an error in his earlier
work with batteries, Joule reintroduced the motor and the concept
of mechanical work. Now the link to steam engineering is re-
established, and simultaneously Joule's papers begin, for the
first time, to read like investigations of energy relations. But
even in 1843 the resemblance to energy conservation is incomplete.
Only as Joule traced still other new "connexions" during the years
1844 to 1847 does his theory really encompass the views of such
disparate figures as Faraday, Mayer, and Helmholtz. Starting
from an isolated problem, Joule had involuntarily traced much of
the connective tissue between the new nineteenth-century discoveries. As he did so, his work was linked increasingly to that of
the other pioneers, and only when many such links had appeared
did his discovery resemble energy conservation.

Joule's work shows that energy conservation could be discovered by starting from a single conversion process and tracing
the network. But, as we have already indicated, that is not the
only way in which conversion processes could effect the discovery
of energy conservation. C. F. Mohr, for example, probably drew
his initial concept of conservation from a source independent of
the new conversion processes, but then used the new discoveries
to clarify and elaborate his ideas. In 1839, close to the end of
a long and often incoherent defense of the dynamical theory of
heat, Mohr suddenly burst out: "Besides the known 54 chemical
elements, there is, in the nature of things, only one other agent,
and that is called force; it can appear under various circumstances as motion, chemical affinity, cohesion, electricity,
light, heat, and magnetism, and from any one of these types of
phenomena all the others can be called forth." A knowledge of
energy conservation makes the import of these sentences clear.
But in the absence of such knowledge, they would have been almost
meaningless except that Mohr proceeded immediately to two systematic pages of experimental examples. The experiments were, of
course, just the new and old conversion processes listed above,
the new ones in the lead, and they are essential to Mohr's argument. They alone specify his subject and show its close similarity to Joule's.

Mohr and Joule illustrate two of the ways in which conversion processes could affect the discoverers of energy conservation. But, as my final example from the works of Faraday and
Grove will indicate, these are not the only ways. Though Faraday
and Grove reached conclusions much like Mohr's, their route to
the conclusions includes none of the same sudden leaps. Unlike
Mohr, they seem to have derived energy conservation directly from
the experimental conversion processes that they had already
studied so fully in their own researches. Because their route is

continuous, the homomorphism of energy conservation with the new conversion processes appears most clearly of all in their work.

In 1834, Faraday concluded five lectures on the new discoveries in chemistry and galvanism with a sixth on the "Relations of Chemical Affinity, Electricity, Heat, Magnetism, and other powers of Matter." His notes supply the gist of this last lecture in the words: "We cannot say that any one [of these powers] is the cause of the others, but only that all are connected and due to one common cause." To illustrate "the connection," Faraday then gave nine experimental demonstrations of "the production of any one [power] from another, or the conversion of one into another." Grove's development seems parallel. In 1842 he included a remark almost identical with Faraday's in a lecture with the significant title, "On the Progress of Physical Science." In the following year he expanded this isolated remark into his famous lecture series, *On the Correlation of Physical Forces*. "The position which I seek to establish in this Essay is," he said, "that [any one] of the various imponderable agencies . . . viz., Heat, Light, Electricity, Magnetism, Chemical Affinity, and Motion, . . . may, as a force, produce or be convertible into the other[s]; thus heat may mediately or immediately produce electricity, electricity may produce heat; and so of the rest."

This is the concept of the universal convertibility of natural powers, and it is not, let us be clear, the same as the notion of conservation. But most of the remaining steps proved to be small and rather obvious. All but one, to be discussed below, can be taken by applying to the concept of universal convertibility the perennially serviceable philosophic tags about the equality of cause and effect or the impossibility of perpertual motion. Since any power can produce any other *and be produced by it*, the equality of cause and effect demands a uniform quantitative equivalence between each pair of powers. If there is no such equivalence, then a properly chosen series of conversions will result in the creation of power, that is, in perpetual motion. In all its manifestations and conversions, power must be conserved. This realization came neither all at once, nor fully to all, nor with complete logical rigor. But it did come.

*   *   *

Nevertheless, the view which Grove and Faraday derived from conversion processes is not identical with what scientists now call the conservation of energy, and we must not underestimate the importance of the missing element. Grove's *Physical Forces* contains the layman's view of energy conservation. In an expanded and revised form it proved to be one of the most effective and sought after popularizations of the new scientific law. But this role was achieved only after the work of Joule, Mayer, Helmholtz, and their successors had provided a full quantitative substructure for the conception of force correlation. Anyone who has worked through a mathematical and numerical treatment of energy conservation may well wonder whether, in the absence of such substructure, Grove would have had anything to popularize. The "measurable relation to a given standard" of the various physical forces is an essential ingredient of energy conservation as we know it, and neither Grove, Faraday, Roget, nor Mohr was able even to approach it.

The quantification of energy conservation proved, in fact, insuperably difficult for those pioneers whose principal intellectual equipment consisted of concepts related to the new conversion processes. Grove thought he had found the clue to quantification in Dulong and Petit's law relating chemical affinity and heat. Mohr believed he had produced the quantitative relationship when he equated the heat employed to raise the temperature of water 1° with the static force necessary to compress the same water to its original volume. Mayer initially measured force by the momentum which it could produce. These random leads were all totally unproductive, and of this group only Mayer succeeded in transcending them. To do so he had to use concepts belonging to a very different aspect of nineteenth-century science, an aspect to which I previously referred as the concern with engines, and whose existence I shall now take for granted as a well-known by-product of the Industrial Revolution. As we examine this aspect of science, we shall find the main source of the concepts--particularly of mechanical effect or work--required for the quantitative formulation of energy conservation. In addition, we shall find a multitude of experiments and of qualitative conceptions so closely related to energy conservation that they collectively provide something very like a second and independent route to it.

Let me begin by considering the concept of work. Its discussion will provide relevant background as well as opportunity for a few essential remarks on a more usual view about the sources of the quantitative concepts underlying energy conservation. Most histories or pre-histories of the conservation of energy imply that the model for quantifying conversion processes was the dynamical theorem known almost from the beginning of the eighteenth century as the conservation of *vis viva*. That theorem has a distinguished role in the history of dynamics, and it also turns out to have been a special case of energy conservation. It could have provided a model. Yet I think the prevalent impression that it did so is misleading. The conservation of *vis viva* was important to Helmholtz's derivation of energy conservation, and a special case (free fall) of the same dynamical theorem was ultimately of great assistance to Mayer. But these men also drew significant elements from a second generally separate tradition-- that of water, wind, and steam engineering--and that tradition is all important to the work of the other five pioneers who produced a quantitative version of energy conservation.

There is excellent reason why this should be so. *Vis viva* is mv^2, the product of mass by the square of velocity. But until a late date that quantity appears in the works of none of the pioneers except Carnot, Mayer, and Helmholtz. As a group the pioneers were scarcely interested in energy of motion, much less in using it as a basic quantitative measure. What they did use, at least those who were successful, was $f \cdot s$, the product of force times distance, a quantity known variously under the names mechanical effect, mechanical power, and work. That quantity does not, however, occur as an independent conceptual entity in the dynamical literature. More precisely it scarcely occurs there until

1820 when the French (and only the French) literature was suddenly
enriched by a series of theoretical works on such subjects as the
theory of machines and of industrial mechanics. These new books
did make work a significant independent conceptual entity, and
they did relate it explicitly to *vis viva*. But the concept was
not invented for these books. On the contrary it was borrowed
from a century of engineering practice where its use had usually
been quite independent of both *vis viva* and its conservation.
That source within the engineering tradition is all that the pioneers of energy conservation required and as much as most of them
used.

*   *   *

Because the concern with engines and the nineteenth-century
conversion discoveries embrace most of the new technical concepts
and experiments common to more than a few of the discoverers of
energy conservation, this study of simultaneous discovery might
well end here. But a last look at the papers of the pioneers
generates an uncomfortable feeling that something is still missing, something that is not perhaps a substantive element at all.
This feeling would not exist if all the pioneers had, like Carnot
and Joule, begun with a straightforward technical problem and
proceeded by stages to the concept of energy conservation. But
in the cases of Colding, Helmholtz, Liebig, Mayer, Mohr, and
Séguin, the notion of an underlying imperishable metaphysical
force seems prior to research and almost unrelated to it. Put
bluntly, these pioneers seem to have held an idea capable of becoming conservation of energy for some time before they found
evidence for it. The factors previously discussed in this paper
may explain why they were ultimately able to clothe the idea and
thus to make sense of it. But the discussion does not yet sufficiently account for the idea's existence. One or two such cases
among the twelve pioneers might not be troublesome. The sources
of scientific inspiration are notoriously inscrutable. But the
presence of major conceptual lacunae in six of our twelve cases
is surprising. Though I cannot entirely resolve the problem it
presents, I must at least touch upon it.

We have already noted a few of the lacunae. Mohr jumped
without warning from a defense of the dynamical theory of heat to
the statement that there is only one force in nature and that it
is quantitatively unalterable. Liebig made a similar leap from
the duty of electric motors to the statement that the chemical
equivalents of the elements determine the work retrievable from
chemical processes by either electrical or thermal means. Colding
tells us that he got the idea of conservation in 1839, while still
a student, but withheld announcement until 1843 so that he might
gather evidence. The biography of Helmholtz outlines a similar
story. Séguin confidently applied his concept of the convertibility of heat and motion to steam engine computations, even
though his single attempt to confirm the idea had been totally
fruitless. Mayer's leap has repeatedly been noted, but its full
size is not often remarked. From the light color of venous blood
in the tropics, it is a small step to the conclusion that less
internal oxidation is needed when the body loses less heat to the

environment. Crawford had drawn that conclusion from the same
evidence in 1778. Laplace and Lavoisier, in the 1780's, had balanced the same equation relating inspired oxygen to the body's
heat losses. A continuous line of research relates their work to
the biochemical studies of respiration made by Liebig and Helmholtz in the early 1840's. Though Mayer apparently did not know
it, his observation of venous blood was simply a rediscovery of
evidence for a well known, though controversial, biochemical
theory. But that theory was not the one to which Mayer leaped.
Instead Mayer insisted that internal oxidation must be balanced
against *both* the body's heat loss *and* the manual labor the body
performs. To this formulation, the light color of tropical venous
blood is largely irrelevant. Mayer's extension of the theory
calls for the discovery that lazy men, rather than hot men, have
light venous blood.

The persistent occurrence of mental jumps like these suggests
that many of the discoverers of energy conservation were deeply
predisposed to see a single indestructible force at the root of
all natural phenomena. The predisposition has been noted before,
and a number of historians have at least implied that it is a
residue of a similar metaphysic generated by the eighteenth-century controversy over the conservation of *vis viva*. Leibniz,
Jean and Daniel Bernoulli, Hermann, and Du Châtelet, all said
things like, "*Vis* [*viva*] never perishes; it may in truth appear
lost, but one can always discover it again in its effects if one
can see them." There are a multitude of such statements, and
their authors do attempt, however crudely, to trace *vis viva* into
and out of non-mechanical phenomena. The parallel to men like
Mohr and Colding is very close. Yet eighteenth-century metaphysical sentiments of this sort seem an implausible source for the
nineteenth-century predisposition we are examining. Though the
technical *dynamical* conservation theorem has a continuous history
from the early eighteenth century to the present, its metaphysical
counterpart found few or no defenders after 1750. To discover
the *metaphysical* theorem, the pioneers of energy conservation
would have had to return to books at least a century old. Neither
their works nor their biographies suggest that they were significantly influenced by this particular bit of ancient intellectual
history.

Statements like those of both the eighteenth-century Lieb-
nizians and the nineteenth-century pioneers of energy conservation can, however, be found repeatedly in the literature of a
second philosophical movement, *Naturphilosophie*. Positing organism as the fundamental metaphor of their universal science, the
Naturphilosophen constantly sought a single unifying principle
for all natural phenomena. Schelling, for example, maintained
"that magnetic, electrical, chemical, and finally even organic
phenomena would be interwoven into one great association . . .
[which]extends over the whole of nature." Even before the discovery of the battery he insisted that "without doubt only a
single force in its various guises is manifest in [the phenomena
of] light, electricity, and so forth." These quotations point to
an aspect of Schelling's thought fully documented by Brehier and
more recently by Stauffer. As a *Naturphilosoph*, Schelling con-

stantly sought out conversion and transformation processes in the science of his day. At the beginning of his career chemistry seemed to him the basic physical science; from 1800 on he increasingly found in galvanism "the true border-phenomenon of both [organic and inorganic] natures." Many of Schelling's followers, whose teaching dominated German and many neighboring universities during the first third of the nineteenth century, gave similar emphasis to the new conversion phenomena. Stauffer has shown that Oersted--a *Naturphilosoph* as well as a scientist--persisted in his long search for a relation between electricity and magnetism largely because of his prior philosophical conviction that one must exist. Once the interaction was discovered, electromagnetism played a major role in Hebart's further elaboration of the scientific substructure of *Naturphilosophie*. In short, many *Naturphilosophen* drew from their philosophy a view of physical processes very close to that which Faraday and Grove seem to have drawn from the new discoveries of the nineteenth century.

   Naturphilosophie could, therefore, have provided an appropriate philosophical background for the discovery of energy conservation. Furthermore, several of the pioneers were acquainted with at least its essentials. Colding was a protegé of Oersted's. Liebig studied for two years with Schelling, and though he afterwards described these years as a waste, he never surrendered the vitalism he had then imbibed. Hirn cited both Ocken and Kant. Mayer did not study *Naturphilosophie*, but he had close student friends who did. Helmholtz's father, an intimate of the younger Fichte's and a minor *Naturphilosoph* in his own right, constantly exhorted his son to desert strict mechanism. Though Helmholtz himself felt forced to excise all philosophical discussion from his classic memoir, he was able to 1881 to recognize important Kantian residues that had escaped his earlier censorship.

*   *   *

   This preliminary discussion of simultaneous discovery must end here. Comparing it with the sources, primary and secondary, from which it derives, makes apparent its incompleteness. Almost nothing has been said, for example, about either the dynamical theory of heat or the conception of the impossibility of perpetual motion. Both bulk large in standard histories, and both would require discussion in a more extended treatment. But if I am right, these neglected factors and others like them would not enter a fuller discussion of simultaneous discovery with the urgency of the three discussed here. The impossibility of perpetual motion, for example, was an essential intellectual tool for most of the pioneers. The ways in which many of them arrived at the conservation of energy cannot be understood without it. Yet recognizing the intellectual tool scarcely contributes to an understanding of simultaneous discovery because the impossibility of perpetual motion had been endemic in scientific thought since antiquity. Knowing the tool was there, our question has been: Why did it suddenly acquire a new significance and a new range of application? For us, that is the more significant question.

   The same argument applies in part to my second example of neglected factors. Despite Rumford's deserved fame, the dynamical

theory of heat had been close to the surface of scientific consciousness almost since the days of Francis Bacon. Even at the
end of the eighteenth century, when temporarily eclipsed by the
work of Black and Lavoisier, the dynamical theory was often described in scientific discussions of heat, if only for the sake
of refutation. To the extent that the conception of heat as
motion figured in the work of the pioneers, we must principally
understand why that conception gained a significance after 1830
that it had seldom possessed before. Besides, the dynamical theory did not figure very largely. Only Carnot used it as an essential stepping stone. Mohr leaped from the dynamical theory to
conservation, but his paper indicates that other stimuli might
have served as well. Grove and Joule adhered to the theory but
show substantially no dependence on it. Holtzmann, Mayer, and
Séguin opposed it--Mayer vehemently and to the end of his life.
The apparently close connections between energy conservation and
the dynamical theory are largely retrospective.

Compare these two neglected factors with the three we have
discussed. The rash of conversion discoveries dates from 1800.
Technical discussions of dynamical engines were scarcely a recur-
rent ingredient of scientific literature before 1760 and their
density increased steadily from that date. *Naturphilosophie*
reached its peak in the first two decades of the nineteenth century. Furthermore, all three of these ingredients, except possibly the last, played important roles in the research of at least
half the pioneers. That does not mean that these factors explain
either the individual or collective discoveries of energy conservation. Many old discoveries and concepts were essential to the
work of all the pioneers; many new ones played significant roles
in the work of individuals. We have not and shall not reconstruct
the causes of all that occurred. But the three factors discussed
above may still provide the fundamental constellation, given the
question from which we began: Why, in the years 1830 to 1850, did
so many of the experiments and concepts required for a full statement of energy conservation lie so close to the surface of scientific consciousness?

V. The Fate of Energy--Narrative

A. Field Theory

Field theory was born from the researches of Michael Faraday.
As early as the 1820's he had remarked the peculiar nature of
what he called the "magnetic curves" or lines of force. His work
in electricity had led him to view the electrostatic line of force
as a line of charged, polarized particles reaching out from a
charged body to whatever terminus was available--a wall, another
body, or what have you. The electrostatic energy was not on the
charged body but in the line of charged particles surrounding the
body. The magnetic line of force was both like and unlike its
electrostatic cousin. Its real existence was proved both by the
pattern of iron filings formed around a magnet and by the current

generated when a conducting wire was moved through the space surrounding the magnet. That the condition was one of strain appeared evident to Faraday to whom this current was the result of
the relief of strain. The rotation of the plane of polarized
light by strong magnetic forces also indicated the presence of
strain. The question that immediately rose in Faraday's mind was
what was being strained? The conventional answer for the time
would have been the ether. Faraday, however, had spent his entire
career seeking to eliminate hypothetical substances from natural
philosophy, and he was not prepared to admit a hypothetical ether.
In an extraordinary lecture at the Royal Institution in 1846,
Faraday suggested that the lines of force were simply there. They
were strains in space itself. If this were admitted, then Faraday
felt that the various kinds of line of force were sufficient to
take care of all electric and magnetic phehomena. Furthermore,
he even put forward the daring idea that light was nothing else
but the vibration of electromagnetic lines of force. [See p.227 .].
    Faraday's later work on magnetism helped him to clarify his
ideas. In particular, he saw that a permanent magnet consisted
of the bar of iron *and* the lines of force that surrounded it.
The energy of the magnet was in the space surrounding the iron,
just as the energy of a voltaic cell was in the wires that connected the terminals. Field theory was built upon this concept
of energy spread out in space, rather than concentrated in the
momentum or kinetic energy of a particle. The advantages of this
view over action-at-a-distance ideas was stressed by Faraday in a
lecture at the Royal Institution in 1857. A body, A, of ordinary
matter he saw as causing strain in space which radiated out from
A as gravitational lines of force. At any distance from A, there
would be a specific strain in space which would be the gravitational force exerted by A at that point. If there were another
body, B, at that point then the strains induced by B interacting
with those from A would bring A and B together according to the
law of gravitational action first enunciated by Newton.
    Faraday's ideas, paradoxically enough, were too abstract for
his contemporaries. Paradoxically, because Faraday was a mathematical illiterate and could not express himself in the language
par excellence of abstraction. It was the young Scot, James
Clerk Maxwell (1831-79) who first attempted to translate Faraday's
ideas systematically into the language of mathematical physics.
He was able to deal with lines of force mathematically by assuming them to be tubes filled with an ideal fluid whose pressure
varied according to a simple law. After obtaining mathematical
expressions for the energies associated with these tubes of force,
Maxwell could and did dispense with the ideal fluid and moved on
to a consideration of electrodynamics. In the 1860's and 1870's
he gradually developed a system of equations and concepts which
enabled him to treat the whole (almost) of electrical phenomena
in terms of the creation and relief of strains in the luminiferous
ether. Maxwell, unlike Faraday, could not do without the ether
and in his theory the ether moved center stage. To Maxwell and
his colleagues, it seemed only natural that a strain must exist
in *something* and that thing must be the ether. The ether was
made almost manifest by what Maxwell called the displacement cur-

rent. Faraday, it may be remembered, had argued that an electric
current was the result of the rapid buildup and breakdown of
strain in a conductor. If a circuit were not complete, but contained a gap such as that found between the plates of a condenser,
then the question was what occurred between the two condenser
plates? Maxwell extended Faraday's argument to the momentary
"current" created when such a circuit was closed. The ether between the plates was thrown into a state of strain, just as if
the current had begun. The strain was only relieved when the
circuit was broken. This "current" at the making and breaking of
the circuit was the displacement current. The displacement current, the lines of force and the ether permitted Maxwell to analyze electromagnetic phenomena with a finesse hitherto unattain-
able. His great *Treatise on Electricity and Magnetism* (1873)
gathered together the electrical investigations of the nineteenth
century and presented them, in a relatively coherent fashion,
within the framework of the concept of the electromagnetic field
--i.e., strains in the ether. All this was done with complete
mathematization and quantification so that even the most mathematical of physicists were impressed. Electricity and magnetism
were now reduced to strains or transverse vibrations in the ether.
Since light was also assumed to be a transverse vibration in the
ether, and since Faraday had already suggested that light was a
vibration of the electromagnetic lines of force, it was not particularly daring of Maxwell to consider light to be electromagnetic radiation through the ether. Support for this view came
from the fact that the calculation for the rate of propagation of
electromagnetic radiation showed that it was very close to the
known value of the speed of light. When, in 1887, Heinrich Hertz
(1857-94) discovered radio waves, in every respect but wave length
identical to light, the point was taken as proven.
     The ether which had been pulled into the nineteenth century
to handle waves of light now appeared to be the fundamental substance in the universe. The attempt was even made to account for
ponderable matter by ether "smoke-rings" after Hermann von Helmholtz had shown mathematically that such closed rings would be
stable in an ideal, frictionless fluid such as the ether was
assumed to be. Although this atomic model ultimately had to be
abandoned, it was symptomatic of the thought of the time. It
seemed as though the dream of the old Hellenic philosophers was
almost within grasp. The basic substance underlying physical
reality was not, as Thales had thought, water but ether. In the
1890's, the editor of the prestigious German scientific journal,
the *Annalen der Physik*, could write a work entitled *The Physics
of the Ether* which could and did account for all physics but that
small and messy area dealing with the relations of particles of
ponderable matter with one another.
     By the 1890's, the importance of the ether in contemporary
physics had also begun to bother a number of the keener minds in
science. The ether, after all, remained totally undetectable and
it was possible to ask if *The Physics of the Ether* should not be
classified as fiction under ghost stories. In particular, there
ought to be some effect of motion of the Earth through the ether.
Or, if the ether moved with the Earth, that effect, too, should

be detectable. In the 1850's, Hippolyte Fizeau had done a number
of experiments on this problem but had been unable to find any
evidence for an ether "wind." In 1887, in Cleveland, Ohio two
Americans--Albert A. Michelson (1852-1931) and Edward W. Morley
(1838-1923) performed an even more delicate and accurate series
of experiments but also failed to detect any ether "wind" or the
effects that would be expected if the ether moved with the Earth.
This was clearly a disturbing situation for it seemed obvious
that the ether either moved with the Earth or did not move with
the Earth. One *should* be able to find out which statement was
true through clever experiments.

Not everyone worried about this problem, however, and for
most physicists, physics was in great shape. The ether seemed
about as real as anything you couldn't detect could be; Maxwell's
equations permitted one to predict and calculate effects over an
increasingly wide range, and field theory appeared adequate to
handle almost any problem. The fact that it could not yet deal
satisfactorily with such phenomena as atomic radiation and the
radiative energy of black bodies was not cause for abandoning the
ether. These effects would undoubtedly be reduced to order by
the next generation of physicists. It is always worth repeating
the story of Lord Kelvin addressing an assemblage of physicists
in the 1890's and pointing out that all that remained for the
next generation to do was to measure everything to the next deci-
mal place. This, on the eve of the discovery of radium, X-rays
and the quantum of action!

B. Kinetic Theory

The notion that heat was the result of the "intestine motion"
of the particles of bodies goes back at least as far as Francis
Bacon in the early seventeenth century. The mechanical philosophers of the Scientific Revolution generally subscribed to the
idea and Gottfried Wilhelm Leibnitz put forward the notion that
this "intestine motion" could be quantified as the *vis viva* or mv^2
of these particles. The concept was a seductive one and a number
of natural philosophers in the eighteenth and early nineteenth
centuries tried their hands at making it into a coherent theory.
In 1738 Daniel Bernoulli in his *Hydrodynamica* had attempted to
deal with molecular kinetic energies and this work is generally
acknowledged to be the first serious treatise on the subject. It
was, however, a century ahead of its time. Moleculae were still
confined to the realm of metaphysics, there being no physical
parameters that could be assigned them. More importantly, Bernoulli's work appeared just before Black's researches on heat
established the material theory of heat as a fluid. The phenomenon of latent heat can be more easily visualized as the result
of the physical combination of two substances--heat + matter--
than as the result of varying degrees of kinetic energy among
molecules. Even Count Rumford's famous experiments on the heat
developed by friction in boring cannon could not shake the conviction that heat was a substance, not a motion. Further attempts
in Bernoulli's tradition by John Herapath and J. J. Waterston in

the early nineteenth century fell on deaf ears. No one was interested in a kinetic solution to a problem that did not exist.
Heat was a fluid and that was that.

The material theory of heat began to crumble in the 1830's
and finally fell in the 1840's. An indirect, but important blow,
fell on caloric with the investigation of radiant heat. William
Herschel had discovered the "heating rays" of the Sun or the
infra-red rays in 1800. Further investigations, especially by
Macedonio Melloni (1798-1854), revealed that radiant heat was, in
every way, similar to light. Thomas Thomson in his textbook on
chemistry had used this similarity to prove the materiality of
heat for Thomson was a good corpuscularian. By the 1830's, however, most scientists were convinced of the undulatory nature of
light and, consequently, were willing to accept the undulatory
nature of radiant heat. At least in this area, caloric disappeared.

It disappeared, as well, in ordinary heat processes when it
became clear in the early 1840's that the quantity of caloric did
not remain constant when work was done. The work of James Prescott Joule here was of fundamental importance. Joule not only
proved that heat was converted into work and vice versa but, in
an increasingly accurate series of experiments, he was able to
measure the mechanical equivalent of heat with fair precision.
The adherents of the caloric theory were now faced with the prospect of admitting the annihilation of a material substance. None
were willing to do this and the caloric theory was rather abruptly
abandoned. There was not, however, anything that could immediately take its place. The kinetic theory was a fair time in being
born.

The problem consisted in determining what was kinetic in the
kinetic theory of heat. It is not immediately obvious that trans-
lational motion is the best thing to assume in order to account
for heat. Sir Humphry Davy had earlier suggested rotational motion of molecules, and Joule modified this model by assuming an
atmosphere of electricity around each molecule. The rotation of
this atmosphere was heat and as a body got hotter, the atmospheres
rotated more rapidly, thereby increasing in size, and leading to
expansion of the body as a whole.

By 1850, Joule had abandoned his electrodynamic molecules
and accepted, instead, a true kinetic theory in which expansion
and gas pressure were the result of the collisions of innumerable
rapidly-moving molecules. From this rather simple model, Joule
was able to deduce the average velocities of gas molecules and to
calculate the specific heat of a gas. The work of Thomas Graham
on gas diffusion, done in the 1840's, gave an experimental standard against which Joule's calculations could be checked and
Joule showed that his calculations on velocities were in accord
with experiment. The same could not be said for the calculation
of specific heats where Joule's deductions were wide of the experimental mark. This problem was to vex and stimulate physicists for two generations, to be solved only with the development
of quantum mechanics in the twentieth century.

Joule's work established the kinetic theory as a respectable
hypothesis that could be developed by respectable physicists.

Since he had also demolished the caloric theory, there was little choice left to those who were interested in thermodynamics. The 1850's, '60's, and '70's witnessed the rapid development of kinetic theory, particularly in the hands of James Clerk Maxwell, Rudolf Clausius and Ludwig Boltzmann (1844-1906). It is impossible to separate their contributions for these three men carried on a dialogue of extreme fertility from the late 1850's until Maxwell's death in 1879.

Maxwell initiated the theoretical conversation in 1859, with his first paper entitled "Illustrations of the Dynamical Theory of Gases." It was in this paper that Maxwell introduced his famous distribution curve for velocities of gas molecules. It would appear that this introduction of a probabilistic argument into a mechanical system was inspired by a book review by Sir John Hershel in 1850 of a book on statistics. The combination of statistics, probability and kinetic theory was to have a brilliant future as statistical mechanics. In 1859, however, Maxwell was still working within the familiar confines of ordinary mechanics and derived his distribution curve from what he thought were good hard-headed physical arguments.

Rudolf Clausius was quick to appreciate what Maxwell was about and, agreeing with Maxwell's distribution of velocities, showed how it was possible, as well, to calculate the mean free path of a molecule. With the velocity distribution curve and the mean free path available, the question of specific heats appeared worthy of attack again. No progress could be made if gases were assumed to be composed of single atoms or elastic spheres. If the molecule of gases was assumed to be diatomic, however, the calculated specific heat came closer to that measured experimentally. It is surely no coincidence that the acceptance of diatomic gas molecules (which violated Berzelius' electrostatic model for chemical bonding) came in kinetic theory in 1860 and that, similarly, the acceptance of Avogadro's hypothesis in chemistry in which diatomic molecules were required dates from the same year. The chemists, we may assume, found Avogadro's hypothesis the only way out of their peculiar dead end but it must have encouraged them to know that physicists were able to live with molecules composed of two similar atoms. The introduction of complex molecules was a mixed blessing, however, for it also introduced complexities into the calculations. Kinetic theory which had started out as a rather simple three-dimensional billiard game, was becoming mathematically forbidding.

The most conspicuous area of increasing complexity revolved around the meaning to be assigned to various mathematical functions. We have already had occasion to mention the function $\int dQ/T$ which Clausius had discovered in his thermodynamic work. What, specifically, did it mean in gases? And how could it be related to the theory of gases as a mechanical system following the laws of Newtonian mechanics? Entropy, as the function was named, could be considered as a measure of the physical disorder of a system. Thus the Second Law of Thermodynamics which states that the entropy of the universe constantly tends to increase can be restated physically to mean that the degree of disorder in the universe is constantly on the increase. If the Second Law holds,

then the end of the world, not its beginning, will be chaos or
total disorder. Since no energy can be made available from total
disorder, the result will be the famous "Heat death" of the nineteenth century in which all physical processes will cease since
there is no available energy to drive them.

The Heat death had a certain romantic appeal to the *fin de
siècle* despondency that was then popular, but it also raised some
serious questions in physics. If the Second Law were valid, then
physicists were faced with a real problem. The kinetic theory
was a classical mechanical system and mechanical systems, by definition since the time of Newton, were reversible. But if entropy
constantly increased, then, by definition, the kinetic processes
were irreversible. Something was obviously wrong somewhere. It
was Ludwig Boltzmann who removed the difficulty. Whereas Maxwell
had introduced probability theory almost casually into his calculations, Boltzmann showed that probability theory was essential
to the very structure of kinetic theory. Entropy was now interpreted as an overwhelming probability, not an absolute and iron-
clad law. Thus, Boltzmann showed that there was a function, W
(for Wahrscheinlichkeit = probability) which gave a probability
for reversibility. For example, W can give a measure of the
probability that all the molecules in the table upon which this
book rests may all suddenly be moving upwards at the same time
and that the table will levitate. The probability, needless to
say, is vanishingly small but it is finite and it is enough to
restore reversibility. Should all the molecules move upwards,
that would be a state of greater order than the random distribution of directions of motion. Entropy, in this case, would decrease. The Heat death, for any readers who are anxious about it,
is not the inevitable fate of the universe!

The achievement of Maxwell, Clausius and Boltzmann was prodigious. Kinetic theory had been developed by them into a highly
sophisticated and mathematically complicated system of inestimable
use in the understanding of microprocesses and molecular physics.
By its means, it was even possible to begin to probe the structure
of molecules and penetrate to the atomic realm. By the 1890's,
Lord Kelvin could confidently state what the sizes of atoms were.
He could also define temperature in terms of the kinetic energy
of these atoms and molecules. Those entities--heat, temperature,
atoms, molecules--which had been mere spectres of reality at the
opening of the century were now handled with the same confidence
with which one treated billiard balls or other common objects.
But, as usually happens, the more one penetrated into the finer
structure of the entities upon which the theory was based, the
more puzzling this structure became. The most perplexing area
was that of the atomic structure that became manifest in the
spectra of the elements. The concept of diatomic molecules gave
some help, although it also presented problems. Suppose the two
atoms of a diatomic molecule could vibrate back and forth along
the line joining their centers. Such vibrations ought to set up
waves in the ether and one ought to get the production of light.
Such light, we might assume, ought to be of all wave lengths
possible from an oscillator of molecular size. But, the spectra
of the elements were not bands of light. Instead they were

specific, narrowly defined, rays. Furthermore, some of the frequencies indicated that the oscillator producing them was of smaller size that the constituent atoms of the moleculae.

In the 1890's, the kinetic theory, thermodynamics and field theory came together in this problem of the production of radiant energy. Kinetic theory had accustomed people to deal with particulate oscillators; thermodynamics had provided excellent guidelines for the deduction of the intensity and partition of energies under various conditions; field theory had pointed the way to the understanding of the mechanism of ether radiation. The three parts ought to fit together. To everyone's increasing horror, they didn't! Expedient after expedient was tried and failed. Time was to show that the only way out was the radical one of a second scientific revolution.

VI. The Fate of Energy--Field Theory Readings

A. Michael Faraday

Michael Faraday was the major architect of field theory. Central to his conceptions was the idea of the line of force. In the two selections that follow,* Faraday reveals the importance of the line of force in his theories and his speculations.

Thoughts on Ray-vibrations. (1846)

To Richard Phillips, Esq.

Dear Sir,

At your request I will endeavour to convey to you a notion of that which I ventured to say at the close of the last Friday-evening Meeting, incidental to the account I gave of Wheatstone's electro-magnetic chronoscope; but from first to last understand that I merely threw out as matter for speculation, the vague impressions of my mind, for I gave nothing as the result of sufficient consideration, or as the settled conviction, or even probable conclusion at which I had arrived.

The point intended to be set forth for consideration of the hearers was, whether it was not possible that the vibrations which in a certain theory are assumed to account for radiation and radiant phænomena may not occur in the lines of force which connect particles, and consequently masses of matter together; a notion which as far as it is admitted, will dispense with the æther, which, in another view, is supposed to be the medium in which these vibrations take place.

You are aware of the speculation which I some time since uttered respecting that view of the nature of matter which con-

---

*M. Faraday, "Thoughts on Ray Vibrations," in *Experimental Researches*, III, pp. 447-52; "On the Physical Character of the Lines of Magnetic Force," in *ibid.*, pp. 407-12, 417-22, 424-26, 437.

siders its ultimate atoms as centers of force, and not as so many little bodies surrounded by forces, the bodies being considered in the abstract as independent of the forces and capable of existing without them. In the latter view, these little particles have a definite form and a certain limited size; in the former view such is not the case, for that which represents size may be considered as extending to any distance to which the lines of force of the particle extend: the particle indeed is supposed to exist only by these forces, and where they are it is. The consideration of matter under this view gradually led me to look at the lines of force as being perhaps the seat of the vibrations of radiant phænomena.

Another consideration bearing conjointly on the hypothetical view both of matter and radiation, arises from the comparison of the velocities with which the radiant action and certain powers of matter are transmitted. The velocity of light through space is about 190,000 miles a second; the velocity of electricity is, by the experiments of Wheatstone, shown to be as great as this, if not greater: the light is supposed to be transmitted by vibrations through an æther which is, so to speak, destitute of gravitation, but infinite in elasticity; the electricity is transmitted through a small metallic wire, and is often viewed as transmitted by vibrations also. That the electric transference depends on the forces or powers of the matter of the wire can hardly be doubted, when we consider the different conductibility of the various metallic and other bodies; the means of affecting it by heat or cold; the way in which conducting bodies by combination enter into the constitution of non-conducting substances, and the contrary; and the actual existence of one elementary body, carbon, both in the conducting and non-conducting state. The power of electric conduction (being a transmission of force equal in velocity to that of light) appears to be tied up in and dependent upon the properties of the matter, and is, as it were, existent in them.

I suppose we may compare together the matter of the æther and ordinary matter (as, for instance, the copper of the wire through which the electricity is conducted), and consider them as alike in their essential constitution; *i.e.* either as both composed of little nuclei, considered in the abstract as matter, and of force or power associated with these nuclei, or else both consisting of mere centres of force, according to Boscovich's theory and the view put forth in my speculation; for there is no reason to assume that the nuclei are more requisite in the one case than in the other. It is true that the copper gravitates and the æther does not; but that cannot indicate the presence of nuclei in the copper more than in the æther, for of all the powers of matter gravitation is the one in which the force extends to the greatest possible distance from the supposed nucleus, being infinite in relation to the size of the latter, and reducing that nucleus to a mere centre of force. The smallest atom of matter on the earth acts directly on the smallest atom of matter in the sun, though they are 95,000,000 of miles apart; further, atoms which, to our knowledge, are at least nineteen times that distance, and indeed, in cometary masses, far more, are in a similar way tied together by the lines of force extending from and belonging to each. What is there in the condition of the particles of the supposed æther, if there be even only *one* such particle between us and the sun, that can in subtility and extent compare to this?

Let us not be confused by the *ponderability* and *gravitation* of heavy matter, as if they proved the presence of the abstract nuclei; these are due not to the nuclei, but to the force superadded to them, if the nuclei exist at all; and, if the *æther* particles be without this force, which according to the assumption. is the case, then they are more material, in the abstract sense, than the matter of this our globe; for matter, according to the assumption, being made up of nuclei and force, the æther particles have in this respect proportionately more of the nucleus and less of the force.

On the other hand, the infinite elasticity assumed as belonging to the particles of the æther, is as striking and positive a force of it as gravity is of ponderable particles, and produces in its way effects as great; in witness whereof we have all the varieties of radiant agency as exhibited in luminous, calorific, and actinic phænomena.

Perhaps I am in error in thinking the idea generally formed of the æther is that its nuclei are almost infinitely small, and that such force as it has, namely its elasticity, is almost infinitely intense. But if such be the received notion, what then is left in the æther but force or centres of force? As gravitation and solidity do not belong to it, perhaps many may admit this conclusion; but what are gravitation and solidity? certainly not the weight and contact of the abstract nuclei. The one is the consequence of an *attractive* force, which can act at distances as great as the mind of man can estimate or conceive; and the other is the consequence of a *repulsive* force, which forbids for ever the contact or touch of any two nuclei; so that these powers or properties should not in any degree lead those persons who conceive of the æther as a thing consisting of force only, to think any otherwise of ponderable matter, except that it has more and other *forces* associated with it than the æther has.

In experimental philosophy we can, by the phænomena presented, recognize various kinds of lines of force; thus there are the lines of gravitating force, those of electro-static induction, those of magnetic action, and others partaking of a dynamic character might be perhaps included. The lines of electric and magnetic action are by many considered as exerted through space like the lines of gravitating force. For my own part, I incline to believe that when there are intervening particles of matter (being themselves only centres of force), they take part in carrying on the force through the line, but that when there are none, the line proceeds through space. Whatever the view adopted respecting them may be, we can, at all events, affect these lines of force in a manner which may be conceived as partaking of the nature of a shake or lateral vibration. For suppose two bodies, A B, distant from each other and under mutual action, and therefore connected by lines of force, and let us fix our attention upon one resultant of force, having an invariable direction as regards space; if one

of the bodies move in the least degree right or left, or if its
power be shifted for a moment within the mass (neither of these
cases being difficult to realise if A and B be either electric or
magnetic bodies), then an effect equivalent to a lateral disturbance will take place in the resultant upon which we are fixing
our attention; for, either it will increase in force whilst the
neighbouring resultants are diminishing, or it will fall in force
as they are increasing.

It may be asked, what lines of force are there in nature
which are fitted to convey such an action and supply for the
vibrating theory the place of the æther? I do not pretend so
answer this question with any confidence; all I can say is, that
I do not perceive in any part of space, whether (to use the common phrase) vacant or filled with matter, anything but forces and
the lines in which they are exerted. The lines of weight or
gravitating force are, certainly, extensive enough to answer in
this respect any demand made upon them by radiant phænomena; and
so, probably, are the lines of magnetic force: and then who can
forget that Mossotti has shown that gravitation, aggregation,
electric force, and electro-chemical action may all have one common connection or origin; and so, in their actions at a distance,
may have in common that infinite scope which some of these actions
are known to possess?

The view which I am so bold as to put forth considers, therefore, radiation as a high species of vibration in the lines of
force which are known to connect particles and also masses of
matter together. It endeavours to dismiss the æther, but not the
vibration. The kind of vibration which, I believe, can alone
account for the wonderful, varied, and beautiful phænomena of
polarization, is not the same as that which occurs on the surface
of disturbed water, or the waves of sound in gases or liquids,
for the vibrations in these cases are direct, or to and from the
centre of action, whereas the former are lateral. It seems to me,
that the resultant of two or more lines of force is in an apt condition for that action which may be considered as equivalent to a
lateral vibration; whereas a uniform medium, like the æther, does
not appear apt, or more apt than air or water.

The occurrence of a change at one end of a line of force
easily suggests a consequent change at the other. The propagation
of light, and therefore probably of all radiant action, occupies
time; and, that a vibration of the line of force should account
for the phænomena of radiation, it is necessary that such vibration should occupy time also. I am not aware whether there are
any data by which it has been, or could be ascertained whether
such a power as gravitation acts without occupying time, or whether lines of force being already in existence, such a lateral
disturbance of them at one end as I have suggested above, would
require time, or must of necessity be felt instantly at the other
end.

As to that condition of the lines of force which represents
the assumed high elasticity of the æther, it cannot in this respect be deficient: the question here seems rather to be, whether
the lines are sluggish enough in their action to render them
equivalent to the æther in respect of the time known experimentally to be occupied in the transmission of radiant force.

The æther is assumed as pervading all bodies as well as space: in the view now set forth, it is the forces of the atomic centres which pervade (and make) all bodies, and also penetrate all space. As regards space, the difference is, that the æther presents successive parts or centres of action, and the present supposition only lines of action; as regards matter, the difference is, that the æther lies between the particles and so carries on the vibrations, whilst as respects the supposition, it is by the lines of force between the centres of the particles that the vibration is continued. As to the difference in intensity of action within matter under the two views, I suppose it will be very difficult to draw any conclusion, for when we take the simplest state of common matter and that which most nearly causes it to approximate to the condition of the æther, namely the state of rare gas, how soon do we find in its elasticity and the mutual repulsion of its particles, a departure from the law, that the action is inversely as the square of the distance!

And now, my dear Phillips, I must conclude. I do not think I should have allowed these notions to have escaped from me, had I not been led unawares, and without previous consideration, by the circumstances of the evening on which I had to appear suddenly and occupy the place of another. Now that I have put them on paper, I feel that I ought to have kept them much longer for study, consideration, and, perhaps, final rejection; and it is only because they are sure to go abroad in one way or another, in consequence of their utterance on that evening, that I give them a shape, if shape it may be called, in this reply to your inquiry. One thing is certain, that any hypothetical view of radiation which is likely to be received or retained as satisfactory, must not much longer comprehend alone certain phænomena of light, but must include those of heat and of actinic influence also, and even the conjoined phænomena of sensible heat and chemical power produced by them. In this respect, a view, which is in some degree founded upon the ordinary forces of matter, may perhaps find a little consideration amongst the other views that will probably arise. I think it likely that I have made many mistakes in the preceding pages, for even to myself, my ideas on this point appear only as the shadow of a speculation, or as one of those impressions on the mind which are allowable for a time as guides to thought and research. He who labours in experimental inquiries knows how numerous these are, and how often their apparent fitness and beauty vanish before the progress and development of real natural truth.

I am, my dear Phillips,
Ever truly yours,
M. Faraday.

Royal Institution,
April 15, 1846.

On the Physical Character of the Lines of Magnetic Force. (1852)

3243. I have recently been engaged in describing and defining the lines of magnetic force . . . , *i.e.* those lines which are indicated in a general manner by the disposition of iron filings or small magnetic needles, around or between magnets; and I have

shown, I hope satisfactorily, how these lines may be taken as
exact representants of the magnetic power, both as to disposition
and amount; also how they may be recognized by a moving wire in a
manner altogether different in principle from the indications
given by a magnetic needle, and in numerous cases with great and
peculiar advantages. The definition then given had no reference
to the physical nature of the force at the place of action, and
will apply with equal accuracy whatever that may be; and this
being very thoroughly understood, I am now about to leave the
strict line of reasoning for a time, and enter upon a few speculations respecting the physical character of the lines of force,
and the manner in which they may be supposed to be continued
through space. We are obliged to enter into such speculations
with regard to numerous natural powers, and, indeed, that of
gravity is the only instance where they are apparently shut out.

3244. It is not to be supposed for a moment that speculations of this kind are useless, or necessarily hurtful, in natural
philosophy. They should ever be held as doubtful, and liable to
error and to change; but they are wonderful aids in the hands of
the experimentalist and mathematician. For not only are they
useful in rendering the vague idea more clear for the time, giving
it something like a definite shape, that it may be submitted to
experiment and calculation; but they lead on, by deduction and
correction, to the discovery of new phænomena, and so cause an
increase and advance of real physical truth, which, unlike the
hypothesis that led to it, becomes fundamental knowledge not subject to change. Who is not aware of the remarkable progress in
the development of the nature of light and radiation in modern
times, and the extent to which that progress has been aided by
the hypotheses both of emission and undulation? Such considerations form my excuse for entering now and then upon speculations;
but though I value them highly when cautiously advanced, I consider it as an essential character of a sound mind to hold them
in doubt; scarcely giving them the character of opinions, but
esteeming them merely as probabilities and possibilities, and
making a very broad distinction between them and the facts and
laws of nature.

3245. In the numerous cases of force acting at a distance,
the philosopher has gradually learned that it is by no means sufficient to rest satisfied with the mere fact, and has therefore
directed his attention to the manner in which the force is transmitted across the intervening space; and even when he can learn
nothing sure of the manner, he is still able to make clear distinctions in different cases, by what may be called the affections of the lines of power; and thus, by these and other means,
to make distinctions in the nature of the lines of force of different kinds of power as compared with each other, and therefore
between the powers to which they belong. In the action of gravity, for instance, the line of force is a straight line as far as
we can test it by the resultant phænomena. It cannot be deflected, or even affected, in its course. Neither is the action in
one line at all influenced, either in direction or amount, by a
like action in another line; *i.e.* one particle gravitating toward
another particle has exactly the same amount of force in the same

direction, whether it gravitates to the one alone or towards myriads of other like particles, exerting in the latter case upon each one of them a force equal to that which it can exert upon the single one when alone: the results of course can combine, but the direction and amount of force between any two given particles remain unchanged. So gravity presents us with the simplest case of attraction; and appearing to have no relation to any physical process by which the power of the particles is carried on between them, seems to be a pure case of attraction or action at a distance, and offers therefore the simplest type of the cases which may be like it in that respect. My object is to consider how far magnetism is such an action at a distance; or how far it may partake of the nature of other powers, and lines of which depend, for the communication of force, upon intermediate physical agencies. . . .

3246. There is one question in relation to gravity, which, if we could ascertain or touch it, would greatly enlighten us. It is, whether gravitation requires *time*. If it did, it would show undeniably that a physical agency existed in the course of the line of force. It seems equally impossible to prove or disprove this point; since there is no capability of suspending, changing, or annihilating the power (gravity), or annihilating the matter in which the power resides.

3247. When we turn to radiation phænomena, then we obtain the highest proof, that though nothing ponderable passes, yet the lines of force have a physical existence independent, in a manner, of the body radiating, or of the body receiving the rays. They may be turned aside in their course, and then deviate from a straight into a bent or a curved line. They may be affected in their nature so as to be turned on their axis, or else to have different properties impressed on different sides. Their sum of power is limited; so that if the force, as it issues from its source, is directed on to or determined upon a given set of particles, or in a given direction, it cannot be in any degree directed upon other particles, or into another direction, without being proportionately removed from the first. The lines have no dependence upon a second or reacting body, as in gravitation; and they require time for their propagation. In all these things they are in marked contrast with the lines of gravitating force.

3248. When we turn to the electric force, we are presented with a very remarkable general condition intermediate between the conditions of the two former cases. The power (and its lines) here requires the *presence* of two or more acting particles or masses, as in the case of gravity; and cannot exist with one only, as in the case of light. But though two particles are requisite, they must be in an *antithetical* condition in respect of each other, and not, as in the case of gravity, alike in relation to the force. The power is now dual; there it was simple. Requiring two or more particles like gravity, it is unlike gravity in that the power is limited. One electro-particle cannot affect a second, third and fourth, as much as it does the first; to act upon the latter its power must be proportionately removed from the former, and this limitation appears to exist as a necessity in the dual character of the force; for the two states, or places, or directions of force must be equal to each other.

3249. With the electric force we have both the static and dynamic state. I use these words merely as names, without pretending to have a clear notion of the physical condition which they seem meaningly to imply. Whether there are two fluids or one, or any fluid of electricity, or such a thing as may be rightly called a current, I do not know; still there are well-established electric conditions and effects which the words *static*, *dynamic*, and *current* are generally employed to express; and with this reservation they express them as well as any other. The lines of force of the *static* condition of electricity are present in all cases of induction. They terminate at the surfaces of the conductors under induction, or at the particles of non-conductors, which, being electrified, are in that condition. They are subject to inflection in their course . . . , and may be compressed or rarefied by bodies of different inductive capacities . . . ; but they are in those cases affected by the intervening matter; and it is not certain how the line of electric force would exist in relation to a perfect vacuum, *i.e.* whether it would be a straight line, as that of gravity is assumed to be, or curved in such a manner as to show something like physical existence separate from the mere distant actions of the surfaces or particles bounding or terminating the induction. No condition of *quality* or *polarity* has as yet been discovered in the line of static electric force; nor has any relation of *time* been established in respect of it.

3250. The lines of force of dynamic electricity are either limited in their extent, as in the lowering by discharge, or otherwise of the inductive condition of static electricity; or endless and continuous, as closed curves in the case of a voltaic circuit. Being definite in their amount for a given source, they can still be expanded, contracted, and deflected almost to any extent, according to the nature and size of the media through which they pass, and to which they have a direct relation. It is probable that matter is always essentially present; but the hypothetical æther may perhaps be admitted here as well as elsewhere. No condition of quality or polarity has as yet been recognised in them. In respect of *time*, it has been found, in the case of a Leyden discharge, that time is necessary even with the best conductors; indeed there is reason to think it is as necessary there as in the cases dependent on bad conducting media, as, for instance, in the lightning flash.

3251. Three great distinctions at least may be taken among these cases of the exertion of force at a distance; that of gravitation, where propagation of the force by physical lines through the intermediate space is not supposed to exist; that of radiation, where the propagation does exist, and there the propagating line or ray, once produced, has existence independent either of its source, or termination; and that of electricity, where the propagating process has intermediate existence, like a ray, but at the same time depends upon both extremities of the line of force, or upon conditions (as in the connected voltaic pile) equivalent to such extremities. Magnetic action at a distance

has to be compared with these. It may be unlike any of them; for
who shall say we are aware of all the physical methods or forms
under which force is communicated? It has been assumed, however,
by some, to be a pure case of force at a distance, and so like
that of gravity; whilst others have considered it as better represented by the idea of streams of power. The question at present
appears to be, whether the lines of magnetic force have or have
not a physical existence; and if they have, whether such physical
existence has a static or dynamic form. . . .

3252. The lines of magnetic force have not as yet been
affected in their *qualities*, *i.e.* nothing analogous to the polarization of a ray of light or heat has been impressed on them. A
relation between them and the rays of light when polarized has
been discovered . . . ; but it is not of such a nature as to give
proof as yet, either that the lines of magnetic force have a separate existence, or that they have not; though I think the facts
are in favour of the former supposition. The investigation is an
open one, and very important.

3253. No relation of *time* to the lines of magnetic force
has as yet been discovered. That iron requires *time* for its magnetization is well known. Plücker says the same is the case for
bismuth, but I have not been able to obtain the effect showing
this result. If that were the case, then mere space with its
æther ought to have a similar relation, for it comes between bismuth and iron . . . ; and such a result would go far to show that
the lines of magnetic force have a separate physical existence.
At present such results as we have cannot be accepted as in any
degree proving the point of *time*; though if that point were
proved, they would most probably come under it. It may be as
well to state, that in the case also of the moving wire or conductor . . . , time is required. There seems no hope of touching
the investigation by any method like those we are able to apply
to a ray of light, or to the current of the Leyden discharge; but
the mere statement of the problem may help toward its solution.

*   *   *

3264. I have not referred in the foregoing considerations
to the view I have recently supported by experimental evidence,
that the lines of force, considered simply as representants of
the magnetic power . . . , are closed curves, passing in one part
of their course through the magnet, and in the other part through
the space around it. These lines are identical in their nature,
qualities and amount, both within the magnet and without. If to
these lines, as formerly defined . . . , we add the idea of physical existence, and then reconsider such of the cases which have
just been mentioned as come under the new idea, it will be seen
at once that the probability of curved external lines of force,
and therefore of the physical existence of the lines, is as great,
and even far greater, than before. For now no back action in the
magnet could be supposed; and the external relation and dependence
of the polarities . . . would, if it were possible, be even more
necessary than before. Such a view would tend to give, but not
necessarily, a dynamic form to the idea of magnetic force; and
its close relation to dynamic electricity is well known. . . .

This I will proceed to examine; but before doing so, will again look for a moment at static electric induction, as a case of the dual powers in mutual dependence by curved lines of force, but with these lines terminated, and not existing as closed circuits. An electric conductor polarized by induction, or an insulated, unconnected, rectilineal, voltaic battery presents such a case, and resembles a magnet in the disposition of the external lines of force. But the sustaining action (as regards the induction) being dependent upon the necessary relation of the opposite dual conditions of the force, is external to the conductor, or the battery; and in such a case, if the conductor or battery be separated in the middle, no charge appears there, nor any origin of new lines of inductive force. This is, no doubt, a consequence of the fact, that the lines of static inductive force are not continued internally; and, at the same time, a cause why the two divided portions remain in opposite states or absolutely charged. In the magnet such a division *does* develop new external lines of force; which being equal in amount to those dependent on the original poles, shows that the lines of force are continuous through the body of the magnet, and with that continuity gives the necessary reason why no absolute charge of northness or southness is found in the two halves.

3265. The well-known relation of the electric and magnetic forces may be thus stated. Let two rings, in planes at right angles to each other, represent them. . . . If a current of electricity be sent round the ring E in the direction marked, then lines of magnetic force will be produced, correspondent to the polarity indicated by a supposed magnetic needle places at NS, or in any other part of the ring M to which such a needle may be supposed to be shifted. As these rings represent the lines of electro-dynamic force and of magnetic force respectively, they will serve for a standard of comparison. I have elsewhere called the electric current, or the line of electro-dynamic force, "an axis of power having contrary forces exactly equal in amount in contrary directions". . . . The line of magnetic force may be described in *precisely the same terms*; and these two axes of power, considered as right lines, are perpendicular to each other; with this additional condition, which determines their mutual direction, that they are separated by a right line perpendicular to both. The meaning of the words above, when applied to the electric current, is precise, and does not imply that the forces are contrary *because* they are in reverse directions, but are *contrary in nature*; the turning one round, end for end, would not at all make it resemble the other; a consideration which may have influence with those who admit electric fluids, and endeavour to decide whether there are one or two electricities.

3266. When these two axes of power are compared, they have some remarkable correspondences, especially in relation to their position at right angles to each other. As a physical fact, Ampère and Davy have shown, that an electric current tends to elongate itself; and, so far, that may be considered as marking a character of the *electric* axis of power. When a free magnetic needle near the end of a bar-magnet first points and then tends to approach it, I see in the action a character of the contrary kind in the *magnetic* axis of power; for the lines of magnetic force, which, according to my recent researches, are common to the magnet and the needle . . . , are shortened, first by the motion of the needle when it points, and again by the action which causes the needle to approach the magnet. I think I may say, that all the other actions of a magnet upon magnets, or soft iron, or other paramagnetic and diamagnetic bodies are in harmony with the same effect and conclusions.

3267.   Again:--like electric currents, or lines of force, or axes of power, when placed side by side, attract each other. This is well known and well seen, when wires carrying such currents are placed parallel to each other. But like magnetic axes of power or lines of force repel each other: the parallel case to that of the electric currents is given, by placing two magnetic needles side by side with like poles in the same direction; and by the use of iron filings, numerous pictorial representations . . . of the same general result may be obtained.

3268.   Now these effects are not merely *contrasts* continued through two or more different relations, but they are contrasts which *coincide* when the position of the two axes of power at right angles to each other are considered. . . . The tendency to *elongate* in the electric current, and the tendency to *lateral* separation of the magnetic lines of force which surround that current, are both tendencies in the same direction, though they seem like contrasts, when the two axes are considered out of their relation of mutual position; and this, with other considerations to be immediately referred to, probably points to the intimate physical relation, and it may be, to the oneness of condition of that which is apparently two powers or forms of power, electric and magnetic. In that case many other relations, of which the following are some forms, will merge in the same result. Thus, unlike magnetic lines, when end on, repel each other, as when similar poles are face to face; and unlike electric currents, if placed in the same relation, stop each other; or if raised in intensity, when thus made static, repel each other. Like electric currents or lines of force, when end on to each other, coalesce; like magnetic lines of force similarly placed do so too. . . . Like electric currents, end to end, do not add their sums; but whilst there is no change in quantity, the intensity is increased. Like magnetic lines of force, similarly placed do not increase each other, for the power then also remains the same . . . : perhaps some effect correspondent to the gain of intensity in the former case may be produced, but there is none as yet distinctly recognised. Like electric currents, side by side, add the quantities together; a case supplied either by uniting several batteries by their like ends, or comparing a large plate battery with a small one. Like magnetic lines of force do the same. . . .

3269.   The mutual relation of the magnetic lines of force and the electric axis of power has been known ever since the time of Œrsted and Ampère. This, with such considerations as I have endeavoured to advance, enables us to form a guess or judgement, with a certain degree of probability, respecting the nature of the lines of magnetic force. I incline to the opinion that they have a physical existence correspondent to that of their analogue,

the electric lines; and having that notion, am further carried on
to consider whether they have a probable dynamic condition, analogous to that of the electric axis to which they are so closely
and, perhaps, inevitably related, in which case the idea of magnetic currents would arise; or whether they consist in a state of
tension (of the æther?) round the electric axis, and may therefore
be considered as static in their nature. Again and again the idea
of an *electro-tonic* state . . . has been forced on my mind; such
a state would coincide and become identified with that which would
then constitute the physical lines of magnetic force. Another
consideration tends in the same direction. I formerly remarked
that the magnetic equivalent to *static* electricity was not known;
for if the undeveloped state of electric force correspond to the
like undeveloped condition of magnetic force, and if the electric
current or axis of electric power correspond to the lines of magnetic force or axis of magnetic power, then there is no known
magnetic condition which corresponds to the static state of the
electric power. . . . Now assuming that the physical lines of
magnetic force are currents, it is very unlikely that such a link
should be naturally absent; more unlikely, I think, than that the
magnetic condition should depend upon a state of tension; the
more especially as under the latter supposition, the lines of
magnetic power would have a physical existence as positively as
in the former case, and the curved condition of the lines, which
seems to me such a necessary admission, according to the natural
facts, would become a possibility.

3270. The considerations which arise during the contemplation of the phænomena and laws that are made manifest in the
mutual action of magnets, currents of electricity, and *moving
conductors* . . . , are, I think, altogether in favour of the
physical existence of the lines of magnetic force. When only a
single magnet is employed in such cases, and the use of iron or
paramagnetic bodies is dismissed, then there is no effect of attraction or repulsion or any ordinary magnetic result produced.
The phænomena may all very fairly be looked upon as purely electrical, for they are such in character; and if they coincide with
magnetic actions (which is no doubt the case), it is probably because the two actions are one. But being considered as electrical actions, they convey a different idea of the condition of the
field where they occur, to that involved in the thought of magnetic action at a distance. When a copper wire is placed in the
neighbourhood of a bar-magnet, it does not, as far as we are
aware (by the evidence of a magnetic needle or other means), disturb in the least degree the disposition of the magnetic forces,
either in itself or in surrounding space. When it is moved across
the lines of force, a current of electricity is developed in it,
or tends to be developed; and I have every reason to believe,
that if we could employ a perfect conductor, and obtain a perfect
result, it would be the full equivalent to the force, electric or
magnetic, which is exerted in the place occupied by the conductor.
But, as I have elsewhere observed . . . , this current, having
its full and equivalent relation to the magnetic force, can hardly
be conceived of as having its entire foundation in the mere fact
of motion. The motion of an external body, otherwise physically

indifferent, and having no relation to the magnet, could not be-
get a physical relation such as that which the moving wire presents. There must, I think, be a previous state, a state of
tension or a static state, as regards the wire, which, when motion
is superadded, produces the dynamic state or current of electricity. This state is sufficient to constitute and give a physical
existence to the lines of magnetic force, and permit the occurrence of curvature or its equivalent external relation of poles,
and also the various other conditions, which I conceive are incompatible with mere action at a distance, and which yet do exist
amongst magnetic phænomena.

3271. All the phænomena of the moving wire seem to me to
show the physical existence of an atmosphere of power about a
magnet, which, as the power is antithetical, and marked in its
direction by the lines of magnetic force, may be considered as
disposed in sphondyloids, determined by the lines or rather shells
of force. As the wire intersects the lines within a given sphondyloid external to the magnet, a current of electricity is generated, and that current is definite and the same for any or every
intersection of the given sphondyloid. . . .

* * *

3276. The magnet, with its surrounding sphondyloid of power,
may be considered as analogous in its condition to a voltaic battery immersed in water or any other electrolyte; or to a gymnotus
. . . or torpedo, at the moment when these creatures, at their
own will, fill the surrounding fluid with lines of electric force.
I think the analogy with the voltaic battery so placed, is closer
than with any case of *static* electric induction, because in the
former instance the physical lines of electric force may be traced
both through the battery and its surrounding medium, for they form
continuous curves like those I have imagined within and without
the magnet. The direction of these lines of electric force may
be traced, experimentally, many ways. A magnetic needle freely
suspended in the fluid will show them in and near to the battery,
by standing at right angles to the course of the lines. Two
wires from a galvanometer will show them; for if the line joining
the two ends in the fluid be at right angles to the lines of electric force (or the currents), there will be no action at the
galvanometer; but if oblique or parallel to these lines, there
will be deflection. A plate, or wire, or ball of metal in the
fluid will show the direction, provided any electrolytic action
can go on against it, as when a little acetate of lead is present
in the medium, for then the electrolysis will be a maximum in the
direction of the current or line of force, and nothing at all in
the direction at right angles to it. The same ball will disturb
and inflect the lines of electric force in the surrounding fluid,
just as I have considered the case to be with paramagnetic bodies
amongst magnetic lines of force. . . . No one I think will doubt
that as long as the battery is in the fluid, and has its extremities in communication by the fluid, lines of electric force having
a physical existence occur in every part of it, and the fluid
surrounding it.

3277. I conceive that when a magnet is in free space, there
is such a medium (magnetically speaking) around it. That a vacuum

has its own magnetic relations of attraction and repulsion is
manifest from former experimental results . . . ; and these place
the vacuum in relation to material bodies, not at either extremity
of the list, but in the *midst* of them, as, for instance, between
gold and platina . . . , having other bodies on either side of
it. What that surrounding magnetic medium, deprived of all material substance, may be, I cannot tell, perhaps the æther. I incline to consider this outer medium as *essential* to the magnet;
that it is that which relates the external polarities to each
other by curves lines of power; and that these must be so related
as a matter of necessity. Just as in the case of the battery
above, there is no line of force, either in or out of the battery,
if this relation be cut off by removing or intercepting the conducting medium;--or in that of static electric induction, which
is impossible until this related state be allowed . . . ;--so I
conceive, that without this external mutually related condition
of the poles, or a related condition of them to other poles. sustained and rendered possible in like manner, a magnet could not
exist; an absolute northness or southness, or an unrelated northness or southness, being as impossible as an absolute or an unrelated state of positive or negative electricity. . . .

3278. In this view of a magnet, the medium or space around
it is as essential as the magnet itself, being a part of the true
and complete magnetic system. There are numerous experimental
results which show us that the relation of the lines to the surrounding space can be varied by occupying it with different substances; just as the relation of a ray of light to the space
through which it passes can be varied by the presence of different bodies made to occupy that space, or as the lines of electric
force are affected by the media through which either induction or
conduction takes place. This variation in regard to the magnetic
power may be considered as depending upon the aptitude which the
surrounding space has to effect the mutual relation of the two
external polarities, or to carry onwards the physical line of
force; and I have on a former occasion in some degree considered
it and its consequences, using the phrase *magnetic conduction* to
represent the physical effect . . . produced by the presence
either of paramagnetic or diamagnetic bodies.

*　　*　　*

3298. Perhaps both magnetic attraction and repulsion, in
all forms and cases, resolve themselves into the differential action . . . of the magnets and substances which occupy space, and
modify its magnetic power. A magnet first originates lines of
magnetic force; and then, if present with another magnet, offers
in one position a very free conduction of the new lines, like a
paramagnetic body; or if restrained in the contrary position,
resists their passage, and resembles a highly diamagnetic substance. So, then, a source of magnetic lines being present, and
also magnets or other bodies affecting and varying the conducting
power of space, those bodies which can convey onwards the most
force, may tend, by differential actions, with the others present,
to take up the position in which they can do so the most freely,
whether it is by pointing or by approximation; the best conductor

passing to the place of strongest action . . . , whilst the worst retreats from it, and so the effects both of attraction and repulsion be produced. The tendency of the lines of magnetic force to shorten . . . would be consistent with such a notion. The result would occur whether the physical lines of force were supposed to consist in a dynamic or a static state. . . .

3299. Having applied the term *line of magnetic force* to an abstract idea, which I believe represents accurately the nature, condition, direction, and comparative amount of the magnetic forces, without reference to any physical condition of the force, I have now applied the term *physical line of force* to include the further idea of their physical nature. The first set of lines I *affirm* upon the evidence of strict experiment. . . . The second set of lines I advocate, chiefly with a view of stating the question of their existence; and though I should not have raised the argument unless I had thought it both important, and likely to be answered ultimately in the affirmative, I still hold the opinion with some hesitation, with as much, indeed, as accompanies any conclusion I endeavour to draw respecting points in the very depths of science, as for instance, regarding one, two or no electric fluids; or the real nature of a ray of light, or the nature of attraction, even that of gravity itself, or the general nature of matter.

Royal Institution, March 6, 1852.

B.   James Clerk Maxwell and Field Theory

The man who really interpreted Faraday to the scientific community was James Clerk Maxwell. His great treatise on electricity and magnetism was an elaboration and mathematization of Faraday's ideas (as well as many of his own) which laid the firm foundations for field theory. In a lecture at the Royal Institution of Great Britain,* Maxwell explained the new theory to a lay audience in 1873.

LIV.   *On Action at a Distance.*

I have no new discovery to bring before you this evening. I must ask you to go over very old ground, and to turn your attention to a question which has been raised again and again ever since men began to think.

The question is that of the transmission of force. We see that two bodies at a distance from each other exert a mutual influence on each other's motion. Does this mutual action depend on the existence of such third thing, some medium of communication, occupying the space between the bodies, or do the bodies act on each other immediately, without the intervention of anything else?

---

*James Clerk Maxwell, "On Action at a Distance," in *Proc. Roy. Inst.*, vol. 7 (1873-75), pp. 44-47, 50-53.

The mode in which Faraday was accustomed to look at phenomena of this kind differs from that adopted by many other modern inquirers, and my special aim will be to enable you to place yourselves at Faraday's point of view, and to point out the scientific value of that conception of *lines of force* which, in his hands, became the key to the science of electricity.

When we observe one body acting on another at a distance, before we assume that this action is direct and immediate, we generally inquire whether there is any material connection between the two bodies; and if we find strings, or rods, or mechanism of any kind, capable of accounting for the observed action between the bodies, we prefer to explain the action by means of these intermediate connections, rather than to admit the notion of direct action at a distance.

Thus, when we ring a bell by means of a wire, the successive parts of the wire are first tightened and then moved, till at last the bell is rung at a distance by a process in which all the intermediate particles of the wire have taken part one after the other. We may ring a bell at a distance in other ways, as by forcing air into a long tube, at the other end of which is a cylinder with a piston which is made to fly out and strike the bell. We may also use a wire; but instead of pulling it, we may connect it at one end with a voltaic battery, and at the other with an electro-magnet, and thus ring the bell by electricity.

Here are three different ways of ringing a bell. They all agree, however, in the circumstance that between the ringer and the bell there is an unbroken line of communication, and that at every point of this line some physical process goes on by which the action is transmitted from one end to the other. The process of transmission is not instantaneous, but gradual; so that there is an interval of time after the impulse has been given to one extremity of the line of communication, during which the impulse is on its way, but has not reached the other end.

It is clear, therefore, that in many cases the action between bodies at a distance may be accounted for by a series of actions between each successive pair of a series of bodies which occupy the intermediate space; and it is asked, by the advocates of mediate action, whether, in those cases in which we cannot perceive the intermediate agency, it is not more philosophical to admit the existence of a medium which we cannot at present perceive, than to assert that a body can act at a place where it is not.

To a person ignorant of the properties of air, the transmission of force by means of that invisible medium would appear as unaccountable as any other example of action at a distance, and yet in this case we can explain the whole process, and determine the rate at which the action is passed on from one portion to another of the medium.

Why then should we not admit that the familiar mode of communicating motion by pushing and pulling with our hands is the type and exemplification of all action between bodies, even in cases in which we can observe nothing between the bodies which appears to take part in the action?

Here for instance is a kind of attraction with which Professor Guthrie has made us familiar. A disk is set in vibration, and is then brought near a light suspended body, which immediately begins to move towards the disk, as if drawn towards it by an invisible cord. What is this cord? Sir W. Thomson has pointed out that in a moving fluid the pressure is least where the velocity is greatest. The velocity of the vibratory motion of the air is greatest nearest the disk. Hence the pressure of the air on the suspended body is less on the side nearest the disk than on the opposite side, the body yields to the greater pressure, and moves toward the disk.

The disk, therefore, does not act where it is not. It sets the air next it in motion by pushing it, this motion is communicated to more and more distant portions of the air in turn, and thus the pressures on opposite sides of the suspended body are rendered unequal, and it moves towards the disk in consequence of the excess of pressure. The force is therefore a force of the old school--a case of *vis a tergo*--a shove from behind.

The advocates of the doctrine of action at a distance, however, have not been put to silence by such arguments. What right, say they, have we to assert that a body cannot act where it is not? Do we not see an instance of action at a distance in the case of a magnet, which acts on another magnet not only at a distance, but with the most complete indifference to the nature of the matter which occupies the intervening space? If the action depends on something occupying the space between the two magnets, it cannot surely be a matter of indifference whether this space is filled with air or not, or whether wood, glass, or copper, be placed between the magnets.

Besides this, Newton's law of gravitation, which every astronomical observation only tends to establish more firmly, asserts not only that the heavenly bodies act on one another across immense intervals of space, but that two portions of matter, the one buried a thousand miles deep in the interior of the earth, and the other a hundred thousand miles deep in the body of the sun, act on one another with precisely the same force as if the strata beneath which each is buried had been non-existent. If any medium takes part in transmitting this action, it must surely make some difference whether the space between the bodies contains nothing but this medium, or whether it is occupied by the dense matter of the earth or of the sun.

But the advocates of direct action at a distance are not content with instances of this kind, in which the phenomena, even at first sight, appear to favour their doctrine. They push their operations into the enemy's camp, and maintain that even when the action is apparently the pressure of contiguous portions of matter, the contiguity is only apparent--that a space *always* intervenes between the bodies which act on each other. They assert, in short, that so far from action at a distance being impossible, it is the only kind of action which ever occurs, and that the favourite old *vis a tergo* of the schools has no existence in nature, and exists only in the imagination of schoolmen.

The best way to prove that when one body pushes another it does not touch it, is to measure the distance between them. Here are two glass lenses, one of which is pressed against the other by means of a weight. By means of the electric light we may obtain on the screen an image of the place where the one lens presses against the other. A series of coloured rings is formed on the screen. These rings were first observed and first explained by Newton. The particular colour of any ring depends on the distance between the surfaces of the pieces of glass. Newton formed a table of the colours corresponding to different distances, so that by comparing the colour of any ring with Newton's table, we may ascertain the distance between the surfaces at that ring. The colours are arranged in rings because the surfaces are spherical, and therefore the interval between the surfaces depends on the distance from the line joining the centres of the spheres. The central spot of the rings indicates the place where the lenses are nearest together, and each successive ring corresponds to an increase of about the 4000th part of a millimètre in the distance of the surfaces.

The lenses are now pressed together with a force equal to the weight of an ounce; but there is still a measurable interval between them, even at the place where they are nearest together. They are not in optical contact. To prove this, I apply a greater weight. A new colour appears at the central spot, and the diameters of all the rings increase. This shews that the surfaces are now nearer than at first, but they are not yet in optical contact, for if they were, the central spot would be black. I therefore increase the weights, so as to press the lenses into optical contact.

But what we call optical contact is not real contact. Optical contact indicates only that the distance between the surfaces is much less than a wavelength of light. To shew that the surfaces are not in real contact, I remove the weights. The rings contract, and several of them vanish at the centre. Now it is possible to bring two pieces of glass so close together, that they will not tend to separate at all, but adhere together so firmly, that when torn asunder the glass will break, not at the surface of contact, but at some other place. The glasses must then be many degrees nearer than when in mere optical contact.

Thus we have shewn that bodies begin to press against each other whilst still at a measurable distance, and that even when pressed together with great force they are not in absolute contact, but may be brought nearer still, and that by many degrees.

Why, then, say the advocates of direct action, should we continue to maintain the doctrine, founded only on the rough experience of a pre-scientific age, that matter cannot act where it is not, instead of admitting that all the facts from which our ancestors concluded that contact is essential to action were in reality cases of action at a distance, the distance being too small to be measured by their imperfect means of observation?

If we are ever to discover the laws of nature, we must do so by obtaining the most accurate acquaintance with the facts of nature, and not by dressing up in philosophical language the loose opinions of men who had no knowledge of the facts which throw most light on these laws. And as for those who introduce ætherial, or other media, to account for these actions, without any direct evidence of the existence of such media, or any clear understanding of how the media do their work, and who fill all space three and four times over with æthers of different sorts, why the less these men talk about their philosophical scruples about admitting action at a distance the better.

*　　*　　*

No man ever more conscientiously and systematically laboured to improve all his powers of mind than did Faraday from the very beginning of his scientific career. But whereas the general course of scientific method then consisted in the application of the ideas of mathematics and astronomy to each new investigation in turn, Faraday seems to have had no opportunity to acquiring a technical knowledge of mathematics, and his knowledge of astronomy was mainly derived from books.

Hence, though he had a profound respect for the great discovery of Newton, he regarded the attraction of gravitation as a sort of sacred mystery, which, as he was not an astronomer, he had no right to gainsay or to doubt, his duty being to believe it in the exact form in which it was delivered to him. Such a dead faith was not likely to lead him to explain new phenomena by means of direct attractions.

Besides this, the treatises of Poisson and Ampère are of so technical a form, that to derive any assistance from them the student must have been thoroughly trained in mathematics, and it is very doubtful if such a training can be begun with advantage in mature years.

Thus Faraday, with his penetrating intellect, his devotion to science, and his opportunities for experiments, was debarred from following the course of thought which had led to the achievements of the French philosophers, and was obliged to explain the phenomena to himself by means of a symbolism which he could understand, instead of adopting what had hitherto been the only tongue of the learned.

This new symbolism consisted of those lines of force extending themselves in every direction from electrified and magnetic bodies, which Faraday in his mind's eye saw as distinctly as the solid bodies from which they emanated.

The idea of lines of force and their exhibition by means of iron filings was nothing new. They had been observed repeatedly, and investigated mathematically as an interesting curiosity of science. But let us hear Faraday as himself, as he introduces to his reader the method which in his hands became so powerful. "It would be a voluntary and unnecessary abandonment of most valuable aid if an experimentalist, who chooses to consider magnetic power as represented by lines of magnetic force, were to deny himself the use of iron filings. By their employment he may make many conditions of the power, even in complicated cases, visible to the eye at once, may trace the varying direction of the lines of force and determine the relative polarity, may observe in which direction the power is increasing or diminishing, and in complex systems may determine the neutral points, or places where there is neither polarity nor power, even when they occur in the midst of powerful magnets. By their use probable results may be seen at once, and many a valuable suggestion gained for future leading experiments."

Experiment on Lines of Force.

In this experiment each filing becomes a little magnet. The poles of opposite names belonging to different filings attract each other and stick together, and more filings attach themselves to the exposed poles, that is, to the ends of the row of filings. In this way the filings, instead of forming a confused system of dots over the paper, draw together, filing to filing, till long fibres of filings are formed, which indicate by their direction the lines of force in every part of the field.

The mathematicians saw in this experiment nothing but a method of exhibiting at one view the direction in different places of the resultant of two forces, one directed to each pole of the magnet; a somewhat complicated result of the simple law of force.

But Faraday, by a series of steps as remarkable for their geometrical definiteness as for their speculative ingenuity, imparted to his conception of these lines of force a clearness and precision far in advance of that with which the mathematicians could then invest their own formulæ.

In the first place, Faraday's lines of force are not to be considered merely as individuals, but as forming a system, drawn in space in a definite manner so that the number of the lines which pass through an area, say of one square inch, indicates the intensity of the force acting through the area. Thus the lines of force become definite in number. The strength of a magnetic pole is measured by the number of lines which proceed from it; the electro-tonic state of a circuit is measured by the number of lines which pass through it.

In the second place, each individual line has a continuous existence in space and time. When a piece of steel becomes a magnet, or when an electric current begins to flow, the lines of force do not start into existence each in its own place, but as the strength increases new lines are developed within the magnet or current, and gradually grow outwards, so that the whole system expands from within, like Newton's rings in our former experiment. Thus every line of force preserves its identity during the whole course of its existence, though its shape and size may be altered to any extent.

I have no time to describe the methods by which every question relating to the forces acting on magnets or on currents, or to the induction of currents in conducting circuits, may be solved by the consideration of Faraday's lines of force. In this place they can never be forgotten. By means of this new symbolism, Faraday defined with mathematical precision the whole theory of electro-magnetism, in language free from mathematical technicalities, and applicable to the most complicated as well as the simplest cases. But Faraday did not stop here. He went on from the conception of geometrical lines of force to that of physical lines of force. He observed that the motion which the magnetic or electric force tends to produce is invariably such as to shorten the lines of force and to allow them to spread out laterally from each other. He thus perceived in the medium a state of stress, consisting of a tension, like that of a rope, in the direction of the lines of force, combined with a pressure in all directions at right angles to them.

This is quite a new conception of action at a distance, reducing it to a phenomenon of the same kind as that action at a distance which is exerted by means of the tension of ropes and the pressure of rods. When the muscles of our bodies are excited by that stimulus which we are able in some unknown way to apply to them, the fibres tend to shorten themselves and at the same time to expand laterally. A state of stress is produced in the muscle, and the limb moves. This explanation of muscular action is by no means complete. It gives no account of the cause of the excitement of the state of stress, nor does it even investigate those forces of cohesion which enable the muscles to support this stress. Nevertheless, the simple fact, that it substitutes a kind of action which extends continuously along a material distance from each other, induces us to accept it as a real addition to our knowledge of animal mechanics.

For similar reasons we may regard Faraday's conception of a state of stress in the electro-magnetic field as a method of explaining action at a distance by means of the continuous transmission of force, even though we do not know how the state of stress is produced.

But one of Faraday's most pregnant discoveries, that of the magnetic rotation of polarised light, enables us to proceed a step farther. The phenomenon, when analysed into its simplest elements, may be described thus:--Of two circularly polarised rays of light, precisely similar in configuration, but rotating in opposite directions, that ray is propagated with the greater velocity which rotates in the same direction as the electricity of the magnetizing current.

It follows from this, as Sir W. Thomson has shewn by strict dynamical reasoning, that the medium when under the action of magnetic force must be in a state of rotation--that is to say, that small portions of the medium, which we may call molecular vortices, are rotating, each on its own axis, the direction of this axis being that of the magnetic force.

Here, then, we have an explanation of the tendency of the lines of magnetic force to spread out laterally and to shorten themselves. It arises from the centrifugal force of the molecular vortices.

The mode in which electromotive force acts in starting and stopping the vortices is more abstruse, though it is of course consistent with dynamical principles.

We have thus found that there are several different kinds of work to be done by the electro-magnetic medium if it exists. We have also seen that magnetism has an intimate relation to light, and we know that there is a theory of light which supposes it to consist of the vibrations of a medium. How is this luminiferous medium related to our electro-magnetic medium?

It fortunately happens that electro-magnetic measurements have been made from which we can calculate by dynamical principles the velocity of propagation of small magnetic disturbances in the supposed electro-magnetic medium.

This velocity is very great, from 288 to 314 millions of

metres per second, according to different experiments. Now the
velocity of light, according to Foucault's experiments, is 298
millions of metres per second. In fact, the different determinations of either velocity differ from each other more than the
estimated velocity of light does from the estimated velocity of
propagation of small electro-magnetic disturbance. But if the
luminiferous and the electro-magnetic media occupy the same place,
and transmit disturbances with the same velocity, what reason
have we to distinguish the one from the other? By considering
them as the same, we avoid at least the reproach of filling space
twice over with different kinds of æther.

Besides this, the only kind of electro-magnetic disturbances
which can be propagated through a non-conducting medium is a disturbance transverse to the direction of propagation, agreeing in
this respect with what we know of that disturbance which we call
light. Hence, for all we know, light also may be an electro-
magnetic disturbance in a non-conducting medium. If we admit
this, the electro-magnetic theory of light will agree in every
respect with the undulatory theory, and the work of Thomas Young
and Fresnel will be established on a firmer basis than ever, when
joined with that of Cavendish and Coulomb by the key-stone of the
combined sciences of light and electricity--Faraday's great discovery of the electro-magnetic rotation of light.

The vast interplanetary and interstellar regions will no
longer be regarded as waste places in the universe, which the
Creator has not seen fit to fill with the symbols of the manifold
order of His kingdom. We shall find them to be already full of
this wonderful medium; so full, that no human power can remove it
from the smallest portion of space, or produce the slightest flaw
in its infinite continuity. It extends unbroken from star to
star; and when a molecule of hydrogen vibrates in the dog-star,
the medium receives the impulses of these vibrations; and after
carrying them in its immense bosom for three years, delivers them
in due course, regular order, and full tale into the spectroscope
of Mr Huggins, at Tulse Hill.

But the medium has other functions and operations besides
bearing light from man to man, and from world to world, and giving evidence of the absolute unity of the metric system of the
universe. Its minute parts may have rotatory as well as vibratory motions, and the axes of rotation form those lines of magnetic force which extend in unbroken continuity into regions which
no eye has seen, and which, by their action on our magnets, are
telling us in language not yet interpreted, what is going on in
the hidden underworld from minute to minute and from century to
century.

And these lines must not be regarded as mere mathematical
abstractions. They are the directions in which the medium is exerting a tension like that of a rope, or rather, like that of our
own muscles. The tension of the medium in the direction of the
earth's magnetic force is in this country one grain weight on
eight square feet. In some of Dr Joule's experiments, the medium
has exerted a tension of 200 lbs. weight per square inch.

But the medium, in virtue of the very same elasticity by
which it is able to transmit the undulations of light, is also

able to act as a spring. When properly wound up, it exerts a
tension, different from the magnetic tension, by which it draws
oppositely electrified bodies together, produces effects through
the length of telegraph wires, and when of sufficient intensity,
leads to the rupture and explosion called lightning.

These are some of the already discovered properties of that
which has often been called vacuum, or nothing at all. They enable us to resolve several kinds of action at a distance into actions between contiguous parts of a continuous substance. Whether
this resolution is of the nature of explication or complication,
I must leave to the metaphysicians.

VII.   The Fate of Energy--Kinetic Theory Readings

A.   James Clerk Maxwell

*James Clerk Maxwell was one of the major architects of
kinetic theory, as well as of field theory. In 1859, Maxwell
read a paper* on the dynamical theory of gases to the British
Association for the Advancement of Science at Aberdeen in which
he laid out certain of the fundamental concepts of the new view
of molecular processes.*

PART I.

On the Motions and Collisions of Perfectly Elastic Spheres.

So many of the properties of matter, especially when in the
gaseous form, can be deduced from the hypothesis that their minute
parts are in rapid motion, the velocity increasing with the temperature, that the precise nature of this motion becomes a subject of rational curiosity. Daniel Bernouilli, Herapath, Joule,
Krönig, Clausius, &c. have shewn that the relations between pressure, temperature, and density in a perfect gas can be explained
by supposing the particles to move with uniform velocity in
straight lines, striking against the sides of the containing vessel and thus producing pressure. It is not necessary to suppose
each particle to travel to any great distance in the same straight
line; for the effect in producing pressure will be the same if
the particles strike against each other; so that the straight
line described may be very short. M. Clausius has determined the
mean length of path in terms of the average distance of the particles, and the distance between the centres of two particles
when collision takes place. We have at present no means of ascertaining either of these distances; but certain phenomena, such as
the internal friction of gases, the conduction of heat through a
gas, and the diffusion of one gas through another, seem to indi-

---

*James Clerk Maxwell, "Illustrations of the Dynamical Theory of
Gases," in *The Scientific Papers of James Clerk Maxwell*, 2 vols.
(Cambridge, 1890), pp. 377-82.

cate the possibility of determining accurately the mean length of path which a particle describes between two successive collisions. In order to lay the foundation of such investigations on strict mechanical principles, I shall demonstrate the laws of motion of an indefinite number of small, hard, and perfectly elastic spheres acting on one another only during impact.

If the properties of such a system of bodies are found to correspond to those of gases, an important physical analogy will be established, which may lead to more accurate knowledge of the properties of matter. If experiments on gases are inconsistent with the hypothesis of these propositions, then our theory, though consistent with itself, is proved to be incapable of explaining the phenomena of gases. In either case it is necessary to follow out the consequences of the hypothesis.

Instead of saying that the particles are hard, spherical, and elastic, we may if we please say that the particles are centres of force, of which the action is insensible except at a certain small distance, when it suddenly appears as a repulsive force of very great intensity. It is evident that either assumption will lead to the same results. For the sake of avoiding the repetition of a long phrase about these repulsive forces, I shall proceed upon the assumption of perfectly elastic spherical bodies. If we suppose those aggregate molecules which move together to have a bounding surface which is not spherical, then the rotatory motion of the system will store up a certain proportion of the whole *vis viva*, as has been shewn by Clausius, and in this way we may account for the value of the specific heat being greater than on the more simple hypothesis.

On the Motion and Collision of Perfectly Elastic Spheres.

Prop. I. Two spheres moving in opposite directions with velocities inversely as their masses strike one another; to determine their motions after impact.

Let P and Q be the position of the centres at impact; AP, BQ the directions and magnitudes of the velocities before impact; Pa, Qb the same after impact; then, resolving the velocities parallel and perpendicular to PQ the line of centres, we find that the velocities parallel to the line of centres are exactly reversed, while those perpendicular to that line are unchanged. Compounding these velocities again, we find that the velocity of each ball is the same before and after impact, and that the directions before and after impact lie in the same plane with the line of centres, and make equal angles with it.

Prop. II. To find the probability of the direction of the velocity after impact lying between given limits.

In order that a collision may take place, the line of motion of one of the balls must pass the centre of the other at a distance less than the sum of their radii; that is, it must pass through a circle whose centre is that of the other ball, and radius (s) the sum of the radii of the balls. Within this circle every position is equally probable, and therefore the probability of the distance from the centre being between r and $r + dr$ is

$$\frac{2r\,dr}{s^2}.$$

Now let ϕ be the angle APa between the original direction and the direction after impact, then $APN = \frac{1}{2}\phi$, and $r = s \sin \frac{1}{2}\phi$, and the probability becomes

$$\frac{1}{2} \sin \phi\,d\phi.$$

The area of a spherical zone between the angles of polar distance ϕ and $\phi + d\phi$ is

$$2\pi \sin \phi\,d\phi;$$

therefore if ω be any small area on the surface of a sphere, radius unity, the probability of the direction of rebound passing through this area is

$$\frac{\omega}{4\pi};$$

so that the probability is independent of ϕ, that is, all directions of rebound are equally likely.

Prop. III. Given the direction and magnitude of the velocities of two spheres before impact, and the line of centres at impact; to find the velocities after impact.

Let OA, OB represent the velocities before impact, so that if there had been no action between the bodies they would have been at A and B at the end of a second. Join AB, and let G be their centre of gravity, the position of which is not affected by their mutual action. Draw GN parallel to the line of centres at impact (not necessarily in the plane AOB). Draw aGb in the plane AGN, making $NGa = NGA$, and $Ga = GA$ and $Gb = GB$; then by Prop. I. Ga and Gb will be the velocities relative to G; and compounding these with OG, we have Oa and Ob for the true velocities after impact.

By Prop. II. all directions of the line aGb are equally probable. It appears therefore that the velocity after impact is compounded of the velocity of the centre of gravity, and of a velocity equal to the velocity of the sphere relative to the centre of gravity, which may with equal probability be in any direction whatever.

If a great many equal spherical particles were in motion in a perfectly elastic vessel, collisions would take place among the particles, and their velocities would be altered at every collision; so that after a certain time the *vis viva* will be divided among the particles according to some regular law, the average number of particles whose velocity lies between certain limits being ascertainable, though the velocity of each particle changes at every collision.

Prop. IV. To find the average number of particles whose velocities lie between given limits, after a great number of collisions among a great number of equal particles.

Let N be the whole number of particles. Let x, y, z be the components of the velocity of each particle in three rectangular directions, and let the number of particles for which x lies between x and $x + dx$, be $Nf(x)dx$, where $f(x)$ is a function of x to be determined.

The number of particles for which y lies between y and $y + dy$ will be $Nf(y)dy$; and the number for which z lies between z and $z + dz$ will be $Nf(z)dz$, where f always stands for the same function.

Now the existence of the velocity x does not in any way affect that of the velocities y or z, since these are all at right angles to each other and independent, so that the number of particles whose velocity lies between x and $x + dx$, and also between y and $y + dy$, and also between z and $z + dz$, is

$$Nf(x)f(y)f(z)\,dx\,dy\,dz.$$

If we suppose the N particles to start from the origin at the same instant, then this will be the number in the element of volume $(dx\,dy\,dz)$ after unit of time, and the number referred to unit of volume will be

$$Nf(x)f(y)f(z).$$

But the directions of the coordinates are perfectly arbitrary, and therefore this number must depend on the distance from the origin alone, that is

$$f(x)f(y)f(z) = \phi(x^2 + y^2 + z^2).$$

Solving this functional equation, we find

$$f(x) = Ce^{Ax^2}, \qquad \phi(r^2) = C\,e^{Ar^2}.$$

If we make A positive, the number of particles will increase with the velocity, and we should find the whole number of particles infinite. We therefore make A negative and equal to $-\dfrac{1}{a^2}$, so that the number between x and $x + dx$ is

$$NCe^{-\frac{x^2}{a^2}}dx.$$

Integrating from $x = -\infty$ to $x = +\infty$, we find the whole number of particles,

$$NC\sqrt{\pi}a = N, \quad \therefore\ C = \frac{1}{a\sqrt{\pi}},$$

$f(x)$ is therefore

$$\frac{1}{a\sqrt{\pi}}\,e^{-\frac{x^2}{a^2}}.$$

Whence we may draw the following conclusions:--

1st. The number of particles whose velocity, resolved in a certain direction, lies between x and $x + dx$ is

$$N\,\frac{1}{a\sqrt{\pi}}\,e^{-\frac{x^2}{a^2}}dx\dots\dots\dots\dots\dots\dots\ (1).$$

2nd. The number whose actual velocity lies between v and $v + dv$ is

$$N \ \frac{4}{a^3 \sqrt{\pi}} \ v^2 e^{-\frac{v^2}{a^2}} dv \dots\dots\dots\dots\dots\dots (2).$$

3rd. To find the mean value of v, add the velocities of all the particles together and divide by the number of particles; the result is

$$\text{mean velocity} = \frac{2a}{\sqrt{\pi}} \ \dots\dots\dots\dots\dots\dots (3).$$

4th. To find the mean value of v^2, add all the values together and divide by N,

$$\text{mean value of } v^2 = \tfrac{3}{2} a^2 \dots\dots\dots\dots\dots\dots (4).$$

This is greater than the square of the mean velocity, as it ought to be.

It appears from this proposition that the velocities are distributed among the particles according to the same law as the errors are distributed among the observations in the theory of the "method of least squares." The velocities range from 0 to ∞, but the number of those having great velocities is comparatively small. In addition to these velocities, which are in all directions equally, there may be a general motion of translation of the entire system of particles which must be compounded with the motion of the particles relatively to one another. We may call the one the motion of translation, and the other the motion of agitation.

B.   Rudolf Clausius

*One of the most fertile dialogues in the history of science is the one that took place between Maxwell and Rudolf Clausius. After Maxwell had published his paper on the dynamic theory of gases, Clausius took up the problem and clarified a number of the obscure portions of Maxwell's treatment.**

I.   *Definition of the case to be considered.*

§ 1.   We will suppose a quantity of gas between two parallel plane surfaces of infinite size, each of which is maintained at a constant temperature. If the temperature of one surface is higher than that of the other, a transference of heat from one surface to the other will take place, through the medium of the gas, by the continual passage of heat from the warmer surface into the

*R. Clausius, "On the Conduction of Heat by Gases," *Phil. Mag.*, 4th Ser., vol. 23 (1862), pp. 420-25, 429-31; "On the Second Fundamental Theorem of the Mechanical Theory of Heat," *Phil. Mag.*, 4th Ser., vol. 35 (1868), pp. 405-8, 415-19.

gas, its advance from one layer to the next within the gas itself, and its being at last given up by the gas to the colder surface. As it is our object to consider here only that movement of heat which is caused by conduction, and not that which might be occasioned by currents of gas produced by the warmer portions being specifically lighter than the colder, we will suppose the action of gravity entirely excluded: this is approximately the case when the two surfaces are horizontal and the hotter is above, for then no currents can arise.

If both surfaces are kept for a considerable time at constant temperatures, a state of equilibrium is at length established in the gas, of such a kind that the temperature remains invariable at each point within it, but is different at different points--the heat being so distributed that, in any plane parallel to the two limiting surfaces, the temperature is the same at every point, but that it continually decreases according to a definite law in the direction from the warmer to the colder surface. A definite and constant flow of heat through the gas then takes place.

It is this stationary condition of the gas that we have to consider, and to endeavour to determine the amount of the flow of heat which goes on owing to the conductive properties of the gas.

§ 2. We will suppose a straight line drawn between the two surfaces and perpendicular to them, and we will assume this as the axis of abscissæ: the temperature within the gas is then a function of the abscissa x; and if, in order to be able at once to form a definite conception, we assume that the first surface, where the abscissa has its smallest value, is the warmest, the temperature diminishes within the gas as the value of x increases. With the density of the gas the case is reversed, for in a state of equilibrium the density of the gas must be higher in proportion as the temperature of the gas is lower; it is therefore a function of x whose value increases with that of x.

We will assume at starting that the gaseous molecules fly about irregularly in all directions, and accordingly strike and rebound from each other, now in one place, now in another, and also that the velocity of their motion is greater the higher the temperature. Let us now suppose a plane cutting the space filled with gas, and parallel to the surfaces by which this space is bounded; then during a unit of time a great number of molecules will pass from the negative to the positive side of this plane, and *vice versâ*. The molecules which pass from the negative to the positive side have a greater average velocity than those which pass from the positive to the negative side, since, according to our assumption, the temperature is higher, and therefore the moving velocity of the molecules greater, on the negative side of the plane than on the positive side. The total *vis viva* which traverses the plane in a unit of time in the positive direction is therefore greater than that which traverses it in the negative direction; and if we strike out, as compensating each other, equal quantities which traverse it in opposite directions, we still obtain a certain excess of *vis viva* traversing the plane in the positive direction. *Vis viva* and heat being regarded as synonymous, the amount of *vis viva* thus passing through the plane constitutes the heat-stream mentioned in the last section, which we call conduction of heat, and which we have to consider in the sequel*.

II. *Behaviour of the molecules emitted from an infinitely thin stratum.*

§ 3. We will begin by considering somewhat more closely the nature of the motions of the individual molecules.

We will suppose two parallel planes to be placed perpendicularly to the axis of x and infinitely near to each other, so as to enclose an infinitely thin stratum. Since molecules are continually flying through this stratum in all directions, it must sometimes happen that two molecules strike each other within it and then rebound again. For the sake of shortness we will call these molecules, which, after having lost their previous motions by the impact, leave the stratum again with different motions, the *molecules emitted from the stratum*; and we will now fix our attention upon their motions.

These motions differ very much from each other; and we must distinguish between variations of two kinds, occasioned by two mutually independent causes, and therefore susceptible of being separately considered. The one kind consists of those irregular variations which always prevail in the molecular motions called heat, and which would therefore also occur if the gas were of uniform temperature and density throughout. They arise from various accidental inequalities accompanying the individual impacts: we will designate them *accidental* variations. The other kind of variations is caused by the circumstance of the gas not having an equal temperature and density throughout. These variations depend in a definite manner upon the laws which govern the differences of temperature and density existing in different parts of the gas: we will call them *normal* variations.

It is the latter which have especially to be considered in the conduction of heat, and we will therefore direct our attention first of all to them.

The cause of their occurrence depends, in the case before us, upon the fact that when two molecules, coming from different sides, strike each other within the stratum, the molecule which comes from the warmer side has in general a greater velocity than the one which comes from the cooler side. The magnitude of this difference is determined by the distances from the stratum in

---

* According to what is said above, we take account only, in considering conduction, of the heat which is inherent in the molecules themselves, and is communicated by one molecule to another solely by their impact. But besides this, each molecule radiates heat, which is transmitted by the æther, and is partially absorbed by other molecules on its way; so that there is thus also a transmission of heat from one molecule to another. The communication of heat in this way, in the case of bodies of such low radiating and absorbing powers as the gases, can, however, scarcely be reckoned as conduction, since the great distances which the rays of heat may traverse without being absorbed gives it an entirely different character. In any case, however, it is allowable to consider separately each of these two ways in which heat moves; and we shall accordingly in the sequel always speak of the *conduction of heat* in this sense.

question of the points at which the said molecules commenced their
motions; and since the distances through which the molecules move
between each two impacts are in general very small, this difference must also be very small, so that we can regard the mean value
of this difference as a magnitude of the same order with the mean
excursions (*Weglänge*) of the molecules. We must now try to determine what influence this difference, existing before the impacts,
exerts upon the motions after the impacts.

§ 4.   The behaviour of two impinging molecules is not in
every respect the same as that of two elastic spheres; but we can
nevertheless in many respects obtain a useful insight into the
behaviour of molecules by starting from the consideration of elastic spheres. The mutual action of two impinging elastic spheres
is very comprehensively treated by Maxwell in the memoir already
mentioned. I will here only quote a few principles, which may,
however, be considered as sufficiently well known without my
doing so.

When two elastic spheres move with equal velocity in opposite
directions, and with their centres in the same straight line, so
that they strike each other centrally, they rebound from each
other in such a manner that each sphere moves back with the same
velocity in the direction of the point from which it came. But
if the spheres move, before the impact, still in opposite directions, but with their centres in two parallel straight lines instead of in the same straight line, and so that the spheres consequently impinge excentrically, they rebound again with equal
velocities, their centres again move in opposite directions in
two parallel straight lines; but the direction of these straight
lines is not the same as that of the straight lines in which the
centres moved before the impact. The new direction depends upon
the position on the two surfaces of the point of contact; and
since the spheres may strike each other on an infinite number of
different points of their surfaces, the rebound may also take
place in an infinite number of different directions; and it can
be easily shown that *each possible direction in space is equally
likely for the motions of the spheres after the impact.*

Let it now be assumed, as a general case, that the two equal
spheres move before the impact *with any velocities whatever and
in any directions whatever.* We will decompose the motion of each
sphere into two components. We will take as the first component
the motion of the common centre of gravity of the two spheres;
the second component must then be the motion of the two spheres
in question relatively to their common centre of gravity. The
former motion is equal and in the same direction for both spheres;
the latter motion is equal and opposite for the two spheres. The
former is not altered by the impact; the latter, on the other
hand, is altered exactly in the same way as it would be if it
existed alone and there were no common motion. In relation to
it, what has already been said of the case of two spheres moving
in parallel straight lines, and which assume various directions
after impact, according to the point at which they strike each
other, is applicable. It thus becomes evident how far the motions
after impact, of molecules which impinge upon each other irregularly, are dependent upon their motions before impact, and how

far they are independent of them. *The motion of each sphere consists of two components, the first of which is entirely determined, both as to magnitude and direction, by the motions before impact, and the second of which has also a determinate magnitude, but may have an infinite number of different directions, every direction in space being equally probable with every other.*

§ 5.   In applying this result to the impacts which occur among the molecules, we may assume that here also only that portion of the motion possessed before impact by two impinging molecules remains unchanged in magnitude and direction which is common to both molecules, that is, the motion of their common centre of gravity; while the direction of the second component of their motions may be altered in so many ways that it may with equal probability assume any direction in space whatever.

Let us now consider the whole number of molecules which impinge upon each other in one unit of time within the infinitely thin stratum spoken of in § 3.   The motions which they possess *before* the impact have already been discussed in § 3: all possible directions are represented among their motions; but the molecules coming from the warmer side have in general somewhat greater velocities than those which come from the colder side.   Since, according to our assumption, the temperature diminishes as x increases, the warmer side is the negative side, that is, the one on which x has a smaller value than it has in the stratum: hence the molecules which pass from the negative to the positive side have in general greater velocities than those which pass from the positive to the negative side, so that, compounding the motions of all impinging molecules, we obtain a certain small momentum in the direction of positive x.

This common momentum remains unaltered by the impacts; but at the same time a complete change occurs in the directions of the motions, in so far that the molecules are impelled in all directions without distinction.   If therefore the motion were, before the impacts, unequally distributed in the various directions (the number of molecules moving in certain directions being greater than the number moving in other directions, or their velocities being different), we must nevertheless assume that all these inequalities would be equalized by the impacts; and that, excepting the general motion in the direction of positive x, no distinction between the different directions would remain, but that all directions would be equally represented among the new motions.

It thus becomes easy to give a definite representation of the state of motion of the molecules emitted from the stratum, if, instead of regarding the velocities of the *separate* molecules, we content ourselves with knowing the *mean* velocity for each direction.   First, let the molecules be conceived as moving equally in all directions, so that an equal number of molecules, and all with the same velocity, move in each direction, and then let a small component motion in the direction of positive x, equal for all the molecules, be conceived as added to all these motions.   The directions and velocities of the motions will be thereby somewhat changed; and the system of motion so modified represents the motions of the molecules emitted from the stratum*.

*   *   *

III.   *Behaviour of the molecules simultaneously existing in an infinitely thin stratum.*

§ 8. We will suppose two planes placed perpendicularly upon the axis of x, and with the abscissæ x and $x + dx$, whereby we obtain again, as in the foregoing section, an infinitely thin stratum; but we will now consider, not the molecules *emitted* from this stratum, but the molecules which *exist in it simultaneously*.

If the gas has the same temperature and density throughout, the motions would be such that an equal number of molecules would move in all directions, and that the velocities would be equal. But in the case before us, where the temperature and density are functions of x, this uniformity does not occur.

To determine the *velocities* of the molecules, let us choose any direction which makes with the axis of x an angle whose cosine is μ, and let us consider the molecules which move in this direction. Before such a molecule enters our infinitely thin stratum with the abscissa x, it has in general traversed a certain distance since its last impact. If this distance be called s, the abscissa of the point where the last impact occurred willl be $x - \mu s$; which expression determines the velocity of the molecule, since, according to the assumptions made above, the velocity with which a molecule is impelled after an impact depends only upon the abscissa of the point of impact, and upon the direction of its motion. We have above denoted the velocity as a function of x and μ, by U, and we may accordingly in this case, in which a molecule is impelled from a point whose abscissa is $x - \mu s$, denote its velocity by V, and write

$$V = U - \frac{dU}{dx}\,\mu s + \frac{1}{2}\frac{d^2U}{dx^2}\,\mu^2 s^2 - \ldots \quad \ldots \ldots \quad (9)$$

The distance s is not the same for all the molecules in our stratum which have a determinate direction, so that their velocities are also somewhat unequal. We may hereafter denote the arithmetical mean of a magnitude whose value, in the particular cases which occur, is various, by making a horizontal stroke over the symbol which represents the particular values of the magnitude, so that $\overline{V}$ shall represent the mean value of V, and $\overline{s}$ and $\overline{s^2}$ the mean values of s and s^2. We may then write

$$\overline{V} = U - \frac{dU}{dx}\,\mu\overline{s} + \frac{1}{2}\frac{d\,U}{dx}\,\mu^2\overline{s^2} - \ldots \quad \ldots \ldots \quad (10)$$

In this expression it is to be observed that the magnitude $\overline{s^2}$ is not equivalent to $(\overline{s})^2$, but that it must be specially determined. Thence it also follows that the mean values of the powers

---

* In the memoir quoted above (Phil. Mag. S. 4. vol. xx.), Maxwell, in determining the conduction of heat, has disregarded the circumstance that the molecules emitted from a stratum have an excess of positive momentum, but has tacitly assumed in his calculations that the molecules are emitted equally in all directions.

V^2, V^3, &c. are not quite equal to the corresponding powers of the mean value $\overline{V}$. We must, in fact, in order to obtain this mean value, start from the equation (9) and, after having squared it, cubed it, &c., then put the mean values for s, s^2, &c. We thus obtain

$$\left.\begin{aligned}
\overline{V^2} &= U^2 - 2U\frac{dU}{dx}\mu\overline{s} + \left[U\frac{d^2U}{dx^2} + \left(\frac{dU}{dx}\right)^2\right]\mu^2\overline{s^2} - \ldots, \\
\overline{V^3} &= U^3 - 3U^2\frac{dU}{dx}\mu\overline{s} + \left[\frac{3}{2}U^2\frac{d^2U}{dx^2} + 3U\left(\frac{dU}{dx}\right)^2\right]\mu^2\overline{s^2} - \ldots, \\
\overline{V^4} &= \&c.
\end{aligned}\right\} \tag{11}$$

The differences between the magnitudes $\overline{V^2}$, $\overline{V^3}$, &c., and the magnitudes $(\overline{V})^2$, $(\overline{V})^3$, &c., which latter are obtained by squaring, cubing, &c., equation (10), occur, as will be seen, first in those terms which are of the second degree in relation to the length of the excursion s; and as these excursions are, on the average, very small quantities, the differences are also very small.

§ 9. It now becomes necessary to determine the values of $\overline{s}$ and $\overline{s^2}$ with greater exactness.

To this end, we will first examine the behaviour of these magnitudes when the temperature and density of the given quantity of gas are uniform throughout, and will afterwards superadd the modification due to the inequality of temperature and density.

Considering, then, all the molecules which are contained at any given time in a stratum of a gas whose temperature and density are everywhere the same, we ask ourselves, how great are the distances which the several molecules have traversed between their last impact and the moment at which we consider them. The likelihood that a molecule has traversed a distance lying between s and $s + ds$, between its last impact and the moment fixed upon, is just as great as the likelihood of its traversing an equal distance between this moment and its next impact; and the likelihood of the latter event can be easily expressed.

If, from a given moment of time, a large number of molecules be supposed to move through the gas with an equal velocity, their motion will cause each of them sooner or later to impinge upon other molecules; and if z denote the number of molecules which traverse the distance s without striking against other molecules, z must diminish according to a definite ratio as s increases. If we saw that the probability of one molecule striking another while traversing the infinitely small distance ds is αds, then of the number z which have traversed the distance s without impediment, the number $z\alpha ds$ will be taken up during the next portion of their course ds, and the decrement of z will hence be represented by the equation

$$dz = -z\alpha ds;$$

whence it follows that, putting Z for the initial value of z when $s = 0$,

$$z = Ze^{-\alpha s}.$$

This value being substituted for z in the product $z\alpha ds$, gives the expression

$$Ze^{-\alpha s}\alpha ds$$

for the number of molecules the length of whose excursions lies
between s and $s + ds$.

In order now to obtain the mean length of all the excursions,
it is only needful to multiply the last expression by s, then to
integrate from $s = 0$ to $s = \infty$, and to divide the integral by the
whole number Z. This gives

$$\bar{s} = \int_0^\infty se^{-\alpha s}\alpha ds = \frac{1}{\alpha}. \quad \ldots \ldots \ldots \quad (12)$$

This expression applies primarily to the mean length of the
distances moved through by the molecules between the point of
time in question and their next impact; but it can also be directly used for the distances the molecules have moved through
between their last previous impact and the instant in question,
for the distances before any given point of time must, on the
average, be equal to the distances after it.

*   *   *

XLVII. *On the Second Fundamental Theorem of the Mechanical Theory
of Heat; a Lecture delivered before the Forty-first Meeting of
the German Scientific Association, at Frankfort on the Maine,
September 23, 1867.* By R. Clausius, *Professor of Physics in
the University of Würzburg.*

Having been honoured with a requisition to deliver a discourse to the present general meeting of the Association, I have
felt it incumbent upon me to choose as my theme, not the result
of any special investigation, but some subject of wide application and general interest. I will therefore take the liberty of
giving, as briefly and in as easily intelligible a form as possible, an account of the theorem known as the Second Fundamental
Theorem of the Mechanical Theory of Heat, which forms one of the
two great principles whereon this whole theory is based. It is
obvious that it is impossible for me upon the present occasion to
present this theorem in a mathematical form, or to give a strict
proof of its truth, and to follow out individually its numerous
applications; all I can do is to place its meaning and its connexion with the first fundamental theorem of the mechanical theory
of heat in a clear light, and perhaps to illustrate by a few examples the conclusions which may be deduced from it.

It is well known that rather more than twenty years ago, following upon the isolated and more general statements of various
earlier authors, Mayer of Heilbronn distinctly asserted, and
Joule of Manchester proved to demonstration by his experimental
investigations, that there exists between mechanical work and
heat a connexion of such a kind that mechanical work can be obtained by the expenditure of heat, and, conversely, heat can be
produced by the expenditure of work, there being under all circumstances one constant ratio between the quantity of heat and the

amount of work. This principle, known as the *principle of the Equivalence of Heat and Work*, formed the starting-point of the rapid development which the mechanical theory of heat has undergone in recent times.

In connexion with this principle, I may be allowed to make a remark which may contribute to facilitate the exposition of what follows.

When work is produced with accompanying expenditure of heat, or heat is produced while work is expended, this may be briefly expressed by saying that heat is transformed into work, or work into heat. Two such magnitudes, capable of being converted one into the other, so that one of them may serve to replace the other, will naturally often require to be considered together; in a mathematical sense, they must be regarded as of the same kind, and occasions will often arise when it is needful to add them together or subtract them one from the other. In such cases considerable inconvenience arises from the circumstance that heat and work are measured by reference to different standards. The unit of work is taken, as is well known, as the product of unit-weight into unit-length, or, for example, on the French metrical system as one kilogrammetre; whereas we are accustomed to take as the unit of heat the quantity of heat which is required to raise the temperature of unit-weight of water from 0° to 1°C. While employing these units, we cannot at once speak of the sum of heat and work; in order to make the sum we must either reduce the work to heat-units, or the heat to work-units. When this is done we always obtain complicated expressions such as these,—"the sum of the heat and the thermal equivalent of the work," or "the sum of the work and the mechanical equivalent of the heat."

On this account I have produced to introduce, as well as work, a second magnitude, which, while still representing work, expresses it in terms, not of the above-mentioned mechanical unit, but in terms of the unit of heat, and therefore so that that amount of work is taken as the unit of work which is equivalent to the thermal unit. For work, when thus measured, I have proposed the name *Ergon*. The principle that heat can be converted into ergon and ergon into heat, then, still holds good just as for work, and we have at the same time the simple relation that the quantities of heat and ergon which are mutually convertible, and which can therefore replace each other, are expressed by the same numbers. Another convenience is that quantities of heat and ergon can be added together or subtracted from one another without any previous reduction having to be performed upon either the one or the other.

We will consequently in the following discussion always speak of ergon instead of work, and will accordingly call the first fundamental theorem the *Theorem of the Equivalence of Heat and Ergon*.

When once this theorem had been propounded and been confirmed by experiment, it very quickly became generally known; and we may often find that people who have only a superficial acquaintance with the mechanical theory of heat suppose that it is the sole foundation of this theory. Such a view of it is indicated, for example, by the name which the mechanical theory of heat often goes by in France, namely, *la théorie de l'équivalent mécanique de la chaleur*. There is, however, a second theorem, not included in the first, but one which requires to be separately proved, and which is of as much importance as the other, inasmuch as both theorems together constitute the complete foundation of the mechanical theory of heat.

The fact that this second theorem is less known than the first, and, especially in popular expositions of the mechanical theory of heat, is sometimes passed over in complete silence, is chiefly due to its being much more difficult to understand than the first theorem, since in expounding it we are obliged to discuss conceptions which are then introduced for the first time, and to institute quantitative comparisons between processes which have not previously been considered as mathematical magnitudes. I believe, however, that when once the necessary mode of viewing the subject has become familiar, the second fundamental theorem will appear just as simple and natural as the first.

I will now try to set before you the processes with which we are here concerned, in such a manner that the new kind of comparison may present itself spontaneously as a necessary consequence, and that thus the second fundamental theorem may be clearly seen to be established as well as the first.

If we examine the conditions under which heat can be transformed into ergon, and, conversely, ergon into heat, we find, in the first place, that the commonest and simplest process is the following. The heat which exists in material bodies tends to alter their condition. It tends to expand them, to render solid bodies liquid and gaseous, and, as we may likewise add, to resolve chemical compounds into their elements. In all these cases the effect of the heat consists in loosening or completely dissolving the connexion which exists between the molecules or atoms, and in separating to the greatest possible distance such molecules as are already completely disconnected from each other.

In order to be able to express this action shortly, I have introduced a magnitude which denotes the extent to which this separation and parting of its smallest particles, which it is the tendency of heat to effect, has already been carried in the case of any body. This magnitude I call the *Disgregation* of the body. The disgregation of a body is consequently, among the three states of aggregation, least in the solid state, greater in the liquid state, and greatest of all in the gaseous state. In the last condition it can still be increased by the molecules separating further from each other--that is, by the gas expanding to a larger volume. In like manner, the decomposition of a chemically compound body into its elements is in general accompanied by an increase of disgregation.

By help of this conception the effect of heat can be simply expressed by saying that *heat tends to increase the disgregation of bodies*.

But in order that the disgregation of a body may be increased, resistances must in most cases be overcome, and resistances of two different kinds. In the first place, in order partially or completely to destroy the connexion between the molecules, the forces with which the molecules mutually attract each other must be overcome; and in the second place, there are commonly, in addition to these internal forces, other external forces which act upon the body from without. Thus, for example, in order that a body subject to external pressure may expand, this pressure, which opposes an increase of volume, must be overcome. Accordingly heat, when it causes increase of disgregation, must perform internal and external ergon in overcoming the opposing forces. In the performance of this ergon, heat is used up; and thus *the increase of disgregation involves conversion of heat into ergon.* Conversely, in order to diminish disgregation, ergon (and in general both internal and extenal ergon) must be expended; since the forces which in the former case were overcome by heat must now in their turn overcome it. In this process heat is produced; and we consequently arrive at the result that, *when disgregation is diminished, ergon is transformed into heat.*

*   *   *

It has been said above that the two fundamental theorems of the mechanical theory of heat are very similar to each other. I must now, however, direct attention to an essential difference, the existence of which indicates a very remarkable characteristic of all natural processes. In the foregoing considerations from which we deduced the second fundamental theorem, it was made a condition throughout that all the changes that occurred should be *reversible*--that is, that they should take place in such a way that the reverse changes should be capable of occurring under the same conditions. We must now put to ourselves the question, what results should we arrive at if this condition were abandoned?

Let us examine, in the first place, the alteration of the disgregation of a body, connecting our considerations, as before, with the case of a perfect gas which undergoes a change of volume.

If a gas expands and at the same time overcomes at every instant the greatest possible external pressure that its expansive force enables it to overcome, so that its pressure and the resistance are always equal to each other, or at least so nearly equal that the excess of one over the other may be disregarded, then, by the application of the same external force as the gas overcame during its expansion, it can be compressed again to its original volume, all the phenomena taking place during the compression in the inverse direction from what they did during the expansion, but otherwise in the same way. This kind of expansion of a gas is, accordingly, reversible.

The expansion of a gas may, however, take place in a different manner. Let us suppose a vessel in which the gas is contained. and let us assume that this vessel is suddenly put into communication with a second empty vessel; a portion of the gas will then pass into the empty vessel until the pressure in both vessels has become equal. The gas has then expanded without overcoming any external force; but we cannot restore it to its former volume without the application of an external force. In this case, therefore, the expansion of the gas has taken place in an unreversible manner.

The final result of the expansion is in both cases so far the same, that the disgregation of the gas has been increased to a certain extent; but in the one case, where a resistance had to be overcome, heat was transformed into ergon, while in the other case, where there was no resistance to overcome, no ergon was done, and accordingly no heat was transformed into ergon. If, on the other hand, it is required to compress the gas again and so to diminish its disgregation, it is not possible to do this otherwise than in such a way that ergon is transformed into heat. But since the transformation of ergon into heat is a positive transformation, and that of heat into ergon a negative transformation, the above result may be expressed as follows:--A diminution of disgregation, which is a negative transformation, cannot take place without a simultaneous positive transformation; while it is possible, on the contrary, for an increase of disgregation, which is a positive transformation, to take place without a negative transformation.

Let us now consider the second kind of transformation, or the transformation of heat into ergon, or *vice versâ*, in relation to the same point.

In order that heat may be transformed into ergon, it is necessary, as we have already seen, that either an increase of disgregation should take place, or if this does not occur, as in the case of cyclical processes, a certain further quantity of heat must be transferred from a hotter to a colder body. But since increase of disgregation and passage of heat from a hotter to a colder body are positive transformations, it follows that the negative transformation of heat into work is necessarily connected with a simultaneous positive transformation.

On the other hand, the positive transformation of ergon into heat can quite well take place without any simultaneous negative transformation. When, for example, force is expended in overcoming the resistance of friction, heat is produced, and thus ergon is transformed into heat without its being at all needful that any negative transformation should take part in the process. In like manner, the resistance of the air and the resistance to conduction which an electric current has to overcome in a conductor comport themselves in the same way as the resistance of friction.

Consequently the proposition holds good of the second kind of transformation also, that the negative transformation of heat into ergon cannot occur without a simultaneous positive transformation, but that the positive transformation of ergon into heat can take place without a simultaneous negative transformation.

Finally, we have still to consider the third kind of transformation, or the passage of heat from one temperature to another.

In order that heat may be transferred from a colder to a hotter body, it is a necessity that a positive transformation should form a part of the same process, as indeed we have seen already, in connexion with cyclical processes, that such a transference of heat involves the transformation of ergon into heat. The inverse transference of heat from a hotter to a colder body, on the contrary, can go on entirely by itself, as it does, for example, when heat passes from a hotter to a colder body by radiation or conduction.

Hence in this case also, just as in the two previous ones, the negative transformation cannot occur withour a positive transformation; but the positive transformation can occur without a negative transformation.

When two transformations are equal in magnitude but of opposite signs, we agreed above to say that they *compensate* each other. Accordingly, we may enunciate the following theorem in reference to all the three kinds of transformations:--*Negative transformations can take place only when they are compensated, but positive transformations can occur even if uncompensated*; or, shorter still, *Uncompensated transformations can never be anything but positive.*

This peculiar relation is met with in every change that occurs in nature; for the case of an alteration being completely reversible, so that the sum of all the transformations involved in it is exactly zero, is merely the limiting case of an infinite number of possible cases, just as zero itself is the lower limit of all positive magnitudes. When we consider the universe, keeping this relation in mind, we arrive at a very remarkable conclusion.

One hears it often said that in this world everything is a circuit. While in one place and at one time changes take place in one particular direction, in another place and at another time changes go on in the opposite direction; so that the same conditions constantly recur, and in the long run the state of the world remains unchanged. Consequently, it is said, the world may go on in the same way for ever.

When the first fundamental theorem of the mechanical theory of heat was established, it may probably have been regarded as an important confirmation of this view. Hitherto, when discussing this theorem, we have spoken only of heat and ergon; but it must be observed that we may regard the word "heat" as also including light; and the conception of "ergon" is very much more comprehensive still. Chemical action, the effects of electrical and magnetic forces, the production and cessation of motion, whether it be the progressive, rotatory, or vibratory motion of ponderable masses, or whether it be the motion of electricity, may all, so far as they are here considered, be represented as ergon. We are consequently dealing with a theorem that applies to all natural phenomena.

Helmholtz, who at once recognized this general significance of the theorem, and established it clearly and convincingly in his beautiful essay on this subject by applying the theorem to the various branches of physics, gave to the theorem, when thus extended as widely as possible, the name of the *Theorem of the Conservation of Force*, for which it would perhaps be a little better to say the *Theorem of the Conservation of Energy.*

When the object is to make it express a general fundamental law of the universe, this theorem may be put into some such form as the following:--*One form of Energy can be transformed into another form of Energy, but the quantity of Energy is thereby never diminished; on the contrary, the total amount of Energy existing in the universe remains just as constant as the total amount of Matter in the universe.*

Notwithstanding that the truth of this theorem is beyond a doubt, and that it expresses the unchangeableness of the universe in a certain very important respect, we should yet be going too far were we to assume that it affords a confirmation of the view according to which the whole condition of the universe is represented as unchangeable, and all involved in never-ending cycles. The second fundamental theorem of the mechanical theory of heat contradicts this view most distinctly.

As was said above, the common rule holds good for all the endlessly manifold changes which go on in the world, that transformations in opposite directions do not necessarily occur in equal numbers, but that the difference can only be on one determinate side, namely, so that the positive transformations preponderate over the negative. Hence it follows that the condition of the universe must gradually change more and more in a certain particular direction.

The ergon which the forces of nature are capable of performing, and which is contained in the existing motions of the bodies which make up the system of the universe, will be gradually converted more and more into heat. The heat, inasmuch as it always tends to pass from hotter to colder bodies, and so to equalize existing differences of temperature, will gradually acquire a more and more uniform distribution, and a certain equilibrium will be attained even between the radiant heat existing in the æther and the heat existing in material bodies. Lastly, in relation to their molecular arrangement, material bodies will get nearer to a certain condition in which, regard being had to the existing temperature, the total disgregation is the greatest possible.

I have endeavoured to express the whole of this process by means of one simple theorem, whereby the condition towards which the universe is gradually approaching is distinctly characterized. I have formed a magnitude which expresses the same thing in relation to transformations that energy does in relation to heat and ergon--that is, a magnitude which represents the sum of all the transformations which must have taken place in order to bring any body or system of bodies into its present condition. I have called this magnitude *Entropy*. Now in all cases in which the positive transformations exceed the negative an increase of entropy occurs. Hence we must conclude that in all the phenomena of nature the total entropy must be ever on the increase and can never decrease; and we thus get as a short expression for the process of transformation which is everywhere unceasingly going on the following theorem:--

The entropy of the universe tends towards a maximum.

The more the universe approaches this limiting condition in which the entropy is a maximum, the more do the occasions of further changes diminish; and supposing this condition to be at last completely attained, no further change could evermore take place, and the universe would be in a state of unchanging death.

Albeit the present condition of the universe is still very far removed from this limiting condition, and the approach to it is so slow that all such periods as we speak of as historical are but a very short span in comparison with the immeasurable periods that the universe requires for comparatively very slight modifications, it yet remains an important result that a law of nature should have been discovered which allows us to conclude with certainty that everything in the universe does not occur in cycles, but that it changes its condition continually in a certain direction, and thus tends towards a limiting condition.

VIII.   The Development of Chemical Science

A.   From Taxonomy to Explanation in Chemistry

Lavoisier's revolution in chemistry cleared away a good deal of debris that had clogged the intellectual pores of chemistry. By classifying chemical compounds according to their composition and by introducing a new nomenclature that reflected that composition, Lavoisier and his French associates made it possible to organize the relatively vast amount of chemical knowledge into a manageable science.   It was now possible to communicate easily within the chemical profession and to be precise about new chemical processes.   What Lavoisier's chemistry did not do was to make it any easier to understand what was going on in any given chemical reaction.   If A reacted with B, or if AB and CD together formed AC and BD, this could be described in precise language. But what actually went on in the reaction was not only impossible to tell but was not even considered to be a legitimate question to ask.

Lavoisier's immediate successors were not content to leave it at that.   Already in the last years of the eighteenth century, the question of the proportions in which bodies combined had come to the fore.   Claude-Louis Berthollet (1748-1822), noting that proportions in certain "compounds" such as what we would today call alloys and solutions could range over wide values for the amount of each constituent present, insisted that chemical compounds were not precise proportions of the substances involved. Moreover, even where specific compounds were concerned, Berthollet discovered that a reaction could be "driven" further in one direction if large amounts of one reagent were used.   This latter observation was the basis for the law of Mass Action.

Berthollet's results and his interpretation of them were challenged by Louis Proust (1754-1826) who insisted that chemical compounds *always* had exactly the same weight of their constituents present.   When the weight differed, the compounds formed were different.   Using the sulfates of copper (cupric and cuprous), Proust proved his point with abundant experimental evidence.   The Law of Definite Proportions provided the fundamental law for the development of analytical chemistry in the early nineteenth century.   The development of analytical chemistry, in turn, permitted chemists to test new theories with some rigor.

Looking backward, the enunciation of the atomic theory seems to be the natural consequence of the Law of Definite Proportions. After all if there are two compounds of A and B, and if the weights of A in these two compounds are as 1 to 2, then it seems only elementary to assume that the first compound consisted of one atom of A and one atom of B (or AB) and the second of two atoms of A and one of B (or A_2B).   But, the train of thought to arrive at this conclusion was not as simple as this example might lead one to believe.   First of all, one had to believe in the real existence of atoms and Lavoisier had already stated that this was philosophically impossible.   Then one had to assume that all atoms of the same element were exactly alike, especially in weight.   This was no trivial assumption.   After all, no one knew what made an atom of gold, say, an atom of gold. Was it its shape? Was it is weight? Was it the presence of "hooks" or other instruments by which it could combine with other atoms? No one could say but it should be noted that common weight was not an obvious characteristic by which chemical species could or should be classified. This is why John Dalton's work was original and not merely the revival of an atomic doctrine as old as Democritus. By focusing on atomic weights and by showing that the relative weights of atoms could be determined in the laboratory, Dalton gave a physical reality to the atomic theory that it had not possessed before. [See p. 164.]

The enunciation of the atomic theory had surprisingly little effect on chemistry at the moment. Chemists were leery of anything that smelled of metaphysics, having just escaped from a metaphysical labyrinth. Atoms, in spite of their relative weights, still smacked of the metaphysical. And, who really needed them? Equivalent weights were just as good for analytical chemistry and equivalent weights were actual, real, tangible things that could be determined in any laboratory. So, for many chemists, the atomic theory was an interesting hypothesis but one that was potentially dangerous and, therefore, to be handled with great circumspection. Better by far to stick to *real* things. Take Gay-Lussac's Law of Combining Volumes, for example. The fact that gases combined in simple volumetric relations was an undoubted fact. Two volumes of hydrogen combined with one volume of oxygen to produce two volumes of water vapor. Those were the facts. The minute these facts were translated into atomic fancies, however, their clarity disappeared. If Dalton were right that water was a binary compound, HO, then there must be half the number of atoms of hydrogen per unit volume as there were oxygen atoms. Why that should be so was inexplicable. Or, if there were an equal number of hydrogen atoms, then water must be H_2O, but then the molecules of water occupied a space different from that of their constituent atoms. For, if, say, one volume contains 10 atoms, then 2 vols contain 20 atoms. So, 20 atoms of hydrogen combine with 10 atoms of oxygen to produce 10 molecules of water (H_2O) but these 10 molecules occupy *twice* the space as 10 atoms of either oxygen or hydrogen.

In 1811, Amadeo Avogadro, arguing essentially from considerations of heat--namely that gases at the same temperature contained caloric atmospheres around each molecule or atom of equal (caloric) densities--suggested that equal volumes of gases at the same temperature contained equal numbers of particles. The only possible way for this to be the case is to assume that the particles of hydrogen and of oxygen are compound particles made up of two atoms of each element. Thus, and only thus, will the equation balance.

$$20 \ H_2 + 10 \ O_2 \rightarrow 20 \ H_2O$$

$$2 \text{ vols.} + 1 \text{ vol.} \rightarrow 2 \text{ vols.}$$

The logic of this analysis appears so simple and convincing that it is difficult to believe that Avogadro's hypothesis was rejected. Yet it was, and the reasons for the rejection show how slippery the atomic doctrine could be. One of Dalton's earliest

disciples was the Swedish chemist Jöns Jacob Berzelius (1779-1848)
who realized that the atomic theory could provide chemistry with
a conceptual device of great utility. Berzelius set the standard
for the first half of the nineteenth century in the determination
of atomic weights. His accuracy as an analytical chemist gave
him great prestige amongst chemists and he used this prestige to
combat Avogadro's hypothesis.

One of the attractions of the atomic theory to Berzelius was
that it provided the basis for a simple mechanical model of chemical processes. As we have already noted, it was Berzelius who
combined the facts of electrochemistry with the atomic theory to
set out a theory of chemical combination. Atoms contained the
two electrical fluids in varying amounts (except for oxygen which
was totally electronegative). Chemical reactions took place between elements of opposite net electrical charge. The chemical
bond, in short, was an electrostatic one and only those reactions
could occur in which the resulting compound was held together by
electrostatic forces. This theory was a powerful one and illuminated the chemical facts of the day with some power. But, it also
made the very idea of an O_2 or H_2 molecule ridiculous. An atom
of oxygen was filled with negative electricity. It must repel
another oxygen atom powerfully and could never associate with it
with the intimacy necessary to produce an oxygen molecule. Hence,
Avogadro's hypothesis, though interesting, must be wrong and it
was rejected for two generations.

The results of this rejection only gradually became clear.
In inorganic chemistry, where, for most simple compounds the bonds
are, in fact, electrostatic or ionic, Berzelius' system worked
quite well. And, atomic weights could be worked out for all the
univalent elements. The result was the rapid development of inorganic chemistry in the 1820's and 1830's. Faraday's work on
electrochemistry, also falling within the framework of ionic bonding, further clarified the relations between elements, even though
Faraday did not accept Berzelius' theory. By the 1850's, there
was a solid science based upon Dalton, Berzelius and Faraday but
it was confined to the inorganic realm. When it came to organic
chemistry, things were in very bad shape. By the 1850's there
was a growing despair amongst organic chemists that they would
never be able to do more than analyze and classify the growing
number of organic compounds.

The trouble with organic chemistry was that it was so unbe-
lievably complicated. What had worked so well for inorganic
chemistry simply did not apply here. Analytical chemists soon
showed that most organic compounds were composed of carbon and
hydrogen, with some oxygen, nitrogen and phosphorus thrown in.
The number of substances that were made up simply of carbon and
hydrogen was already too large to fit into the classification
scheme of Lavoisier. The -ic and -ous or -ate and -ite endings
devised by the French chemists to indicate degree of saturation
simply made no sense. Was a C_3H_8 an -ic and a C_2H_6 an -ous compound? Clearly neither was correct. Nor, it might be added,
could one even be sure whether the C was C_3 or C_6 since the atomic
weight of carbon was notoriously difficult to determine. No wonder, then, that organic chemists were desperate. There were only

a few, rare, shafts of sunlight to light up the organic landscape. Early in the century, Gay-Lussac had discovered that cyanogen-- C_2N_2--acted as though it were a stable assemblage of atoms. The C_2N_2 radical appeared to act like the elements themselves in inorganic chemistry. When Justus Liebig (1803-73) and Friedrich Wöhler (1800-1882) discovered the Benzoyl radical (C_6H_5O) in the 1830's, there was a brief hope that organic chemistry might turn out to be the chemistry of radicals. The hope was dashed when it was discovered that there were reactions in which it was impossible to isolate any radicals. The radical theory nevertheless continued to be part of organic thinking.

The most important crisis in organic chemistry in the early nineteenth century did not come from the failure of the radical theory. It came out of a social incident and shook the very foundations of the science. In 1833, Louis Philippe, King of the French, held a magnificent soirée in the Tuileries Palace. To light the affair, the King ordered the new, beautifully white candles, bleached by chlorine. The evening was a disaster. The candles burned with a black smoke and acrid fumes that sent everyone into fits of coughing. The King asked Jean-Baptiste Dumas (1800-1884) to discover what had happened. Dumas could not believe what his researches indicated. All his evidence appeared to indicate that the chlorine from the bleach replaced hydrogen in the organic molecules of which the candles were composed. To announce that chlorine, a most electronegative element, could replace hydrogen, the model of electropositivity, was to risk the thunders of the Jove of Sweden, Berzelius. Dumas was not prepared to take that risk and attempted to evade the clear conclusion to which his data led. A younger contemporary and former student of Dumas, Auguste Laurent (1808-53), was willing to grasp the nettle grimly and argue that chlorine was substituted for the hydrogen in the molecule. This implied that there should be other substitution reactions and Laurent was not slow in producing them. The substitution reaction soon became an important instrument in theoretical organic chemistry for chlorine could be easily tracked down in molecules. Laurent now suggested that there was a nucleus or fundamental radical upon which chlorine could be substituted for hydrogen. Laurent's nucleus became the *type* in the hands of another chemist and Laurent's collaborator, Charles Gerhardt (1816-56). Gerhardt insisted that there were four basic nuclei or types in organic chemistry as follows: hydrogen, hydrochloric acid, water and ammonia. They can be represented as:

$$\left. \begin{array}{c} H \\ H \end{array} \right\} \qquad \left. \begin{array}{c} H \\ Cl \end{array} \right\} \qquad \left. \begin{array}{c} H \\ H \end{array} \right\} O \qquad \left. \begin{array}{c} H \\ H \\ H \end{array} \right\} N$$

From these types, compounds could be derived by substituting elements or radicals. Thus, for example, the series of simple alcohols took on a new simplicity when represented according to the theory of types.

$$\left. \begin{array}{c} H \\ H \end{array} \right\} O \qquad \left. \begin{array}{c} CH_3 \\ H \end{array} \right\} O \qquad \left. \begin{array}{c} C_2H_5 \\ H \end{array} \right\} O \qquad \left. \begin{array}{c} C_3H_7 \\ H \end{array} \right\} O$$

$$\text{water} \qquad\quad \text{methyl} \qquad\quad \text{ethyl} \qquad\qquad \text{propyl}$$
$$\text{alcohol} \qquad\quad \text{alcohol} \qquad\quad \text{alcohol}$$

More importantly, the theory of types could predict compounds, such as acetic anhydride,

$$\left. \begin{array}{l} C_2H_3O \\ C_2H_3O \end{array} \right\} O$$

or greatly clarify reactions, as in the production of ether.

$$\left. \begin{array}{l} C_2H_5 \\ K \end{array} \right\} O \ + \ \left. \begin{array}{l} C_2H_5 \\ I \end{array} \right\} \ \rightarrow \ KI \ + \ \left. \begin{array}{l} C_2H_5 \\ C_2H_5 \end{array} \right\} O$$

Although both Laurent and Gerhardt disclaimed any desire to represent real structures, it is, nevertheless, quite clear that the theory of types implied a structure. As long as it was not pushed beyond the simple examples we have presented here, it worked well. But in more complicated cases, it broke down. Another clue, also implicit in the theory of types, was to provide the thread by which the exit from the labyrinth could be discovered. In the water type above, it is obvious that the oxygen has two "hooks" upon which two radicals can hang. In the ammonia type, nitrogen has three "hooks." In 1852, Edward Frankland (1825-99) who had been investigating organo-metallic compounds suggested that elements had only a limited and specific number of "hooks." The doctrine of valency, for such it was, when applied to carbon suddenly created order out of chaos. Auguste Kekulé (1829-96) first investigated the consequences of attributing four bonds to the carbon atom. Archibald Couper in England and Alexander Butlerov in Russia hit upon the idea at the same time and together the three men created structural chemistry. The tetravalent carbon atom became the firm foundation upon which a rational organic chemistry could now be built. The simultaneous acceptance of Avogadro's principle also permitted the atomic weight of carbon to be determined so that actual structural formulae could now be written. The later insight by Kekulé (1866) that benzene could be represented by a ring provided the last element necessary for the basic understanding of both chain and aromatic hydrocarbons.

It should be noted that a considerable price was paid for this enlightenment. It was very handy to know of the tetravalent carbon bond but it was also necessary to announce that no one had the faintest idea what that bond was. This was especially true in ring structures where apparent double bonds had to be simply ignored. The problem was not solved until recent decades with resonance theory and its dependence upon quantum mechanics.

The final step in the understanding of organic compounds came with the creation of stereochemistry. The difference between structural and stereochemistry is that structural chemistry allows one to see how the atoms in a compound are arranged and stereochemistry permits the correlation of structure with chemical qualities.

The founder of stereochemistry was Louis Pasteur (1822-95). In 1848, Pasteur laboriously separated the crystals of tartaric acid by hand. On one hand were crystals of one kind; on the other were their mirror images. When the two types of crystals were dissolved together, the resultant solution had no effect upon the plane of a ray of plane polarized light. If solutions were made of the one kind of crystal, and another solution made of its mirror image, the plane of a ray of polarized light was rotated one way by the one solution and the other way by the second. Pasteur drew the conclusion that crystal asymmetry implied molecular asymmetry and this was the fundamental idea of stereochemistry. It was an idea whose time, however, had not yet come. It was not until after the basic mysteries of organic chemistry had been removed that chemists could take seriously the notion that chemists could actually determine where atoms were in a molecule. In the 1870's Achille LeBel (1847-1930) and Jacobus Henricus Van't Hoff (1852-1911) systematically explored Pasteur's concept and showed how it was both possible to determine where atoms were and to correlate atomic position with chemical qualities [see p. 285.].

By the 1880's, organic chemistry was thriving and the major difficulties were to be found in the inorganic area. The problem of solutions of salts and their reactions in electrochemistry was particularly acute. Faraday's conceptualization of electrochemistry had failed the test of time. He had insisted that the constituents of electrolytes--ions--were never free from attachment to one another even though they migrated by one another in an electrochemical cell. Later researches, particularly those of Wilhelm Hittorf (1824-1914), Rudolf Clausius and Friedrich W. Kohlrausch (1840-1910) clearly pointed to the conclusion that ions were free particles in an electrolyte. But a free chlorine particle or a free sodium particle simply could not exist in an aqueous solution. A way out of this difficulty was discovered by Svante Arrhenius (1859-1927) in 1887. He simply supposed that the ions of sodium and chlorine were charged particles, rather than neutral atoms. The charges, then, were responsible for the fact that sodium did not act like sodium. In 1885, Van't Hoff had conceived of a dilute solution as resembling a gas and obeying laws precisely similar to the gas laws, in osmosis. The combination of Van't Hoff's and Arrhenius' views led to the ionic theory of dissociation. Solutions were composed of dissociated molecules whose constituent charged particles migrated under the influence of an electric field. Although there were still a number of theoretical difficulties to be overcome and a number of skeptics to be converted, the ionic theory provided a necessary clarification of this area. Furthermore, the charged ion could be used to advantage in other areas of inorganic chemistry, such as the bonding structure of complex inorganic salts.

One final development in the chemistry of the nineteenth century remains to be detailed. Although the evolution of chemistry was clearly from classification to explanation, the power of classification should not be underestimated. In the hands of a master, it could turn into a powerful tool for the analysis of matter and for the laying of a strong foundation for chemistry.

One of the characteristics of chemistry in the first half of the nineteenth century was the multiplication of the number of known elements. This was made possible by the refinement of analytical techniques and the discovery of new elements was, at first, a kind of exhilarating game which guaranteed immortality in the history of science. But as the number of elements in-

creased, so did the unease with which every new announcement was
greeted. Chemists had reluctantly given up the old monist dream
that all matter was basically one. It had, to be sure, been revived in 1815 when Dr. William Prout published an anonymous article in which he argued that all elements were combinations of
hydrogen. But the dream vanished when Berzelius showed that the
atomic weight of chlorine was 35.5, hydrogen being 1. The multiplication of elements, however, seemed to be carrying things too
far to the other extreme. Was it absolutely necessary to have
fifty, sixty or more separate elements having no connection with
one another? No, surely. There must be some underlying plan
that would destroy the seeming   individuality of the elements.
In 1819, Johann Wilhelm Dobereiner (1780-1849) called attention
to similarities that existed between selected triads of elements.
Thus chlorine, bromine and iodine, although clearly elementary,
nevertheless had very similar chemical properties. They appeared
to be connected somehow, but Dobereiner was at a loss to discover
what the connection was. Later, in the 1850's John Newlands
(1838-98) tried arranging the known elements in horizontal rows
by atomic weight, by putting elements of similar chemical properties under one another. The arrangement led him to a table in
which the horizontal row consisted of seven elements and the re-
current properties fell in the eighth place. Newlands thus called
these periods octaves, a term which guaranteed their rejection.
This seeming rebirth of wild Pythagoreanism in staid Victorian
England was rejected out of hand. At the meeting of the Chemical
Society in which he announced his "discovery," Newlands was asked
sarcastically by one of the members if he had tried arranging the
elements in order according to their initial letter! But, there
was clearly something there and others picked up where Newlands
left off. Success came in 1869. Dimitri Mendeléef (1834-1907)
while composing a textbook on inorganic chemistry for use in the
schools of Russia, took up the problem. His approach differed
subtly but importantly from that of Newlands. The vertical similarities were, by now, so obvious that they could not be ignored.
But Mendeleef recognized, as well, that chemical qualities changed
rather gradually with increasing atomic weight. With this clue
in hand, Mendeleef now proceeded with great daring. When an element of next higher atomic weight differed significantly chemically from its predecessor, Mendeleef inserted a blank space
between the two elements to signify that an element as yet undiscovered was to fill that space. He even went so far as to predict
the properties of these elements. Thus his periodic table was
not merely an arrangement but a research guide to undiscovered
elements. When these elements were discovered, Mendeleef's courage was justified and the Periodic Table was born.

Beyond bringing order into the growing list of elements, the
Periodic Table had important implications for the atomic theory.
Periodicity of properties suggested periodicity of structure.
But atoms, by their very name, were not supposed to have struc-
tures. By the 1880's, there was too much evidence converging from
different directions to permit the preservation of the concept
of the chemical atom in Daltonian terms. In 1859, Bunsen and
Kirchhoff published a paper calling attention to the fact that

elements emitted characteristic light spectra. By the 1880's, these line spectra were assumed to be emitted by subatomic oscillators and this implied that atoms had parts. So, too, did the ionic theory. So, too, did the Periodic Table. Both physicists and chemists were prepared for the discovery of atomic parts, and matter theory had evolved to the point at the end of the nineteenth century where chemists and physicists were both looking for much the same things. The oscillator that produced the physicist's atomic spectrum might also be found to carry the charge of ions. In this sense, at least, chemistry and physics had moved close to one another during the nineteenth century. It was to take more than a half-century, however, for this closeness to turn into a sound marriage.

B. Newland's Octaves

John Alexander Reina Newlands (1837-1898) had been trained as a chemist at the Royal college of Chemistry. He was an experienced analytical chemist to whom the atomic weights of the elements were, literally, his daily companions. It was as an analytical chemist that he was struck by certain periodic similarities in the qualities of the chemical elements. All that seemed necessary was to discover the periodicity. In a series of paper published in the Chemical News* *he reported upon his discovery of this periodicity.*

On Relations among the
Equivalents.

To the Editor.

Sir,--In addition to the facts stated in my late communication, may I be permitted to observe that if the elements are arranged in the order of their equivalents, calling hydrogen 1, lithium 2, glucinum 3, boron 4, and so on (a separate number being attached to each element having a distinct equivalent of its own, and where two elements happen to have the same equivalent, both being designated by the same number), it will be observed that elements having consecutive numbers frequently either belong to the same group or occupy similar positions in different groups, as in the following examples:--

		No.		No.		No.		No.		No.	
Group	*a*	N	6	P	13	As	26	Sb	40	Bi	54
"	*b*	O	7	S	14	Se	27	Te	42	Os	50
"	*c*	Fl	8	Cl	15	Br	28	I	41	—	—
"	*d*	Na	9	K	16	Rb	29	Cs	43	Tl	52
"	*e*	Mg	10	Ca	17	Sr	30	Pa	44	Pb	53

Chemical News, vol. 10 (August 20, 1864), pp. 94-95; vol. 12 (August 18, 1865), p. 83; vol. 12 (August 25, 1865), pp. 94-95; vol. 13 (March 9, 1866), p. 113.

Here the difference between the number of the lowest member of a group and that immediately above it is 7; in other words, the eighth element starting from a given one is a kind of repetition of the first, like the eighth note of an octave in music. The differences between the numbers of the other members of a group are frequently twice as great; thus in the nitrogen group, between N and P there are seven elements; between P and As, 13; between As and Sb, 14; and between Sb and Bi, 14.

In conclusion, I may remark that just as we have several examples of the apparent existence of triads, the extremities of which are known, whilst their centres are wanting (such as the metals of the platinum group, which may be conceived to be the extremities of three distinct triads, and perhaps also silver and gold may be related to each other in this manner), so we may look upon certain of the elements, e.g. Mn, Fe, Co, Ni, and Cu, as the centres of triads, the extremes of which are at present unknown, or, perhaps, in some instances only unrecognised.

I am, &c.,

August 8, 1864.   John A. R. Newlands.

On the Law of Octaves

To the Editor of the Chemical News.

Sir,--With your permission, I would again call attention to a fact pointed out in a communication of mine, inserted in the Chemical News for August 20, 1864.

If the elements are arranged in the order of their equivalents, with a few slight transpositions, as in the accompanying table, it will be observed that elements belonging to the same group usually appear on the same horizontal line.

No.	No.	No.	No.	No.	No.	No.	No.
H 1	F 8	Cl 15	Co & Ni 22	Br 29	Pd 36	I 42	Pt & Ir 50
Li 2	Na 9	K 16	Cu 23	Rb 30	Ag 37	Cs 44	Tl 53
G 3	Mg 10	Ca 17	Zn 25	Sr 31	Bd 38	Ba & V 45	Pb 54
Bo 4	Al 11	Cr 19	Y 24	Ce & La 33	U 40	Ta 46	Th 56
C 5	Si 12	Ti 18	In 26	Zr 32	Sn 39	W 47	Hg 52
N 6	P 13	Mn 20	As 27	Di & Mo 34	Sb 41	Nb 48	Bi 55
O 7	S 14	Fe 21	Se 28	Ro & Ru 35	Te 43	Au 49	Os 51

(Note.--Where two elements happen to have the same equivalent, both are designated by the same number.)

It will also be seen that the numbers of analogous elements generally differ either by 7 or by some multiple of seven; in other words, members of the same group stand to each other in the same relation as the extremities of one or more octaves in music. Thus, in the nitrogen group, between nitrogen and phosphorus there are 7 elements; between phosphorus and arsenic, 14; between arsenic and antimony, 14; and lastly, between antimony and bismuth, 14 also.

This peculiar relationship I propose to provisionally term the "Law of Octaves."   I am, &c.

John A. R. Newlands, F.C.S.

Laboratory, 19, Great St. Helen's, E.C., August 8, 1865.

On the Cause of Numerical Relations
among the Equivalents.

To the Editor.

Sir,--By way of addition to my last letter, I will, with
your permission, endeavour to show that all the numerical relations among the equivalents pointed out by M. Dumas and others,
including the well-known triads, are merely arithmetical results
flowing from the existence of the "law of octaves," taken in connection with the fact of the equivalents forming a series of numbers approaching to the natural order, as may be observed by an
inspection of the following table:--

Symbol.	No.	Eq.	Eq. ÷ No.	Symbol.	No.	Eq.	Eq. ÷ No.
H	1	1	1	Br	29	80	2.758
Li	2	7	3.5	Rb	30	85	2.833
G	3	9	3	Sr	31	87.5	2.823
Bo	4	11	2.75	Zr	32	89.5	2.797
C	5	12	2.4	Ce	33	92	2.788
N	6	14	2.333	Di	34	96	2.824
O	7	16	2.286	Ro	35	104	2.971
F	8	19	2.375	Pd	36	106.5	2.958
Na	9	23	2.555	Ag	37	108	2.919
Mg	10	24	2.4	Cd	38	112	2.947
Al	11	27.5	2.5	Sn	39	118	3.026
Si	12	28	2.333	U	40	120	3
P	13	31	2.385	Sb	41	122	2.975
S	14	32	2.286	I	42	127	3.024
Cl	15	35.5	2.367	Te	43	129	3
K	16	39	2.437	Cs	44	133	3.023
Ca	17	40	2.353	Ba	45	137	3.044
Ti	18	50	2.778	Ta	46	138	3
Cr	19	52.5	2.763	W	47	184	3.915
Mn	20	55	2.75	Nb	48	195	4.062
Fe	21	56	2.667	Au	49	196	4
Co	22	58.5	2.659	Pt	50	197	3.94
Cu	23	63.5	2.761	Os	51	199	3.902
Yt	24	64	2.667	Hg	52	200	3.846
Zn	25	65	2.6	Tl	53	203	3.83
In	26	72	2.769	Pb	54	207	3.833
As	27	75	2.778	Bi	55	210	3.818
Se	28	79.5	2.839	Th	56	238	4.25

In this table the first column of figures gives the numbers
of the elements; the second, their equivalents; and the third,
the product obtained by dividing the equivalent of an element by
its number. It will be seen that the number of an element is
nearly equal to its equivalent divided by a certain sum, which
varies, however, as we ascend the scale, thus:--

From 4 to 17, the No. = Eq. ÷ 2.5
From 18 to 34, the No. = Eq. ÷ 2.75
From 35 to 46, the No. = Eq. ÷ 3
From 47 to 56, the No. = Eq. ÷ 4

Now, as the equivalents correspond more or less closely in their rate of increase to the numbers of the elements, anything that is true of the latter must, with a certain amount of latitude, be true of the former also; and, therefore, if the number of one element is the mean of those of two others (whether belonging to the same group or not), its equivalent will also be the mean of their equivalents.

Thus the number of Ti, 18, is the mean of those of F, 8, and Se, 28, and the equivalent of Ti = 50 is also the mean of those of F = 19 and Se = 79.5, thus:--

$$\frac{19 + 79.5}{2} = 49.25.$$

This is only one example of many that I might adduce of elements, whether analogous or not, possessing intermediate numbers, and also intermediate equivalents.

Now, in conformity with the "law of octaves," elements belonging to the same group generally have numbers differing by seven or by some multiple of seven,--that is to say, if we begin with the lowest member of a group, calling it 1, the succeeding members will have the numbers 8, 15, 22, 29, 36, &c., respectively.

But 8 is the mean between 1 and 15; 15 is the mean between 8 and 22; 22 is the mean between 15 and 29, &c., and, therefore, as an arithmetical result of the "law of octaves," the number of an element is often the exact mean of those of two others belonging to the same group, and consequently its equivalent also approximates to the mean of their equivalents.

The real triad exists in the numbers of analogous elements, as a consequence of their differing by some multiple of a regularly recurring number, viz. 7. The triad of M. Dumas is only an approximation to the former, and is due to the partial concordance between the equivalents of the elements and their respective numbers.

A similar train of reasoning will explain why it is that on deducting the equivalent of the lowest member of a group from that immediately above it we obtain a constant number (about 16). For we find that if, instead of taking elements of the same group (that is, elements whose numbers differ by 7), we perform a similar calculation with elements whose numbers differ by 8 or 9, &c., we obtain in each case numbers quite as constant as in the above. The difference of about 16 merely expresses the average difference for an interval of seven elements in the lower part of the scale of equivalents.

The above remarks are merely offered as an attempt to indicate, in a general manner, the mode in which the existence of arithmetical relations among the equivalents may, at any rate, be partially explained.

I am, &c.,

August 15, 1865.   John A. R. Newlands.

Extract from Report of Meeting of the
Chemical Society, March 1, 1866. Professor
A. W. Williamson in the Chair.

Mr. John A. R. Newlands read a paper entitled "The Law of
Octaves, and the Causes of Numerical Relations among the Atomic
Weights." The author claims the discovery of a law according to
which the elements analogous in their properties exhibit peculiar
relationships, similar to those subsisting in music between a note
and its octave. Starting from the atomic weights on Cannizzaro's
system, the author arranges the known elements in order of succession, beginning with the lowest atomic weight (hydrogen) and
ending with thorium (= 231.5); placing, however, nickel and cobalt, platinum and iridium, cerium and lanthanum, &c., in positions of absolute equality or in the same line. The fifty-six
elements so arranged are said to form the compass of eight octaves, and the author finds that chlorine, bromine, iodine, and
fluorine are thus brought into the same line, or occupy corresponding places in his scale. Nitrogen and phosphorus, oxygen
and sulphur, &c., are also considered as forming true octaves.
The author's supposition will be exemplified in Table II., shown
to the meeting, and here subjoined:--

Table II.--Elements Arranged in Octaves.

No.	No.	No.	No.	No.	No.	No.	No.
H 1	F 8	Cl 15	Co & Ni 22	Br 29	Pd 36	I 42	Pt & Ir 50
Li 2	Na 9	K 16	Cu 23	Rb 30	Ag 37	Cs 44	Os 51
G 3	Mg 10	Ca 17	Zn 24	Sr 31	Cd 38	Ba & V 45	Hg 52
Bo 4	Al 11	Cr 19	Y 25	Ce & La 33	U 40	Ta 46	Tl 53
C 5	Si 12	Ti 18	In 26	Zr 32	Sn 39	W 47	Pb 54
N 6	P 13	Mn 20	As 27	Di & Mo 34	Sb 41	Nb 48	Bi 55
O 7	S 14	Fe 21	Se 28	Ro & Ru 35	Te 43	Au 49	Th 56

Dr. Gladstone made objection on the score of its having been
assumed that no elements remain to be discovered. The last few
years had brought forth thallium, indium, caesium, and rubidium,
and now the finding of one more would throw out the whole system.
The speaker believed there was as close an analogy subsisting between the metals named in the last vertical column as in any of
the elements standing on the same horizontal line.

Professor G. F. Foster humorously inquired of Mr. Newlands
whether he had ever examined the elements according to the order
of their initial letters? For he believed that any arrangement
would present occasional coincidences, but he condemned one which
placed so far apart manganese and chromium, or iron from nickel
and cobalt.

Mr. Newlands said that he had tried several other schemes
before arriving at that now proposed. One founded upon the specific gravity of the elements had altogether failed, and no relation could be worked out of the atomic weights under any other
system than that of Cannizzaro.

C. Dimitri Mendeléef

It was Dimitri Ivanovich Mendeléef who was ultimately successful in discovering the true relationship between the elements. His periodic table finally sorted things out so that chemists could see clearly what their ultimate building blocks were and how they were related to one another.*

The Relation between the Properties and Atomic Weights of the
Elements.

. . . In undertaking to prepare a textbook called "Principles of Chemistry," I wished to establish some sort of system of simple bodies in which their distribution is not guided by chance, as might be thought instinctively, but by some sort of definite and exact principle. We previously saw that there was an almost complete absence of numerical relations for establishing a system of simple bodies, but in the end any system based on numbers which can be determined exactly will deserve preference over systems which do not have numerical support, since the former leave little room for arbitrary choices. The numerical data for simple bodies are limited at the present time. If for some of them the physical properties are determined with certainty, yet this applies only to a very small number of the elementary bodies. For example, such properties as optical, or even electrical or magnetic, ones, cannot in the end serve as a support for a system because one and the same body can show different values for these properties, depending on the state in which they occur. In this regard, it is enough to recall graphite and diamond, ordinary and red phosphorus, and oxygen and ozone. Not only do we not know the density in the vapor state for most of them, by which to determine the weight of the particles of the simple bodies, but this density is subject to alteration exactly like those polymeric alterations which have been noted for complex bodies. Oxygen and sulfur show this effect positively, but the relations between nitrogen, phosphorus, and arsenic offer further confirmation because these similar elements have particle weights of N_2, P_4, and As_4, unequal in the number of atoms among themselves. A number of the properties of the simple bodies must change with these polymeric changes. Thus we cannot be sure that for any element, even for platinum, there may not occur another state, and the location of an element in a system based on its physical properties would then be changed. Besides this, anyone understands that no matter how the properties of a simple body may change in the free state, *something* remains constant, and when the elements form compounds, this *something* has a material value and establishes the characteristics of the compounds which include the given element. In this respect, we know only one constant peculiar to an element, namely, the atomic weight. The size of the atomic weight, by the very essence of

---

*D. I. Mendeléef, "The Relation between the Properties and Atomic Weights of the Elements," in *A Source Book in Chemistry, 1400-1900* by Henry M. Leicester and Herbert S. Klickstein (McGraw Hill, 1952), pp. 439-42, 443-44.

the matter, is a number which is not related to the state of division of the simple body but to the material part which is common to the simple body and all its compounds. The atomic weight belongs not to coal or the diamond, but to carbon. The property which Gerhardt and Cannizzaro determined as the atomic weight of the elements is based on such a firm and certain assumption that for most bodies, especially for those simple bodies whose heat capacity in the free state has been determined, there remains no doubt of the atomic weight, such as existed some years ago, when the atomic weights were so often confused with the equivalents and determined on the basis of varied and often contradictory ideas.

This is the reason I have chosen to base the system on the size of the atomic weights of the elements.

The first attempt which I made in this way was the following: I selected the bodies with the lowest atomic weights and arranged them in the order of the size of their atomic weights. This showed that there existed a period in the properties of the simple bodies, and even in terms of their atomicity the elements followed each other in the order of arithmetic succession of the size of their atoms:

Li = 7; Be = 9.4; B = 11;　C = 12; N = 14; O = 16;　F = 19
Na = 23; Mg = 24; Al = 27.4; Si = 28; P = 31; S = 32; Cl = 35.3
K = 39; Ca = 40; .... Ti = 50; V = 51 ....

In the arrangement of elements with atoms greater than 100, we meet an entirely analogous continuous order:

Ag = 108; Cd = 112; Ur = 116; Sn = 118; Sb = 122; Te = 128; I = 127.

It has been shown that Li, Na, K, and Ag are related to each other, as are C, Si, Ti, Sn, or as are N, P, V, Sb, etc. This at once raises the question whether the properties of the elements are expressed by their atomic weights and whether a system can be based on them. An attempt at such a system follows.

In the assumed system, the atomic weight of the element, unique to it, serves as a basis for determining the place of the element. Comparison of the groups of simple bodies known up to now according to the weights of their atoms leads to the conclusion that the distribution of the elements according to their atomic weights does not disturb the natural similarities which exist between the elements but, on the contrary, shows them directly. . . .

All the comparisons which I have made in this direction lead me to conclude that *the size of the atomic weight determines the nature of the elements*, just as the weight of the molecules determines the properties and many of the reactions of complex bodies. If this conclusion is confirmed by further applications of this approach to the study of the elements, then we are near an epoch in understanding the existing differences and the reasons for the similarity of elementary bodies.

I think that the law established by me does not run counter to the general direction of natural science, and that until now it has not been demonstrated, although already there have been hints of it. Henceforth, it seems to me, there will be a new interest in determining atomic weights, in discovering new elementary bodies, and in finding new analogies between them.

I now present one of many possible systems of elements based on their atomic weights. It serves only as an attempt to express those results which can be obtained in this way. I myself see that this attempt is not final, but it seems to me that it clearly expresses the applicability of my assumptions to all combinations of elements whose atoms are known with certainty. In this I have also wished to establish a general system of the elements. Here is this attempt:

			Ti = 50	Zr = 90	? = 180
			V = 51	Nb = 94	Ta = 182
			Cr = 52	Mo = 96	W = 186
			Mn = 55	Rh = 104,4	Pt = 197,4
			Fe = 56	Ru = 104,4	Ir = 198
		Ni = Co = 59		Pd = 106,6	Os = 199
H = 1			Cu = 63,4	Ag = 108	Hg = 200
	Be = 9,4	Mg = 24	Zn = 65,2	Cd = 112	
	B = 11	Al = 27,4	? = 68	Ur = 116	Au = 197?
	C = 12	Si = 28	? = 70	Sn = 118	
	N = 14	P = 31	As = 75	Sb = 122	Bi = 210?
	O = 16	S = 32	Se = 79,4	Te = 128?	
	F = 19	Cl = 35,5	Br = 80	J = 127	
Li = 7	Na = 23	K = 39	Rb = 85,4	Cs = 133	Tl = 204
		Ca = 40	Sr = 87,6	Ba = 137	Pb = 207
		? = 45	Ce = 92		
		?Er = 56	La = 94		
		?Yt = 60	Di = 95		
		?In = 75,6	Th = 118?		

Periodic table according to D. I. Mendeléev, 1869.

. . . In conclusion, I consider it advisable to recapitulate the results of the above work.

1. Elements arranged according to the size of their atomic weights show clear *periodic* properties.

2. Elements which are similar in chemical function either have atomic weights which lie close together (like Pt, Ir, Os) or show a uniform increase in atomic weight (like K, Rb, Cs). The uniformity of such an increase in the different groups is taken from previous work. In such comparisons, however, the workers did not make use of the conclusions of Gerhardt, Regnault, Cannizzaro, and others who established the true value of the atomic weights of the elements.

3. Comparisons of the elements or their groups in terms of size of their atomic weights establish their so-called "atomicity" and, to some extent, differences in chemical character, a fact which is clearly evident in the group Li, Be, B, C, N, O, F, and is repeated in the other groups.

4. The simple bodies which are most widely distributed in nature have small atomic weights, and all the elements which have small atomic weights are characterized by the specificity of their properties. They are therefore the typical elements. Hydrogen, as the lightest element, is in justice chosen as typical of itself.

5. The *size* of the atomic weight determines the character
of the element, just as the size of the molecule determines the
properties of the complex body, and so, when we study compounds,
we should consider not only the properties and amounts of the elements, not only the reactions, but also the weight of the atoms.
Thus, for example, compounds of S and Te, Cl and I, etc., although
showing resemblances, also very clearly show differences.

6. We should still expect to discover many *unknown* simple
bodies; for example, those similar to Al and Si, elements with
atomic weights of 65 to 75.

7. Some *analogies* of the elements are discovered from the
size of the weights of their atoms. Thus uranium is shown to be
analogous to boron and aluminum, a fact which is also justified
when their compounds are compared.

The purpose of my paper will be entirely attained if I succeed in turning the attention of investigators to the same relationships in the size of the atomic weights of nonsimilar elements, which have, as far as I know, been almost entirely neglected until now. Assuming that in problems of this nature lies
the solution of one of the most important questions of our science,
I myself, as my time will permit, will turn to a comparative study
of lithium, beryllium, and boron.

*   *   *

And now, in order to clarify the matter further, I wish to
draw some conclusions as to the chemical and physical properties
of those elements which have not been placed in the system and
which are still undiscovered but whose discovery is very probable.
I think that until now we have not had any chance to foresee the
absence of these or other elements, because we have had no order
for their arrangement, and even less have we had occasion to predict the properties of such elements. An established system is
limited by its order of known or discovered elements. With the
periodic and atomic relations now shown to exist between all the
atoms and the properties of their elements, we see the possibility
not only of noting the absence of some of them but even of determining, and with great assurance and certainty, the properties of
these as yet unknown elements; it is possible to predict their
atomic weight, density in the free state or in the form of oxides,
acidity or basicity, degree of oxidation, and ability to be reduced and to form double salts and to describe the properties of
the metalloorganic compounds and chlorides of the given element;
it is even possible also to describe the properties of some compounds of these unknown elements in still greater detail. Although at the present time it is not possible to say when one of
these bodies which I have predicted will be discovered, yet the
opportunity exists for finally convincing myself and other chemists of the truth of those hypotheses which lie at the base of
the system I have drawn up. Personally, for me these assumptions
have become so strong that, as in the case of indium, there is
justification for the ideas which are based on the periodic law
which lies at the base of all this study.

Among the ordinary elements, the *lack* of a number of *ana-
logues of boron and aluminum* is very striking, that is, in group

III, and it is certain that we lack an element of this group immediately following aluminum; this must be found in the even, or
second, series, immediately after potassium and calcium. Since
the atomic weights of these latter are near 40, and since then in
this row the element of group IV, titanium, Ti = 50, follows,
then the atomic weight of the missing element should be nearly 45.
Since this element belongs to an even series, it should have more
basic properties than the lower elements of group III, boron or
aluminum, that is, its oxide, R_2O_3, should be a stronger base.
An indication of this is that the oxide of titanium, TiO_2, with
the properties of a very weak acid, also shows many signs of
being clearly basic. On the basis of these properties, the oxide
of the metal should still be weak, like the weakly basic properties of titanium dioxide; compared to aluminum, this oxide should
have a more strongly basic character, and therefore, probably, it
should not decompose water, and it should combine with acids and
alkalis to form simple salts; ammonia will not dissolve it, but
perhaps the hydrate will dissolve weakly in potassium hydroxide,
although the latter is doubtful, because the element belongs to
the even series and to a group of elements whose oxides contain a
small amount of oxygen. I have decided to give this element the
preliminary name of *ekaboron*, deriving the name from this, that
it follows boron as the first element of the even group, and the
syllable *eka* comes from the Sanskrit work meaning "one." Eb = 45.
Ekaboron should be a metal with an atomic volume of about 15, because in the elements of the second series, and in all the even
series, the atomic volume falls quickly as we go from the first
group to the following ones. Actually, the volume of potassium is
nearly 50, calcium nearly 25, titanium and vanadium nearly 9, and
chromium, molybdenum, and iron nearly 7; thus the specific gravity
of the metal should be close to 3.0, since its atomic weight = 45.
The metal will be nonvolatile, because all the metals in the even
series of all the groups (except group I) are nonvolatile; hence
it can hardly be discovered by the ordinary method of spectrum
analysis. It should not decompose water at ordinary temperature,
but at somewhat raised temperatures it should decompose it, as do
many other metals of this series which form basic oxides. Finally, it will dissolve in acids. Its chloride $EbCl_3$ (perhaps
Eb_2Cl_6), should be a volatile substance but a salt, since it
corresponds to a basic oxide. Water will act on it as it does on
the chlorides of calcium and magnesium, that is, ekaboron chloride
will be a hygroscopic body and will be able to evolve hydrogen
chloride without having the character of a hydrochloride. Since
the volume of calcium chloride = 49 and that of titanium chloride
= 109, the volume of ekaboron chloride should be close to 78, and
therefore its specific gravity will probably be about 2.0. Ekaboron oxide, Eb_2O_3, should be a nonvolatile substance and probably
should not fuse; it should be insoluble in water, because even
calcium oxide is very slightly soluble in water, but it will probably dissolve in acid. Its specific volume should be about 39,
because in the series potassium oxide has a volume of 35, CaO =
18, TiO = 20, and CrO_3 = 36; that is, considered on the basis of
a content of one atom of oxygen, the volume quickly falls to the
right, thus, for potassium = 35, for calcium = 18, for titanium =
10, for chromium = 12, and therefore the·volume for ekaboron oxide

ontaining one atom of oxygen should be nearly 13, and so the formula Eb_2O_3 should correspond to a volume of about 39, and therefore anhydrous ekaboron oxide will have a specific gravity close to 3.5. Since it is a sufficiently strong base, this oxide should show little tendency to form alums, although it will probably give alum-forming compounds, that is, double salts with potassium sulfate. Finally, ekaboron will not form metalloorganic compounds, since it is one of the metals of an even series. Judging by the data now known for the elements which accompany cerium, none of them belong in the place which is assigned to ekaboron, so that this metal is certainly not one of the members of the cerium complex which is now known.

D. Molecular Qualities

1. J. H. van't Hoff and J. A. Le Bel

The discovery of the tetravalency of carbon provided the necessary information for the suggestion that chemical qualities might be the result of the location of atoms in space, as well as caused by the nature of the elements in a compound themselves. Le Bel and van't Hoff developed this idea. *

HISTORICAL.

Original Enunciation of the Theory.

The theory of what is known as the 'asymmetric carbon atom' originated simultaneously in France and Holland, and was enunciated independently by two chemists, and we think it desirable to quote the chief part of the text of the two original memoirs as they were given by their authors.

In the Bulletin of the Chemical Society of Paris, November, 1874, p. 337, J. A. Le Bel expressed his conceptions in the following manner:--

'On the relations which exist between the atomic formulae of organic bodies and the rotatory power of their solutions.

'We have hitherto possessed no certain rule which allows us to predict whether or not the solution of a substance should manifest rotatory power (in respect of polarised light). It was simply known that the derivatives of an active substance were in general also active; but it was often observed that rotatory power might disappear in certain derivatives, and even in the more immediate derivatives, while it was preserved in derivatives much more remote. Starting from considerations of a purely geometric character I have arrived at the expression of a more general law. Before giving the reasoning by which I have arrived at this law, I propose to give the data on which it is founded, and finally to discuss the verifications furnished by the present

---

*J. H. van't Hoff, *Chemistry in Space*, trans. and edited by J. E. Marsh (Oxford, 1891), pp. 1-13.

state of our chemical knowledge.

'The researches of Pasteur and others have completely established the correlation existing between molecular dissymmetry and
rotatory power. If the dissymmetry only exists in the crystalline
molecule the crystal alone will be active; if, on the other hand,
it belongs to the chemical molecule, rotatory power will be manifested in solution often, and also by the crystal, if the structure admits of its perception, as is the case with sulphate of
strychnine and the alum of amylamine. There are, moreover, mathematical proofs of the necessary existence of this correlation,
which we may consider an absolutely ascertained fact.

'In the reasoning which follows we shall not take into account the dissymmetries which might result from a possible orientation possessed by the atoms and monatomic radicals in space; as
a consequence of considering them equivalent to spheres or material points, equal if the atoms or the radicals are equal, and
different if they are different. This restriction is justified
by the fact that without recourse to such orientation it has become possible to account for all the cases of isomerism hitherto
observed, and the discussion at the close of this memoir will show
that the appearance of rotatory power can be equally well predicted without recourse to the hypothesis just mentioned.

'*First general principle*.--Let us consider a molecule of a
chemical compound having the formula MA_4: M being a simple or complex radical combined with four atoms A, capable of replacement
by substitution. Let us replace three of them by simple or complex monatomic radicals different from A and also from each other;
the body obtained will be unsymmetrical. In other words, the
group of radicals RR'R"A if considered as material points, being
each different, forms by itself a structure not superposable on
its image reflected in a mirror, and the residue M cannot re-
establish symmetry. In general, therefore, we may assert that
when a body is derived from the original type MA_4 by the substitution of three atoms A by three new atoms or radicals of different kinds its molecule will by unsymmetrical, and it will exhibit
rotatory power.

'But there are two exceptional cases distinct in character.

'(1) If the molecular type has a plane of symmetry containing
the four atoms A, the substitution of these by radicals (which we
must consider as not capable of orientation) can in no way alter
the symmetry in respect of this plane, and in such instances the
whole series of substitution products will be inactive.

'(2) The last radical replacing A may consist of the same
atoms as all the rest of the group into which it enters, and
these two equal groupings may have on polarised light either a
neutralising effect, or an effect of increased activity: if the
former is the case, the body will be inactive. Now it is possible that this arrangement may be met with in the case of a derivative of an active unsymmetrical body where there is but little
difference in constitution, and we shall see later a remarkable
instance of this.

'*Second general principle*.--If in the fundamental type we
substitute only two radicals R, R', there may be symmetry or not
according to the constitution of the primitive type MA_4. If this

molecule had originally a plane of symmetry passing through the
two atoms of A which have been replaced by R and R', this plane
will remain a plane of symmetry after the substitution; and the
body obtained will be inactive. From our knowledge of the constitution of certain simple types we are able to assert that certain
bodies derived from them by two replacements will be inactive.

'Again, if it happens not only that a single substitution
furnishes only one derivative, but also that two and even three
substitutions only furnish one and the same chemical isomer, we
are obliged to admit that the four atoms A occupy the angles of a
regular tetrahedron, whose planes of symmetry are identical with
those of the whole molecule MA_4; in this case also no bisubsti-
tuted body can have rotatory power.

'*Application to saturated bodies of the fatty series.*--All
the saturated bodies of the fatty series are derived from marsh
gas CH_4 by replacement of the hydrogen by different radicals.
Provided that the atoms of hydrogen are not in the same plane, a
supposition on which the very existence of active trisubstituted
bodies is based, we can apply the first general principle and
assert that the substitution of three different radicals will
furnish active bodies, and whenever in the constitutional or typical formula of a substance we meet with one carbon atom combined
with three monatomic radicals different from each other and from
hydrogen, we ought to find it an active body.

'Further, as marsh gas never furnishes more than one derivative
by two substitutions, we can apply the second general principle and assert that such derivatives are never active. Hence
whenever we meet with a carbon atom combined with two atoms of
hydrogen or with two identical radicals, such a body ought not to
manifest rotatory power. Let us now review the active bodies of
the fatty series (as such are instanced the lactic, malic, tartaric, and amylic groups, and the group of sugars).

'*Fatty bodies with two free atomicities.*--We have not yet
taken into account active unsaturated bodies, for we do not include in this class bodies obtained by the substitution of an
active radical in an unsaturated inactive body, such as, for example, valerate of allyl.

'We have only to examine the case where the double linking
of the unsaturated body is due to the disappearance of some of
the radicals, the unsymmetrical grouping of which caused rotatory
power in the corresponding saturated body. Since all the bodies
with two free atomicities are derived from ethylene, it is to
this latter we must, if possible, apply the general principles
which we have previously employed.

'We shall neglect the case where the four atoms of hydrogen
may not have determinate positions one to another, for it is clear
that their replacement could not furnish unsymmetrical bodies.
If, on the contrary, these relative positions are fixed, we can
apply to ethylene the same reasoning as to marsh gas.

'If the four atoms of hydrogen lie in the same plane, which
is a possible case of equilibrium, there will be no trisubstituted
active derivative; nevertheless, we do not know examples of well-
studied bodies derived from ethylene by three different substitutions, and we are therefore unable to solve this question at
present.

'As to the second general principle, it is not applicable to ethylene, for the formula $CH_2 = CH_2$ shows that by two substitutions chemically different isomers are obtained. This is not opposed to the possibility of the atoms being in the same plane, in which case the derivatives by two substitutions will be inactive. In any other case, to explain the isomerism of the ethylene derivatives, we must suppose the hydrogen atoms placed at the angles of a hemihedral quadratic pyramid superposable on its image $\frac{P}{2}$, and we should obtain by two substitutions two isomers, one of which would be symmetrical, and the other unsymmetrical. These isomers will be both symmetrical if the two substituted radicals are the same, as is the case with maleic and fumaric acids. It will suffice, therefore, to study the optical character of two disubstituted derivatives, such as the amylene of active amyl alcohol $CH_2 = C = \frac{CH_3}{C_2H_5}$, and its isomer $CH_3 - CH = CH - C_2H_3$, to decide whether the four atoms of hydrogen are or are not in the same plane.

'*Aromatic Series*.--All chemists agree in considering that the atoms of hydrogen in benzene occupy fixed positions, we cannot then consider, as we did in the case of saturated bodies, a part of the molecule of benzene as a single material point; but this restrictive hypothesis will still hold in the case of the radicals or groups which replace hydrogen in benzene. The geometrical hypotheses which account for the isomerism of the aromatic series have already been discussed elsewhere; they assume that the atoms of hydrogen are situated at the six equal angles of a rhombohedron or at those of a right prism on an equilateral triangular base. A simple geometrical reasoning shows that in either arrangement by two different substitutions there are obtained an unsymmetrical and two different symmetrical isomers; the existence of an active dymene which has been announced confirms these hypotheses which we will not discuss further.

'Without ascribing to the atoms of hydrogen in benzene any particular grouping, we can apply the first general principle to any three atoms of hydrogen whatever, provided they do not occupy a plane of symmetry of the whole molecule.

'Hence it follows that we shall discover active bodies whenever three atoms of hydrogen at least are replaced by different radicals. We find this inference realised in a large number of bodies of the camphor series.

'The case is not the same for spirit of turpentine; we know that this is derived, as also the camphor series, from paracymene, in which the radicals methyl and propyl occupy the positions 1 and 4 in Kekulé's hexagon, and as this is a plane of symmetry of benzene we have the reason why cymene is inactive. Now spirit of turpentine is derived from cymene by the substitution of two H_2 groups for two atoms of hydrogen; if these occupy the positions 2 and 6 or 3 and 5, symmetrical with regard to the plane of symmetry passing through 1 and 4, we shall have inactive isomers; on the other hand we shall have active isomers (terebenthene and camphene) if they occupy positions not symmetrical one to another, as 2 and 5 or 2 and 3; and one might apply the same reasoning to the other isomers of terebenthene.

'We see what amount of interest is attached to the study of active aromatic compounds, and how necessary it is that chemists who are dealing with bi- and tri-substituted derivatives of benzene capable of being active should attempt the separation of their dextro- and laevo-rotatory isomers. We will proceed to show that the bodies obtained by synthesis consist in fact of equal proportions of these isomers.

'*Theorem.*--When an unsymmetrical body is formed in a reaction where there are present originally only symmetrical bodies, there will be formed in equal quantities two isomers of inverse symmetry.

'This is not necessarily true for unsymmetrical compounds formed in presence of active bodies themselves, or traversed by circularly polarised light, or, in short, submitted to some cause which is favourable to the formation of one of the unsymmetrical isomers. Such conditions are exceptional; and generally in the case of bodies synthetically prepared those which are active must necessarily be overlooked unless the chemist takes pains to separate the mixed isomeric products of which the combined action on polarised light is neutral. We have a striking example of this in the case of tartaric acid, for neither the dextro nor the laevo acid has ever been obtained directly by synthesis, but always the active acid or racemic acid which is a combination of equal parts of dextro and laevo acid.'

In a Dutch pamphlet, published in September, 1874, I expressed my own opinions as follows:--

'*A treatise on a system of atomic formulae in three dimensions and on the relation between rotatory power and chemical constitution.*

'I propose to offer certain ideas in a preliminary note in order to profit by the discussion which may follow.

'The atomic formulae at present in use are incapable of interpreting certain instances of isomerism: this defect which is becoming more and more evident is due perhaps to the absence of precise conceptions as to the relative positions of the atoms.

'Dealing in the first instance with organic bodies, if we suppose that the four affinities of carbon act in the same plane and in directions perpendicular to each other, the number of isomers derivable from methane CH_4 is as follows: none in the cases CH_3R and $CH(R)_3$; two in the cases $CH_2(R)_2$, CH_2RR_1 and $CHR_2(R)_2$; and three in the cases $CHR_1R_2R_3$ and $CR_1R_2R_3R_4$; this number is evidently larger than we are as a matter of fact acquainted with.

'On the other hand, if we grant that the affinities of the carbon atom are directed towards the angles of a regular tetrahedron, of which this atom occupies the centre, there results a marked coincidence between the theory and the facts. According to this hypothesis the number of isomers becomes as follows:--

'No isomers in the cases CH_3R_1, $CH_2(R_1)_2$, $CH_2R_1R_2$ and $CHR_2(R)_2$; the case alone $CHR_1R_2R_3$, or more generally $CR_1R_2R_3R_4$, allows the prediction of isomerism; in other words,--If the four affinities of the carbon atom are saturated by four different groups, we obtain two tetrahedrons of which one is the nonsuperposable image of the other, that is to say, we have to deal with two different structural formulae in space. Consequently according to this hypothesis the compounds $CR_1R_2R_3R_4$ possess a different character from that of the compounds $C(R_1)_2R_2R_3$, $C(R_1)_3R_2$ or $C(R_1)_4$, a difference which is not explained by atomic formulae in their present form.

'In offering this first conclusion it appears to me possible to show that the compounds containing an atom of carbon combined with four different groups, which I will call an "asymmetric" atom, are in a special manner characterised as much by the fact of isomerism as by their peculiar properties. This fact offers a serious obstacle to the application of the constitutional formulae hitherto employed.

'First Part.--I. *Relation between the asymmetric carbon atom and rotatory power.*

'(a) Every carbon compound which in solution rotates the plane of polarised light contains an asymmetric carbon atom.

'To justify this statement it is only necessary to pass in review the active bodies of ascertained constitution (as such may be quoted the lactic, tartaric, camphoric groups, and the group of sugars).

'(b) The derivatives of optically active bodies lose their rotatory power if the asymmetry of the carbon atom disappears. This in general does not take place otherwise. (The examples quoted apply here.)

'(c) On reviewing the compounds which contain an asymmetric carbon atom, it is clear that proposition (a) can not be taken in a converse sense, that is to say, that a compound of such a nature acts necessarily on polarised light; we can explain this by the following considerations:--

'(1) The compounds in question may be composed of an inactive mixture of two oppositely active isomers.

'(2) The rotatory power may have escaped notice owing to its feebleness or the want of solubility of the compound.

'(3) The presence of an asymmetric carbon atom may of itself be an insufficient condition, and not only the difference of the groups, but also their nature should be taken into consideration.

'However that may be, the above observations show that a relation may exist between atomic constitution and rotatory power, which may serve in default of better arguments to explain the following cases:--

'(1) Active amyl alcohol,
$(CH_3)(C_2H_6)CH.CH_2OH$,

'(2) Inactive citric acid,
$(CH_2CO_2H)_2COH.CO_2H$.

'(3) Most simple active compounds,
the alcohol $CH_3CH.OHC_2H_5$,
the acid $CH_3CH(CO_2H)C_2H_5$,
diatomic alcohol $CH_3CH.OHCH_2OH$,
the hydrocarbon $CH_3C_2H_5CHC_3H_7$,
the aromatic hydrocarbon $CH_3C_2H_5CHC_6H_5$.

'(4) Prediction of inactive series,
hydrocarbons of the normal series $CH_3(CH_2)_3CH_3$.
Primary alcohols and the corresponding acids derived
from the normal hydrocarbons.

'(5) Prediction of the possibility of separating the body CHBrClI into two isomers oppositely active.

'II. *Relation between the asymmetric carbon atom and the number of isomers.*

'Possibly the presence of asymmetric carbon is insufficient of itself to produce rotatory power; yet its presence must, according to the hypothesis proposed, lead to an isomerism manifesting itself in some way or other, an isomerism which can predict double the number of bodies foreseen by the use of present formulae if it deals with one asymmetric atom, and many more in the case of several such atoms. In fact, it appears possible to point out compounds exhibiting the apparent anomaly in question, which Wislicenus has called geometrical isomerism, insisting on the evident insufficiency of existing hypotheses, though without offering a more satisfactory explanation.

'(As applicable examples may be instanced dibrom- and isodibrom-succinic acids, citra-, ita- and mesabromo-pyrotartaric, and citra-, ita- and mesamalic acids.)

'Second Part.--I have hitherto dealt with the application of this hypothesis to saturated bodies (excepting always certain benzene derivatives); for the sake of completeness it is necessary to deal with:--

'*The influence of the new conception on the series of unsaturated bodies having two free atomicities.*

'To represent the double bond between two carbon atoms, we suppose two tetrahedrons having one of their edges common, so that the four groups R_1, R_2, R_3, R_4 combined respectively to the two atoms of carbon occupy the free angles, and are situated in one plane.

'If all the groups R_1, R_2, R_3, R_4 are identical, or if there is equality only between R_1 and R_2, R_3 and R_4, there will be only one relative position possible; if, on the other hand, R_1 and R_2 are different, and at the same time R_3 and R_4, no matter whether the groups R_1 and R_3, or R_2 and R_4 are identical or not, there will be two different relative positions enabling us to predict a case of isomerism not interpretable by the aid of the ordinary atomic formulae.

'From a study of the subject it seems that the following compounds are instances of this isomerism (as such are given, fumaric and maleic acids, bromo- and isobromomaleic, citra- ita- and mesaconic, crotonic and isocrotonic, chloro- and isochlorocrotonic acids).

'Third Part.--It only remains to consider compounds having a triple bond between the carbon atoms, for example, acetylene. Such compounds may be represented by two tetrahedrons which have three angles in common, the groups combined with the two carbon atoms occupying the free angles. It is clear that in this case the hypothesis entails no considerations other than follow from the formulae in use.

'Finally, I think I am entitled to observe that:--

'(1) The new hypothesis leaves no phenomenon unexplained that the theories in use are capable of interpreting.

'(2) Certain properties and certain isomerisms hitherto unexplained are explicable by the new hypothesis.

'(3) The observation as to bodies which in solution are optically active has some analogy with that of Rammelsberg in the case of active crystals. This scientist, starting from the researches of Herschell and Pasteur, asserts that the property of rotating the ray of polarised light in the solid state is accompanied by the existence of two crystalline forms, each the non-superposable image of the other. It is plain that we are here dealing with a relative position of molecules in the active crystal perfectly analogous to that of the atomic groupings in the active molecule, a position which entails the absence of a plane of symmetry in the active crystals mentioned by Rammelsberg, and also in the tetrahedrons representing, according to my hypothesis, the molecules endowed with rotatory power.'

2. Hermann Kolbe

Not all chemists were favorably struck by the idea of chemistry being reduced to solid geometry. To many, the very existence of atoms was in doubt; now to insist that chemical qualities resulted from the orientation of these quasi-metaphysical particles in space was too much. Hermann Kolbe (1818-84), Professor of Chemistry at Leipzig gave voice to his objections to this new departure in chemistry. *

'In a paper published lately . . . I have ascribed as one of the causes of the present decay of chemical research in Germany the lack of general and at the same time thorough chemical training, since no small fraction of our chemical professors are working to the great detriment of the science. In consequence of this, a miserable speculative philosophy, useless in reality, while apparently deep and ingenious, is springing up like a rank growth. Fifty years ago this was swept away and its place taken by exact scientific research. At the present time, however, it is again being rescued from the lumber-room of man's erratic speculations, by certain pseudo-philosophers seeking to thrust it forward surreptitiously, like some fashionably and gorgeously attired female, intruding into good society which is not her place.

'If any one supposes that I exaggerate this evil, I recommend him to read, if he has the patience, the recent fanciful publication of Messrs. Van't Hoff and Hermann on "Die Lagerung der Atome im Raume." This paper, like many others, I should have been content to ignore had not a distinguished chemist taken it under his protection and warmly recommended it as a performance of merit.

'A Dr. J. H. Van't Hoff, of the Veterinary College, Utrecht, appears to have no taste for exact chemical research. He finds it a less arduous task to mount his Pegasus (evidently borrowed from the Veterinary College) and to soar to his Chemical Parnassus, there to reveal in his "La Chimie dans l'Espace" how he

*J. H. van't Hoff, *ibid.*, pp. 15-18.

finds the atoms situated in the world's space.

'His hallucinations met with but little encouragement from the prosaic chemical public. Dr. F. Hermann, assistant at the Agricultural Institute of Heidelberg, therefore undertook to give them further publicity by means of a German edition, which bears the title "Die Lagerung der Atome im Raume."

'It is not possible, even cursorily, to criticise this paper, since its fanciful nonsense carefully avoids any basis of fact, and is quite unintelligible to the calm investigator. To obtain, however, some idea of what may have been in the minds of the authors, it will suffice to read the two following paragraphs. The pamphlet begins with the words:--

'"Our modern chemical theory has two weak points. It does not express itself either as to the relative position of the atoms in the molecule or as to their methods of movement."

'The second paragraph at the top of page 35 in the memoir runs as follows:--

'"In the asymmetric carbon atom we have a medium distinguished by the screw-like arrangement (sic) of its smallest parts, the atoms!"

'In view of the objection that it is unfair to quote isolated passages without giving the context, I can only refer to the memoir itself. Anybody can then satisfy himself that these passages with the context or without are equally absurd and unintelligible.

'It is characteristic of the present time with its poverty in and hatred for criticism, that two chemists almost unknown, one from a veterinary college and the other from an agricultural institute, should on the deepest and possibly insoluble problems of chemistry, especially the question of the position of the atoms in space, give their opinions with an amount of assurance and undertake the solution of these questions with an amount of audacity such as to astound the true investigator.

'I should, as I have said, have taken no notice of this matter, had not Wislicenus oddly enough prefaced the pamphlet, and not by way of a joke but in all seriousness warmly recommended it as a serviceable performance, on which account many a young inexperienced chemist might be led astray and set some store by these baseless and superficial speculations.

'Wislicenus delivers himself in his preface as follows:--

'"I was obliged to express the opinion that the facts compelled me to explain the difference between isomeric molecules of the same structural formulae by the different position of their atoms in space."

'It is one of the signs of the times that modern chemists hold themselves bound and consider themselves in a position to give an explanation for everything, and when their knowledge fails them to make use of supernatural explanations. Such a treatment of scientific subjects, not many degrees removed from a belief in witches and from spirit-rapping, even Wislicenus considers permissible. He thus continues--

'"We are indebted to Van't Hoff for his having performed this serivce in a perfectly definite and in the happiest manner," &c.

'Herewith Wislicenus makes it clear that he has gone over from the camp of the true investigators to that of the speculative philosophers of ominous memory, who are separated. by only thin "medium" from Spiritualism.'

3. *Van't Hoff and Le Bel opened up new vistas in organic chemistry. They did little in their work on stereochemistry, however, to explain the ordinary actions of molecules in inorganic chemistry. New insights into chemical activity here came from the enunciation of the ionic theory of dissociation in the 1880s. Van't Hoff again played a crucial role here with his work on osmotic pressure. It is described below in the lecture that he gave upon receipt of the Nobel Prize for Chemistry in 1901.**

Although the investigations on which I am about to speak were carried out 15 years ago, I am going to begin by describing still earlier studies--those which, in fact, formed the basis of my own. These studies concern the experimental determination of osmotic pressure.

What is osmotic pressure? When a solution, e.g. of sugar in water, is separated from the pure solvent--in this case water--by a membrane which allows water but not sugar to pass through it, then water forces its way through the membrane into the solution. This process naturally results in greater pressure on that side of the membrane to which the water is penetrating, i.e. to the solution side.

This pressure is osmotic pressure.

It is thanks to this osmotic pressure that the sap of the oak-tree rises to the topmost twigs. This pressure was known to exist as long ago as the beginning of the 19th century, but it is only somewhat more than 20 years ago since this phenomenon has been the subject of precise measurements. It was the botanist Pfeffer who first measured this pressure in 1877 by making a membrane which satisfied the following three conditions: It was permeable to water, impermeable to sugar, and it withstood the by no means negligible pressure to which it was subjected.

Osmotic forces are in fact unexpectedly great: with a 1% sugar solution they are equal to no less than 2/3 atm.

Thus, Pfeffer measured osmotic pressure but he was unable to find the relation between the value of this pressure and the concentration of the solution, its temperature, etc. He put this problem to the celebrated physicist Clausius in Bonn, but he, too, failed to discover any regular interrelations. Pfeffer's results therefore remained in a specialized botanical paper, thus escaping the notice of scientists in other fields.

The importance of a solution of this problem becomes clear when one remembers the vital role played by osmotic pressure in plant and animal life. The membranes of the cell are in fact

---

**Nobel Lectures, Chemistry*, Elsevier Pub. Co., Amsterdam, 1966, pp. 5-10.

permeable to water but not to substances dissolved in the cell fluid. Osmotic pressure can therefore develop in the cells. It was the botanist Hugo de Vries in particular who emphasized its importance to plant life: Such pressure (turgor) must exist in the plant cells, if they are not to wither; in other words it is essential for growth. Thus, plants wither not only when they lose water through evaporation but also when they are surrounded by an aqueous solution of common salt, potassium chloride, magnesium chloride, sugar or other substance, if the solution is of higher osmotic pressure, whereas they do not wilt if the osmotic pressure is lower. The critical point can be very accurately determined with the aid of a microscope, and thus De Vries found a method of establishing how concentrated a solution must be if it is to have the same osmotic pressure as the plant cells, i.e. if it is to be «isotonic» with them.

Donders and Hamburger then discovered that osmotic pressure plays no less important a part in animal than in plant life. The life of the higher animals stands or falls with the erythrocytes. These are cells which in relation to the osmotic pressure of the liquid surrounding them behave in a manner similar to plant cells, i.e. if the external osmotic pressure is too great, then a phenomenon similar to wilting occurs. And at that time it was particularly remarkable that solutions found to be isotonic in this respect were also isotonic for the plant cell.

Lastly, in chemistry osmotic pressure is very important because, among other things, it can be related directly to what is known as chemical affinity. In the binding of water of crystallization, for instance, one can imagine that natural gypsum, the chemical formula of which is $CaSO_4 \cdot 2H_2O$, binds its water of crystallization in almost the same way as the plant cell holds water within itself, and the force with which this takes place can be measured in the same way as De Vries measured the osmotic force of cells. If a piece of transparent selenite is placed successively in aqueous solutions of increasing concentration of any substance, then there finally comes a point at which the gypsum can no longer retain its water but gives it up to the solution of greater osmotic pressure: «it wilts». The force with which gypsum binds its water can therefore be measured directly by osmotic pressure.

So much for the earlier work.

In the subsequent study of processes in this field the law around which the prize-winning work centred was now discovered.

It was found namely that with sufficiently dilute solutions the osmotic pressure was the same as the gas pressure, i.e. the pressure which the dissolved substance would exert as gas. To some extent this is obvious: Just as one imagines the gas pressure P to arise as a result of the movement of molecules and of their collisions with the walls (Fig. 1), so can one imagine the osmotic pressure p to arise as a result of the collisions of the dissolved molecules with the semi-permeable membrane (Fig. 2) surrounded by the solvent (denoted by shading).

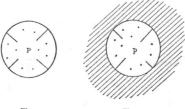

Fig. 1.   Fig. 2.

However, independently of an anyway hypothetical conception on
the cause of this pressure, it was found that under the same circumstances, i.e. with the same number of molecules in the same
volume and at the same temperature, the pressures also were the
same. This can be expressed mathematically by the equation

$$p = P \qquad (1)$$

osmotic pressure = gas pressure. From this formula it is possible
to calculate theoretically the value found by Pfeffer: 2/3 atm.
for a 1% sugar solution.

It was found, however, that a relatively small group of solu-
tions--all of them aqueous--of acids, bases and salts, which are
known as electrolytes, e.g. solutions of sodium chloride or potassium chloride (i.e. mostly those which were investigated first),
constituted an exception. In the case of these the law did not
apply. The osmotic pressure was i times greater than the theoretical value, and consequently the following formula was for a
time used for these exceptions:

$$p = iP \qquad (2)$$

We shall be returning to this point later. In the case of the
non-electrolytes this reduces to (1), since $i = 1$. Now let us
apply the basic relationship and consider the so-called chemical
equilibrium. A distinction must be made between complete and incomplete reactions, according to the final state in which a chemical reaction results. After dynamite has been exploded not the
slightest trace of the original substance is found. The reaction
is complete. In other cases, however, the reaction ceases before
complete transformation--for instance, where methanol and formic
acid are converted into water and methyl formate according to the
equation:

$$CH_4O + CH_2O_2 = H_2O + C_2H_4O_2$$

A similar formula might also be drawn up for the dynamite explosion. In the reaction which has just been formulated, however,
only 2/3 of the possible quantity of the products on the right
side are formed. The reason for this is that not only are methyl
formate and water produced from methanol and formic acid, but

that conversely methanol and formic acid are produced again from
methyl formate and water. This can be illustrated in the formula
by introducing the sign for a reversible reaction instead of the
sign of equality:

$$CH_4O + CH_2O_2 \rightleftarrows H_2O + C_2H_4O_2$$

Such transformations, then, take place in either direction: the
final state being known as *chemical equilibrium.*

The laws governing this chemical equilibrium in the case of
dissolved substances can now be deduced by using the basic relationship for osmotic pressure.

The first of these,

for non-electrolytes: $\qquad \Sigma \, n \, \log p = K \qquad$ (3a)
for electrolytes: $\qquad \Sigma \, ni \, \log p = K \qquad$ (3b)

determines the quantity of the product which will form in a given
volume from given quantities with substances reacting with one
another, provided that a single so-called equilibrium constant,
K, is known.

Since the value i enters into this formula in the case of
electrolytes, we see that it plays an important part in the relevant laws of equilibrium.

In the second law

$$\frac{dK}{dt} = \frac{W}{2T^2} \qquad (4)$$

we find yet another factor affecting the equilibrium, namely the
temperature T (so-called absolute temperature). W is the quantity
of heat evolved during the reaction.

Finally, in the last formula

$$K = -\frac{A}{2T} \qquad (5)$$

allowance is also made for the quantity of work done during a
chemical reaction, e.g. a dynamite explosion, the quantity being
linked with the equilibrium constants.

Following this brief mathematical excursion we will now turn
to some of the results which were subsequently obtained by means
of these formulae.

I.   The molecular weight of dissolved substances is now easy
to determine. Fifteen years ago it was possible to assess the
molecular weight of gaseous substances only. By means of osmotic
pressure it is now also possible to determine the molecular weight
of dissolved substances. But it is not only liquids which have
come into the range of molecular weight determination. In addition, homogeneous mixtures, e.g. isomorphic mixtures of solid substances are comparable to solutions, and the laws of osmosis can
therefore be extended to solid substances. Consequently, it is
now possible to determine molecular weight not only in the
gaseous, but also in the liquid and in the solid state of aggre-

gation. The problem of molecular weight determination has thus to a certain extent been solved.

The results are very interesting. It has often been thought that during the transition from the gaseous to the liquid phase several gas molecules unite to form a liquid molecule, and that the molecules in the solid state of aggregation consist of still larger complexes. In reality, however, the situation is very simple. It is in fact only in exceptional cases that in a liquid or solid state of aggregation, molecules consisting of two gas molecules of the substance have been found, whereas nothing like a substance which forms aggregates of three gas molecules has yet been found for certain.

II. Equation (2) was at first the critical point in the theory. I should not have had the pleasure of giving this lecture if Professor Arrhenius had not succeeded in demonstrating the cause of these exceptions and therefore in reducing Equation (2) to (1).

III. We need go no further into Equation (3a). It coincides essentially with the law of mass action formulated by the two Norwegians Guldberg and Waage, except with regard to i and n (number of molecules participating in the reaction).

IV. Equation (4) links the chemical equilibrium constant K with the heat W evolved by the reaction. It can of course be tested experimentally, and has indeed been confirmed experimentally.

A corollary to this law shows how the chemical equilibrium varies with temperature--namely how, as the temperature increases, more of the one compound is formed at the expense of the other, or vice versa. This corollary can be stated as follows: At low temperature the greater yield is always of that product whose formation is accompanied by evolution of heat.

In most cases, in fact, the equilibrium at ordinary temperature has shifted so far in favour of those products which are situated on one side of the arrows in the chemical formula that no trace of the products on the other side can be detected. An example of this is the formation of water from a mixture of oxygen and hydrogen, the so-called oxyhydrogen gas. At ordinary temperature the equilibrium is so much on the side of the water that the oxyhydrogen gas cannot be detected at all. At higher temperatures there is a shift towards the gas; a measurable equilibrium between water, oxygen, and hydrogen is established. The above-mentioned formula thus embraces the dissociation processes which were studied by Deville and Deprez.

V. It is only very recently that it has been possible to test Equation (5) experimentally. Bredig and Knüpfer have determined K from the equilibrium and have also determined by chemical methods the work done during the reaction.

In conclusion a timely remark. Whereas application of the laws of osmosis has proved very fruitful in the field of chemistry, what De Vries and Donders emphasized 15 years ago, namely that osmotic pressure plays a fundamental role in plant and animal life, has since been fully confirmed as well. The determination of osmotic pressure and of the associated lowering of the freezing-point of solutions is already frequently of great importance in physiology and medicine, e.g. in the study of disease. However, the peculiar discovery made very recently by Loeb is the most important one of all. This scientist has been studying the problem of fertilization, which is bound up so closely with the problem of life, and he has found that the eggs of sea urchins will develop as a result of the temporary action of a specific osmotic pressure brought about by solutions of potassium chloride, magnesium chloride, sugar, etc.

4. *The real architect of the ionic theory was Svante Arrhenius (1859-1927). In 1904, he presented an account of his discoveries and ideas before an audience at the Royal Institution of Great Britain.* *

Development of the Theory of Electrolytic Dissociation

The law of multiple proportions is one of the foundations on which modern chemistry is built. Another such is Avogadro's law which states that equal volumes of different gases at the same temperature and pressure contain the same number of molecules. This theory, which dates from the beginning of the nineteenth century, first met with strong opposition and it was its great value in explaining the new discoveries within the rapidly expanding field of organic chemistry that resulted in its universal adoption in the middle of last century after Cannizzaro had acted vigorously in its favour.

Meanwhile there were certain problems to be overcome before Avogadro's law could be accepted. It was found, for example, that the molecular volume of ammonium chloride, NH_4Cl, in the gaseous state is greater than would be supposed on the basis of its chemical composition. This led to the assumption that the molecules of NH_4Cl in the gaseous form are partly broken down into ammonia, NH_3, and hydrochloric acid, HCl. Von Pebal and Von Than were able to prove that this does in fact occur. They used an apparatus shown in Fig. 1. Two tubes were placed one inside the other by means of a cork. The outer tube was sealed at its open end; the inner tube was open and contained at C, on top of an asbestos partition, a piece of NH_4Cl. The top was heated in an air bath so that the piece of NH_4Cl slowly volatilized. At the same time a stream of hydrogen was admitted through the two glass tubes D and E. Ammonia diffuses through porous walls at a faster rate than the hydrochloric acid. If the NH_4Cl gas partly breaks down in this way to form ammonia and hydrochloric acid, it is reasonable to expect that there should be an excess of the latter above the porous asbestos partition and an excess of ammonia below it. Von Pebal showed this to be so. The stream of hydrogen from D gave

*Proc. R. I., 1904.

an acid reaction with litmus paper at A, and the stream from E gave an alkaline reaction, likewise on litmus paper, at B. It was then objected that the breakdown might be caused by the asbestos partition or by the hydrogen. Von Than therefore made a partition of NH_4Cl and replaced the hydrogen by nitrogen, but with the same result.

These experiments were performed in 1862 and 1864. They were based on the theory of dissociation which had been worked out in 1857 by Sainte-Claire-Deville and elaborated by his pupils. From time immemorial use had been made of the fact that at high temperature limestone gives off carbon dioxide to form quicklime. This and similar processes were studied by Sainte-Claire-Deville. He found that the same law applies to the pressure of carbon dioxide above limestone as to the pressure of water vapour above evaporating water at different temperatures. These fundamental studies are basic to the theory of dissociation which has since played an increasingly important part in chemistry and, in a manner of speaking, created a wide bridge between the physical and chemical sciences.

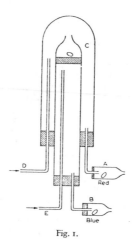

Fig. 1.

At almost the same time we find in Clausius' work on the electrical conductivity of salt solutions the first inklings of an idea that salts and other electrolytes are capable of partial dissociation when dissolved in water. Buff had found that even the least electrical force is sufficient to drive a current through a salt solution. According to Grotthus' conception, which at that time was generally accepted, the electrical current passes through a solution in such a way that the conducting molecules, e.g. of potassium chloride (KCl), separate into their ions, which recombine in the following manner. Firstly, when the current sets in, the pole A becomes positive and the pole B negative. All the conducting KCl molecules arrange themselves with their positive K ions turned towards the negative pole B and their negative Cl ions towards the positive pole A. Next a chlorine ion is liberated at A and a potassium ion at B, and the other ions combine again, the K ion in the first molecule capturing the Cl ion in the second molecule, and so on (Fig. 2). The molecules then turn under the influence of the electrical force to give us stage 3 and splitting can take place anew. That is Grotthus' view; it presupposes continuous splitting and recombination of the salt molecules.

Since these exchanges of ions between the molecules take place under the influence of the least electrical force, Clausius concluded that they must occur also when there is no electrical force acting, in other words, irrespective of whether current

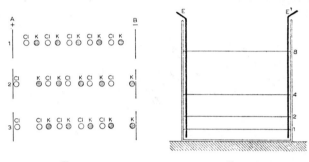

Fig. 2.   Fig. 3.

passes through the liquid. In support of this hypothesis he pointed out that in fact as early as 1852 Williamson, in his epoch-making theory of the formation of esters, assumed a similar exchange of constituents between the molecules. Clausius held that during the exchange of ions it would sometimes, although extremely rarely, occur that an ion remained free in the solution for a short time. At least, such an assumption is quite consistent with the mechanical theory of heat as developed at that time by Krönig, Maxwell, Clausius and others.

Meanwhile Bouty and particularly Kohlrausch devised methods to determine the electrical conductivity of salt solutions. In 1884 I gave a paper dealing with this subject. I had found that if a solution of, say, zinc sulphate is diluted, its conductivity per molecule, or what is termed its molal conductance, does not increase infinitely but only as far as a certain limit. We can visualize an experiment carried out in the following manner (Fig. 3). Into a parallel-walled vessel are inserted very close to two opposite sides two amalgamated zinc plates, E and E'. A layer of zinc sulphate solution is introduced extending from the horizontal bottom of the vessel to the line 1. The conductivity is assumed now to be k_1. After this has been measured, sufficient water is added so that after the solution has been stirred the level reaches 2 which is as far above 1 as 1 from the bottom. The

302

conductivity is then found to have increased and have a value k_2.
When the volume is doubled in the same way by the addition of pure
water, level 4 is reached and the conductivity is greater than in
the foregoing case, let us say k_4. We can continue in this way
and the conductivity increases but ultimately at a lower rate than
at the beginning. A final value of k_∞ is thus reached. This is
best illustrated by the following diagram which shows Kohlrausch's
more recent determinations (Figs. 4 and 5). Here the dilutions
are the abscissa and are given in gram-equivalents per litre.
The molal conductance at 18°C is the ordinate and given in
thousandth of units (ohm).
    I explained these experimental results in the following man-
ner. The conductance is governed by the rate at which the ions
(Zn and SO_4) of the molecules ($ZnSO_4$) are carried through the

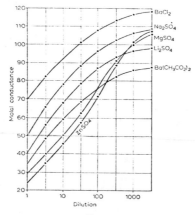

Fig. 4.

liquid by the electrical force, i.e. the potential difference
between E and E'. If this potential difference is assumed constant, the rate is determined solely by the friction which the
ions during their passage through the liquid set up on the surrounding molecules. Since at strong dilutions these are almost
exclusively water molecules, there is reason to suppose that the
molal conductance will remain constant and independent of the
dilution, assuming of course, that all $ZnSO_4$ molecules participate
in the conduction of the electricity. As the experiment now shows
that the molal conductance increases with the dilution to a very
high value--1,000 water molecules or more to each molecule of
$ZnSO_4$--we arrive at the hypothesis that not all but only some of
the $ZnSO_4$ molecules participate in the conduction of the electricity. This participation grows with the dilution in the same
ratio as the molal conductance k. With continuously increasing
dilution, the molal conductance approximates more and more to the
limit value k_∞ which is the point at which all molecules conduct

electricity. The conducting part of the molecules is termed the
active part. It can clearly be calculated as the quotient of
$k : k_\infty$.

 If this concept had only been applicable to accounting for
the phenomenon of electrical conductivity, its value would not
have been particularly great. An examination of the numerical
values adduced by Kohlrausch and others for the electrical conductivity of acids and bases as compared with Berthelot's and
Thomson's measurements of their relative strengths in terms of
their chemical effect showed me that the acids and bases with the
greatest conductivity are also the strongest. I was thus led to
the assumption that the electrically active molecules are also
chemically active, and that conversely the electrically inactive

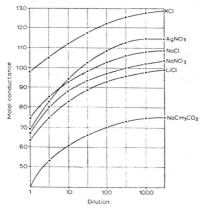

Fig. 5.

molecules are also chemically inactive, relatively speaking at
least. In this connection I would like to mention Gore's remarkable experiment which can readily be explained by the new concept.
Concentrated hydrochloric acid, which is free from water, has no
effect on oxides or carbonates. It happens that hydrochloric acid
in this form is very nearly incapable of conducting electrical
current whereas its aqueous solutions have very good conductivity.
The pure hydrochloric acid thus contains no active molecules, or
extremely few, and this agrees very closely with Gore's experiment. In the same way we can explain the fact that concentrated
sulphuric acid can be stored in a sheet iron vessel without damage
to the latter, although this is impossible with the dilute acid.

 An unexpected conclusion may be drawn from this concept. Because all electrolytes in an extremely dilute state are completely
active, the weak acids must increase in strength when diluted and
approach that of the strongest acids. Shortly afterwards this
proved to be in agreement with the experiments carried out by
Ostwald.

The Norwegian research scientists Guldberg and Waage had developed a theory according to which the strength of different acids could be measured by their capacity of displacing, in solutions, another acid as well as by their capacity of increasing the speed of certain chemical reactions. In conformity with this we can suppose that the speed of a reaction produced by an acid is proportional to the number of active molecules in it. I had only a few experiments by Berthelot to demonstrate this law, but in 1884 Ostwald published a large number of observations which proved that this conclusion was correct.

The most far-reaching conclusion from the conception of active molecules was the explanation of heat of neutralization. As it is much simpler to understand this by means of the theory of electrolytic dissociation, I will therefore anticipate it for this case. According to this theory strong acids and bases, as well as salts, are in extreme dilution almost completely dissociated into their ions, i.e. HCl into H^+ and Cl^-, NaOH into Na^+ and OH^-, and NaCl into Na^+ and Cl^-. On the other hand, water is hardly dissociated at all. The reaction of neutralization of a strong acid with a strong base, e.g. HCl with NaOH, both greatly diluted, can therefore be expressed by the following equation:

$$(H^+ + Cl^-) + (Na^+ + OH^-) = (Na^- + Cl^-) + HOH$$

or

$$H^+ + OH^- = HOH$$

This equation is equivalent to the formation of water from its two ions, H^+ and OH^-, and is evidently independent of the nature of the strong acid and the strong base. The development of heat in any reaction of this kind must therefore always be the same for equivalent quantities of any strong acids and bases. Actually, it has been found that in every case this is 13,600 calories (at 18°C). This constancy of neutralization heat is the most law-abiding phenomenon which has been discovered in thermochemistry.

The question now arose in what respect the active state of the electrolytes differs from the inactive state. I gave an answer to this question in 1887. At this time Van't Hoff had formulated his far-reaching law that the molecules in greatly diluted solutions obey the laws which apply to the gaseous state if gas pressure in liquids is merely replaced by the osmotic pressure. As Van't Hoff demonstrated, the osmotic pressure of a solute can be far more easily determined by measuring the freezing point of its solution than directly. However, both the direct measurements carried out by De Vries and the freezing points of electrolytic solutions showed a much higher osmotic pressure than would have been expected from the chemical formula. For instance, whilst the solution of one gram-molecule (mole) of ethyl alcohol, $C_2H_5OH = 46$ grams, in one litre of water gives a freezing point of -1.85°C, according to Van't Hoff's calculations a solution of one mole of sodium chloride, $NaCl = 58.5$ grams in one litre of water gives a freezing point of $-3.26°C = -1.75 \times 1.85°C$. This characteristic could be explained in the same way as the «abnormal» density of gaseous ammonium chloride, i.e. by supposing a partial dissociation--up to 75%--of the sodium chloride molecules. On this assumption, therefore, the solution contains 0.25 moles of NaCl, 0.75 moles of Cl and 0.75 moles of Na, a total of 1.75 moles, and has a corresponding effect regarding the depression of the freezing point. We have seen in what way we can calculate from the electrical conductivity the number of active molecules in the same solution of sodium chloride, and from Kohlrausch's measurements we find exactly the same number, i.e. 0.75. This strengthens the conception that the active molecules in the salt NaCl have split up into the ions Na^+ and Cl^-. These are absolutely free and they appear in the solutions exactly like other molecules. In the same way I calculated by both methods the degree of dissociation in all the electrolytes which had been determined at the time--there were about 80 of them--and I found that there was a very good agreement between the two different methods of determination. In some cases the agreement was not so good and I therefore carried out new analyses of these bodies and some others. The new analyses were all completely in agreement with the theoretical assumptions.

Fig. 6 shows the freezing points of some solutions of salts and non-conductors. The abscissa of the diagram shows the concentration of the bodies in the solutions, while the ordinate shows

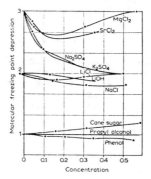

Fig. 6.

the molecular depression of the freezing point divided by 1.85. The figure shows us that all the curves of the non-conductors--in this instance cane sugar, propyl alcohol and phenol--converge towards unity with decreasing concentration as one would expect, since no dissociation takes place. With higher concentrations variations from the simple law take place. As examples of electrolytes consisting of two ions, LiOH, NaCl and LiCl have been selected; their curves all converge towards value 2. As electrolytes consisting of three ions K_2SO_4, Na_2SO_4, $MgCl_2$ and $SrCl_2$ have been selected; all these curves converge on value 3 for great dilution.

As I had accepted this explanation, which seemed to chemists to be most adventurous, I had to investigate whether it would agree chemically and physically with experience obtained. The most general and far-reaching point of all this is that the properties of a highly diluted electrolytic solution are composed of the different ions of which the electrolyte consists. It was already known that this was the case in many instances, and Valson had for this purpose drawn up tables of their so-called moduli. By comparing the one modulus value--for the negative ion--with the other--for the positive ion--we can calculate the properties of each of the electrolytes consisting of the ions in the table. In this way we can deal with the specific weight (Valson), the molecular conductivity (Kohlrausch), the internal friction (Arrhenius), the capillary attraction (Valson), the compressibility (Röntgen and Schneider), the refraction exponent (Gladstone), the natural polarization rotation (Oudemans), the magnetic polarization rotation (Perkin and Jahn), the magnetism (Wiedemann) and all the other properties of the electrolytes which have so far been adequately studied.

The most significant of these properties are those we use in chemical analysis. As is well-known, it is in general true that chlorides yield a white deposit (silver chloride) with silver salts. It used to be said, therefore, that silver salts were reagents for chlorine. Now we say that silver ions are reagents for chlorine ions. This expression is better than the older one, as indeed some such silver salts, e.g. potassium silver cyanide and many other silver compounds which do not contain silver ions, on the one hand, and all chlorine compounds, e.g. potassium chlorate and many organic chlorides which do not contain chlorine ions, on the other hand, do not give this characteristic reaction. The experiment succeeds only with such silver and chlorine compounds which are split to a noticeable degree into silver and chlorine ions. Ostwald has dealt comprehensively with this question and in this way has produced a rational presentation of the general phenomena of analytical chemistry. To this sphere there also belongs the poisonous effect of certain salts, which can be regarded as a separate physiological-chemical reaction of the chemical compounds.

5. *Not every chemist accepted the assumptions that Arrhenius made about the ionic state. Could electrically charged particles* really *exist as isolated individuals in solution without recombining with one another? And did it make any sense to treat solutions as gases when the two states were so obviously different? These were fundamental questions, raised most insistently by the English organic chemist, Henry E. Armstrong. In order to challenge the ionic theory, Armstrong had to develop a theory of solutions in general, and of water in particular, that was quite at variance with accepted notions.* *

---

*Henry E. Armstrong, *Essays on the Art and Principles of Chemistry*, New York, n.d. .

The Origin of Osmotic Effects

Hydronodynamic Change in
Aqueous Solutions

From 1885 onwards, in communications to this Society and
elsewhere, I have advocated an electrolytic explanation of chemical change, reciprocally a chemical explanation of electrolysis,
in which no assumption is made beyond the ordinary canons of
chemical belief. I have reason to think that, even now, my conception is in no way understood. I also can but recognise that I
have not yet presented my full case.

The following statement is an attempt to show that a simple
explanation may be given of the operations involved in the dissolution of "salts" in water, of the same mathematical form as the
ionic dissociation hypothesis, accounting equally well for electrical and osmotic peculiarities, which has the advantage that it
is in harmony with general chemical experience. Although in most
part but a repetition of arguments already advanced, the statement
is more comprehensive and definite than any previous attempt; the
consequences, particularly with respect to water, may prove to be
not without application in other fields of inquiry.

Much of the difficulty, in any theoretical advance, is due
to the force of prejudice and of dictated belief. The great obstacle, apparently, in arriving at an acceptable solution of the
problem of chemical change (including electrolysis) has been the
constant association of the symbol OH_2 with "water" and the disre-
gard of the determining part played by "water"; "water," moreover,
has an undeserved reputation for "neutrality." Actually, the
symbol is only representative of the molecule in dry steam. The
term water should be confined to the liquid. To give emphasis to
this contention, I have applied the name *Hydrone* to the simple
unit-molecule symbolised as OH_2, choosing this ketonic term ad-
visedly, instead of *Hydrol*, because of the special significance
of *ol* in chemical nomenclature.

My one postulate is, that not only are electrolysis and chemical change inseparable reciprocal effects--the conditions which
determine the one inevitably involve the other--but that change
takes place and only takes place in a system of three components,
such as is known to constitute a voltaic-couple.

The picture I would draw of water and of aqueous solutions
is as follows. Water is a complex mixture, in proportions which
vary with the temperature, of the fundamental molecule, *hydrone*
(OH_2), with molecules of various polymorphs, perhaps.

Hydrone is the volatile component of water and the vapour-
pressure may be regarded as the relative measure of the proportion
in which it is present. Whether the liquid contain any other
directly volatile constituent is an open question: as the relative

density of the vapour from (not of) water is greater than 9 near
to the boiling point, some molecules of greater mass than that of
hydrone are contained in the gas.

The proportion of hydrone molecules in ordinary water must
be small. If water were but a collocation of molecules of hydrone,
the boiling-point of the liquid would be far lower--its freezing
point would also be much lower. Even if it contained any considerable proportion of hydrone molecules, its boiling point would
be lower.

If any substance be dissolved in water, the physical properties of the liquid are proportionately altered, not always in the
same molecular ratio but to an extent which depends upon the nature of the compound dissolved; potential electrolytes produce the
greater effect per molecule. Apparently, the effect is in no way
mechanical, i.e., solvent and solute do not merely become mixed
together and the molecules separated by mutual (mechanical) interference; the process is inductive and chemical throughout.

Non-electrolytes all produce the same effect per molecule,
whatever their molecular magnitude, in raising the osmotic attractive power of water and, at the same time, of lowering its vapour
pressure. The negative pressure developed within the liquid is
such that apparently a gramme-molecular-proportion of hydrone is
taken out of action as volatile constituent per gramme-molecular-
proportion of the *non-electrolyte* dissolved; each molecule of the
solute appears to "anchor" a molecule of hydrone, yet in some
special way which enables this still to preserve its attractive
power for molecules of its own kind. The effect of potential
electrolytes is greater, to an extent depending upon the valency
and character of the constituent radicles; "salts" of the type
X'R', in very dilute solution, may produce an effect double that
proper to a single molecule and the effect of salts containing
radicles of higher valency than unity may be still greater.

Solutions of such "salts" are electrolytic conductors and
chemically are not only active but, when two salts in a solution
(a reciprocal salt pair) interact (the Williamson change), the
change is practically immediate in its occurrence.

No binary hydrogen compound in the liquid state is an electrolyte *per se*. The facts are such that we are justified in
assuming that compounds such as hydrogen chloride and hydrone, in
the liquid state, would be without trace of conductivity and inactive chemically, *if pure*--although, probably, water, as we know
it, would then have no existence. I use the word pure in the
ideal sense of free from impurity, recognising no degrees of purity but only of impurity.

How, then, does conductivity arise when hydrogen chloride is
dissolved in water? Even the two simple molecules (both potential
electrolytes) would not *interact* when in contact; at most, it may
be supposed, they would merely

2.   HCl $\longleftrightarrow$ OH$_2$

form a couple in which they exercised an inductive attractive
effect (contact difference of potential) upon one another but
nothing more. Such an effect might cause the withdrawal (neutrali-

sation) of hydrone (the fall of vapour pressure is evidence of such fixation) but the osmotic activity acquired by the solution cannot well be accounted for by the occurrence.

Suppose, however, that a conducting circuit could be and were formed by the conjunction of such a couple with the two independent molecules and that electrolytic change took place; this might be of the following order:

3.

$$
H_2O \longrightarrow \underset{\substack{H \\ Cl \\ O \\ H_2}}{} ClH \rightleftharpoons H_2O \underset{\substack{H \\ Cl \\ O \\ H_2}}{} ClH
$$

$$
H_2O \underset{H}{\overset{Cl}{<}} \quad + \quad \underset{\substack{H \\ | \\ Cl \\ | \\ OH}}{ClH}
$$

$$
\quad\quad\quad a \quad\quad b
$$

$$
H_2O \underset{OH}{\overset{H}{<}} \quad + \quad \underset{\substack{Cl \\ | \\ Cl \\ | \\ H}}{ClH}
$$

$$
\quad\quad\quad c \quad\quad d
$$

If it cannot be admitted that a voltaic couple could be thus constituted, the intervention of some third component must be postulated: if not an "impurity," the walls of the containing vessel, alternatively, *dissolved gas*, may be called into service and should suffice.

The extent to which change takes place reversibly, in the two directions indicated, must be left open to decision. The production in electrolysis of chlorine alone from strong solutions but together with oxygen from weak solutions may conceivably be due to the preponderance of system *d* in the former. The rapid increase of the assumed "molecular" conductivity of the hydrogen chloride, as the concentration is diminished, however, is an indication that the more steady state *ab*, eventually *ac*, is rapidly reached.

In these electrolytic changes the primary molecules engaged would be *distributed* upon one another. In the reciprocal complexes thus formed, the affinity of the constituent radicles, *inter se*, would be less strong than in the original simple molecules: thus the chlorine would be but weakly held by the oxygen in the muriated complex *a*, the hydroxyl but weakly by the chlorine in the hydrol *b*. On the other hand, the residual affinity of the chlorine atom would be greater than that of chlorine in hydrogen chloride and that of the oxygen in the hydrols greater than that of oxygen in hydrone. Each such distributed system would be eminently attractive to hydrone.

If change take place in the manner suggested, the number of "distributed" active systems produced can only be equal to the number of molecules of the solute: some further change must therefore be postulated to account for the ultimate apparent "doubling" of the molecular influence of the solute--for the enhanced effect produced by the potential electrolyte.

Assuming that change took place to an ever-increasing extent, as the solution became more and more dilute, in a direction

involving the rupture of the "couple" shown along the dotted lines
in the following equation,

$$4. \quad
\begin{array}{l}
\text{ClH} \;\vdots\; \text{OH} \quad \text{H} \\
\cdots\;|\cdots\cdots\cdots\cdots|\;\cdots \\
\text{H}_2\text{O} \qquad \text{HO}\!-\!\text{ClH} \\
\quad| \qquad\qquad\; \vdots \\
\quad\text{H} \qquad\qquad\; \vdots
\end{array}
= \text{H}_2\text{O}\!\!<\!\!\begin{array}{l}\text{H}\\\text{OH}\end{array} + 2\text{ClH} + \text{OH}_2,$$

hydronol would be formed in an increasing proportion relatively
to the hydrone chloride *a*.

In a sufficiently dilute solution, ultimately, two osmoti-
cally active, reciprocal molecules would be produced, at the expense of each single molecule of the chloride: in other words,
the single molecule of the potential electrolyte, hydrogen chloride, would apparently have double the effect of a single molecule
of a non-electrolyte.

Assuming that electrolysis involve the interaction of two
diverse "distributed" systems, under the influence of an electromotive force, the (molecular) conductivity of the dissolved chloride would also be at its maximum in the fully diluted liquid.

The formation of the all but neutral polyhydrones present in
water together with the highly active molecules of hydrone and
hydronol is to be pictured as taking place in a similar manner,
by condensation from several molecules of hydrone, under the influence of the primary distributed systems discussed above.
Apparently, molecules of hydrone, like atoms of carbon, have a
natural tendency to "fall or fit together" in certain ways, which
may well be similar. In fact, if the carbon atom be represented
by a pyramid of four equal spheres--corresponding with its quadri-
valency--the molecule of hydrone may be represented by a like
model in which two of the spheres are taken to represent the oxygen atom and the other two the two hydrogen atoms.

A similar structure may be assigned to the metallic ammonias
without assuming that the metal in these compounds has a specially
high valency. The partial or complete inertness of the negative
radicle in many of these is better explained in this way than by
current assumptions.

The distribution of a substance in water, in the manner set
forth, must involve a reduction in the proportion of hydrone molecules. That fresh molecules are supplied to take their place by
dissociation of the polyhydrones is not to be supposed, as vapour
pressure falls as the solution becomes more concentrated; apparently, the polyhydrones are hydrolysed and reduced to hydrone
only in response to the demand made when the proportion of salt
is increased. It follows that the composition of the "water" in
a solution must vary not only as the temperature changes but also
with the concentration--the relative proportions in which the
several constituents are present must be changed.

That the affinity of the solution for hydrone increases with
the concentration is clear, however, from the increase in osmotic
activity. This osmotic activity is to be attributed, as indicated above, to the reciprocal distributed systems: in a dilute
solution of hydrogen chloride, for example, to the molecules of

muriated hydrol and of hydronol, $HCl\hspace{-0.3em}<\hspace{-0.3em}\begin{smallmatrix}H\\OH\end{smallmatrix}$ and $H_2O\hspace{-0.3em}<\hspace{-0.3em}\begin{smallmatrix}H\\OH\end{smallmatrix}$

Each such system has unit effect: if the solution be placed in contact with water, molecules of hydrone are attracted from the water, one molecule by each unit system, the result being that the complex is held in check and neutralised.

The pressure is exercised by the hydrone molecules thus controlled. In other words, the osmotic pressure is due to the directed oscillatory impacts of molecules of hydrone, not of molecules of the dissolved substance: it is rather to be regarded as of the order of hydraulic than of gaseous pressure.

The most striking fact in connection with the behaviour of non-electrolytes is their unit-effect per molecule. Thus the osmotic effect of a molecule of alcohol, $C_2H_5 \cdot OH$ is the same as that of the complex molecule of cane-sugar, $C_{12}H_{14}O_3(OH)_8$. The influence of the molecule is, in a sense, polar: apparently it is exercised from a single centre. Some inductive influence is at work, in the complex hydroxy-compound, preventing effective hydrolation at contiguous hydroxy-groups and favouring it at some one dominant centre--perhaps at the etheric linkage between the two C_6 complexes.

This conception must be extended to other solvents in which no "distributive" action is possible, which develop no special activity in the dissolved substance such as is produced on dissolving electrolytes in water. All solvents probably are to be regarded as mixtures of simple molecules with complexes formed by the association of several of these units. The proportion of simple molecules present must be a fixed one in every liquid and if equilibrium be disturbed by the fixation of the unit molecule by that of the solute the solution will be attractive of such molecules to the extent required to meet the deficiency.

As the interacting molecules in an aqueous solution are the complexes formed primarily from molecules of hydrone, the variations in the rate of change, not only as the composition of the solution is varied but also as the temperature is varied, will be proportional to the number of molecules of hydrone available. The conclusion arrived at by Adrian Brown and Worley that the variation in the entry of "water" into the barley grain is coincident with the variation in the vapour-pressure of water--*i.e.*, the proportion of escaping molecules of hydrone--is in harmony with this assumption. It also provides an explanation of the uniform variation of the rate of chemical change in solution enunciated by Harcourt and Esson, expressed by the relation

$$K/K' = (TT')^m,$$

KK' being the rates of change at absolute temperatures TT' respectively, m being a number peculiar to each condition of change which expresses the ratio of dK/K to dT/T. This was originally stated by them in 1895 in the form

$$\frac{K_t}{K_0} = \left(\frac{273 + t}{273}\right)^m$$

and is obviously but the gas law in disguise.

We are in no way at the end of the study of liquids. H. B. Baker's recent observations on the effect of drying benzene very thoroughly in raising its boiling point are an indication that the properties we are in the habit of assigning to liquids may be, in a considerable degree, influenced even by a minute impurity. In all liquids change of state involves chemical change.

Water in particular has still to be appreciated. If the influence of a "salt" in determining change be as suggested, the production of water from hydrone--being a chemical process--is dependent upon the presence of a potential electrolyte: there would be no condensation of the gas in the absence of such a conditioning agent. It has long been held, on the basis of Aitkin's observations, that the formation of raindrops in the upper atmosphere is due to the presence of nuclei. The supposition was at first made that these might be mere dust particles; of late meteorologists have contended that only "hygroscopic" materials are effective as nuclei. It is safe to assert that the nucleus must be a potential electrolyte.

The electrical discharge developed in the division of large drops--apparently the origin of thunderstorms--may be regarded as the consequence of a change in the composition of the water as the drop divides. The evaporation from a drop is said to be in excess of that from the same plane surface, the more the smaller the drop. If this be so, it may be supposed that the proportion of hydrone is greater in drops than in a mass of water and that the proportion is the greater the smaller the drop. Attention has been drawn by G. C. Simpson also to the presence of water drops in the upper atmosphere at temperatures far below the freezing-point of ordinary water; maybe this is possible, because the "water" in such drops, being different in composition from ordinary water, richer in its volatile constituent hydrone, is less easily frozen. This same argument is probably of consequence--at least to be kept in mind--in any discussion of the influence of moisture in chemical change at catalytic surfaces, particularly in cases in which a certain critical minimum proportion has maximum effect.

I have spoken of *pure water* as an ideal which cannot be realized, because of the impossibility of excluding impurity and of condensing pure hydrone. If pure water were obtained, it would be different from the water we know in not a few particulars.

The conclusions arrived at in this communication are summarised in the following proportions:

1. "Water" is a complex saturated with the "gas" *hydrone*, OH_2. Primarily, hydrone is the sole potentially "active" constituent but it becomes actually active only under conditions which suffice to determine electrolytic change. Pure water would be inert--but this is and must ever be an ideal.

2. The vapour pressure either of water or of a solution is the measure of the proportion of *free* hydrone molecules present in the liquid. The diminution of the pressure when a substance is dissolved in water, therefore, is a proof that the molecules of hydrone are concerned in the change and are thereby diminished in proportion.

3. Although the vapour pressure is lowered in presence of any solute, the solution acquires attractive properties. The internal activity is increased whilst external activity is diminished. Non-electrolytes all have unit effect per molecular proportion; potential electrolytes have at least twice this effect, in sufficiently dilute solutions.

4. The effect produced may be ascribed to an interaction of molecules of the solute and those of hydrone. From non-electrolytes (under the influence of conducting impurity) a simple hydrol is formed, $M{<}^H_{OH}$, only a single molecule of hydrone being "distributed" upon the molecule of the solute, whatever its magnitude.

5. In the case of potential electrolytes, a reciprocal interchange of the radicles of the salt and of hydrone is to be postulated. Not only is the solute hydrolated but it is itself distributed upon hydrone, the salt $\overset{+}{R}{'}\overset{-}{X}{'}$ giving rise initially to the reciprocal systems

$$RX{<}^H_{OH} \quad \text{and} \quad H_2O{<}^R_X$$

6. As the concentration is lowered, under the influence of hydrone, the complex $RX{<}^H_{OH}$ is more and more converted into hydronol, $H_2O{<}^H_{OH}$. Ultimately the solution contains the solute only in the form $H_2O{<}^R_X$, together with an equal number of molecules of hydronol. The solute then has maximum (bimolecular) effect.

7. The "distributed" reciprocal complexes, including hydronol, are the electro-chemical agents in a solution. The negative radicle in such complexes has greater residual affinity than it has in the original simple molecules; it is specially attractive of hydrone and, therefore, hydrone is attracted into the solution when it is in contact with water.

Each complex attracts a single hydrone molecule, the molecules thus brought into the solution serving to restore the hydrone equilibrium.

8. The osmotic pressure manifest in an aqueous solution is the hydraulic pressure exercised by the extra molecules of hydrone attracted into it by the distributed complexes, one by each complex, acting as though they were present in the gaseous state. In short, the osmotic pressure developed within an aqueous solution, whatever the solute, has its origin in one and the same cause and is properly spoken of as *Hydronodynamics*--if the word be permissible; indeed, this term may be used as expressive of the general activity of water, *electro-chemical and osmotic*.

6.   *Discussions of the nature of ions and of solutions and of all
     the fundamental concepts of chemistry were characteristic of
     the last decade of the nineteenth century.   There were even
     those who seriously suggested that the very central feature
     of chemical science in the nineteenth century--the atomic
     theory--had outlived its utility.   The foremost advocate of
     the anti-atomic view was the great German chemist and his-
     torian of chemistry, Wilhelm Ostwald (1853-1932).   In 1904,
     he spelled out his ideas before an interested audience at the
     Chemical Society of London.**

Elements and Compounds.

From what store of ideas will a modern chemist derive the new
materials for a new answer to the old question? A physicist will
have a ready answer: he will construct the elements in a *mechanical* way, or, if he is of the most modern type, he will use *electricity* as timber. The chemist will look on these structures
with due respect indeed, but with some reserve. Long experience
has convinced chemists (or at least some of them) that every
hypothesis taken from another science ultimately proves insufficient. They are adapted to express certain sides of his, the
chemist's, facts, but on other not less important sides they fail,
and the end is inadequacy. Learning by this experience, he makes
a rule to use only chemical material for this work, and according
to this rule I propose to proceed.

Hence, like Dumas, I put the question: what are the most important achievements of the chemistry of our day? I do not hesitate to answer: *chemical dynamics* or the theory of the progress
of chemical reactions and the theory of chemical equilibrium.
What answer can chemical dynamics give to the old question about
the nature of the chemical elements?

The answer to this question sounds most remarkable; and to
impress you with the importance I ascribe to this investigation,
I will mention the result at once: *It is possible, to deduce from
the principles of chemical dynamics all the stoichiometrical laws;
the law of constant proportions, the law of multiple proportions and
the law of combining weights.* You all know that up to the present
time it has only been possible to deduce these laws by help of the
atomic hypothesis. Chemical dynamics has, therefore, made the
atomic hypothesis unnecessary for this purpose and has put the
theory of the stoichiometrical laws on more secure ground than
that furnished by a mere hypothesis.

I am quite aware that in making this assertion I am stepping
on somewhat volcanic ground. I may be permitted to guess that
among this audience there are only very few who would not at once
answer, that they are quite satisfied with the atoms as they are,
and that they do not in the least want to change them for any
other conception. Moreover, I know that this very country is the
birthplace of the atomic hypothesis in its modern form, and that

---

**Lectures Delivered Before the Chemical Society: Faraday Lectures,
1869-1928.* London, 1928, pp. 187-201.

only a short time ago the celebration of the centenary of the
atomic hypothesis has reminded you of the enormous advance which
science has made in this field during the last hundred years.
Therefore I have to make a great claim on your unbiassed scientific receptivity. But still I do not hesitate one moment to lay
the results of my work before you. For I feel quite sure that I
shall find this receptivity unrestricted; and, moreover, I shall
reap another advantage. For I also feel assured that you will
offer me the severest criticism which I shall be able to find
anywhere. If my ideas should prove worthless, they will be put
on the shelf here more quickly than anywhere else, before they can
do harm. If, on the contrary, they should contain anything sound,
they will be freed here in the most efficacious way from their in-
exact and inconsistent components, so as to take the shape fittest
for lasting use in science. And now let us go into the matter.

The first concept we start from is *equilibrium*. In its
original meaning, this word expresses the state of a balance when
two loads are of the *same weight*. Later, the conception was
transferred to forces of all kinds, and designates the state when
the forces neutralise one another in such a way that *no motion*
occurs. As the result of the so-called chemical forces does not
show itself as a motion, the use of the word has to be extended
still further to mean that *no variation* occurs in the properties
of the system. In its most general sense, *equilibrium denotes a
state independent of time.*

For the existence of such a state it is above all necessary
that temperature and pressure shall remain constant; in consequence of this, volume and entropy remain constant too. Now it
is a most general experimental law, that the possibility of such
a state, independent of time, is dependent on the *homogeneity* of
the system. In non-homogeneous bodies, as, for instance, in a
solution of different concentrations in different places, or in
a gaseous mixture of different composition in different places,
equilibrium cannot exist, and the system will change spontaneously
into a homogeneous state. We can therefore limit our consideration to this state, and we shall consider only bodies or systems
of bodies in equilibrium, and, consequently, homogeneous.

Perhaps the possibility of the existence of water in contact
with water-vapour might be considered contradictory to this statement, because we have here two different states and no homogeneity.
Here we meet with the new concept created by Willard Gibbs, namely,
that of a *phase*.

Systems of this kind are formed of homogeneous bodies indeed,
but of more than one. The water in our system is homogeneous in
itself, and the vapour too, and equilibrium cannot exist until
both are homogeneous. But there is a possibility that a finite
number of different homogeneous bodies can exist together without
disturbing one another. In such a system we must have the same
temperature and the same pressure everywhere, but the specific
volume and the specific entropy may change from one body to the
other.

We call a *phase* every part of the system where these specific
properties exhibit the same value. It is not necessary that a
phase should be connected to one body only; it may be distributed

over any number of parts. In this way the millions of globules of
butter in milk form only *one* phase, and the watery solution of
casein and milk-sugar forms a second phase: milk is a two-phase
system.

*Every system consisting of only one phase has two degrees of
freedom.* This law involves only the assumption that the sole
forms of energy involved in the system are heat and volume-energy;
we exclude from consideration any effects due to gravitation,
electricity, surface-tension, &c. This law is connected with the
famous phase rule of Willard Gibbs, but is not identical with it,
for it contains no mention at all of the so-called components of
the system. Indeed, the law is valid in the same way for any pure
chemical element, for example, oxygen, or for any mixture, for
example, a glass of whisky and water. If you allow to the latter
only one phase, it is impossible to change it in more than two
ways, namely, in pressure and temperature.

The existence of such a body in the shape of only one phase
is generally limited. If the pressure be lowered at constant
temperature, a liquid or a solid will change at last into a gas.
Lowering of temperature will change a gas into a liquid and a
liquid into a solid. For every one-phase system it is possible
to determine a "sphere of existence." This sphere is not necessarily limited on all sides; for gases we do not expect a limit
on the side of low pressures and high temperatures, nor for solids
on the side of high pressures and low temperatures. But on certain sides every phase has its limits, and most of these limits
are experimentally accessible.

What will happen if we exceed the limit of existence of a
phase? The answer is most simple: *a new phase will be formed.*
The spheres of existence of the different phases therefore limit
one another, and the boundary-lines represent the interdependent
values of temperature and pressure for the possibility of the co-
existence of both phases.

By granting the co-existence of two phases we lose therefore
one degree of freedom. At the same time a new variation has
arisen from the ratio between the masses of the two phases. For
we must not suppose that this ratio is without influence on the
state; indeed we find here two radically different cases.

The most general case is, that during the transformation of
one phase into another the properties of both are continually
changing, and the state of every phase is therefore dependent on
the ratio of the two masses. By evaporating sea-water at constant
temperature the density of the residue grows continually higher,
while the pressure, and therefore the density, of the vapour goes
on decreasing. If, however, we evaporate distilled water, we do
not find any change in the properties of the residue and of the
vapour during the whole transmutation.

Bodies of the first description we will call *solutions*, and
of the second, *hylotropic bodies.* You will be inclined to call
the latter substances or chemical individuals, and indeed both
concepts are most nearly related. However, the concept of a
hylotropic body is somewhat broader than that of a substance.
But the possibility of being changed from one phase into another
without variation of the properties of the residue and of the new

phase is indeed the most characteristic property of a substance or chemical individual, and all our methods of testing the purity of a substance or of preparing a pure one can be reduced to this one property; any one may readily convince himself of this by investigating any such method in the light of this description. . . .

What is the general process of change in a solution while it is being vaporised? The answer is quite distinct: *the residue is always less volatile* than the original solution, and *the distillate more volatile*. If there were an example of a solution behaving in the contrary way, then the process of vaporisation at constant temperature would be an explosive one. For the vapour begins to form at a given pressure; if by this the vapour-pressure of the residue were lowered, the vaporisation would continue of itself at a continually accelerated rate until all the liquid would be vaporised at once. It would be, in other words, a *labile* equilibrium. These equilibria are, however, only mathematical fictions, and have no experimental existence. If, on the contrary, the residue has a lower vapour-pressure, then the process is self-limiting, and shows the characteristics of a *stable* equilibrium. With hylotropic bodies we have an *indifferent* equilibrium, because the state is independent of the progress of the transmutation. . . .

It is possible in every case, to separate solutions into a finite number of hylotropic bodies.

From the components, we can compose the solution again with its former properties. This is also a general experimental law; if exceptions seem to exist, it is only because the case is not one of true equilibrium. Still we may limit our consideration to those cases where the law holds good. Then we have a relation between the properties of any solution, and the nature and relative quantity of its hylotropic components, which admits of only one interpretation. Every solution of distinct properties has also a distinct composition and *vice versâ*.

If we consider for simplicity's sake solutions of only *two* components, we may represent any property as depending upon the composition in a rectangular co-ordinate system, the abscissæ giving the composition and the ordinates the value of the property considered. In this way, we get a continuous line of a shape dependent on the particular case chosen.

If we consider the boiling points of all solutions formed by two hylotropic components, the most simple forms of curves (indeed the only experimental ones known) are given by the types I, II, and III, Fig. 3. For any solution, for example, the solution with the abscissa *a*, we can foretell its variation on distillation by the slope of the curve. For as the residue must be less volatile, the residue will change to the ascending side of the curve. This is for I and III to the right, for II to the left side of the diagram. The change of the *distillate* is the opposite.

If we try to apply this criterion to the points *m* of the curve II and III, where there is a maximum and a minimum of the boiling point, we arrive at no decisive answer, for if the boiling point is already the highest possible it cannot rise, and if it is the lowest possible, it cannot fall. We are forced therefore to conclude that the boiling point cannot change at all, that is,

318

that this special solution must behave as a hylotropic body.

This is a well-known theorem of Gibbs and Konovaloff, to wit, that a maximum or a minimum, generally spoken of as a *distinguishing point* in the boiling curve, is necessarily connected with the

Fig. 3.

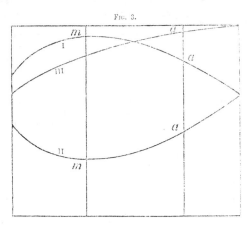

property of distilling without change in the composition of the solution. A similar law holds good for the transitions from liquid to solid and from solid to gas.

Now this looks like a contradiction; while a few minutes ago we placed solutions in a class exclusive of hylotropic bodies, we have here solutions, that is, mixtures, which behave like hylotropic substances. But the contradiction vanishes if we consider a series of boiling-point curves corresponding with various pressures. We then find that the composition at the distinguishing point does not remain constant under different pressures, but shifts to one side, with alteration of pressure. This fundamental fact was discovered and experimentally developed in an admirable way by Sir Henry Roscoe, and has since proved a most important criterion in recognising a chemical individual.

By drawing curves corresponding with various pressures, we get therefore generally the diagram shown in Fig. 4, the loci of the distinguishing points forming one curve. Between the infinite possibilities of the shape of this curve we have a distinguishing case again, the case that the curve is a *vertical straight line*. This means that the composition is independent of the pressure. *When this is the case, we call this hylotropic body a substance or a chemical individual.*

Therefore we conclude that a connection exists between solutions and chemical compounds or substances; the latter being a distinguishing case of the former. On the other hand, we get an exact definition: *a substance or a chemical individual is a body, which can form hylotropic phases within a finite range of temperature and pressure.*

Such substances can often be produced from other substances

in the same way as a solution is, namely, by putting them together. If that can be done, we may infer from our definition
that there exists a definite ratio between the components, independent of temperature and pressure between certain limits.

Fig. 4.

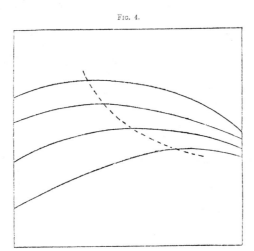

Now, *this is essentially the law of definite proportions*,
the first of the stoichiometrical laws. We have deduced, therefore, the law of constant proportions from the concept of the
chemical individual.

As you have seen, this deduction is extremely simple; the
constancy of composition is a natural consequence of the mode of
preparation and purification of chemical substances.

If we exceed the limits of temperature and pressure, where
the body behaves as a hylotropic one, it assumes the properties
of a solution, that is, its distinguishing point begins shifting
in composition when the temperature is changed. Then it becomes
possible to separate the body into its components, and we call
this state the state of dissociation of the substance in question.
In our graphic representation, the hitherto straight vertical
line of distinguishing points turns sideways, Fig. 5.

Most substances behave in this way, but there are substances
which have never been transformed into solutions or whose sphere
of existence covers all accessible states of temperature and pressure. Such substances we call elements. In other words, *elements
are substances which never form other than hylotropic phases.*

From this we may conclude that every body is finally trans-
formable into elements, and into only *one definite set of elements.*
For the most general case is a solution. Every solution can be
separated into a finite number of hylotropic components, and
these again can generally be transferred into a state when they
behave like solutions and can be separated further. Finally, the

components remain hylotropic through the whole range of temperature and pressure, that is, they are elements.

From the fact that the relation between a compound substance
and its elements admits of only one qualitative and quantitative
interpretation, we derive the conclusion that the resolution of

Fig. 5.

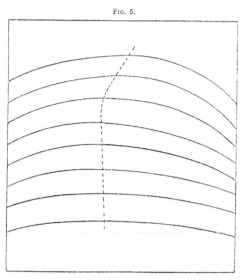

any substance into its elements must always lead to the same elements in the same proportion. Here we find the source of the law
of the *conservation of the elements*. This law is not generally
expressed as a special stoichiometrical law, because we tacitly
infer it from the atomic hypothesis. But it is truly an empirical law, and we see that it is not only a consequence of the
atomic hypothesis, but also a consequence of the experimental
definition of an element and of our methods of obtaining elements. . . .

Now there are still two stoichiometrical laws to be deduced,
namely, the law of multiple proportions and the law of combining
weights. I prefer to invert the order, and first to deduce the
second law. It expresses the fact that it is possible to ascribe
to each element a certain relative weight in such a way that every
combination between the elements can be expressed by these weights
or their multiples.

We suppose three elements, A, B, and C, given, which may
form binary combinations, AB, BC, and AC, and besides these a
ternary combination, ABC; there shall be but one combination of
every kind. Now we begin by forming the combination AB; for this
purpose, we must take a certain invariable ratio between the
weights of A and B, according to the already proved law of constant proportions. Now we combine AB with C and get the ternary

compound ABC. There will be a certain ratio, too, between AB and C, and we can, if we put A as unity, assign to B and C certain numbers describing their combining weights relatively to A.

Now we begin to combine A with C forming AC, and then we form the ternary combination, ACB from AC and B. According to our law of a relation between elements and compounds, which can be interpreted only in one way, ACB cannot be different from ABC, and, in particular, it must show the same ratio between the relative weights of its elements. Therefore, the ratio of the weights of A and C in forming the combination AC cannot be other than that expressed by the relative combining weights already found in the first way. In other words, it is possible to compute the composition of the hitherto unknown combination AC, from analyses of the combinations AB and ABC. In the same way, we can compute the composition of the unknown combination BC, by the help of the numbers obtained by the analyses of two other combinations of the same elements. To resume: the combining weights relatively to A regulate all other possible compounds between the elements concerned. But this is nothing else than the general stoichiometrical law of combining weights for we can extend our considerations without difficulty to any number of elements.

Lastly, it is easy to deduce the law of multiple proportions from the law of combining weights. If no compounds can be formed except according to their combining weights, then, if there are two different compounds between A and B, we can form the one containing more of B either directly from A and B, or indirectly, combining first A and B to form the lower compound and then combining this with more of B. In applying the law of combining weights, we conceive that the weight of B in the higher compound must be twice its weight in the lower. The same consideration may be repeated, and finally we get the result, that instead of double the combining weight, *any multiple* of it may occur in combinations, but no other ratio.

If we cast a backward glance on the mental operations we have performed in the last two deductions, we recognise the method, the application of which has made the two laws of energetics so fruitful. In the same manner as the difference between the whole and the available energy is independent of the nature of the path between the same limiting points, the product of the chemical action between a number of given elements is independent of the way in which they are combined. If we compare two different ways, we get an equation between the characteristics of the two ways, and this is equivalent to a new law. In our case, this new law is the law of combining weights.

I will put the same idea into somewhat different words. By stating the equation between any two ways, we can get any number of different equations, each representing a new way as an experimental fact. Now, in order that all these equations shall be consistent, there must be some general law regulating the characteristics of the equations. For the consistency of the several equations in the case under discussion, the existence of specific combining weights, independent of the several combinations, is the necessary condition.

This is the main point of the considerations I wish to lay before you this evening. There are some secondary questions as to isomerides or allotropic states of substances, and there are

other similar questions, but it would lead us too far to consider
them one by one. I have investigated them on the same basis, and
I can assure you that I have nowhere found an insurmountable
difficulty or an impassable contradiction. All these facts find
their proper place in the frame of the same general ideas.

Let me still add some words about the *nature of the elements*,
as considered from my point of view. I wish to lay great stress
on the fact that here, too, I find myself on the same ground as
that on which Faraday has built his general concepts during his
whole scientific career. There is only one difference, due to
the development of science. Faraday ever held up the idea that
we know matter only by its forces, and that if we take the forces
away, there will remain no inert carrier, but really nothing at
all. As Faraday still clung to the atomic hypothesis, he was
forced to express this idea by the conception that the atoms are
only mathematical points whence the forces emerge, or where the
directions of the several forces intersect; here his view coincided with that of Boscovich.

In the language of modern science I express these ideas by
stating: *what we call matter is only a complex of energies which
we find together in the same place*. We are still perfectly free,
if we like, to suppose either that the energy fills the space
homogeneously, or in a periodic or grained way; the latter assumption would be a substitute for the atomic hypothesis. The decision between these possibilities is a purely experimental question.
Evidently there exist a great number of facts--and I count the
chemical facts among them--which can be completely described by a
homogeneous or non-periodic distribution of energy in space.
Whether there exist facts which cannot be described without the
periodic assumption, I dare not decide for want of knowledge;
only I am bound to say that I know of none.

Taking this general point of view, in what light do we regard the question of the elements? We will find the answer, if
we remember that the only difference between elements and compounds consists in the supposed impossibility of proving the so-
called elements to be compounds. We are therefore led to ask for
the general energetic properties underlying the concept of a
chemical individual, whether element or compound.

The answer is most simple. The reason why it is possible to
isolate a substance from a solution is that the available energy
of the substance *is a minimum*, compared with that of all adjacent
bodies. I will not develop this thesis at length, for it is a
well-known theorem in energetics or thermodynamics. I will only
recall the fact that a minimum of vapour-pressure is always
accompanied by a minimum of available energy; and we have already
seen that a minimum of vapour-pressure or a maximum of boiling-
point is the characteristic of a hylotropic body or chemical
individual.

This granted, we proceed to the question regarding the differences between the several substances. Expressed in the most
general way, we find these differences connected with differences
in their *specific energy content*. Temperature and pressure are
not specific, for we can change them at will. Specific volume
and specific entropy, on the contrary, are not changeable at will;

every substance has its own values of these. We may take therefore these values as the characteristics of the different substances. How many of such characteristics exist I cannot tell.
Only for simplicity's sake I will assume that two of them are
sufficient. As I will take care not to deduce any conclusions
from this number, we shall not be led into error by accepting it.

We place these two characteristics in a system of planar
coordinates; then the several elements will be represented by
single points in the plane. We lay the plane horizontally and
raise from these points ordinates, representing the available
energy of each element. Between the points of the elements in
the plane are situated the points of all possible solutions, filling up the whole plane. Each of these solutions will also have
its available energy, and all the corresponding points in space
will form a continuous surface. The form of this surface can be
described in a general way. For as each *element* has its point in
a *relative minimum*, the surface as a whole will have a shape like
the ceiling of a cavern full of hanging stalactites, the end of
each stalactite representing an element.

How can we pass from one element to another? Evidently not
otherwise than by going over the higher parts of the surface, or
the passes separating each stalactite from its neighbours. This
can only be done by accumulating an appropriate amount of available energy in the element to be changed. Now the concentration
of energy is a task we cannot accomplish *ad libitum*, for the possibility very soon ends. Think, for example, of compressing a
gas into a given space. Up to some ten thousand atmospheres the
work of compression will go on smoothly, but after that every
metal begins to flow like a liquid and you cannot proceed further.
With the concentration of electric or any other energy the task
is similar and so we come to the conclusion that the concentration of energy can be pushed to only a very limited extent. The
application of this result to our question about elements is
simple enough: we cannot get over the pass between two stalactites
because we cannot attain the necessary concentration of energy.

From the history of science we learn that these considerations contain at least some truth, for the isolation of the elements has ever been dependent upon the power of concentrating
energy available at that time. The most brilliant example is the
application of the voltaic pile to the isolation of the alkali
metals by Humphry Davy.

Still I must confess that these last considerations are in a
very embryonic state, and I should not have brought them before
you if an unexpected application had not lately made itself manifest. Some years ago I explained these views to my old friend
Sir William Ramsay, when he asked me how the idea of elements
fitted into my conceptions of energy. Then I forgot all about it
until Sir William reminded me of it, saying that his perplexing
discovery of the transmutation of radium into helium might conceivably find some explanation in this way. This I am convinced
of, and the considerations may be pictured in the following
manner.

In the corner of our cavern where the elements with the highest combining weight are assembled, the stalactites are very

short; and at last they are not really stalactites, but rather
regions of different slope in the sloping ceiling. In our cavern,
a drop of water furnishes generally a picture of the stability of
the elements. While hanging at the end of a true stalactite,
more or less work must be done to raise the drop over the pass
until it flows down another stalactite. But in this corner it
will flow of its own accord, and only delay for a short time on
the nearly horizontal portions in the ceiling.

Such elements will have only a *temporary existence*. Now we
are sure that for the transmutation of one element into another,
enormous amounts of energy would be required, for the concentrations of energy as yet available have proved themselves insufficient for this purpose. We may expect, therefore, that enormous
amounts of energy will be liberated if such an unstable element
changes into a stable one. This accounts for the extraordinary
quantity of energy developed by radium during its existence. The
fact that radium changes into helium, an element with an excep-
tionally long stalactite (for it is impossible to get even any
combination of helium) makes us expect indeed such an unusually
great development of energy as is found to occur.

IX. From Natural History to Biology

A. The Foundation of Scientific Physiology

The word biology was coined in the early nineteenth century
to represent the sciences of life. At the time, however, there
was considerable doubt over whether the phenomena of life could
ever be reduced to scientific terms. Zoology and botany were, of
course, studies of long standing but they were not sciences in
the sense that the nineteenth century understood the term. The
purpose of zoology and botany was to compile natural histories
and provide a system of classification that would permit zoologists and botanists to make some taxonomic sense out of the bur-
geoning number of known animal and plant species. The eighteenth
century had borne eloquent witness to this approach. The multi-
volumed works of Linnaeus and Buffon graced the library shelves
of the learned and provided the bookish with at least a nodding
acquaintance with animate nature. But this was hardly science in
the same sense that celestial mechanism or optics were sciences.
The one was firmly founded on mathematical analysis; the other
was based upon repeatable experiments. Neither mathematics or
experiment seemed applicable to living matter and so it seemed
that natural history would just have to do.

There is some irony in the fact that the person who, in many ways, led the way to the experimental physiology of the nineteenth century was one of those who believed that the phrase "science of life" was a necessary contradiction in terms. Xavier Bichat (1771-1802) was a physician in Paris who devoted his brief life to the study of pathology. He defined life as the sum of the forces resisting death, an epigram of doubtful utility to the physiologist. Yet, it did serve as a theoretical framework for his ideas. Life, Bichat felt, was necessarily the product of vital forces that were not amenable to scientific treatment. These forces were constantly changing for life, itself, was constant change. Like Heraclitus before him, Bichat felt that one could never understand something unless it remained constant long enough to subject it to a meaningful scientific analysis. He used the common medical example of a patient's urine to make his point. What can urinalysis indicate? This will depend upon when the sample is taken. The urine is different before eating from what it is afterwards. It is different when the patient has a fever. It is different at different times of day. In short, it is impossible even to define "normal" urine to be used as a standard and without such a standard, urinalysis was meaningless. The same reasoning applied to all other aspects of life, leading to the conclusion that no science of life, properly speaking, was possible. This did not mean, for Bichat, that no knowledge of the living state could be had. Quite the contrary; certain things could be known and Bichat merely wished investigators to focus upon these and leave the dream of a science of life alone. What could be known was normal and abnormal anatomy and pathology. The latter was fundamental, for through pathology Bichat felt that a solid foundation could be created for a rational medical art. Pathology was the study of diseased organs. The pathologist must first understand what a healthy organ does. Then, in disease, there will be a malfunction of the diseased organ and this malfunction, as J. B. Morgagni had already pointed out in the eighteenth century, will be correlated with organic lesions. The doctor, after a post-mortem, by examining the organs can then understand the clinical symptoms of disease in terms of the specific malfunction of a specific organ. In practical terms, this meant that a physician was given a slightly better chance of predicting the course of a disease and could inform a patient's relatives what he died of. In terms of the advance of physiology, however, it was of central importance. In order to understand malfunction, the pathologist had to lay bare the physiology of the organs of the body. The opportunity to observe an organ in action, in the days before anaesthetics, rarely occurred. So, the key to organic function was anatomy. From structure, function could be deduced. Given the quality of microscopes at the end of the eighteenth century, anatomy had still to be mainly concerned with structures visible to the naked eye. What Bichat saw was a variety of organs made up of different tissues, of which he distinguished 21 varieties. Each tissue, he insisted, had a peculiar life of its own and organ function was determined by the tissues of which it was composed. The vital force was what coordinated all these individual "tissue lives" to preserve the life of the organism. By breaking life down into the sum of the functions of the tissues, Bichat made it possible to study living processes without running into the fog of vitalism at every step. Thus, the paradox mentioned earlier may be resolved. The totality of life —tho life of the organism as a whole--was dependent upon the coordinating faculty of the vital force and thus could not be analyzed experimentally. The life of an organ, however, was the result of the vital properties of its constituent tissues, and this life could be analyzed and understood. Physiology, understood in these terms, could become at least a descriptive science.

Bichat's approach was both revolutionary in that it insisted upon the possibility of gaining scientific knowledge of life processes, and conservative, in that it reserved a central place to the vital force. His younger contemporary, François Magendie (1783-1855) wished to push Bichat's views to the more revolutionary conclusion that the living organism was merely a machine of extraordinary complexity. It was, therefore, completely deterministic in its functioning and, as such, as susceptible to experimental investigation as any system in inorganic nature. Magendie's career was spent proving this point and he made fundamental contributions to physiology while doing so.

It was Magendie who really created the art of experimentation on living animals. This was a very unpleasant business in the early 1800's for the lack of anaesthesia forced the physiologist to inflict pain on his experimental subjects. Not everyone could stand the screams and obvious suffering of dogs, cats and rabbits. Magendie could, and was often accused of sadism for he insisted upon repeating his experiments past the point where most of his contemporaries were satisfied with his results.

Magendie's first important investigation was upon the action of strychnine as a poison. He first showed that no matter how the poison was introduced into the body, by mouth or by injection, the result was always convulsions and death. If the brain were severed from the spinal cord, the convulsion still ensued but if the spinal cord were destroyed, no convulsions resulted. Hence, the poison acted on the spinal cord. The rapidity with which the poison took effect convinced Magendie that it was transported by the blood·stream, and not, as was generally believed, by the lymphatic system. To prove this, he injected the poison into a dog's leg connected to the body by only one vein and one artery. The dog went into convulsions and died, and the theory was proved.

An even more elegant use of experiment to prove a physiological point was in Magendie's investigation of the mechanism of vomiting. The simple common-sense view (still held today by most people) was that the stomach rejected bad food by contracting violently and expelling its own contents. Magendie administered strong emetics to animals whose stomachs were exposed and observed that the stomach remained passive during the act of vomiting. It was the diaphragm which pressed upon the stomach, forcing it to empty. To make the point obvious, Magendie removed a stomach from one of his experimental animals and substituted a pig's bladder for it. There could be no doubt about the passivity of the bladder yet it could be emptied when a substance such as *nux vomica* was injected into the animal. Thus, by the 1820's, Magendie had clearly demonstrated that experiment could be applied to living organisms and that experimental results were repeatable. The necessary framework for a science of physiology had been created.

Magendie, himself, went on to fill in the blank spaces bordered by his experimental framework. He demonstrated conclusively, what Sir Charles Bell in England had deduced from anatomy, that the nerves emerging from the anterior and posterior roots of the spinal cord had different functions. The anterior nerves, when stimulated, caused motion; the posterior nerves, when stimulated, caused pain. This work opened up the field of neurophysiology which made giant strides in the next decades. Magendie also produced a clue that was later to lead to important advances in the general theory of physiology. In his work on vomiting, Magendie discovered that vomiting could be induced by stimulation of the vagus nerve. It could also be induced by injection of a poison such as *nux vomica*. This implied (and Magendie did not follow up the implication) a more generalized control over internal matters than a mere simple mechanical response. The stomach could be emptied by acting upon a nerve or by introducing a substance into the bloodstream. There must, then, be some kind of overall physiological control of individual organs exercised by the body. The nature of this control was to be discovered by Magendie's pupil and assistant, Claude Bernard (1818-1878).

Magendie's main physiological work was done between 1809 and 1825. Bernard's great discoveries were made in the late 1840's and 1850's. In the years in between, a powerful new tool was added to the physiologist's instruments of research. It was in those years that organic chemistry, particularly analytical organic chemistry, made great strides and became useful to the physiologist. Its utility was particularly important in the field of the physiology of nutrition and digestion. The question, here, was of great antiquity going back at least as far as Anaxagoras. What was in the food that men and animals ate and how was it converted into men and animals? Anaxagoras, it may be remembered, thought that food consisted of small pieces of flesh, blood and bone. Digestion was merely the sorting out and allocation of these pieces to the proper part of the body. Very little progress on the problem had been made between the fifth century A.D. and 1800. There had been a certain amount of speculation about digestion and even some new facts. Paracelsus had argued with his usual vehemence that digestion was the result of the chemical activity of an *archaeus* or alchemical spirit resident in the stomach. Reaumur, in the eighteenth century, had proved that the stomach did act chemically on food by forcing his pet vulture to regurgitate ingested food and then examining it. That was about all that was known, however, until the nineteenth century.

The facts of digestion were enlarged in the 1820's as the result of a hunting accident. In 1822, a young Canadian trapper, Alexis St. Martin, accidentally was wounded in the stomach by a musket ball. He was treated by Dr. William Beaumont. When the wound healed, it left a hole into St. Martin's stomach cavity, making it impossible for him to digest food unless the hole were plugged. Beaumont, a frontier doctor in a wilderness community in the Michigan woods, realized that he had a physiological specimen available that not even the best laboratories of Europe could equal. He performed a series of simple but classic experiments on digestion that involved inserting various foods into the stomach, withdrawing them after various periods of time and noting their disintegration. He carefully tabulated the effects of temperature, alcohol and rage on digestion. Moreover, by collecting digestive juices, Beaumont was able to duplicate the digestive process *in vitro*, thus proving that digestion was a purely physico-chemical process which did not rely upon a vital force associated only with living tissue. If digestion were merely a physico-chemical process, then it ought to be amenable to study by chemists. In the 1830's, Justis Liebig turned his attention to the problem of nutrition and digestion. Although Liebig believed in a vital force, he nevertheless also believed that chemistry could lay bare the mechanism of vital processes.

Liebig's approach was rather gross, involving a material balance of intake and excretion. His analogy was the crude one of a steam engine. Man took in fuel plus other nutrient in the form of plant and animal matter. The fuel was burned up, and what was useless was excreted. Since all parts of the body, by chemical analysis, contained nitrogen, Liebig assumed that proteins alone supplied this need and constructed a series of diets around this "fact." Carbohydrates were the source of fuel for the physiological engine. Excess carbohydrate was turned into fat. Thus food served essentially three purposes. Protein provided nitrogen for body tissues; carbohydrate provided energy and also provided fat for future use. These results could be (and, indeed, were) produced by the analysis of dead tissue, not living organisms. What remained to be determined was the processes by which foodstuffs were actually turned into flesh and energy. It was in this area of the physiology of digestion that Claude Bernard made his first important discoveries.

In 1816, Magendie had performed the first experiments in animal nutrition. He fed three dogs on foods containing no nitrogen and the dogs died. Some elements, clearly, were essential to life. But what about compounds? Could the body synthesize these, or was it dependent for certain of these upon outside sources? One of the "fuels" most easily utilized by the body was sugar. Bernard early became interested in the digestion of sugar in the body. He showed that pancreatic juice aided in the breakdown of starch into sugar but what happened to the sugar when once formed remained a mystery. If a sugar solution were injected into the bloodstream it could not be utilized by the body and was excreted in the urine. Yet, if an animal were fed a sugar-free diet or starved, a form of sugar--glucose--was found in the portal vein leading from the liver. This suggested to Bernard that the sugar was somehow coming from the liver. By ligating the portal vein, he was able to test this hypothesis. Sugar did appear in the blood on the side of the ligation nearest the vein. It could be assumed, and Bernard assumed, that one function of the liver was to store sugar. The assumption was wrong and Bernard discovered

his error by accident. His usual procedure for testing for sugar
had been to remove the liver and flush it out with water, testing
the solution for sugar. One day, however, he was unable to complete the tests and had to leave the flushed liver for some hours.
It came as a surprise, therefore, when Bernard returned to the
laboratory to discover that the liver was filled with glucose.
It had obviously been producing glucose all the while Bernard had
been gone. Pursuing the subject further, Bernard found that the
liver does not store sugar. Rather, it makes sugar from a starch-
like carbohydrate which he christened glycogen. Glycogen is insoluble, thus facilitating its storage in an aqueous environment.
The release of sugar depended upon a series of complicated stimuli for Bernard soon found that the release of sugar from the
liver was apparently controlled by the vagus nerve. Wounding of
this nerve caused an excess of sugar to appear in the blood and
in the urine. As with Magendie's researches on vomiting, a physiological process was found to depend upon nervous action. This
time, however, it affected the presence or absence of a substance
produced by an organ of the body. If the vital principle regulated and coordinated the vital activity of organs, it appeared
as though the instruments of that coordination were the nerves.
And, the mechanism was subject to experimental investigation.

Besides his work on the glycogenic function of the liver,
Bernard did fundamental work on the action of certain poisons,
particularly curare. The coordinative function of the nerves
also stimulated further research. Bernard knew that many branches
of the sympathetic or vasomotor nerves followed the arteries.
Pathologists knew that lesions in the mixed trunks of the main
nerves caused cooling of the part served by the respective trunks.
Now, Bernard argued, if only the sympathetic nerve fibres were
cut, then the same cooling should be produced. Cutting the cervi-
cal sympathetic nerve of a rabbit, to Bernard's surprise, produced
dilation of the blood vessels and increased warmth on the side of
the head. Stimulation of the cut nerve produced constriction and
coolness. Blood flow, too, was controlled by the nerves. Bernard
mistakenly felt that even the rate of oxidation in the affected
tissue was under nervous guidance, and this contributed to an
idea that Bernard was developing. It was the concept of the
milieu intérieur, or internal environment. It was a literally
revolutionary idea for it ran directly counter to the main concept of life entertained up to that point. To return to Bichat,
Bernard would argue that the variability of the nature of urine
did not indicate the capricious variability of living tissue.
Quite the contrary! The variability of the urine was merely the
external sign of the attempts of the body to keep the internal
environment *constant*. The purpose of many, if not most, of the
organs of the body was to preserve the *milieu intérieur* within
very narrow limits of chemical variability. Changes in this
milieu triggered reactions which were intended to restore equilibrium. The nerves were only one of the means for this restoration. Later biochemical messengers, such as hormones, were to
enrich the concept of the *milieu intérieur*. The organism as a
whole, as Bernard left the idea, was an amazingly complicated,
self-adjusting and sophisticated machine, but a machine, never-

theless. As such, as Magendie had insisted, it could be dealt with scientifically.

B. The Scientific Basis of Classification

As we have noted, the problem of a comprehensive taxonomy was increasingly acute in the early nineteenth century. There were so many species of living organisms that no system yet devised was able to provide a truly rational basis of classification. There was clearly the feeling that some important clue to the Creation was being ignored. That that clue was common ancestry is apparent from the fact that the idea of evolution became explicit at just this time. The German Nature Philosophers, the English polymath Erasmus Darwin (1731-1802) and the French botanist and invertebrate zoologist, Jean Baptiste de Lamarck (1744-1829) all devised an evolutionary theory within a few short years of one another. If plant and animal species were connected *genetically* then the task of taxonomy was to discover the family relationships between species. Taxonomy, then, would be based upon real biological facts and not on possibly fictitious biological similarities and analogies. The trouble was that no one (or practically no one) took these evolutionary ideas seriously. Part of the reason, as we shall see, was that the mechanisms proposed for species change were unsatisfactory to most people. By and large, however, the rejection of evolutionary hypotheses came about because these theories appeared flatly to contradict Scripture. The Book of Genesis is about as plain and unequivocal on this subject as it is possible to be. Creation took six days. God created the plants on the third day, some animals on the fourth day, and the rest of the animals plus man on the sixth day. Since the Bible provided a reasonably complete genealogy from Adam down to historic times, it was possible to compute the date of creation. This had been done in the seventeenth century when Archbishop Ussher announced to an astonished world that God had begun creation of the universe at 6 A.M., October 6, 4004 B.C.

This combination of the explicit story of animal and plant creation and a rigid date of creation made it impossible for an evolutionary theory based on natural laws to survive. No theory could both combat Scriptural authority on creation and work out evolution of species with only six thousand years of time in which such evolution could take place. So other factors had to be called upon. The German Nature philosophers used the protean energies of the vital principle as the driving force behind evolution. It was the vital force which caused organisms to grow and evolve into species at a rate which, to modern eyes, is extremely rapid. Lamarck called upon a chemistry that was already obsolete to effect his transformations of species. The imponderable fluids, particularly heat and electricity, were the principles of form in living organisms. When these fluids concentrated in an organ, as they did when that organ was used a great deal, the organ underwent a change in form and a new species arose when the change in form was large enough. Neither of these suggestions were upheld by facts of history or observation. Napoleon's expedition to Egypt, for example, had revealed that species still alive had not changed significantly since the time of the Pharaohs. Since the time that had elapsed was almost as much time as there was, failure to detect change in this case appeared to refute any evolutionary hypothesis.

Two things served to pave the way for the acceptance of the fact of evolution. The development of geology in the first half of the nineteenth century made it very difficult to adhere to the chronology of the Bible. The development of paleontology also made it difficult to believe in a single act of vital creation. Breaking with orthodoxy on these two fundamental points opened the door to naturalistic systems in which only natural forces were at work.

The problem of the evolution of the Earth had intrigued men since Greek times. Christian thought had generally attempted to reconcile Christian doctrine with observation. The presence of oyster shells in the Alpine passes, for example, could be explained by the flood, even though men like Leonardo da Vinci preferred to believe that the waters had covered the Alps for more time than Scripture allowed. The first serious attempts to account for the Earth's formation and later development in completely natural terms came in the eighteenth century. George Louis Leclerc, Comte de Buffon (1707-88) devised a geological time scale based on the supposition that the Earth had been formed by the collision of a comet with the Sun. Basing his calculations on the rate of cooling of a large mass of iron, Buffon figured that the age of the Earth was to be figured in the hundreds of thousands of years, a figure far larger than that allowed by Scripture. Buffon's work was condemned and burned by the Catholic Church in France.

In Saxony, in the eighteenth century, a really serious attempt was made by Abraham Gottlob Werner (1749-1817) to reconcile the facts of geology (or at least, of mineralogy) with Scripture. Geological formations, Werner taught, were the results of the flood. Strata are the precipitates that settled out of the waters that covered the Earth as the waters receded. Where the waters receded to, Werner left unexplained. This Neptunist theory, as it was called, successfully accounted for those geological formations that were the result of sedimentation but forced Werner and his followers to perform some rather extraordinary mental gyrations. Granite, for example, is notably insoluble and it is difficult to imagine how it precipitated from anything. It is also found in veins that appear as though they had been forced into other rocks under conditions of tremendous heat and pressure. All this Werner ignored, primarily because Saxony displayed few examples of granitic rocks.

When Werner's doctrines were exported, however, this insufficiency was made manifest. The center of France is marked with extinct volcanoes and it was only natural, therefore, for French geologists to call attention to the relevance of volcanic activity in the shaping of the Earth's crust. Scotland is a land of granitic crags and it is no coincidence that Werner's most severe critic was the Scot, James Hutton (1726-97).

In many ways, Hutton's most important contribution to geology was his definition of it as a science. If one looked at the

Earth purely as a scientist, Hutton insisted, there was no evidence that it ever had a beginning or would ever come to an end. Creation, therefore, was a theological condition imposed on geology by nongeologists. It had no place in the *science* of geology, whatever might be its status in religion. The task of the geologist was not to reconcile Scripture with geology but to account for the present structure of the Earth in terms of natural forces. For Hutton, the most important force was heat. Granite he saw as being the result of heat and pressure. Columnar basalt, one of the most striking of all geological structures, Hutton argued was the result of the cooling of molten basalt, not precipitation from a primeval sea. The Vulcanist school, founded by Hutton, not only opposed the Neptunists but also challenged all those who insisted upon introducing supernatural causes into geology.

Perhaps the most successful attempt at preserving the traditional orthodoxy was that made by Georges Cuvier (1769-1832), the creator of paleontology and modern comparative anatomy. Cuvier was a devout Protestant as well as a superb paleontologist and he must have been severely torn by the conflict between his faith and his science. By the early decades of the nineteenth century, paleontology had shown conclusively that fossils were the organic remains of animals and that most, if not all, the fossil animals were extinct. Cuvier's observations in the Paris Basin had made these conclusions inescapable. They had also created somewhat of a dilemma for Cuvier. If fossil animals were extinct and if species were immutable, then where did the present fauna of the Earth come from? They could not be descended from the fossil species nor was there any evidence for more than one set of animals created by God. Cuvier suggested that God, when He revealed himself through Scripture, had held back the whole truth from the primitive Hebrew tribes. His mission, after all, was to teach them morality, not paleontology and so Scripture was not literally true. There had been, Cuvier supposed, not one but a series of creations in which God filled the Earth with animals and then destroyed them in sudden cataclysms. The fossil record bears witness to these successive catastrophes. Scripture records only the *last* creation when God, after having warmed up, so to speak, with the earlier creations, was able to turn out His masterpiece, Man. Thus Cuvier could accept a considerable antiquity for the Earth and still preserve the integrity of Scripture. Species remained immutable and taxonomy remained a tangled mess.

In spite of attempts to save Scripture, the science of geology made steady headway, culminating in the publication of Charles Lyell's *Principles of Geology*, the first volume of which appeared in 1830. Lyell put together an enormous number of geological facts and organized them under the banner of Hutton's doctrine that we must account for geological features by the forces of nature now in action. This doctrine of the uniformity of action of natural forces over time was known as Uniformitarianism. It forced a drastic revision of the geological time scale. If gorges and mountains and other geological features had to be accounted for by the erosion of rivers, winds and rain or by the slow elevation of land, then the Earth must be millions of years old, not thousands. And, if the Earth were millions of years old, then very slow processes of change in plants and animals might account for the appearance of seemingly new species. Charles Darwin took Lyell's first volume with him when H.M.S. Beagle sailed from Plymouth harbor on December 27, 1831.

In 1831, there was no one less likely than Charles Darwin to be selected as a person who would cause one of the greatest intellectual revolutions in the history of mankind. Darwin was then 22 years old and a failure at everything he had yet tried. He was a dropout from a medical education at Edinburgh and had studied for a ministry in which he did not believe at Cambridge. His sole passions were hunting and a kind of aimless collection of animal specimens. The voyage of the Beagle was to transform him into a first-rate naturalist in whom the idea of the evolution of species was to gestate for two decades.

It is customary to point out that the idea of evolution was "in the air" and so it was. Even though Darwin was no great scholar at this point, he could hardly have missed hearing of his grandfather's ideas. But this was certainly not enough to persuade him of the fact of evolution even though it might have helped him to look for evidence of it. This stimulus the voyage of the Beagle provided [see p. 3 61]. It was only two years after his return to England in 1835 that he began the systematic collection of evidence for the existence of evolution. The mechanism, however, escaped him. This, too, was "in the air" of England at the time. The social revolution caused by the Industrial Revolution had forced a good deal of writing on economics and social welfare, among which was the Rev. Thomas Malthus' *Essay on Population*. The most recent scholarship on Darwin claims that Darwin had already stumbled on the idea of food pressure serving as a selection mechanism before he read Malthus although Darwin later said that it was Malthus' *Essay* which gave him the thought. In any case, the idea was not a terribly complicated or difficult one. Malthus had argued that population increased geometrically whereas food supply, at best, could only increase arithmetically. The result was that population always outran food and so millions of human beings were condemned to death by starvation. Wars, famines, and natural catastrophes were blessings in disguise since they kept population down. The same pressures ought to exist in Nature and this pressure was what allowed species ultimately to evolve. Starting from the observation that, in nature, individuals all differed slightly from one another, Darwin argued that these slight differences could be crucial. Thus a difference in neck length of one inch, in times of severe drought, could make the difference between life and death in an animal that browsed on trees. Over the course of millennia these slight variations, if favorable to individuals, would accumulate to produce new species. The above example would illustrate how the giraffe got its long neck.

For twenty years, Darwin patiently collected data, did research, and prepared for the great work he would ultimately write. He knew perfectly well that his *magnum opus* would be the center of controversy and so kept putting off the writing of it while his pile of evidence grew and grew. In 1858, he received a letter from a young naturalist, Alfred Russell Wallace (1823-1913) to-

gether with a memoir by Wallace on evolution through natural selection. Wallace, too, had read Malthus -and had worked out his
evolutionary theory while lying ill with fever in Malaya. We can
well imagine Darwin's emotions when he read this paper and realized that he had been forestalled. Darwin was scrupulously honest
and was intent upon publishing Wallace's paper without letting
the scientific world know that he, too, had been working on the
same problem and had far more data to support the theory than
Wallace did. Fortunately, Darwin was persuaded by friends to
accompany Wallace's paper with a short article of his own to
stake his partial claim to the subject, and then to put his evidence together into a book. The result was *The Origin of Species*
which appeared in November of 1859. It was an instant best seller
in spite of its dense subject matter and rather flat prose. But
those who bought it knew that they were purchasing an intellectual
bomb destined to destroy the age-old belief in man's special
place in Nature. To a certain extent, they were disappointed but
only because Darwin did not explicitly and in detail apply his
theory to man. Implicitly, however, man was made into the final
product of evolution from lower animals and everyone knew it. At
the 1860 meeting of the British Association for the Advancement
of Science at Oxford, Samuel Wilberforce, Bishop of Oxford asked
Thomas Henry Huxley, Darwin's defender, if he would care to tell
the expectant audience upon which of his parent's sides he was
descended from apes. Huxley replied that he would rather be descended from apes than prostitute his intellect as the Bishop had
just done. The sally was one that Huxley relished but it did not
adequately take into account the effect of Darwin's theory. If
Darwin were correct and men were animals, would this knowledge
not lead them sooner or later to act like animals? For the moral
Victorians, this was not a pleasant prospect to contemplate.
Fortunately, it was not until the twentieth century that such
fears were to be realized.

Darwin steadfastly refused to be drawn into polemical arguments. Books poured from his pen, all illustrating one or the
other of themes first stated in *The Origin of Species*. In 1871
the other shoe finally dropped with the publication of *The Descent
of Man* in which human evolution was explicitly described. Other
treatises, ranging from earthworms to orchids, illustrated various
aspects of the doctrine of evolution by natural selection. In
all these works, Darwin put his passion for the collection of
specimens and facts to excellent use and, like the coral reefs
upon which he had earlier written a treatise, the general structure of his thought emerged. Evolution by natural selection
turned the Victorian world upside down. The old argument from
Design, used almost complacently, to prove the existence of a
beneficent Deity was shown to be faulty. Design disappeared to
be replaced by adaptation and adaptation was the result of blind
chance. Mechanism was carried to its ultimate in Darwin for Nature, herself, was revealed to be nothing but a gigantic winnowing
machine. Successful adaptations survived while unsuccessful variations were rapidly and blindly sorted out and discarded. The
final step in stripping man of his divinity was taken. Copernicus
had started it by removing the Earth from the center of the uni-

verse where God had put it. Scientific Law had gradually displaced the actions of God in the physical world. Now, on the
largest scale imaginable, scientific law displaced divine purpose
with regard to life. And man who had prided himself for so long
upon being made in the image of God suddenly saw the face of a
grinning ape staring back at him from his evolutionary past. For
men like Huxley, this was a liberation from a tradition which
seemed to stifle Truth and bind men to the dead forms of orthodoxy. To others, it was the opening of a new Pandora's box in
which new evils were loosed upon mankind. Through it all, Darwin
preserved his aloofness. The books continued to appear and the
order of nature was transformed.

Not everyone could accept the new order with the philosophic
calmness of a Darwin or the enthusiasm of a Huxley. Although the
fact of evolution appeared established for men of science beyond
all reasonable doubt, the mechanism of natural selection did not
seem adequate to explain evolutionary changes. Take, for example,
the evolution of the wing. A wing that did not permit an organism
to fly was clearly of no use. But, the changes envisioned by natural selection were small, almost imperceptible. Of what use
was an imperceptible skin fold that might, in millennia, turn
into a full-fledged wing? "None, whatsoever" answered those who
desperately wished not to believe in natural selection. The
exquisite adaptations that naturalists were now quick to produce,
also seemed incapable of being created by a blind, mechanical
process. And so, although purpose and design had been thrown out
the front door of natural history, it now crept in through the
back window. In the 1880's, Lamarck's ideas were revived. Neo-
Lamarckianism insisted (as had Darwin) upon the inheritance of
acquired characteristics and, more importantly, upon the purposeful adaptation of organisms to their environment. It was not
until the middle of the twentieth century that natural selection
was finally accepted as an adequate evolutionary mechanism by
most biologists.

Although the Darwinian theory remained controversial for
decades after its inception, there was one area in which it served
to clarify all issues immediately. Taxonomy was now seen clearly
to be a question of genetic descent. The actual lines of descent
might be terribly difficult to discern, but if they could be discovered, the result was a classificatory mechanism of enormous
power. Taxonomists might have doubts about the efficacy of natural selection but without evolution they were helpless.

C. Evolution--Lamarckian or Darwinian?

1. Towards Evolutionary Theory

a. Jean Baptiste de Lamarck's Zoological Philosophy

(1) From *Zoological Philosophy**

The idea of the evolution of species had a long history by the time Lamarck turned his attention to the problem in the late eighteenth century. Empedocles in the fifth century B.C. had suggested a crude evolutionary scheme and a number of evolutionary speculations had been forthcoming in the eighteenth century. What distinguished Lamarck from his predecessors was both the depth of his knowledge of zoology and botany and the penetration of his insight into the influence of the interaction of organisms with their environment. In his Zoological Philosophy *which appeared in 1809, he considered the problem of evolution and its mechanism in detail.*

Preface.

Experience in teaching has made me feel how useful a philosophical zoology would be at the present time. By this I mean a body of rules and principles, relative to the study of animals, and applicable even to the other divisions of the natural sciences; for our knowledge of zoological facts has made considerable progress during the last thirty years.

I have in consequence endeavoured to sketch such a philosophy for use in my lessons, and to help me in teaching my pupils; nor had I any other aim in view. But in order to fix the principles and establish rules for guidance in study, I found myself compelled to consider the organisation of the various known animals, to pay attention to the singular differences which it presents in those of each family, each order, and especially each class; to compare the faculties which these animals derive according to its degree of complexity in each race, and finally to investigate the most general phenomena presented in the principal cases. I was therefore led to embark upon successive inquiries of the greatest interest to science, and to examine the most difficult of zoological questions.

How, indeed, could I understand that singular degradation which is found in the organisation of animals as we pass along the series of them from the most perfect to the most imperfect, without enquiring as to the bearings of so positive and so remarkable a fact, founded upon the most convincing proofs? How could I avoid the conclusion that nature had successively produced the different bodies endowed with life, from the simplest

*J. B. Lamarck, *Zoological Philosophy*, translated with an introduction, by Hugh Elliot (London, 1914), pp. (in order of reproduction), 1-2, 186-88, 201-2, 205, 211-13, 38-40, 54-55, 106-8, 112-13, 119-20.

worm upwards? For in ascending the animal scale, starting from the most imperfect animals, organisation gradually increases in complexity in an extremely remarkable manner.

I was greatly strengthened in this belief, moreover, when I recognised that in the simplest of all organisations there were no special organs whatever, and that the body had no special faculty but only those which are the property of all living things. As nature successively creates the different special organs, and thus builds up the animal organisation, special functions arise to a corresponding degree, and in the most perfect animals these are numerous and highly developed.

These reflections, which I was bound to take into consideration, led me further to enquire as to what life really consists of, and what are the conditions necessary for the production of this natural phenomenon and its power of dwelling in a body. I made the less resistance to the temptation to enter upon this research, in that I was then convinced that it was only in the simplest of all organisations that the solution of this apparently difficult problem was to be found. For it is only the simplest organisation that presents all the conditions necessary to the existence of life and nothing else beyond, which might mislead the enquirer.

The conditions necessary to the existence of life are all present in the lowest organisations, and they are here also reduced to their simplest expression. It became therefore of importance to know how this organisation, by some sort of change, had succeeded in giving rise to others less simple, and indeed to the gradually increasing complexity observed throughout the animal scale. By means of the two following principles, to which observation had led me, I believed I perceived the solution of the problem at issue.

Firstly, a number of known facts proves that the continued use of any organ leads to its development, strengthens it and even enlarges it, while permanent disuse of any organ is injurious to its development, causes it to deteriorate and ultimately disappear if the disuse continues for a long period through successive generations. Hence we may infer that when some change in the environment leads to a change of habit in some race of animals, the organs that are less used die away little by little, while those which are more used develop better, and acquire a vigour and size proportional to their use.

Secondly, when reflecting upon the power of the movement of the fluids in the very supple parts which contain them, I soon became convinced that, according as this movement is accelerated, the fluids modify the cellular tissue in which they move, open passages in them, form various canals, and finally create different organs, according to the state of the organisation in which they are placed.

Arguing from these two principles, I looked upon it as certain that, firstly, the movement of the fluids within animals--a movement which is progressively accelerated with the increasing complexity of the organisation--and, secondly, the influence of the environment, in so far as animals are exposed to it in spreading throughout habitable places, were the two general causes

which have brought the various animals to the state in which we
now see them.

                    *   *   *

        Whatever may be the state of organisation of a body and of
its essential fluids, active life could assuredly not exist in
that body without a special cause capable of exciting its vital
movements. Whatever hypothesis we may form in this matter, we
are always obliged to recognise that some special cause must be
present for the active manifestations of life. Now it can no
longer be doubted that this cause which animates living bodies is
to be found in the environment of those bodies, and thus varies
in intensity according to places, seasons, and climates. It is
in no way dependent on the bodies which it animates, it exists
before they do and remains after they have been destroyed. Lastly, it stimulates in them the movements of life, so long as the
state of these bodies allows; and it ceases to animate them when
that state opposes obstacles to the performance of the movements
which it stimulates.
        In the most perfect animals this exciting cause of life is
developed within themselves, and suffices to animate them up to a
certain point; but it still needs the co-operation of that provided by the environment. In the other animals, and in all plants
it is altogether external to them; so that they can only obtain
it from their environment.
        When these interesting facts have been ascertained and set-
tled, we shall enquire how the first outlines of organisation come
to be formed, how spontaneous generation can have occurred and in
what part of the two series of living bodies.
        If, indeed, bodies which possess life are really productions
of nature, she must have had and still have the faculty of producing some of them spontaneously. She must then have endowed them
with the faculty of growth, multiplication and increasing complexity of organisation and the power of varying according to
time and circumstances. She must have done this if all those
that we now observe are really the products of her power and
efforts.
        After recognising the necessity for these acts of direct
creation, we must enquire which are the living bodies that nature
may produce spontaneously, and distinguish them from those which
only derive their existence indirectly from her. Assuredly the
lion, eagle, butterfly, oak, rose, do not derive their existence
immediately from nature; they derive it as we know from individuals like themselves who transmit it to them by means of reproduction; and we may be sure that if the entire species of the lion
or oak chanced to be destroyed in those parts of the earth where
they are now distributed, it would be long before the combined
powers of nature could restore them.
        I propose then to show what is the method apparently used by
nature for forming, in favourable places and conditions, the most
simply organised living bodies and through them the most perfect
animals; how these fragile animals, which are the mere rudiments
of animality directly produced by nature, have developed, multiplied and become varied; how at length, after an infinite series

of generations, the organisation of these bodies has advanced in complexity and has extended ever more widely the animal faculties of the numerous resulting races.

We shall find that every advance made in complexity of organisation and in the faculties arising from it has been preserved and transmitted to other individuals by means of reproduction, and that by this procedure maintained for very many centuries nature has succeeded in forming successively all the living bodies that exist.

We shall see, moreover, that all the faculties without exception are purely physical, that is, that each of them is essentially due to activities of the organisation; so that it will be easy to show how, from the humblest instinct, the origin of which can be easily ascertained, nature has attained to the creation of the intellectual faculties from the most primitive to the most highly developed. . . .

If we wish to grasp the chain of physical causation which brought living bodies into existence, we must pay attention to the principle which I embody in the following proposition:

It is to the influence of the movements of various fluids in the more or less solid substances of our earth that we must attribute the formation, temporary preservation, and reproduction of all living bodies observed on its surface, and of all the transformations incessantly undergone by the remains of these bodies.

*　　*　　*

Chapter II.

Of Life, What It Consists of, and the Conditions of Its Existence in a Body.

. . . Life when studied in living bodies is exclusively due to the relations existing between the three following objects: the parts of the body adapted for containing liquids, the contained liquids moving in them, and the exciting cause of such movements and changes as are carried out.

Whatever efforts we may make by the most profound thought and meditation to decide as to what life consists of, we shall necessarily be compelled to fall back on the principle just enunciated as soon as we pay attention to the teaching of observation on the matter; in fact, life consists of nothing else.

A comparison drawn between life and a watch in active movement is inadequate, to say the least of it; for in the watch there are only two main points to consider: (1) the wheels and machinery of movement; (2) the spring which by its tension and elasticity keeps up the movement so long as that tension continues.

But in a living body, instead of two chief points for study, there are three: (1) the organs or supple containing parts; (2) the essential contained fluids which are always in motion; (3) lastly, the exciting cause of vital movements, from which arises the action of the fluid on the organs and the reaction of the organs on the fluids. It is then purely from the relations between these three objects that the movements, changes, and all the phenomena of life result.

In order to improve the comparison between a watch and a living body we should have to compare the exciting cause of organic movements with the spring of the watch, and regard the supple containing parts, together with the essential contained fluids, as the machinery of the movement in question.

It will then be clear, in the first place, that the spring (exciting cause), is the essential motive power, without which the whole remains inactive, and that its variations of tension must be the cause of the variations of energy and rapidity of movements.

In the second place, it will be obvious that the machinery of movement (the organs and essential fluids) must be in a state and arrangement suitable for the performance of the movements which it has to carry out; hence, when this machinery gets out of order the effective power of the spring is lost.

From this point of view the parallel is complete; a living body may be compared with a watch; and I can easily show the close accuracy of this comparison by reference to known facts and observations.

As to the machinery of movement, its existence and faculties are now well known, as also most of the laws which control its various functions.

But as to the spring, the essential motive power and originator of all movements and activities, it has hitherto escaped the researches of observers: I believe, however, that I shall be able to describe it in the next chapter, in such a way that it cannot in future be neglected.

But first let us continue the enquiry as to what essentially constitutes life.

Seeing that life in a body results exclusively from the relations existing between the containing parts in an appropriate condition, the contained fluids moving in them, and the exciting cause of the movements, activities and reactions which take place, we may include what essentially constitutes life in the following definition.

Life, in the parts of any body which possesses it, is an order and state of things which permit of organic movements; and these movements constituting active life result from the action of a stimulating cause which excites them.

* * *

Conditions essential to the Existence of the Order and Structure of a Body in order that it may possess Life.

First condition. No body can possess life unless it consists essentially of two kinds of parts, viz. supple containing parts and contained fluid substances.

As a matter of fact, no body that is perfectly dry can be alive, nor can any body whose parts are fluid be in possession of life. The first condition essential to life in a body therefore is that it should consist of a mass with two kinds of parts, the one solid and containing, but soft and more or less cohesive, the other fluid and contained.

Second condition. No body can possess life unless its containing parts are cellular tissue or formed out of cellular tissue.

Cellular tissue, as I shall show, is the matrix in which all the organs of living bodies have been successively formed; and the movement of fluids in this tissue is the means adopted by nature for the gradual creation and development of these organs.

Every living body is thus essentially a mass of cellular tissue in which more or less complex fluids move more or less rapidly; so that if the body is very simple, that is, has no special organs, it appears homogeneous and consists only of cellular tissue containing fluids which are slowly moving; but if its organisation is complex, all its organs without exception are invested in cellular tissue down to their smallest parts, and are even essentially formed of it.

Third condition. No body can possess active life except when an exciting cause of its organic movements works within it. Without the impulse of this active stimulus, the solid containing parts of an organised body would be inert, the contained fluids would remain at rest, organic movements would not take place, no vital function would be carried out, and consequently active life would not exist.

*   *   *

Of the Exciting Cause of Organic Movements.

We have seen that life is a natural phenomenon which itself produces several others, and that it results from the relations existing between the supple containing parts of an organised body and the contained fluids of that body. We cannot conceive the production of this phenomenon, that is to say, the presence and continuance of the movements constituting active life, unless we imagine a special exciting cause of these movements, a force which animates the organs, controls the activities and all the organic functions,--a spring, in short, of which the permanent though variable tension is the driving energy of all vital movements.

There can be no doubt that the visible fluids of a living body and the solid parts which contain them are irrelevant to the cause that we are here seeking. All these parts together constitute the machinery of movement, if I may revert to the parallel already drawn; and it is not the function of any of them to supply the force in question, that is, the motive power or exciting cause of the movements of life.

We may be certain that if there were no special cause to stimulate and maintain orgasm and irritability in the supple and containing parts of animals, and to produce in plants an obscure orgasm by promoting direct movement of their contained fluids, the blood of animals which have a circulation and the transparent whitish-serum of those that have not, would remain at rest and would rapidly decompose together with the solid parts.

In the same way, if there were no exciting cause of vital movements, if there were no force or spring to endow a body with active life, the sap and special fluids of plants would remain

motionless, would degenerate and be exhaled, and finally compass
the death and desiccation of these living bodies.

The ancient philosophers felt the necessity for a special
exciting cause of organic movements; but not having sufficiently
studied nature, they sought it beyond her; they imagined a vital
principle, a perishable soul for animals, and even attributed the
same to plants; thus in place of positive knowledge, which they
could not attain from want of observations, they created mere
words to which are attached only vague and unreal ideas.

Whenever we abandon nature, and give ourselves up to the fantastic flights of our imagination, we become lost in vagueness,
and our efforts culminate only in errors. The only knowledge
that it is possible for us to acquire is and always will be confined to what we have derived from a continued study of nature's
laws; beyond nature all is bewilderment and delusion: such is my
belief.

If it were true that it is really beyond our powers to ascertain the exciting cause of organic movements, it would be none
the less obvious that such a cause exists and that it is physical,
since we can observe its effects and nature has all the means of
producing it. Do we not know that it spreads and maintains movement in all bodies, and that none of the objects submitted to nature's laws really possesses an absolute stability?

I do not wish to go back to the consideration of first causes,
nor of all the movements and changes observed in physical bodies
of all kinds. We shall confine ourselves to a study of the immediate recognised causes acting on living bodies, and we shall see
that they are quite sufficient to maintain in these bodies the
movements constituting life, so long as the appropriate order of
things is not destroyed.

It would doubtless be impossible to ascertain the exciting
cause of organic movement if the subtle, invisible, uncontainable,
incessantly moving fluids which constitute it were not disclosed
to us in a great variety of circumstances; if we had not proofs
that the whole environment in which all living bodies dwell are
permanently filled with them; lastly, if we did not know positively that these invisible fluids penetrate more or less easily
the masses of all these bodies and stay in them for a longer or
shorter time; and that some of them are in a constant state of
agitation and expansion, from which they derive the faculty of
distending the parts in which they are insinuated, of rarefying
the special fluids of the living bodies that they penetrate, and
of communicating to the soft parts of these same bodies, an ere-
thism or special tension which they retain so long as their condition is favourable to it.

But it is well known that the question at issue is not insoluble; for no part of the earth inhabited by a living beings is
destitute of caloric (even in the coldest regions), of electricity, of magnetic fluids, etc. These fluids, some of which are
expansive and the others agitated in various ways, are incessantly
undergoing more or less regular displacements, renewals or replacements and perhaps in the case of some of them there may
actually be a genuine circulation.

We do not yet know how numerous may be these subtle invisible fluids which are distributed in constant agitation throughout the environment. But we do perceive in the clearest manner that these invisible fluids penetrate every organised body and there accumulate with constant agitation, finally escaping in turn after being retained for a longer or shorter period. They thus stimulate movements and life, when they come in contact with an order of things permitting of such results.

With regard to such of these invisible fluids as chiefly constitute the exciting cause under consideration, two of them appear to us to be the essential elements of this cause, viz. caloric and the electric fluid. They are the direct agents which produce orgasm and the internal movements which in organised bodies constitute and maintain life.

Caloric appears to be that of the two exciting fluids in question which causes and maintains the orgasm of the supple parts of living bodies; and the electric fluid is apparently that which provides the cause of the organic movements and activities of animals.

My justification for this division of the faculties assigned to the two fluids in question is based on the following principles.

In inflammations, the orgasm acquires an excessive energy which is at length even destructive of the parts. This is clearly in consequence of the extreme heat developed in inflamed organs: it is, then, especially to caloric that the orgasm must be attributed.

The rapidity of the movements of caloric throughout the bodies which it penetrates is very far from equalling the extraordinary speed of the movements of the electric fluid. Hence this latter fluid must be the cause of the movements and activities of animals; it must be more particularly the genuine exciting fluid.

It is possible, however, that other active invisible fluids combine with the two already named in the composition of the exciting cause; but what appears to me beyond question is that caloric and electricity are the two chief components, and perhaps even the only components of this cause.

*   *   *

We learn from a number of facts that, according as the individuals of one of our species change their abode, climate, habits, or manner of life, they become subject to influences which little by little alter the consistency and proportions of their parts, their shape, properties and even their organisation; so that in course of time everything in them shares in these mutations.

In the same climate, very different habitats and conditions at first merely cause variations in the individuals exposed to them; but in course of time the continued change of habitat in the individuals of which I speak, living and reproducing in these new conditions, induces alterations in them which become more or less essential to their being; thus, after a long succession of generations these individuals, originally belonging to one species, become at length transformed into a new species distinct from the first.

Suppose, for example, that the seeds of a grass or any other plant that grows normally in a damp meadow, are somehow conveyed first to the slope of a neighbouring hill where the ground although higher is still rich enough to allow the plant to maintain its existence. Suppose that then, after living there and reproducing itself many times, it reaches little by little the dry and almost barren ground of a mountain side. If the plant succeeds in living there and perpetuating itself for a number of generations, it will have become so altered that botanists who come across it will erect it into a separate species. . . .

To assist us to a judgment as to whether the idea of species has any real foundation, let us revert to the principles already set forth; they show:

(1) That all the organised bodies of our earth are true productions of nature, wrought successively throughout long periods of time.

(2) That in her procedure, nature began and still begins by fashioning the simplest of organised bodies, and that it is these alone which she fashions immediately, that is to say, only the rudiments of organisation indicated in the term *spontaneous generation*.

(3) That, since the rudiments of the animal and plant were fashioned in suitable places and conditions, the properties of a commencing life and established organic movement necessarily caused a gradual development of the organs, and in course of time produced diversity in them as in the limbs.

(4) That the property of growth is inherent in every part of the organised body, from the earliest manifestations of life; and then gave rise to different kinds of multiplication and reproduction, so that the increase of complexity of organisation, and of the shape and variety of the parts, has been preserved.

(5) That with the help of time, of conditions that necessarily were favourable, of the changes successively undergone by every part of the earth's surface, and, finally, of the power of new conditions and habits to modify the organs of living bodies, all those which now exist have imperceptibly been fashioned such as we see them.

(6) That, finally, in this state of affairs every living body underwent greater or smaller changes in its organisation and its parts; so that what we call species were imperceptibly fashioned among them one after another and have only a relative constancy, and are not as old as nature.

*   *   *

As a result of the rapid multiplication of the small species, and particularly of the more imperfect animals, the multiplicity of individuals might have injurious effects upon the preservation of races, upon the progress made in perfection of organisation, in short, upon the general order, if nature had not taken precautions to restrain that multiplication within limits that can never be exceeded.

Animals eat each other, except those which live only on plants; but these are liable to be devoured by carnivorous animals.

We know that it is the stronger and the better equipped that eat the weaker, and that the larger species devour the smaller. Nevertheless, individuals rarely eat others of the same race as themselves; they make war on different races.

The multiplication of the small species of animals is so great, and the succession of generations is so rapid, that these small species would render the globe uninhabitable to any others, if nature had not set a limit to their prodigious multiplication. But since they serve as prey to a multitude of other animals, and since the duration of their life is very short and they are killed by any fall of temperature, their numbers are always maintained in the proper proportions for the preservation of their own and other races.

As to the larger and stronger animals, they might well become dominant and have bad effects upon the preservation of many other races if they could multiply in too large proportions; but their races devour one another, and they only multiply slowly and few at a time; and this maintains in their case also the kind of equilibrium that should exist.

Lastly, man alone, considered apart from all that is special to him, seems to be able to multiply indefinitely, for his intelligence and powers protect him from any limit of multiplication due to the voracity of any animal. He exercises a supremacy over them, so that instead of having to fear the larger and stronger races of animals, he is capable rather of extinguishing them, and he is continually keeping down their numbers.

But nature has given him numerous passions which unfortunately develop with his intelligence, and thus set up a great obstacle to the extreme multiplication of individuals of his species.

It seems, in fact, that man is himself responsible for continually keeping down the numbers of his kind; for I have no hesitation in saying that the earth will never be covered by the population that it might support; several of its habitable regions will always be sparsely populated in turns, although the period of these fluctuations are, so far as we are concerned, immeasurable.

By these wise precautions, everything is thus preserved in the established order; the continual changes and renewals which are observed in that order are kept within limits that they cannot pass; all the races of living bodies continue to exist in spite of their variations; none of the progress made towards perfection of organisation is lost; what appears to be disorder, confusion, anomaly, incessantly passes again into the general order, and even contributes to it; everywhere and always the will of the Sublime Author of nature and of everything that exists is invariably carried out.

Before devoting ourselves to showing the degradation and simplification existing in the organisation of animals, when we proceed according to custom from the most complex to the simplest, let us examine their true arrangement and classification, as well as the principles employed for this purpose. It will then be easier for us to recognise the proofs of the degradation in question.

*   *   *

Of the Influence of the Environment on the Activities and Habits
of Animals, and the Influence of the Activities and Habits
of These Living Bodies in Modifying Their Organisation and
Structure.

. . . The influence of the environment as a matter of fact is
in all times and places operative on living bodies; but what makes
this influence difficult to perceive is that its effects only become perceptible or recognisable (especially in animals) after a
long period of time. . . .

In the preceding chapter we saw that it is now an unquestion-
able fact that on passing along the animal scale in the opposite
direction from that of nature, we discover the existence, in the
groups composing this scale, of a continuous but irregular degradation in the organisation of animals, an increasing simplification in their organisation, and, lastly, a corresponding diminution in the number of their faculties.

This well-ascertained fact may throw the strongest light
over the actual order followed by nature in the production of all
the animals that she has brought into existence, but it does not
show us why the increasing complexity of the organisation of animals from the most imperfect to the most perfect exhibits only
an *irregular gradation,* in the course of which there occur numerous anomalies or deviations with a variety in which no order is
apparent.

Now on seeking the reason of this strange irregularity in the
increasing complexity of animal organisation, if we consider the
influence that is exerted by the infinitely varied environments
of all parts of the world on the general shape, structure and
even organisation of these animals, all will then be clearly explained.

It will in fact become clear that the state in which we find
any animal, is, on the one hand, the result of the increasing complexity of organisation tending to form a regular gradation; and,
on the other hand, of the influence of a multitude of very various
conditions ever tending to destroy the regularity in the gradation
of the increasing complexity of organisation.

I must now explain what I mean by this statement: *the environment affects the shape and organisation of animals,* that is to
say that when the environment becomes very different, it produces
in course of time corresponding modifications in the shape and
organisation of animals.

It is true if this statement were to be taken literally, I
should be convicted of an error; for, whatever the environment
may do, it does not work any direct modification whatever in the
shape and organisation of animals.

But great alterations in the environment of animals lead to
great alterations in their needs, and these alterations in their
needs necessarily lead to others in their activities. Now if the
new needs become permanent, the animals then adopt new habits
which last as long as the needs that evoked them. This is easy
to demonstrate, and indeed requires no amplification.

It is then obvious that a great and permanent alteration in
the environment of any race of animals induces new habits in these
animals.

Now, if a new environment, which has become permanent for some race of animals, induces new habits in these animals, that is to say, leads them to new activities which become habitual, the result will be the use of some one part in preference to some other part, and in some cases the total disuse of some part no longer necessary.

Nothing of all this can be considered as hypothesis or private opinion; on the contrary, they are truths which, in order to be made clear, only require attention and the observation of facts.

*   *   *

Now the true principle to be noted in all this is as follows:

1. Every fairly considerable and permanent alteration in the environment of any race of animals works a real alteration in the needs of that race.

2. Every change in the needs of animals necessitates new activities on their part for the satisfaction of those needs, and hence new habits.

3. Every new need, necessitating new activities for its satisfaction, requires the animal, either to make more frequent use of some of its parts which it previously used less, and thus greatly to develop and enlarge them; or else to make use of entirely new parts, to which the needs have imperceptibly given birth by efforts of its inner feeling; this I shall shortly prove by means of known facts.

Thus to obtain a knowledge of the true causes of that great diversity of shapes and habits found in the various known animals, we must reflect that the infinitely diversified but slowly changing environment in which the animals of each race have successively been placed, has involved each of them in new needs and corresponding alterations in their habits. This is a truth which, once recognised, cannot be disputed. Now we shall easily discern how the new needs may have been satisfied, and the new habits acquired, if we pay attention to the two following laws of nature, which are always verified by observation.

First Law.

In every animal which has not passed the limit of its development, a more frequent and continuous use of any organ gradually strengthens, develops and enlarges that organ, and gives it a power proportional to the length of time it has been so used; while the permanent disuse of any organ imperceptibly weakens and deteriorates it, and progressively diminishes its functional capacity, until it finally disappears.

Second Law.

All the acquisitions or losses wrought by nature on individuals, through the influence of the environment in which their race has long been placed, and hence through the influence of the predominant use or permanent disuse of any organ; all these are preserved by reproduction to the new individuals which arise,

*provided that the acquired modifications are common to both sexes,
or at least to the individuals which produce the young.*

*   *   *

*The frequent use of any organ, when confirmed by habit, in-
creases the functions of that organ, leads to its development and
endows it with a size and power that it does not possess in animals which exercise it less.*

We have seen that the disuse of any organ modifies, reduces
and finally extinguishes it. I shall now prove that the constant
use of any organ, accompanied by efforts to get the most out of
it, strengthens and enlarges that organ, or creates new ones to
carry on functions that have become necessary.

The bird which is drawn to the water by its need of finding
there the prey on which it lives, separates the digits of its
feet in trying to strike the water and move about on the surface.
The skin which unites these digits at their base acquires the
habit of being stretched by these continually repeated separations
of the digits; thus in course of time there are formed large webs
which unite the digits of ducks, geese, etc., as we actually find
them. In the same way efforts to swim, that is to push against
the water so as to move about in it, have stretched the membranes
between the digits of frogs, sea-tortoises, the otter, beaver,
etc.

On the other hand, a bird which is accustomed to perch on
trees and which springs from individuals all of whom had acquired
this habit, necessarily has longer digits on its feet and differently shaped from those of the aquatic animals that I have just
named. Its claws in time become lengthened, sharpened and curved
into hooks, to clasp the branches on which the animal so often
rests.

We find in the same way that the bird of the water-side which
does not like swimming and yet is in need of going to the water's
edge to secure its prey, is continually liable to sink in the mud.
Now this bird tries to act in such a way that its body should not
be immersed in the liquid, and hence makes its best efforts to
stretch and lengthen its legs. The long-established habit acquired by this bird and all its race of continually stretching
and lengthening its legs, results in the individuals of this race
becoming raised as though on stilts, and gradually obtaining long,
bare legs, denuded of feathers up to the thighs and often higher
still. . . .

We note again that this same bird wants to fish without wet-
ting its body, and is thus obliged to make continual efforts to
lengthen its neck. Now these habitual efforts in this individual
and its race must have resulted in course of time in a remarkable
lengthening, as indeed we actually find in the long necks of all
water-side birds.

If some swimming birds like the swan and goose have short
legs and yet a very long neck, the reason is that these birds
while moving about on the water acquire the habit of plunging
their head as deeply as they can into it in order to get the
aquatic larvae and various animals on which they feed; whereas
they make no effort to lengthen their legs.

(2) From *Histoire naturelle des animaux san vertèbres**

In a later work on the natural history of invertebrate animals, Lamarck summed up the cause of evolution in four laws.

First law. Life, by its own forces, tends continually to
increase the volume of every body which possesses it and to extend
the dimensions of its parts up to a point determined by itself.
Second law. The creation of a new organ in an animal body is
the result of a newly produced need which continues to be felt
and of a new motion which this need causes to arise and to continue.
Third law. The development of organs and their power of
action are constantly in direct proportion to the use of these
organs.
Fourth law. Everything that has been acquired, imprinted or
changed in the organization of individuals during the course of
their lives, is preserved in reproduction and transmitted to the
new individuals which come from those in whom these changes have
taken place.

b. Georges Cuvier, Genesis and Geology

The single most important scientific obstacle to the acceptance of a theory of evolution was that of time. It was here that Scripture seemed to present an insuperable problem. God, in the beginning, according to the Book of Genesis, had created the earth and all its creatures in six days. Man made his appearance during this period and his history was both continuous and known since then. The number of generations between the Creation and the beginning of independent historical evidence could be determined precisely; one simply added up all the "begats" with which Genesis abounds. Indeed, if one were willing to make a few simple assumptions about the length of a generation, and work in such obvious anomalies as Methusaleh's 969 year life, it was possible to calculate the date of the Creation itself. This was what Archbishop Ussher of Ireland did in the seventeenth century. The world, he declared, was created in 4004 B.C. If this were so, then all Lamarck's ingenious arguments were worthless for there was simply not enough time for the change in habits which accompanied the change in habitat to effect transformation of species.

By the beginning of the nineteenth century, even the most devout were beginning to doubt the literal truth of the Scriptural account. The geological record seemed to require a greater period of time than that allowed by the Bible. There were essentially two courses open to the man who was both devout and a geologist. He could argue that the Bible was not intended as a scientific treatise and should not, therefore, be taken literally on scien-

*J. B. Lamarck, *Histoire naturelle des animaux sans vertèbres* (Paris, 1815), vol. 1, p. 181.

tific matters. Or, he could maintain that the Bible was literally true, but did not contain the whole truth. God gave to the early Hebrews only enough knowledge of the origins and workings of His universe to impress them properly with His power. One could, therefore, go beyond Genesis to discover what really happened. This was the course chosen by Georges Cuvier (1769-1832), one of the greatest paleontologists in the history of science. In his Essay on the Theory of the Earth,* *Cuvier set out clearly to refute Lamarck. His weapon was geology and in his hands it was a weapon to be taken seriously.*

Proofs that Revolutions have been numerous.

If we institute a more detailed comparison between the various strata and those remains of animals which they contain, we shall soon discover still more numerous differences among them, indicating a proportional number of changes in their condition. The sea has not always deposited stony substances of the same kind. It has observed a regular succession as to the nature of its deposits; the more ancient the strata are, so much the more uniform and extensive are they; and the more recent they are, the more limited are they, and the more variation is observed in them at small distances. Thus the great catastrophes which have produced revolutions in the basin of the sea, were preceded, accompanied, and followed by changes in the nature of the fluid and of the substances which it held in solution; and when the surface of the seas came to be divided by islands and projecting ridges, different changes took place in every separate basin.

Amidst these changes of the general fluid, it must have been almost impossible for the same kind of animals to continue to live:--nor did they do so in fact. Their species, and even their genera, change with the strata; and although the same species occasionally recur at small distances, it is generally the case that the shells of the ancient strata have forms peculiar to themselves; that they gradually disappear, till they are not to be seen at all in the recent strata, still less in the existing seas, in which, indeed, we never discover their corresponding species, and where several even of their genera are not to be found; that, on the contrary, the shells of the recent strata resemble, as it respects the genus, those which still exist in the sea; and that in the last formed and loosest of these strata there are some species which the eyes of the most expert naturalist cannot distinguish from those which at present inhabit the ocean.

In animal nature, therefore, there has been a succession of changes corresponding to those which have taken place in the chemical nature of the fluid; and when the sea last receded from our continent, its inhabitants were not very different from those which it still continues to support.

*   *   *

*Georges Cuvier, Essay on the Theory of the Earth, 4th ed. (Edinburgh, 1822), pp. 12-13, 15-17, 114-19, 121-22, 149-51, 173-75.

Proofs that the Revolutions have been sudden.

These repeated irruptions and retreats of the sea have nei-- ther been slow or gradual; most of the catastrophes which have occasioned them have been sudden; and this is easily proved, especially with regard to the last of them, the traces of which are most conspicuous. In the northern regions it has left the carcases of some large quadrupeds which the ice had arrested, and which are preserved even to the present day with their skin, their hair, and their flesh. If they had not been frozen as soon as killed they must quickly have been decomposed by putrefaction. But this eternal frost could not have taken possession of the regions which these animals inhabited except by the same cause which destroyed them;* this cause, therefore, must have been as sudden as its effect. The breaking to pieces and overturnings of the strata, which happened in former catastrophes, shew plainly enough that they were sudden and violent like the last; and the heaps of *debris* and rounded pebbles which are found in various places among the solid strata, demonstrate the vast force of the motions excited in the mass of waters by these overturnings. Life, therefore, has been often disturbed on this earth by terrible events-- calamities which, at their commencement, have perhaps moved and overturned to a great depth the entire outer crust of the globe, but which, since these first commotions, have uniformly acted at a less depth and less generally. Numberless living beings have been the victims of these catastrophes; some have been destroyed by sudden inundations, others have been laid dry in consequence of the bottom of the seas being instantaneously elevated. Their races even have become extinct, and have left no memorial of them except some small fragment which the naturalist can scarcely recognize.

*   *   *

Proofs that the extinct Species of Quadrupeds are not Varieties of the presently existing Species.

The following objection has already been started against my conclusions. Why may not the presently existing races of mammiferous land-quadrupeds be mere modifications or varieties of those ancient races which we now find in the fossil state, which modifications may have been produced by change of climate and other local circumstances, and since raised to the present excessive difference, by the operation of similar causes during a long succession of ages?

This objection may appear strong to those who believe in the indefinite possibility of change of forms in organized bodies, and

*The two most remarkable phenomena of this kind, and which must for ever banish all idea of a slow and gradual revolution, are the rhinoceros discovered in 1771 in the banks of the *Vilhoui*, and the elephant recently found by M. Adams near the mouth of the *Lena*. This last retained its flesh and skin, on which was hair of two kinds; one short, fine, and crisped, resembling wool, and the other like long bristles. The flesh was still in such high preservation, that it was eaten by dogs.

think that during a succession of ages, and by alterations of habitudes, all the species may change into each other, or one of them give birth to all the rest. Yet to these persons the following answer may be given from their own system: If the species have changed by degrees, as they assume, we ought to find traces of this gradual modification. Thus, between the *palæotherium* and the species of our own days, we should be able to discover some intermediate forms; and yet no such discovery has ever been made. Since the bowels of the earth have not preserved monuments of this strange genealogy, we have a right to conclude, That the ancient and now extinct species were as permanent in their forms and characters as those which exist at present; or at least, That the catastrophe which destroyed them did not leave sufficient time for the production of the changes that are alleged to have taken place.

In order to reply to those naturalists who acknowledge that the varieties of animals are restrained by nature within certain limits, it would be necessary to examine how far these limits extend. This is a very curious inquiry, and in itself exceedingly interesting under a variety of relations, but has been hitherto very little attended to. It requires that we should define accurately what is, or ought to be, understood by the word species, which may be thus expressed:--*A species comprehends all the individuals which descend from each other, or from a common parentage, and those which resemble them as much as they do each other.* Thus the different races which they have generated from them are considered as varieties but of one species. Our observations, therefore, respecting the differences between the ancestors and the descendants, are the only rules by which we can judge on this subject; all other considerations being merely hypothetical, and destitute of proof. Taking the word *variety* in this limited sense, we observe that the differences which constitute this variety depend upon determinate circumstances, and that their extent increases in proportion to the intensity of the circumstances which occasion them.

Upon these principles it may be observed, that the most superficial characters are the most variable. Thus colour depends much upon light; thickness of hair upon heat; size upon abundance of food, &c. In wild animals, however, even these varieties are greatly limited by the natural habits of the animal, which does not willingly migrate from the places where it finds in sufficient quantity what is necessary for the support of its species, and does not even extend its haunts to any great distances, unless it also finds all these circumstances conjoined. Thus, although the wolf and the fox inhabit all the climates from the torrid to the frigid zone, we hardly find any other differences among them, through the whole of that vast space, than a little more or a little less beauty in their furs. I have compared the skulls of foxes from the most northern regions and from Egypt with those of France, and found no differences but what might naturally be expected in different individuals. The most savage animals, especially those which are carnivorous, being confined within narrower limits, vary still less; and the only difference between the hyena of Persia and that of Morocco, consists in a thicker or a thinner mane.

While animals which subsist upon herbage feel the influence
of climate a little more extensively, because there is added to
it the influence of food, both in regard to its abundance and its
quality.   Thus the elephants of one forest are larger than those
of another; their tusks also grow somewhat longer in places where
their food may happen to be more favourable for the production of
the substance of ivory.   The same may take place in regard to the
horns of stags and reindeer.   But let us examine two elephants
the most dissimilar that can be conceived, we shall not discover
the smallest difference in the number and articulations of the
bones, the structure of the teeth, &c.

Besides, the species of herbivorous animals, in their wild
state, seem more restrained from migrating and dispersing than
the carnivorous species, being influenced both by climate and by
the kind of nourishment which they need.

Nature appears also to have guarded against the alterations
of species which might proceed from mixture of breeds, by influencing the various species of animals with mutual aversion from
each other.   Hence all the cunning and all the force that man is
able to exert is necessary to accomplish such unions, even between
species that have the nearest resemblances.   And when the mule-
breeds that are thus produced by these forced conjunctions happen
to be fruitful, which is seldom the case, this fecundity never
continues beyond a few generations, and would not probably proceed
so far, without a continuance of the same cares which excited it
at first.   Thus we never see in a wild state intermediate productions between the hare and the rabbit, between the stag and the
doe, or between the martin and the weasel.   But the power of man
changes this established order, and contrives to produce all these
intermixtures of which the various species are susceptible, but
which they would never produce if left to themselves.

*   *   *

The most remarkable effects of the influence of man are produced upon that animal which he has reduced most completely under
subjection.   Dogs have been transported by mankind into every part
of the world, and have submitted their actions to his entire direction.   Regulated in their sexual unions by the pleasure or ca-
price of their masters, the almost endless variety of dogs differ
from each other in colour; in length and abundance of hair, which
is sometimes entirely wanting; in their natural instincts; in
size, which varies in measure as one to five, amounting, in some
instances, to more than a hundred fold in bulk; in the forms of
their ears, noses, and tails; in the relative length of their
legs; in the progressive development of the brain in several of
the domesticated varieties, occasioning alterations, even in the
form of the head; some of them having long slender muzzles with a
flat forehead; others having short muzzles, with the forehead
convex, &c. insomuch that the apparent differences between a
mastiff and a water spaniel, and between a greyhound and a pug-
dog, are even more striking than between almost any of the wild
species of a genus.   Finally, and this may be considered as the
maximum of known variation in the animal kingdom, some races of
dogs have an additional claw on each hind foot, with corresponding

bones of the tarsus; as there sometimes occur in the human species some families that have six fingers on each hand. Yet, in
all these varieties, the relations of the bones with each other
remain essentially the same, and the form of the teeth never
changes in any perceptible degree, except that in some individuals one additional false grinder occasionally appears, sometimes on the one side, and sometimes on the other.

It follows from these observations, that animals have certain fixed and natural characters, which resist the effects of
every kind of influence, whether proceeding from natural causes
or human interference; and we have not the smallest reason to
suspect that time has any more effect upon them than climate.

*   *   *

*Proofs, from traditions, of a great Catastrophe,
and subsequent renewal of Human Society.*

From all that has been said, it may be seen that nature
every where distinctly informs us that the commencement of the
present order of things cannot be dated at a very remote period;
and it is very remarkable, that mankind every where speak the same
language with nature, whether we consult their natural traditions
on this subject, or consider their moral and political state, and
the intellectual attainments which they had made at the time when
they began to have authentic historical monuments. For this purpose we may consult the histories of nations in their most ancient
books, endeavouring to discover the real facts which they contain,
when disengaged from the interested fictions which often render
the truth obscure.

The Pentateuch has existed in its present form at least ever
since the separation of the ten tribes under Jeroboam, since it
was received as authentic by the Samaritans as well as by the
Jews; and this assures us of the actual antiquity of that book
being not less than two thousand eight hundred years. Besides
this, we have no reason to doubt of the book of Genesis having
been composed by Moses, which adds five hundred years to its antiquity.

Moses and his people came out of Egypt, which is universally
allowed by all the nations of the west to have been the most an-
ciently civilized kingdom on the borders of the Mediterranean.
The legislator of the Jews could have no motive for shortening
the duration of the nations, and would even have disgraced himself
in the estimation of his own, if he had promulgated a history of
the human race contradictory to that which they must have learnt
by tradition in Egypt. We may therefore conclude, that the Egyp-
tians had at this time no other notions respecting the antiquity
of the human race than are contained in the book of Genesis. And,
as Moses establishes the event of an universal catastrophe, occasioned by an eruption of the waters, and followed by an almost
entire renewal of the human race, and as he has only referred it
to an epoch fifteen or sixteen hundred years previous to his own
time, even according to those copies which allow the longest interval, it must necessarily have occurred rather less than five
thousand years before the present day.

*   *   *

Concluding Reflections.

I am of opinion, then, . . . --That, if there is any circumstance thoroughly established in geology, it is, that the crust of our globe has been subjected to a great and sudden revolution, the epoch of which cannot be dated much farther back than five or six thousand years ago; that this revolution had buried all the countries which were before inhabited by men and by the other animals that are now best known; that the same revolution had laid dry the bed of the last ocean, which now forms all the countries at present inhabited; that the small number of individuals of men and other animals that escaped from the effects of that great revolution, have since propagated and spread over the lands then newly laid dry; and consequently, that the human race has only resumed a progressive state of improvement since that epoch, by forming established societies, raising monuments, collecting natural facts, and constructing systems of science and of learning.

Yet farther,--That the countries which are now inhabited, and which were laid dry by this last revolution, had been formerly inhabited at a more remote era, if not by man, at least by land animals; that, consequently, at least one previous revolution had submerged them under the waters; and that, judging from the different orders of animals of which we discover the remains in a fossil state, they had probably experienced two or three irruptions of the sea.

These alternate revolutions form, in my opinion, the problem in geology that is most important to be solved, or rather to be accurately defined and circumscribed; for, in order to solve it satisfactorily and entirely, it were requisite that we should discover the cause of these events,--an enterprise involving difficulties of a very different nature.

c. Charles Lyell's Expansion of Geological Timespan

For those geologists who looked exclusively to the geological record for the history of the earth and insisted that Scripture was not a reliable scientific guide, there was the way marked out at the end of the eighteenth century by the great Scotch geologist, James Hutton (1726-97). According to Hutton, there was no evidence from geology that the earth had even been created. It was just there and the function of geology was not to worry about its origins but to understand its transformations. These transformations were not to be explained by calling in super-natural events like the Noachian flood, but by appealing to those forces which could be observed at work in the contemporary world. Thus the history of the earth was uniform with its present condition; the doctrine was known as Uniformitarianism. His greatest successor was Charles Lyell (1797-1875) who seized upon Hutton's insight and proceeded to buttress it with hosts of geological facts. The first volume of his magistral Principles of Geology *appeared* *in 1830.* It was taken with him aboard H.M.S. Beagle by Charles Darwin in 1831 when he set out on the voyage which was to lead him to the theory of natural selection.*

We have seen that, during the progress of geology, there have been great fluctuations of opinion respecting the nature of the causes to which all former changes of the earth's surface are referrable. The first observers conceived that the monuments which the geologist endeavours to decipher, relate to a period when the physical constitution of the earth differed entirely from the present, and that, even after the creation of living beings, there have been causes in action distinct in kind or degree from those now forming part of the economy of nature. These views have been gradually modified, and some of them entirely abandoned in proportion as observations have been multiplied, and the signs of former mutations more skilfully interpreted. Many appearances, which for a long time were regarded as indicating mysterious and extraordinary agency, are finally recognized as the necessary result of the laws now governing the material world; and the discovery of this unlooked for conformity has induced some geologists to infer that there has never been any interruption to the same uniform order of physical events. The same assemblage of general causes, they conceive, may have been sufficient to produce, by their various combinations, the endless diversity of effects, of which the shell of the earth has preserved the memorials, and, consistently with these principles, the recurrence of analogous changes is expected by them in time to come.

*   *   *

The establishment, from time to time, of numerous points of identification, drew at length from geologists a reluctant admission, that there was more correspondence between the physical constitution of the globe, and more uniformity in the laws regulating the changes of its surface, from the most remote eras to the present, than they at first imagined. If, in this state of the science, they still despaired of reconciling every class of geological phenomena to the operations of ordinary causes, even by straining analogy to the utmost limits of credibility, we might have expected, that the balance of probability at least would now have been presumed to incline towards the identity of the causes. But, after repeated experience of the failure of attempts to speculate on different classes of geological phenomena, as belonging to a distinct order of things, each new sect persevered systematically in the principles adopted by their predecessors. They invariably began, as each new problem presented itself, whether relating to the animate or inanimate world, to assume in their theories, that the economy of nature was formerly governed by rules quite independent of those now established. Whether they endeavoured to account for the origin of certain igneous rocks, or to explain the forces which elevated hills or excavated val-

*Charles Lyell, Principles of Geology, 3 vols. (London, 1830-32), I, pp. 75, 85-89, 165-66.

leys, or the causes which led to the extinction of certain races of animals, they first presupposed an original and dissimilar order of nature; and when at length they approximated, or entirely came round to an opposite opinion, it was always with the feeling, that they conceded what they were justified *a priori* in deeming improbable. In a word, the same men who, as natural philosophers, would have been greatly surprised to find any deviation from the usual course of Nature *in their own time*, were equally surprised, as geologists, not to find such deviations at every period of the past.

The Huttonians were conscious that no check could be given to the utmost licence of conjecture in speculating on the causes of geological phenomena, unless we can assume invariable constancy in the order of Nature. But when they asserted this uniformity without any limitation as to time, they were considered, by the majority of their contemporaries, to have been carried too far, especially as they applied the same principle to the laws of the organic, as well as of the inanimate world.

We shall first advert briefly to many difficulties which formerly appeared insurmountable, but which, in the last forty years, have been partially or entirely removed by the progress of science; and shall afterwards consider the objections that still remain to the doctrine of absolute uniformity.

In the first place, it was necessary for the supporters of this doctrine to take for granted incalculable periods of time, in order to explain the formation of sedimentary strata by causes now in diurnal action. The time which they required theoretically, is now granted, as it were, or has become absolutely requisite, to account for another class of phenomena brought to light by more recent investigations. It must always have been evident to unbiassed minds, that successive strata, containing, in regular order of superposition, distinct beds of shells and corals, arranged in families as they grow at the bottom of the sea, could only have been formed by slow and insensible degrees in a great lapse of ages; yet, until organic remains were minutely examined and specifically determined, it was rarely possible to prove that the series of deposits met with in one country was not formed simultaneously with that found in another. But we are now able to determine, in numerous instances, the relative dates of sedimentary rocks in distant regions, and to show, by their organic remains, that they were not of contemporary origin, but formed in succession. We often find, that where an interruption in the consecutive formation in one district is indicated by a sudden transition from one assemblage of fossil species to another, the chasm is filled up, in some other district, by other important groups of strata. The more attentively we study the European continent, the greater we find the extension of the whole series of geological formations. No sooner does the calendar appear to be completed, and the signs of a succession of physical events arranged in chronological order, than we are called upon to intercalate, as it were, some new periods of vast duration. A geologist, whose observations have been confined to England, is accustomed to consider the superior and newer groups of marine strata in our island as modern, and such they are, comparatively

speaking; but when he has travelled through the Italian peninsula
and in Sicily, and has seen strata of more recent origin forming
mountains several thousand feet high, and has marked a long series
both of volcanic and submarine operations, all newer than any of
the regular strata which enter largely into the physical structure
of Great Britain, he returns with more exalted conceptions of the
antiquity of some of those modern deposits, than he before entertained of the oldest of the British series. We cannot reflect on
the concessions thus extorted from us, in regard to the duration
of past time, without foreseeing that the period may arrive when
part of the Huttonian theory will be combated on the ground of
its departing too far from the assumption of uniformity in the
order of nature. On a closer investigation of extinct volcanos,
we find proofs that they broke out at successive eras, and that
the eruptions of one group were often concluded long before others
had commenced their activity. Some were burning when one class
of organic beings were in existence, others came into action when
different races of animals and plants existed,--it follows, therefore, that the convulsions caused by subterranean movements,
which are merely another portion of the volcanic phenomena, occurred also in succession, and their effects must be divided into
separate sums, and assigned to separate periods of time; and this
is not all:--when we examine the volcanic products, whether they
be lavas which flowed out under water or upon dry land, we find
that intervals of time, often of great length, intervened between
their formation, and that the effects of one eruption were not
greater in amount than that which now results during ordinary
volcanic convulsions. The accompanying or preceding earthquakes,
therefore, may be considered to have been also successive, and to
have been in like manner interrupted by intervals of time, and
not to have exceeded in violence those now experienced in the
ordinary course of nature. Already, therefore, may we regard the
doctrine of the sudden elevation of whole continents by paroxysmal
eruptions as invalidated; and there was the greatest inconsistency
in the adoption of such a tenet by the Huttonians, who were anxious to reconcile former changes to the present economy of the
world. It was contrary to analogy to suppose, that Nature had
been at any former epoch parsimonious of time and prodigal of
violence--to imagine that one district was not at rest while another was convulsed--that the disturbing forces were not kept
under subjection, so as never to carry simultaneous havoc and
desolation over the whole earth, or even over one great region.
If it could have been shown, that a certain combination of circumstances would at some future period produce a crisis in the
subterranean action, we should certainly have had no right to
oppose our experience for the last three thousand years as an
argument against the probability of such occurrences in past ages;
but it is not pretended that such a combination can be foreseen.
In speculating on catastrophes by water, we may certainly anticipate great floods in future, and we may therefore presume that
they have happened again and again in past times. The existence
of enormous seas of fresh-water, such as the North American lakes,
the largest of which is elevated more than six hundred feet above
the level of the ocean, and is in parts twelve hundred feet deep,

is alone sufficient to assure us, that the time will come, however distant, when a deluge will lay waste a considerable part of the American continent. No hypothetical agency is required to cause the sudden escape of the confined waters. Such changes of level, and opening of fissures, as have accompanied earthquakes since the commencement of the present century, or such excavation of ravines as the receding cataract of Niagara is now effecting, might breach the barriers. Notwithstanding, therefore, that we have not witnessed within the last three thousand years the devastation by deluge of a large continent, yet, as we may predict the future occurrence of such catastrophes, we are authorized to regard them as part of the present order of Nature, and they may be introduced into geological speculations respecting the past, provided we do not imagine them to have been more frequent or general than we expect them to be in time to come.

* * *

The geologist who yields implicit assent to the truth of these principles, will deem it incumbent on him to examine with minute attention all the changes now in progress on the earth, and will regard every fact collected respecting the causes in diurnal action, as affording him a key to the interpretation of some mystery in the archives of remote ages. Our estimate, indeed, of the value of all geological evidence, and the interest derived from the investigation of the earth's history, must depend entirely on the degree of confidence which we feel in regard to the permanency of the laws of nature. There immutable constancy alone can enable us to reason from analogy, by the strict rules of induction, respecting the events of former ages, or, by a comparison of the state of things at two distinct geological epochs, to arrive at the knowledge of general principles in the economy of our terrestrial system.

The uniformity of the plan being once assumed, events which have occurred at the most distant periods in the animate and inanimate world will be acknowledged to throw light on each other, and the deficiency of our information respecting some of the most obscure parts of the present creation will be removed. For as by studying the external configuration of the existing land and its inhabitants, we may restore in imagination the appearance of the ancient continents which have passed away, so may we obtain from the deposits of ancient seas and lakes an insight into the nature of the subaqueous processes now in operation, and of many forms of organic life, which, though now existing, are veiled from our sight. Rocks, also produced by subterranean fire in former ages at great depths in the bowels of the earth, present us, when upraised by gradual movements, and exposed to the light of heaven, with an image of those changes which the deep-seated volcano may now occasion in the nether regions. Thus, although we are mere sojourners on the surface of the planet, chained to a mere point in space, enduring but for a moment of time, the human mind is not only enabled to number worlds beyond the unassisted ken of mortal eye, but to trace the events of indefinite ages before the creation of our race, and is not even withheld from penetrating into the dark secrets of the ocean, or the interior of the solid

globe; free, like the spirit which the poet described as animating the universe,
——————ire per omnes
Terrasque tractusque maris, cœlumque profundum.

d. Charles Darwin and Evolution

Charles Darwin (1809-82) was born into a family of intellectual mavericks. His father was a prosperous country doctor who clearly entertained strong and sometimes idiosyncratic opinions on almost every subject. His grandfather, Erasmus Darwin (1731-1802), had published a number of works on natural history among which were two treatises dealing with the evolution of higher animals from lower organisms. Darwin later insisted that he had not been influenced by his grandfather's work, but at least he had been prepared to entertain the idea of evolution at a time when it was anathema to most naturalists.

Darwin's own intellectual brilliance was a long time appearing. In his youth and early manhood, he gave little evidence of what was to come. He did mediocre work at school and drifted aimlessly at both the University of Edinburgh and Cambridge. Until the age of 21, his only discernible talent was as a crack shot and his passions were directed almost entirely at the hunting of snipe, grouse and pheasant. All this was to change with his experience as naturalist on H.M.S. Beagle which set out from Plymouth for South America on an oceanographic mission in 1831. In South America and especially at the Galapagos Archipelago off the coast of Peru, Darwin had the opportunity to observe all the variety of nature and to speculate upon it.

Darwin's first scientific love had been geology and Lyell provided him with a perspective from which he could view the history of the earth. His own geological forays in South America revealed to him the extent of the fossil record. His observations of living flora and fauna impressed upon him the conditions of survival in the wild and the sheer exuberance of creation in the tropics struck him forcefully with the problem of the origin of species. From his five years with the Beagle were to come most of the questions which the Origin of Species *set out to answer. The result was to be a scientific revolution comparable only to the revolution created by Copernicus, Kepler, Galileo and Newton in the seventeenth century. It transformed man's view of the universe and his estimate of his own place in it.*

(1) Charles Darwin, *On the Origin of Species by Means of Natural Selection or The Preservation of Favoured Races in the Struggle for Life**

The green octavo volume which appeared in London bookstalls in November, 1859 bearing the above title was the bombshell which

---

*Charles Darwin, *On the Origin of Species* . . . (London, 1859), pp. 3-6, 60-64, 87-88, 90-94, 484-90.

*Darwin lobbed into the seemingly placid waters of mid-Victorian
England. It was but the first explosion in what was to be a battle that raged into the twentieth century. The first stage was
deceptive; it merely amounted to the claim that species were not
immutable and that changes took place by a mechanism called
"natural selection" by Darwin. This was controversial, but hardly
something the modern reader would expect to upset a whole society.
Yet the Victorians saw perfectly clearly what was at stake. It
was far more than how a giraffe got his neck or how a duck got
webbed feet. It was the nature of man himself, his morality, the
very foundations of civilized society which were involved. The
reader should recognize this and read with it in mind. Natural
selection was a mechanical process, without mind or morality.
Perhaps the universe itself had no need of either. Man, himself,
then would be merely the product of the blind forces of nature, a
nature "red in tooth and claw." What, then, would become of the
glorious illusion that man was made in the image of God? And how
would civilization survive this fall from divine grace into the
pit where only the fit would survive?*

In considering the Origin of Species, it is quite conceivable
that a naturalist, reflecting on the mutual affinities of organic
beings, on their embryological relations, their geographical distribution, geological succession, and other such facts, might come
to the conclusion that each species had not been independently
created, but had descended, like varieties, from other species.
Nevertheless, such a conclusion, even if well founded, would be
unsatisfactory, until it could be shown how the innumerable species inhabiting this world have been modified, so as to acquire
that perfection of structure and coadaptation which most justly
excites our admiration. Naturalists continually refer to external
conditions, such as climate, food, &c., as the only possible cause
of variation. In one very limited sense, as we shall hereafter
see, this may be true; but it is preposterous to attribute to
mere external conditions, the structure, for instance, of the
woodpecker, with its feet, tail, beak, and tongue, so admirably
adapted to catch insects under the bark of trees. In the case of
the misseltoe, which draws its nourishment from certain trees,
which has seeds that must be transported by certain birds, and
which has flowers with separate sexes absolutely requiring the
agency of certain insects to bring pollen from one flower to the
other, it is equally preposterous to account for the structure of
this parasite, with its relations to several distinct organic
beings, by the effects of external conditions, or of habit, or of
the volition of the plant itself.
The author of the 'Vestiges of Creation' would, I presume,
say that, after a certain unknown number of generations, some
bird had given birth to a woodpecker, and some plant to the misseltoe, and that these had been produced perfect as we now see
them; but this assumption seems to me to be no explanation, for
it leaves the case of the coadaptations of organic beings to each
other and to their physical conditions of life, untouched and unexplained.

It is, therefore, of the highest importance to gain a clear insight into the means of modification and coadaptation. At the commencement of my observations it seemed to me probable that a careful study of domesticated animals and of cultivated plants would offer the best chance of making out this obscure problem. Nor have I been disappointed; in this and in all other perplexing cases I have invariably found that our knowledge, imperfect though it be, of variation under domestication, afforded the best and safest clue. I may venture to express my conviction of the high value of such studies, although they have been very commonly neglected by naturalists.

From these considerations, I shall devote the first chapter of this Abstract to Variation under Domestication. We shall thus see that a large amount of hereditary modification is at least possible; and, what is equally or more important, we shall see how great is the power of man in accumulating by his Selection successive slight variations. I will then pass on to the variability of species in a state of nature; but I shall, unfortunately, be compelled to treat this subject far too briefly, as it can be treated properly only by giving long catalogues of facts. We shall, however, be enabled to discuss what circumstances are most favourable to variation. In the next chapter the Struggle for Existence amongst all organic beings throughout the world, which inevitably follows from their high geometrical powers of increase, will be treated of. This is the doctrine of Malthus, applied to the whole animal and vegetable kingdoms. As many more individuals of each species are born than can possibly survive; and as, consequently, there is a frequently recurring struggle for existence, it follows that any being, if it vary however slightly in any manner profitable to itself, under the complex and sometimes varying conditions of life, will have a better chance of surviving, and thus be *naturally selected*. From the strong principle of inheritance, any selected variety will tend to propagate its new and modified form.

This fundamental subject of Natural Selection will be treated at some length in the fourth chapter; and we shall then see how Natural Selection almost inevitably causes much Extinction of the less improved forms of life, and induces what I have called Divergence of Character. In the next chapter I shall discuss the complex and little known laws of variation and of correlation of growth. In the four succeeding chapters, the most apparent and gravest difficulties on the theory will be given: namely, first, the difficulties of transitions, or in understanding how a simple being or a simple organ can be changed and perfected into a highly developed being or elaborately constructed organ; secondly, the subject of Instinct, or the mental powers of animals; thirdly, Hybridism, or the infertility of species and the fertility of varieties when intercrossed; and fourthly, the imperfection of the Geological Record. In the next chapter I shall consider the geological succession of organic beings throughout time; in the eleventh and twelfth, their geographical distribution throughout space; in the thirteenth, their classification or mutual affinities, both when mature and in an embryonic condition. In the last chapter I shall give a brief recapitulation of the whole work, and a few concluding remarks.

No one ought to feel surprise at much remaining as yet unexplained in regard to the origin of species and varieties, if he makes due allowance for our profound ignorance in regard to the mutual relations of all the beings which live around us. Who can explain why one species ranges widely and is very numerous, and why another allied species has a narrow range and is rare? Yet these relations are of the highest importance, for they determine the present welfare, and, as I believe, the future success and modification of every inhabitant of this world. Still less do we know of the mutual relations of the innumerable inhabitants of the world during the many past geological epochs in its history. Although much remains obscure, and will long remain obscure, I can entertain no doubt, after the most deliberate study and dispassionate judgment of which I am capable, that the view which most naturalists entertain, and which I formerly entertained--namely, that each species has been independently created--is erroneous. I am fully convinced that species are not immutable; but that those belonging to what are called the same genera are lineal descendants of some other and generally extinct species, in the same manner as the acknowledged varieties of any one species are the descendants of that species. Furthermore, I am convinced that Natural Selection has been the main but not exclusive means of modification.

*　　*　　*

Struggle for Existence

Before entering on the subject of this chapter, I must make a few preliminary remarks, to show how the struggle for existence bears on Natural Selection. It has been seen in the last chapter that amongst organic beings in a state of nature there is some individual variability; indeed I am not aware that this has ever been disputed. It is immaterial for us whether a multitude of doubtful forms be called species or sub-species or varieties; what rank, for instance, the two or three hundred doubtful forms of British plants are entitled to hold, if the existence of any well-marked varieties be admitted. But the mere existence of individual variability and of some few well-marked varieties, though necessary as the foundation for the work, helps us but little in understanding how species arise in nature. How have all those exquisite adaptations of one part of the organisation to another part, and to the conditions of life, and of one distinct organic being to another being, been perfected? We see these beautiful co-adaptations most plainly in the woodpecker and missletoe; and only a little less plainly in the humblest parasite which clings to the hairs of a quadruped or feathers of a bird; in the structure of the beetle which dives through the water; in the plumed seed which is wafted by the gentlest breeze; in short, we see beautiful adaptations everywhere and in every part of the organic world.

Again, it may be asked, how is it that varieties, which I have called incipient species, become ultimately converted into good and distinct species, which in most cases obviously differ from each other far more than do the varieties of the same species? How do those groups of species, which constitute what are called distinct genera, and which differ from each other more than do the species of the same genus, arise? All these results, as we shall more fully see in the next chapter, follow inevitably from the struggle for life. Owing to this struggle for life, any variation, however slight and from whatever cause proceeding, if it be in any degree profitable to an individual of any species, in its infinitely complex relations to other organic beings and to external nature, will tend to the preservation of that individual, and will generally be inherited by its offspring. The offspring, also, will thus have a better chance of surviving, for, of the many individuals of any species which are periodically born, but a small number can survive. I have called this principle, by which each slight variation, if useful, is preserved, by the term of Natural Selection, in order to mark its relation to man's power of selection. We have seen that man by selection can certainly produce great results, and can adapt organic beings to his own uses, through the accumulation of slight but useful variations, given to him by the hand of Nature. But Natural Selection, as we shall hereafter see, is a power incessantly ready for action, and is as immeasurably superior to man's feeble efforts, as the works of Nature are to those of Art.

We will now discuss in a little more detail the struggle for existence. In my future work this subject shall be treated, as it well deserves, at much greater length. The elder De Candolle and Lyell have largely and philosophically shown that all organic beings are exposed to severe competition. In regard to plants, no one has treated this subject with more spirit and ability than W. Herbert, Dean of Manchester, evidently the result of his great horticultural knowledge. Nothing is easier than to admit in words the truth of the universal struggle for life, or more difficult-- at least I have found it so--than constantly to bear this conclusion in mind. Yet unless it be thoroughly engrained in the mind, I am convinced that the whole economy of nature, with every fact on distribution, rarity, abundance, extinction, and variation, will be dimly seen or quite misunderstood. We behold the face of nature bright with gladness, we often see superabundance of food; we do not see, or we forget, that the birds which are idly singing round us mostly live on insects or seeds, and are thus constantly destroying life; or we forget how largely these songsters, or their eggs, or their nestlings, are destroyed by birds and beasts of prey; we do not always bear in mind, that though food may be now superabundant, it is not so at all seasons of each recurring year.

I should premise that I use the term Struggle for Existence in a large and metaphorical sense, including dependence of one being on another, and including (which is more important) not only the life of the individual, but success in leaving progeny. Two canine animals in a time of dearth, may be truly said to struggle with each other which shall get food and life. But a plant on the edge of a desert is said to struggle for life against the drought, though more properly it should be said to be dependent on the moisture. A plant which annually produces a thousand seeds, of which on an average only one comes to maturity, may be more truly said to struggle with the plants of the same and other kinds which already clothe the ground. The missletoe is dependent on the apple and a few other trees, but can only in a far-fetched sense be said to struggle with these trees, for if too many of these parasites grow on the same tree, it will languish and die. But several seedling missletoes, growing close together on the same branch, may more truly be said to struggle with each other. As the missletoe is disseminated by birds, its existence depends on birds; and it may metaphorically be said to struggle with other fruit-bearing plants, in order to tempt birds to devour and thus disseminate its seeds rather than those of other plants. In these several senses, which pass into each other, I use for convenience sake the general term of struggle for existence.

A struggle for existence inevitably follows from the high rate at which all organic beings tend to increase. Every being, which during its natural lifetime produces several eggs or seeds, must suffer destruction during some period of its life, and during some season or occasional year, otherwise, on the principle of geometrical increase, its numbers would quickly become so inordinately great that no country could support the product. Hence, as more individuals are produced than can possibly survive, there must in every case be a struggle for existence, either one individual with another of the same species, or with the individuals of distinct species, or with the physical conditions of life. It is the doctrine of Malthus applied with manifold force to the whole animal and vegetable kingdoms; for in this case there can be no artificial increase of food, and no prudential restraint from marriage. Although some species may be now increasing, more or less rapidly, in numbers, all cannot do so, for the world would not hold them.

There is no exception to the rule that every organic being naturally increases at so high a rate, that if not destroyed, the earth would soon be covered by the progeny of a single pair. Even slow-breeding man has doubled in twenty-five years, and at this rate, in a few thousand years, there would literally not be standing room for his progeny. Linnæus has calculated that if an annual plant produced only two seeds--and there is no plant so unproductive as this--and their seedlings next year produced two, and so on, then in twenty years there would be a million plants. The elephant is reckoned to be the slowest breeder of all known animals, and I have taken some pains to estimate its probable minimum rate of natural increase: it will be under the mark to assume that it breeds when thirty years old, and goes on breeding till ninety years old, bringing forth three pair of young in this interval; if this be so, at the end of the fifth century there would be alive fifteen million elephants, descended from the first pair.

* * *

Sexual Selection.--Inasmuch as peculiarities often appear under domestication in one sex and become hereditarily attached to that sex, the same fact probably occurs under nature, and if so, natural selection will be able to modify one sex in its func-

tional relations to the other sex, or in relation to wholly different habits of life in the two sexes, as is sometimes the case
with insects. And this leads me to say a few words on what I
call Sexual Selection. This depends, not on a struggle for existence, but on a struggle between the males for possession of
the females; the result is not death to the unsuccessful competi-
tor, but few or no offspring. Sexual selection is, therefore,
less rigorous than natural selection. Generally, the most vigorous males, those which are best fitted for their places in nature,
will leave most progeny. But in many cases, victory will depend
not on general vigour, but on having special weapons, confined to
the male sex. A hornless stag or spurless cock would have a poor
change of leaving offspring. Sexual selection by always allowing
the victor to breed might surely give indomitable courage, length
to the spur, and strength to the wing to strike in the spurred
leg, as well as the brutal cock-fighter, who knows well that he
can improve his breed by careful selection of the best cocks.
How low in the scale of nature this law of battle descends, I
know not; male alligators have been described as fighting, bel-
lowing, and whirling round, like Indians in a war-dance, for the
possession of the females; male salmons have been seen fighting
all day long; male stag-beetles often bear wounds from the huge
mandibles of other males. The war is, perhaps, severest between
the males of polygamous animals, and these seem oftenest provided
with special weapons. The males of carnivorous animals are already well armed; though to them and to others, special means of
defence may be given through means of sexual selection, as the
mane to the lion, the shoulder-pad to the boar, and the hooked
jaw to the male salmon; for the shield may be as important for
victory, as the sword or spear.

*　　*　　*

Illustrations of the action of Natural Selection.--In order
to make it clear how, as I believe, natural selection acts, I
must beg permission to give one or two imaginary illustrations.
Let us take the case of a wolf, which preys on various animals,
securing some by craft, some by strength, and some by fleetness;
and let us suppose that the fleetest prey, a deer for instance,
had from any change in the country increased in numbers, or that
other prey had decreased in numbers, during that season of the
year when the wolf is hardest pressed for food. I can under such
circumstances see no reason to doubt that the swiftest and slim-
mest wolves would have the best chance of surviving, and so be
preserved or selected,--provided always that they retained
strength to master their prey at this or at some other period of
the year, when they might be compelled to prey on other animals.
I can see no more reason to doubt this, than that man can improve
the fleetness of his greyhounds by careful and methodical selection, or by that unconscious selection which results from each
man trying to keep the best dogs without any thought of modifying
the breed.
　　Even without any change in the proportional numbers of the
animals on which our wolf preyed, a cub might be born with an innate tendency to pursue certain kinds of prey. Nor can this be

thought very improbable; for we often observe great differences
in the natural tendencies of our domestic animals; one cat, for
instance, taking to catch rats, another mice; one cat, according
to Mr. St. John, bringing home winged game, another hares or rabbits, and another hunting on marshy ground and almost nightly
catching woodcocks or snipes. The tendency to catch rats rather
than mice is known to be inherited. Now, if any slight innate
change of habit or of structure benefited an individual wolf, it
would have the best chance of surviving and of leaving offspring.
Some of its young would probably inherit the same habits or structure, and by the repetition of this process, a new variety might
be formed which would either supplant or coexist with the parent-
form of wolf. Or, again, the wolves inhabiting a mountainous
district, and those frequenting the lowlands, would naturally be
forced to hunt different prey; and from the continued preservation of the individuals best fitted for the two sites, two varieties might slowly be formed. These varieties would cross and
blend where they met; but to this subject of intercrossing we
shall soon have to return. I may add, that, according to Mr.
Pierce, there are two varieties of the wolf inhabiting the Cat-
skill Mountains in the United States, one with a light greyhound-
like form, which pursues deer, and the other more bulky, with
shorter legs, which more frequently attacks the shepherd's flocks.

Let us now take a more complex case. Certain plants excrete
a sweet juice, apparently for the sake of eliminating something
injurious from their sap: this is effected by glands at the base
of the stipules in some Leguminosæ, and at the back of the leaf
of the common laurel. This juice, though small in quantity, is
greedily sought by insects. Let us now suppose a little sweet
juice or nectar to be excreted by the inner bases of the petals
of a flower. In this case insects in seeking the nectar would
get dusted with pollen, and would certainly often transport the
pollen from one flower to the stigma of another flower. The
flowers of two distinct individuals of the same species would thus
get crossed; and the act of crossing, we have good reason to believe (as will hereafter be more fully alluded to), would produce
very vigorous seedlings, which consequently would have the best
chance of flourishing and surviving. Some of these seedlings
would probably inherit the nectar-excreting power. Those individual flowers which had the largest glands or nectaries, and which
excreted most nectar, would be oftenest visited by insects, and
would be oftenest crossed; and so in the long-run would gain the
upper hand. Those flowers, also, which had their stamens and
pistils placed, in relation to the size and habits of the particular insects which visited them, so as to favour in any degree
the transportal of their pollen from flower to flower, would
likewise be favoured to selected. We might have taken the case
of insects visiting flowers for the sake of collecting pollen instead of nectar; and as pollen is formed for the sole object of
fertilisation, its destruction appears a simple loss to the plant;
yet if a little pollen were carried, at first occasionally and
then habitually, by the pollen-devouring insects from flower to
flower, and a cross thus effected, although nine-tenths of the
pollen were destroyed, it might still be a great gain to the

plant; and those individuals which produced more and more pollen, and had larger and larger anthers, would be selected.

When our plant, by this process of the continued preservation or natural selection of more and more attractive flowers, had been rendered highly attractive to insects, they would, unintentionally on their part, regularly carry pollen from flower to flower; and that they can most effectually do this, I could easily show by many striking instances. I will give only one--not as a very striking case, but as likewise illustrating one step in the separation of the sexes of plants, presently to be alluded to. Some holly-trees bear only male flowers, which have four stamens producing rather a small quantity of pollen, and a rudimentary pistil; other holly-trees bear only female flowers; these have a full-sized pistil, and four stamens with shrivelled anthers, in which not a grain of pollen can be detected. Having found a female tree exactly sixty yards from a male tree, I put the stigmas of twenty flowers, taken from different branches, under the microscope, and on all, without exception, there were pollen-grains, and on some a profusion of pollen. As the wind had set for several days from the female to the male tree, the pollen could not thus have been carried. The weather had been cold and boisterous, and therefore not favourable to bees, nevertheless every female flower which I examined had been effectually fertilised by the bees, accidentally dusted with pollen, having flown from tree to tree in search of nectar. But to return to our imaginary case: as soon as the plant had been rendered so highly attractive to insects that pollen was regularly carried from flower to flower, another process might commence. No naturalist doubts the advantage of what has been called the "physiological division of labour;" hence we may believe that it would be advantageous to a plant to produce stamens alone in one flower or on one whole plant, and pistils alone in another flower or on another plant. In plants under culture and placed under new conditions of life, sometimes the male organs and sometimes the female organs become more or less impotent; now if we suppose this to occur in ever so slight a degree under nature, then as pollen is already carried regularly from flower to flower, and as a more complete separation of the sexes of our plant would be advantageous on the principle of the division of labour, individuals with this tendency more and more increased, would be continually favoured or selected, until at last a complete separation of the sexes would be effected.

*   *   *

When the views entertained in this volume on the origin of species, or when analogous views are generally admitted, we can dimly foresee that there will be a considerable revolution in natural history. Systematists will be able to pursue their labours as at present; but they will not be incessantly haunted by the shadowy doubt whether this or that form be in essence a species. This I feel sure, and I speak after experience, will be no slight relief. The endless disputes whether or not some fifty species of British brambles are true species will cease. Systematists will have only to decide (not that this will be easy) whether any form be sufficiently constant and distinct from other forms, to be capable of definition; and if definable, whether the differences be sufficiently important to deserve a specific name. This latter point will become a far more essential consideration than it is at present; for differences, however slight, between any two forms, if not blended by intermediate gradations, are looked at by most naturalists as sufficient to raise both forms to the rank of species. Hereafter we shall be compelled to acknowledge that the only distinction between species and well-marked varieties is, that the latter are known, or believed, to be connected at the present day by intermediate gradations, whereas species were formerly thus connected. Hence, without quite rejecting the consideration of the present existence of intermediate gradations between any two forms, we shall be led to weigh more carefully and to value higher the actual amount of difference between them. It is quite possible that forms now generally acknowledged to be merely varieties may hereafter be thought worthy of specific names, as with the primrose and cowslip; and in this case scientific and common language will come into accordance. In short, we shall have to treat species in the same manner as those naturalists treat genera, who admit that genera are merely artificial combinations made for convenience. This may not be a cheering prospect; but we shall at least be freed from the vain search for the undiscovered and undiscoverable essence of the term species.

The other and more general departments of natural history will rise greatly in interest. The terms used by naturalists of affinity, relationship, community of type, paternity, morphology, adaptive characters, rudimentary and aborted organs, &c., will cease to be metaphorical, and will have a plain signification. When we no longer look at an organic being as a savage looks at a ship, as at something wholly beyond his comprehension; when we regard every production of nature as one which has had a history; when we contemplate every complex structure and instinct as the summing up of many contrivances, each useful to the possessor, nearly in the same way as when we look at any great mechanical invention as the summing up of the labour, the experience, the reason, and even the blunders of numerous workmen; when we thus view each organic being, how far more interesting, I speak from experience, will the study of natural history become!

A grand and almost untrodden field of inquiry will be opened, on the causes and laws of variation, on correlation of growth, on the effects of use and disuse, on the direct action of external conditions, and so forth. The study of domestic productions will rise immensely in value. A new variety raised by man will be a far more important and interesting subject for study than one more species added to the infinitude of already recorded species. Our classifications will come to be, as far as they can be so made, genealogies; and will then truly give what may be called the plan of creation. The rules for classifying will no doubt become simpler when we have a definite object in view. We possess no pedigrees or armorial bearings; and we have to discover and trade the many diverging lines of descent in our natural genealogies, by characters of any kind which have long been inherited.

Rudimentary organs will speak infallibly with respect to the nature of long-lost structures. Species and groups of species, which are called aberrant, and which may fancifully be called living fossils, will aid us in forming a picture of the ancient forms of life. Embryology will reveal to us the structure, in some degree obscured, of the prototypes of each great class.

When we can feel assured that all the individuals of the same species, and all the closely allied species of most genera, have within a not very remote period descended from one parent, and have migrated from some one birthplace; and when we better know the many means of migration, then, by the light which geology now throws, and will continue to throw, on former changes of climate and of the level of the land, we shall surely be enabled to trace in an admirable manner the former migrations of the inhabitants of the whole world. Even at present, by comparing the differences of the inhabitants of the sea on the opposite sides of a continent, and the nature of the various inhabitants of that continent in relation to their apparent means of immigration, some light can be thrown on ancient geography.

The noble science of Geology loses glory from the extreme imperfection of the record. The crust of the earth with its embedded remains must not be looked at as a well-filled museum, but as a poor collection made at hazard and at rare intervals. The accumulation of each great fossiliferous formation will be recognised as having depended on an unusual concurrence of circumstances, and the blank intervals between the successive stages as having been of vast duration. But we shall be able to gauge with some security the duration of these intervals by a comparison of the preceding and succeeding organic forms. We must be cautious in attempting to correlate as strictly contemporaneous two formations, which include few identical species, by the general succession of their forms of life. As species are produced and exterminated by slowly acting and still existing causes, and not by miraculous acts of creation and by catastrophes; and as the most important of all causes of organic change is one which is almost independent of altered and perhaps suddenly altered physical conditions, namely, the mutual relation of organism to organism,-- the improvement of one being entailing the improvement or the extermination of others; it follows, that the amount of organic change in the fossils of consecutive formations probably serves as a fair measure of the lapse of actual time. A number of species, however, keeping in a body might remain for a long period unchanged, whilst within this same period, several of these species, by migrating into new countries and coming into competition with foreign associates, might become modified; so that we must not overrate the accuracy of organic change as a measure of time. During early periods of the earth's history, when the forms of life were probably fewer and simpler, the rate of change was probably slower; and at the first dawn of life, when very few forms of the simplest structure existed, the rate of change may have been slow in an extreme degree. The whole history of the world, as at present known, although of a length quite incomprehensible by us, will hereafter be recognised as a mere fragment of time, compared with the ages which have elapsed since the first creature, the progenitor of innumerable extinct and living descendants, was created.

In the distant future I see open fields for far more important researches. Psychology will be based on a new foundation, that of the necessary acquirement of each mental power and capacity by gradation. Light will be thrown on the origin of man and his history.

Authors of the highest eminence seem to be fully satisfied with the view that each species has been independently created. To my mind it accords better with what we know of the laws impressed on matter by the Creator, that the production and extinction of the past and present inhabitants of the world should have been due to secondary causes, like those determining the birth and death of the individual. When I view all beings not as special creations, but as the lineal descendants of some few beings which lived long before the first bed of the Silurian system was deposited, they seem to me to become ennobled. Judging from the past, we may safely infer that not only living species will transmit its unaltered likeness to a distant futurity. And of the species now living very few will transmit progeny of any kind to a far distant futurity; for the manner in which all organic beings are grouped, shows that the greater number of species of each genus, and all the species of many genera, have left no descendants, but have become utterly extinct. We can so far take a prophetic glance into futurity as to foretel that it will be the common and widely-spread species, belonging to the larger and dominant groups, which will ultimately prevail and procreate new and dominant species. As all the living forms of life are the linear descendants of those which lived long before the Silurian epoch, we may feel certain that the ordinary succession by generation has never once been broken, and that no cataclysm has desolated the whole world. Hence we may look with some confidence to a secure future of equally inappreciable length. And as natural selection works solely by and for the good of each being, all corporeal and mental endowments will tend to progress towards perfection.

It is interesting to contemplate an entangled bank, clothed with many plants of many kinds, with birds singing on the bushes, with various insects flitting about, and with worms crawling through the damp earth, and to reflect that these elaborately constructed forms, so different from each other, and dependent on each other in so complex a manner, have all been produced by laws acting around us. These laws, taken in the largest sense, being Growth with Reproduction; Inheritance which is almost implied by reproduction; Variability from the indirect and direct action of the external conditions of life, and from use and disuse; a Ratio of Increase so high as to lead to a Struggle for Life, and as a consequence to Natural Selection, entailing Divergence of Character and the Extinction of less-improved forms. Thus, from the war of nature, from famine and death, the most exalted object which we are capable of conceiving, namely, the production of the higher animals, directly follows. There is grandeur in this view of life, with its several powers, having been originally breathed into a few forms or into one; and that, whilst this planet has

gone cycling on according to the fixed law of gravity, from so
simple a beginning endless forms most beautiful and most wonderful have been, and are being, evolved.

(2) Charles Darwin, *The Descent of Man**

In the Origin of Species, *Darwin carefully refrained from
applying the theory of evolution to the origin of mankind. He
could not have been unaware, however, of the fact that others
would do what he had not and that a good part of the storm raised
by the* Origin *was precisely because it did cast doubt upon man's
traditional unique place in nature. In 1871, Darwin took the
logical next step; he applied the theory of natural selection to
the origin of mankind. Henceforth, for those who accepted his
argument, man was to be considered solely as the result of a long
evolution from more primitive forms, not as a special creature
with special attributes linking him to a Divinity. Darwin even
went so far as to derive the foundations of morality from natural
selection!*

Rate of Increase.--Civilised populations have been known
under favourable conditions, as in the United States, to double
their number in twenty-five years; and according to a calculation
by Euler, this might occur in a little over twelve years. At the
former rate the present population of the United States, namely,
thirty millions, would in 657 years cover the whole terraqueous
globe so thickly, that four men would have to stand on each square
yard of surface. The primary or fundamental check to the continued increase of man is the difficulty of gaining subsistence and
of living in comfort. We may infer that this is the case from
what we see, for instance, in the United States, where subsistence is easy and there is plenty of room. If such means were
suddenly doubled in Great Britain, our number would be quickly
doubled. With civilised nations the above primary check acts
chiefly by restraining marriages. The greater death-rate of infants in the poorest classes is also very important; as well as
the greater mortality at all ages, and from various diseases, of
the inhabitants of crowded and miserable houses. The effects of
severe epidemics and wars are soon counterbalanced, and more than
counterbalanced, in nations placed under favourable conditions.
Emigration also comes in aid as a temporary check, but not to any
great extent with the extremely poor classes.

There is reason to suspect, as Malthus has remarked, that
the reproductive power is actually less in barbarous than in civilised races. We know nothing positively on this head, for with
savages no census has been taken; but from the concurrent testimony of missionaries, and of others who have long resided with
such people, it appears that their families are usually small,

---

*Charles Darwin, *The Descent of Man, and Selection in Relation to
Sex*, 2 vols. (London, 1871), Vol. I, pp. 131-36, 154-57, 162-66.

and large ones rare. This may be partly accounted for, as it is believed, by the women suckling their infants for a prolonged period; but it is highly probable that savages, who often suffer much hardship, and who do not obtain so much nutritious food as civilised men, would be actually less prolific. I have shewn in a former work, that all our domesticated quadrupeds and birds, and all our cultivated plants, are more fertile than the corresponding species in a state of nature. It is no valid objection to this conclusion that animals suddenly supplied with an excess of food, or when rendered very fat, and that most plants when suddenly removed from very poor to very rich soil, are rendered more or less sterile. We might, therefore, expect that civilised men, who in one sense are highly domesticated, would be more prolific than wild men. It is also probable that the increased fertility of civilised nations would become, as with our domestic animals, an inherited character: it is at least known that with mankind a tendency to produce twins runs in families.

Notwithstanding that savages appear to be less prolific than civilised people, they would no doubt rapidly increase if their numbers were not by some means rigidly kept down. The Santali, or hill-tribes of India, have recently afforded a good illustration of this fact; for they have increased, as shewn by Mr. Hunter, at an extraordinary rate since vaccination has been introduced, other pestilences mitigated, and war sternly repressed. This increase, however, would not have been possible had not these rude people spread into the adjoining districts and worked for hire. Savages almost always marry; yet there is some prudential restraint, for they do not commonly marry at the earliest possible age. The young men are often required to show that they can support a wife, and they generally have first to earn the price with which to purchase her from her parents. With savages the difficulty of obtaining subsistence occasionally limits their number in a much more direct manner than with civilised people, for all tribes periodically suffer from severe famines. At such times savages are forced to devour much bad food, and their health can hardly fail to be injured. Many accounts have been published of their protruding stomachs and emaciated limbs after and during famines. They are then, also, compelled to wander much about, and their infants, as I was assured in Australia, perish in large numbers. As famines are periodical, depending chiefly on extreme seasons, all tribes must fluctuate in number. They cannot steadily and regularly increase, as there is no artificial increase in the supply of food. Savages when hardly pressed encroach on each other's territories, and war is the result; but they are indeed almost always at war with their neighbours. They are liable to many accidents on land and water in their search for food; and in some countries they must suffer much from the larger beasts of prey. Even in India, districts have been depopulated by the ravages of tigers. . . .

If we look back to an extremely remote epoch, before man had arrived at the dignity of manhood, he would have been guided more by instinct and less by reason than are savages at the present time. Our early semihuman progenitors would not have practised infanticide, for the instincts of the lower animals are never so

perverted as to lead them regularly to destroy their own offspring. There would have been no prudential restraint from marriage, and the sexes would have freely united at an early age.
Hence the progenitors of man would have tended to increase rapidly, but checks of some kind, either periodical or constant, must
have kept down their numbers, even more severely than with existing savages. What the precise nature of these checks may have
been, we cannot say, any more than with most other animals. . . .
No doubt in this case and in all others, many checks concur, and
different checks under different circumstances; periodical
dearths, depending on unfavorable seasons, being probably the
most important of all. So it will have been with the early progenitors of man.

Natural Selection.--We have now seen that man is variable in
body and mind; and that the variations are induced, either directly or indirectly, by the same general causes, and obey the same
general laws, as with the lower animals. Man has spread widely
over the face of the earth, and must have been exposed, during
his incessant migrations, to the most diversified conditions.
The inhabitants of Tierra del Fuego, the Cape of Good Hope, and
Tasmania in the one hemisphere, and of the Arctic regions in the
other, must have passed through many climates and changes their
habits many times, before they reached their present homes. The
early progenitors of man must also have tended, like all other
animals, to have increased beyond their means of subsistence;
they must therefore occasionally have been exposed to a struggle
for existence, and consequently to the rigid law of natural selection. Beneficial variations of all kinds will thus, either occasionally or habitually, have been preserved, and injurious ones
eliminated. I do not refer to strongly-marked deviations of
structure, which occur only at long intervals of time, but to
mere individual differences. We know, for instance, that the
muscles of our hands and feet, which determine our powers of movement, are liable, like those of the lower animals, to incessant
variability. If then the ape-like progenitors of man which inhabited any district, especially one undergoing some change in
its conditions, were divided into two equal bodies, the one half
which included all the individuals best adapted by their powers
of movement for gaining subsistence or for defending themselves,
would on an average survive in greater number and procreate more
offspring than the other and less well endowed half.

*   *   *

. . . In this chapter we have seen that as man at the present
day is liable, like every other animal, to multiform individual
differences or slight variations, so no doubt were the early progenitors of man; the variations being then as now induced by the
same general causes, and governed by the same general and complex
laws. As all animals tend to multiply beyond their means of subsistence, so it must have been with the progenitors of man; and
this will inevitably have led to a struggle for existence and to
natural selection. This latter process will have been greatly
aided by the inherited effects of the increased use of parts;
these two processes incessantly reacting on each other. It

appears, also, as we shall hereafter see, that various unimportant characters have been acquired by man through sexual selection. An unexplained residuum of change, perhaps a large one, must be left to the assumed uniform action of those unknown agencies, which occasionally induce strongly-marked and abrupt deviations of structure in our domestic productions.

Judging from the habits of savages and of the greater number of the Quadrumana, primeval men, and even the ape-like progenitors of man, probably lived in society. With strictly social animals, natural selection sometimes acts indirectly on the individual, through the preservation of variations which are beneficial only to the community. A community including a large number of well-endowed individuals increases in number and is victorious over other and less well-endowed communities; although each separate member may gain no advantage over the other members of the same community. With associated insects many remarkable structures, which are of little or no service to the individual or its own offspring, such as the pollen-collecting apparatus, or the sting of the worker-bee, or the great jaws of soldier-ants, have been thus acquired. With the higher social animals, I am not aware that any structure has been modified solely for the good of the community, though some are of secondary service to it. For instance, the horns of ruminants and the great canine teeth of baboons appear to have been acquired by the males as weapons for sexual strife, but they are used in defence of the herd or troop. In regard to certain mental faculties the case, as we shall see in the following chapter, is wholly different; for these faculties have been chiefly, or even exclusively, gained for the benefit of the community; the individuals composing the community being at the same time indirectly benefited.

It has often been objected to such views as the foregoing, that man is one of the most helpless and defenceless creatures in the world; and that during his early and less well-developed condition he would have been still more helpless. The Duke of Argyll, for instance, insists that "the human frame has diverged from the structure of brutes, in the direction of greater physical helplessness and weakness. That is to say, it is a divergence which of all others it is most impossible to ascribe to mere natural selection." He adduces the naked and unprotected state of the body, the absence of great teeth or claws for defence, the little strength of man, his small speed in running, and his slight power of smell, by which to discover food or to avoid danger. To these deficiencies there might have been added the still more serious loss of the power of quickly climbing trees, so as to escape from enemies. Seeing that the unclothed Fuegians can exist under their wretched climate, the loss of hair would not have been a great injury to primeval man, if he inhabited a warm country. When we compare defenceless man with the apes, many of which are provided with formidable canine teeth, we must remember that these in their fully-developed condition are possessed by the males alone, being chiefly used by them for fighting with their rivals; yet the females which are not thus provided, are able to survive.

In regard to bodily size or strength, we do not know whether man is descended from some comparatively small species, like the chimpanzee, or from one as powerful as the gorilla; and, therefore, we cannot say whether man has become larger and stronger, or smaller and weaker, in comparison with his progenitors. We should, however, bear in mind that an animal possessing great size, strength, and ferocity, and which, like the gorilla, could defend itself from all enemies, would probably, though not necessarily, have failed to become social; and this would most effectually have checked the acquirement by man of his higher mental qualities, such as sympathy and the love of his fellow-creatures. Hence it might have been an immense advantage to man to have sprung from some comparatively weak creature.

The slight corporeal strength of man, his little speed, his want of natural weapons, &c., are more than counterbalanced, firstly by his intellectual powers, through which he has, whilst still remaining in a barbarous state, formed for himself weapons, tools, &c., and secondly by his social qualities which lead him to give aid to his fellow-men and to receive it in return. No country in the world abounds in a greater degree with dangerous beasts than Southern Africa; no country presents more fearful physical hardships than the Arctic regions; yet one of the puniest races, namely, the Bushmen, maintain themselves in Southern Africa, as do the dwarfed Esquimaux in the Arctic regions. The early progenitors of man were, no doubt, inferior in intellect, and probably in social disposition, to the lowest existing savages; but it is quite conceivable that they might have existed, or even flourished, if, whilst they gradually lost their brute-like powers, such as climbing trees, &c., they at the same time advanced in intellect. But granting that the progenitors of man were far more helpless and defenceless than any existing savages, if they had inhabited some warm continent or large island, such as Australia or New Guinea, or Borneo (the latter island being now tenanted by the orang), they would not have been exposed to any special danger. In an area as large as one of these islands, the competition between tribe and tribe would have been sufficient, under favourable conditions, to have raised man, through the survival of the fittest, combined with the inherited effects of habit, to his present high position in the organic scale.

* * *

. . . When two tribes of primeval man, living in the same country, came into competition, if the one tribe included (other circumstances being equal) a greater number of courageous, sympathetic, and faithful members, who were always ready to warn each other of danger, to aid and defend each other, this tribe would without doubt succeed best and conquer the other. Let it be borne in mind how all-important, in the never-ceasing wars of savages, fidelity and courage must be. The advantage which disciplined soldiers have over undisciplined hordes follows chiefly from the confidence which each man feels in his comrades. Obedience, as Mr. Bagehot has well shewn, is of the highest value, for any form of government is better than none. Selfish and contentious people will not cohere, and without coherence nothing can be effected. A tribe possessing the above qualities in a high degree would spread and be victorious over other tribes; but in the course of time it would, judging from all past history, be in its turn overcome by some other and still more highly endowed tribe. Thus the social and moral qualities would tend slowly to advance and be diffused throughout the world.

But it may be asked, how within the limits of the same tribe did a large number of members first become endowed with these social and moral qualities, and how was the standard of excellence raised? It is extremely doubtful whether the offspring of the more sympathetic and benevolent parents, or of those which were the most faithful to their comrades, would be reared in greater number than the children of selfish and tracherous parents of the same tribe. He who was ready to sacrifice his life, as many a savage has been, rather than betray his comrades, would often leave no offspring to inherit his noble nature. The bravest men, who were always willing to come to the front in war, and who freely risked their lives for others, would on an average perish in larger number than other men. Therefore it seems scarcely possible (bearing in mind that we are not here speaking of one tribe being victorious over another) that the number of men gifted with such virtues, or that the standard of their excellence, could be increased through natural selection, that is, by the survival of the fittest.

Although the circumstances which lead to an increase in the number of men thus endowed within the same tribe are too complex to be clearly followed out, we can trace some of the probable steps. In the first place, as the reasoning powers and foresight of the members became improved, each man would soon learn from experience that if he aided his fellow-men, he would commonly receive aid in return. From this low motive he might acquire the habit of aiding his fellows; and the habit of performing benevolent actions certainly strengthens the feeling of sympathy, which gives the first impulse to benevolent actions. Habits, moreover, followed during many generations probably tend to be inherited.

But there is another and much more powerful stimulus to the development of the social virtues, namely, the praise and the blame of our fellow-men. The love of approbation and the dread of infamy, as well as the bestowal of praise or blame, are primarily due, as we have seen in the third chapter, to the instinct of sympathy; and this instinct no doubt was originally acquired, like all the other social instincts, through natural selection. At how early a period the progenitors of man, in the course of their development, became capable of feeling and being impelled by the praise or blame of their fellow-creatures, we cannot, of course, say. But it appears that even dogs appreciate encouragement, praise, and blame. The rudest savages feel the sentiment of glory, as they clearly show by preserving the trophies of their prowess, by their habit of excessive boasting, and even by the extreme care which they take of their personal appearance and decorations; for unless they regarded the opinion of their comrades, such habits would be senseless.

They certainly feel shame at the breach of some of their lesser rules; but how far they experience remorse is doubtful. I was at first surprised that I could not recollect any recorded

instances of this feeling in savages; and Sir J. Lubbock states
that he knows of none. But if we banish from our minds all cases
given in novels and plays and in death-bed confessions made to
priests, I doubt whether many of us have actually witnessed remorse; though we may have often seen shame and contrition for
smaller offences. Remorse is a deeply hidden feeling. It is incredible that a savage, who will sacrifice his life rather than
betray his tribe, or one who will deliver himself up as a prisoner
rather than break his parole, would not feel remorse in his in-
most soul, though he might conceal it, if he had failed in a duty
which he held sacred.

We may therefore conclude that primeval man, at a very remote period, would have been influenced by the praise and blame
of his fellows. It is obvious, that the members of the same tribe
would approve of conduct which appeared to them to be for the
general good, and would reprobate that which appeared evil. To
do good unto others--to do unto others as ye would they should do
unto you,--is the foundation-stone of morality. It is, therefore,
hardly possible to exaggerate the importance during rude times of
the love of praise and the dread of blame. A man who was not impelled by any deep, instinctive feeling, to sacrifice his life
for the good of others, yet was roused to such actions by a sense
of glory, would by his example excite the same wish for glory in
other men, and would strengthen by exercise the noble feeling of
admiration. He might thus do far more good to his tribe than by
begetting offspring with a tendency to inherit his own high character.

With increased experience and reason, man perceives the more
remote consequences of his actions, and the self-regarding virtues, such as temperance, chastity, &c., which during early times
are, as we have before seen, utterly disregarded, come to be highly esteemed or even held sacred. I need not, however, repeat what
I have said on this head in the third chapter. Ultimately a highly complex sentiment, having its first origin in the social instincts, largely guided by the approbation of our fellow-men,
ruled by reason, self-interest, and in later times by deep religious feelings, confirmed by instruction and habit, all combined,
constitute our moral sense or conscience.

2. Modern Interpretations of Evolution

a. The Mechanism of Evolution: Lamarckian or Darwinian?

*One of the more striking aspects of the history of modern
evolutionary theory is the contrast in the treatment given Lamarck's and Darwin's theories of evolution. Except for one sharp
exchange between Cuvier and one of Lamarck's disciples in 1830,
Lamarck's theories seemed to arouse little controversy or even
interest. After Cuvier's attack, the tendency was simply to ignore him. Darwin's theory, on the other hand, called forth a
series of attacks and massive defense by fellow biologists. What
was the difference between the two theories and why was Darwin's
so much more successful in spite of the fact that it contained*

many difficulties. And which, in the long run, is right? Are Darwinism and Lamarckism, in fact, mutually exclusive as most modern biologists insist?

(1) From Charles Coulston Gillispie's "Lamarck and Darwin in the History of Science"*

Charles Gillispie is Professor of the History of Science at Princeton University. It is as a historian that he views the respective places of Darwin and Lamarck in the history of biological thought. What advantage did Darwinism have over Lamarckism?

Most students will agree that Darwin's work had two aspects, empirical and theoretical. First, it definitively established the mutability of organic species in their descent out of the past. Secondly, it explained these variations by the concept of natural selection. Religious fundamentalists might deny the fact of evolution. But this reaction was intellectually trivial, and where philosophical offense was taken it was rather the view of the world implicit in the theory of natural selection which wounded humane sensibilities more deeply, and which was repudiated as inadmissible or meaningless or both, for the two complaints come down to the same thing and turn on the eternal question of what a scientific explanation really says.

There is, perhaps, a certain inconsequence which besets controversy of this sort. Having rejected Darwin's evolutionary principles, most of his opponents thought it worthwhile to impugn his originality. Among moralists Samuel Butler, and among scientists (though for different reasons) the French, put it about that Lamarck had had everything essential to an evolutionary biology. And it would be difficult indeed to claim the fact of the evolutionary variation of species as a Darwinian discovery. It is true that Darwin disposed of a greater fund of species than had Lamarck. Moreover, the seating of the chronology of earth history in paleontological indices gave biologists by way of return the succession of species in geological time. It was for lack of this information that Lamarck had had to establish his order in the scale of increasing morphological complexity.

It is to be doubted, however, whether the uniformitarian philosophy of Charles Lyell was as essential to Darwin's success as is usually said, or as I once said myself. For Lamarck had been his own Lyell. His *Hydrogéologie* prepared the ground for his theory of evolution with a uniformitarian earth history as uncompromising as Lyell's, if not so well founded. More generally, it might be argued—indeed, I do argue—that in the relative cogency with which the two theories organize actual biological information, Lamarck's presentation in the great *Histoire naturelle des animaux sans vertèbres* is the more interesting and

*Charles Coulston Gillispie, "Lamarck and Darwin in the History of Science," *American Scientist*, 46 (1958), pp. 388-93, 394-97, 402-9.

elegant. It is analytical and informs a systematic taxonomy, whereas Darwin simply amassed detail and pursued his argument through the accumulated observations in a naturalist's common-place-book. To be single-minded and relentless is not necessarily to be systematic, and the merit of Darwin's approach must be sought elsewhere.

Nevertheless, despite the greater formal elegance of La-marck's ultimate presentation, his theory failed to compel assent. It scarcely even won attention. Those most competent to judge, Lamarck's own scientific colleagues, treated his ventures into theory as the embarrassing aberrations of a gifted observer, to be passed over in silence. "I know full well," he once observed bitterly, "that very few will be interested in what I am going to propose, and that among those who do read this essay, the greater part will pretend to find in it only systems, only vague opinions, in no way founded in exact knowledge. They will say that: but they will not write it." Cuvier and Lamarck were able to work together in actual taxonomy. But they could never agree on the structure of nature.

No such humiliating judgment of irrelevance awaited Darwin's theory. (Even though my argument is that Darwin's original con-tribution was the theory and not the evidence, I shall in the interests of economy perpetuate the injustice which makes Wal-lace's role in the history of science little more than an object lesson in the agonizing generosity of creative minds.) Huxley's description of his own reaction is well known. Once stated, the force of the concept leapt out at him like the pattern from the pieces of the puzzle of adaptation, so that all he could say to himself was, "How extremely stupid not to have thought of that." The right answer, it presented itself in that combination of un-expectedness and irresistibility which has often been the hallmark of a truly new concept in scientific history.

One sometimes reads, however, that the force of Darwin's ideas derived from their mechanistic character in an age which identified the scientific with the mechanistic. I cannot think this quite correct. The one thing Darwin did not, and could not, specify was the mechanism of variation or heredity. All he could do was postulate its naturalistic mode. Ultimately, of course, his hypothesis was vindicated by discoveries in genetics of a materialistic character. But that is quite another matter--the *bête-machine* belongs to the 18th century (or to the 20th), but not to the 19th. It was through no metaphor or analogy that Dar-win prevailed. He prevailed because his work turned the study of the whole of living nature into an objective science. In the un-likely guise of a Victorian sermon on self-help in nature, on profit and loss, on progress through competition, there was clothed nothing less than a new natural philosophy, as new in its domain as Galileo's in physics. Darwin, indeed, abolished the distinction which had divided biology from physics at least since Newton, and which rested on the supposition (or defense) that the biologist must characteristically study the nature and the wisdom of the whole rather than the structure of the parts.

II

Lamarck, too, conveyed a philosophy of nature in his theory of the development of life, but it stands in the same relationship to Darwin's as does Hegel's historical dialectic to that of Marx. It is no compliment to Lamarck's own conception of his lifework, therefore, to make him out an unappreciated forerunner of Darwin. I recently asked a friend who is a biologist specializing in evolution what he and his colleagues understood by Lamarckism, and the first thing he said was the inheritance of acquired characteristics, and after that a lingering temptation in biology generally to indulge in an "Aristotelian vitalism." Now, vitalism and the mode of acquisition and transmission of variations were, indeed, the points on which scientific discussion of evolution turned in the later decades of the 19th century before the establishment of modern genetics. And it is most natural that biologists should have looked upon Lamarck in the perspective of their science, which takes the shape of evolution from Darwin. But in doing so they have first missed and then misrepresented the point of Lamarck's work, which was neither Aristotelian nor vitalistic, and which instead was meant to establish, not simply the subordinate fact of transmutation, but a view of the world. For Lamarck's theory of evolution was the last attempt to make a science out of the instinct, as old as Heraclitos and deeply hostile to Aristotelian formalization, that the world is flux and process, and that science is to study, not the configurations of matter, nor the categories of form, but the manifestations of that activity which is ontologically fundamental as bodies in motion and species of being are not. . . .

For Lamarck began as a theorist and only ended as a taxonomist. The great *Histoire naturelle des animaux sans vertèbres* appeared between 1815 and 1822. It is presented as exemplifying the evolutionary theory, which was already fully developed in *Philosophie zoologique*, published in 1809. But Lamarck had first adumbrated the notion of transmutation of living species in his course at the *Muséum d'histoire naturelle* in 1800. The date is significant. Since we know that in 1797 he still believed in the immutability of species, this interval of three years has always been taken as the critical and creative period in Lamarck's life, when he revolutionized his concepts and founded evolutionary thought. The circumstance is curious for another reason. Although Lamarck was fifty-seven years old in 1800, he was only beginning his career as a zoologist. Since 1793 when, known to science only as a botanist, he was appointed to the new chair of zoology at the reorganized *Muséum*, his thoughts had been absorbed by writings on chemistry, geology, and meteorology. These interests still figure in *Philosophie zoologique*, and are usually ignored by scientific readers. . . .

Concise statement was never Lamarck's own way. It is, nevertheless, possible to abstract from Part I of *Philosophie zoologique* a summary of the evolutionary theory in its final form. In living nature, according to this zoological philosophy, inheres a plastic force--indeed living nature *is* a plastic force--forever producing all varieties of animals from the most rudimentary

to the most advanced by the progressive differentiation and perfection of their organization. If this action of organic nature
were omnipotent, the sequence would be altogether regular, a perfect continuum of organic forms from protozoa to man. But the
innate tendency to complication is not the only factor at work.
Over against it, constraining it into certain channels of necessity which we mistakenly take for natural species, works the influence of the physical environment. The dead hand of inorganic
nature causes discontinuities in what the organic drive toward
perfection would alone achieve. These appear as gaps between the
forms of life. Changes in the environment lead to changes in
needs; changes in needs produce changes in behaviour; changes in
behaviour become new habits which may lead to alterations in particular organs and ultimately in general organization. But the
environment cannot be said to act directly on life. On the contrary, in Lamarck only life can act, for life and activity are
ultimately one. Rather, the environment is a shifting set of
circumstances and opportunities to which the organism responds
creatively, not precisely as the expression of its will (although
Lamarck's admirers interpreted him in that fashion) but as an
expression of its whole nature as a living thing. And it was
rather as a consequence than as a statement of his view of nature
that Lamarck laid down two corollaries which he described as laws:
that of the development or decay of organs through use or disuse,
and that of the inheritance of the characteristics acquired by
organisms in reacting to the environment.
    According to Lamarck himself, *Philosophie zoologique* was the
elaboration of an earlier work, *Recherches sur l'organisation des
corps vivants* of 1802. Here, too, the main evolutionary principles may all be found, though it is even less possible than in the
later work to take them for the point of the argument. The body
of the treatise is devoted to physiology and psychology, and the
theory of evolution appears as a preface. Moreover, the emphasis
is different. The position is rather that species do not exist
than that they are mutable. What interested Lamarck at this stage
in the development of his opinions was the whole tableau of the
animal series. We are to see it, not as the chain or ladder, but
as the escalator of being. For nature is constantly creating life
at the bottom. And life fluids are ever at work differentiating
organs and complicating and perfecting structures. And there is
a perpetual circulation of organic matter up the moving staircase
of existence, and of its lifeless residue spilling as chemical
husks back down the other side, the inorganic side. Here, too,
Lamarck states laws. But they are different laws from those of
1809. They generalize the facts, not about evolution in time, but
about the whole zoological scale of being, which exists both in
time and at any time. The first law states that there is indeed
a regular series in nature, and the second that it resides, not
in species, but in organic "masses" which he defined as the life
stuff distributed among the different systems of organization.
    Moving back again, two years this time to the inaugural lec-
ture of 1800, in which Lamarch first spoke of transmutation, one
meets with yet another emphasis. He there advanced the evolutionary thesis, so he tells us, as a pedagogical device, by which to

lead his students' minds back down the path which nature herself had followed in (so to say) producing them. Consistently enough, he presents the animal series as a study in degradation, not development. The theses of 1802 do appear, as do most of the evolutionary principles of 1809, but they occur only as very summary propositions in support of the main contention. This is that natural history must begin with the fundamental distinction between living and non-living bodies, between organic and physical nature.

Now, not only was this the argument of Lamarck's debut as a zoologist. It was also the argument of his final assault upon the new chemistry, the *Mémoires de physique et d'histoire naturelle* of 1797, in which he referred in passing to the unchanging character of species. The *Mémoires* resumed the attack which as a young man he had launched twenty years before in the *Recherches sur les causes des principaux faits physiques*. The central dynamical proposition is that which he later developed into the escalator of being: that all inorganic composites are residues of life processes, perpetually repairing the decay and disintegration which are all that physical nature holds in the way of process, and as perpetually doomed by mortality in their drive to bring living order to a world of chaotic physical necessity. Returning for a moment to *Philosophie zoologique*, this is perfectly consistent with the theory of evolution, in which irregularities in the animal scale mark the casualties in the conflict between organism and the brute environment. This relationship between organic nature as order and physical nature as disorder, a situation of both opposition and dependence, is fundamental to Lamarck's thought which in this respect is almost dialectical.

Nor is the inconsistency on species other than trivial. In a short essay of 1802, Lamarck himself tells us how he came to alter his view on what he then saw as a detail. All he did between 1797 and 1800 was to assimilate the question of animal species—or rather their nonexistence—to that of species in general. For in Lamarck the word has not lost its broader connotations. It still carries the sense of all the forms into which nature casts her manifold productions in all three kingdoms (or rather in both divisions). He had long been impressed with the perpetual crumbling decay of the surface of the earth. He had long shared Daubenton's opinion that there are no permanent species among minerals. The only entities in inorganic nature are the "*molécules intégrantes*" and the masses which form in the play of circumstance and universal attraction.

This makes a striking parallel to the view that Lamarck came to hold of the living world. In both organic and inorganic nature, there is nothing but process linking the individual—the particular animal, the particular molecule—and the system of organization—mammalian quadruped, granitic structure—into which it is temporarily set. This explains Lamarck's pleasure in the concept of masses as links in the double chain of systems along which materials move, from mollusc to man, from limestone to granite. It is natural enough to think of the principle of granite as mass. What Lamarck did was to think of the principle of mammal in the same fashion. For the notion was still very widespread in the

18th century that minerals are molded by some plastic force, that they are bred in the womb of the earth. Lamarck did not express this old instinct. But he cannot have been unaware of it, and it is implicit in his chemistry, where he refused to believe that a molecule can be "as ancient as the world." And the interest of this chemistry is that in asserting the indefinite variability of chemical composition, it contained the germ of what, when it was transferred to natural history, was to become Lamarck's evolutionary theory.

In Paris, Lamarck complained, the chemists teach that the integral molecule of every compound is invariant, and consequently that it is as old as nature. It followed that species are constant among minerals. As for himself, he was convinced that the integral molecule of every compound can change in its nature, that is to say in the number and proportion of the principles which constitute it. To deny this is to deny the phenomena of chemistry--the fermentations, the dissolutions, the combustions-- which leave the molecules in some different condition.

Furthermore, if attention be turned from evolutionary natural history to the other aspects of the *Philosophie zoologique*, the physiology and psychology, these too emerge as derivative from an archaic chemistry of qualities, both in manner and substance. The cardinal principle of this chemistry was that only life can synthesize. Conversely, in the life process the physiology of growth consists in retention during youth of what is needed from the materials which the organism passes through its system. Aging and death follow on the progressive hardening of the pliant organs by their lifelong digestion of the environment. Later on, Lamarck adapted his principle of an equilibrium balancing life against mass to provide evolution with a mechanism. It was analogous to erosion, no doubt because Lamarck was writing his uniformitarian treatise on geology at the time when he first put forward his evolutionary view of life. The property of life fluids is to wear away new channels, new reservoirs, and new organs in the soft tissues, and thereby to differentiate structures and specialize functions. The individual organism silts up after a time and dies, but it leaves more highly complicated descendants.

Lamarck's first scientific essay was a chemical treatise of 1776. It contains an interesting note. In order to explain physically the origin and mechanism of the universe (and he aspired to nothing less), we need to understand three things: the cause of matter, the cause of life, and the case of that activity everywhere manifest. Having dealt, therefore, with Lamarck's views on the origin and essence of matter and organism, let us turn briefly to the third problem of this trilogy, the problem of activity. In all his chemistry Lamarck attached primary importance to the element of fire. Later on he was to attack oxygen as a perfectly gratuitous postulate. Not only has it never been seen, but combustion is explicable as the action of fire, which can be seen in the act of burning or shimmering over a hot stove or a tile roof in the sun of a summer day. But this was not simply a disagreement over the most common chemical reaction. For fire is the principle of activity. It exists in many states, of which Lamarck undertook, characteristically enough, a taxonomy. In the fixed state, in coal, wood, or what will burn, fire is the principle of combustion. Conflagration is fire in its state of violent expansion, penetrating the pores of a burning body and ripping it to shreds. Evaporation occurs when fire in a state of moderate expansion surrounds molecules of water and bears them upward, so many tiny molecular balloons, to rejoin the clouds where the specific gravity of the water molecule encased in its light shell of fire balances that of air. (Lamarck also aspired to found the science of meteorology.) Finally--not to follow fire into all its states--there is a natural state, to which fire strives ever to return. And all the phenomena of light and heat, all the effects of sun and atmosphere, are manifestations of fire in its different states, forever striving to regain that which is natural.

Nor did Lamarck ever abandon his commitment to fire. It provided him with a physical basis of feeling and of life itself, and this will make clear the mistake of those who have taken him for a vitalist. His dichotomy of organic and inorganic nature provides no escape into transcendentalism, and that has always been the door through which vitalists have slipped from science into mystery. Life is a purely physical phenomenon in Lamarck, and it is only because science has (quite rightly) left behind his conception of the physical that he has been systematically misunderstood and assimilated to a theistic or vitalistic tradition which in fact he held in abhorrence. In his view spontaneous generation was no continuing miracle. Life was activated by the stirring of fluids. Lamarck hinted that this process is quickened by fire, and on the mechanism of sentience he was explicit. Its physical basis is the nervous fluid, the same substance as the electrical fluid, which itself is only a special state of fire. The pyrotic theory, therefore, embraces matter, life, and activity and in that theory lay the common origin of the three aspects of the *philosophie zoologique*--its psychology, its physiolog', and its evolutionary view of species. . . .

Lamarck's philosophy, therefore, is no anticipa ion of Darwin but a medley of dying echoes: a striving toward perf ction; an organic principle of order over against brute natur ; a life process as the organism digesting its environment; a 'rimacy of fire, seeking to return to its own, a world as flux and as becoming.

*   *   *

IV

What fundamental scientific generalization ever came into the world in so unassuming a guise as Darwin's theory of evolution? Is there any "great book" about which one secretly feels so guilty as *On the Origin of Species*? None in the history of science gives me, at any rate, such uphill work with students. There is, perhaps, a certain cruelty about student judgments, arising from the failure of skeptical young minds to perceive greatness where the scholar and the teacher say it resides. But to have to test our own enthusiasms according to our power to impart them may, perhaps, help maintain a sense of proportion, or at least force us to examine the grounds of what we say. If facts be faced, neither does a truly compelling interest shine spontaneously out of the law of falling bodies, or Newton's laws, or Lavoisier's theory of combustion. But there at least, the teacher is assisted by the arresting force of Galileo's vision of science, by the daemonic quality of Newton's genius, or by the dramatic shadow of Lavoisier's destiny. Darwin gives one no such help. He claims for himself not power of abstract thought, but the worthiest and dullest of intellectual virtues--patience, accuracy, devotion. His might be taken as the classic illustration of what Duhem meant when he described the English mind in science as weak and comprehensive. Nothing in the history of science is more familiar than his theory, or than the steps which led him to it by way of the Galapagos Islands and Malthusian political economy.

Like the law of falling bodies, the theory of natural selection is so widely taken for granted that its magnitude is not on the face of it apparent. And rather than rehearse it once again, it may perhaps set Darwin off to better advantage to consider briefly what his theory did not do and what it forbade others to do. For Darwin's opponents--the serious ones, not the theologians, who were only pathetic--did not deny the fact of evolutionary variation. But they did want things from biology which science cannot give without ceasing to be science and becoming moral or social philosophy. And this perspective will make apparent the justice of the judgment which attributes to Darwin the importance for biology that Newton has for physics, so that his rather numbing humility becomes, not the attribute of inferiority, but only the quality fitted to a science in which observation plays a larger role than abstract formalization.

Both Newton and Darwin, to begin with, were criticized for ingratitude to their predecessors. This is not just a question of scholarly manners: once the theory--gravitation, natural selection--is repudiated, then what is left is the evidence--the inverse square relationship, the fact of variation--which intellectual property might indeed be claimed for predecessors. But in both cases the theory was rejected, not as mistaken, but as meaningless. For Newton and Darwin had a way of simply accepting the phenomena as given. They excluded reason and purpose, according to this complaint, not in any dogmatic or positive way, but simply as an abdication of judgment which prevents philosophy from coming to grips with science.

Fontenelle, for example, dismissed Newton's geometric manner of proof on the same grounds that led Darwin's critics to deny merit to the concept of fitness in the organism. These are not scientific demonstrations, say the critics. Nor can they be, because they come out precisely even. They are simply tautologies which circle through the phenomena right back to their starting point. What is causation in Newton and what in Darwin?--only a formless sequence of results extending backward or outward endlessly into a metaphysical limbo. Newton purports to unite his system with the principle of gravity, and Darwin with the principle of natural selection. But if either is asked what causes gravity, or what causes the variations that are selected, he does not know. Nor did the theory depend upon his trying to say. Indeed, its success hinged precisely on dropping that question. Of Darwin, too, it could be said, "Hypotheses non fingo," and in the

same sense in which it is true of Newton: not as a sterile assertion of empiricism, but as a statement that theories (speculations
are another matter) must just embrace the evidence. . . .

Biological romanticism never made much impression in the world
of English letters, where Samuel Butler and Shaw have been the
most widely read of Darwin's critics. In their case, too, a comparison with certain themes of the 18th-century Enlightenment is
instructive, for it makes clear that the question is no biological
discussion, but simply the continuing expression of a moral resentment which wants more out of nature than science finds there. To
read Diderot and Butler together is a curious experience, itself
almost a vindication of Butler's *Unconscious Memory*. For one has
the impression that this and Butler's other writings upon nature
were products of his own rather painful and labored reflection,
and yet how unoriginal they are! These, for example, are the four
principles of Butler's *Life and Habit*: "The oneness of personality
between parents and offspring; memory on the part of offspring of
certain actions which it did when in the persons of its fore-
fathers; the latency of that memory until it is rekindled by a
recurrence of the associated ideas; and the unconsciousness with
which habitual actions come to be performed." Butler follows
Diderot's route out of atomistic materialism: "It is more coherent
with our other ideas, and therefore more acceptable, to start with
every molecule as a living thing, and then deduce death as the
breaking up of an association or corporation, than to start with
inanimate molecules and smuggle life into them; and, . . . therefore, what we call the inorganic world must be regarded as up to a
certain point living, and instinct, within certain limits, with
consciousness, volition, and power of concerted action."

But from the point of view of one who admires the intellectual achievements of science, it is Shaw rather than Butler who,
by contrast to his pretensions, seems drastically diminished in
stature by his ventures into scientific criticism. The famous
preface to *Back to Methuselah* presents clichés with the air of
lordly malice that Shaw knew how to assume as the right of a superior intelligence which did not mind pointing to its own per-
versity. But it was an intelligence which, far from transcending
science, had never given itself the trouble to understand the
force or limitations of scientific demonstrations, and in the perspective of history, Shaw on Darwin will surely find a place side
by side with Bellarmine and the papal jury setting the astronomers
right about natural philosophy. It does not appear that Shaw ever
thought to ask the biologists whether natural selection was true.
It was simply "a blasphemy, possible to many for whom Nature is
nothing but a casual aggregation of inert and dead matter, but
eternally impossible to the spirits and souls of the righteous."
Darwin is forbidden to banish mind from the universe: "For 'Natural Selection' has no moral significance: it deals with that part
of evolution which has no purpose, no intelligence, and might more
appropriately be called accidental selection, or better still,
Unnatural Selection, since nothing is more unnatural than an accident. If it could be proved that the whole universe had been produced by such Selection, only fools and rascals could bear to
live." And the Shavian word on evolution, therefore, is in fact

only a diatribe, another expression of the anti-vivisectionism--
and in a certain sense the vegetarianism--of a personality whose
Rousseauist attitude to nature involved more of sentimental hostility to intellect (as to any aristocracy) than is generally
appreciated.

With this background in mind, one might almost have predicted
that the latest thrust back to Lamarckism would have occurred in a
Marxist context. And though the science of genetics will, unlike
certain geneticists, survive its misadventures in the Soviet
Union, this episode should stand as a warning that ideas have consequences, and that to succumb to the very natural and often well-
intentioned temptation to bend science to the socializing or the
moralizing of nature is to invite its subjection to social authority, which is to say to politics. For your moralist knows what
kind of nature he wants science to give him, and if it does not,
he will either, like Shaw, repudiate it, or if like Lysenko he
has the power, he will change it. Once again, as in Diderot, as
in Goethe, as in Lamarck, resentment of mathematics (which expresses quantity and not the good) reveals the moralist beneath
the natural philosopher--the Michurin school rejects in principle
the mathematicization of biology in favor of the autonomy of
organism. Lysenko's purported findings may, therefore, be taken
as the nadir of the history of Lamarckism, and (one hopes) the
end of the story. For in his demagoguery the humane view of nature is vulgarized by way of a humanitarian naturalism into the
careerist's opportunity. But there is nothing new about it. It
is only the most recent expression of that pattern of resistance
to science which has attended its entire history in reaction
against the objectification of nature.

V

So far as the intellectual and cultural significance of evolutionary theory is concerned, therefore, Darwin had no predecessor in Lamarck. Lamarck's theory of evolution belongs to the
contracting and self-defeating history of subjective science, and
Darwin's to the expanding and conquering history of objective
science. In the concept of natural selection, Darwin put an end
to the opposition between mechanism and organism through which the
humane view of nature, ultimately the Greek view, had found refuge
from Newton in biology. Lamarck's theory, on the other hand,
originated as the transfer to natural history of that old view for
which Lavoisier had made chemistry, the science of matter, uninhabitable. It is for this reason that Darwin was the orderer of
biological science, as Newton was of physics and Galileo of mechanics. He was the first to frame objective concepts widely
enough to embrace the whole range of phenomena studied by his
science. And it may be worthwhile to consider the theory of natural selection analytically for a moment, in order to specify what
were the elements of its success, and how it was that, schemati-
cally speaking, Darwinian evolutionary theory stands in the same
relation to Lamarckian in the overall structure of the history of
science as does Galilean to Aristotelian mechanics.

In mechanics Galileo achieved objectivity by accepting motion as natural, and considering its quantity as something to be measured independently of the moving body. This he accomplished by treating time as a dimension, after which motion in physics is no longer taken as a substantial change. In Darwin--to begin drawing out the parallel--natural selection treats that sort of change which expresses itself in organic variation in the same way. Instead of explaining variation, he begins with it as a fundamental fact of nature. Variations are assumed to occur at random, requiring no further explanation and presupposing no causative agent for science to seek out. This is what opened the breach through which biology could follow physics into objectivity, because it introduced the distinction, which Darwin was the first to make, between the origin of variations and their preservation. Variations arise by chance. But they are preserved according as they work more or less effectively in objective circumstance. In Lamarck, on the other hand, the two problems are handled as a single question, which in effect is begged by its solution in the inheritance of acquired characteristics. Lamarck, therefore, could no more have distinguished the study of variations from the study of the organism as a whole than the impetus school could separate motion from the missile.

In another and even more impressive respect, Darwinian evolutionary change is analytically analogous to Galilean motion. There is direction in it, whereas in Lamarck's formulation life simply circles endlessly through nature. . . . Quite generally, in fact, Darwin's work, though not of course quantitative in result, was nevertheless quantitative in method and manner of thought. Thus, that he began with the Malthusian ratio was of far more significance for his success than was the question of its validity. It was, indeed, of utmost significance. What selection does in Darwin is to determine the quantity of living beings which can survive in any given set of objective circumstances. This aspect of the approach is more evident, perhaps, in Wallace's essay than in Darwin's more diffuse account. For example:

> Wild cats are prolific and have few enemies: why then are they never as abundant as rabbits?
> The only intelligible answer is, that their supply of food is more precarious. It appears evident, therefore, that so long as a country remains physically unchanged, the numbers of its animal population cannot materially increase. If one species does so, some others requiring the same kind of food must diminish in proportion. . . . It is, as we commenced by remarking, "a struggle for existence," in which the weakest and least perfectly organized must always succumb.

. . . It has sometimes been remarked as a paradox that it should have been Darwin (and Wallace), the old-fashioned naturalists, and not the embryologists or physiologists of the continental laboratories, who brought the revolution in biology. But the reason is clear. It does not lie in the nature of their empirical contributions. It lies in the nature of their reasoning, which was concerned with quantity and circumstance. This is why it was they who liberated biology from its limiting dependence on classification and dissection, with the gulf between bridged insubstantially by that metaphor of goal-directed organism which the evidence never could control. . . .

Darwin and Lamarck, therefore, speak their parts in that endless debate between atoms and the continuum, the multiplicity of events and the unity of nature, which is what has given the history of science its dialectic since its opening in Greece. Who seeks unity in nature believes in the continuum. Nor is it simply the wrong side, for it has been espoused by men worthy of attention: by Plato and Descartes, by Goethe and Einstein. For Lamarck the rational continuum resided in life. This was the root of his opposition to atomizing chemistry and of his emanationist evolutionary theory. At a time when he still believed in the immutability of species, he nevertheless expressed opposition to the Linnaean system, hostility to which is the touchstone of romantic or metamorphosizing tendencies in taxonomy as a rejection of atomism is in physics.

. . . It is a mistake . . . to say with Cassirer that Darwin brought becoming within the pale of science. What he did was to treat that whole range of nature which had been relegated to becoming rather as a problem in being, an infinite set of objective situations reaching back through time. He treated scientifically the historical evidence for evolution, which had been marshalled often enough before him but more as a travesty than an extension of science. . . . The Darwinian theory of evolution turned the problem of becoming into a problem of being and permitted the eventual mathematicization of that vast area of nature which until Darwin had been protected from logos in the wrappings of process.

b. Darwinism Today.

(1) From Julian Huxley's *Evolution, the Modern Synthesis**

Julian Huxley (1887-) is the grandson of Thomas Henry Huxley, "Darwin's bulldog," the great defender of Darwinism in the nineteenth century. Julian is an eminent biologist who has devoted his scientific life to the expansion and exposition of the Darwinian synthesis. In one of his more famous works, Evolution, the Modern Synthesis, *Huxley spells out the modern evaluation of Darwinism.*

The Theory of Natural Selection
1. The Theory of Natural Selection

Evolution may lay claim to be considered the most central and the most important of the problems of biology. For an attack upon it we need facts and methods from every branch of the science --ecology, genetics, paleontology, geographical distribution, embryology, systematics, comparative anatomy--not to mention reinforcements from other disciplines such as geology, geography, and mathematics.

Biology at the present time is embarking upon a phase of synthesis after a period in which new disciplines were taken up in turn and worked out in comparative isolation. Nowhere is this movement towards unification more likely to be valuable than in this many-sided topic of evolution; and already we are seeing the first-fruits of the re-animation of Darwinism.

By Darwinism I imply that blend of induction and deduction which Darwin was the first to apply to the study of evolution. He was concerned both to establish the fact of evolution and to discover the mechanism by which it operated; and it was precisely because he attacked both aspects of the problem simultaneously, that he was so successful. On the one hand he amassed enormous quantities of facts from which inductions concerning the evolutionary process could be drawn; and on the other, starting from a few general principles, he deduced the further principle of natural selection.

It is as well to remember the strong deductive element in Darwinism. Darwin based his theory of natural selection on three observable facts of nature and two deductions from them. The first fact is the tendency of all organisms to increase in a geometrical ratio. The tendency of all organisms to increase is due to the fact that offspring, in the early stages of their existence, are always more numerous than their parents; this holds good whether reproduction is sexual or asexual, by fission or by budding, by means of seeds, spores, or eggs. The second fact is that, in spite of this tendency to progressive increase, the numbers of a given species actually remain more or less constant.

---

*Julian Huxley, *Evolution, the Modern Synthesis*, Science Editions, (New York: John Wiley & Sons, Inc., 1964), pp. 13-20, 22-28.

The first deduction follows. From these two facts he deduced the struggle for existence. For since more young are produced than can survive, there must be competition for survival. In amplifying his theory, he extended the concept of the struggle for existence to cover reproduction. The struggle is in point of fact for survival of the stock; if its survival is aided by greater fertility, an earlier breeding season, or other reproductive function, these should be included under the same head.

Darwin's third fact of nature was variation: all organisms vary appreciably. And the second and final deduction, which he deduced from the first deduction and the third fact, was Natural Selection. Since there is a struggle for existence among individuals, and since these individuals are not all alike, some of the variations among them will be advantageous in the struggle for survival, others unfavourable. Consequently, a higher proportion of individuals with favourable variations will on the average survive, a higher proportion of those with unfavourable variations will die or fail to reproduce themselves. And since a great deal of variation is transmitted by heredity, these effects of differential survival will in large measure accumulate from generation to generation. Thus natural selection will act constantly to improve and to maintain the adjustment of animals and plants to their surroundings and their way of life.

A few comments on these points in the light of the historical development of biology since Darwin's day will clarify both his statement of the theory and the modern position in regard to it.

His first fact has remained unquestioned. All organisms possess the potentiality of geometric increase. We had better perhaps say *increase of geometric type*, since the ratio of offspring to parents may vary considerably from place to place, and from season to season. In all cases, however, the tendency or potentiality is not merely to a progressive increase, but to a multiplicative and not to an additive increase.

Equally unquestioned is his second fact, the actual constancy of numbers of any species. As he himself was careful to point out, the constancy is only approximate. At any one time, there will always be some species that are increasing in their numbers, others that are decreasing. But even when a species is increasing, the actual increase is never as great as the potential: some young will fail to survive. Again, with our much greater knowledge of ecology, we know to-day that many species undergo cyclical and often remarkably regular fluctuations, frequently of very large extent, in their numbers. But this fact, although it has certain interesting evolutionary consequences, does not invalidate the general principle.

The first two facts being accepted, the deduction from them also holds: a struggle for existence, or better, a struggle for survival, must occur.

The difficulties of the further bases of the theory are greater, and it is here that the major criticisms have fallen. In the first place, Darwin assumed that the bulk of variations were inheritable. He expressly stated that any which were not inheritable would be irrelevant to the discussion; but he continued in the assumption that those which are inheritable provide an adequate reservoir of potential improvement.

As Haldane has pointed out, the decreased interest in England in plant-breeding, caused by the repeal of the Corn Laws, led Darwin to take most of his evidence from animal-breeders. This was much more obscure than what the plant-breeders in France had obtained: in fact Vilmorin, before Darwin wrote, had fully established the roles of heritable and non-heritable variation in wheat.

Thus in Darwin's time, and still more in England than in France, the subject of inheritance was still very obscure. In any case the basic laws of heredity, or, as we should now say, the principles of genetics, had not yet emerged. In a full formulation of the theory of Natural Selection, we should have to add a further fact and a further deduction. We should begin, as he did, with the fact of variation, and deduce from it and our previous deduction of the struggle for existence that there must be a *differential survival* of different types of offspring in each generation. We should then proceed to the fact of inheritance. *Some* variation is inherited: and that fraction will be available for transmission to later generations. Thus our final deduction is that the result will be a differential transmission of inherited variation. The term Natural Selection is thus seen to have two rather different meanings. In a broad sense it covers all cases of differential survival: but from the evolutionary point of view it covers only the differential transmission of inheritable variations.

Mendelian analysis has revealed the further fact, unsuspected by Darwin, that recombination of existing genetic units may both produce and modify new inheritable variations. And this, as we shall see later, has important evolutionary consequences.

Although both the principle of differential survival and that of its evolutionary accumulation by Natural Selection were for Darwin essentially deductions, it is important to realize that, if true, they are also facts of nature capable of verification by observation and experiment. And in point of fact differential mortality, differential survival, and differential multiplication among variants of the same species are now known in numerous cases.

The criticism, however, was early made that a great deal of the mortality found in nature appeared to be accidental and non-selective. This would hold for the destruction of the great majority of eggs and larvae of prolific marine animals, or the death of seeds which fell on stony ground or other unsuitable habitats. It remains true that we require many more quantitative experiments on the subject before we can know accurately the extent of non-selective elimination. Even a very large percentage of such eliminations, however, in no way invalidates the selection principle from holding for the remaining fraction. The very fact that it is accidental and non-selective ensures that the residue shall be a random sample, and will therefore contain any variation of selective value in the same proportions as the whole population. It is, I think, fair to say that the fact of differential survival of different variations is generally accepted, although it still requires much clarification, especially on the quantitative side. In other words, natural selection within the bounds of the single generation is an active factor in biology.

2. The Nature of Variation

The really important criticisms have fallen upon Natural Selection as an evolutionary principle, and have centred round the nature of inheritable variation.

Darwin, though his views on the subject did not remain constant, was always inclined to allow some weight to Lamarckian principles, according to this the effects of use and disuse and of environmental influences were supposed to be in some degree inherited. However, later work has steadily reduced the scope that can be allowed to such agencies: Weismann drew a sharp distinction between soma and germplasm, between the individual body which was not concerned in reproduction, and the hereditary constitution contained in the germ-cells, which alone was transmitted in heredity. Purely somatic effects, according to him, could not be passed on: the sole inheritable variations were variations in the hereditary constitution.

Although the distinction between soma and germplasm is not always so sharp as Weismann supposed, and although the principle of Baldwin and Lloyd Morgan, usually called Organic Selection, shows how Lamarckism may be simulated by the later replacement of adaptive modifications by adaptive mutations, Weismann's conceptions resulted in a great clarification of the position. It is owing to him that we to-day classify variations into two fundamentally distinct categories--modifications and mutations (together with new arrangements of mutations, or recombinations). Modifications are produced by alterations in the environment (including modifications of the internal environment such as are brought about by use and disuse), mutations by alterations in the substance of the hereditary constitution. The distinction may be put in a rather different but perhaps more illuminating way. Variation is a study of the differences between organisms. On analysis, these differences may turn out to be due to differences in environment (as with an etiolated plant growing in a cellar as against a green one in light; or a sun-tanned sailor as against a pale slum-dweller); or they may turn out to be due to differences in hereditary constitution (as between an albino and a green seedling in the same plot, or a negro and a white man in the same city); or of course to a simultaneous difference both in environment and in constitution (as with the difference in stature between an undernourished pigmy and a well-nourished negro). Furthermore, only the latter are inherited. We speak of them as genetic differences: at their first origin they appear to be due to mutations in the hereditary constitution. The former we call modifications, and are not inheritable.

The important fact is that only experiment can decide between the two. Both in nature and in the laboratory, one of two indistinguishable variants may turn out to be due to environment, the other to genetic peculiarity. A particular shade of human complexion may be due to genetic constitution making for fair complexion plus considerable exposure to the sun, or to a genetically dark complexion plus very little tanning: and similarly for stature, intelligence, and many other characters.

This leads to a further important conclusion: characters as such are not and cannot be inherited. For a character is always the joint product of a particular genetic composition and a particular set of environmental circumstances. Some characters are much more stable in regard to the normal range of environmental variation than are others--for instance, human eye-colour or hairform as against skin-colour or weight. But these too are in principle similar. Alter the environment of the embryo sufficiently, and eyeless monsters with markedly changed brain-development are produced. . . .

Actually, every character is dependent on a very large number (possibly all) of the genes in the hereditary constitution: but some of these genes exert marked differential effects upon the visible appearance. Both rose- and single-comb fowls contain all the genes needed to build up a full-sized comb: but "rose" genes build it up according to one growth-pattern, "single" genes according to another.

This principle is of great importance. For instance, up till very recently the chief data in human genetics have been pedigrees of abnormalities or diseases collected by medical men. And in collecting these data, medical men have usually been obsessed with the implications of the ideas of "character-inheritance". When the character has not appeared in orthodox and classical Mendelian fashion they have tended to dismiss it with some such phrase as "inheritance irregular", whereas further analysis might have shown a perfectly normal *inheritance* of the gene concerned, but an irregular *expression* of the character, dependent on the other genes with which it was associated and upon differences in environment.

This leads on to a further and very vital fact, namely, the existence of a type of genetic process undreamt of until the Mendelian epoch. In Darwin's day biological inheritance meant the reappearance of similar characters in offspring and parent, and implied the physical transmission of some material basis for the characters. What would Darwin or any nineteenth-century biologist say to facts such as the following, which now form part of any elementary course in genetics? A black and an albino mouse are mated. All their offspring are grey, like wild mice: but in the second generation greys, blacks, and albinos appear in the ratio 9:3:4. Or again, fowls with rose-comb and pea-comb mated together produce nothing but so-called walnut combs: but in the next generation, in addition to walnut, rose, and pea, some single combs are produced.

To the biologist of the Darwinian period the production of the grey mice would have been not inheritance, but "reversion" to the wild type, and the reappearance of the blacks and whites in the next generation would have been "atavism" or "skipping a generation". Similarly the appearance of single combs in the fowl cross would have been described as reversion, while the production of walnut combs would have been regarded as some form of "sport."

*   *   *

3. The Eclipse of Darwinism

The death of Darwinism has been proclaimed not only from the pulpit, but from the biological laboratory; but, as in the case of Mark Twain, the reports seem to have been greatly exaggerated, since to-day Darwinism is very much alive.

The reaction against Darwinism set in during the nineties of last century. The younger zoologists of that time were discontented with the trends of their science. The major school still seemed to think that the sole aim of zoology was to elucidate the relationship of the larger groups. Had not Kovalevsky demonstrated the vertebrate affinities of the sea-squirts, and did not comparative embryology prove the common ancestry of groups so unlike as worms and molluscs? Intoxicated with such earlier successes of evolutionary phylogeny, they proceeded (like some Forestry Commission of science) to plant wildernesses of family trees over the beauty-spots of biology.

A related school, a little less prone to speculation, concentrated on the pursuit of comparative morphology within groups. This provides one of the most admirable of intellectual trainings for the student, and has yielded extremely important results for science. But if pursued too exclusively for its own sake, it leads, as Radl has pithily put it in his *History of Biological Theories*, to spending one's time comparing one thing with another without ever troubling about what either of them really is. In other words, zoology, becoming morphological, suffered divorce from physiology. And finally Darwinism itself grew more and more theoretical. The paper demonstration that such and such a character was or might be adaptive was regarded by many writers as sufficient proof that it must owe its origin to Natural Selection. Evolutionary studies became more and more merely case-books of real or supposed adaptations. Late nineteenth-century Darwinism came to resemble the early nineteenth-century school of Natural Theology. Paley *redivivus*, one might say, but philosophically upside down, with Natural Selection instead of a Divine Artificer as the *Deus ex machina*. There was little contact of evolutionary speculation with the concrete facts of cytology and heredity, or with actual experimentation.

A major symptom of revolt was the publication of William Bateson's *Materials for the Study of Variation* in 1894. Bateson had done valuable work on the embryology of *Balanoglossus*; but his sceptical and concrete mind found it distasteful to spend itself on speculations on the ancestry of the vertebrates, which was then regarded as the outstanding topic of evolution, and he turned to a task which, however different it might seem, he rightly regarded as piercing nearer to the heart of the evolutionary problems. Deliberately he gathered evidence of variation which was discontinuous, as opposed to the continuous variation postulated by Darwin and Weismann. The resultant volume of material, though its gathering might fairly be called biassed, was impressive in quantity and range, and deeply impressed the more active spirits in biology. It was the first symptom of what we may call the period of mutation theory, which postulated that large mutations, and not small "continuous variations", were the raw material of evolution, and actually determined most of its course, selection being relegated to a wholly subordinate position. . . .

Bateson did not hesitate to draw the most devastating conclusions from his reading of the Mendelian facts. In his Presidential Address to the British Association in 1914, assuming first that change in the germplasm is always by large mutation and secondly that all mutation is loss, from a dominant something to a recessive nothing, he concluded that the whole of evolution is merely an unpacking. The hypothetical ancestral amoeba contained --actually and not just potentially--the entire complex of life's hereditary factors. The jettisoning of different portions of this complex released the potentialities of this, that, and the other group and form of life. Selection and adaptation were relegated to an unconsidered background. . . .

It was in this period, immediately prior to the war, that the legend of the death of Darwinism acquired currency. The facts of Mendelism appeared to contradict the facts of paleontology, the theories of the mutationists would not square with the Weismannian views of adaptation, the discoveries of experimental embryology seemed to contradict the classical recapitulatory theories of development. Zoologists who clung to Darwinian views were looked down on by the devotees of the newer disciplines, whether cytology or genetics, *Entwicklungsmechanik* or comparative physiology, as old-fashioned theorizers; and the theological and philosophical antipathy to Darwin's great mechanistic generalization could once more raise its head without fearing too violent a knock.

But the old-fashioned selectionists were guided by a sound instinct. The opposing factions became reconciled as the younger branches of biology achieved a synthesis with each other and with the classical disciplines: and the reconciliation converged upon a Darwinian centre.

It speedily became apparent that Mendelism applied to the heredity of all many-celled and many single-celled organisms, both animals and plants. The Mendelian laws received a simple and general interpretation: they were due in the first place to inheritance being particulate, and in the second place to the particles being borne on the chromosomes, whose behaviour could be observed under the microscope. Many apparent exceptions to Mendelian rules turned out to be due to aberrations of chromosome-behaviour. Segregation and recombination, the fundamental Mendelian facts, are all but universal, being co-extensive with sexual reproduction; and mutation, the further corollary of the particulate theory of heredity, was found to occur even more widely, in somatic tissues and in parthenogenetic and sexually-reproducing strains as well as in the germtrack of bisexual species. Blending inheritance as originally conceived was shown not to occur, and cytoplasmic inheritance to play an extremely subsidiary role.

The Mendelians also found that mutations could be of any extent, and accordingly that apparently continuous as well as obviously discontinuous variation had to be taken into account in discussing heredity and evolution. The mathematicians found that biometric methods could be applied to neo-Mendelian postulates, and then become doubly fruitful. Cytology became intimately linked with genetics. Experimental embryology and the study of growth illuminated heredity, recapitulation, and paleontology. Ecology and systematics provided new data and new methods of approach to the evolutionary problem. Selection, both in nature and in the laboratory, was studied quantitatively and experimentally. Mathematical analysis showed that only particulate inheritance would permit evolutionary change: blending inheritance, as postulated by Darwin, was shown by R. A. Fisher to demand mutation-rates enormously higher than those actually found to occur. Thus, though it may still be true in a formal sense that, as such an eminent geneticist as Miss E. R. Saunders said at the British Association meeting in 1920, "Mendelism is a theory of heredity: it is not a theory of evolution", yet the assertion is purely formal. Mendelism is now seen as an essential part of the theory of evolution. Mendelian analysis does not merely explain the distributive hereditary mechanism: it also, together with selection, explains the progressive mechanism of evolution.

Biology in the last twenty years, after a period in which new disciplines were taken up in turn and worked out in comparative isolation, has become a more unified science. It has embarked upon a period of synthesis, until to-day it no longer presents the spectacle of a number of semi-independent and largely contradictory sub-sciences, but is coming to rival the unity of older sciences like physics, in which advance in any one branch leads almost at once to advance in all other fields, and theory and experiment march hand-in-hand. As one chief result, there has been a rebirth of Darwinism. . . .

The Darwinism thus reborn is a modified Darwinism, since it must operate with facts unknown to Darwin; but it is still Darwinism in the sense that it aims at giving a naturalistic interpretation of evolution, and that its upholders, while constantly striving for more facts and more experimental results, do not, like some cautious spirits, reject the method of deduction.

Hogben disagrees with this conclusion. He accepts the findings of neo-Mendelism and the mathematical conclusions to be drawn from them; but, to use his own words, "the essential difference between the theory of natural selection expounded by such contemporary writers as J. B. S. Haldane, Sewall Wright, and R. A. Fisher, as contrasted with that of Darwin, resides in the fact that Darwin interpreted the process of artificial selection in terms of a theory of 'blending inheritance' universally accepted by his own generation, whereas the modern view is based on the Theory of Particulate Inheritance. The consequences of the two views are very different. According to the Darwinian doctrine, evolution is an essentially continuous process, and selection is essentially creative in the sense that no change would occur if selection were removed. According to the modern doctrine, evolution is discontinuous. The differentiation of varieties or species may suffer periods of stagnation. Selection is a destructive agency."

Accordingly, Hogben would entirely repudiate the title of Darwinism for the modern outlook, and would prefer to see the term Natural Selection replaced by another to mark the new connotations it has acquired, although on this latter point he is prepared to admit the convenience of retention.

These objections, coming from a biologist of Hogben's calibre, must carry weight. On the other hand we shall see reason in later chapters for finding them ungrounded. In the first place, evolution, as revealed in fossil trends, *is* "an essentially con-

tinuous process". The building-blocks of evolution, in the shape
of mutations, are, to be sure, discrete quanta of change. But
firstly, the majority of them (and the very great majority of
those which survive to become incorporated in the genetic constitution of living things) appear to be of small extent; secondly,
the effect of a given mutation will be different according to the
combinations of modifying genes present; and thirdly, its effect
may be masked or modified by environmental modification. The net
result will be that, for all practical purposes, most of the variability of a species at any given moment will be continuous, however accurate are the measurements made; and that most evolutionary
change will be gradual, to be detected by a progressive shifting
of a mean value from generation to generation.

In the second place, the statement that selection is a destructive agency is not true, if it is meant to imply that it is
merely destructive. It is also directive, and because it is directive, it has a share in evolutionary creation. Neither mutation nor selection alone is creative of anything important in
evolution; but the two in conjunction are creative.

Hogben is perfectly right in stressing the fact of the important differences in content and implication between the Darwinism
of Darwin or Weismann and that of Fisher or Haldane. We may,
however, reflect that the term *atom* is still in current use and
the supposedly indivisible units having been divided. This is
because modern physicists still find that the particles called
atoms by their predecessors do play an important role, even if
they are compound and do occasionally lose or gain particles and
even change their nature. If this is so, biologists may with a
good heart continue to be Darwinians and to employ the term Natural Selection, even if Darwin knew nothing of mendelizing mutations, and if selection is by itself incapable of changing the
constitution of a species or a line.

c. Modern Lamarckism

(1) From Sir Alistair Hardy, *The Living Stream**

*Sir Alistair Hardy is one of Great Britain's foremost living
naturalists. In 1963 he was invited to give the Gifford Lectures
on Science, Natural History and Religion at the University of
Aberdeen. The Gifford Lectures have frequently been the medium
for those who objected to the reduction of biology to mechanics
with its consequent banishment of spirit and God from the universe. Sir Alistair Hardy follows in this tradition. He stresses
aspects of Lamarck's evolutionary theory which, he feels, still
have relevance to the modern biologist. These aspects permit him
to salvage purpose of a kind from the modern destruction of a
purposeful universe.*

---

*Sir Alistair Hardy, *The Living Stream: A Restatement of Evolution
Theory and Its Relation to the Spirit of Man* (London: Collins, St.
James Place, 1965), pp. 41-42, 56-58, 73-75, 96-97, 124, 169-72,
177-78.

Early Streams of Evolutionary Thought

Today, as I briefly reminded you at the end of the last lecture, it is being realised that with the development of modern man organic evolution has passed into a new phase of operation-- one which is almost as striking an innovation as the beginning of life itself. It is what Sir Julian Huxley has called the psycho-social phase or what Teilhard de Chardin means by the emergence of his "noösphere". It is characterised by what Waddington calls the working of the socio-genetic system; by this he means that evolution is no longer proceeding just by the transference of the physical genetical material--the hereditary genes--but by the handing on and development of ideas. Acquired knowledge is continually passed on: at first it was transmitted in speech, then in writing, next in printed books, and now in all manner of new means of communication. It is constantly being added to by experience. We see emerging a new element in our stream of life: the verbal inheritance of acquired experience and ideas.

In this and the next lecture I want very briefly to discuss the development of the ideas concerning the mechanism of the evolutionary process. It is important that we should be clear just how the present-day views have been built up. . . .

Yet again, there is another reason for recounting what to some will be a familiar story, for it provides an excellent illustration of this new phase in the nature of the living stream; in it we see the emergence, conflict, rejection or survival of various ideas which are thrown up as it flows along in time. Few lines of thought, considering the short time since its acceptance, have affected history more.

In this lecture I want to follow the growth of the idea of evolution up to and including the publication of Darwin's *Origin of Species*. This is the period which shows us the emergence of the two great rival doctrines: that of Darwin and the earlier one of Lamarck. We must be quite sure about the implications of each, for about one at least there has been, and still is, a good deal of misunderstanding; it is well to clear this up as soon as possible.

* * *

Turning . . . to France, we come to the great Lamarck (1744-1829). . . . He first put forward his evolutionary views in his *Philosophie Zoologique* in 1809 when he enunciated two laws, but subsequently in 1816 in his *Histoire des Animaux sans Vertèbres* he enlarged the statement of his theory into four laws. (There is thus, unfortunately, some confusion as to what some writers mean by referring to his first or second laws.)

These propositions may be stated as follows:

> *First Law.*--Life by its internal forces tends continually to increase the volume of every body that possesses it, as well as to increase the size of all the parts of the body up to a limit which it brings about.
>
> *Second Law.*--The production of a new organ or part results from a new need or want, which continues to be felt, and from the new movement which this need initiates and causes to continue.

Third Law.--The development of organs and their force or power of action are always in direct relation to the employment of these organs.

Fourth Law.--All that has been acquired or altered in the organisation of individuals during their life is preserved by generation, and transmitted to new individuals which proceed from those which have undergone these changes.

This theory, which for a time was the greatest rival to the later Darwinian doctrine, has so often been misunderstood. Its main feature is that changes in the *habits* of animals can bring about evolutionary change. So often writers have misrepresented him in supposing that he believed in the direct effect of the environment. He only believed in this in regard to plants and the very lowest animals; for the majority of animals he definitely denies this. For him the real cause of evolutionary change springs from the animal's behaviour. It was Buffon . . . who believed in the direct effect of the environment, *not* Lamarck; although it is true that he (Lamarck) believed that changes in behaviour may often be *brought about* by changes in the environment. Let me give another translation from Lamarck to make this quite clear.

Great changes in environment bring about changes in the habits of animals. Changes in their wants necessarily bring about parallel changes in their habits. If new wants become constant or very lasting, they form new habits, the new habits involve the use of new parts, or a different use of old parts, which results finally in the production of new organs and the modification of old ones.

We know now that the suggested mechanism which Lamarck postulated for bringing about structural change--*i.e.* the development of some parts of the body through greater employment or the reduction of others through less frequent use, with such changes being inherited--has now been disproved. Unfortunately with the dismissal of his particular mechanism the majority of biologists also threw aside Lamarck's conception of the importance of new habits in bringing about evolutionary change, because they could not see how such a principle could possibly work. It is this idea, but with a Darwinian mechanism, which I hope to show will return into the main evolutionary theory and then Lamarck, I believe, will have the credit for his brilliant insight into this vital part of the process. Lamarck curiously enough always avowed himself a materialist; yet his theory was essentially one linked to the behavioural side of life, and, consequently, with what some would regard as a form of vitalism.

* * *

In his first edition of the *Origin* Darwin relied almost entirely on natural selection to bring about the evolutionary change. In his sixth edition of 1872, however, he had come to admit the importance of the use and disuse effect (which was Lamarck's theory) and on p. 395 summarises his views thus:

> This [evolution] has been affected chiefly through the natural selection of numerous successive, slight, favourable variations; aided in an important manner by the inherited effects of use and disuse of parts; and in an unimportant manner, that is in relation to adaptive structures, whether past or present, by the direct action of external conditions and by variations which seem to us in our ignorance to arise quite spontaneously.

It is certainly interesting to note this change when we remember that in 1844 he wrote to Hooker saying "Heaven defend me from Lamarck's nonsense" and in other letters of the same period he refers to Lamarck's work as "veritable rubbish" and "an absurd though clever book". This weakening of his position in regard to natural selection was due to a criticism published in 1867. Not much general notice of this objection, however, was taken until much later, and for this reason I postpone an account of it (p. 79); nevertheless it affected Darwin deeply. Wallace was clearly shocked at Darwin's retreat. . . .

Wallace's *Darwinism* was not published until 1889 so that in the 1870's Lamarck's doctrine, following the change in Darwin's outlook, was being accepted and came next in importance to natural selection. Let me just remind those who are not biologists of the essential difference between the two theories. As a striking illustration, because perhaps slightly ridiculous, let me take the giraffe, which was an example used by Lamarck himself. The giraffe, as everyone knows, lives in the park-like savannah country of Africa, where it feeds on the foliage of the tall trees which are separated by stretches of grassland. Lamarck explains their long necks and long front legs by their continual craning upwards to get their food; he thought that, over vast periods of time, this stretching of the necks and legs had gradually led to an increase in their length. Darwin, on the theory of natural selection, would explain it in quite a different way. We see how the trees in any park containing cattle are browsed off in a perfectly level fashion showing us just how high the cattle can reach to get their food. In the case of the giraffe, according to Darwin, if there should be competition for such food, and if there is some variation in the length of the neck and legs amongst the population, then those with the shorter necks will tend to be starved, whilst their more lofty brothers and sisters survive. If such chance variations in the length of neck are inherited, then as the process is repeated again and again over hundreds and thousands of years, there must be a gradual evolution leading to the grotesque forms of today, provided of course that the animal as a whole remains as a reasonably efficient organism. (It must indeed be near the limit of that efficiency now.)

In those days, in the 1870's, you could take your choice between these two views and many people tended to prefer the Lamarckian doctrine because they could not bring themselves to believe that the whole act of creation was brought about by the ruthless, almost mechanical, selection of small chance variations. . . .

*   *   *

There are, of course, many other aspects of evolution theory which I cannot touch on in this one lecture; but one of these must be mentioned here, for without it the present position cannot be properly understood. Once more the stream of ideas surprises us; only within the last twenty years, have most biologists grasped what we now recognise as one of the basic principles of the whole process. I refer to the nature of a species.

As several writers have pointed out, although Darwin called his great book *The Origin of Species*, he did not, strictly speaking, deal with the problem of speciation--of just how individual species do in fact originate; he dealt with the general principles of evolution. He did not recognise any real distinction between species and varieties on the one hand or between species and genera on the other; he regarded the development of such categories as one gradual general process with the distinction between them only a matter of classificatory convenience. Hardly any one, until Ernst Mayr published his *Systematics and the Origin of Species* in 1942, really understood that the species was a unique unit, having quite a different significance in the evolutionary system from that of any other category.

For a long time naturalists had accepted what had been called the practical species concept which Darwin held: he wrote in the *Origin of Species:* "In determining whether a form should be ranked as a species or a variety, the opinion of naturalists having sound judgement and wide experience seems the only guide to follow." We now realise that the species is something which is not just a matter of judgement but has a quite definite *objective reality*. I cannot here develop the modern theory of speciation; I merely want to point out that this is a recent and important development in evolution theory. The crux of the matter is this. An inter-breeding population of animals (or plants) may happen to become divided by a geographical barrier (or other means of isolation) into two quite separate groups, so that, with the passage of time, the members of one, by the action of selection under somewhat different conditions, may come to differ from those of the other; so if eventually the two populations should come in contact with one another again, and if they should now be so different, either in structural or behavioural character that they will no longer interbreed, then we shall have two new species in place of the former one. This is how the *real steps* in evolutionary change take place. It was, indeed, the separation of the slightly different forms of life on the Galapagos Islands which had impressed Darwin so much and it was Wallace who made a special study of such isolation in his splendid book *Island Life*. It was not, however, until eighty years after Darwin's masterpiece was published that Mayr made us all realise exactly how the origin of species did in fact take place. Thus, in *his* book, he told us how this true conception of the species had actually first been expressed, some ten years before Darwin ever went to the Galapagos, by the naturalist Leopold von Buch in a description of the fauna and flora of the Canary Islands published in 1825 (and then forgotten!):

> The individuals of a genus spread out over the continents,
> move to far-distant places, form varieties (on account of

differences of the localities, of the food, and the soil),
which owing to their segregation [geographical isolation]
cannot interbreed with other varieties and thus be returned to the original main type. Finally these varieties become constant and turn into separate species.
Later they may reach again the range of other varieties
which have changed in a like manner, and the two will now
no longer cross and thus they behave as "two very different species".

Again we may marvel how such a clear and simple statement on so
important an issue can have lain unnoticed for so long. . . .

* * *

There can no longer, I think, be any doubt that selection
acting upon the small random changes in the inherited nuclear
material is the main *physical* mechanism of evolutionary change.
Looked at just like this, I agree that it appears to be an intensely materialistic process. Here at the end of the fourth lecture I might seem that I was coming down on the side of the
mechanists. I have presented the case as I believe it is seen by
the majority of biologists of today. I am sure that the main features of the process I have outlined are true, but I am also sure
they are not the whole of the process. Undoubtedly the physical
environment and the action of predators, as we have just seen, are
powerful forces of selection; there is, however, I believe, another equally powerful agent, and whether this can be explained
in mechanistic terms I very much doubt. . . .

* * *

When I was President of the Zoology Section of the British
Association at their meeting in Newcastle-upon-Tyne in 1949 I took
as the subject of my address "Zoology outside the Laboratory".
After discussing several lines of field work I went on as follows:

A still more important contribution that field zoology can
make to evolutionary theory is to throw more light on the
part played by Organic Selection. The gene combinations
which are best suited to the *habits* of the animal may tend
to survive in preference to those which do not give such
full scope to the animal's pattern of behaviour. This
idea of Organic Selection, which was put forward independently by Baldwin and Lloyd Morgan at the turn of the century, has been almost forgotten until quite recently.
This possible selection of structural variations by habit
as opposed to the selection of other variations by the
environment may indeed be a factor of importance. It is
in effect similar to that postulated by Lamarck but
brought about on Darwinian lines. External Natural Selection must of course be important, but if Organic Selection
can be shown to be a really significant factor, it may
well alter our way of looking at evolution as a whole.
The relative importance of the two forms of selection must
be the subject both of experiment and of more research
into the habits and behaviour of animals in nature.

I had thought that I might have started a discussion on the relative potencies of these two forms of selection; but I was disappointed. It has taken me some time to realise that there appears to be a curious, I might almost say psychological, block preventing the majority of biologists with whom I have discussed the matter from really appreciating the point I have been trying to make, or even being interested in what they quickly dismiss as the "Baldwin Effect: a principle of only minor importance." In part no doubt it has been my lack of explanatory skill, but I think now that there have been two other reasons for their failure to grasp the possible significance of selection by change of behaviour. One I have already dealt with: the imagined bogy of Lamarckism; the other is that so many people still think of evolution in terms of individuals rather than of populations. Of course the process is mediated by the variations in the gene complexes of the individuals and a differential mortality among them; but it is the populations which are evolving not the individuals. The effect I am discussing is essentially a population effect.

When I have previously discussed the matter I have, I think, usually been misunderstood. I would therefore ask you to excuse me if I appear perhaps to be needlessly over-labouring one or two points. I want to be quite certain of making clear a distinction which some people evidently seem to find a somewhat subtle and almost unreal one; it is one which to me, however, appears to be of paramount importance.

I will first of all state the proposition in the simplest terms. If a population of animals should change their habits (no doubt often on account of changes in their surroundings such as food supply, breeding sites, etc., but also sometimes due to their exploratory curiosity discovering new ways of life, such as new sources of food or new methods of exploitation) then, sooner or later, variations in the gene complex will turn up in the population to produce small alterations in the animal's structure which will make them more efficient in relation to their new behaviour pattern; these more efficient individuals will tend to survive rather than the less efficient, and so the composition of the population will gradually change. This evolutionary change is one caused *initially* by a change in behaviour.

As an illustration of what I mean let me use the example I gave when I discussed the matter at a meeting of the Linnean Society in 1956. If birds of a particular species, originally feeding on insects from the surface of the bark of trees, found, in a time of shortage, that they could get more prey by probing into or under the bark, then they might develop a change of habit which, by being copied by other members of the species, could gradually spread through the whole population. In recent years we have seen two examples of such new habits spreading across the country: firstly the opening of milk bottles--first the cardboard tops, then the metal tops--spreading, apparently by copying right through the tit populations of Europe, and secondly the spread across England of the attack on *Daphne* seeds by green-finches. Now to return to our birds probing into the bark for insects; if this new habit became well established and more profitable to the bird than mere pecking off the surface, then any members of the population with a gene complex giving a beak slightly better adapted to such probing would have a better chance of survival than those less well equipped. A new shape of beak would be evolved as a result of a change of habit. I went on to say (*loc. cit.*): "The same will apply to any other changes of habit as when an animal turns to digging for its food, diving into the water for fish and so on; in any population those gene complexes which modify particular organs to give a better expression to the new habit, will, in the long run, supplant those which produced organs less efficient in satisfying its needs."

Now most people with whom I discuss this say that I am talk-ing about pure Darwinism and seem to imply that I am just making a fuss about nothing. This is where I disagree and insist that there is a real if somewhat subtle difference: a difference which it is essential that we should understand if we are to appreciate the true nature of the living stream--the evolutionary process. To try and make clear this point I must return for a moment to the different kinds of selection.

We can classify the forms of selection in various ways; most people when thinking of Darwinism think of two main types: selec-tion by other organisms, including both predators and competitors, and selection by the inanimate environment. The first kind is usually subdivided into inter- and intra-specific selection, *i.e.* one of competition and combat between different species and the other of rivalry between members of the same species. In the last lecture we saw examples of the powers of predator selection. Examples of the second kind of selection, that of the physical environment, are obvious, such as species of mammals with thicker fur being selected by survival in colder regions or races of wing-less flies left surviving on small oceanic islands because those with normal wings are blown away to destruction. Undoubtedly these kinds of selection account for a great deal of adaptation and evolutionary change. I would, however, make another kind of division between the forms of selection. I would distinguish all the foregoing kinds under a super heading of *external* selective agencies, meaning those acting from outside the organisms con-cerned, *i.e.* the selective forces acting from both the animate and inanimate environments; and in contrast to these I would place an *internal* selective force due to the behaviour and habits of the animal itself. Much of behaviour--all instinctive behaviour--is, of course, governed by the gene complex; in addition however there are the kind of changes in behaviour to which I have just referred: new modes of action which spread through the population and are maintained in higher vertibrates by tradition before they become converted by assimilation into instinctive action. . . .

Now because a change of habit is usually occasioned by changes in the environment, it is generally supposed, I think, that any selection due to such a habit change is one differing only in degree, but not in kind, from the other forms of selec-tion just discussed. This for me is the crux of the whole issue; I think they are radically different. I realise, of course, that it is the differential mortality in the population which brings about the survival of the more efficient type of beak, for exam-ple, and this is obviously mediated by factors in the external

world killing off a higher proportion of the less efficient forms;
nevertheless the real initiating agent in the process is the new
behaviour pattern, the *new habit*.   I believe the case for regarding this "behavioural" type of selection as different in kind
from the rest can be maintained.   A new habit, as Lamarck said,
is frequently the result of some environmental change and this
may make this kind of selection seem similar to the other kinds.
But among vertebrates, it must often be the restless, exploring
and perceiving animal that discovers new ways of living, new
sources of food, just as the tits have discovered the value of
the milk bottles. . . .

*   *   *

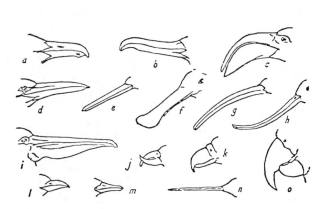

A selection of beaks of birds of various habits: *a*, herring gull; *b*, frigate bird; *c*, flamingo;
d, gannet; *e*, snipe; *f*, spoonbill; *g*, curlew; *h*, avocet; *i*, pelican; *j*, cross-bill; *k*, eagle;
l, swallow; *m*, spotted flycatcher; *n*, humming-bird; *o*, parrot.

Now in fig. 56 let us look at the diversity of beaks among
birds in general.   Can it really be maintained that it is *more
likely* that random mutations forced these different groups of
birds to their different modes of life, rather than that they developed different habits and that such differences in feeding led
gradually to beaks better and better adapted to their ways of
life?   Surely it must be admitted that it is change of habit which
is the dominating factor influencing such selection.   Now if we
had been looking at a chart showing not the forms of beaks but
the legs and feet of these birds would we not have come to a similar conclusion?

When I had mentioned my hypothetical birds pecking at insects
on the bark of trees in the 1956 discussion at the Linnean Society
already referred to, and then talked of tits opening milk bottles,
someone half jokingly said "and eventually I suppose we shall have
a race of tits with beaks like tin-openers!"   Exactly.   If milk
bottles were some curious hard-covered organic objects and a

species of tit specialised on them for food, then if "the bottles"
with the thicker "caps" tended to survive, who could doubt that
in time there would be evolved both thicker and thicker "caps"
and more specialised tin-opener-like beaks for dealing with them?

D.   The Cell Theory and Heredity

The third major area of biological advance in the nineteenth
century was that of microbiology. The reason for the lateness of
this development is quite clear: until the nineteenth century,
microscopes were so poor that they could not be trusted. The
major fault lay in the inability to eliminate chromatic aberra-
tion. This meant that every object viewed under a microscope was
surrounded by either a red or a blue halo which prevented anyone
from seeing micro-structures with any degree of accuracy.
All this changed when, in 1837, Giovan Battista Amici
(1784-1863) utilized the hemispheric objective lens that permitted
the first clear microscopic views. The further development of
the microscope was rapid and by mid-century there were made available instruments of superior and trustworthy caliber. The development of the microscope naturally stimulated the development of
micro-techniques. Again, by mid-century, these techniques made
it possible to obtain a micro-section of plant or animal tissue
and, through the use of a few, newly developed stains, bring out
the structure of these tissues. The increasing sophistication of
staining techniques, and the use of increasingly sophisticated
optical systems (oil-immersion lenses, polarized light, etc.)
permitted cytologists in the second half of the nineteenth century
to investigate the fine-structure of living cells. And this, in
turn, provided basic clues to the mechanism of heredity and held
out the promise of revealing the secret of life itself. Further
developments in the twentieth century such as the electron microscope, have come close to fulfilling this promise.
In the early 1800's, as we have seen, the possibility of
penetrating very far into the secret of life seemed remote, indeed. Even Bichat's identification of tissues as the basic units
of life was not found to be of much help. Physiology developed
quite well without having to concern itself over the basic unit
(if any) of living matter.
The development of the cell theory transformed physiology by
providing both a new dimension and the basic physiological building block. Like most generalizations, it grew slowly and was
built by a number of hands. The first use of the term cell goes
back to Robert Hooke's observations of cork in the seventeenth
century. Unicellular organisms had been studied by Leeuwenhoek
in the same century but it occurred to no one to take seriously
the idea that these tiny utricles could be considered the basis
of life. In the early nineteenth century, even with the bad
microscopes then available, the ubiquity of the cell began to
become obtrusive. The French botanist, Henri Dutrochet (1776-
1847) succeeded in making preparations of plant cells and in
studying them between 1824 and 1830. Dutrochet sought, unsuc-
cessfully, to discover similar structures in animals. The

English botanist, Robert Brown (1773-1858) remarked in 1831 on the presence of the cell nucleus in the epidermis of orchids. In 1833, he reported that this body was present in the "celluler" tissue of many plants and threw out the suggestion that the nucleus, somehow, was an essential part of plant tissues.

It was not until the late 1830's that a formal cell theory was proposed. It was the result of the collaboration of Matthias Jakob Schleiden (1804-81), a botanist, and Theodor Schwann (1810-83), a physiologist. Schleiden had early come under the influence of *Naturphilosophie*, and particularly the writings of Lorenz Oken. Oken, as early as 1805, had played with the idea of a fundamental living polyp out of which all living tissues were composed. Schleiden, in studying the development of the embryo and endosperm within the embryo sac in higher plants, witnessed what he thought must be the creation of Oken's basic polyp. Further investigation convinced him that the whole plant was composed of cells which, like Oken's polyps, were endowed with vitality. Schleiden discussed his new idea with Schwann, then a student of Johannes Müller, the founder of German physiology. Schwann, who had been working on notochord development in tadpoles, recognized the similarity between what Schleiden described in plants and what he observed in tadpoles. Expanding his researches, Schwann was able to show that all animal tissues he examined were composed of cells. Like Schleiden, he was eager to accept the cell as the ultimate living unit, but for different reasons. Schleiden was a vitalist for whom the cell was the center of a vital force. Schwann was a mechanist who was intent upon destroying the idea that an organism was an inert object, animated by a vital force imposed upon it. This was the view held by Johannes Müller and Schwann was delighted to prove his teacher wrong. An organism, for Schwann, was the sum of the physiological activity of its constituent cells. This physiology, Schwann was convinced, could be understood in physico-chemical terms. It might be mentioned parenthetically that Müller was amazingly successful in turning out students whose disagreements with his theories led to fundamental advances in physiology. Another student, Hermann Helmholtz, wrote his epoch-making paper on conservation of energy to leave no room for a vital principle and Emil du Bois-Reymond was a creator of neuro-physiology in spite of Müller's beliefs that nervous activity must defy scientific analysis.

Schleiden and Schwann's cell theory provided a kind of atomic basis for physiology. Their theory of cell formation from a nutrient soup called the cytoblastema, however, was completely wrong and soon discarded. In the 1840's it was shown that cells arose only from other cells, leading to Rudolf Virchow's famous dictum *Omni cellula e cellula* (All cells come from cells).

It was Virchow who showed the utility of cell theory for medicine. His work on *Cellular Pathology* which was first published in 1858 provided a new foundation for the study of disease. Virchow was overenthusiastic when he insisted that all diseases were ultimately diseases of cells and showed up by causing changes in cell structure. This ignored, because it was still unknown, the role of bacteria in disease but it did serve to focus attention on such maladies as cancer in which cellular changes did signal the onset and progress of the disorder.

By the 1860's, cells were generally recognized as the fundamental units of life. Knowledge of cell structure and cell function, it was felt, would lead to knowledge of fundamental living processes. Further development of the study of cells led in three separate directions. The germ theory of disease was an offshoot of the study of cells; histology, or the study of tissues, became the physiology of cells; and, finally, the mysteries of heredity and reproduction appeared to be contained in the study of the sex cells produced by the reproductive organs.

The development of the germ theory of disease is a familiar one whose bare outlines need only be sketched here. Ideas of contagion through microorganisms go back at least as far as Fracostoro in the sixteenth century. It was not until the nineteenth century, however, that there was any evidence to support the ideas. The study of fermentation is at the origin of the germ theory. As early as 1838, the Baron Cagniard de Latour (1777-1859) had published a paper in which he argued that the fermentation of sugar was caused by the microorganisms that made up yeast. His view was ridiculed by Liebig and Wöhler who insisted that fermentation was a strictly chemical process requiring no vital activity whatsoever. In the 1860's, the subject was taken up again by Louis Pasteur. Pasteur studied a whole series of fermentations and proved that each specific kind of fermentation depended upon a specific kind of microorganism. It is not a great leap from this position to the one that suggests that specific diseases are caused by specific microbes. To prove the point was another matter. Pasteur did it with anthrax, a plague that periodically decimated the cattle and sheep herds of France. Anthrax bacilli could be cultured and Pasteur soon discovered that after successive generations of culture at a certain temperature, they lost their virulence but retained their ability to convey immunity. The great test came on May 31, 1881. Pasteur inoculated 25 sheep with his attenuated culture of anthrax. Then these 25 sheep and 25 uninoculated ones were infected with anthrax bacilli. On June 2, the 25 uninoculated sheep were dead; the 25 protected by Pasteur were browsing peacefully. The point was proven. Certain diseases, at least, were caused by single celled organisms. The cell theory was not only the clue to life but to health as well. The techniques devised by Pasteur for the attenuation of cultures were applicable to a number of bacterial diseases. In 1881, Pasteur attacked a disease whose cause he could not isolate or see under the microscope--rabies. Rabies is caused by a virus but virology is a science of the twentieth century and Pasteur was only partly successful. The existence of viruses, however, opened up a whole new area of research which, in the twentieth century, was to lead to the unraveling of the puzzle of heredity.

The problem of the inheritance of characteristics from parents, again, was one of great antiquity. Aristotle had wrestled with it and even Darwin who was no microbiologist had had a fling at it. Nothing much could be done until some of the main facts of reproduction became known.

The egg is an obvious part of reproduction in cases where eggs are obvious. It was not until 1827 that the mammalian egg was actually observed by Karl Ernst von Baer (1792-1876). The role of the sperm cell was also gradually discovered at the same period. Jean-Louis Prévost (1790-1850) and the chemist J. B. Dumas performed a series of simple but elegant experiments which showed that spermatozoa were necessary for the fertilization of frogs' eggs. If the seminal fluid were filtered before it was placed in contact with the eggs, no fertilization took place. It was not, however, until the 1870's that the actual penetration of a sperm cell into an egg was observed and the fact discovered that one, and only one, sperm cell fertilized an egg. The significance of this fact was not clear, even after Flemming had taken note of meiosis (the halving of the chromosomes in sex-cell development) and the fusion of nuclei in 1882.

The vital clue to the mechanism of heredity was produced by an obscure Austrian monk, Gregor Mendel (1822-84), in the years 1858 to 1865. Mendel chose the ordinary pea plant (not sweet peas as is often reported) as his experimental subject. Pea plants vary in certain ways. Some are tall, some are short; some have wrinkled peas, some smooth. Mendel bred his plants to gain pure lines and then crossed them, taking careful note of the characteristics of the offspring. The results were surprising. Instead of opposite characteristics blending, they remained separate. Thus, suppose a plant has a characteristic A whose opposite may be designated a (tallness and shortness, for example). If an A plant is bred with an a, the results in the first generation will be all A. If this generation is then interbred, the famous Mendelian ratio will emerge. Three-quarters of the offspring of this generation will be A, but one-quarter will be a. The only way Mendel could account for this was to assume that some factor that accounted for A and a was transmitted and retained in the offspring as a whole unit. Thus, in the cells of the first generation, there were both A and a factors but the a was dominated by A. In the second generation, there would be recombinations of factors to produce AA, Aa and aa and it could be shown by simple mathematics that the ratio would be 1:2:1. But since Aa and AA were indistinguishable as plants, the ratio of A characteristic to a would be 3:1.

By implication, these factors would have to be contained in the individual sex cells. Mendel, however, was no microbiologist and he was unable to pursue his researches further. He did publish his results in the early 1860's but they fell on deaf ears. No one was yet prepared to admit either the atomic nature of heredity nor the application of mathematical statistics to biology.

In spite of the general ignorance of Mendel's results, further research on the structure of cells led men up to the point where they almost grasped an acceptable hereditary theory. The chromosomes were discovered in 1880 because of their unique ability to take up basic dyes and their optical prominence led to their intensive study. The discovery of both meiosis and mitosis indicated that the chromosomes played some part in the hereditary process but the ignorance of Mendel's work prevented researchers from realizing exactly what. In the 1880's, August Weismann (1834-1914) developed a theory of heredity based upon the absolute separation of somatic cells and germ cells. For Weismann,

the two were completely different and he used this difference to
"prove" the impossibility of the inheritance of acquired characteristics. In a famous experiment, he cut off the tails of thirty
generations of mice only to have the thirty-first generation born
with tails. Weismann triumphantly announced the results, ignoring
the fact that Lamarck had laid out rather specific conditions for
the inheritance of acquired characteristics which had not been
fulfilled in Weismann's experiment. Be that as it may, Weismann
then proceeded to devise a theory of a germ plasm in which the
chromosomes played an important role. He located hereditary factors on the chromosomes and tried to build a kind of mosaic theory
of inheritance around them. Each factor contributed to the development of the embryo by laying down its tissue according to the
master plan and inheritance was nothing but the unfolding of this
mosaic. Weismann's theory gave birth to the new science of *Entwicklungsmechanik* or development mechanics. This science was intended to put all the pieces together and finally lay bare the
details of precisely how the hereditary factors controlled each
step of the development of the embryo. The triumph of mechanism
was at hand when, finally, the formation of the organism could be
understood in mechanical terms. It seems appropriate, therefore,
to close this section with the work of Hans Driesch (1867-1941).
Driesch was one of the leading practitioners of *Entwicklungsmechanik* until he made the startling discovery that almost any part
of the "mosaic" had the potential to develop into a fully-formed
embryo. This was a peculiar kind of "mechanics" in which each
part seemingly had the ability to become the whole and Driesch
set out to destroy *Entwicklungsmechanik* as a false science. He
revived vitalism just at the moment in the history of biology
when mechanism appeared triumphant. His challenge to the mechanists in biology was to set almost all the important questions
that the twentieth century biologists were to ask.
Thus, in spite of the triumphs of evolution theory, germ theory
and cell theory, the nineteenth century closed on biology with
the large question of the ultimate nature of life still left
unanswered.

E.   Mechanism and Vitalism in Biology

1.   Theodore Schwann and Cell Theory*

*The enunciation of cell theory in 1838 provided a firm mate-
rial basis for the study of life. In the hands of one of the co-
authors of the theory, Theodor Schwann, the cell theory also
appeared to exile vitalism from biology. Schwann's treatment was
entirely mechanistic and seemed to turn cell physiology into a
physico-chemical science.*

---

*T. Schwann, *Microscopical Researches into the accordance in the
Structure and Growth of Animals and Plants*, trans. by Henry
Smith (London, 1847), pp. 1-8, 161-63, 165-72, 175-77, 186-93.

Although plants present so great a variety of external form, yet they are no less remarkable for the simplicity of their internal structure. This extraordinary diversity in figure is produced solely by different modes of junction of simple elementary structures, which, though they present various modifications, are yet throughout essentially the same, namely, *cells*. The entire class of the Cellular plants consists only of cells; many of them are formed solely of homogeneous cells strung together, some of even a single cell. In like manner, the Vascular plants, in their earliest condition, consist merely of simple cells; and the pollen-granule, which, according to Schleiden's discovery, is the basis of the new plant, is in its essential parts only a cell. In perfectly-developed vascular plants the structure is more complex, so that not long since, their elementary tissues were distinguished as cellular and fibrous tissue, and vessels or spiral-tubes. Researches on the structure, and particularly on the development of these tissues, have, however, shown that these fibres and spiral-tubes are but elongated cells, and the spiral-fibres only spiral-shaped depositions upon the internal surface of the cells. Thus the vascular plants consist likewise of cells, some of which only have advanced to a higher degree of development. The lactiferous vessels are the only structure not as yet reduced to cells; but further observations are required with respect to their development. According to Unger they in like manner consist of cells, the partition-walls of which become obliterated.

Animals, which present a much greater variety of external form than is found in the vegetable kingdom, exhibit also, and especially the higher classes in the perfectly-developed condition, a much more complex structure in their individual tissues. How broad is the distinction between a muscle and a nerve, between the latter and cellular tissue, (which agrees only in name with that of plants,) or elastic or horny tissue, and so on. When, however, we turn to the history of the development of these tissues, it appears, that all their manifold forms originate likewise only from cells, indeed from cells which are entirely analogous to those of vegetables, and which exhibit the most remarkable accordance with them in some of the vital phenomena which they manifest. *The design of the present treatise is to prove this by a series of observations.*

It is, however, necessary to give some account of the vital phenomena of vegetable cells. Each cell is, within certain limits, an Individual, an independent Whole. The vital phenomena of one are repeated, entirely or in part, in all the rest. These Individuals, however, are not ranged side by side as a mere Aggregate, but so operate together, in a manner unknown to us, as to produce an harmonious Whole. The processes which go forward in the vegetable cells, may be reduced to the following heads: 1, the production of new cells; 2, the expansion of existing cells; 3, the transformation of the cell-contents, and the thickening of the cell-wall; 4, the secretion and absorption carried on by cells.

The excellent researches of Schleiden, which throw so much light upon this subject, form the principal basis for my more minute observations on these separate vital phehomena.

First, of the production of new cells. According to Schleiden, in Phænogamous plants, this process always (except as regards
the cells of the Cambium,) takes place within the already mature
cells, and in a most remarkable manner from out of the well-known
cell-nucleus. . . .

The following is Schleiden's description of the origin of
the cells from the cytoblast. So soon as the cytoblasts have attained their full size, a delicate transparent vesicle, the young
cell, rises upon their surface, and is placed upon the flat cytoblast like a watch-glass upon a watch. It is at this time so
delicate that it dissolves in distilled water in a few minutes.
It gradually expands, becomes more consistent, and at length so
large, that the cytoblast appears only as a small body inclosed
in one of the side walls. The portion of the cell-wall which covers the cytoblast on the inner side, is, however, extremely delicate and gelatinous, and only in rare instances to be observed;
it soon undergoes absorption together with the cytoblast, which
likewise becomes absorbed in the fully-developed cell. The cytoblasts are formed free within a cell, in a mass of mucus-granules,
and the young cells lie also free in the parent cell, and assume,
as they become flattened against each other, the polyhedral form.
Subsequently the parent cell becomes absorbed. . . .

The expansion of the cell when formed, is, either regular on
all sides, in which case it remains globular, or it becomes polyhedral from flattening against the neighbouring cells, or it is
irregular from the cell growing more vigorously in one or in
several directions. . . .

With regard to the changes which the cell-contents and cell-
wall undergo during vegetation, I only take into consideration the
thickening of the latter, as I have but a few isolated observations upon the transformations of the contents of animal cells,
which however indicate analogous changes to those of plants. The
thickening of the cell-walls takes place, either by the deposition
from the original wall, of substances differing from, or more
rarely, homogeneous with it, upon the internal surface of the
cell, or by an actual thickening of the substance of the cell-
wall. . . .

In all these processes each cell remains distinct, and maintains an independent existence. . . .

After these preliminary remarks we pass on to animals. The
similarity between some individual animal and vegetable tissues
has already been frequently pointed out. Justly enough, however,
nothing has been inferred from such individual points of resemblance. Every cell is not an analogous structure to a vegetable
cell; and as to the polyhedral form, seeing that it necessarily
belongs to all cells when closely compacted, it obviously is no
mark of similarity further than in the circumstance of densely
crowded arrangement. An analogy between the cells of animal tissues and the same elementary structure in vegetables can only be
drawn with certainty in one of the following ways: either, 1st, by
showing that a great portion of the animal tissues originates
from, or consists of cells, each of which must have its particular
wall, in which case it becomes probable that these cells correspond to the cellular elementary structure universally present in

plants; or, 2dly, by proving, with regard to any one animal tissue consisting of cells, that, in addition to its cellular structure, similar forces to those of vegetable cells are in operation in its component cells; or, since this is impossible directly, that the phenomena by which the activity of these powers or forces manifests itself, namely, nutrition and growth, proceed in the same or a similar manner in them as in the cells of plants. I reflected upon the matter in this point of view in the previous summer, when, in the course of my researches upon the terminations of the nerves in the tail of the Larvæ of frogs, I not only saw the beautiful cellular structure of the Chorda Dorsalis in these lawvæ, but also discovered the nuclei in the cells. J. Müller had already proved that the chorda dorsalis in fishes consists of separate cells, provided with distinct walls, and closely packed together like the pigment of the Choroid. The nuclei, which in their form are so similar to the usual flat nuclei of the vegetable cells that they might be mistaken for them, thus furnished an additional point of resemblance. As however the importance of these nuclei was not known, and since most of the cells of mature plants exhibit no nuclei, the fact led to no farther result. J. Müller had proved, with regard to the cartilage-corpuscles discovered by Purkinje and Deutsch in several kinds of cartilage, from their gradual transition into larger cells, that they were hollow, thus in a more extended sense of the word, cells; and Miescher also distinguishes an especial class of spongy cartilages of a cellular structure. Nuclei were likewise known in the cartilage-corpuscles. Müller, and subsequently Meckauer, having observed the projection of the cartilage-corpuscles at the edge of a preparation, it became very probable that at least some of them must be considered as cells in the restricted sense of the word, or as cavities inclosed by a membrane. Gurlt also, when describing one form of permanent cartilage, calls them vesicles. I next succeeded in actually observing the proper wall of the cartilage-corpuscles, first in the branchial cartilages of the frog's larvæ, and subsequently also in the fish, and also the accordance of all cartilage-corpuscles, and by this means in proving a cellular structure, in the restricted sense of the word, in all cartilages. During the growth of some of the cartilage-cells, a thickening of the cell-walls might also be perceived. Thus was the similarity in the process of vegetation of animal and vegetable cells still further developed. Dr. Schleiden opportunely communicated to me at this time his excellent researches upon the origin of new cells in plants, from the nuclei within the parent-cell. The previously enigmatical contents of the cells in the branchial cartilages of the frog's larvæ thus became clear to me; I now recognized in them young cells, provided with a nucleus. Mechauer and Arnold had already found fat-vesicles in the cartilage-corpuscles. As I soon afterwards succeeded in rendering the origin of young cells from nuclei within the parent-cells in the branchial cartilages very probable, the matter was decided. Cells presented themselves in the animal body having a nucleus, which in its position with regard to the cell, its form and modifications, accorded with the cytoblast of vegetable cells, a thickening of the cell-wall took place, and the formation of young cells within the parent-cell

from a similar cytoblast, and the growth of these without vascular
connexion was proved. This accordance was still farther shown by
many details; and thus, so far as concerned these individual tissues, the desired evidence, that these cells correspond to the
elementary cells of vegetables was furnished. I soon conjectured
that the cellular formation might be a widely extended, perhaps a
universal principle for the formation of organic substances. Many
cells, some having nuclei, were already known; for example, in the
ovum, epithelium, blood-corpuscles, pigment, &c. &c. It was an
easy step in the argument to comprise these recognized cells under
one point of view; to compare the blood-corpuscles, for example,
with the cells of epithelium, and to consider these, as likewise
the cells of cartilages and vegetables, as corresponding with each
other, and as realizations of that common principle. This was the
more probable, as many points of agreement in the progress of development of these cells were already known.

*　*　*

Section III.

Review of the Previous Researches--The Formative
Process of Cells--The Cell Theory.

The two foregoing sections of this work have been devoted to
a detailed investigation of the formation of the different tissues
from cells, to the mode in which these cells are developed, and to
a comparison of the different cells with one another. We must now
lay aside detail, take a more extended view of these researches,
and grasp the subject in its more intimate relations. The principal object of our investigation was to prove the accordance of
the elementary parts of animals with the cells of plants. But the
expression "plant-like life" (pflanzen-ähnliches Leben) is so
ambiguous that it is received as almost synonymous with growth
without vessels; and it was, therefore, explained at page 6 that
in order to prove this accordance, the elementary particles of
animals and plants must be shown to be products of the same formative powers, because the phenomena attending their development are
similar; that all elementary particles of animals and plants are
formed upon a common principle. Having traced the formation of
the separate tissues, we can more readily comprehend the object
to be attained by this comparison of the different elementary
particles with one another, a subject on which we must dwell a
little, not only because it is the fundamental idea of these researches, but because all physiological deductions depend upon a
correct apprehension of this principle.

When organic nature, animals and plants, is regarded as a
Whole, in contradistinction to the inorganic kingdom, we do not
find that all organisms and all their separate organs are compact
masses, but that they are composed of innumerable small particles
of a definite form. These elementary particles, however, are subject to the most extraordinary diversity of figure, especially in
animals; in plants they are, for the most part or exclusively,
cells. This variety in the elementary parts seemed to hold some
relation to their more diversified physiological function in animals, so that it might be established as a principle, that every

diversity in the physiological signification of an organ requires
a difference in its elementary particles; and, on the contrary,
the similarity of two elementary particles seemed to justify the
conclusion that they were physiologically similar. It was natural
that among the very different forms presented by the elementary
particles, there should be some more or less alike, and that they
might be divided, according to their similarity of figure, into
fibres, which compose the great mass of the bodies of animals,
into cells, tubes, globules, &c. The division was, of course,
only one of natural history, not expressive of any physiological
idea, and just as a primitive muscular fibre, for example, might
seem to differ from one of areolar tissue, or all fibres from
cells, so would there be in like manner a difference, however
gradually marked between the different kinds of cells. It seemed
as if the organism arranged the molecules in the definite forms
exhibited by its different elementary particles, in the way required by its physiological function. It might be expected that
there would be a definite mode of development for each separate
kind of elementary structure, and that it would be similar in
those structures which were physiologically identical, and such a
mode of development was, indeed, already more or less perfectly
known with regard to muscular fibres, blood-corpuscles, the ovum
(see the Supplement), and epithelium-cells. The only process common to all of them, however, seemed to be the expansion of their
elementary particles after they had once assumed their proper
form. The manner in which their different elementary particles
were first formed appeared to vary very much. In muscular fibres
they were globules, which were placed together in rows, and coa-
lesced to form a fibre, whose growth proceeded in the direction
of its length. In the blood-corpuscles it was a globule, around
which a vesicle was formed, and continued to grow; in the case of
the ovum, it was a globule, around which a vesicle was developed
and continued to grow, and around this again a second vesicle was
formed.

The formative process of the cells of plants was clearly explained by the researches of Schleiden, and appeared to be the
same in all vegetable cells. So that when plants were regarded
as something special, as quite distinct from the animal kingdom,
one universal principle of development was observed in all the
elementary particles of the vegetable organism, and physiological
deductions might be drawn from it with regard to the independent
vitality of the individual cells of plants, &c. But when the
elementary particles of animals and plants were considered from a
common point, the vegetable cells seemed to be merely a separate
species, co-ordinate with the different species of animal cells,
just as the entire class of cells was co-ordinate with the fibres,
&c., and the uniform principle of development in vegetable cells
might be explained by the slight physiological difference of their
elementary particles.

The object, then, of the present investigation was to show,
that the mode in which the molecules composing the elementary
particles of organisms are combined does not vary according to the
physiological signification of those particles, but that they are
everywhere arranged according to the same laws; so that whether a

muscular fibre, a nerve-tube, an ovum, or a blood-corpuscle is to be formed, a corpuscle of a certain form, subject only to some modifications, a cell-nucleus, is universally generated in the first instance; around this corpuscle a cell is developed, and it is the changes which one or more of these cells undergo that determine the subsequent forms of the elementary particles; in short, that there is one common principle of development for all the elementary particles of organisms.

*   *   *

. . . It was, in fact, shown that the elementary parts of most tissues, when traced backwards from their state of complete development to their primary condition are only developments of cells, which so far as our observations, still incomplete, extend, seemed to be formed in a similar manner to the cells compared in the first section. As might be expected, according to this principle the cells, in their earliest stage, were almost always furnished with the characteristic nuclei, in some the pre-existence of this nucleus, and the formation of the cell around it was proved, and it was then that the cells began to undergo the various modifications, from which the diverse forms of the elementary parts of animals resulted. Thus the apparent difference in the mode of development of muscular fibres and blood-corpuscles, the former originating by the arrangement of globules in rows, the latter by the formation of a vesicle around a globule, was reconciled in the fact that muscular fibres are not elementary parts co-ordinate with blood-corpuscles, but that the globules composing muscular fibres at first correspond to the blood-corpuscles, and are like them, vesicles or cells, containing the characteristic cell-nucleus, which, like the nucleus of the blood-corpuscles, is probably formed before the cell. The elementary parts of all tissues are formed of cells in an analogous, though very diversified manner, so that it may be asserted, *that there is one universal principle of development for the elementary parts of organisms, however different, and that this principle is the formation of cells.* This is the chief result of the foregoing observations.

The same process of development and transformation of cells within a structureless substance is repeated in the formation of all the organs of an organism, as well as in the formation of new organisms; and the fundamental phenomenon attending the exertion of productive power in organic nature is accordingly as follows: *a structureless substance is present in the first instance, which lies either around or in the interior of cells already existing; and cells are formed in it in accordance with certain laws, which cells become developed in various ways into the elementary parts of organisms.*

The development of the proposition, that there exists one general principle for the formation of all organic productions, and that this principle is the formation of cells, as well as the conclusions which may be drawn from this proposition, may be comprised under the term *cell-theory*, using it in its more extended signification, whilst in a more limited sense, by theory of the cells we understand whatever may be inferred from this proposition with respect to the powers from which these phenomena result.

But though this principle, regarded as the direct result of these more or less complete observations, may be stated to be generally correct, it must not be concealed that there are some exceptions, or at least differences, which as yet remain unexplained. Such, for instance, is the splitting into fibres of the walls of the cells in the interior of the chorda dorsalis of osseous fishes, which was alluded to at page 14. Several observers have also drawn attention to the fibrous structure of the firm substance of some cartilages. In the costal cartilages of old persons for example, these fibres are very distinct. They do not, however, seem to be uniformly diffused throughout the cartilage, but to be scattered merely here and there. I have not observed them at all in new-born children. It appears as if the previously structureless cytoblastema in this instance became split into fibres; I have not, however, investigated the point accurately. Our observations also fail to supply us with any explanation of the formation of the medullary canaliculi in bones, and an analogy between their mode of origin and that of capillary vessels, was merely suggested hypothetically. The formation of bony lamellæ around these canaliculi, is also an instance of the cytoblastema assuming a distinct form. But we will return presently to an explanation of this phenomenon that is not altogether improbable. In many glands, as for instance, the kidneys of a young mammalian fœtus, the stratum of cells surrounding the cavity of the duct, is enclosed by an exceedingly delicate membrane, which appears to be an elementary structure, and not to be composed of areolar tissue. The origin of this membrane is not at all clear, although we may imagine various ways of reconciling it with the formative process of cells. (These gland-cylinders seem at first to have no free cavity, but to be quite filled with cells. In the kidneys of the embryos of pigs, I found many cells in the cylinders, which were so large as to occupy almost the entire thickness of the canal. In other cylinders, the cellular layer, which was subsequently to line their walls, was formed, but the cavity was filled with very pale transparent cells, which could be pressed out from the free end of the tube.)

These and similar phenomena may remain for a time unexplained. Although they merit the greatest attention and require further investigations, we may be allowed to leave them for a moment, for history shows that in the laying down of every general principle, there are almost always anomalies at first, which are subsequently cleared up.

The elementary particles of organisms, then, no longer lie side by side unconnectedly, like productions which are merely capable of classification in natural history, according to similarity of form; they are united by a common bond, the similarity of their formative principle, and they may be compared together and physiologically arranged in accordance with the various modifications under which that principle is exhibited. In the foregoing part of this work, we have treated of the tissues in accordance with this physiological arrangement, and have compared the different tissues with one another, proving thereby, that although different, but similarly formed, elementary parts may be grouped together in a natural-history arrangement, yet such a classifica-

420

tion does not necessarily admit of a conclusion with regard to
their physiological position, as based upon the laws of development. Thus, for example, the natural-history division, "cells,"
would, in a general sense, become a physiological arrangement
also, inasmuch as most of the elementary parts comprised under it
have the same principle of development; but yet it was necessary
to separate some from this division; as, for instance, the germinal vesicle, all hollow cell-nuclei, and cells with walls composed
of other elementary parts, although the germinal vesicle is a cell
in the natural-history sense of the term. It does not correspond
to an epithelium-cell, but to the nucleus of one. The difference
in the two modes of classification was still more remarkable in
respect to fibres. The mode of their origin is most varied, for,
as we saw, a fibre of areolar tissue is essentially different
from a muscular fibre; while, on the other hand, a whole primitive muscular fasciculus is identical in its mode of origin with
a nervous fibre, and so on. The existence of a common principle
of development for all the elementary parts of organic bodies
lays the foundation of a new section of general anatomy, to which
the term *philosophical* might be applied, having for its object--
firstly, to prove the general laws by which the elementary parts
of organisms are developed; and, secondly, to point out the different elementary parts in accordance with the general principle
of development, and to compare them with one another.

Survey of Cell-Life.

The foregoing investigation has conducted us to the principle
upon which the elementary parts of organized bodies are developed,
by tracing these elementary parts, from their perfected condition,
back to the earlier stages of development. Starting now from the
principle of development, we will reconstruct the elementary parts
as they appear in the matured state, so that we may be enabled to
take a comprehensive view of the laws which regulate the formation
of the elementary particles. We have, therefore, to consider--
1, the cytoblastema; 2, the laws by which new cells are generated
in the cytoblastema; 3, the formative process of the cells themselves; 4, the very various modes in which cells are developed
into the elementary parts of organisms.

Cytoblastema.--The cytoblastema, or the amorphous substance
in which new cells are to be formed, is found either contained
within cells already existing, or else between them in the form
of intercellular substance. The cytoblastema, which lies on the
outside of existing cells, is the only form of which we have to
treat at present, as the cell-contents form matter for subsequent
consideration. Its quantity varies exceedingly, sometimes there
is so little that it cannot be recognized with certainty between
the fully-developed cells, and can only be observed between those
most recently formed; for instance, in the second class of tissues; at other times there is so large a quantity present, that
the cells contained in it do not come into contact, as is the case
in most cartilages. The chemical and physical properties of the
cytoblastema are not the same in all parts. In cartilages it is
very consistent, and ranks among the most solid parts of the body;

in areolar tissue it is gelatinous; in blood quite fluid. These
physical distinctions imply also a chemical difference. The cytoblastema of cartilage become converted by boiling into gelatine,
which is not the case with the blood; and the mucus in which the
mucus-cells are formed differs from the cytoblastema of the cells
of blood and cartilage. The cytoblastema, external to the existing cells, appears to be subject to the same changes as the cell-
contents; in general it is a homogeneous substance; yet it may
become minutely granulous as the result of a chemical transformation, for instance, in areolar tissue and the cells of the shaft
of the feather, &c. As a general rule, it diminishes in quantity,
relatively with the development of the cells, though it seems that
in cartilages there may be even a relative increase of the cytoblastema proportionate to the growth of the tissue. The physiological relation which the cytoblastema holds to the cells may be
twofold: first, it must contain the material for the nutrition of
the cells; secondly, it must contain at least a part of what remains of this nutritive material after the cells have withdrawn
from it what they required for their growth. In animals, the
cytoblastema receives the fresh nutritive material from the blood-
vessels; in plants it passes chiefly through the elongated cells
and vascular fasciculi; there are, however, many plants which
consist of simple cells, so that there must also be a transmission of nutrient fluid through the simple cells; blood-vessels and
vascular fasciculi are, however, merely modifications of cells.

Laws of the generation of new cells in the cytoblastema.--
In every tissue, composed of a definite kind of cells, new cells
of the same kind are formed at those parts only where the fresh
nutrient material immediately penetrates the tissue. On this depends the distinction between organized or vascular, and unorga-
nized or non-vascular tissues. In the former, the nutritive
fluid, the liquor sanguinis, permeates by means of the vessels
the whole tissue, and therefore new cells originate throughout
its entire thickness. Non-vascular tissues, on the contrary,
such as the epidermis, receive the nutritive fluid only from the
tissue beneath; and new cells therefore originate only on their
under surface, that is, at the part where the tissue is in connexion with organized substance. So also in the earlier period
of the growth of cartilage, while it is yet without vessels new
cartilage-cells are formed around its surface only, or at least
in the neighbourhood of it, because the cartilage is connected
with the organized substance at that part, and the cytoblastema
penetrates from without. We can readily conceive this to be the
case, if we assume that a more concentrated cytoblastema is requisite for the formation of new cells than for the growth of those
already formed. . . . The difference in the growth of animals and
plants also rests upon the same law. In plants, the nutritive
fluid is not so equably distributed throughout the entire tissues,
as it is in the organized tissues of animals, but is conveyed in
isolated fasciculi of vessels, widely separated from one another,
more after the manner of bone. These fasciculi of vessels are
also observed to be surrounded with small (most likely younger)
cells, so that, in all probability, the formation of their new

cells also takes place around these vessels, as it does in bones around the medullary canaliculi. . . .

General phenomena of the formation of cells. Round corpuscles make their appearance after a certain time in the cytoblastema which, in the first instance, is structureless or minutely granulous. These bodies may either be cells in their earliest condition (and some may be recognized even at this stage), that is, hollow vesicles furnished with a peculiar structureless wall, cells without nuclei, or they may be cell-nuclei or the rudiments of cell-nuclei, round which cells will afterwards be formed. . . .

*   *   *

. . . The formative process of the nucleus may, accordingly, be conceived to be as follows: A nucleolus is first formed; around this a stratum of substance is deposited, which is usually minutely granulous, but not as yet sharply defined on the outside. As new molecules are constantly being deposited in this stratum between those already present, and as this takes place within a precise distance of the nucleolus only, the stratum becomes defined externally, and a cell-nucleus having a more or less sharp contour is formed. The nucleus grows by a continuous deposition of new molecules between those already existing, that is, by intussusception. If this go on equally throughout the entire thickness of the stratum, the nucleus may remain solid; but if it go on more vigorously in the external part, the latter will become more dense, and may become hardened into a membrane, and such are the hollow nuclei. The circumstance of the layer generally becoming more dense on its exterior, may be explained by the fact that the nutritive fluid is conveyed to it from the outside, and is therefore more concentrated in that situation. Now if the deposition of the new molecules between the particles of this membrane takes place in such a manner that more molecules are deposited between those particles which lie side by side upon its surface than there are between those which lie one beneath another in its thickness, the expansion of the membrane must proceed more vigorously than its increase in thickness, and therefore a constantly increasing space must be formed between it and the nucleolus, whereby the latter remains adherent to one side of its internal surface. . . .

When the nucleus has reached a certain stage of development, the cell is formed around it. The following appears to be the process by which this takes place. A stratum of substance, which differs from the cytoblastema, is deposited upon the exterior of the nucleus. . . . In the first instance this stratum is not sharply defined externally, but becomes so in consequence of the progressive deposition of new molecules. The stratum is more or less thick, sometimes homogeneous, sometimes granulous; the latter is most frequently the case in the thick strata which occur in the formation of the majority of animal cells. We cannot at this period distinguish a cell-cavity and cell-wall. The deposition of new molecules between those already existing proceeds, however, and is so effected that when the stratum is thin, the entire layer--and when it is thick, only the external portion--becomes gradually consolidated into a membrane. . . .

Immediately that the cell-membrane has become consolidated, its expansion proceeds as the result of the progressive reception of new molecules between the existing ones, that is to say, by virtue of a growth by intussusception, while at the same time it becomes separated from the cell-nucleus. We may therefore conclude that the deposition of the new molecules takes place more vigorously between those which lie side by side upon the surface of the membrane, than it does between those which lie one upon another in its thickness. The interspace between the cell-membrane and cell-nucleus is at the same time filled with fluid, and this constitutes the cell-contents. . . .

*　　*　　*

Theory of the Cells.

The whole of the foregoing investigation has been conducted with the object of exhibiting from observation alone the mode in which the elementary parts of organized bodies are formed. Theoretical views have been either entirely excluded, or where they were required (as in the foregoing retrospect of the cell-life), for the purpose of rendering facts more clear, or preventing subsequent repetitions, they have been so presented that it can be easily seen how much is observation and how much is argument. But a question inevitably arises as to the basis of all these phenomena; and an attempt to solve it will be more readily permitted us, since by making a marked separation between theory and observation the hypothetical may be clearly distinguished from that which is positive. An hypothesis is never prejudicial so long as we are conscious of the degree of reliance which may be placed upon it, and of the grounds on which it rests. Indeed it is advantageous, if not necessary for science, that when a certain series of phenomena is proved by observation, some provisional explanation should be conceived that will suit them as nearly as possible, even though it be in danger of being overthrown by subsequent observations; for it is only in this manner that we are rationally led to new discoveries, which either establish or refute the explanation. It is from this point of view I would beg that the following theory of organization may be regarded; for the inquiry into the source of development of the elementary parts of organisms is, in fact, identical with the theory of organized bodies.

The various opinions entertained with respect to the fundamental powers of an organized body may be reduced to two, which are essentially different from one another. The first is, that every organism originates with an inherent power, which models it into conformity with a predominant idea, arranging the molecules in the relation necessary for accomplishing certain purposes held forth by this idea. Here, therefore, that which arranges and combines the molecules is a power acting with a definite purpose. A power of this kind would be essentially different from all the powers of inorganic nature, because action goes on in the latter quite blindly. A certain impression is followed of necessity by a certain change of quality and quantity, without regard to any purpose. In this view, however, the fundamental power of the organism (or the soul, in the sense employed by Stahl) would, inasmuch as it works with a definite individual purpose, be much more nearly allied to the immaterial principle, endued with consciousness which we must admit operates in man.

The other view is, that the fundamental powers of organized bodies agree essentially with those of inorganic nature, that they work altogether blindly according to laws of necessity and irrespective of any purpose, that they are powers which are as much established with the existence of matter as the physical powers are. It might be assumed that the powers which form organized bodies do not appear at all in inorganic nature, because this or that particular combination of molecules, by which the powers are elicited, does not occur in inorganic nature, and yet they might not be essentially distinct from physical and chemical powers. It cannot, indeed, be denied that adaptation to a particular purpose, in some individuals even in a high degree, is characteristic of every organism; but, according to this view, the source of this adaptation does not depend upon each organism being developed by the operation of its own power in obedience to that purpose, but it originates as in inorganic nature, in the creation of the matter with its blind powers by a rational Being. We know, for instance, the powers which operate in our planetary system. They operate, like all physical powers, in accordance with blind laws of necessity, and yet is the planetary system remarkable for its adaptation to a purpose. The ground of this adaptation does not lie in the powers, but in Him, who has so constituted matter with its powers, that in blindly obeying its laws it produces a whole suited to fulfil an intended purpose. We may even assume that the planetary system has an individual adaptation to a purpose. Some external influence, such as a comet, may occasion disturbances of motion, without thereby bringing the whole into collision; derangements may occur on single planets, such as a high tide, &c., which are yet balanced entirely by physical laws. As respects their adaptation to a purpose, organized bodies differ from these in degree only; and by this second view we are just as little compelled to conclude that the fundamental powers of organization operate according to laws of adaptation to a purpose, as we are in inorganic nature.

The first view of the fundamental powers of organized bodies may be called the *teleological*, the second the *physical* view. An example will show at once, how important for physiology is the solution of the question as to which is to be followed. If, for instance, we define inflammation and suppuration to be the effort of the organism to remove a foreign body that has been introduced into it; or fever to be the effort of the organism to eliminate diseased matter, and both as the result of the "autocracy of the organism," then these explanations accord with the teleological view. For, since by these processes the obnoxious matter is actually removed, the process which effects them is one adapted to an end; and as the fundamental power of the organism operates in accordance with definite purposes, it may either set these processes in action primarily, or may also summon further powers of matter to its aid, always, however, remaining itself the "primum movens." On the other hand, according to the physical view, this is just as little an explanation as it would be to say, that the motion of the earth around the sun is an effort of the fundamental power of the planetary system to produce a change of seasons on the planets, or to say, that ebb and flood are the reaction of the organism of the earth upon the moon.

In physics, all those explanations which were suggested by a teleological view of nature, as "horror vacui," and the like, have long been discarded. But in animated nature, adaptation--individual adaptation--to a purpose is so prominently marked, that it is difficult to reject all teleological explanations. Meanwhile it must be remembered that those explanations, which explain at once all and nothing, can be but the last resources, when no other view can possibly be adopted; and there is no such necessity for admitting the teleological view in the case of organized bodies. The adaptation to a purpose which is characteristic of organized bodies differs only in degree from what is apparent also in the inorganic part of nature; and the explanation that organized bodies are developed, like all the phenomena of inorganic nature, by the operation of blind laws framed with the matter, cannot be rejected as impossible. Reason certainly requires some ground for such adaptation, but for her it is sufficient to assume that matter with the powers inherent in it owes its existence to a rational Being. Once established and preserved in their integrity, these powers may, in accordance with their immutable laws of blind necessity, very well produce combinations, which manifest, even in a high degree, individual adaptation to a purpose. If, however, rational power interpose after creation merely to sustain, and not as an immediately active agent, it may, so far as natural science is concerned, be entirely excluded from the consideration of the creation.

But the teleological view leads to further difficulties in the explanation, and especially with respect to generation. If we assume each organism to be formed by a power which acts according to a certain predominant idea, a portion of this power may certainly reside in the ovum during generation; but then we must ascribe to this subdivision of the original power, at the separation of the ovum from the body of the mother, the capability of producing an organism similar to that which the power, of which it is but a portion, produced: that is, we must assume that this power is infinitely divisible, and yet that each part may perform the same actions as the whole power. If, on the other hand, the power of organized bodies reside, like the physical powers, in matter as such, and be set free only by a certain combination of the molecules, as, for instance, electricity is set free by the combination of a zinc and copper plate, then also by the conjunction of molecules to form an ovum the power may be set free, by which the ovum is capable of appropriating to itself fresh molecules, and these newly-conjoined molecules again by this very mode of combination acquire the same power to assimilate fresh molecules. The first development of the many forms of organized bodies--the progressive formation of organic nature indicated by geology--is also much more difficult to understand according to the teleological than the physical view.

Another objection to the teleological view may be drawn from the foregoing investigation. The molecules, as we have seen, are not immediately combined in various ways, as the purpose of the organism requires, but the formation of the elementary parts of organic bodies is regulated by laws which are essentially the same for all elementary parts. One can see no reason why this should be the case, if each organism be endued with a special power to frame the parts according to the purpose which they have to fulfil: it might much rather be expected that the formative principle, although identical for organs physiologically the same, would yet in different tissues be correspondingly varied. This resemblance of the elementary parts has, in the instance of plants, already led to the conjecture that the cells are really the organisms, and that the whole plant is an aggregate of these organisms arranged according to certain laws. But since the elementary parts of animals bear exactly similar relations, the individuality of an entire animal would thus be lost; and yet precisely upon the individuality of the whole animal does the assumption rest, that it possesses a single fundamental power operating in accordance with a definite idea.

Meanwhile we cannot altogether lay aside teleological views if all phenomena are not clearly explicable by the physical view. It is, however, unnecessary to do so, because an explanation, according to the teleological view, is only admissible when the physical can be shown to be impossible. In any case it conduces much more to the object of science to strive, at least, to adopt the physical explanation. And I would repeat that, when speaking of a physical explanation of organic phenomena, it is not necessary to understand an explanation by known physical powers, such, for instance, as that universal refuge electricity, and the like; but an explanation by means of powers which operate like the physical powers, in accordance with strict laws of blind necessity, whether they be also to be found in inorganic nature or not.

We set out, therefore, with the supposition that an organized body is not produced by a fundamental power which is guided in its operation by a definite idea, but is developed, according to blind laws of necessity, by powers which, like those of inorganic nature, are established by the very existence of matter. As the elementary materials of organic nature are not different from those of the inorganic kingdom, the source of the organic phenomena can only reside in another combination of these materials, whether it be in a peculiar mode of union of the elementary atoms to form atoms of the second order, or in the arrangement of these conglomerate molecules when forming either the separate morphological elementary parts of organisms, or an entire organism. We have here to do with the latter question solely, whether the cause of organic phenomena lies in the whole organism, or in its separate elementary parts. If this question can be answered, a further inquiry still remains as to whether the organism or its elementary parts possess this power through the peculiar mode of combination of the conglomerate molecules, or through the mode in which the elementary atoms are united into conglomerate molecules.

We may, then, form the two following ideas of the cause of organic phenomena, such as growth, &c. First, that the cause resides in the totality of the organism. By the combination of the molecules into a systematic whole, such as the organism is in every stage of its development, a power is engendered, which enables such an organism to take up fresh material from without, and appropriate it either to the formation of new elementary parts, or to the growth of those already present. Here, therefore, the cause of the growth of the elementary parts resides in the totality of the organism. The other mode of explanation is, that growth does not ensue from a power resident in the entire organism, but that each separate elementary part is possessed of an independent power, an independent life, so to speak; in other words, the molecules in each separate elementary part are so combined as to set free a power by which it is capable of attracting new molecules, and so increasing, and the whole organism subsists only by means of the reciprocal action of the single elementary parts. So that here the single elementary parts only exert an active influence on nutrition, and totality of the organism may indeed be a condition, but is not in this view a cause.

In order to determine which of these two views is the correct one, we must summon to our aid the results of the previous investigation. We have seen that all organized bodies are composed of essentially similar parts, namely, of cells; that these cells are formed and grow in accordance with essentially similar laws; and, therefore, that these processes must, in every instance, be produced by the same powers. Now, if we find that some of these elementary parts, not differing from the others, are capable of separating themselves from the organism, and pursuing an independent growth, we may thence conclude that each of the other elementary parts, each cell, is already possessed of power to take up fresh molecules and grow; and that, therefore, every elementary part possesses a power of its own, an independent life, by means of which it would be enabled to develop itself independently, if the relations which it bore to external parts were but similar to those in which it stands in the organism. The ova of animals afford us examples of such independent cells, growing apart from the organism. It may, indeed, be said of the ova of higher animals, that after impregnation the ovum is essentially different from the other cells of the organism; that by impregnation there is something conveyed to the ovum, which is more to it than an external condition for vitality, more than nutrient matter; and that it might thereby have first received its peculiar vitality, and therefore that nothing can be inferred from it with respect to the other cells. But this fails in application to those classes which consist only of female individuals, as well as with the spores of the lower plants; and, besides, in the inferior plants any given cell may be separated from the plant, and then grow alone. So that here are whole plants consisting of cells, which can be positively proved to have independent vitality. Now, as all cells grow according to the same laws, and consequently the cause of growth cannot in one case lie in the cell, and in another in the whole organism; and since it may be further proved that some cells, which do not differ from the rest in their mode of growth, are developed independently, we must ascribe to all cells an independent vitality, that is, such combinations of molecules as occur in any single cell, are capable of setting free the power by which it is enabled to take up fresh molecules. The cause of nutrition and growth resides not in the organism as a whole, but in the separate elementary parts--the cells. The failure of growth in the case of any particular cell, when separated from an organized body, is as slight an objection to this theory, as it is an objection against the independent vitality of a bee, that it cannot continue long in existence after being separated from its swarm. The manifestation of the power which resides in the cell depends upon conditions to which it is subject only when in connexion with the whole (organism).

2. Johannes Müller and Physiology

*Schwann's views on vital phenomena may well be contrasted with those of his mentor, Johannes Müller.**

Prolegomena
on General Physiology.

Physiology is the science which treats of the properties of organic bodies, animal and vegetable, of the phenomena they present, and of the laws which govern their actions. Inorganic substances are the objects of other sciences,--physics and chemistry.

In entering upon the study of physiology, the first point to be ascertained regards the distinctions between these two great classes of bodies--the organic and the inorganic,--and the following questions suggest themselves for discussion:--Do organic and inorganic substances differ in their material composition? and if the phenomena presented by them are obviously different, are the forces or principles on which these phenomena depend, also different; or are the forces which give rise to the phenomena of the organic kingdom merely modifications of those which produce physical and chemical actions?

1. Of Organic Matter.

Nothing analogous to sensation, nutrition, or generation, is observed in inanimate nature, and nevertheless the matter which composes organic bodies consists of precisely the same elements as inorganic matter. In examining the composition of organic bodies, it is true, we meet with substances--the proximate principles, or *principes immédiats*--which are peculiar to them, and cannot be produced artificially by any chemical process; such are fibrin, albumen, gelatin, &c. But all these substances may be reduced by chemical analysis to the same simple elements which constitute minerals. Of these simple substances, all entering into the composition of inorganic bodies, there are fifty-two. In organic bodies there have been discovered but eighteen.

The elementary substances which are met with in plants are:--

---

*Johannes Müller, *Elements of General Physiology*, trans. by W. Baly (Philadelphia, 1843), pp. 13-17, 19-22, 26-28, 31, 33-35, 44.

```
 1. Carbon,      ⎫
 2. Oxygen,      ⎬ their most essential components.
 3. Hydrogen,    ⎭
 4. Nitrogen,      found less frequently.
 5. Phosphorus, ⎫  .  . principally in vegetable albumin and gums, especially
 6. Sulphur,    ⎭         in the tetradynamia, combined with nitrogen.
 7. Potassium,     .  . almost universally.
 8. Sodium,        .  . principally in marine plants.
 9. Calcium,       .  . almost universally.
10. Aluminium,     .  . rarely.
11. Silicium,
12. Magnesium,    occurring rarely.
13. Iron,       ⎫ .      . frequently.
14. Manganese,  ⎭
15. Chlorine.
16. Iodine,     ⎫ occurring in marine plants.
17. Bromine,    ⎭
```

The same substances, with the exception of aluminium, are met with likewise in the animal kingdom. Here sodium is more frequent, potassium less frequent than in plants; iodine and bromine occur in some marine animals.

In man and the higher animals the components are:--

```
 1. Oxygen,
 2. Hydrogen,
 3. Carbon,
 4. Nitrogen,
 5. Sulphur,      met with principally in the hair, albumen, and brain.
 6. Phosphorus,   .   .   .   .   . in the bones, teeth, and brain.
 7. Chlorine,   ⎫
 8. Fluorine,   ⎪
 9. Potassium,  ⎬  .   .   .   .   . in the teeth and bones.
10. Sodium,     ⎪
11. Calcium,    ⎪
12. Magnesium,  ⎭
13. Manganese,  ⎫ found in the hair.
14. Silicium,   ⎭
15. Iron,         .  . in the blood, pigmentum nigrum, and crystalline lens.
```

Copper also has been found by Meissner, and more recently by Sarzeau in plants. Beecher asserts that he has found gold also in the ashes of tamarinds.

The number of the elements which enter into their composition, constitutes, then, the first difference between organic and inorganic bodies. All the elementary substances found in the inorganic kingdom do not enter into the composition of organic bodies; and some are even inimical to their life.

The mode in which the elements are combined forms a second distinguishing character; and the peculiarity of organic matter depends probably on the following circumstances, first pointed out by Berzelius and Fourcroy:--

1. In mineral substances the elements are always combined in a binary manner; thus, two elementary substances unite together, and this binary compound unites again with another simple substance, or with another binary compound. For example, carbonate

of ammonia is constituted of carbon, oxygen, hydrogen, and nitrogen, combined as follows:--

Carbon,
Oxygen, } unite to form carbonic acid,
Hydrogen,
Nitrogen, } .   .   . ammonia,

which again unite to form carbonate of ammonia.

In minerals the elementary substances are never observed to
combine three or four together, so as to form a compound in which
each element is equally united with all the others. This, however,
is the case in organic bodies. Oxygen, hydrogen, carbon, and
nitrogen, the same elements which by binary combination formed
inorganic substances, unite together, each with all the others,
and form the peculiar proximate principles of organic beings.
These compounds are termed ternary, or quaternary, according to
the number of elements composing them. Vegetable mucus, starch,
and adipose matter are ternary compounds of oxygen, carbon, and
hydrogen: gum, albumen, fibrin, animal mucus, and resin are quaternary compounds, their fourth ingredient being nitrogen.

A doubt has recently been thrown upon this theory of the composition of organic substances; but there is still great probability in its favour, more particularly with reference to the higher
organic compounds, such as albumen, fibrin, &c. Though it is
certainly true that there are products formed from organic matter,
which have a binary constitution; such, for example, is alcohol,
which is a compound of ether and water.

It must at any rate, however, be admitted, that the mode in
which the ultimate elements are combined in organic bodies, as
well as the energies by which the combination is effected, are
very peculiar; for, although they may be reduced by analysis to
their ultimate elements, they cannot be regenerated by any chemical process. Berard, Proust, Dobereiner, and Hatchett believe,
indeed, that they have succeeded in producing organic compounds
by artificial processes; but their results have not been sufficiently confirmed. Woehler's experiments afford the only trustworthy instances of the artificial formation of these substances;
as in his procuring urea and oxalic acid artificially. Urea, however, can be scarcely considered as organic matter, being rather
an excretion than a component of the animal body. In the mode of
combination of its elements it has not perhaps the characteristic
properties of organic products.

2. Another essential distinction pointed out by Berzelius
is, that in organic products the combining proportions of their
elements do not observe a simple arithmetical ratio. Thus, for
example, among the large number of different fatty matters which
Chevreul has examined, many, according to his experiments, differ
only by fractional parts in the numerical proportions of their
atoms.

3. Organic bodies, animal and vegetable, consist chiefly of
combustible matter, which, except in the acids, is constituted of
carbon and hydrogen, combined with oxygen in quantity not sufficient to saturate the other elements.

Their tendency to decomposition.--The matter forming organic
bodies has a constant tendency to undergo decomposition; it is

only the continuance of life which preserves it: even during life the balance which maintains its elements in their peculiar combination, may be destroyed by the agency of certain simple inorganic bodies, or binary compounds of these, as we witness in the cauterisation of parts of the living body. At some period or other, this change necessarily ensued spontaneously in every living being; the state of influence which maintains the elements in their peculiar combinations becomes more and more feeble, and is, at length, no longer able to counteract the tendency of these elements to form binary compounds among themselves and with other simple substances in the atmosphere around them. Organic matter is thus annihilated, and with it the organized being of which it formed part. In ceasing to present the phenomena of life, it falls under the influence of the laws which govern the formation of chemical compounds; presenting the phenomena of fermentation and putrefaction, and giving origin to a foul smell when the substance contained much nitrogen. Chemical compounds, we know, are regulated by the intrinsic properties and the elective affinity of the substances uniting to form them; in organic bodies, on the contrary, the power which induces and maintains the combination of their elements does not consist in the intrinsic properties of these elements, but something else, which not only counteracts their affinities, but effects combinations conformably to laws of its own operation. Light, heat, and electricity, it is true, influence the compositions and decompositions going on in organic bodies; as they do those in inorganic bodies; but nothing justifies us in regarding, without further inquiry, any one of the imponderables,--heat, light, and electricity,--as the ultimate cause of vital actions.

After the cessation of life, organic substances always undergo decomposition, if the conditions necessary for the exertion of chemical affinity are present. The products of this decomposition are nitrogen and hydrogen, (which partly escape in a free state,) water, carbonic acid, carburetted hydrogen, olefiant gas, ammonia, cyanogen, prussic acid, phosphuretted hydrogen, and hydrosulphuric acid; while in some cases the elements reunite in different proportions so as to form a new organic compound, as in the production of sugar from starch in the saccharine fermentation. Sometimes from one organic substance two new compounds are generated, --one organic, the other inorganic,--as in vinous fermentation, during which carbonic acid and alcohol are formed from sugar. Decomposition does not commence in the bodies of animals and plants immediately after their death. This Gmelin explains, by supposing that the conditions necessary for the exertion of elective affinity are not then present, just as several inorganic substances require a certain temperature for their decomposition.

The conditions more or less necessary for the spontaneous decomposition of organic matter, are moisture, the access of atmospheric air, and a certain temperature. The first is absolutely necessary: organic substances when perfectly dry, do not undergo decomposition at the ordinary temperature of the atmosphere. Air is also often necessary, but not always: moist animal tissues suffer decomposition even when atmospheric air is excluded, (for example, by immersion in fluid mercury,) although the presence of air facilitates putrefaction in the highest degree, even more than oxygen alone. A certain temperature is always necessary.

The gaseous products of the decomposition of animal matter, and of the human body in particular, are carbonic acid, sometimes nitrogen, hydrogen, sulphuretted hydrogen, phosphuretted hydrogen, and ammonia. Acetic acid is also formed, and sometimes nitric acid. The solid matter that remains, consists of the carbonaceous substances, which decompose more slowly, and of the fixed mineral ingredients, earths, oxides, and salts, which with the carbonaceous substances form the soil (*humus*.) Several parts of the bodies of man and animals immersed in water, or buried in certain situations, even without the access of water, undergo a peculiar change in their being converted into a substance, named adipocire. Berzelius is of opinion, that the fibrin, albumen, and colouring matter of the blood, as well as the adipose matter, may be converted into this substance; while Gay Lussac and Chevreul state that the fat, which can be extracted from fresh animal textures by chemical processes, equals in quantity the adipocire generated by putrefaction in water, and they infer, therefore, that the fat merely is converted into adipocire, while the other tissues are destroyed.

*　　*　　*

The simplest forms in which organic matter appears, are now to be considered.

The first form is that of complete solution. There are many fluids containing organic matter, in which no visible molecules can be discovered; such, for instance, is the serum of blood until it is subjected to the influence of heat, galvanism, or different chemical agents. A part of the animal matter of the lymph and chyle is also in the state of solution.

The second form is the state of softness which the solid organised tissues present, and which is peculiar to organic beings. The tissues derive their properties of extensibility and flexibility from the water, which constitutes four-fifths of their weight; although they cannot be said to be wet, and do not impart their water to other substances so as to moisten them. This water, as Berzelius remarks, appears not to be chemically combined in them; for it is gradually given off by evaporation, and can be extracted at once by strong pressure between blotting-paper. When deprived of its water, animal matter becomes wholly insusceptible of vitality; except in the case of some of the lower animals, which, as well as some plants, revive when again moistened. According to Chevreul, pure water alone can reduce organized substances to this state of softness; although salt water, alcohol, ether, and oil are also imbibed by dry animal textures. Moist animal tissues, by virtue of their porosity, allow soluble matters, which come into contact with them, to be dissolved by the water which they contain, and which fills their pores; if the matters are already in solution, they are imparted by their solutions to the water of the tissues. Gaseous substances are taken up in the same way. Matters, also, which are contained in solution in one tissue, are rapidly imparted to other tissues which can dissolve them. The laws of the attraction of substances in solution, the laws governing the uniform distribution of miscible fluids, are therefore also applicable in the case of moist animal tissues.

Organic substances are, during life, never crystallised, and the excreted matters of animals which are crystallizable, viz. urea, lithic acid, and some fatty matters, are never found crystallized in the living tissues, except in their diseased states, although crystallized mineral substances are sometimes observed in the cells of plants.

The organic matter frequently appears in the form of microscopic molecules. These organic molecules are observed sometimes in fluids: such are the red particles of the blood which in man measure from $\frac{1}{3700}$ to $\frac{1}{4600}$ of an inch; the globules of the chyle which measure $\frac{1}{7199}$ of an inch, according to Prevost and Dumas; and those of the saliva, which measure $\frac{1}{2770}$ of an inch, according to Weber. The small bodies contained in the chyle, milk, and bile, are globular; those of the blood are, in mammalia, round, but flattened; and in birds, reptiles, amphibia, and fishes, oval as well as flattened. The blood corpuscules always consist of a nucleus inclosed in an outer envelope. The globules of coagulated albumen and fibrin are less distinct. Many of the tissues even of organized bodies, particularly of animals, appear to consist of molecules aggregated in the form of fibres, lamellæ, and membranes. These molecules are most distinct in the brain, and in the embryo, for instance, in the germinal membrane of the ovum; in other tissues, it is by no means certain that the appearance of molecules, observed under the microscope, is not an illusion produced merely by inequalities of the surface. The opaque part of the germinal membrane in the ovum of the bird is evidently composed of globules of considerable size, which are visible with a simple lens, and are perfectly similar to the globules of the yolk; but even the vessels which are distributed through the germinal membrane are, according to my observations, formed of an incomparably finer matter; as are also the central transparent part of the germinal membrane, the *area pellucida*, and the embryo itself. It appears, indeed, that the germinal membrane is formed by the attraction and aggregation of the globules of the yolk; but all the parts developed in this germinal membrane are produced by solution of these globules, and conversion of them into a matter in which no elementary particles can be distinctly recognised, and of which the molecules must, at any rate, be beyond comparison more minute than the globules of the yolk and germinal membrane.

The ultimate muscular fibre in the frog is from five to eight times more minute than the red particles of its blood, and more minute even than the nuclei of these red particles; the thickness of the muscular fibre of the frog and in Mammalia is nearly the same, while the size of the red particles of the blood in the two is very different. The diameter of the ultimate nervous fibre in Mammalia is, according to my observation, twice or three times less than that of their blood corpuscules, and is greater than that of the nuclei of the blood corpuscules. In the frog, the primitive nervous fibre has only $\frac{1}{8}$th the diameter of its blood corpuscules, and is therefore much smaller than the nucleus of the blood corpuscule. I have not been able to satisfy myself that the nervous fibrils consist of globules arranged in a linear form.

They certainly present successive inequalities, but these inequalities are not regular. In fine, this theory of the composition of
tissues by the aggregation of globules, which are supposed to be
more than $\frac{1}{2000}$ of a line in diameter, is rendered exceedingly improbable by the discovery of Ehrenberg, that monads, which themselves do not measure more than $\frac{1}{2000}$ of a line, have compound
organs. On account of the difficulty of distinguishing by the
microscope between inequalities and globules, this theory still
remains a mere hypothesis. At any rate, the organic molecules are
merely the most minute forms in which the compound organic matter
appears; they are not the atoms of the organic combination. The
hypothesis that all the tissues of the animal body are, in their
perfect state, composed of globules aggregated together in different forms, is now known to be wholly incorrect. The nervous
fibres, for instance, are delicate tubes of perfectly smooth and
homogeneous structure, enclosing a fine granular substance. The
cellular tissue, when perfectly developed, consists of smooth
cylindrical fibres. The interesting discovery has been made, however, that most probably all tissues are originally developed from
bodies of similar form, the primary or formative cells, as will
be explained hereafter.

   Source of organic matter.--It is only in organic bodies themselves that the peculiar force which animates them is observed.
It is manifested only in the organic compounds produced in these
bodies; the mere accidental coming together of the elementary components is not capable of producing organic matter. Fray, it is
true, asserts that he has observed the formation of microscopic
Infusoria in pure water; and Gruithuisen says, that he has seen a
gelatinous membrane form in infusions of granite, chalk, and mar-
ble, and infusory animalcules subsequently appear in this membrane. The fact observed by Retzius is also remarkable; namely,
that a peculiar kind of Conferva was generated in a solution of
muriate of baryta in distilled water, which had been kept half a
year in a bottle closed with a glass stopper. But, in these remarkable cases, it is certain that either the vessels, or the
water, contained organic matter, however small may have been the
quantity; and, according to the experiments of Schultze, the most
minute particles of organic matter in the form of dust are sufficient, under favourable circumstances, to produce the phenomena
which have been regarded as instances of equivocal generation.

   Even animals themselves have not the power of generating organic matter out of simple inorganic elements or binary compounds,
but grow by the assumption of matter already organized, whether
animal or vegetable;--they have the power of preserving organic
compounds and of converting one into another, but they cannot
produce them. Plants, on the contrary, seem to be able not merely
to assimilate the organic matter of animals and vegetables; but
also to generate it from simple elementary bodies and their compounds, such as carbonic acid and water, although the presence of
some organic matter in the soil in which plants grow, is necessary. It seems impossible to deny this production, by plants, of
organic matter from inorganic compounds; for, unless such were the
case, the nutriment on the earth would be constantly decreasing in
quantity, since animal and vegetable matters are being incessantly

converted by combustion, putrefaction, &c. into binary compounds.

The organic matter formed by plants, or that contained in plants and animals, and modified by them, is capable of again forming a part of other living beings, when tak·n into them and subjected to their vital forces. In this manner all the organic matter which is spread over the surface of the earth, originates in living beings. Death, that is, the extinction of the power which produces and maintains organic compounds, annihilates the individual; while the organic matter which formed this individual, as long as it is not reduced to binary compounds, is still capable of receiving new life, or, in other words, of nourishing other living bodies.

*   *   *

Origin of organic matter and of the organic force.--In the production of Infusoria there is no new formation of organic matter; the previous existence of organic beings is presupposed. Organic matter is never produced spontaneously. Plants alone seem to have the power of generating ternary or organic compounds from binary or inorganic compounds; while animals are nourished only by organic matter, which they cannot generate from binary compounds, and consequently their existence presupposes that of the vegetable kingdom. How organic beings were originally produced, and how organic matter became endowed with a force which is absolutely necessary to its formation and preservation, but which is manifested only in it, are questions beyond the compass of our experience and knowledge to determine. The difficulty is not removed by saying that the organic force has resided in the organic matter from eternity, as if organic force and organic matter were only different ways of regarding the same object: for, in fact, the organic or vital phenomena are presented only by a certain combination of the elements; and even organic matter, itself susceptible of life, is reduced to inorganic compounds as soon as the cause of the vital phenomena, namely, the vital force, ceases to exist in it. This problem, however, is not a subject of experimental physiology, but of philosophy. Conviction in philosophy and in natural science have entirely different bases; the first suggestion here, therefore, is, not to be led away from the field of rational experiment. We must be content to know that the forces which give life to organic bodies are peculiar, and then examine more closely their properties.

II. Of Organism and Life.

Organised beings are composed of a number of essential and mutually dependent dissimilar parts.--The manner in which their elements are combined, is not the only difference between organic and inorganic bodies; there is in living organic matter a principle constantly in action, the operations of which are in accordance with a rational plan, so that the individual parts which it creates in the body, are adapted to the design of the whole; and this it is which distinguishes organism. Kant says, "The cause of the particular mode of existence of each part of a living body resides in the whole, while in dead masses each part contains this cause within itself." This explains why a mere part separated

from an organised whole generally does not continue to live; why,
in fact, an organised body appears to be one and indivisible. And
since the different parts of an organised body are heterogeneous
members of one whole, and essential to its perfect state, the
trunk cannot live after the loss of one of these parts.

It is only in very simple animals or plants which possess a
certain number of similar parts, or where the dissimilar parts are
repeated in each successive segment of the individual, that the
body can be divided, and the two portions, each still possessing
all the essential parts of the whole, though in smaller number,
continue to live. Branches of plants separated from the trunk,
being planted, form new individuals. The different parts of
plants are so similar, that they are convertible one into another,
branches into roots, and stamens into petals. This is the case
also with some simple polypes. The experiments of Trembley,
Roesel, and others, prove that portions of a divided polype will
continue to grow until each half becomes a perfect animal. In the
same way some worms, as the Naïdes, in which each segment contains
nearly the same essential parts,--the intestine, nerves, and
blood-vessels,--have been observed to propagate by spontaneous
division. Bonnet states, that he has seen this new growth and reproduction in the portions of a divided earthworm: but this animal, when thus divided, could not continue to live; for neither
portion would contain all the parts essential to the whole.

In the higher animals, and in man, there are certain organs,
--that is, parts differing in their properties and functions,--
which cannot be removed without destruction of life, and of our
idea of the whole; and such organs also only occur singly, as
brain, spinal marrow, lungs, heart, and intestinal canal. Other
parts, on the contrary, which are not members essentially necessary to our idea of the whole being, or which are several in number, may be removed with impunity: no part, however, of one of the
higher animals can continue to live when separated from the body,
for no one part contains all the organs essential to the whole.
The ovum, the germ itself, alone possesses this power; for, at the
time of its separation from the parent animal, the vital force has
not formed in it the essential parts of the whole; and yet it becomes developed into a new integral being. There is, then, a
unity in the organism, to which its composition of dissimilar
parts is subordinate. From the facts above stated, however, it
appears that organised bodies are not absolutely indivisible; they
may, indeed, always be divided, and still retain their properties,
if each portion contains the essential heterogeneous members of
the whole, and in the generation even of the highest animals and
plants a division takes place.

Inorganic bodies are divisible in a much more extended sense,
without the parts losing the chemical properties of the whole;
they may be divided (to use the common expression) *ad infinitum*,--
that is, according to the atomic theory, into the ultimate atoms
which, on account of their minuteness, elude the senses; and in
chemical compounds, into molecules which are formed of the different component atoms, and which are likewise not recognisable by
the senses. To this character of inorganic bodies, however, crystals form an exception, since they cannot be reduced by division

to their ultimate particles without losing some of the properties.

* * *

The organic force is creative.--Hitherto, I have examined
merely that peculiarity of organised bodies which consists in
their being systems of dissimilar organs, the existence of each
of which has its source, not in itself, but in the entire system,
as Kant expressed it. *The organic force*, which resides in the
whole, and on which the existence of each part depends, has however also the property of generating from organic matter the individual organs necessary to the whole. Some have believed that
life,--the active phenomena of organised bodies,--is only the result of the harmony of the different parts--of the mutual action,
as it were, of the wheels of the machine,--and that death is the
consequence of a disturbance of this harmony. This reciprocal
action of parts on each other evidently exists; for respiration
in the lungs is the cause of the activity of the heart, and the
motion of the heart at every moment sends blood, prepared by
respiration, to the brain, which thus acquires the power of animating all other organs, and again gives occasion to the respiratory movements. The external impulse to the whole machinery is
the atmospheric air, in respiration. Any injury to one of the
principal moving powers in the mechanism, any considerable lesion
of the lungs, heart, or brain, may be the cause of death; hence
these organs have been named the *atria mortis*. But the harmonious
action of the essential parts of the individual subsists only by
the influence of a force, the operation of which is extended to
all parts of the body, which does not depend on any single organ,
and which exists before the harmonising parts, these being, in
fact, formed by it during the development of the embryo. The
germ is "potentially" the whole animal; during the development of
the germ, the essential parts which constitute the "actual" whole
are produced. The development of the separate parts out of the
simple mass is observable in the incubated egg. We are not to
suppose, however, that the germ is the miniature of the future
being with all its organs, as Bonnet and Haller believed; it is
merely "*potentially*" this being, with the specific vital force of
which it is endued, and which it becomes "*actually*" by development, and by the production of the organs essential to the active
state of the "*actual*" being. For the germ itself is formed merely
of amorphous matter, and a high magnifying power is not necessary
to distinguish the earliest rudiments of the separate organs; on
the contrary, these are from their first appearance distinct and
pretty large, but simple; so that the later-complicated state of
a particular organ can be seen to arise by transformation from
its simple rudiment. These remarks are now no longer mere opinions, but facts; and nothing is more distinct than the development
of glands from the intestinal tube, and of the intestinal tube
itself from a portion of the germinal membrane.

* * *

Nature of the organic force.--The unity resulting from the
combination of the organising force with organic matter could be

better conceived, if it were possible to prove that the organising
force and the phenomena of life are the result, manifestation, or
property of a certain combination of elements. The difference of
animate or inanimate organic matter would then consist, in that
state of combination of the elements, which is necessary to life,
having in the latter undergone some change. Reil has stated this
bold theory in his famous treatise on the "vital energy," which
some physiologists,--Rudolphi, for example,--regard as a masterpiece, on which the principles of physiology must be founded.

Reil refers organic phenomena to original difference in the
composition and form of organic bodies. Differences in composition and form are, according to his theory, the cause of all the
variety in organised bodies, and in their endowments. But if
these two principles be admitted, still the problem remains un-
solved; it may still be asked, how the elementary combination acquired its form, and how the form acquired its elementary combination. Into the composition of the organic matter of the living
body there must enter an unknown (according to Reil's theory,
subtile material) principle, or the organic matter must maintain
its properties by the operation of some unknown forces. Whether
this principle is to be regarded as an imponderable matter, or as
a force or energy, is just as uncertain as the same question is
in reference to several important phenomena in physics; physiology
in this case is not behind theother natural sciences, for the
properties of this principle, as displayed in the functions of the
nerves, are nearly as well known as those of light, caloric, and
electricity, in physics.

At all events, the mobility of the organic principle is certain: its motion is evident in innumerable vital phenomena. Parts
frozen, stiff, and deprived of sensation and motion, are observed
gradually to recover animation, which extends into them from the
borders of the living parts. This passage of the vital principle
from one part to another, is still more manifest on the removal
of pressure from a nerve, after that state has been produced in
which the limb is said to be "asleep." The fibrin effused in inflammation on the surface of an organ, is observed to become endowed with life and organisation. This same organic principle
exerts its influence even beyond the surface of an organ, as is
shown by the changes produced in the animal matter contained in
the vessels, for instance, in the lymph and chyle, which latter
fluid during its progress through the lacteals acquires new properties: by the coats of the blood-vessels, again, the organic
principle exerts an influence on the blood, in maintaining its
fluidity; for, out of the vessels the blood coagulates under almost all circumstances, unless it has undergone some chemical
change. Lastly, I may with Autenrieth adduce that property of
animal tissues, by virtue of which vital energy is at one time
withdrawn from them, and then again imparted to them, and is often
quickly accumulated in one organ. I do not think, with Hunter,
that it is the influence of the vital energy which in an unincu-
bated egg preserves the yolk and white from putrefaction; but it
is certain, that an extravasated, enclosed, or morbidly collected
fluid, even morbid animal matter, as pus, is preserved from putrefaction longer in the living body than out of it; which does not

arise merely from the exclusion of air, since, when the vital
powers are low, blood and pus rapidly undergo decomposition even
in the body. From all these facts the existence of a force which
is often rapid in its action, and is capable of extending from one
part to another, or of an imponderable matter, is evident; nevertheless we are by no means justified in regarding it as identical
with the known imponderable matters, or general physical forces,--
caloric, light, and electricity, a resemblance to which is disproved by a close investigation. The researches on the so-called
animal magnetism at first promised to throw some light on this
enigmatical principle, or imponderable matter. It was thought
that, by one person laying his hand upon, or passing it along the
surface of another, and by other procedures, remarkable effects
were produced, arising from the overflow of the animal magnetic
fluid; some indeed have imagined that by certain operations they
could produce accumulation of this hypothetic fluid. These tales,
however, are a lamentable tissue of falsehood, deception, and
credulity; and from them we have only learned how incapable most
medical men are of instituting an experimental investigation, how
little idea they have of a logical criticism, which in other natural sciences has become a universal method. There is no single
fact relating to this doctrine which is free from doubt, except
the certainty of endless deceptions; and in the practice of medicine there is also no fact which can be connected with these wonders, except the often repeated, but still unconfirmed accounts
of the cure of paralysis by investing the limbs with the bodies of
animals just killed, and the willingly credited fables of the
restoration of youth to the old and diseased, by their being in
the proximity and exposed to the exhalation of healthy children,
and *vice versâ*.

We have thus seen that organic bodies consist of matters
which present a peculiar combination of their component elements--
a combination of three, four, or more to form one compound, which
is observed only in organic bodies, and in them only during life.
Organised bodies moreover are constituted of organs,--that is, of
essential members of one whole,--each member having a separate
function, and each deriving its existence from the whole: and they
not merely consist of these organs, but by virtue of an innate
power they form them within themselves. Life, therefore, is not
simply the result of the harmony and reciprocal action of these
parts; but it is first manifested in a principle, or imponderable
matter which is in action in the substance of the germ, enters
into the composition of the matter of this germ, and imparts to
organic combinations properties which cease at death.

* * *

The power of generating organic from mineral compounds cannot, however, be entirely denied to plants; for, were it not for
this power, the vegetable and animal kingdoms would soon perish.
The unceasing destruction of organic bodies presupposes the formation by plants of new organic matter from binary compounds and
elementary substances.

Now, by the growth and propagation of organised bodies, the
organic force seems to be multiplied; for, from one being many

others are produced, and from these in their turn many more; while, on the other hand, with the death of organised bodies the organic force also seems to perish. But the organic force is not merely transmitted from one individual to another,--on the contrary, a plant, after producing yearly the germs of very many productive individuals, may still remain capable of the same production. Hence the source of the increase of the organic or vital force would likewise seem to lie in the organisation of new matter; and, if this be admitted, we must suppose that plants, while they form new organic matter from inorganic substances under the influence of light and caloric, are also endowed with the power of increasing the organic force from unknown external sources, and that animals also in their turn generate the organic force from their nutriment under the influence of the vital stimuli, and distribute it to the germs during propagation. Whether, during life, the organic force, as well as the organic matter, is constantly suffering destruction, is quite unknown. Thus much, however, seems certain, that, at the death of organic bodies, the vital force is resolved into its general natural causes, from which it appears to be generated anew by plants. If this increase of the vital principle in existing organised bodies from unknown sources in the external world be rejected, the apparently endless multiplication of the vital force in the processes of growth and propagation, must be regarded as a mere evolution of germs encased one within another, or it must be admitted that the division of the organic force which takes place in propagation does not weaken its intensity; a supposition which appears absurd. But the fact would still remain, that, by the death of organised bodies, organic force is constantly becoming inert, or resolved into its general physical causes.

3. C. Cagniard-Latour on Fermentation

The battle over cells and their function could be narrowed down to the specific function of certain cells. The process of fermentation had fascinated man for ages. In 1838, at the same time that Schleiden and Schwann were suggesting the cell theory, Baron Charles Cagniard-Latour published an article* on vinous fermentation in which he argued that fermentation was the result of the vital activity of cells of yeast.

Memoir on Vinous Fermentation

In the year VIII [1800], the class of physical and mathematical sciences of the Institute proposed the following question as the subject of a prize: What are the qualities which, in vegetable and animal matters, distinguish those which serve as a ferment from those which permit the action of fermentation? The

---

*C. Cagniard-Latour, "Mémoir sur la fermentation vineuse," *Annales de chimie et de physique*, 2nd Ser., 68 (1838), pp. 206-22. Translated by L. Pearce Williams.

prize was a medal of the value of one kilogram of gold, that is, a little more than three thousand francs; this prize was again proposed in the year X [1802] but it as well as those of all the other classes was then withdrawn in the year XII [1804] as the result of an unexpected event which deprived the institute of the funds which provided for these prizes.

The question of fermentation having remained without a solution can thus still be considered as interesting as it was at the time when it was the object of a competition. Therefore, believing that the competition was directed principally toward the most important fermentation, that is to say that which converts sugared material into alcohol and carbonic acid or, in a word, vinous fermentation, I began to follow out a series of researches on this point but proceeded differently than before by studying the phenomena of this action with the aid of a microscope.

Chemists know that if a sugar solution is mixed with fresh yeast from beer and the mixture is introduced into a flask which may even be closed, as for example a flask which has a Wolf's tube at the top, and if this flask is then heated to around twenty-five degrees centigrade, at the end of a few moments ordinarily there will begin a fermentation whose progress will continue to increase rapidly if the proportion of yeast is rather large. In the same circumstances, vinous fermentation does not take place even after a long time if the solution does not contain any yeast and if the sugar in the solution is pure.

It seemed proper, then, first of all to make a microscopic examination of the material which has the property of making the sugar ferment. This examination led me to recognize that the granules of which yeast is composed have a globular form, from which I concluded that they are probably organized beings.

No matter how closely I observed these globules, which are in general simple, transparent, spherical or very slightly oblong and almost without color, I never saw them perform any movements which might be considered as exterior signs of volition. On the other hand, the globules of yeast, as I will soon show, can make their appearance in a liquid where there has been previously no sign of vinous fermentation. Now, since these bodies are of a globular form, that is to say other than crystalline, are produced in a mucous liquid which, before undergoing transformation shows no sign of such globules and since these bodies appeared to have no locomotive motion, the microscopists would ordinarily consider them simple, as vegetables. . . .

One can, therefore, regard it as very probable that the globules of yeast are organized creatures and that they belong to the vegetable kingdom. These conjectures, moreover, as we shall see, seem to be confirmed by a number of observations which I shall point out a little later on.

But these plants, if one can give such a name to simple vesicules, are extremely small. Among the globules of diverse dimensions of which yeast is composed, the diameter of those which appear to have reached the final stage of their development does not ordinarily exceed a hundredth of a millimeter. They are, moreover, for the most part, smaller than this so that in a cubic millimeter of yeast in the form of a paste, there are probably at least a million of these globular individuals.

Assuming that the globules of yeast must have the faculty of reproducing themselves, I performed a number of experiments to check this. The first, which were done on a small scale failed, but this was not the case with two others that I did, one on a vat of porter must of about 10 hectoliters given to me by M. Leperdriel, proprietor of the English brewery at number 19 avenue de Neuilly and the other on a smaller quantity of similar must.

[From my observations] the principle results are: 1. that the globules of the yeast, rise to the surface by reason of the gas which they cause to be disengaged from the beer must and many of these globules remain entangled in the abundant foam produced by the fermentation. The globules are easily visible in the foam because of their characteristic lustre. 2. that these globules diminish in volume as they act upon the beer must and by this contraction they very probably emit some kind of seeds or reproductive bodies since it does not take long to discover new globules in the must, that is to say, nebulous or less visible globules although they are large enough to see with the microscope; these globules are not perceived right off and they offer this particularity that they appear to have the ability to reproduce themselves by budding or prolongations of their own tissue and are thus able to form multiple globules, that is to say, grouped by two by three and sometimes in greater number which as can be seen seems to confirm my hypothesis that the globules of yeast are organized and that they belong to the vegetable kingdom.

Having found it rather extraordinary that the globules of yeast which are mature are deprived of the power of regenerating themselves by extensions of their own tissue, while younger individuals enjoyed this faculty, I asked M. Turpin if he knew if an analogous difference had been observed in regard to other microscopic products made up of isolated globules but according to this Academician, it would seem that my observation has nothing new in it.

[I also] noticed upon examining the examples of porter which are carefully drawn from the barrel every hour that at the end of the first hour, after the yeast has been put in it, the must already contains double globules, that is to say, on each one can perceive a secondary and smaller globule; that a little later, this latter appears to have grown since on many couples the two globules had about the same size; that finally the fourth sample contained only double globules. I would add that to assure myself that these couples were composed of globules attached together and not merely close to one another, I knocked on the glass covering the globules which were placed under the microscope with a small pointed needle and these shocks, although they produced considerable agitation among the globules, in no case destroyed the connections; but it would seem that as these bodies become older they separate naturally since they are in general, simple, in commercial yeast, as I have already pointed out. This later separation can only be attributed to a vital action far from the idea it seems to me that the formation of the globules can be considered as a simple effect of crystallization or of albuminous coagulation since in the course of many of the fermentations that I have observed with beer yeast there existed cases where it was possible to distinguish a number of granules in certain of the globules and sometimes a round or oval spot located centrally or laterally which after the separation of which we are speaking could be presumed to be the scar or umbilical mark.

I have assumed that yeast, although containing nitrogen, belongs to the vegetable kingdom by basing myself principally on the fact that the globules of which it is composed do not have the power of locomotion. On this point, it has been objected that certain animals are deprived of similar motions and it would appear possible to assume that among the microscopic animalcules there must be analogous creatures and that perhaps the globules of ferment are of this kind. But it appears rather improbable that yeast belongs to the animal kingdom, properly speaking, when one considers: 1. that the substance when it acts on sugar loses its nitrogen according to the discovery made long ago by M. Thenard (*Annales de chimie*, year XI, p. 313), and 2., that all vegetables in their rudimentary state yield ammonia directly on distillation and, moreover, that nitrogenous matter can thus be eliminated entirely from them and leave behind only the vegetable tissue. . . .

I would add that having attentively followed the various changes that take place in the juice of white currants which have been filtered and then closed up in a flask tightly stoppered by a cork, I noticed that a few days after the juice was put into the flask there were a number of animalcules, even rather large, which appeared in the liquid but, no matter how active they were they soon began to languish when the vinous fermentation began and did not take long to disappear which again seems to rule out the idea that the globules of the ferment can be from the animal kingdom. . . .

The globules of the ferment are susceptible, it would seem, to very rapid development because a very little of must from the barrel, of which I spoke earlier, having been examined eight hours after being taken from the yeast already showed an increase of 300 times in the field of the microscope, that is, eighty to a hundred globules whereas, immediately after the introduction of the yeast there were only about eighteen.

Moreover after all the must that the porter barrel had been able to produce is collected it is found that this quantity was about seven times the weight of the yeast employed which agrees as we can see with the results of my microscopical examination.

According to the rapidity with which this multiplication takes place, it is reason to believe that the increase is principally the result of the reproduction of the globules of the yeast, that is to say, from the globules which find themselves in a liquid which contains an aliment which is proper to favor this reproduction. No brewer is ignorant of the fact that beer must ordinarily produce a weight of yeast greater than the ferment used to start the fermentation; but it has been supposed that this augmentation came about principally from a precipitation of vegetable albumin contained in the must and this explanation would seem to be supported by the fact that porter must and the must of strong beers in general produce more yeast than that of ordinary beer.

But although beer must is a medium in which the reproduction

of globules of the ferment can take place very easily, this is not
the same it would seem as simple sugar solutions since the yeast
in acting upon these solutions does not increase in weight and
moreover as is well known, it loses its activity.

Wishing to find the cause of this gradual impoverishment, I
examined with a microscope a yeast with which I had successively
caused two fermentations of sugar in closed vessels and I saw that
this yeast, which moreover was not really a very strong ferment,
contained a certain quantity of amorphous detritus no doubt coming
from disorganized globules and that the globules whose form could
still be distinguished had, in general, become dull and their con-
tours had altered. It would thus seem that if yeast, after having
acted on sugar, is less active although it has lost only part of
its weight, it is because it contains fewer healthy globules or
those endowed with vitality and from this one can conclude that
it is very probably by some effect of their vegetation that the
globules of the ferment destroy the equilibrium of the constituent
principles of the sugar and thus lead slowly to its conversion
into alcohol and carbonic acid. We should add that these globules
appear to be vegetables which do not perish from lack of water
since yeast dried in the air as is well known even after a long
time does not lose its power to be a good ferment.

M. Gay-Lussac, in the reprint of his memoir on fermentation,
remarks on the subject of vinous fermentation that it still appears to be one of the most mysterious operations of chemistry,
above all because it only takes place successively (*Annales de
chimie*, 1810). Now it can be judged how correct the reflection
of this scientist is, since according to my researches we are led
to believe that vinous fermentation results from a vegetative
phenomenon.

This same scientist shows by the results of diverse experiments that oxygen exercises a great influence on the development
of fermentation in certain liquids, notably grape juice but that
if oxygen is necessary for the commencement of fermentation it is
not so for its continuation. According to this discovery and
other considerations, among others that beer yeast can produce
the fermentation of sugared matter without the influence of oxygen, M. Gay-Lussac is of the opinion that the ferment must be
solid in a great number of substances, but in a state quite specifically different from that of beer yeast.

In order to gain some clue as to this difference, I performed
the following experiment whose results, as we shall see, seems to
prove that the opinion of this scientist is well founded.

I squeezed a grape enclosed in a bell jar filled with hydrogen gas and preserved its juice for 15 days over mercury. At the
end of this time, I examined a little of the sediment which had
fallen from the juice with a microscope and found it almost amorphous; but, in a similar examination, after I had introduced a
little oxygen into the bell jar and stimulated the vinous fermentation of the grape must, I found many globules in the sediment.
One is thus tempted to suspect, 1., that the seeds of these little
vegetables form a part of the sediment, 2., that they do not ger-
minate when they are enclosed in the skin of the grape, and 3.,
that this germination takes place as soon as they are exposed to

the influence of the oxygen gas and that it is by the beginning of this development that they become susceptible to act as beer yeast.

At this point, I should like to recall a fact that M. Thenard having filtered the juice of currants which had just been pressed out of the fruits, collected on the filter a substance which contained almost a sixth of its weight of ferment, although it had been submitted to a number of washings before being used in a sugar solution; thus according to this result and those of my microscopic observations on ferments, there is no longer room for doubt that the globules observed in the sediment of grape juice of which I spoke were formed, if not all, at least in part, from the elements contained in the material of the sediment.

According to what I have pointed out earlier on the reproduction of the globules of yeast in porter must, it seems that this can no longer be put in doubt. However a learned physicist has objected that, according to M. Milne-Edwards, one can produce a similar apparition of globules simply by heating the white of an egg which has been mixed with water. He added that it would then seem possible to suppose that the yeast was a nitrogenous matter formed by the coagulation of some vegetable-animal material contained in the beer must and that consequently the globules of which it is composed have no more real vital organization than those produced by the action of heat on egg white.

In order to clarify this point, I placed a mixture of 50 grams of water and one gram of egg white in a capsule on a sand bath heated to 90 degrees centigrade. When a part of the albumin was coagulated by the heat, I lifted out the capsule and, after cooling it, examined with a microscope a little of the very thin film which had formed on the surface of the liquid. I did find that this film contained a kind of globules; their diameter was, on the average, about 100th of a millimeter, but they all had, in general, some kind of crystalloid form and in none of them did I distinguish granules or the umbilical spot. It thus seems to me that the objection that I have just mentioned is not sufficient to authorize one to believe that the globules of the ferment are analogous to those of coagulated egg white.

Moreover, I allowed some porter must to ferment in a closed apparatus spontaneously, that is to say, without adding yeast. Now one would expect, according to M. Thenard's experiments upon which I shall remark in a moment, that this must, although well filtered, would produce a sediment of yeast by its fermentation. In examining this sediment with the microscope I found that it was composed of globules analogous to those of ordinary yeast. Now, this fermentation took place more slowly than that produced in breweries, and according to the hypothesis in which these globules should be formed by a sort of albuminous coagulation, some of them should have been very large or at least slightly crystalloid-- something like the globules of the coagulated egg white--but this did not happen. Moreover, it was found that in this sediment the globules are not generally of equal sizes as in ordinary yeast, which is again favorable to the supposition of some organization for it is clear that in a ferment produced in a long period of time the globules ought to be of different ages.

I performed the same experiments with a flask that I had previously filled with carbonic acid. The fermentation developed a little later, but nevertheless, the sediment obtained had about the same microscopic appearances.

It is known according to M. Thenard's experiments that the juice of ripe fruits and, in general, the fluids which undergo vinous fermentation, lay down sediments enjoying the same properties as yeast (*Annales de chimie*, year XI). It is also known that a solution of sugar in which some egg white has been mixed can undergo vinous fermentation and produce a sediment of yeast, given a temperature of about 35 degrees over a certain period of time.

From these analogies, I thought that similar sediments ought to show the same traces of organization under the microscope as those of beer yeast; I therefore performed a number of fermentations in closed vessels, namely on the juice of currants, grape juice, and juice of the prune, as well as on a solution of sugar in which egg white had been mixed, liquids which had been filtered before being introduced into their respective flasks. By examining the sediments obtained, I recognized that each of these sediments was composed in large part of globules analogous to those of beer yeast, results which, as can be seen, are in a remarkable accord with the observation of M. Thenard.

Everyone who is continually occupied with fermentation on a large scale, namely brewers and the distillers of grain alcohol, know that in spite of all the care that they bring to their operations, the results of them are extremely variable. These irregularities, themselves, would seem to be in favor of the hypothesis that vinous fermentation is brought about by bodies endowed with life because who does not know how many ways such bodies can be affected.

It is also known by M. Thilorier's work that carbonic acid can become solid by a certain degree of cooling and that in this state of condensation its temperature is very much lower than that which causes mercury to freeze. This ingenious and clever experimenter was kind enough to put at my disposal a certain amount of his solidified acid and I mixed this with dry yeast reduced to a very fine powder. This yeast, although it had thus been exposed to an extremely low temperature, that is to say of -60 degrees centigrade or more below zero, was no less proper to decompose sugar again as actively as the similar yeast powder which had not been submitted to this refrigeration.

A little while ago I had some fresh yeast frozen by a temperature of 5 degrees centigrade with a certain quantity of water and I again found that after this refrigeration it could still act on solutions of sugar as did ordinary fresh yeast.

Conclusion

I have looked at the principal works which treat vinous fermentation and in none of them have I seen that the microscope has been used to study the phenomena upon which it depends.

This essay, as one can judge by the researches which I have just mentioned, will be useful since it has furnished a number of new observations from which the principal results that can be drawn are: 1, that beer yeast, this ferment which is in such use and which, for this reason, should be examined very closely, is a mass of little globular bodies capable of reproducing themselves, and thus organized beings, and not a simple organic or chemical substance as has been supposed; 2, that these bodies seem to belong to the vegetable kingdom and regenerate themselves in two different ways, and 3, that they seem to act on a solution of sugar only so long as they are in the vital state: from which it can be concluded that it is very probably by some effect of their vegetation that they are able to disengage carbon dioxide from this solution and convert the solution into a spirituous liquor. I would like to remark, further, that yeast, considered as an organized matter, perhaps merits the attention of physiologists in this sense, 1, that it can be born and develop in certain circumstances with great rapidity even in the middle of carbonic acid as in the brewers' barrels; 2, that its mode of reproduction presents particularities of a kind which have not been observed in other microscopical products composed of isolated globules and 3, that it does not die by a very considerable refrigeration nor by deprivation of water.

Finally, to conclude, I would add that the question formerly proposed by the Institute appears to be resolved now according to the results that I have just reported and diverse others that I have given out during the years 1835 and 1836 to the Philomathic Society since they lead to the conclusion that in general ferments, or at least those which produce vinous fermentation by means of yeast, are composed of organized bodies which are microscopically very simple and that the matter upon which they act to create fermentation are substances which are purely chemical since they are, as everyone knows, sugar and the compounds that resemble it.

4. Liebig and Wöhler on Vinous Fermentation

Cagniard-Latour's paper was not well received in certain quarters. In many ways it represented a serious challenge to a whole movement in science which had been striving to get away from the influence of vital forces or of living tissues when dealing with what seemed to be clear chemical problems. Cagniard-Latour was not, necessarily, a vitalist but to reduce fermentation to the action of living organisms smacked of vitalism and his article and views were immediately attacked. The leading opponent of such views was Justus Liebig (1803-73) in Germany and it was Liebig, together with his colleague, Friedrich Wöhler (1800-1882) who leapt into the breach that Cagniard-Latour's paper seemed to open in the wall of materialist chemistry.

Their attack was an oblique one and was intended to ridicule rather than to refute the new position on fermentation. In an anonymous article* in Liebig's Annalen der Pharmacie, *Liebig and Wöhler parodied Cagniard-Latour's paper in rather vulgar terms.*

---

*(Anonymous), "The Secret of Vinous Fermentation Revealed," *Annalen der Pharmacie*, 29 (1839), pp. 100-104. Translated by L. Pearce Williams.

The Secret of Spirituous Fermentation Revealed
[J. Liebig & F. Wöhler]

I am on the point of developing a new theory of vinous fermentation. I have been led to the clue to this hitherto incomprehensible decomposition in the simplest way in the world and consider it completely solved. This discovery also proves how simple are the means which Nature utilizes in order to produce the most marvelous phenomena. I owe it to the use of an excellent microscope which was made according to the specifications of the famous Ehrenberg and exported by the great instrument maker Pistorius.

Powdered brewer's yeast mixed with water is seen under this instrument to dissolve into infinitely small globules which are hardly 1/300 of a line in diameter, and into fine threads which are unmistakably a kind of albumin. When these globules are put into sugar water, it is observed that they are really the eggs of animals; they swell up, burst, and there then develops little animals which multiply with unbelievable speed and in a most unusual way. The form of these animals is unlike that of the 600 kinds described up to this time. They have the form of a Beindorf distilling flask (without the cooling coil). The nose is a kind of siphon covered with fine bristles of 1/200 line in diameter; no teeth or eyes could be detected. What stands out are a stomach, intestine, anus (a pink colored point) and the organs for the excretion of urine. From the moment when they burst out of the egg, they can be seen to imbibe the sugar from the solution which soon arrives in the stomach. In a moment it is digested; this digestion is detectable by the immediate and inevitable evacuation of excrement. In a word, these animals gobble sugar, discharge alcohol from their intestinal canal and carbon dioxide from their urinary organ. The bladder, when full, has the shape of a Champagne bottle, when empty, that of a small button. Another process can also be observed. In the animals' insides a gas bubble forms which increases in size some ten times and then, by means of a screw-shaped tube which the animal controls by a circular shaped muscle, the bubble is finally passed out. I think it extremely likely that the process here is the same as when electricity is conducted through a metal wire; as everyone knows, according to the most famous physicists, magnetism is created in this case and, instead of following the shortest path, if not hindered, (for this is a natural law) it takes a spiral path. I consider this as a proof that, as Döbereiner and Schweigger have shown, Magnetism and Electricity equally play a role in fermentation. This observation here proves the justice of their rather weakly supported views.

Without pursuing these hypotheses further, we can notice that a specifically light fluid pours upwards unceasingly from the anus of these animals, and from their huge genitalia there spurts, in a very rapid burst, a stream of carbon dioxide.

When the solution is heated to the boiling point, the fermentation ceases since the animals will be killed at high temperatures. If sulphuric acid, too much alcohol, a mineral acid or pyroligneous acid are added, they will also be killed and the fermentation will thereby be interrupted. If the amount of water in the solution is too small, i.e., if the sugar concentration is too high, then, as is known, fermentation doesn't start. This occurs because these little beings cannot excrete, or can excrete only with great difficulty in dense fluids and they therefore die of indigestion because of the failure of this movement. In order to give an idea of the digestive strength of these animals, I refer to Thenard's results in which he found that 3 parts of beer yeast (in a dry state) was able to decompose 200 parts of sugar into alcohol. Thus the weight of the excrement voided by these animals in 18 hours is almost 66 times the weight of the animals themselves.

The effect of etheric mustard oil on these animals is noteworthy. If a mustard seed is put into the fermenting liquid, their vitality is lessened and, after a moment, they appear lifeless. But, with the access of air, after a few hours they recover and the fermentation begins again with its earlier vigor. This action is very similar to that with oil of anise, whose fumes are known to knock out fleas, until the evaporation of the oil stops it.

I have noticed that solanin acts as an emetic on these infusoria. When solanin is put into a sugar solution undergoing fermentation, the animals all draw together vertically and a fluid, which is undoubtedly the fusel oil from potatoes, flows from their siphons. The Fusel Oil of whiskey and brandy appear differently as a kind of sweat through the hide. There now remains only one important question to resolve--namely, what these animals, with their incomparable hunger for sugar, really assimilate to keep their bodies going. This is also now clear. The above-mentioned fine threads of albumen which are produced by the nitrogen containing part of the animals, are absorbed and assimilated with a bite of sugar.

Most extraordinary is the chemical composition of these animals. I took a sample of 0.4375 grams (containing 50,000 million in number) and subjected it to ordinary analysis with copper oxide. The tests showed that they contain the four elements in the same proportions as is found (by Müller) in albumen, ether and carbon dioxide.

This does not really remove all the difficulties involved in their digestive processes, for there still remains the mystery of how the yeast leads to fermentation. As soon as the animals can find no more sugar, they digest themselves. . . . Everything is digested, down to the egg which passes undigested through the intestine and one finally ends up with yeast capable of initiating fermentation. This is the seed of the animals which remains. The final cadavers of the animals are decomposed in ammonia with a bit of acetic acid. The weight of the eggs at the end of the fermentation is understandably a little less than at the beginning.

The numerical results, as well as illustrations of the form of these animals will follow in a special paper.

5. *It was work on fermentation that led Louis Pasteur (1822-1895)
    to the Germ Theory of disease. Pasteur was trained as a
    chemist but was led, early in his career, to study fermenta-
    tion in beer and wine. He knew Cagniard-Latour's work and
    appreciated its importance. In an article on the Germ Theory,
    he recalls the path he took in his epoch-making researches.**

The Germ Theory and Its Application to Medicine and Surgery
by Louis Pasteur with the collaboration of MM. Joubert and
Chamberland.

All the sciences gain by supporting one another. When, following my first communications on fermentations in 1857-1858, it
was shown that ferments, properly speaking, are living beings;
that the germs of microscopic organisms are abundant on the surface of all objects in the atmosphere and in water; that the
hypothesis of spontaneous generation is chimerical; that wines,
beer, vinegar, blood, urine and all the fluids of the animal
economy suffer none of their common changes when in contact with
pure air, medicine and surgery were the recipients of new clear
ideas. A French doctor, Dr. Davaine, was the first to apply
these principles to medicine in 1863.

Our researches in the last year have not cleared up the
etiology of putrefaction or septicemia as much as those of anthrax. We have rendered it very probable that septicemia is
caused by the presence and the multiplication of a microscopic
organism, but the rigorous demonstration of this important conclusion has not yet been accomplished. In order to affirm experimentally that a microscopic organism is really the agent of sickness and of contagion, I see no other way in the actual state of
our science than to submit the *microbe* (the new and happy expression proposed by M. Sedillot) to the method of successive cultures
outside the living animal. In twelve such cultures, each only of
a volume of ten cubic centimeters, the original droplet is diluted
as much as if it had been placed in a volume of liquid equal to
the total volume of the earth. It is precisely this kind of proof
to which M. Joubert and I have submitted the anthrax bacterium.
After having cultivated it a large number of times in a liquid
deprived of all virulence, with each culture having as its seed a
droplet of the preceding culture, we have shown that the product
of the last culture was capable of multiplying itself and of
acting in the bodies of animals by giving them anthrax with all
the symptoms of this disease.

This is the proof which we consider to be beyond question--
that *anthrax is an illness caused by bacteria.*

As for the bacteria of septicemia, our researches have not
brought the same conviction. It was in order to fill in this gap
that we undertook these experiments. To achieve this aim we
attempted the culture of the septic bacteria taken from an animal

---

*Louis Pasteur, *Oeuvres de Pasteur*, Vol. 6, Paris, 1933. "The
Germ Theory and Its Application to Medicine and Surgery," trans.
by L. Pearce Williams. Pp. 112-122, 124.

which had died of septicemia. It is worth remarking that all our first experiments failed in spite of the variety of the culture media which we used: urine, yeast water, meat bouillon, etc.

Our liquids did not remain sterile, but most often we obtained a microscopic organism which had no relation to the septic bacillus, having the very common form of a rosary of small spherical beads of an extreme tenuity and without any kind of virulence. It was, it seemed to us, an impurity sowed at the same time as the septic bacillus in our cultures and of which the germ passed into the intestines, which are always inflamed and distended in septicemic animals, and then into the abdominal serum from which we originally took the culture of septic bacilli. If this hypothesis of the impurity of our cultures is true, we should be able to obtain the pure septic bacilli by looking for it in the blood of the heart of an animal recently dead of septicemia. This is what happened, but a new difficulty arose. All our cultures became sterile. Moreover, this sterility was joined to the loss of the virulence of the inoculation in the liquid in the culture.

We then conceived that the septic bacilli must be an organism which was exclusively anaerobic and that the sterility of our inoculated liquids must be the result of the bacilli being killed by the oxygen of the air which is dissolved in these liquids. The Academy may perhaps remember that I have stated similar facts on the bacilli of butyric fermentation which not only live without air but which are killed by the air.

It was thus necessary to cultivate the septic bacilli either in a vacuum or in the presence of inert gases such as carbon dioxide. The facts answered to our expectations: the septic bacilli developed easily in a perfect vacuum and with an equal facility in the presence of pure carbon dioxide.

These results had a necessary corollary. In exposing a liquid filled with septic bacilli to the contact of pure air, one should kill the bacilli and suppress all virulence. This is exactly what happens. If one places a few drops of septic serum, spread out in a very thin film in a tube lying horizontally, then in less than half a day the liquid will become absolutely inoffensive even if it were at such a virulent point at the beginning that it would bring about death by inoculation with a very small fraction of a drop.

There's more than this: all the bacilli which fill the liquid completely in the form of moving threads will be destroyed and disappear. After the action of the air, all that is found are fine, amorphous granulations, which cannot be used to make a culture and will not communicate any illness whatsoever. One might say that the air burns up the bacilli.

If it is terrifying to think that life might be at the mercy of the multiplication of these infinitely small creatures, it is just as consoling to hope that science will not remain forever impotent before such enemies when one can see . . . that simple contact with the air is sometimes sufficient to destroy them.

But if oxygen destroys the bacilli, how can septicemia exist since atmospheric air is present everywhere? How can blood, exposed to the contact of the air, become septic from the dust contained in the air?

Everything is hidden, obscure, and open to discussion when the cause of phenomena is ignored; everything is clear when one possesses it. What we have said is only true of a septic liquid .filled with adult bacilli dividing by fission; things are different when the bacilli are transformed into their germs, that is to say, into shining corpuscles described and illustrated for the first time in my "Studies on the disease of silkworms" which dealt with the bacilli of worms dead from the illness called *flacherie*. Only the adult bacilli disappear and are burned and lose their virulence in contact with the air; the germ corpuscles in these conditions are preserved, always ready for new cultures and new inoculations.

All this does not yet resolve the difficulty of knowing how septic germs can exist on the surface of objects, floating in the air and in water. Where do these corpuscles arise? Well! Nothing is easier than the production of these germs in spite of the presence of air in contact with septic liquids.

Let one take from the abdominal serum filled with septic bacilli all those which are in the process of generating by division and then expose this liquid to the contact of the air as we have just shown, with the only precaution, however, of giving it a certain thickness if only one centimeter, and in a few hours here is the strange phenomenon which one witnesses. In the upper layers, the oxygen is absorbed which becomes manifest by the change in the color of the liquid. There the bacilli die and disappear. In the deeper layers, on the contrary, at the bottom of this centimeter of depth of septic liquid that we have supposed to be in our experiment, the bacilli, protected against the action of oxygen by their brothers who perish above them, continue to multiply by division; then, little by little, they pass to the state of germ corpuscles with the resorption of the rest of the body of the thread-like bacillus. Then, in place of moving threads of all sizes, whose length often surpasses the field of the microscope, there is only to be seen a dust of lustrous points, isolated or enveloped with an amorphous gangue, which is barely visible. And there is formed a latent life of germs, no longer fearing the destructive action of the oxygen; there, I say, is the septic powder and we are armed now with the knowledge which just before seemed to us so obscure. We can understand the infection of putrescible liquids by the dust of the atmosphere; we can understand the permanence of putrid maladies at the surface of the earth.

I hope the Academy will permit me to bring out one of the principal theoretical consequences of these curious results before abandoning them. At the beginning of these researches, since they have really just started, although already a new world has revealed itself, what should one ask with the greatest insistence? It is the peremptory proof that there exist transmissible contagious infectious diseases whose causes reside essentially and uniquely in the presence of microscopic organisms. It is the proof that, for a certain number of sicknesses, one must forever abandon the idea of spontaneous virulence--the idea of contagion and of infectious elements being born suddenly in the bodies of men and of animals and ready to give rise to those illnesses

which will then propagate themselves under forms which are identical to them. These are all opinions that are fatal to medical
progress and that have encouraged the gratuitous hypotheses of
spontaneous generation, of albuminoid material ferments, of hemi-
organism, of archbiosis, and all the other conceptions which have
no foundation in observation.

What one ought to look for in these cases is the proof
that alongside our bacilli there is not any independent virulence
which is unique to the liquid or solid matters and that finally
that the bacilli are not simply an epiphenomenon of the sickness
of which they are the necessary companion. Now what do we see in
the results that I have just made known? We see a septic liquid,
taken at a certain moment, such that the bacilli are not yet
transformed into germs, lose all virulence by simple contact with
the air, and conserve, on the contrary, this virulence when exposed to the air if only the condition has been met that it has a
certain thickness during a few hours. In the first case, after
the loss of virulence with contact with the air, the liquid is
incapable of any restoration of virulence by means of culture; but
in the second case, it retains and can propagate once again this
virulence even after it has been exposed to the contact of the
air. It is thus not possible to sustain the argument that beyond
and alongside the adult bacilli or their germs, there is a virulent matter which loses its virulence at the same time that the
adult bacillus dies because this supposed matter ought equally,
then, to lose its virulence when the bacilli are transformed into
germs and are exposed to the contact of the air. Since, in this
case, the virulence persists, this can only be the result of the
exclusive presence of the germ corpuscles. There is only one
hypothesis possible for the existence of a virulent matter in the
soluble state; it is that such a matter, which would be in insufficient quantity to kill in our experiments of inoculation, would
immediately be furnished by the bacilli themselves while they are
in the process of propagation in the body of the living animal.
But what difference does this make since this hypothesis supposes
the earlier and necessary existence of the bacilli.

This supposition has in fact been made and in order to confirm it an innumerable number of works have been undertaken on
the other side of the Rhine.

Dr. Panum, today professor at Copenhagen, and following him
a large number of German physiologists stopped at the idea that
putrefaction develops in matters which are submitted to a double
poison that neither cooking nor a repeated distillation over many
hours can affect in its properties, no more than chemical reactions of this kind are capable of suppressing the effects of mor-
phine or of strychnine. This chemical poison is called by the
name of Sepsine by Dr. Burgmann and those who follow him along
this route. We have looked for this poison in the muscles and in
the liquids of the bodies of animals dead of septicemia; we have
not, up to now, discovered it and we believe that we have the
explanation of the facts observed by the German physiologists.
The details into which it would be necessary to enter to show
this clearly would take me far beyond the limits of this communication.

I have often pointed out before this Academy that there exist microscopic ferment beings with diverse physiological properties from the *micoderma aceti* which are essentially aerobic, to beer yeast which is both aerobic and anaerobic and I have often insisted on the point that life, which manifests itself even during a very short time without having to utilize free oxygen gas, immediately brings about the phenomena of fermentation.

In the bacilli of septicemia we meet a microbe which is exclusively anaerobic since it can only develop in a vacuum or in the presence of inert gases. Therefore it ought to be a ferment. This is exactly the case. While the multiplication of the bacillus goes on by division, its life is accompanied by a disengagement of carbon dioxide, of hydrogen gas, of a little nitrogen and very small quantities of putrid gases. These gases only cease to be produced at the moment when the bacillus transforms itself into germ corpuscles.

The gaseous disengagement during the life of the bacillus explains the very rapid swelling of animals dead of septicemia and the enphysematic state of conjunctive tissue, particularly at certain points of the body, the groin and the armpit, where inflammation is sometimes excessive.

I ought to add immediately that all of the bacilli are not anaerobic; that one of the most commonly found frequently at the surface of infusions of organic vegetable matter exposed to the air, is a very supple bacillus very rapid in its movements and exclusively aerobic. It absorbs oxygen and exhales carbon dioxide in almost equal volumes, thus recalling the physiology of the anthrax bacilli. Pressed by time, I would only like to point out this bacillus in passing since it has given us the occasion for a number of observations which are well worthy of notice. This bacillus is inoffensive. Introduced under the skin, it only causes local disorders of little importance. In comparing this innocuousness to the virulence of the septic bacillus, it seems logical to believe that the different modes of life for these two bacilli, as one is aerobic and the other anaerobic, explains the opposition of their actions on the body. But the effect of the anthrax bacillus which is also essentially aerobic and nevertheless terrible does not permit such a supposition to be upheld. If this aerobic bacillus is inoffensive it is because it cannot live at the temperature of the animal body. Around 38° its movements and reproduction are suspended and, once inoculated, it disappears under the skin as though it were digested so to speak.

Scientific novelties often struggle against prejudices. What difference does it make, some people have cried, your bacteria and your bacilli! Don't we see infinitely small beings multiplying everywhere? Do we not see them in abundance on the linen of bandages, and even covering wounds which are in process of healing? Can there be the least danger from them? But what infinitely small beings do you speak of, I will answer? We have just shown that alongside the most dangerous bacilli there exist innocent ones and certainly these latter are far from being the only microbes which are deprived of all virulence.

Conducted by the knowledge of the cause of the innocuousness of the aerobic bacillus of which I have just spoken, to institute

a number of experiments on the limits of resistance of microscopic
beings to diverse temperatures, and having recognized that the
anthrax bacillus does not develop or only with great difficulty
at temperatures of 43-44° in certain liquid cultures, we thought
that this might be the explanation of a well known fact which is
nevertheless mysterious, namely, that certain animals are immune
to the anthrax disease. In our experiments of last year it was
impossible to give *anthrax* to chickens. Might not the temperature
of around 42 degrees of these fowl, joined to vital resistance,
oppose the development of the anthrax bacteria in the bodies of
these animals? If this conjecture had any grounds, we ought to
be able to give anthrax to chickens rather easily by lowering
their body temperature. The success of the experiment was immediate. As soon as one inoculates a chicken with anthrax bacteria
and places the legs into water at 25°, which is sufficient to
lower the temperature of the whole bodies to 37-38°, the animals
become susceptible to anthrax and in 24 or 30 hours the chicken
dies with its whole body invaded by the anthrax bacteria. Certain inverse experiments have already given us favorable results,
that is to say, that by raising the temperature of animals which
contract anthrax we have been able to preserve them from this
horrible disease which today has no cure.

To increase or limit the great power of these infinitely
small bodies and to confound the mystery of their action by a
simple change of temperature is one of the most important facts
necessary to show what can be attained by the efforts of science,
even in the study of the most obscure diseases.

Let us return to our septic bacillus and compare it to the
anthrax bacteria in regard to the formation of its germs in order
to reinforce in people's minds this conviction that microscopic
organisms have various physiological properties and it is necessary to pay attention to their most diverse manifestations.

Some precise experiments have taught us that the septic
bacillus can not only live and reproduce in the most perfect
vacuum as in the purest carbon dioxide, but that it there yields
its germs and that free oxygen gas is not necessary for their
formation. On the contrary, the anthrax bacteria in the vacuum
or in carbon dioxide finds it absolutely impossible, not only to
live as we already know, but to transform itself into germ corpuscles. This last research is, however, one of the most delicate. If there remains the slightest bit of air in the tubes in
which the vacuum is made and in which the anthrax bacteria are
cultured, germ corpuscles will appear to such a point that the
most perfect mercury pumps are often insufficient to prevent the
phenomenon. We have found it necessary to combine the use of the
vacuum of these pumps with that of liquids which absorb the most
feeble traces of oxygen before being able to convince ourselves
that the anthrax bacteria is essentially aerobic at every moment
in its existence. What a difference there is, therefore, between
the septic bacillus and this bacterium and is it not remarkable
to see such beings multiply in the animal organization even though
they are so dissimilar in their mode of nutrition!

Another question of no less interest is that of knowing if
the germ corpuscles of the septic bacillus, whether formed in a

vacuum or in pure carbon dioxide, do not have need of small quantities of oxygen in order to regain their vitality. Physiology today knows of no germination without the contact of air. Well! Nevertheless, experiments prove that the germs of the septic bacillus are absolutely sterile in contact with oxygen no matter what the proportion of this gas may be; always with the condition that there is a certain ratio between the volume of the air and the number of the germs, for these first germinations, removing the air which is in solution, can become a protection for the germs that remain and it is thus that the septic bacillus can propagate itself even in the presence of small quantities of air although such a propagation is impossible if the air flows through the culture.

A curious therapeutic observation now presents itself. Let us suppose a wound exposed to the contact of the air and in a condition of putridity leading to simple septicemia in the person who has been operated upon, that is, without any other complication than that which results from the development of the septic bacillus. Well, theoretically at least, the best thing one can do to prevent death in this case would be to wash the wound ceaselessly with a common aerated water or to have atmospheric air flow over its surface. The adult septic bacilli in process of division would perish with the contact of the air; as for their germs, they will all be sterile. Moreover, one ought to be able to bring to the surface of the wound, air filled with septic bacilli or to wash the wound with water which contains billions of these germs in suspension without, by that, causing the slightest septicemia in this case. But in such conditions, a single bloody scab, a single fragment of dead skin lodged in a corner of the wound, protected from the oxygen of the air and surrounded by carbon dioxide gas, even though it may be a very thin layer, will give rise immediately to septic germs in less than twenty-four hours, an infinity of bacilli will regenerate themselves by division and be capable of creating a mortal septicemia in short order. . . .

. . . We have said that the septic bacillus is formed of small moving threads. This is, in particular, the aspect under which it is met in the abdominal serum or in the muscles of animals dead of septicemia but it is often associated both in the muscles and above all in the muscles of the abdomen with very small bodies that are generally immobile having a lenticular form. These lentil-shaped bodies, which sometimes carry a germ corpuscle at one of their extremities, were for a long time an embarrassment and a mystery to us. Our attempts at culture have happily shown us that they are nothing less than one of the forms of the septic bacillus. Sometimes the lens shaped body terminated on one side by an elongated appendix thus taking the form of the pendulum of a clock. We have also seen the septic bacillus in the form of little short rods, either fat or pockmarked, but what is the most surprising is the facility with which the septic bacillus can reproduce without showing the slightest movement, a facility which is accompanied by a great diminution of virulence although this latter does not seem to be absent. For a long time we thought that we were dealing with two or more septic bacilli of different forms and different virulences and that in our cultures we were

obtaining the more or less complete separation of these diverse
bacilli. This is not true. We have only met one bacillus in
septicemia itself; the media in which it has been cultivated
causes it to change form to facilitate its propagation and its
virulence.

The best proof that we have had to do only with one bacillus
in our cultures which have been constantly repeated is that the
last cultures have been capable of being restored to the virulence
of the first by changing the liquids of these cultures. If you
reproduce the septic bacillus in Liebig Bouillon 10, 20, 30 times
and then substitute for the Bouillon a bloody serum containing a
little bit of fibrous coagulants, the new culture will furnish a
very septic bacillus which will kill, for example, with one two
thousandth of a drop, and the blood and the serum of the dead
animal will acquire right there a virulence infinitely greater
still with the forms and the habitual motion of the septic bacillus.

Given these preceding facts how premature, in the present
state of our knowledge, are the classifications and the nomencla-
tures proposed for the beings which can change their form and
their properties so much by a simple change in exterior conditions. . . .

If I had the honor of being a surgeon, convinced as I am of
the dangers caused by the germs of microbes present on the surface of all objects, particularly in hospitals, not only would I
use only instruments of an absolute cleanliness, but after having
washed my hands with the greatest care and passing them rapidly
through a flame (which does not really create any inconvenience
any more than that suffered by the smoker who tosses a glowing
coal from one hand to the other) I would only use gauze, bandages,
or sponges which have been previously exposed in air at a temperature of 130-150°. I would never use any water except that which
had been raised to a temperature of 110-120 degrees. All this is
very practicable. In this way I would only have to fear the germs
in suspension in the air around the bed of the sick person but
observation shows us every day that the number of these germs is
insignificant, so to speak, when compared to those which are to
be found in the dust on the surface of bodies or in even the most
limpid ordinary water. And moreover nothing prevents one from
employing antiseptic processes of bandaging. But, joined to the
precautions that I indicate, these processes would be singularly
simplified. Dilute carbolic acid, without any inconvenience because of its causticity, for the hands or lungs of the surgeon
could be easily and advantageously substituted for caustic carbolic acid.

6. *In the early 1880's, a lively debate took place between Robert Koch (1843-1910), the great German microbiologist and the discoverer of the tuberculosis bacillus, and Louis Pasteur. The debate revolved around Pasteur's researches on rabies and gives some idea of the tone and methods of scientific discourse in the late nineteenth century.*

Robert Koch

I can characterize the point of view from which I speak in a few words. It is not yet demonstrated that all infectious diseases are caused by parasitic microorganisms; this is why it is necessary in each particular case to furnish the proof of the parasitic character of the illness. The first step on the road to this demonstration is a minute examination of all the tissues of the body modified by the disease in order to establish the presence of parasites, their distribution in different organs and their relationship with the tissues. It goes without saying that for this research one must use all the means of investigation which modern microscopical technique has at its disposal. Not only the tissues but the humours, the lymph, blood, etc. must be examined with a microscope in their fresh state, with and without the use of reagents, then dessicated in a dessicator and treated by different processes of staining: the harder pieces must be sliced into very fine slices with the aid of a microtome and the preparations thus obtained submitted to a microscopic examination in which one uses proper lighting and the best system of lenses. It is only when, in this way, enough information of a precise nature has been gained on the presence of microorganisms in the parts of the body changed by illness, on the regions where these microorganisms can be observed clearly either, for example in the lungs, in the spleen, in the blood of the heart, and so on that one should even attempt to state the pathogenic nature of these microorganisms and their role as the cause of the illness in question. With this in mind, microorganisms are cultivated in pure culture media and when, in this way, they are found to be unencumbered by all the particles of the sick organism that might adhere to them, they are inoculated into animals of the same species as those in which the illness has been observed or at least into animals in which this sickness exists in a recognizable way. In order to make my thoughts clear by use of an example, let me recall what has happened with tuberculosis. First of all it was demonstrated by microscopical examination that the organs showing by tuberculosis lesions contained the *bacillus* which is characterized by specific reactions with certain dyestuffs; these *bacillus* [*sic*] were then isolated in cultures and great care was taken to collect them in organs where they were not adulterated by being mixed with other bacteria; finally, tuberculosis was reproduced by inoculating with the product of the cultures a great number of animals belonging to a number of various species all of which were known to be receptive to tuberculosis. Another very instructive example is furnished by erysipelas in man. It has been known for a long time that in those people who are

afflicted with this illness the cutaneous lymphatic vessels constantly contain micrococci. But it was not demonstrated by this
fact that these micrococci were the cause of erysipelas. Now,
recently, Fehleisen has succeeded in culturing these micrococci
with thin sheets of skin taken from people with erysipelas. Great
care was taken against all possible adulteration of the cultures
inoculated by the bacteria which were accidentally to be found on
the surface of this external tissue. By inoculating man with the
products of the culture he was able to develop a typical erysipelas. Since then there is no longer any doubt that these micrococci are the cause of erysipelas and this illness has a parasitic
origin.

M. Pasteur has deviated noticeably from this method of investigation as I have described it and which is the only one
which corresponds to the actual state of the science.

First of all, M. Pasteur begins with the conviction that all
contagious diseases are parasitic, caused by microbes and he does
not consider it indispensable to follow the first of the conditions that I have laid down,namely, the demonstration of the
presence of microorganisms in the body and the study of the conditions under which these microorganisms exist. For, if I may
use an example, M. Pasteur does not say if in the disease which
he calls the *new malady of rabies*, he has looked for the presence
of specific micrococci in the organs and, in particular, in the
sublingual glands of the child who, having succumbed to rabies,
served as the point of departure for the inoculation experiments
of this French scientist. In this case, precisely such a research
should have been an indispensable thing for it is known that in
rabies the sublingual glands contain the infectious principle
and, since in ordinary circumstances there are no bacteria to be
met with in these glands, it is in them that are to be found the
best chances of discovering the presumed microbes and in a state
of perfect purity. Now, when he attempted to transmit rabies from
the cadaver of the child to animals, M. Pasteur utilizes as his
inoculation material saliva itself, rather than the tissue of the
sublingual glands: it is well known that this liquid contains
innumerable bacteria of various species and among others, as
M. Vulpian and Sternberg have demonstrated, pathogenic bacteria
even in men in a state of health. It is in this same way that
M. Pasteur has proceeded with the illness that he calls *typhoid
fever of horses*. He does not examine the edematic swellings of
the skin and of the intestine nor the swollen spleen; he does not
tell us either if the blood of the sick animals or those that
have already died contains the characteristic microbes. M. Pasteur is content to inoculate the mucous which runs from the nostrils of a dead animal, which mucous is, without doubt, like
saliva, adulterated by many other bacteria. . . .

The methods followed by M. Pasteur must then be called in-
exact because as we have just shown they neglect to make use of
microscopic examination, because inoculations are conducted with
impure substances of all kinds, because they utilize for these
inoculations animals which are not proper to the researches.
These methods cannot, then, lead to certain results. When, following this, M. Pasteur allows himself to be influenced in the

interpretation of his results by prejudices and when he then
arrives at marvelous conceptions concerning the symptoms and the
disease manifestations in cadavers or observed in animals in
experiments, one ought for these reasons to be less inclined to
reproach him. M. Pasteur is not a doctor and one should not require from him the same kind of exact judgments on pathological
processes and morbid symptoms. This is really the duty of his
medical collaborators to be put on guard against such gross errors
as those which were brought to light by the conception of the
sickness of rabbit developed by inoculation of the nasal mucous
of horses. This horse illness, (typhoid fever) according to the
researcher Schütz, belongs in the group of erysipelatic processes
and has absolutely nothing in common with the typhoid fever of
man. Similarly the sickness developed (in the rabbit) by inoculation with nasal mucous (of sick horses) is, as has already been
said, identical to rabbit septicemia because of the characteristic form in an 8 of its microbe and because of the rapidity of
the mortal effects of this latter; it has absolutely nothing to
do with typhoid fever. Now M. Pasteur, seduced by this name of
typhoid fever of horses chosen completely by accident, seems to
represent this illness as a true typhoid affliction, even as an
affliction similar to or identical to the typhoid fever of man.
In effect, he insists particularly, on the fact that infected
rabbits present Peyer's swollen plaques principally in the neigh-
borhood of the ileocoecal valve and that the animals succumbed in
the space of 24 hours to a *true typhoid fever*. He gives no indication how he diagnosed this typhoid fever which does not even
last 24 hours; but without more information, the thing in its
totality seems very odd to say the least, because up to now no
typhoid fever of a rabbit is known nor, in a general way, do we
know of a typhoid fever of one day's duration. This typhoid fever
of the rabbit which lasts one day, like the rabies of the rabbit
of equal duration discovered by MM. Lannelongue and Raynaud, like
syphilis in the pig, recently described by Martineau and Hamonic,
all of which manifest themselves by the appearance of the bacillus
in the blood 24 hours after the inoculation, are all things which
are formally contradictory to all the experimental facts and dominant ideas of our science today; they are only fit to destroy the
confidence in etiological researches that has gradually been
built up. For the future of this new branch of science, it would
be wished that errors of this kind could be corrected as soon as
they occur or simply forgotten. There is real reason for astonishment that a Revue edited with such care as the *Annales d'hygiène
publique* could announce in one of its last numbers (No. 9, p.
301), in the most serious fashion that M. Pasteur has succeeded
in culturing the bacteria of typhoid fever (of the horse) which
must have raised the idea in the minds of all the readers that he
was concerned with bacteria of true typhus, that is to say, of
typhoid fever.

Louis Pasteur

In 1881 you attacked my works hastily and lightly in the
first volume of the collection of the *Imperial German Sanitary*

Office. At Geneva on September 5, 1882 I refuted your errors in passing. It is deplorable that you then refused a public discussion. I would wish a debate in which we could face one another in the presence of competent judges, but I accept these different conditions.

You say that in the congress at Geneva I did not bring forth any scientific novelty. Really monsieur! A general method of attenuation of viruses by simple exposure to the action of the oxygen of the air, knowledge of new microbes, clues to the conditions of their attenuation which vary according to their respective properties--all that has nothing which seems new to you! It is true that in the German pamphlet that I will cite you have said that the attenuation of viruses is a fable and the probable effect of some adulteration of my cultures or due to the presence of a foreign germ on the needle which was used for vaccination.

Regardless of how accustomed I may be to contradictions of all kinds I must say that I was somewhat disconcerted in reading in your brochure that "in the study of a sickness, I do not look for microbes, I do not worry about knowing where they are and that I leave aside in every specific case, the demonstration of their parasitic character."

One must really have these lines before him in order to persuade himself that they have been written.

It is thus, you continue with assurance, that Pasteur does not say if he has, in this illness that he describes as a new illness of rabies, explored the organs of the child who succumbed to rabies and who served him as the point of departure for his experiments of inoculation and, above all, if he looked with a microscope in the sublingual glands for the presence of the specific microbe.

I find here again, monsieur, a new example of the means of discussion that you have already used in 1881; you accuse me of errors that I have not committed; you combat them and brilliantly reveal your triumph. Where have you read a work of mine relative to a "new illness of rabies"? No doubt in some secondary work.

No, monsieur, I have never affirmed that I have found a new illness of rabies. I have said, and I repeat, that I have found a new sickness which was obtained for the first time by the saliva of a child dead of rabies, that this saliva, or rather the mucous from the mouth, when inoculated to rabbits caused them to die rapidly by the presence of a microbe that no one before us has pointed out for I write in my name and in name of my three collaborators, MM. Chamberland, Roux and Thuillier. This microscopic organism I have described; I have indicated the lesions that it causes; I have demonstrated that this microbe, although pathogenic for dogs and rabbits and although present in the oral mucous of people who die of rabies has, however, no relation whatsoever with the etiology of this latter disease; and that finally it is to be met with habitually in the mouths of children dead of common ailments and equally in the saliva of adult persons who are completely healthy. This is what I said and it would have been easy for you to have seen it. You continue imperturbably

"Pasteur, when he tried to transmit the rabies from the cadaver of this child to animals, used, not the tissue itself of the sublingual gland, but saliva; now it is known that this latter contains an incalculable number of diverse bacteria, notably as Vulpian and Sternberg have shown, pathogenic bacteria which occur even in the saliva of healthy people. . . ."

You are therefore ignorant, monsieur, of the fact that rabic saliva was the only substance in which the presence of rabic virus had been proven and that still, today, the presence of this virus in the glands is contested; this is not the only thing I would like to point out to you. I would simply like to show you that you possess the art of mixing up things and confounding dates, that MM. Vulpian and Sternberg did not discover, but merely confirmed, the former report of the existence of a pathogenic microbe in the saliva of people who were completely healthy. . . .

Since you are clearly concerned to take from me part of the credit for the discovery of the new microbe in the saliva and the illness that it causes, you gratuitously state that this sickness is identical to the rabbit septicemia of Davaine which is completely wrong. Since you had the prudence not to give any proof of your assertion I will not stop there.

Your general method of argument is to be seen in the manner in which you present what I said on another new microbe, namely, that which we have found in the foamy matter which flows from the nostrils of a horse dead of the affliction called typhoid fever of the horse.

Why do you have me say that at Geneva I spoke of the discovery of a microbe of typhoid fever of horses? It was quite to the contrary. I mentioned expressly that I was going to leave to one side the question of whether our microbe, in spite of its origin, played any part whatsoever in the cause of this disease. You know perfectly well that my paper at Geneva had as its main object to give some examples of attenuation of virus by the influence of the oxygen of the air and that for one of these examples I took the microbe whose origin I had just pointed out. You state besides, without the slightest proof, that this fourth microbe is identical with the pathogenic microbe in the saliva. This is a new error on your part. These two microbes differ physiologically between one another as much as it is possible to do so. On the day when you will become enlightened on this point and on all these other points which have preceded it, I will be at your disposition before a congress or before a commission whose members you may even designate. If you accept my proposition, you will perhaps not continue to maintain the tone of assurance reflected in the terms that I have chosen from your brochure.

7.   T. H. Huxley's Review of Cell Theory

A more serious criticism of the cell theory was that leveled against it by Thomas Henry Huxley.*

. . . As Schwann himself well expresses it:
"An hypothesis is never hurtful, so long as one bears in mind the amount of its probability, and the grounds upon which it is formed. It is not only advantageous, but necessary to science, that when a certain cycle of phenomena have been ascertained by observation, some provisional explanation should be devised as closely as possible in accordance with them; even though there be a risk of upsetting this explanation by further investigation; for it is only in this way that one can rationally be led to new discoveries, which may either confirm or refute it." (p. 221.)
The value of an hypothesis may, in fact, be said to be twofold--to the original investigator, its worth consists more in what it suggests than in what it teaches; let it be enunciated with perspicuity, so that its logical consequences may be clearly deduced, and made the base of definite questions to nature--questions to which she must answer yes or no--and of its absolute truth or falsehood, he recks little: for the mass of men, again, who can afford no time for original research, and for the worker himself, so far as respects subjects with which he is not immediately occupied, some system of artificial memory is absolutely necessary. This want is supplied by some "appropriate conception" which, as Dr. Whewell would say, "colligates" the facts--ties them up in bundles ready to hand--by some hypothesis, in short. Doubtless the truer a theory is,--the more "appropriate" the colligating conception,--the better will it serve its mnemonic purpose, but its absolute truth is neither necessary to its usefulness, nor indeed in any way cognizable by the human faculties. Now it appears to us that Schwann and Schleiden have performed precisely this service to the biological sciences. At a time when the researches of innumerable guideless investigators, called into existence by the tempting facilities offered by the improvement of microscopes, threatened to swamp science in minutiæ, and to render the noble calling of the physiologist identical with that of the 'putter-up' of preparations, they stepped forward with the cell-theory as a colligation of the facts. To the investigator, they afforded a clear basis and starting-point for his inquiries; for the student, they grouped together immense masses of details in a clear and perspicuous manner. Let us not be ungrateful for what they brought. If not absolutely true, it was the truest thing that had been done in biology for half a century.
But who seeks for absolute truth? Flattering as they were to our vanity, we fear it must be confessed that the days of the high *a priori* road are over. . . .

*   *   *

*Thomas Henry Huxley, "The Cell Theory [Review]," in *The Scientific Memoirs of Thomas Henry Huxley*, Vol. 1 (London, 1898), pp. 249, 253-59, 277-78.

Schleiden and Schwann teach implicitly that the primary histological elements (cells) are independent, anatomically and physiologically; that they stand in the relation of *causes* or *centres*, to organization and the "organizing force;" and that the whole organism is the result of the union and combined action of these primarily separate elements. Wolff, on the other hand, asserts that the primary histological elements (cells too, but not always defined in the same way) are not either anatomically or physiologically independent; that they stand in the relation of *effects* to the organizing or vital force (vis essentialis); and that the organism results from the "differentiation" of a primarily homogeneous whole into these parts. Such a doctrine is, in fact, a most obvious and almost a necessary development of the doctrine of epigenesis in general. To one who had worked out the conclusion, that the most complex, grosser, animal or vegetable organizations, arise from a semi-fluid and homogeneous mass, by the continual and successive establishment of differences in it, it would be only natural to suppose that the method of nature, in that finer organization which we call histological, was the same; and that as the organ is developed by the differentiation of cells, so the cells are the result of the differentiation of inorganic matter. If the organism be not constituted by the coalescence of its organs and tissues in consequence of their peculiar forces, but if, on the other hand, the organism exists before its organs and tissues, and evolves them from itself,--is it not probable that the organs and tissues also, are not produced by the coalescence of the cells of which they are composed, in consequence of *their* peculiar forces, but, contrariwise, that the cells are a product of the differentiation of something which existed before them?

For Schwann the organism is a beehive, its actions and forces resulting from the separate but harmonious action of all its parts (compare Schwann, l. c., p. 229). For Wolff it is a mosaic, every portion of which expresses only the conditions under which the formative power acted and the tendencies by which it was guided.

We have said above, not without a full consciousness of the responsibility of the assertion, that we believe the cell-theory of Schleiden and Schwann to be based upon erroneous conceptions of structure, and to lead to errors in physiology, and we beg now to offer some evidence in favour of these views. We need not stop to prove, what must be familiar to every one who is acquainted with Schwann's work, that in making his comparison of animal with vegetable structures, he rests wholly upon Schleiden's statements concerning the development, and upon the commonly prevalent views with respect to the anatomy, of the latter.

It is clear, then, that however logically consequent Schwann's work may be in itself, its truth and the justice of its nomenclature will depend upon that of these latter views and statements. Schwann took these for granted, and if they were untrue he has been trusting to a rotten reed. Such, we fear, has indeed been the case. Schwann's botanical data were:

1. The prevalent notion of the anatomical independence of the vegetable cell, considered as a separate entity.

2. The prevalent conception of the structure of the vegetable
   cell.
3. The doctrine of the mode of its development.

Each of these, as assumed by Schwann, and as taught by Schleiden, has since, we shall endeavour to show, been proved to be
erroneous. We will take them *seriatim*.

1. The first observer who, aided by the microscope, turned
his attention to the structure of plants, was the versatile Hooke,
and, as might be expected, the most noticeable thing to his mind
was the existence of the innumerable cavities or "cells" scattered
through their substance. Malpighi, the first proper botanical
histologist, found that the walls of these vesicles were separa-
ble, that they could be isolated from one another, and therefore,
doubtless urged more by the obvious convenience of the phraseol-
ogy, than by any philosophical consideration upon the subject, he
gave each the definite name of "utriculus," and regarded it as an
independent entity. Of course it was a natural consequence that
the plant should be regarded as constituted by the *union and
coalescence* of a great number of these entities.

Grew, who if all scandal be true, is so much indebted to
Malpighi, did not appropriate this view among other things; on the
other hand, he compared the utricles to the cavities in the foam
of beer; and subsequently Wolff propounded the idea, that the
cells were cavities in a homogeneous substance, as we have mentioned above. In modern times, the most important defender of
this mode of regarding the matter has been Mirbel, who (escaping
the error of Wolff, that the cavities of the cells communicate)
endeavoured to demonstrate its truth, by tracing the formation of
the cambium; but, at the time when Schwann wrote, it must be considered to have been wholly discredited, the opposite view having
one of its strongest supporters in the caustic Schleiden himself
--as, indeed, would necessarily be the case, from the tendency of
his researches upon phytogenesis. As we shall see below, however,
Schleiden was quite wrong in his ideas of cell-development--and
we have therefore merely to consider the purely anatomical arguments for the independence of the cell. Now these amount, however
various their disguise, to nothing more than this--that, by certain chemical or mechanical means, a plant may be broken up into
vesicles corresponding with the cavities which previously existed
in it: of course no one denies this fact; but of what value is it?
Is the fact that a rhombohedron of calcareous spar breaks up, if
pounded, into minute rhombohedrons, any evidence that those mi-
nuter ones were once independent, and formed the larger by their
coalescence? Is the circumstance that wood itself tears up into
fibres, any evidence that it was formed by the coalescence of
fibres? Assuredly not; for every hand-book will tell us that
these fibres are the result of a metamorphosis of quite different
parts. Is it not perfectly clear, that the behaviour of a body
under mechanical or chemical influences, is simply an evidence of
the disposition of the lines of greatest cohesion or affinity
among its particles *at the time being*, and bears not in the
slightest degree upon the question as to what these lines indicate; whether they are the remains of an ancient separation among
heterogeneous parts, or the expression of a recent separation

which has arisen in a homogeneous whole? So that, if the walls
of the cells were really, as distinct from one another as is commonly supposed, it would be no argument for their vital independence: but they are not so. Von Mohl has shown that, in the great
majority of cases, the assumption of the existence of a so-called
intercellular substance, depends simply on imperfect chemical investigation, that there exists no real line of demarcation between
one cell and another, and that wherever cells have been separated,
whether mechanically or chemically, there is evidence that the
continuous cellulose substance has been torn or in some way destroyed. In young tissues--such, for instance, as the cambium,
or the base of a leaf, we have been quite unable to detect the
least evidence of the existence of any line of demarcation between
the cells; the cellulose substance forms a partition between cavity and cavity, which becomes evenly blue throughout by the action
of sulphuric acid and iodine, and which certainly, even under the
highest powers, exhibits no symptom of any optical difference; so
that, in this state, vegetable tissue answers pretty closely to
Wolff's idea. It is a homogeneous cellulose-yielding, transparent
substance, containing cavities, in which lie peculiar vesicular
bodies, into whose composition much nitrogen enters. It will be
found a great aid if in the present confused state of terminology
the reader will accept two new denominations for these elementary
parts, which express nothing but their mutual relation. To the
former, and to everything which answers to it, we shall throughout
the present article give the name of *Periplast*, or periplastic
substance; to the latter, that of *Endoplast*. So far, then, from
the utricles or cells in the plant, being anatomically distinct,
we regard it as quite certain that that portion which corresponds
with the periplast, forms a continuous whole through the entire
plant.

2. In 1837-8, each utricle of the plant was considered to
have the following composition. In the first place, there was
the cellulose cell-wall, or the portion of periplast answering to
any particular endoplast; secondly, there were the cell-contents,
a substance of not very defined nature, which occupied the cavity
of the cell; and thirdly, there was the *nucleus*, a body to whose
occurrence attention was first drawn, as is well known, by our
own illustrious botanist, Robert Brown. He, however, cautiously
remarked only its very general occurrence, without pretending to
draw any inference from the fact; while Schleiden made the belief
in its existence, in all young tissues, the first article of the
faith botanical. This is, however, most certainly incorrect;
there is no trace of a nucleus in many Algæ, such as Hydrodictyon,
Vaucheria, Caulerpa; in the leaf of Sphagnum, nor in young germi-
nating Ferns.

Whatever opinion may be entertained upon this head, there is
one point quite certain--the enumeration of the elements of the
vegetable-cell given above is incomplete; there being one, and
that the most important, which is omitted. We refer to the
primordial utricle, which was only discovered by Von Mohl in 1844.
This is a nitrogenous membrane, which always lies in close contact
with the periplast, and forms, in fact, an included vesicle, within which the "contents" and the nucleus lie. Instead, therefore,

of the endoplast consisting merely of contents and a nucleus, it is a vesicle containing the two latter, when they exist at all; and they are of subordinate importance, for while, as we have seen, a nucleus and formed contents may be absent in young or even fully formed tissues, the primordial utricle is invariably present in the young structures, and often persists until they have attained their full size. Since, then, the functions of the vegetable "cell" can be effectually carried on by the primordial utricle alone; since the "nucleus" has precisely the same chemical composition as the primordial utricle; and since, in some cases of cell-division, new nuclei are seen to arise in the substance of the endoplast, by a mere process of chemical and morphological differentiation (Von Mohl, l. c., p. 52), it follows, we think, that the primordial utricle must be regarded as the essential part of the endoplast--the protoplasm and nucleus being simply its subordinate, and, we had almost said, *accidental* anatomical modifications.

3. Finally, with respect to Schleiden's observations upon the mode of cell-development, according to which in all cases the new production of vegetable-cells takes place by the development of nuclei, round which the cell-membrane is deposited, subsequently expanding and becoming separated from the nucleus, so as to form a complete cell; we need only say, that they have been long since set aside by the common consent of all observers; in Von Mohl's words (p. 59): "The whole of this account of the relation of the nucleus to the cell-membrane is incorrect." The fact is, that in by far the greater proportion of cases, new cell-development occurs by the division of the previous endoplasts, and the growth or deposition round them and between them, of fresh periplastic substance. The extent of this process of division will be understood, if we remember that all observers now agree in its being the method by which "cell-development" always occurs, except in the embryo-sac of the Phanerogamia, the sporangia of Lichens and of some Algæ and Fungi. The so-called free cell-development of the latter, however, by no means takes place in accordance with Schleiden's views, but by the development of a cellulose membrane (periplast) around a mass of nitrogenous substance (endoplast), which may or may not contain a nucleus; subsequently increasing, *pari passu*, with the periplast. And it is well worthy of consideration, how far the process deserves any distinction, except in degree, from ordinary cell-division, since the new endoplast is only one portion of that of the parent cell, set aside for the purpose of fresh development, while the rest undergoes no corresponding change. However this may be, it may be regarded as quite certain that, leaving out of view the immediate results of sexual reproduction, the whole of the "cells,"--the entirety of the periplasts and endoplasts--of which a plant, whether it be a moss or an oak, are composed, never are independent of one another, and never have been so, at any period of their existence; but that, while the original endoplast of the embryo-cell, from which the plant sprung, has grown and divided into all the endoplasts of the adult, the original periplast has grown at a corresponding rate, and has formed one continuous and connected envelope from the very first. The ground of his com-

parison, therefore, is cut away from under Schwann's feet; every
statement of Schleiden's on which he relied turning out to be
erroneous--as we shall see if we turn to his original comparison
of cartilage with a vegetable tissue (pp. 9-17). Schwann, finding
in cartilage cavities with more or less distinct walls, in each
of which lay a corpuscle, singularly resembling the nucleus of the
vegetable-cell; finding also that the cell-wall was close to this
corpuscle in the younger parts, more distant from it in the older
(p. 24), naturally concluded that he had here, in the animal
world, an exact confirmation of Schleiden's supposed discoveries,
and of course gave to the corpuscle of cartilage the name of
"cytoblast," or "nucleus," as indicating its homology with the
structure of that name, in the plant.

The primordial utricle was, as we have said, not then discovered in the latter, and of course Schwann was not led to look
for anything corresponding to it. Indeed, had he done so, his
search would have been unsuccessful, for the young and unaltered
cartilage cavity contains the corpuscle, and nothing else. The
circumstance, therefore, which Schwann considered to demonstrate
the identity of structure of plants and animals--i.e., the correspondence of the cartilage-corpuscle with the nucleus of the vegetable-cell, and of the chondrin-wall with the cellulose-wall,
would, if it were really the case, be the widest possible ground
of distinction between the two, for it would leave the most important element of the latter, the "primordial utricle," without any
homologue in the animal, and totally unaccounted for.

It is precisely the neglect of this important change in the
whole subject, effected by the discovery of Von Mohl, which has,
we think, led to the confusion which prevails at present, not
only in the comparative, but in the absolute nomenclature of animal histology. Animal physiologists go on using Schwann's nomenclature, forgetting that the whole doctrine of the vegetable-cell,
from which he drew that nomenclature, has been completely upset;
and at present, beyond the mere fact of a common vesicularity at
once period of their existence, one would be led, on opening successively two works on animal and vegetable structure, rather to
predicate their total discrepancy, than any uniformity between
them.

*   *   *

We cannot conclude better than by concisely repeating the
points to which we have attempted to draw attention in the course
of the present article.

We have endeavoured to show that life, so far as it is manifested by structure, is for us nothing but a succession of certain
morphological and chemical phenomena in a definite cycle, of whose
cause or causes we know nothing; and that, in virtue of their invariable passage through these successive states, living beings
have a development, a knowledge of which is necessary to any complete understanding of them. It has been seen that Von Baer enunciated the law of this development, so far as the organs are concerned; that it is a continually increasing differentiation of
that which was at first homogeneous; and that Caspar Friedrich
Wolff demonstrated the nature of histological development to be

essentially the same, though he erred in some points of detail. We have found Schwann demonstrating for the animal, what was already known for the plant—that the first histological differentiation, in the embryo, is into endoplast and periplast, or, in his own phrase, into a "nucleated cell;" and we have endeavoured to show in what way he was misled into a fundamentally erroneous conception of the homologies of these two primitive constituents in plants and animals—that what he calls the "nucleus" in the animal is not the homologue of the "nucleus" in the plant, but of the primordial utricle.

We have brought forward evidence to the effect that this primary differentiation is not a necessary preliminary to further organization—that the cells are not machines by which alone further development can take place, nor, even with Dr. Carpenter's restriction (p. 737), are to be considered as "instrumental" to that development. We have tried to show that they are not instruments, but indications—that they are no more the producers of the vital phenomena than the shells scattered in orderly lines along the sea-beach are the instruments by which the gravitative force of the moon acts upon the ocean. Like these, the cells mark only where the vital tides have been, and how they have acted.

Again, we have failed to discover any satisfactory evidence that the endoplast, once formed, exercises any attractive, metamorphic, or metabolic force upon the periplast; and we have therefore maintained the broad doctrine established by Wolff, that the vital phenomena are not necessarily preceded by organization, nor are in any way the result or effect of formed parts, but that the faculty of manifesting them resides in the matter of which living bodies are composed, as such—or, to use the language of the day, that the "vital forces" are molecular forces.

It will doubtless be said by many, But what guides these molecular forces? Some Cause, some Force, must rule the atoms and determine their arrangement into cells and organs; there must be something, call it what you will—Archæus, "Bildungs-trieb," "Vis Essentialis," Vital Force, Cell-force—by whose energy the vital phenomena in each case are what they are.

We have but one answer to such inquiries: Physiology and Ontology are two sciences which cannot be too carefully kept apart; there may be such entities as causes, powers, and forces, but they are the subjects of the latter, and not of the former science, in which their assumption has hitherto been a mere gaudy cloak for ignorance. For us, physiology is but a branch of the humble philosophy of facts; and when it has ascertained the phenomena presented by living beings and their order, its powers are exhausted. If cause, power, and force mean anything but convenient names for the mode of association of facts, physiology is powerless to reach them. It is satisfactory to reflect, however, that in this comparatively limited sphere the inquiring mind may yet find much occupation.

8. *By the end of the nineteenth century, the rival claims of the evolutionists, pangeneticists and the cell theorists had created a situation of considerable confusion. There was a very strong feeling that the cell was a purely mechanical system whose physiology had only temporarily eluded the keenest searcher but which would yield up its secret if only investigations were carried on for another decade or so. The inability to explain inheritance or variation merely seemed to be a minor consequence of the difficulties encountered in unraveling cell physiology. There was, certainly, a distinct feeling of revulsion towards those vitalistic ideas which, it was thought, had been finally defeated with the cell theory and with cellular pathology.*

   It was onto this scene of rather strident claims which were unsupported by equivalent discoveries, that Hans Driesch (1867-1941) made his appearance in the 1890's. He was a master experimenter who had begun his career as a proponent of the standard theories of biology. In the 1890's, however, he performed a series of experiments which very nicely blew up the theories of Weismann and his experimental collaborator, Wilhelm Roux. In essence, what Driesch showed was that no theory of mechanism could explain heredity or, better yet, the differentiation of tissues from a single, relatively amorphous egg cell. In the Gifford lectures delivered in 1907,* Driesch laid out his philosophy of the organism in which he showed that mechanism was incapable of dealing with biological problems and that the three great problems of biology --heredity, differentiation, and evolution--were not to be solved by the use of crude mechanical analogies.

The Work of Wilhelm Roux

We have already said that an hypothesis about the foundation of individual development was Roux's starting-point. Like Weismann, he supposed that there exists a very complicated structure in the germ, and that nuclear division leads to the disintegration of that structure. He next tried to bring forward what might be called a number of indicia supporting his view.

A close relation had been found to exist in many cases between the direction of the first cleavage furrows of the germ and the direction of the chief planes of symmetry in the adult: the first cleavage, for instance, very often corresponds to the median plane, or stands at right-angles to it. And in other instances, such as have been worked out into the doctrine of so-called "cell-lineages", typical cleavage cells were found to correspond to typical organs. Was not that a strong support for a theory which regarded cellular division as the principal means of differentiation? It is true, the close relations between cleavage and symmetry did not exist in every case, but then there had always happened some specific experimental disturbances, e.g. influences

---

*Hans Driesch, *The Science and Philosophy of the Organism*, 2nd ed., London, 1929, pp. 37-9, 40-42, 86-91, 96-98, 104, 106-7.

of an abnormal direction of gravity on account of a
turning over of the egg, and it was easy to reconcile such cases
with the generally accepted theory on the assumption of what was
called "anachronism" of cleavage.

But Roux was not satisfied with mere indicia; he wanted a
proof, and with this intention he carried out an experiment which
has become very celebrated. With a hot needle he killed one of
the first two blastomeres of the frog's egg after the full accom-
plishment of its first cleavage, and then watched the development
of the surviving cell. A typical half-embryo was seen to emerge--
an organism, indeed, which was as much a half as if a fully-formed
embryo of a certain stage had been cut in two by a razor. It was
especially in the anterior part of the embryo that its "halfness"
could most clearly be demonstrated.

That seemed to be a proof of Weismann's and Roux's theory
of development, a proof of the hypothesis that there is a very
complicated structure which promotes ontogeny by its disintegration, carried out during the cell divisions of embryology by the
aid of the process of nuclear division, the so-called "karyo-
kinesis". But things were far from being decided in a definitive
manner.

The Experiments on the Egg of the Sea-Urchin

Roux's results were published for the first time in 1888;
three years later I tried to repeat his fundamental experiment on
another subject and by a somewhat different method. It was known
from the cytological researches of the brothers Hertwig and Boveri
that the eggs of the common sea-urchin (*Echinus microtuberculatus*)
are able to stand well all sorts of rough treatment, and that, in
particular, when broken into pieces by shaking, their fragments
will survive and continue to segment. I took advantage of these
facts for my purposes. I shook the germs rather violently during
their two-cell stage, and in several instances I succeeded in
killing one of the blastomeres, while the other one was not dam-
aged, or in separating the two blastomeres from one another.

Let us now follow the development of the isolated surviving
cell. It went through cleavage just as it would have done in
contact with its sister-cell, and there occurred cleavage stages
which were just half of the normal ones. The stage, for instance,
which corresponded to the normal sixteen-cell stage, and which,
of course, in my subjects was built up of eight elements only,
showed two micromeres, two macromeres, and four cells of medium
size, exactly as if a normal sixteen-cell stage had been cut in
two; and the form of the whole was that of a hemisphere. So far
there was no divergence from Roux's results.

The development of our Echinus proceeds rather rapidly, the
cleavage being accomplished in about fifteen hours. I quickly
noticed, on the evening of the first day of the experiment, when
the half-germ was composed of about two hundred elements, that
the margin of the hemispherical germ bent together a little, as
if it were about to form a whole sphere of smaller size, and,
indeed, the next morning a *whole* diminutive blastula was swimming
about. I was so much convinced that I should get Roux's morpho-

genetical result in all its features that, even in spite of this whole blastula, I now expected that the next morning would reveal to me the half-organisation of my subject once more; the intestine, I supposed, might come out quite on one side of it, as a half-tube, and the mesenchyme ring might be a half one also.

But things turned out as they were bound to do and not as I had expected; there was a typically *whole* gastrula on my dish the next morning, differing only by its small size from a normal one; and this *small but whole* gastrula was followed by a whole and typical small pluteus-larva.

But of greater importance for our purposes was what followed. I succeeded in pressing the eggs of Echinus between two glass plates, rather tightly, but without killing them; the eggs became deformed to comparatively flat plates of a large diameter. Now, in these eggs all nuclear division occurred at right-angles to the direction of pressure, that is to say, in the direction of the plates, as long as the pressure lasted; but the divisions *began* to occur at right-angles to their former direction, as soon as the pressure ceased. By letting the pressure be at work for different times I therefore, of course, had it quite in my power to obtain cleavage types just as I wanted to get them. If, for instance, I kept the eggs under pressure until the eight-cell stage was complete, I got a plate of eight cells, one beside the other, instead of two rings, of four cells each, one above the other, as in the normal case; but the next cell division occurred at right-angles to the former ones, and a sixteen-cell stage, of two plates of eight cells each, one above the other, was the result. If the pressure continued until the sixteen-cell stage was reached, sixteen cells lay together in one plate, and two plates of sixteen cells each, one above the other, were the result of the next cleavage.

We are not, however, studying these things for cytological but for morphogenetical purposes, and for these the cleavage phenomenon itself is less important than the organogenetic result of it: all our subjects resulted in *absolutely normal* organisms. Now, it is clear that the spatial relations of the different nuclear divisions to each other are anything but normal in the eggs subjected to the pressure experiments; that, so to say, every nucleus has got quite different neighbours if compared with the "normal" case. If that makes no difference, then there *cannot* exist any close relation between the single nuclear divisions and organogenesis at all, and the conclusion we have drawn more provisionally from the whole development of isolated blastomeres has been extended and proved in the most perfect manner. There ought to result a morphogenetic chaos according to the theory of real "evolutio" carried out by nuclear division, if the positions of the single nuclei were fundamentally changed with regard to one another. But now there resulted not chaos, but the normal organisation: therefore it was disproved, in the strictest way, that nuclear divisions have any bearing on the origin of organisation --at least, as far as the divisions during cleavage come into account.

The Morphogenetic "System"

We know from our experimental work that many, if not all, of the elementary organs in ontogeny show one and the same prospective potency distributed equally over their elements. If we now borrow a very convenient term from mechanics, and call any part of the organism which is considered as a unit from any morphogenetic point of view, a morphogenetic "*system*", we may sum up what we have learnt by saying that both the blastoderm of the echinoderms, at least around its polar axis, and also the germlayers of these animals, are "systems" possessing an equal potentiality in all of their elements, or, in short, that they are *equipotential systems*.

But such a term would not altogether indicate the real character of these systems.

Later on, we shall analyse, more carefully than before, the distribution of potencies which are the foundation both of regeneration proper and of adventitious growth, and then we shall see that, in higher plants for instance, there is a certain "system" which may be called the organ proper of restitutions, and which also in each of its elements possesses the same restoring potency; I refer to the well-known *cambium*. This cambium, therefore, also deserves the name of an "equipotential system". But we know already that its potencies are of the *complex* type, that they consist in the faculty of producing the *whole* of such a complicated organisation as a branch or a root, that the term "equipotential system" is here only to signify that such a complicated unit may arise out of each of the cells of the cambium.

The potencies we have been studying in the blastula or gastrula of echinoderms are not of the complex type: our systems are equipotential to the extent that each of their elements may play every *single* part in the totality of what will occur in the whole system; it is to this *single* part that the term "function of the position" relates. We therefore might call our systems equipotential systems with single potencies; or, more shortly, *singular-equipotential* systems.

But even this terminology would fail to touch precisely the very centre of facts: it is not only the simplicity or singularity of their potencies which characterises the rôle of our systems in morphogenesis, but far more important with respect to the production of form are two other leading results of the experimental researches. The proper act to be performed by every element in each actual case is, in fact, a single one, but the potency of any element as such consists in the possibility of *many* single acts: that, then, might justify us in speaking of our systems as "indefinite equipotential", were it not that another reason makes another title seem still more preferable. For the name of indefinite equipotential systems might also be applied to elementary organs, the single potencies of which are awaked to organogenesis by specific formative stimuli, as in the experiments carried out by Spemann and his school, where the reaction of one and the same cell varies according to the stimulus in question. But this is not the case in the system of which we are now speaking. There are, indeed, indefinite singular potencies at work in our systems

during ontogeny; but what happens to arise in every case out of
the totality of the single acts performed by all of the single
equipotential cells is not a sum induced from without, but a unit
guaranteed from within. That is to say, there exists a sort of
inner harmony in every case among the *real products* of our systems, these products being due to the inner forces of the systems
exclusively. The term *harmonious-equipotential system*, therefore,
seems to be the right one to denote them.

We now shall try, first, to analyse to its very extremes the
meaning of the statement that a morphogenetic system is harmonious-equipotential.

The "Harmonious-Equipotential System"

We have an ectoderm of the gastrula of a starfish here before
us; we know that we may cut off any part of it in any direction,
and that nevertheless the differentiation of the ectoderm may go
on perfectly well and result in a typical little embryo, which is
only smaller in its size than it would normally be. It is by
studying the formation of the highly complicated ciliary band
that these phenomena can be most clearly understood.

Now let us imagine our ectoderm to be a cylinder instead of
being approximately a sphere, and let us imagine the surface of
this cylinder unrolled. It will give us a plane of two definite
dimensions, a and b. And now we have all the means necessary for
the analytical study of the differentiation of an harmonious-
equipotential system.

Our plane of the dimensions a and b is the basis of the
normal, undisturbed development; taking the sides of the plane as
fixed localities for orientation, we can say that the actual fate,
the "prospective value" of every element of the plane stands in a
fixed and definite correlation to the length of two lines, drawn
at right-angles to the bordering lines of the plane; or, to speak
analytically, there is a definite actual fate corresponding to
each possible value of x and of y. Now, we have been able to
state by our experimental work, that the prospective value of the
elements of our embryonic organ is not identical with their "prospective potency", or their possible fate, this potency being very
much richer in content than is shown by a single case of ontogeny.
What will be the analytical expression of such a relation?

Let us put the question in the following way: on what factors
does the fate of any element of our system depend in all possible
cases of development obtainable by means of operations? We may
express our results in the form of an equation--

$$p.v.(X) = f(\ . \ . \ . \ ),$$

i.e. "the prospective value of the element X is a function of
. . ."--of what?

We know that we may take off *any* part of the whole, as to
quantity, and that a proportionate embryo will result, unless the
part removed is of a very large size. This means that the prospective value of any element certainly depends on, certainly is
a function of, the *absolute size* of the actually existing part of
our system in the particular case. Let s be the absolute size of

the system in any actual experimental case of morphogenesis: then we may write $p.v.(X) = f(s \ . \ . \ . \ )$. But we shall have to add still some other letter to this s.

The operation of section was without *any* restriction either as to the *amount* of the material removed from the germ or as to the direction of the cut. Of course, in almost every actual case there will be both a definite size of the actual system and a definite direction of the cut going hand-in-hand. But in order to study independently the importance of the variable *direction* alone, let us imagine that we have isolated at one time that part of our system which is bounded by the lines a_1b_1, and at another time an *equal* amount of it which has the lines a_2b_2 as its boundaries. Now, since in both cases a typical small organism may result on development, we see that, in spite of their equal size, the prospective value of every element of the two pieces cut out of the germ may vary even in relation to the direction of the cut itself. Our element, X, may belong to both of these pieces of the same size: its actual fate nevertheless will be different. Analytically, it may be said to change in correspondence to the actual position of the actual boundary lines of the piece itself with regard to the fundamental lines of orientation, a and b; let this actual position be expressed by the letter l, l marking the distance of one of the actual boundary lines of our piece from a or b: then we are entitled to improve our formula by writing $p.v.(X) = f(s, l \ . \ . \ . \ )$ (Fig. II).

But the formula is not yet complete: s and l are what the mathematicians call variables: they may have *any* actual value and there will always be a definite value of $p.v.$, *i.e.* of the actual fate which is being considered; to every value of s and l, which as we know are independent of each other, there corresponds a definite value of the actual prospectivity. Now, of course, there is also a certain factor at work in every actual case of experimental or normal development, which is *not* a variable, but which is the same in all cases. This factor is a something embraced in the prospective potency of our system, though not properly identical with it.

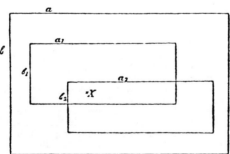

Fig. II.--Diagram to show the Characteristics of an "Harmonious-Equipotential System."

The element X forms part of the systems ab or a_1b_1 or a_2b_2; its prospective value is different in each case.

The prospective potency of our system, that is to say of each of its elements, is the sum total of what can be done equally well by all; but the fact that a typically proportionate development occurs in every possible case, proves that this sum comes into account, not merely as a sum, but as a sort of order: we may call this order the "relation of localities in the absolutely normal case". If we keep in mind that the term "prospective potency" is always to contain this order, or, as we may also call it, this "relative proportionality", which, indeed, was the reason for calling our systems "harmonious", then we may apply it without further explanation in order to signify the *non-variable* factor on which the prospective value of any element of our systems depends; and if we denote the prospective potency, embracing order, by the letter E, we are now able to complete our formula by saying $p.v.(X) = f(s, l, E)$.

The Problem of the Factor E

We turn back again to considerations of a more abstract form. We left our analysis of the differentiation of the harmonious-equipotential systems, and particularly of the phenomena of localisation during this differentiation, at the point where we had succeeded in obtaining an equation as the expression of all those factors on which the prospective value, the actual fate, of any element of our systems depends. $p.v.(X) = f(s, l, E)$ was the short expression of all the relations involved; s and l, the absolute size of the system and the relative position of the element with respect to some fixed points, were independent variables; E was a constant, namely, the prospective potency, with special regard to the proportions embraced by it.

We shall now study the significance of the factor E.

What does this E mean? Is it a short expression merely for an actual sum of elemental agents having a common resultant? And, if so, of what kind are these agents? Or what may E mean, if it can be shown *not* to be a short sign for a mere sum?

No Explanation offered by "Means" or "Formative Stimuli"

For practical purposes it seems better if we modify the statement of our question. Let us put it thus: E is one of the factors responsible, among variables, for the localisation of organic differentiation; what then do we actually know about the causal factors which play a *localising* part in organogenesis? We, of course, have to look back to our well-studied "formative stimuli". These stimuli, be they "external" or "internal", come from without with respect to the elementary organ in which any sort of differentiation, and therefore of localisation, occurs: but in our harmonious systems no localising stimulus comes from without, as was the case, for instance, in the formation of the lens of the eye in response to the optical vesicle touching the skin. We know absolutely that it is so, not to speak of the self-evident fact that the general "means" of organogenesis have no localising value at all.

Some authors have objected to my arguments that the germ,

say in the shape of sixteen cells, might be regarded as a typically ordered physico-chemical system, in which all sorts of
diffusions and other kinds of transport of materials might go on
in a well-regulated pre-established way. Very well--for the case
of *normal* embryology. But there are the results of the experiment! I take away one of the first four cleavage cells: the
result is the normal one. And, if I may add another type of
experiment not yet mentioned, the result is also the normal one
if in the 16-cell stage I take, say, two micromeres, one macro-
mere, and three mesomeres--that is, if I allow development to
start from very "unharmoniously composed" conditions.

In face of such facts, the theory of the well-ordered pre-
established system of surfaces, diffusions, etc., breaks down
completely.

So we see there is nothing to be done, either with the means
or with the formative stimuli; both are entirely unable to account
for those kinds of localisation during differentiation which
appear in our harmonious systems.

It seems to me that there is only one conclusion possible.
If we are going to explain what happens in our harmonious-equipotential systems by the aid of causality based upon the

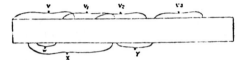

Fig. 14.--An "Harmonious-Equipotential System" of whatever kind.

According to the "machine-theory" of life this system ought to possess a certain
   unknown very complicated machine *in its completeness*:
      (*a*) in its total length,
   and (*b*) in each of the equal volumes v, v_1, v_2, v_3, and so on,
   and (*c*) in each of the unequal volumes w, x, y, and so on,
   and (*d*) in every imaginable volume, no matter of what size.
Therefore the "machine-theory" of life is absurd.

constellation of single physical or chemical factors and events,
there must be some such thing as a machine. Now, just the assumption of the existence of a "machine" proves to be absolutely absurd in the light of the experimental facts. *Therefore there can
be neither any sort of a machine nor any sort of causality based
upon constellation underlying the differentiation of harmonious-
equipotential systems.*

For a machine, typical with regard to the three chief dimensions of space, cannot remain itself if you remove parts of it or
if you rearrange its parts at will.

"Entelechy"

But shall we not give a name to our vitalistic or autonomous
factor E, concerned in morphogenesis? Indeed we will, and it was
not without design that we chose the letter E to represent it
provisionally. The great father of systematic philosophy,

Aristotle, is also to be regarded as the founder of theoretical biology. Moreover, he is the first vitalist in history, for his theoretical biology is throughout vitalism; and a very conscious vitalism indeed, for it grew up in permanent opposition to the dogmatic mechanism maintained by the school of Democritus.

Let us then borrow our terminology from Aristotle, and let that factor in life phenomena which we have shown to be a factor of true autonomy be called *Entelechy*, though without identifying our doctrine with what Aristotle meant by the word ἐντελέχεια. We shall use this word only as a sign of our admiration for his great genius; his word is to be a mould which we have filled and shall fill with new contents. The etymology of the word ἐντελέχεια allows us such liberties, for indeed we have shown that there is at work a something in life phenomena "which bears the end in it-self", ὃ ἔχει ἐν ἑαυτῷ τὸ τέλος.

Our concept of entelechy marks the end of our analysis of individual morphogenesis. Morphogenesis, we have learned, is "epigenesis" not only in the descriptive but also in the theoretical sense: manifoldness in space is produced where no manifoldness was, real "evolutio" is limited to rather insignificant topics. But was there nothing "manifold" previous to morphogenesis? Nothing certainly of an *extensive* character, but there was something else: there was entelechy, and thus we may provisionally call entelechy an "*intensive manifoldness*". That then is our result: not evolutio, but epigenesis--"epigenesis vitalistica".

9. Claude Bernard's Course of Physiology

*Further microscopical work on cells soon established the cell
theory beyond the doubts of even a Huxley. By the 1870's, cells
were acknowledged to be the fundamental units of physiology. In
one of his last lectures,* Claude Bernard indicated how the cell
theory was to be reconciled with his own experimental work in
physiology.*

Up to now we have studied the development of physiological
conceptions of life during antiquity, the middle ages and up to
modern times. We have seen that of all the works that have been supported by the spirit of systems, criticism has left nothing standing. On these ruins the experimental spirit has raised a monument
whose base is solidly founded and whose general plan can perhaps
already be perceived. It now remains to make it known. The work
of historical criticism has been done; what remains is the work
of building, itself. I am therefore going to present to you the
ensemble of the ideas and of the conceptions which should, as I
see it, be dominant today in the life sciences.
These conceptions go back to the end of the last century and
have their origin in the physico-chemical works of Lavoisier and
Laplace and the anatomical works of Bichat. The first attempts
of these great men have been developed and extended by the efforts
of modern experimental physiology.
Even in our period, however, the last vestiges of the systematic spirit are not yet completely destroyed. At the beginning
of this century, for example, the German school of the nature
philosophers with Hegel and Schelling tried to throw one last
obscurity over it. Since then, by a kind of natural reaction,
the philosophical spirit has been banished with too much rigor.
The constellation of experimenters and observers has become infinitely extended. But because of this it is necessary that a
general and a philosophical view should be taken today to reassem-
ble the innumerable materials which have been brought together
and to reveal the main lines of the building which they serve to
raise. It is necessary to recognize the design and the plan of
what is being done blindly, so to speak, by the efforts of this
army of workers which has become so numerous. Systems are certainly dead and no effort should be made to resuscitate them; but
what is lacking perhaps is a general view of the direction of our
science. Having been a witness to this evolution for more than
thirty years, I think it is useful to say to what conceptions
continual meditation on physiological problems and the knowledge
of facts has conducted me.
Modern physiology has two roots, one in anatomy and the other
in the physico-chemical sciences. These two roots bring their
sap to a single trunk. It is wrong that they are separated. If
the manifestations of the living organism obey the laws of physics

---

*Claude Bernard, "Cours de physiologie," *Revue Scientifique*, 10
(1876), pp. 446, 450, 466-67. Translated by L. Pearce Williams.

and of general chemistry, their processes of action are, however,
essentially specific to the organism and derive from its anatomical arrangement. Let us first glance rapidly at the anatomical
constitution of the tissues of living bodies. We will then examine the physico-chemical phenomena special to the organism and
from these two kinds of considerations we will deduce the unique
nature of physiological phenomena.

The explanation of vital phenomena should be looked for in
the cell. Modern opinions on vital phenomena are founded on histology; they have their origin really in the ideas of Bichat. We
have seen that at the beginning of this century Xavier Bichat gave
a powerful stimulus to physiological science by placing the cause
of vital phenomena in the tissues which compose bodies. This attempt at the *decentralization* of life was the first step along a
fertile road, and which has led to our contemporary conception,
to the physiology of anatomical elements.

Bichat founded general anatomy in opposition to descriptive
anatomy. He classified all the parts of the body into a certain
number of groups which constituted the anatomical systems or tissues. And instead of making the organism known by describing its
parts in topographical order *De capite ad calcem*, he began a systematic method which was infinitely more philosophical by bringing
together similar organs wherever they were placed and by studying
them together under the name of body system, glandular system,
nervous system, serous system, etc. . . .

. . . It is now established, thanks to the accumulated work
of the histologists and to a larger conception of cellular evolution that the organism is made up of an assemblage of cells which
are more or less recognizable, modified in diverse degrees, associated together and assembled in different ways. The cell is
thus the unit, the element, of the animal organism as of the vegetable organism.

It is even more than this, it is its *origin*. The phenomena
of generation are known well enough so that one can say that every
living creature comes from an egg or *ovum* which is entirely analogous to a more or less complex cell. The evolution of the cell
has been followed with the greatest care to show that it is the
matrix of the new being: it has been seen to divide, to multiply
itself and thus to constitute a cellular mass (the blastoderm);
at this time the animal in process of formation is only composed
of cells separated by an intercellular substance. It is known
and more will be known each day, how each tissue comes from these
embryonic elements; by what various phases, by what stages the
primitive cells must pass in order to end up in their final and
most complex state.

The end of all these discoveries that we have mentioned by
sketching in their main points is what we originally announced at
the beginning. The major portion of the beings that we call individuals, zoological or botanical, are really societies, or nations, as has been said. What we observe are manifestations of
this social life, that is to say a complex result. What it is
necessary to know is individual life for its manifestations are
the key to the others.

When physiology will permit us to penetrate the mysteries of these individual lives, of the cellular activities, we will better understand the vital phenomena which result from the grouping and the interaction of these activities.

As we have already said, the autonomy of elementary organizations is still respected in their association: the elements can not possess other characters in the state of parts of a complicated being from those which they possess in the isolated and free state. Their autonomy is only limited by particular conditions that the association itself creates. The more complicated this association is, the more the elementary organism is itself modified, the more varied and novel are the manifestations of this assembly of organ, system, or individual.

But there are cases where association is not present or becomes extremely simple and it is then that the cellular properties manifest themselves more clearly. There are cases where the cell does not associate with any other and where it forms, by itself, a complete being, a *monocellular* organism.

Monocellular organisms are to be found in infinite number in the vegetable and animal kingdoms and most often at the frontier of these two areas constituting the intermediary group between plants and animals that Bory de Saint-Vincent has called the *Psychodiary kingdom* and that Haeckel more recently has called the *protist kingdom*.

Even in the most complex organisms there are unicellular elements which preserve their liberty and a sort of independent life such as, for example, the male and female germ cells, blood corpuscles, and leucocytes.

Such are, in short and in a very incomplete manner, the materials brought together by the efforts of anatomists and contemporary physiologists. It is these materials that it is necessary to examine and from which we shall try to deduce a conception of life. The materialists and the spiritualists no longer have a role in this scientific realm. On the other hand, experimenters and men of the laboratory have not yet built up a general and philosophical view of the facts that they have discovered. Thus it seems to me the time has come to attempt this synthesis and to show how *physiological determinism* will erect on this prepared ground a general conception of life and of its manifestations.

The Law of the Constitution of Organisms

We have said that the living organism is an association of organized cells more or less modified and grouped in tissues, in organs and in systems. From the cellular being up to man one meets all the degrees of complication in these groupings. The law of this increasing complication has for a long time remained obscure: today we can perceive it. Anatomical examination was not enough to bring it to light: so long as one remained committed to the idea of form, the reason behind this successive complication, the law which presided over it, remained mysterious. It was by physiology that the solution to the problem was achieved. Here is the idea which it is necessary that we look at.

The most complex organism is a vast mechanism which results from the assemblage of secondary mechanisms. The most perfect animal possesses a circulatory system, a respiratory system, and a nervous system. But these interlocking mechanisms do not exist for themselves as was wrongfully thought before. It is not in these systems that life itself should be localized. They exist not for themselves but for the cells, for the innumerable anatomical elements which form the organic edifice. Their role, their unique reason for being, is to create conditions favorable or necessary to the life of each cell: it is to create for each of these the special medium in which it can grow and function. Thus, nerves, vessels, respiratory organs become evident to the extent that the histological scaffolding becomes complicated, in order to create around each element the milieu and the conditions which are necessary to this element. There are inferior animals without lungs, without blood vessels, without distinct nerves; thus these organs by themselves are not indispensable to the life of the animal: they are only of use for what they do: they give to the organic element the materials which it requires in sufficient measure--water, nourishment, air, heat. It is the result of their work which is indispensable and not the means of execution of this work. They are in living bodies the same as manufacturers or industrial establishments in an advanced society which furnish to the different members of this society the means of clothing themselves, heating themselves, of food and of light. These systems are therefore not essential, they only prepare the scene for the vital power.

Organic perfection does not consist only in the division of physiological work; the law of this perfection is intimately connected to the law of cellular life. Organs are added to organs and systems to systems in order to permit cellular life to continue more smoothly. The task which is imposed on organs and systems is to bring together the conditions of cellular life both qualitatively and quantitatively; this is absolute. In order to accomplish it, different things must be done; there is a larger number of organs and systems to take up these tasks as the organism becomes more complicated and they are less numerous when it is more simple, but the goal is always the same. As for the means, this consists of increasing complexity of anatomical elements and in an increasing functional complication.

What then are these conditions necessary to cellular life? They are the same as those which are necessary to the life of the entire organism.

The life of elementary organisms is a phenomenon which requires two factors: 1 the element itself with its properties; 2 the milieu in which this element exists. There must be a certain compatibility between these two factors: there must be a certain correspondence between them.

In a word, cellular life results in two series of conditions: those conditions *intrinsic* to the cell, and the *extrinsic* conditions or the milieu. We repeat, it is the same as for the entire organism.

Leaving the intrinsic conditions aside for the moment, which is the whole heart of the question, let us deal with the extrinsic conditions.

The extrinsic conditions which must be realized in order to permit each cell to function according to its nature are very numerous, very delicate and variable, if one wishes to speak of them precisely in all their details. It would be necessary to give the history of each cellular individual in order to arrive at this knowledge. If it were reduced to that, the problem would not present any simplicity: it would be a crushing task, impossible to achieve.

Such is not the case. The essential extrinsic conditions instead of being infinitely variable are, to the contrary, very small in number: they are the same for all animal or vegetable cells. This is a capital fact and one on which we cannot insist too much. Nothing demonstrates vital unity better, that is to say the identity of life from one extremity to the other of the scale of creation than this uniformity of conditions necessary to its manifestation. The conditions are: 1, humidity 2, air 3, heat 4, a certain chemical constitution of the nutritive milieu which is always the same.

In order to live, every cell requires the combination of these conditions. It needs water, oxygen, a proper temperature and certain chemical principles, all of these in proportions which are very much alike.

If the cell is free, that is if we are dealing with one of the unicellular beings . . . then in order to live there must be certain conditions in the exterior milieu in which it exists. If instead of a being so simple we are dealing with a creature formed of an assemblage of elementary organisms, of histological elements, then the same result will be attained. The elements which are deeply situated, separated from the cosmic milieu, must find the same indispensable circumstances combined around them in the situation in which they exist. They must have around them a true *interior milieu* where these common conditions can be achieved. The organism as a whole is dominated by this necessity of permitting the access around each cell of water, of air, and of certain chemical nutritive substances at a convenient temperature. The living body must be constructed in such a way that it can satisfy this necessity: and this is why as we said above the circulatory, respiratory and nervous systems appear for they are destined to constitute this milieu and to regulate its use.

I have often insisted on the idea that the existence of the living creature does not take place in the exterior milieu but in the interior milieu. Man, no more than the other creatures who live in the air, does not exist in atmospheric air: aquatic animals do not live in the middle of water, and the terrestrial worm does not live in sand. This is only an appearance which these terms of language made use of. The elementary organism, the truly living constitutive particles, the histological cells are bathed in an *interior milieu* which envelops them and which serves as the intermediary between them and the cosmic milieu. Air, water and the earth form a second envelope, a second milieu in which the true interior milieu finds its nourishment. This latter in the most highly organized animals is the lymph, that is to say the plasma, the liquid part of the blood which penetrates all tissues and constitutes the totality of all the interstitial liquids. It is the expression of all local nutrition and the source and confluence of all elementary exchanges.

It is, in one word, in the milieu in which the elements are submerged that the extrinsic conditions of life are united, that is: water, oxygen, heat and chemical alimentary substances.

Without pursuing this subject on which I have often spoken further and which requires considerable development in order to be treated completely, we can sum up by indicating a few of the general propositions which are the direct consequences of the ideas that we have just presented.

1. Life resides in each organic cell; it is not centralized in any part, in any system or organ of the body. All the systems are constructed with a view towards cellular life. When, in a higher animal the lung, the heart or the brain is suppressed . . . one does not remove a vital principle which has its seat in one or the other of these organs because life can exist without them in simpler organisms; one dislocates the vital mechanism and renders cellular life impossible by the disturbances brought about in the interior milieu which no longer can be properly distributed to the elementary cells of the organism. Le Gallois and Flourens thus committed an error by placing the seat of life in the medulla oblongata because injury to a point in this region bring instantaneous death in higher animals. The explanation is quite otherwise. The injury to the vital center of the medulla oblongata, as Flourens calls it, produces instantaneous death in mammals and birds because it destroys the respiratory center and the oxygen of the air ceases to be carried to the cells of which the organism is composed. The proof of this is that injury to the same vital center does not bring instantaneous death in cold blooded animals which can go a long time without breathing. The same explanation applies to the removal of the heart or of the brain; this mutilation destroys the conditions of cellular life but does not remove any vital principle.

2. General life, that is to say, the total cellular life, not only ceases when one of the systems which distributes the nourishing liquid (the interior milieu) breaks down into its anatomical elements; it is also extinguished when this interior milieu is altered or vitiated; this is the case in the introduction of toxic substances into the circulation. The poison does not act on any vital principle whatsoever, but on one or many cellular elements. It is the same with morbid alterations of the interior milieu. The cells themselves concur in the creation of the milieu in which they live; it is they which prepare the immediate principles which become their nutritive principles: when a cell becomes ill, the milieu is altered and the other cells are themselves affected. The morbific principles are thus produced by the cells and this alters the interior milieu. In the pathological state, as in the normal state, everything is explained by the *consensus* of all the cellular lives living in harmony.

3. However, in the cellular life which constitutes organisms, there is, at one and the same time, autonomy, differentiation and subordination of the anatomical elements. The autonomy of the elements as well as their differentiation gives us the explanation of the variety of vital manifestations. Subordination explains their harmony.

To conclude, everything is made in organisms for cellular life. The respiratory system furnishes oxygen; the digestive

system, nutriment, the circulatory system, the secretions which
assure nutritive renewal. The nervous system itself acts with
the purpose of the harmony of cellular life. We will see that
basically all these organic systems even including the nervous
system which are indispensable to superior beings act to insure
to cellular life the physico-chemical conditions which are necessary to it.

10. August Weismann on the Germ Plasm

*By the 1880's, the problem of inheritance appeared to be
intimately connected with cells. The phenomenon of meiosis and
the prominence of the chromosomes in mitosis suggested that the
mechanism of heredity was to be found within the sex cells.
August Weismann developed a subtle and complicated theory which
he presented in his work,* Das Keimplasm *which was almost immediately translated into English.**

As long as we were under the erroneous impression that the
fertilisation of the ovum by the spermatozoon depended on an *aura
seminalis* which incited the egg to undergo development, we could
only partially explain the fact that the father as well as the
mother is able to transmit characters to the children by assuming
the existence of a *spiritus rector*, contained in the *aura seminalis* which was transferred to the ovum and united with that of
the latter, and thus with it directed the development. The discovery that development is effected by material particles of the
substance of the sperm, the sperm-cells, entering the ovum, opened
the way to a more correct interpretation of this process. We now
know that fertilisation is nothing more than the partial or complete fusion of two cells, the sperm-cell and the egg-cell, and
that normally only *one* of the former unites with *one* of the latter. Fertilisation thus depends on the union of two protoplasmic
substances. Moreover, although the male germ-cell is always very
much smaller relatively than the female germ-cell, we know that
the father's capacity for transmission is as great as the
mother's. The important conclusion is therefore arrived at that
only a small portion of the substance of the ovum can be the actual hereditary substance. Pflüger and Nägeli were the first to
follow out this idea to its logical conclusion, and the latter
observer stated definitely that it is impossible to avoid the
assumption that no more hereditary substance is contained in the
egg-cell than in the male germ-cell, and that consequently the
amount of the substance must be infinitesimal, for the sperm-cell
is, in most cases, many hundred times smaller than the ovum.
The numerous and important results of the investigations of
many excellent observers on the process of fertilisation have now
rendered it almost certain--in my opinion, absolutely so--that by

*August Weismann, *The Germ-Plasm, A Theory of Heredity*, trans. by
W. Newton Parker and Harriet Rönnfeldt (London, 1893), pp. 22-24,
26, 37, 39-40, 42-45, 48-49, 52-54, 56-57, 59-63, 65-67.

far the larger part of the egg-cell does not consist of hereditary substance, and that the latter only constitutes a small portion even of the sperm-cell. From his observations on the egg of the star-fish, Oscar Hertwig had suspected that the essential part of the process of fertilisation consists in the union of the *nuclei* of the egg- and sperm-cells, and as it is now known that the hereditary substance is undoubtedly contained in the nucleus, this view has, in this respect at least, proved to be the right one. It is true that the nucleus of the male cell is always surrounded by a cell-body, and that Strasburger's opinion to the contrary is incorrect. We now know, through the researches of Guignard, that even in Phanerogams a small cell-body surrounds the nucleus, and that a special structure, the 'centrosome,'--which is absolutely essential for the commencement of development,--is contained within it. This structure will be treated of in further detail presently, but I must here lay stress upon my view, that *the 'centrosome' with its 'sphere of attraction' cannot in any case be the hereditary substance, and that it is merely an apparatus for the division of the cell and nucleus.*

Both in animals and plants, however, essentially the same substance is contained in the nucleus both of the sperm-cell and egg-cell:--this is the *hereditary substance of the species*. There can now be no longer any doubt that the view which has been held for years by Strasburger and myself is the correct one, according to which *the nuclei of the male and those of the female germ-cells are essentially similar, i.e., in any given species they contain the same specific hereditary substance.*

The splendid and important investigations carried out by Auerbach, Bütschli, Flemming, and many others, on the detailed processes of nuclear division in general, and those dealing more particularly with the fertilisation of the egg in *Ascaris* by van Beneden, Boveri, and others, have given us the means of ascertaining more definitely what portion of the nucleus is the substance on which heredity depends. As already remarked, this substance corresponds to the 'chromosomes,' those rod-like, looped, or granular bodies which are contained in the nucleus, and which become deeply stained by colouring matters.

As soon as it had been undoubtedly proved that the nucleus, and not the body of the cell, must contain the hereditary substance, the conclusion was drawn that neither the membrane of the nucleus, nor its fluid contents, nor the nucleoli--which latter had been the first to attract attention--could be regarded as such, and that the 'chromatic granules' alone were important in this respect. As a matter of fact several investigators,--Strasburger, Oscar Hertwig, Köllicker, and myself,--reasoning from the same data, arrived at this conclusion independently, within a short time of one another.

It will not be considered uninteresting or superfluous to recapitulate the weighty reasons which force us to this conclusion, for it is clear that it must be of fundamental importance in a theory of heredity to know for certain what the substance is from which the phenomena which are to be explained proceed.

The certainty with which we can claim the 'chromatin granules' of the nucleus as the hereditary substance depends firstly, on the process of amphimixis; and secondly, on that of nuclear division. We know that the process of fertilisation consists essentially in the association of an equal number of chromatin rods from the paternal and maternal germ-cells, and that these give rise to a new nucleus from which the formation of the off-spring proceeds. We also know that in order to become capable of fertilisation each germ-cell must first get rid of half of its nuclear rods, a process which is accomplished by very peculiar divisions. Without entering into further particulars here, amphi-mixis may be described as a process by means of which one-half of the number of nuclear rods is removed from a cell and replaced by an equal number from another germ-cell.

*   *   *

It is evident, as Wilhelm Roux was the first to point out, that the whole complex but wonderfully exact apparatus for the division of the nucleus exists for the purpose of dividing the chromatin substance in a fixed and regular manner, not merely quantitatively, but also in respect of the *different qualities* which must be contained in it. So complicated an apparatus would have been unnecessary for the quantitative division only: if, how-ever, the chromatin substance is not uniform, but is made up of several or many different qualities, each of which has to be di-vided as nearly as possible into halves, or according to some definite rule, a better apparatus could not be devised for the purpose. On the strength of this argument, we may therefore represent *the hereditary substance as consisting of different 'qualities.'* The same conclusion is arrived at on purely theo-retical grounds, as will be shown later on when we follow out the consequences of the process of amphimixis.

For the present it is sufficient to show that the complex mechanism for cell-division exists practically for the sole pur-pose of dividing the chromatin, and that thus the latter is with-out doubt the most important portion of the nucleus. Since, therefore, the hereditary substance is contained within the nu-cleus, *the chromatin must be the hereditary substance.*

*   *   *

The Material Basis of Heredity.

The Germ-Plasm.

1. The Fundamental Units.

Now that the conception of the germ-plasm as the hereditary substance contained in the germ-cells has been fully established, and since it has been shown in general terms that this form of the idioplasm must become changed during ontogeny and converted into the idioplasm of the cells which constitute the mature organism, we must attempt to form some idea of its nature; for it would otherwise be impossible to construct a theory of heredity. In attempting this, we shall for the present entirely neglect the complication due to sexual reproduction, and take as our starting-point a germ-plasm which does not contain the primary constituents of two parents, but those of one only,--that is to say, one which

is constituted just as it would be in a species which had at all
times multiplied asexually.

*   *   *

All those writers who have assumed the existence of units on
which the vital forces of protoplasm depend, have pointed out that
they are not chemical molecules, for the latter do not possess the
power of assimilation and reproduction. Hence it follows that
protoplasm is a complex substance which is not homogeneous, but
which consists of different kinds of molecules. There is therefore no molecule of protoplasm, but we have to imagine that even
in its simplest modifications, protoplasm invariably consists of
groups of molecules, each of which is composed of *different kinds*
of chemical molecules. I shall call these units the *'bearers of
vitality'* ('Lebensträger') or *biophors*,' because they are the
smallest units which exhibit the primary vital forces, viz.,
*assimilation and metabolism, growth, and multiplication by fis-
sion.*

As living protoplasm cannot be subjected to chemical analysis, we cannot describe its chemical constitution more precisely;
but what has so far been determined by the analysis of dead protoplasm certainly indicates that the albuminoids are not the only
bearers of vitality, as has generally been assumed, but that other
substances play a no less important part in living protoplasm,--a
fact which has been insisted on by Hoppe-Seyler and Baumann. Besides albuminoids, compounds containing phosphorus, such as leci-
thin and nuclein, which are not related chemically to albumen, but
enter into combination with it, are known to occur in dead protoplasm; and besides these, protoplasm also contains cholesterin,
which is probably a product of destructive metabolism, and carbohydrates, such as glycogen, starch, inulin, and dextrin, as well
as compounds of potassium. Although we cannot at present guess
from what chemical compounds in living protoplasm these bodies
have been derived, there can be no doubt that 'a relation exists
between them and the vital processes' (Hoppe-Seyler), and that
albumen, or different kinds of albumen, do not alone bring about
the vital processes, but that several other substances, such as
salts, and compounds containing phosphorus, and more particularly
water, are just as essential; in short, life depends simply on the
interaction of molecules, differing chemically from one another,
but *defined* within certain limits.

After long consideration, I have decided to designate such a
group of molecules on which the phenomena of life depend by the
special term *'biophor.'* . . .

*   *   *

. . . The biophors, as bearers of vitality, possess the power
of growth and of multiplication by fission, *just as is the case in
all orders of vital units on which direct observations have been
made*, beginning with the microsomata, which constitute the chromatin of the nucleus, and passing through the chlorophyll granules,
nuclei, and cells, up to the simpler plants and animals. Nägeli's
micellæ also multiply, but the multiplication occurs 'by the free
interposition of new micellæ, similar to, or identical with, those

already present,' in the same manner as he supposed the addition
of new particles to take place in a starch grain, or as crystals
separate from the mother liquor. These new micellæ would certainly have to be formed by an influence, exerted by those already
present, which cannot be further defined. . . .

The biophors play the same part with respect to heredity as
that which de Vries ascribes to his pangenes, *i.e.*, they are the
'bearers of the qualities or 'characters' of the cells;' or more
accurately, *the bearers of the cell-qualities*. As all living
matter consists of biophors, the differences in it can only depend
on the differences in the biophors composing it; an animal cell
containing, for example, transversely striped muscular substance,
or delicate nervous or glandular structures, or again, a vegetable
cell enclosing chlorophyll bodies, must contain several *different*
kinds of biophors of which these various cell-structures are composed, and which constitute the germ-plasm of a species.

There must be a great number of different kinds of biophors,
for otherwise they could not give rise to so great a variety of
cells as exists in the organic world. Nor is it difficult to infer the possibility of an almost unlimited number of different
kinds of biophors from their assumed composition.

As the biophors are not individual molecules, but *groups* of
molecules, nothing prevents us from tracing a large number of
variations in them to the widely varying *number of their molecules*. But even the *chemical constitution of the molecules* is not
by any means necessarily the same in all cases, although the possible fluctuations are certainly confined within certain limits.

Numerous facts show that at any rate in the two main divisions of the organic world, the animal and vegetable kingdoms,
several of the molecules composing the biophors differ chemically
from one another, so that substitutions occur. Whereas glycogen
is a constituent which is never absent from animal protoplasm,
provided that the latter possesses amœboid movement, this carbohydrate has not yet been discovered in plants, in which, as Hoppe-
Seyler suspects, it is probably replaced by amylum, dextrine, or
gum. Similarly, the crystalline proteids in plants, which are
known as aleurone grains, are chemically different from the yolk-
granules in animals.

A difference in the biophors can, moreover, be conceived
without a change in their atomic composition, by regarding as possible a *re-arrangement of the atoms* in the individual molecules.
The molecule of albumin in particular has, according to the conclusions of modern chemistry, a molecular weight of at least 1,000,
so that innumerable isomeric molecules of albumen seem to be conceivable. It is, however, impossible to state how many of them
actually exist.

In order to give as complete an explanation as possible of
the phenomena of heredity with the aid of the biophors, the latter
must be invested with the capacity for a further change, namely,
a rearrangement of the molecules, analogous to the isomeric re-
arrangement of the atoms in a single molecule. This assumption is
not unfounded, inasmuch as several instances of molecular compounds
are known in chemistry, *e.g.*, the double salts and the water of
crystallisation of salts, in which definite numbers of molecules

are always present: this number is even retained in spite of substitution. Thus alum always contains twenty-four molecules of
water of crystallisation, and this evidently indicates a degree of
affinity between the molecules. We shall have to assume this
property for the biophor also, for without it the latter would not
be a real unit at all. We shall, moreover, be able to conclude
that these degrees of affinity are of various kinds, and that the
molecules can combine in many different ways and form groups, so
that isomeric molecular compounds are formed. Such isomeric compounds, however, will possess other properties, just as in the
isomeric arrangement of atoms in the individual molecule; and thus
we conclude that the special properties of a biophor are to be
considered dependent not only on the physico-chemical constitution
of the molecule, but also very essentially on their position and
relation to one another; so that one biophor can be changed into
another by an alteration in the arrangement of its molecules.

According to this statement there are several kinds of biophors, the difference between which depends on either the absolute
relative number of molecules, their chemical constitution (isomerism included), or their grouping; in fact we may say that the
number of possible kinds of biophors is unlimited, just as is the
number of conceivable organic molecules. We shall, at any rate,
meet with no theoretical difficulties on this score, however large
the number of different kinds of biophors may be which we require
to explain the theory of heredity.

*The biophors are not, I believe, by any means mere hypotheti-
cal units; they must exist*, for the phenomena of life must be connected with a material unit of some sort. But since the primary
vital forces--assimilation and growth--do not proceed spontaneously
from either atoms or molecules, there must be a unit of a higher
order from which these forces are developed, and this can only
consist of a group consisting of a combination of dissimilar molecules. I emphasise this particularly, because a theory of heredity
requires so many assumptions which cannot be substantiated that
the few fixed points on which we can rely are doubly valuable.

These biophors constitute *all* protoplasm--the morphoplasm
which is differentiated into the cell-substance, as well as the
idioplasm contained in the nucleus. It will be shown subsequently
in what manner these two kinds of protoplasm differ as regards
their constitution, and I will only remark here that the idioplasm
must have a far more complex structure than the morphoplasm. The
latter, as the cell-substance of a muscle or gland-cell shows, can
assimilate, grow, and also divide, but it is not able to change
into anything *different from itself*. The idioplasm, on the other
hand, is capable of regular change during growth; and ontogeny, or
the development of the individual in multicellular organisms,
depends upon this fact. The two first embryonic cells of an animal arise from the division of the ovum, and continually give rise
to differently constituted cells during the course of embryogeny.
The diversity of these cells must, as I have shown, depend on
changes in the nuclear substance.

It now remains to be considered how we are to imagine this
capacity on the part of the idioplasm for regular and spontaneous
change. The fact in itself is beyond doubt, when once it is

established that the morphoplasm of each cell is controlled, and its character decided, by the idioplasm of the nucleus. The regular changes occurring in the egg-cell and the products of its division in each embryogeny must then be referred to the corresponding changes of the idioplasm. *But what is the nature of these changes, and how are they brought about?*

*   *   *

If, then, each vital unit in all organisms, from the lowest to the highest grade, can only arise by division from another like itself, an answer is given to the question with which we started; and we see that the structures of a cell-body, which constitute the specific character of the cell, cannot be produced by the emitted influence of the nuclear substance, nor by its enzymatic action, but can only arise owing to the migration of material particles of the nucleus into the cell-body. *Hence the nuclear matter must be in a sense a storehouse for the various kinds of biophors which enter into the cell-body and are destined to transform it.* Thus the development of the 'undifferentiated' embryonic cell into a nerve-, gland-, or muscle-cell, as the case may be, is determined in each case by the presence of the corresponding biophors in the respective nuclei, and in due time these biophors will pass out of the nuclei into the cell-bodies, and transform them.

To me this reasoning is so convincing that any difficulties we meet with in the process of determining the nature of the cell hardly come into account. We are still far from being able to describe in detail the entire histological process of the differentiation of a cell. The passage of invisible 'biophors' through the pores of the nuclear membrane is probably just as admissible an assumption as that of the independent power of motion thereby necessitated in these bearers of vitality; but the histological structure of a cell is not completed by the mere emission into the cell-body of a few kinds of biophors with great powers of multiplication. Numerous questions suggest themselves in this connection, all pointing to the fact that forces are at work of which we are at present ignorant. The immigrating biophors are the mere material which forms the histological structure of a cell, only when subjected to the guiding forces--presumably those of attraction and repulsion--which must be located in the biophor.

We can as yet form no more exact conception of this process than we can of the manner in which the biophors already contained in the cell-body behave in respect to those which have migrated into it from the nucleus. Presumably a struggle of the parts occurs, in which the weaker are suppressed and serve as nutritive material for the stronger ones. But although much remains to be decided by future investigation, the main point at issue, at any rate, viz., that the nature of the cell is really decided by the elements of the nucleus, is definitely established. By the nature of the cell must be understood not only the histological structure of the cell as a whole and its mode of reacting to external influences, but more particularly its *mode of division* in respect of time and place. It is true that the cell-*body* itself and its apparatus for division (the centrosome) primarily determine whether a cell is to divide sooner or later, and into equal or unequal parts; but these processes always depend finally on the nucleus, which controls the cell-body and impresses on the latter its definite nature.

*   *   *

The experiments made by Nussbaum and Gruber on the artificial division of Infusoria prove that the nucleus really controls the cell-body. These observers found that only those portions which contained a part of the nucleus were capable of giving rise to a complete animal; the other pieces lived for a time, and then perished. One of Gruber's observations also tends to show that when regeneration of missing parts occurs, the nucleus sends out invisible material particles into the cell-body. He cut a large *Stentor* which was preparing for division transversely into two parts, so that the posterior portion contained no trace of the nucleus, and then observed that regeneration of the missing parts nevertheless took place, especially in the oral region. If the control of the cell depended on the emitted influence of the nucleus, this regeneration would be totally inexplicable; if, however, biophors proceed from the nucleus into the cell-body when regeneration is to take place, this might have already occurred in an animal preparing for division, as this one was before it was artificially divided.

The descendants of unicellular animals are similar to their ancestors: two daughter-cells are produced by the division of the mother-cell, and thus the nuclear substance is always composed of different kinds of biophors. But how does this apply to multicellular forms in which so large a number of different kinds of cells, each presupposing a different structure of the nuclear matter, arises from the germ-plasm of the ovum? Thus we find ourselves brought back to the question asked at the end of the last section:--on what do the regular series of changes in the germ-plasm during ontogeny depend?

3. The Determinants.

As has just been shown, the nuclear matter of an Infusorian must be composed of a great number of different kinds of biophors, each of which corresponds to the primary constituent of a definite portion of the unicellular organism. If the cells of a multicellular animal were represented in the germ-plasm by all the kinds of biophors occurring in them, such an enormous aggregation of biophors would result that, even if they were extremely small, the minute quantity of matter in the germ-plasm would not be able to contain them. It was this consideration more than any other which for many years made me persevere in my attempt to discover an epigenetic theory of heredity. I thought that it must be possible to imagine a germ-plasm which, although higher complex, nevertheless did not consist of such an inconceivably large number of separate particles, but which was of such a structure as to become changed in a regular manner during its growth in the course of ontogeny, and, finally, to yield a large number of different kinds of idioplasm for the control of the cells of the body in a specific manner.

Hatschek, too, has recently put forward the view that 'the egg-cell may be supposed to contain a relatively small number of qualities,' and that this number is not larger than that which is to be assumed in the case of any other histologically differentiated cell of the body. The diversity in structure seen in multicellular organisms is due, in his opinion, to the fact that in spite of the limited diversity as regards the qualities contained within a single cell (including the ovum), a far greater complication of the body as a whole is attained by the variation of these few qualities ('des einen Grundthemas').

If in considering a theory of heredity we had only to deal with an explanation of the transmission of an *unalterable* structure from the parent to the offspring from generation to generation, there would be theoretically no objection to the assumption of such a structure of the germ-plasm. We have, however, to deal with the transmission of parts which are *variable*, and this necessitates the assumption that just as many independent and variable parts exist in the germ-plasm as are present in the fully formed organism. It is impossible that a portion of the body should exhibit an independent variation capable of transmission unless it were represented in the germ-plasm by a special particle, a variation in which is followed by one in the part under consideration. If this were represented, together with other parts of the body, by one particle of the germ-plasm, a change in the latter would be followed by a variation in all the parts of the body determined by it. *The independently and hereditarily variable parts of the body therefore serve as an exact measure for determining the number of ultimate particles of which the germ-plasm is composed: the latter must contain at least as great a number as would be arrived at by such a computation.*

*   *   *

The germ-plasm must consequently be composed of as many units as there are transmissible parts in the body which are independently variable from the germ onwards. Each of these units cannot be smaller than a biophor, and they can therefore not be simple molecules within a biophor; for variation is a biological conception, and a biological element does not presuppose a one that is merely physical.

What parts of the body of a multicellular organism are represented in the germ by special particles of the minimum value of one biophor? Is each cell, or even each part of a cell? Darwin adopted the former, and de Vries the latter of these two alternatives. Darwin's gemmules are germs of *cells,* so that every cell of the body would be represented in the ovum by these units; while de Vries's pangenes are in a sense germs of the characters or structures ('Zellorganen') of the cell. There is no doubt that the hereditary variations in plants and animals manifest themselves in alterations of the individual parts or structures of the cell, and not only in the *number,* relative arrangement, and the changes in the form, size, and nature of the cells as a whole. The variegated varieties of our ornamental plants possess similar cells to those of their ancestral forms, but the green colour of the leaf is absent in certain of the cells: the red tint of the leaves of the copper beech, and other varieties of plants, depends on the red colour of the sap in a certain layer of cells, and this colour is transmissible. The coloured pattern of a butterfly's wing or a bird's plumage depends on cellular elements which were probably all alike in remote ancestors, but which afterwards became gradually changed by hereditary variations in the individual components or in the structure of the cell. Although the entire phyletic transformation of a species does not by any means alone depend on its *intra*-cellular variation, the latter has, nevertheless, constantly accompanied the other variations, and has shared to a greater or less extent in the transformation of the species. Hence it cannot be doubted that even in multicellular forms not only the cells as a whole, but also their parts, are determined from the germ onwards.

It seems therefore impossible to avoid the stupendous assumption that each of the millions of cells in a multicellular organism is represented in the germ-plasm by several or many different kinds of biophors. There is, however, a simple and natural way out of this dilemma, as soon as we inquire whether *every* cell of a plant or an animal is independently variable at all, and whether consequently it must be represented by special elements in the germ-plasm.

I shall designate the cells or groups of cells which are independently variable from the germ onwards as the '*hereditary parts*' or '*determinates*,' and the particles of the germ-plasm corresponding to and determining them, as the '*determining parts*' or '*determinants*.' It is evident that many of the cells in the higher animals are not represented *individually* in the germ-plasm by a determinant. The millions of blood-corpuscles which are formed during the life of a Vertebrate might possibly be controlled in the germ-plasm by a *single* determinant. At any rate no disadvantage to the species would result from this, because the capacity for being independently determined on the part of the individual blood-corpuscles, or even individual thousands of them, would be of no value to the animal. They are not localised: one of them has the same value as another, and their variability therefore might well be controlled from a single point. In conformity with the law of economy, Nature would not have incorporated more determinants than was necessary into the germ-plasm.

* * *

In all the more highly differentiated animals there can be little doubt that the number of determinants is always very much less than that of the cells which are the factors in the process of ontogeny. If we compare this statement with Darwin's assumption of the presence of a gemmule--or rather of several gemmules-- for each cell, it is evident that the germ-plasm is thus to some extent relieved of a burden.

We must not forget, however, that a cell may vary as regards transmission not only as a whole but also in its parts, so that not *one* but several biophors must be assumed for each determinant of a cell or group of cells; we must, in fact, suppose just as many to be present as there are structures in the cell which are variable from the germ onwards. We ought, properly speaking, to speak of these bearers of qualities, which correspond to de Vries's pangenes, as determinants also, for they determine the parts of a cell. As the name of biophor has been given to them, however, it is better to retain this term, and to define a *determinant as a primary constituent of a cell or group of cells*. Thus a determinant is always a group of biophors, and never a single one.

It may now, I believe, be proved without difficulty that the biophors determining a cell not only lie close together in the germ-plasm so as to form a group, but that *they also combine to form a higher unit*. The determinant is not a disconnected mass of different biophors, but *a vital unit of a higher order than the biophor, possessed of special qualities*.

The fact that the determinants must possess the power of multiplication is in itself a sufficient proof of this. We know how greatly the nuclear matter contained in the fertilised egg-cell increases in volume during development, and this can only be due to the multiplication of its vital particles, the biophors. Such a multiplication could never occur with as much precision and regularity as is necessary for the preservation of the character of a certain cell, if the biophors which determine it were scattered at random instead of being definitely separated from those of other cells. Hence the multiplication of the biophors must occur within the fixed limits of the determinant, and must be preliminary to the division of the determinant itself. And consequently the latter is also a vital unit.

In accordance with our assumption, which can scarcely be refused, a single determinant of the germ-plasm frequently controls entire groups of cells: this is a further proof that the determinants as such must multiply. This is only possible if they do so in the process of ontogeny. It is very probable, moreover, that the nucleoplasm of any cell in the body never contains *one* specimen only of the determinant controlling it, but several; otherwise, how could such a cell be visible at all under our microscopes? Biophors, at any rate, are far beyond the limit of vision, and even determinants can hardly come within it.

Thus the assumption made by the gifted propounder of the theory of pangenesis is so far justified. 'Gemmules' of cells really exist, and multiply by fission; but they are not the ultimate vital units, nor are special gemmules of all the cells of the body already present in the germ-plasm.

We have next to deal with the question as to how these two elements of the germ-plasm, which have not been formulated, are instrumental in the process of ontogeny.

4. The Id in Ontogeny.

We can now make an attempt to solve the problem stated at the close of the last section concerning the way in which the germ-plasm is capable of giving rise to the various kinds of idioplasm required in the construction of the organism.

As we have seen, the germ-plasm contains the primary constituents of all the cells in the body in its determinants, and it only remains to inquire how each kind of determinant reaches the right part in the right number. Although we do not know what forces are called into play for this purpose, the elements of the germ-plasm now formulated, and the processes and course of ontogeny, nevertheless enable us to draw certain conclusions as to the structure of the germ-plasm and the nature of the changes it undergoes; and I trust that these conclusions will not lead us too far from the truth.

We can, in the first place, state with certainty that the germ-plasm possesses a *fixed architecture, which has been transmitted historically*. In working out the idea of determinates, it was stated that probably not nearly all the cells of the higher organisms are represented in the germ-plasm by special determinants: possibly all the blood-corpuscles, or the thousands of fibres in a particular muscle, for instance, are represented each by *one* determinant. But it does not therefore follow that all the cells of a similar kind which exist in the body can be represented by *one* common determinant: this would be equivalent to abandoning the conception of determinants altogether. If, for instance, all the transversely striped muscles of a Vertebrate were represented in the germ-plasm by a *single* determinant, each variation in the latter would also produce a corresponding change in *all* the muscles, and the independent variation of which each individual muscle is actually capable would then be impossible.

Several, or even many, similar determinants must therefore exist in the germ-plasm of an animal. Muscle-cells and nerve-cells are repeatedly formed even in the fully developed organism, and, in so far as they can vary individually at all from the germ onwards, will be represented by identical or by very similar determinants in the germ-plasm.

If such *identical* determinants represent a single fixed cell or group of cells, they cannot be situated anywhere in the germ-plasm, nor can they change their position according to varying influences: the determinants must be definitely localised, for otherwise they would not be certain to reach the right cell and the right position in the course of ontogeny. I have already mentioned the olfactory setæ of *Gammarus*, which are situated individually on particular segments of the feeler. Each of these can vary hereditarily, and thus it is necessary to assume special determinants for them in the germ-plasm; these, however, will all be similar to one another. This is also true of the black spots on the wings of certain butterflies, already referred to. In *Lycæna argus*, for instance, there is a spot on that part of the wing which is known to entomologists as 'cell 1 b,' and this spot is independently variable: it may be larger or smaller, and the variations in it can be transmitted quite independently of the numerous other black marks on the wing. The particular spot referred to may have disappeared entirely in another species of *Lycæna*, while a precisely similar spot in 'cell 4' has become much larger. We have also decided indications that homologous parts in the two halves of the body in bilaterally symmetrical animals can vary independently of one another. The human birth-mark mentioned above was always inherited on the left side, and never on the right.

If each determinant occupies a fixed position in the germ-plasm, *it cannot have an indefinite or variable size and form,*

but must form a complete unit by itself, from which nothing can
be removed, and to which nothing can be added. In other words,
we are led to the assumption *of groups of determinants*, each of
which represents a separate vital unit of the third degree, since
it is composed of determinants, which in their turn are made up
of biophors. These are the units which I formulated on different
lines long ago, and to which the name of *ancestral germ-plasms*
was then given. I shall now speak of them as '*ids*,' a term which
recalls the 'idioplasm' of Nägeli.

I assume that just as the individual biophor has other qualities than those of the determinant, which is composed of biophors,
so also does the id possess qualities differing from those of its
component determinants. The fundamental vital properties--growth
and multiplication by division--must however be attributed to the
id as to all vital units. Several reasons, more especially those
furnished by the phenomena of heredity in sexual reproduction,
lead us to assume that the germ-plasm does not consist of a *single*
id, but of several, or even many of them, and this assumption must
be made even in the case of asexual reproduction.

I shall therefore assume that *each idioplasm is composed of
several or many ids, which are capable of growth and multiplication by division*. If animals existed, in the whole series of
ancestors of which sexual reproduction had never occurred, these
ids would be exactly similar to one another. But in all cases
every id of the germ-plasm contains the whole of the elements
which are necessary for the development of all subsequent idic
stages. Theoretically, therefore, *one* id would suffice for
ontogeny.

We assume that *the changes in the id of germ-plasm during
ontogeny* consist merely in a regular disintegration of the determinants into smaller and smaller groups, until finally only *one*
kind of determinant is contained in the cell, viz., that which
has to determine it. It is highly improbable that all the determinants in the id of germ-plasm are carried along through all the
idic stages of the ontogeny. In discussing regeneration and
gemmation later on, I shall have to show that, under certain circumstances, groups of determinants are supplied to certain series
of cells, and that these are not actually required for determining the cells; this arrangement, however, depends, I believe, on
special adaptations, and is not primitive, at any rate not in the
higher animals and plants. Why should Nature, who always manages
with economy, indulge in the luxury of providing all the cells of
the body with the whole of the determinants of the germ-plasm if
a single kind of them is sufficient? Such an arrangement will
presumably only have occurred in cases in which it serves definite purposes. The enormous number of determinants contained in
the germ-plasm also stands in the way of such an assumption, for
in the higher animals they can be reckoned by hundreds of thousands at the very least; and although we may assume that they all
remain in a latent condition in every cell, and so need not interfere with the activity of the determinants which control the cell,
they nevertheless deprive the active determinants--which we must
also suppose to exist in large numbers--of a considerable space.

*   *   *

. . . *The historical transmission of the architecture of the germ-plasm forms the basis of the entire ontogenetic development of the idioplasm.*

If however the id has a right and left half in bilateral animals, we must not thereby infer that it is merely a miniature of the fully formed animal, and that therefore we are once more dealing with the old theory of preformation. Quite apart from all conjectures as to the detailed architecture of the id of germ-plasm, it is at any rate certain that the arrangement of the determinants in it is quite different from that of the corresponding parts in the fully-formed organism. This is proved by a study of development, and need scarcely be treated of in detail here. Any one with a knowledge of animal embryology knows how great a difference there is between the mode of development of the parts from one another in the embryo and their respective relation in the mature organism. The early stages of segmentation of the ovum show that groups of determinants have been formed in the id of germ-plasm, and that these, moreover, correspond to the parts of the body which arise from one another consecutively, though they can have no resemblance to them either in form or in their degree of perfection.

In some worms the two first blastomeres do not give rise respectively to the right and left sides of the body, but to the entire ectoderm and endoderm. In these cases the id of germ-plasm must break up into two groups, one of which contains all the determinants of the ectodermal organs, and the other all those of the endoderm: it is evident that this arrangement has no analogy to that which obtains as regards the organs of the fully-formed animal. If in any species we knew the 'value in primary constituents' ('Anlagenwerth')--if I may use such a term--of each cell in the ontogeny, we could give an approximate representation of the architecture of the germ-plasm; for, beginning with the last formed cells, we could infer the nature of the determinants which must have been contained in each previous mother-cell, passing gradually backwards to the ovum; thus we should reach the two first blastomeres, and finally the egg-cell itself. The groups of determinants which are present at each stage would thus be known, and we might in imagination then arrange them in such a way that it would be possible to picture their disintegration into the respective series of smaller and smaller groups.

Such a representation of the architecture of the id of germ-plasm would, however, never be an accurate one, because its parts must be subjected to incessant slow displacement during the growth of the idioplasm and in the course of development.

This brings us to the *second factor* which takes part in the ontogeny of the idioplasm, viz., the uneven *rate of multiplication of the determinants*. An id of germ-plasm composed entirely of *similar* determinants, would have to retain its original architecture even during vigorous growth and continued division; just as would be the case in one of the lowest forms of life--a Moner-- consisting of a number of identical biophors, which must remain the same throughout all the divisions which it undergoes. In a germ-plasm consisting of a number of different determinants, a perfectly even rate of multiplication cannot be assumed in the case of all of them. For the difference between two determinants depends presumably on the differences in the nature, number, or arrangement of their constituent biophors, and the latter differ again in their molecular structure, *i.e.* in their essential physico-chemical properties. Hence the determinants will behave differently as regards their reaction to external influences,-- more especially in respect of their rate of growth and increase,-- according to their constitution. The same conditions of nutrition will therefore stimulate one to a faster, and another to a slower, growth and corresponding multiplication, and thus an alteration in the proportional numbers in which the individual kinds of determinants are present in the germ-plasm must occur continually in the course of embryogeny; for the latter is connected with a constant growth of the idioplasm, and therefore also with a continual increase of the determinants. This must cause a disarrangement in the architecture of the germ-plasm, in which process the third factor concerned in these changes, viz., *the forces of attraction in the determinants*, may take part.

The assumption of such forces can scarcely be avoided. For it is very probable, *a priori*, that vital units do act upon one another in different degrees, and this view is supported by a consideration of the processes of nuclear division, together with the distribution of the primary constituents in ontogeny.

So far I have not touched upon the question as to what observable parts of the idioplasm are to be regarded as ids. This point cannot be decided with certainty at present, but I have elsewhere expressed the opinion that those rod-like, loop-like, or granular masses of chromatin in the nucleus,--the chromosomes,--are to be considered equivalent, not to single ids, but to series or aggregations of ids. I have therefore proposed to call the chromosomes *idants*, in order to keep up a certain uniformity in the nomenclature. It is probable that the ids correspond to the small granules hitherto called 'microsomata,' which are known to form the individual idants in many animals: we may mention as an example, *Ascaris megalocephala*, as in it the nuclear structure is best known. These microsomata, although lying very close together in *one* row, are nevertheless separated by a thin layer of intermediate substance; the whole idant cannot therefore be equivalent to one id, for the latter is a clearly defined vital unit possessing a fixed architecture, and cannot consist of completely separated parts.

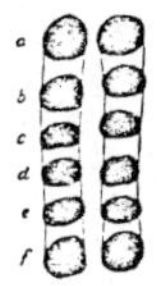

Fig. 2.
Two Idants with their contained Ids of *Ascaris megalocephala*. (After Boveri.)

The great variety as regards size, number, and form of the chromosomes in different species of animals, indicates that they possibly have not always a similar morphological value. As however there is no reason for assuming that the number of ids must always be the same in all species, and as, on the contrary, it is much more probable that their number varies greatly, it is impossible to make use of the above fact as a decisive argument. We can only state that the individual chromosome or idant in all probability represents a different number of ids in different species.

CONCLUSION

It is fitting, at this point, to try and draw together some of the main themes of what has gone before. Perhaps the most important point to make is that the 19th century witnessed two apparently contradictory scientific developments. On the one hand, science became more specialized and narrower so that, by the end of the century, a scientist was not just a physicist or a chemist, but a theoretical physicist or experimental physicist, or an organic chemist or a biochemist, or a mineralogical chemist, and so on. As fields narrowed and deepened, it became impossible for any one scientist to encompass more than his own specialty. Hence, it has often been remarked that the 19th century gave birth to the specialization of the sciences and the final destruction of the old ideal of "natural philosophy." This is true, but it ignores the fact that the sciences were also unified in the 19th century. The principle of the Conservation of Energy and the Second Law of Thermodynamics, just to give the most obvious examples, were not confined to physics. They applied equally well to chemistry and biology and were, in fact, to be of fundamental importance in the development of these, and all other, sciences.

The sciences were also unified in another sense. At the beginning of the 19th century, it was not at all clear how science should proceed. The atomic doctrine was in philosophical disrepute and, as we have seen, there were alternative philosophies of science that wished to dispense with altogether. What happened in the 19th century was the establishment of atomism, not just as a physical theory, but as an explanatory scheme of universal application. The atomic doctrine in chemistry, the atomic hypothesis in kinetic theory, the cell theory in biology and medicine all led to the same philosophical goal: the understanding of complicated processes by the understanding of the nature and activity of the elements upon which these processes depended. By the end of the century, it seemed clear to those who believed that all phenomena were the result of physico-chemical interactions, that the dance of the atoms must ultimately explain everything. It is fair to say that science became physics by 1900.

Finally, we can only note here the extraordinary rise of science in society. When the 19th century began, science was the preserve of a relatively few, generally financially independent, "amateurs" who cultivated it out of curiosity. Their rewards were generally intellectual or honorific. By the end of the century, scientists made up a new estate in modern society. Educational institutions had been created specifically for the creation of scientists and science had begun its permeation of all aspects of modern life. Scientists were now professionals, in great demand in universities and industries. That fact alone has revolutionized the modern world. We do not yet know what its full effect will be upon the lives of ordinary citizens. What we do know is that science has conquered the modern intellectual world. Ideas and concepts are respectable only insofar as they can successfully meet the test of scientific criticism. Older modes of thought have been forced into corners where they battle to survive. This is not to say that the scientific mode of thinking is, in fact, universally applicable or even correct. It merely means that science now sets the standards and other modes must justify themselves with that standard constantly in view. Western Civilization has become, then, the first scientific society in the history of the world.

EPILOGUE

While the attempt to give a picture of the development of the sciences in general must end with 1900, because of limitations of space, it would be unfair to the reader not to consider briefly the revolution in physics that marked the beginning of the twentieth century. Hence this epilogue.

The confident world of physical science in the 1890's was shattered by unexpected events and discoveries in the closing years of the century. Three major lines of development emerged from the confusion and reevaluation which occurred: the atomic theory, the theories of special and general relativity, and the quantum theory. Each of these new areas of work involved experiments and concepts never imagined in the context of nineteenth-century physics. The twentieth century ushered in both a change in subject matter and a fundamental change in the conception of the physical world. Even the major events in these three areas can only be hinted at in a brief account. The narrative soon involves concepts which are outside the range of comprehension of the reader untrained in physical science. Interesting areas of investigation can only be presented to give the reader some perspective as he continues his study in the sciences and the history of science.

A.   The Atomic Theory

The "atom" has had a prominent place in the history of science since the time of the Ancient Atomists, but the definition of the term has changed, as we have seen. The answers to the question, what is an atom, have varied widely, but the need for an answer remained constant. The concept of the atom changed to meet the changing requirements of explanation for physical and chemical phenomena. As the phenomena of the world were observed with greater and more exacting detail, the description of the atom became more complex to meet the increasing demands placed upon it. The Ancient Atomists conceived of the atom as a bit of matter moving in the void. The Newtonians envisioned a hard, massy, impenetrable, billiard-ball-like atom capable of various geometrical groupings to meet explanatory requirements in physics, optics and chemistry. The Daltonian atom added the concept of caloric and also provided the possibility of distinction by atomic weight. This was an atom well suited to the explanation of changes of state and the physical aspects of chemical reactions. The discovery of current electricity produced problems which led to Ampère's "electrodynamic molecule" and the concern with the ether prompted the formulation of the "vortex atom" by Stokes, Kelvin and Tait after 1850. In short, the nineteenth century had available a number of variations on the description of an atom. There was controversy over the type of atomic model most suitable, and there was some argument over the existence of atoms at all, as we have seen, but in the midst of all the activity, the notion of sub-atomic entities had not even occurred. The question of what is an atom was difficult enough, and there had been little reason to worry about the possible complexity of matter at the atomic level.

There had been some hints during the nineteenth century that the atom, whatever it was, had a structure. Evidence from chemistry on the periodicity of the chemical elements implied that atoms might have a structure which varied periodically with increasing atomic weight and position in the newly accepted periodic table. But chemists had many other more pressing problems to concern themselves with.

Faraday's work on electrolysis in the early 1830's also implied the existence of a subatomic entity. His second law of electrolysis states: "the atoms of bodies which are equivalent to each other in their ordinary chemical action have equal quantities of electricity naturally associated with them." But Faraday did not really believe in the existence of atoms and therefore usually spoke in terms of equivalent weights. He did not draw the possible conclusion that since atoms of elements have specific amounts of electricity associated with them in ordinary chemical action, electricity must be atomistic in character.

In 1874, Johnstone Stoney estimated the amount of charge carried by a single atom of hydrogen in electrolysis and called this an electron. It was not until 1881 that Hermann Helmholtz appreciated the implication of Faraday's second law of electrolysis and initiated the search for the carrier of the electrical properties of atoms.

The search for subatomic entities received strong stimulus from two other areas in late century: spectroscopy and the discovery of cathode rays. Observations of solar spectra had yielded a huge number of observations on the "dark lines" which appeared in the spectrum. William Hyde Wollaston (1766-1828) first noticed these dark lines and described them in a paper to the Royal Society of London in 1801. The Bavarian instrument maker, Joseph Fraunhofer (1787-1826) combined a telescope with a prism in order to see the solar spectrum more clearly and noticed, in 1814, that the dark lines had a constant position. Fraunhofer undertook the extended task of mapping the exact position of each "dark line" of the solar spectrum with respect to its visible wavelength. He discovered that the lines were in the same position regardless of whether light came directly from the sun or whether it was reflected from the moon or the planets.

In 1859, two Heidelberg professors, Gustav Kirchhoff (1824-87) and Rubert Bunsen (1811-99) showed that there was an invariable connection between certain lines of the spectrum and certain elements. They discovered this relationship to be fixed, using it to discover two new elements from unidentified spectral lines, caesium and rubidium. Anders Ångström (1814-74) increased the precision of measurement of the position of the lines, using the 10-millionth of a millimeter unit for wavelength which bears his name. He defined the visible region of the spectrum to be from red at 7600 angstroms to violet at 3900 angstroms. The use of photography then made the extension of spectroscopic observations possible, into the infrared on the long wavelength end and into the ultraviolet on the shorter wavelength side.

Until the 1880's, the spectrum of the sun and of the chemical elements had been a curiosity and sometimes a useful tool for research, but it seemed to pose no serious threat to accepted physical theory. There was no theory to account for the spectral lines, but it was assumed that since light consisted of waves in the ether, the lines must be produced by some complex form of atomic oscillation. In 1885, Johann Balmer (1825-98) studied the spectrum produced by hydrogen and declared that the large number of lines produced by this simplest element could not be accounted for in terms of atomic oscillations. Johannes Rydberg (1854-1919) recognized that the various spectra of hydrogen in the visible, infrared and ultraviolet regions of the spectrum could by analyzed into a series of lines. The wavelengths of these series could be represented rather closely by a mathematical formula. It became clear in the 1880's that the special spectral lines produced by every chemical element could not be explained in terms of the ordinary mechanics of vibration of an atom. There must be some more complex structure to account for the production of the spectral lines.

The discovery and investigation of cathode rays lent added impetus to the notion of a complex atomic structure. Glows in vacuum tubes produced by the discharge of electricity through a partially evacuated glass tube had been a curiosity during the first half of the nineteenth century. The color of the glow from the discharge could be varied by changing the kind of gas in the discharge tube. But after the work of Julius Plücker (1801-68) and his pupil Johann Hittorf (1824-1914) these tubes became more than a curiosity because it was determined that the discharge in the tube was accompanied by the emission of some type of an invisible ray from the negative electrode or cathode. Hittorf found that these "rays" were capable of casting the shadow of an opaque body on the wall of the tube. The rays seemed to be emitted in straight lines from the cathode and they produced a fluorescent glow at the point which they struck the glass wall of the tube. Eugen Goldstein (1850-1930) called the "rays" cathode rays in 1876 and Sir William Crookes (1832-1919) undertook an extended investigation of them in England. Sir William was convinced the cathode rays were particles of some type, but scientists on the Continent especially in Germany, as might be expected, considered the rays to be energy emanations in the ether.

The center for the study of cathode rays in England was the famous Cavendish Laboratory in Cambridge, founded in 1874. The Cavendish attracted the finest experimenters and students from all over the world. It was there that J. J. Thomson (1856-1940) took up the problem of the cathode rays and the related subject of the newly discovered X-rays in 1895. Thomson was convinced the cathode rays were composed of many small corpuscles which, after Stoney, he called electrons. He was determined to learn more about these electrons and succeeded in modifying a cathode ray tube in such a way that he could measure the charge to mass ratio of the corpuscles, the famous e/m of the electron. At a Friday Evening Discourse at the Royal Institution on 30 April 1897, Thomson announced that the cathode rays consisted of particles lighter than the lighest atom. Thomson's value for the e/m

ratio for the electron was 10^7. The same ratio for hydrogen was
10^4, so Thomson chose to infer that the charge e was the same but
the electron was 1/1000 the mass of the hydrogen atom. It seemed
very likely that this was the case, but it might well have been
that e was not the same at all. Thomson simply measured the ratio
and assumed the existence of the particle, the electron, with the
specified charge and mass. Many people, primarily Germans, simply
would not agree. It remained for Robert A. Millikan in 1904 to
devise his famous and delicate oil drop experiment to measure the
actual value for e and thereby allow the determination of m from
the e/m ratio. Millikan proved that the lowest common denominator
of the electral charge he was able to measure with his apparatus
was a specific value, 4.774×10^{-10} esu. Thus electric charge was
not continuous like a fluid, but came in discrete units of charge.
The particle which carried the charge was the electron observed
in J. J. Thomson's cathode ray tubes.

Thomson did not wait for Millikan's work to proceed to formulate an atomic model which included the electron. Unlike many
Germans, most Englishmen believed in the existence of atoms and
now electrons. The problem was how to relate this charged particle to the atom? This was a new problem for the atomic theory
because the atom was now to have a structure. In the normal
state, atoms do not have a charge. But electrons appeared to be
parts of matter. They had not only been produced in gas discharge
tubes, but also by irradiating gas with X-rays, and from hot in-
candescent filaments. Thomson devised his atomic model to account
for the inclusion of electrons in matter.

The Thomson atom consisted of a sphere of positive electricity, with electrons embedded in this sphere, like "raisins in a
hot cross bun." It was not a haphazard arrangement. The electrons were grouped in rings, with 5 in the first, 14 in the
second, and 26 in the third ring. This atom was well suited to
account for chemical phenomena. Atoms with filled rings were
inactive. Atoms with missing members of a ring were more chemically active. Oscillations and motions of electrons within the
positive atom provided a partial, qualitative explanation for the
production of the many spectral lines. This was the first atom
with a substructure. But while Thomson was developing his model,
work was being done to provide the means of demonstrating its
deficiencies.

The phenomena of radioactivity provided the means of disprov-
ing the Thomson model. The first X-rays were noticed by W. Röntgen
in 1896. X-ray photographs were taken by Röntgen and sent to the
French Academy of Science in January, 1896. The X-rays appeared
to come from the fluorescent patch on the glass discharge tube,
where cathode rays strike the wall. Henri Becquerel saw the photos
in February 1896 and decided to investigate whether phosphorescent
substances emitted X-rays. While investigating various phosphorescent substances, he discovered to his surprise that the salts
of uranium were capable of affecting a photographic plate, wrapped
tightly so as not to admit light. The uranium salts produced some
type of radiation capable of penetrating opaque substances. Marie
Curie (1867-1934), a poor student in Paris at the time, chose this
new phenomenon of radiation from uranium as the topic for her

doctoral dissertation. There were some observed similarities between X-ray behavior and this new radiation from uranium. Both
were capable of making gases conduct electricity when exposed to
the radiation. This conductivity could be measured by the leaking
of charge from a gold leaf electroscope (see Figure 1).

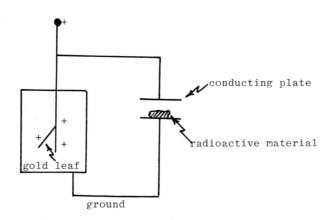

Figure 1

By careful use of this simple device, Marie Curie showed that the
amount of radiation was proportional to the weight of uranium
present. It did not make any difference what compounds of uranium
were used; the effect depended exclusively upon the uranium present. Radio activity, as Marie Curie called the phenomenon, seemed
to be an atomic property of uranium. With this in mind, she began
to investigate other metals to see if they exhibited similar
properties. She discovered that thorium was also radioactive and
that pitchblende, the ore from which uranium was extracted, was
four times as radioactive as pure uranium. Mme Curie reasoned
that the ore must contain some unknown radioactive element responsible for this radioactivity. To prove this idea, she had to
isolate the element and determine its atomic weight. This proved
to be a formidable four-year task. Mme Curie and her husband
Pierre Curie worked with 6 tons of pitchblende to finally produce
one-tenth gram of the new element. In 1902 they announced that
they had isolated a new element, radium, with an atomic weight of
225. The next year, the Curies received the Nobel Prize, along
with Henri Becquerel, for work in the new phenomena of radioactivity.
     At the beginning of the twentieth century, the atomic theory
had important added responsibilities. It must explain the observed

data on the various spectra produced by atoms, the presence of
electrons in the atomic substructure, and the strange production
of radioactive radiations by certain heavy metal atoms. Radioactivity was especially puzzling because it seemed to deny the conservation of energy. Radiation was not affected by temperature
or any other physical or chemical conditions. It occurred with
amazing stability. Radioactive substances such as radium seemed
capable of producing large amounts of heat continuously, without
apparent change of condition.

Stimulating answers to two of these requirements were provided by a brilliant young experimenter from New Zealand, Ernest
Rutherford (1871-1937). Rutherford was attracted to the Cavendish
Laboratory in 1897 by a full scholarship and by the chance to work
with the new phenomenon of radioactivity. Rutherford began by
studying the radiations from uranium salts. He soon discovered
that the radiations given off by uranium were quite different in
their behavior than X-rays. He found there were at least two
types of radiation emitted from uranium salts. The situation had
grown more complex than expected. Rutherford found a less penetrating and a more penetrating kind of radiation given off, which
he called alpha and beta radiation, respectively. He set to work
investigating the properties of alpha radiation and found that
substances absorbed this radiation rather differently. It could
be completely absorbed by a thick sheet of paper or by a few
centimeters of air.

At about the same time beta rays were shown to be similar in
charge to J. J. Thomson's e/m electrons; in fact they seemed to be
electrons. Also a third type of radiation emitted from some
radioactive substances was detected, gamma radiation, shown to be
similar to Röntgen's X-rays. There were now three kinds of radiation emitted by atoms. (See Figure 2.)

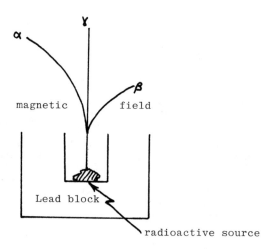

Figure 2

The three behaved differently in a magnetic field. The alpha rays
were bent in one direction, the beta rays were bent strongly in
the opposite direction, and the gamma rays seemed unaffected by
the field.

In September, 1898, Rutherford left Cambridge to take his
first job at the newly created MacDonald Research Laboratory at
McGill University in Montreal. At McGill, Rutherford began his
investigation of the radioactive properties of thorium. Thorium
seemed to produce a kind of inert radioactive gas. After two
years of study and several published articles on thorium, he determined two fundamental questions still to be answered: what was
the nature of the radioactive emanation from thorium and how was
this emanation produced? Rutherford realized that he needed the
help of a chemist to answer these questions, and happily found
Federick Soddy (1877-1956) working as a demonstrator in chemistry
at McGill.

Soddy had recently graduated from Merton College, Oxford
with first class honors in chemistry. He applied for a position
as professor at McGill, but was turned down in favor of an older
man. As a disappointing alternative he accepted a position as
demonstrator. To relieve the boredom of this uninspiring job, he
read widely and prepared a lecture course in "The History of
Chemistry from Earliest Times" as an interesting diversion. Soddy
developed a real interest in alchemy in the process and wrote a
paper "Alchemy and Chemistry" which concluded with a statement of
the importance of the concept of transmutation of the elements in
chemistry. "The constitution of matter," he wrote, "is the province of chemistry, and little, indeed, can be known of this constitution until transmutation is accomplished. This is, as it has
always been, the real goal of the chemist." Soddy saw the problem
of transmutation as a continuing problem in the history of chemistry.

In the fall of 1901, Soddy was asked to give a six-lecture
course on gas analysis. He knew the techniques of gas analysis
and he had worked with the newly discovered inert gas, argon. It
was at this point that the Rutherford-Soddy collaboration began--
Rutherford with his interest in radioactivity and his problems
with thorium, Soddy with his skill in gas analysis and his awareness of the question of transmutation. Rutherford's skill as a
physicist and Soddy's abilities as a chemist combined to produce
the disintegration theory of atoms and the theory of the natural
transmutation of radioactive substances through disintegration.
These formed the basis for radiochemistry. Their short collaboration between 1901 and 1903 resulted in nine papers and a Nobel
prize in chemistry for Rutherford in 1908.

Frederick Soddy's work in the disintegration theory was
usually forgotten after Rutherford's Nobel prize. It is most
probable that Soddy was in fact responsible for the concept of
the transmutation of the elements through disintegration. Rutherford's prize in chemistry read "To Ernst Rutherford, as a reward
for your researches on the disintegration of the elements and the
chemistry of radioactive matters." Rutherford admitted in a
letter to his friend Otto Hahn, "I am very startled at my metamorphosis into a chemist." He claimed the quickest transformation

in nature was his own from physicist to chemist. Soddy was eventually awarded a Nobel Prize in chemistry in 1921 for his work on the displacement law, which related the disintegration theory to the periodic table of the elements.

It was clear by 1905 that the Thomson model of the atom was not an adequate model to meet the demands placed upon it by the new discoveries. A new model was needed and Rutherford did the work to provide one. In 1907 he became professor of physics at Manchester University. He used the excellent laboratory facilities there and two conscientious assistants to begin a new series of experiments on alpha particles. Rutherford designed an experiment to investigate the scattering of alpha particles by matter. He turned over the performance of the experiment to his assistants Geiger and Marsden.

Alpha particles were produced by radium and aimed at a thin sheet of gold foil. The scattering of the particles was observed by means of a scintillation screen; a zinc sulphide screen which flashed when struck by an alpha particle. To everyone's surprise, the angles at which the alpha particles were scattered were much greater than calculations showed they should be. In fact, when the screen was extended to surround the gold foil completely, it was discovered that about one in ten thousand particles actually bounced back. This was incredible and completely inexplicable in terms of the Thomson model of the atom.

In 1910 Rutherford conceived of an atomic model which would explain the alpha scattering. The atom looked like a miniature solar system. The center was a heavy positively charged nucleus with electrons orbiting around the center. This nucleus was capable of deflecting the alpha particles and even causing them to rebound on a direct hit. Rutherford calculated the probability for the alpha particle scattering through various angles, assuming the inverse square law of electrostatic repulsion was operative between the nucleus and the alpha particle. The number of flashes on the scintillation screen could be predicted at various angles; 60 degrees, 120 degrees, 180 degrees, etc. Geiger and Marsden confirmed that the calculations coincided with observational data. It seemed as if the atom was a heavy nucleus with electrons orbiting about it. There were many problems yet to be solved in the atomic theory, but in the meantime a different area of physics was under rapid development and was soon to dramatically affect the atomic theory. This new area of study led to the quantum theory.

B. The Quantum Theory

The quantum theory had its origin in problems associated with the classical theory of electromagnetic radiation. The man responsible for the beginning of the quantum theory was Max Planck (1858-1947). Planck wanted to be a theoretical physicist at a time when most of the activity in the physical sciences was centered about laboratory work. He was fascinated with thermodynamics and with the study of energy relationships. In the 1890's he turned his attention to the great amount of work being done in spectroscopy and in the analysis of electromagnetic radiation

intensities. In 1895 Gustav Kirchhoff discovered a seemingly
simple relationship, that the absorptivity of a substance exactly
equalled its emissivity. The ratio of the total amount of radiant
energy absorbed by a body is equal to the ratio of the amount of
energy emitted by that body, compared to the total amount of energy which falls upon the body. A body which absorbs all the radiant energy which falls upon it would also emit the same amount of
energy. Such a body was called a black body, with an absorptivity
of 1. The absorptivity and emissivity of bodies were functions
of temperature, not of the detailed nature of the bodies themselves. This was rather surprising. It suggested that the spectral distribution of the radiation of a black body depended only
upon temperature. Black bodies at the same temperature should
yield the same spectral distribution of radiation, that is to say
there should be the same amount of radiant energy at each wavelength for every black body at the same temperature. The actual
amount of energy at any particular wavelength would vary according
to whether the temperature of the black body was raised or lowered.
When the temperature was rather low, most energy would be at the
longer wavelengths, such as red and the infrared. As the temperature was increased, the spectral distribution of the radiation
would shift toward the shorter wavelengths. This phenomenon had
been observed and in fact the shift had been mathematically described in 1893 by Wien.

The actual energy distribution for each wavelength could be
easily measured and graphs of the experimental data were easily
plotted (see Figure 3).

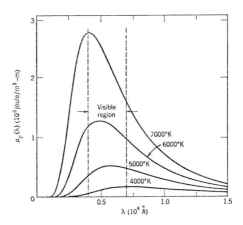

Figure 3. Spectral Distribution of Black Body Radiation

The problem was that even though experimental data abounded, no one in the 1890's had succeeded in finding the theoretical equation which fit that data. Theoretical calculations of what the curve should look like were all failures. Ever since Descartes formulated his analytical geometry with the assumption that each curve on a graph should correspond to a mathematical equation, natural philosophers and mathematicians alike believed this to be true.

The unnatural split between theoretical calculation and experimental evidence was finally reconciled by Max Planck. But his reconciliation was effected by making a very disturbing assumption about the physical situation. Planck's postulate, stated in modern terms, was as follows: "Any physical entity whose single 'coordinate' executes simple harmonic oscillations can possess only total energies E which satisfy the relation $E = nh\nu$, $n = 0, 1, 2, 3 \ldots$, where ν is the frequency of oscillation and h is a universal constant." This means that the emission of energy by an oscillator is limited to only certain levels. Instead of being able to observe the emission of any amount of energy at all, only special levels, given by $e = nh\nu$ will be observed.

When Planck applied this postulate to black body radiation, he was able to derive the theoretical radiation equation which fit the experimentally produced data curves exactly. On October 19, 1900, Planck submitted his radiation formula to the Berlin Physical Society. On December 19, 1900, Planck gave a lecture to the same society to explain the significance of h, the constant in his formula; the "quantum of action" as he called it. The value for h was determined by fitting the theoretical curve to the experimentally produced curves. It turned out to be $h = 6.63 \times 10^{-27}$ erg-sec. This unusual constant needed some explanation. Planck believed that a black body emitted radiation at discrete energy levels, determined by $E = nh\nu$. He believed, as everyone did at that time, that energy was continuous, but the emission process somehow constrained the energy to specific levels; it quantized the energy.

This was a strange situation which conflicted with the classical conception of continuous energy distributions. In normal, large-scale situations, such as pendulum motion, for example, the quantum of action did not seem to have an effect. The energy of such macroscopic mechanical systems was much too large, in comparison to h, to make possible any observation of whether energy in this instance was quantized. Only in systems where the frequency was very large or the energy was so small that it was of the order of $h\nu$, did Planck's postulate seem to take effect. Black body radiation, electron phenomena and light phenomena all fell into the range where the quantum of action must be taken into account.

Albert Einstein (1879-1955) found another instance of the applicability of Planck's constant in 1905. This was a remarkably productive year for Einstein. He published three papers of major significance in three different areas of physics. He solved the problem of Brownian movement and provided the formula for it, he laid the foundations for the special theory of relativity in a paper on electromagnetic theory, and he developed the law for the photoelectric effect. Experiments conducted by Lenard in Germany had shown that electrons could be ejected from the surface of metals by shining light on the surface. Curiously, the velocity of these photoelectrons was independent of the intensity of the light used, but depended only upon the wavelength of the light. Blue light produced photoelectrons with a greater velocity than red light. If the intensity of the light increased, more photoelectrons were ejected from the surface, but their velocity was dependent only upon the wavelength.

The accepted electromagnetic theory was completely incapable of affording an explanation and description of this phenomenon. Einstein argued that the answer lay in the quantum of action. Not only was the emission of energy quantized, but so was the absorption. In fact, Einstein asserted that energy itself was quantized. Energy was quantized into small packets, as described by $e = nh\nu$. In the photoelectric process therefore, each photoelectron absorbed one complete packet of energy. This packet came in the form of a light photon, with energy $h\nu$, ν being the frequency of the incident light. The energy of the photoelectron was given very simply by the equation $E = h\nu - W$, where W is the work function of the metal. W indicated the amount of energy needed for the photoelectron to escape from the surface of the metal, so if the incident light was monochromatic, all of one frequency or color, all the photoelectrons would have the same energy. Einstein's theory of the photoelectric effect was supported experimentally by Robert Millikan in 1916. Einstein's equation matched Millikan's data. The slope of the straight line on the graph which Millikan drew from his data turned out to be exactly equal to Planck's constant. He had performed an experiment which lent strong support to two purely theoretical conceptions.

After 1905, those who agreed with Einstein could no longer conceive of energy as continuous. It was not only emitted and absorbed in discrete bundles, but it was itself discontinuous and quantized. This shocking line of reasoning had obvious implications for all radiation phenomena and for the spectra produced by atoms in particular. The famous Bohr atom was based upon the ideas of energy quanta and it was formulated specifically to explain atomic spectra.

Niels Bohr (1885-1962) modified the Rutherford atomic model in 1913 in ways which would enable it to account for spectral evidence. Bohr stated four completely a priori hypotheses in order to develop his model: 1) an electron moves in a circular orbit about the nucleus under the influence of Coulomb attraction, and obeying the established laws of mechanics; 2) it was only possible for the electron to move in certain special orbits, not any orbit at all; 3) electrons moving in those special orbits maintained a constant energy and did not radiate as Maxwell's theory stated they should; 4) electromagnetic radiation emitted by an atom was the result of an electron moving discontinuously from one allowed orbit to another. The frequency of this radiation was given by $\nu = (E_1 - E_2)/h$, where E_1 was the initial orbit of the electron and E_2 was the new orbit. The h, of course, is Planck's constant.

Bohr's four postulates provided the basis for an atomic model with many advantages; it related directly to Einstein's conception

of the quantization of energy, it incorporated Planck's constant
as a natural part of the model, and it served to account, in part,
for the production of the spectra produced by the hydrogen atom.
But despite its advantages, the Bohr atom had grave deficiencies.
It accounted for the hydrogen atom and singly ionized helium atoms
reasonably well, but it was unsuccessful for more complex elements. It also only provided information on the frequency of
radiation produced, but failed to include the two other important
aspects of radiation, intensity and polarization.

The Bohr atom underwent some very sophisticated tinkering by
many fine physicists in an attempt to make it fit experimental
observations. The decade between 1913 and 1920 was the last
period of serious model building in physics. This was the high
point of the scientific tradition of the nineteenth century, based
on common sense and confidence in what should happen in terms of a
visualizable and physically plausible model. Physics was still
thought to be conceivable in terms of models and in terms of physical concepts derived from common sense experience. In the early
1920's, Bohr himself began to despair that his model would ever
explain more than the simplest radiation phenomena in the most
superficial way. It was at this point that Werner Heisenberg,
Louis de Broglie and Erwin Schrödinger devised a totally new approach to physics which they believed effectively eliminated the
role of common sense and common experience from physics.

In 1925 Heisenberg completely abandoned the idea of ever
devising an atomic model. He developed a theory called matrix
mechanics, based only upon observable properties of radiation:
intensity of spectral lines, frequency of those lines, and polarization. The matrices were constructed on the basis of numbers
derived by experiment. By use of matrix algebra, the matrices
could be manipulated and new values could be determined for frequency, intensity and polarization. It so happened that the numbers which popped out of the matrix algebra fit the observed data
very well.

Heisenberg did his work at the Copenhagen Institute for
Theoretical Physics, founded by Bohr in 1920. Copenhagen soon
became the center for studies in quantum theory, with Bohr,
Heisenberg and the mathematician-physicist Paul Dirac the major
figures. Heisenberg found that his matrices would yield predic-
tions to a good degree of accuracy. The degree, or limit, of
accuracy seemed to be proportional to Planck's constant. The
matrices had no model--just the observed values for radiation.

Meanwhile, Louis de Broglie made another rather startling
assertion: in 1924, De Broglie suggested that electrons, and in
fact matter in general, could have wave-like properties and behave
as waves. De Broglie reasoned that the energy carried by an electron could be related to a frequency associated with the electron.
On the simplest level,

$$E = h\nu \qquad E = \tfrac{1}{2}mv^2$$
$$h\nu = \tfrac{1}{2}mv^2$$
$$\nu = mv^2/2h$$

Each electron, or each particle, with a given energy, should also
have a very specific frequency associated with it.

In 1926, Schrödinger applied De Broglie's theory of electron waves to the hydrogen atom, and obtained an equation which was the basis for wave mechanics. Wave mechanics was able to give a very satisfactory explanation to Bohr's allowed orbits for electrons in the Bohr atom. Each orbit must contain an integral number of electron wavelengths, just as standing waves in violin strings. But even more striking, Schrödinger was able to prove that his wave mechanics was equivalent to Heisenberg's quantum mechanics, despite the different approaches of the two theories.

The agreement of the two theories emphasized a very peculiar situation which hardly needed emphasis. There seemed to be a duality associated with light and matter. Light appeared at times to behave as a wave and at others as a particle. Other work indicated that not only light, but electrons and other particles sometimes behaved like waves. Einstein's paper on the photoelectric effect had placed great emphasis upon photons of light as particle-like, carrying quanta of energy. His paper on Brownian motion had provided support to the people who argued for the particulate nature of matter in the form of atoms and molecules. There was good evidence to believe in quanta of light, photons, quanta of electricity, electrons, and quanta of matter, atoms. But all this emphasis upon particles and quanta was completely ineffectual in explaining the well established phenomena of light diffraction and the new experiments on electron scattering and diffraction. Experiments by Arthur Compton on X-ray diffraction from crystals and by Clinton Davisson on the diffraction of electrons by crystals in 1927, confirmed that X-rays and electrons, as well as photons, exhibited very definite wave-like properties.

By the 1920's, there was evidence to draw the conclusions that photons, X-rays and electrons could be best considered as waves in some circumstances, particles in others; and there were some instances where it made little difference what you considered them to be. This was not a question of one or the other, particle or wave, as it was with Newtonian optics vs. the wave theory at the beginning of the ninetèenth century. Now light and electrons behaved as both, under different conditions of observation.

An answer to this duality was proposed by Max Born. Born suggested that electron waves were not waves in the ordinary, physical, common sense meaning, but were representations of the probability of the electron's presence. The waves, under Born's interpretation, represented not the electron itself, but the probability of finding the electron there, if appropriate efforts were made to look for the electron. Born's "probability waves" suited Schrödinger's wave mechanics very well. They also served to dispel the mystery of why both the wave mechanical and the quantum mechanical formalisms should yield the same results.

The application of the reliance on probability led to a fundamental change in orientation in physical science. For example, the diffraction pattern produced by electrons in the two hole diffraction experiment could be treated in such a way that the pattern was a probability distribution for finding an electron at a point on the viewing screen. If huge numbers of electrons were considered, as they must be in most experimental situations, the results were very accurate. The total results were predictable, i.e., the diffraction pattern not the path of the individual electron. This statistical treatment of the situation eliminated the need for a concern about the motion of individuals. The theory predicted the net results of the distribution pattern of electrons behind the two holes. It told nothing of the motion of the individual electron, nor could it be made to say anything about it.

This was one of the fundamental differences between quantum physics and "classical physics." Nineteenth century statistical laws, such as Boltzmann's statistical mechanics, dealt with large groups of individual events. For classical physics, the aim was to describe the objects as they existed in space and the laws governing their changes with respect to time. The classical statistical treatment dealt with huge groups of individual events. They rested upon individual events which were too numerous to be treated separately.

Quantum physics did away with a concern for individual events and the laws governing those individual events. Statistical laws were given immediately because the individual events of quantum physics were not describable. The events of the first decades of the twentieth century seemed to necessitate this abandonment of the possibility of knowing and describing the individual event. The major reasons were the ones we have described: 1) the wave-particle duality; 2) the emission of spectral lines and the impossibility of knowing which atoms of the large groups of atoms in the sample emitted which spectral line; 3) the emission of radioactive radiation which must be described in terms of the total expected radiation because it was impossible to tell which atom would suddenly emit radiation and undergo natural transformation. These three areas and others were completely outside the realm of classical physics and reinforced the apparent need to abandon individual events in favor of laws for representative samples. As Einstein and Leopold Infeld put it in their book *The Evolution of Physics*, "Quantum physics deals only with aggregations, and its laws are for crowds and not for individuals. . . . We have had to forsake the description of individual cases as objective happenings in space and space; we have had to introduce laws of a statistical nature. These are the chief characteristics of modern quantum physics."

Einstein and Planck, and to a lesser extent and more recently, Schrödinger and De Broglie, were concerned with this reliance upon statistical laws. They believed that nature represented a separate, independent reality in which causal laws for individual events held in detail. For these men, the reliance upon the probabilistic foundations of quantum theory was but a temporary, although extremely effective, phase in the history of science.

Heisenberg, Bohr, Dirac and most quantum physicists disagreed with the hopes for an eventual return to a deterministic world view held by Einstein and Planck. The usual interpretation or "Copenhagen Interpretation" of quantum theory flatly denied the possibility of ever knowing individual events and therefore of ever establishing a determined world picture. They use the Principle of Indeterminacy or Uncertainty as one of the bases for this interpretation. The Uncertainty Principle has many applications and interpretations, but to take one example of an electron, we can never know both the position and the momentum of an electron at the same time, with any amount of precision we desire. This constraint usually takes the form of $pq = h/2\pi$ where p represents the momentum of the electron and q represents the position. This is more than a simple constraint on observation. It is interpreted as a constraint upon our knowledge and is extended to characterize the physical world.

Every attempt we make to get within p of the momentum insures that we will not get within q of the position. On the level of observation, if we fix the exact position of an electron, say by shining photons upon it, we will have little knowledge of the momentum. The act of observation has changed the conditions in an indeterminable way. We cannot know what happened to the electron we observed, nor where it went. If we attempt to set up an experiment to follow it, we have no means of identifying the electron as the one we observed before.

The observer changed the conditions by his act of observation. In this sense, the observer created the reality he saw. The moment of observation of the electron represented a specific instance. But there could be no follow-up to assign connected movements to the electron because the observation changed the situation in an unknowable way. There could be no way to identify individual electrons, nor could there be a way of assessing the amount of disturbance imparted by an observation. This became a very serious change in orientation for physical science. The usual interpretation of quantum theory limited activity to the performance of experiments and the collection of data for specific instances. The world between each separate instance of observation was unknown, and unknowable.

The Copenhagen Interpretation forced a rigidly positivistic attitude upon modern physics. The data collected by observation became the foundation of quantum physics. This represented a very different attitude toward science than that maintained by Einstein, Planck and more recently other physicists like the American, David Bohm. Einstein and Infeld concluded their treatment of quantum mechanics in *The Evolution of Physics* with the following: "With the help of physical theories we try to find our way through the maze of observed facts, to order and understand the world of our sense impressions. We want the observed facts to follow logically from our concept of reality. Without the belief that it is possible to grasp the reality with our theoretical constructions, without the belief in the inner harmony of our world, there could be no science."

The adherents of the Copenhagen interpretation label this search for reality and inner harmony of the world as metaphysics and quite out of place in modern physics. It has no place at all in the quantum theoretical formalism. We will perhaps be in a position to see which orientation toward science is the most fruitful. There have been abundant recent indications that the quantum formalism is incomplete.

C. Relativity Theory

The formulation of the special and general theories of relativity involved work in areas rather removed from atomic theory or quantum theory. The impact of relativity was at least as profound as the other two. The acceptance of relativity led to fundamental changes in the conceptions of space and time, in the concept of mass and energy and in the laws of the conservation of mass and the conservation of energy themselves. Einstein published accounts of his special theory of relativity in 1905 and of his general theory in 1916.

The special theory of relativity began with two assumptions: 1) the velocity of light in vacuo is the same in all coordinate systems moving uniformly, relative to each other; and 2) all the laws of nature are the same in all coordinate systems moving uniformly, relative to each other. The first assumption specified that light had a constant velocity when moving in empty space, quite independent of the motions of the source of the light or of the receiver of the light. This meant that the standard transformation of coordinate systems with respect to one another in terms of the addition or subtraction of uniform velocities could not be applied to light. The second assumption made it impossible to distinguish an absolute uniform motion and therefore an absolute frame of reference. It also raised the question of simultaneity. Two events which were observed to occur simultaneously in one coordinate system may not appear simultaneous with respect to another coordinate system moving uniformly with respect to the first.

Questions of time and measurement took on new importance in the context of special relativity that could not even have been imagined under the old notions of absolute space and time. "We may well imagine," Einstein wrote, "that not only does the moving clock change its rhythm, but also that a moving stick changes its length, so long as the laws of the change are the same for all inertial coordinate systems." Einstein went on to state: "If the velocity of light is the same in all coordinate systems, then moving rods must change their length, moving clocks must change their rhythm, and the laws governing these changes are rigorously determined." Classical physics, and common sense, assumed that the length of meter sticks and the rhythm of clocks did not change. But these were just assumptions. Part of Einstein's great insight consisted in exposing these as assumptions which had been maintained for no sufficient reason. This was another blow to "common sense" notions in the physical sciences. Einstein pointed out that there was no reason to believe that Nature behaved as we expected or wanted her to.

Special theory made use of a set of mathematical transformations called the Lorentz Transformations. Several conclusions were made apparent by these transformations. The "old" classical mechanics was only valid for small velocities and formed the limiting case for the new relativistic mechanics. At great velocities, the new mechanics made clear that resistance to change depended both upon the mass of the body and upon its velocity. As the velocity of a body approached the speed of light, it became increasingly difficult to increase the velocity of that body.

Viewed in another way, energy derived from motion behaves like matter. Energy resisted change of motion. In the special theory, there was no difference between mass and energy. Energy had mass and mass had energy. A continuation of this line of reasoning led to the most widely known equation in the twentieth century: $E = mc^2$. Energy can be related directly to mass, using the constant of the speed of light. In this age of nuclear weapons, the implications of this relationship are obvious to us. These implications were gradually appreciated after 1905 and received the undivided attention of the Manhattan Project during the second World War.

The realization of the relationship between mass and energy made some changes necessary in the understanding of the conservation laws. The laws of the conservation of mass and the conservation of energy were combined into the conservation of mass-energy. Mass could disappear, but always with the exact production of an equivalent amount of energy.

The general theory of relativity applied to all coordinate systems moving arbitrarily with respect to one another. This theory was based on the equivalence between gravitational and inertial mass, and on the deeper understanding of gravitational fields. Einstein worked from 1905 to 1915 in his attempt to devise the general theory. The concept of equivalency was included in the broader statement: "A gravitational field of force at any point of space is in every way equivalent to an artificial field of force resulting from acceleration, so that no experiment can possibly distinguish between them."

The gravitational field took on great significance in the general theory. It had an effect on light and upon the basic geometry of the universe. Euclidian geometry was no longer suitable for a world without absolute space and time and where the shortest distance between two points was not a straight line but the path that light would follow. The broad implications of the general theory might best be hinted at by a humorous remark that Einstein made to a group of reporters in 1919: "If you will not take the answer too seriously and consider it only as a kind of a joke, then I can explain it as follows. It was formerly believed that if all material things disappeared out of the universe, time and space would be left. According to relativity theory, however, time and space disappear together with the things."

Einstein attempted to include all areas of physics into a general physical theory. He spent the rest of his life searching for what was called a unified field theory. He favored a field concept in physics, rather than one which dealt with matter in autonomous bits. Einstein hoped that the concept of field could be extended so that the difference between matter and the field could be eliminated. "We could regard matter as regions in space where the field is extremely strong," he wrote. "In this way a new philosophical background could be created. Its final aim would be the explanation of all events in nature by structure laws valid always and everywhere." In this new physics, field would be the only reality.

The field concept could not be applied to matter, "to regions in which the energy is enormously concentrated." Einstein did not succeed in establishing his theory and physics continued to concern itself with both matter and fields. The theory of relativity did place great emphasis upon the field concept of physics.

Einstein's search was strongly motivated by his belief in the harmony of the world. He believed that scientific theories were the free creations of the human mind rather than inductions from observation and experience. Man progressed from mountain top to mountain top in the search for knowledge of the world; a world in which God revealed himself by harmony. Einstein responded to a presumptuous telegram in 1919 in the following way: "Do you believe in God stop prepaid reply 50 words." "I believe in Spinoza's God who reveals himself in the harmony of all being, not in a God who concerns himself with the fate and actions of men."

Einstein represented a strong contrast in his approach to physical science to that taken by those who adhered to positivism. Einstein's science involved what others called metaphysics as an integral part. His science was wildly speculative and creative, but always subject at last to the test of experiment and observation. He remained firm in his belief in the reality of the physical world and was confident that the statistical laws of quantum theory did not represent the final answers. The search for an understanding of nature was most important, even if that understanding might never be reached.

A BIBLIOGRAPHICAL GUIDE

What follows is, in no sense, a bibliography of the history
of science. Such a bibliography would add a large number of pages
to an already extensive work. What we have tried to do in the
pages that follow is to provide starting points for the reader
who wishes to pursue a subject further. Where possible we have
indicated works that contain extensive bibliographies and we refrained from copying their titles here. Only when we have felt
that works cited elsewhere deserve special mention, either for
their goodness or badness, have we singled them out. What follows, then, is a guide, not a complete map. But it is our hope
that with this guide, the reader can ultimately find his way to
wherever he wishes to go.

I. Some General Aids

The literature in the history of science is enormous for it
encompasses all the works published in the course of the development of science as well as all the studies of science and its
history. There are, fortunately, a number of aids which the student of the history of science can consult when in need of assistance in finding particular references.

The late George Sarton was a pioneer in the history of
science whose most lasting contribution to the field will probably be the bibliographical work he did. His *Horus, A Guide to
the History of Science* (Waltham, Mass., 1952) is a handbook of
first instance for anyone embarking on a serious study of the
subject. Therein, Sarton not only lists basic secondary works,
but also resources such as Museums, Archives, Journals, etc., to
which the researcher may wish to have recourse. For those interested in the history of ancient or medieval science, Sarton's
magistral *Introduction to the History of Science*, 3 vols. in 5
(Baltimore, 1927-47) contains a bibliographical treasury of
science in both East and West down to the end of the fourteenth
century. Sarton also founded the journal, ISIS, now the official
journal of the History of Science Society in the United States.
Since 1913, ISIS has published an annual critical bibliography
which collects titles of books and articles related to the history of science viewed in the widest possible perspective. This
bibliography is now available in a three-volume edition, edited
by M. Whitrow (London, 1971).

Two other useful, general bibliographical guides are F. Russo,
Histoire des sciences et des techniques. Bibliographie (Paris,
1954) and Henry Guerlac, *Science in Western Civilization: A Syl-
labus* (New York, 1952).

Help in locating original papers may be obtained from two
standard reference works. J. C. Poggendorff was, for many years,
the editor of the *Annalen der Physik*. His *Biographisch-litera-
risches Handwörterbuch zur Geschichte der exacted Wissenschaften*,
now ten volumes, lists all "exact" scientists from antiquity to
1931 with a bibliography for each. The biological sciences are
not included. Ernst Gurlt, Agathon Wernich and August Hirsch,

Biographisches Lexikon der hervorragenden Aerzte aller Zeiten und Volker (6 vols., Vienna, 1884-8) revised 5 vol. edition with supplement (Berlin, 1929-35) fills in the gaps left by Poggendorff. Many men of science in the past, particularly those who made contributions to biology, were physicians and their works are to be found here. The *Dictionary of Scientific Biography*, edited by Charles Gillispie, is an invaluable reference work.

In sheer volume of papers produced, the 19th century ranks as a major period in the history of science. To cope with the difficulties produced by the flood of publications, the Royal Society of London sponsored the publication of a *Catalogue of Scientific Papers* which appeared in 19 vols. with a 4 volume subject index (Cambridge, 1867-1925). All scientific areas are covered. The *International Catalogue of Scientific Literature* which was intended to extend the Royal Society's catalogue into the 20th century was a victim of World War I. Some 254 volumes were produced, covering the scientific literature from 1901 to 1913 before the venture was abandoned. There is no general bibliography for the 20th century.

There are a number of general histories of science that the reader may wish to consult to provide a different perspective from that found here. W. C. Dampier Whetham's *A History of Science and its Relations with Philosophy and Religion* (Cambridge, 1929) is old but still valuable for some subjects. E. J. Dijkterhuis, *The Mechanization of the World Picture* (Oxford, 1961) presents a reliable but unexciting account of the development of the physical sciences to the Scientific Revolution. W. P. D. Wightman, *The Growth of Scientific Ideas* (Edinburgh, 1900) and S. F. Mason, *Main Currents of Scientific Thought* (New York, 1953) are both lively and comprehensive in their coverage. Stephen Toulmin and June Goodfield have produced three volumes that cover basic concepts in science. *The Architecture of Matter, The Discovery of Time*, and *The Fabric of the Heavens* are all available in paperback and contain bibliographies.

For special histories, the reader should consult J. L. Dreyer, *A History of Astronomy from Thales to Kepler*, available in paperback and A. Pannekoek, *A History of Astronomy* (New York, 1961). J. R. Partington's multi-volume *A History of Chemistry* (London, 1964-1972) cannot be read as a narrative but contains invaluable bibliographical information. There is no good history of biology. Readers will have to make do with Charles Singer, *A History of Biology* in paperback and Eric Nordenskiold, *The History of Biology* (New York, 1928). Some appreciation for the history of mathematics may be gleaned from D. E. Smith, *History of Mathematics*, 2 vols. in paperback. M. Kline's ambitious *Mathematical Thought from Ancient to Modern Times* (Oxford, 1973) deals with the whole of mathematics in an original and exciting way. Carl Boyer's *The Concepts of the Calculus* (New York, 1949) is a sober and thorough treatment containing an extensive bibliography.

II. Suggestions for further reading: Ancient Science

For the exact sciences in antiquity, there are two standard works. Otto Neugebauer's *The Exact Sciences in Antiquity* (2nd

ed., Providence, R.I., 1957) has already been sampled in the
Readings. B. L. van der Waerden, *Science Awakening* (Groningen,
1954) also treats of the birth of the mathematical sciences and
is written by one of the foremost modern mathematicians. A more
general view is that offered by M. Clagett, *Greek Science in
Antiquity* (New York, 1956) which provides excellent summaries and
short discussions of the major scientific achievements of the
Greeks. Benjamin Farrington's *Greek Science* in paperback looks
at ancient science from the standpoint of a Marxist. It should
be read with some caution but it is both interesting and stimulating. S. Sambursky, *The Physical World of the Greeks* (London,
1956) presents an interesting interpretation of Greek science as
influenced by the Stoic philosophy. The question of the relations
between science and philosophy is treated in a whole host of volumes. The standard source for the pre-Socratics is G. S. Kirk
and J. E. Raven, *The Presocratic Philosophers, A Critical History
with a Selection of Texts* (Cambridge, 1957). The best treatment
of the whole of Greek philosophy, including science up to the time
of Plato, is W. K. C. Guthrie, *A History of Greek Philosophy*, 5
vols. (Cambridge, 1962-78). The work is expected to be completed
in six volumes and to carry the story through the classical period.
R. G. Collingwood, *The Idea of Nature* (Oxford, 1945) is a philosophical history which is particularly good for Greek cosmology
(Part I).

The history of Greek mathematics is covered by T. L. Heath,
Greek Mathematics, 2 vols. (Oxford, 1921). The most recent treatment of Greek astronomy is D. R. Dicks, *Early Greek Astronomy to
Aristotle* (Ithaca, N.Y., 1970). Another volume is promised to
complete the story. Until it appears, the reader should still
consult T. L. Heath, *Aristarchus of Samos* (Oxford, 1913).

Ancient medicine is well treated in a number of works.
Henry O. Sigerist completed only two volumes of his projected
multi-volume *History of Medicine* before his death, but these
carry the story through antiquity (New York, 1951-61). J. H.
Breasted, as we have seen in the Readings, introduced and edited
The Edwin Smith Papyrus (Chicago, 1930). The Hippocratic writings
have been translated in the Loeb Classical Library by W. H. S.
Jones and E. T. Washington, *Hippocrates*, 4 vols. (London and New
York, 1923-31). The reader should be warned that there is a considerable area of doubt over which treatises are to be considered
genuine, but the translations here mentioned certainly can be
recommended as part of the medical culture of antiquity, if not
necessarily Hippocratic. William Heidel's *Hippocratic Medicine*
(New York, 1941) is still worth consulting. The writings of
Ludwig Edelstein are probably the best guides to ancient medicine.
See his *Ancient Medicine* (Baltimore, 1967) as well as *The Hippocratic Oath* (Baltimore, 1943).

Science in Rome has been dealt with exhaustively by William
Stahl in his *Roman Science* (Madison, Wisconsin, 1962). There
does not seem to be much more to say on the subject.

III. Suggestions for further reading:
      The Transmission of Ancient Science

There is almost nothing, in book form, devoted to science in the Byzantine Empire. Some inkling of what went on in the East after the collapse of Rome may be gleaned from J. M. Hussey, *Church and Learning in the Byzantine Empire, 867-1185* (Oxford and London, 1937) and from S. Runciman, *Byzantine Civilization* (London and New York, 1933).

Science in Islam has recently been treated by Nasr whose book has been used extensively in the section on Islamic science. Readers should also consult D. E. Smith and L. C. Karpinski, *The Hindu-Arabic Numerals* (Boston, 1911), E. G. Browne, *Arabian Medicine* (Cambridge, 1921), Donald Campbell, *Arabian Medicine and its Influence on the Middle Ages*, 2 vols. (London, 1926).

The preservation of the remnants of classical science is treated both by Stahl and by M. L. W. Laistner in *Thought and Letters in Western Europe, A.D. 500 to 900* (rev. ed., London, 1957). This work is a rather dry catalogue of names and dates and should be supplemented by the collection of Laistner's essays made by Chester G. Starr entitled *The Intellectual Heritage of the Early Middle Ages* (Ithaca, N.Y., 1957). Early Christian education is discussed well in H. I. Marrou, *A History of Education in Antiquity* (New York, 1956), chapters 9-11.

IV. Suggestions for further reading: Medieval Science

Alistair Crombie's *From Augustine to Galileo*, published in paperback as *Medieval and Early Modern Science*, 2 vols., is the best general treatment of science in general during the Middle Ages. It includes an excellent bibliographical essay at the end of each volume. The same author's *Robert Grosseteste and the Origins of Experimental Science, 1100-1700* (Oxford, 1953) provides a valuable discussion on scientific method in the Middle Ages. Edward Grant, *Physical Science in the Middle Ages* (New York, 1971) provides a competent summary based upon the latest scholarship. It, too, concludes with a bibliographical essay that surveys the literature comprehensively.

From among the books listed in the above bibliographies, we wish to call attention to only a few. Charles Homer Haskins, *The Rise of Universities* (New York, 1923) and *The Renaissance of the Twelfth Century* (Cambridge, Mass., 1927), both now available in paperback, are classics. Lynn White Jr., in his *Medieval Technology and Scoial Change* (Oxford, 1962), has been the most important spokesman for the thesis that the Middle Ages was a period of vital technological innovation and consequent expansion of the practical control of nature. Marshall Clagett has almost single-handed opened up the world of the medieval texts on mechanics to those who do not read medieval Latin. His *The Science of Mechanics in the Middle Ages* (Madison, Wis., 1959) offers both texts and commentaries. The concluding chapters provide the sanest evaluation yet of the place of medieval mechanics within the overall growth of science. *Archimedes in the Middle Ages, The Arabo-Latin Tradition* (Madison, Wis., 1964) documents the existence of a physico-mathematical tradition in the Middle Ages that was to become of primary importance in the Scientific Revolution. Lynn Thorndike's *A History of Magic and Experimental Science*, 8 vols. (New York, 1923-58) is a treasury of bizarre and arcane texts held together by Thorndike's perceptive but somewhat idiosyncratic idea that beneath the skin of most medieval scientists there lurked a magician eager and ready to play Faust. A decade ago, such an interpretation appeared to border on the foolish but the work of D. Walker, *Spiritual and Demonic Magic from Ficino to Campanella* (London, 1958) and of Frances Yates, particularly her *Giordano Bruno and the Hermetic Tradition* (London, 1964) have given new life to Thorndike's approach. Although he is not always to be taken seriously, it would be folly to neglect or ignore him. Finally, Maris Boas' *The Scientific Renaissance, 1450-1630* (London, 1962) traces the development of science during the period of the Renaissance with great skill and clarity. It is based upon the latest scholarship and is eminently readable. Its bibliography nicely supplements those to be found in Crombie and Grant.

V. Suggestions for further reading: The Scientific Revolution

The Scientific Revolution is finally receiving the kind of scholarly attention its importance in the history of Western Civilization warrants. The scholar largely responsible for this was the late Alexandre Koyré whose epoch-making work on Galileo, *Études galiléennes* (Paris, 1939) has never been translated into English. *From the Closed World to the Infinite Universe* (Baltimore, 1957) provides a good idea of Koyré's ideas on the nature and course of the Scientific Revolution. The collection of his essays, *Metaphysics and Measurement* (Cambridge, Mass., 1968), nicely complements *From the Closed World* by permitting Koyré to examine some questions in truly scholarly depth as opposed to the necessarily more popular mode of exposition in his general book. We would offer as a general rule that it is always worth reading anything that Koyré wrote for his was a truly original mind.

Herbert Butterfield's *The Origins of Modern Science* (London, 1950) was also responsible for stimulating scholarly interest in the Scientific Revolution. Butterfield was not trained as an historian of science but as an historian and it was as an historian that he recognized the world-shaking impact of the Scientific Revolution. His little book appeared when most historians of science were preoccupied with specialized monographs and it revealed to them just how important their own discipline was. It, together with Koyré's work, has sparked a number of excellent surveys. The most ambitious of these was Charles Gillispie's *The Edge of Objectivity* (Princeton, 1960), now available in paperback. Gillispie's book is a brilliant history of science since the Scientific Revolution. His interpretation of the nature and course of the evolution of science is a highly personal one with which we do not agree but he illuminates so many problems and raises so many interesting questions in such an original way that we can recommend the book enthusiastically. The reader will easily discover where we disagree with his point of view by simply

comparing our account with his. Gillispie's book concludes with
a selective bibliography which should be consulted. A. Rupert
Hall literally picked up the torch passed him by Butterfield and
offered a masterly survey of the Scientific Revolution in a work
that has now earned its place as the standard work on the subject.
The Scientific Revolution, 1500-1800 (London, 1954) is both solid
and trustworthy. His later *From Galileo to Newton, 1630-1720*
(London, 1963) covers some of the same ground, but with a bit
more spirit and liveliness. His bibliography and notes can also
serve as reliable guides to the literature. We feel about Hall
much as we do about Koyré, that anything he writes is worth reading and so recommend his articles, as well, to our readers.
Richard S. Westfall is a leading scholar of the works of Newton
whose *Force in Newton's Physics* (London and New York, 1971) with
bibliography is a survey of the introduction of the concept of
force into the physics of the 17th century. He has written *The
Construction of Modern Science: Mechanisms and Mechanics* (New
York, 1971) for a popular audience. It, too, contains a bibliography of some value.

One of the debates in which historians of science have engaged over the last few decades is whether the Scientific Revolution was more highly influenced by the changes in philosophy that
marked the end of the 16th century or by the new practices of
technology, particularly navigation and mining. Two works are
fundamental for this debate. E. A. Burtt, *The Metaphysical Foundations of Modern Physical Science* (rev. ed., London, 1932) argued
the first side persuasively and may be said to have prepared the
way for Koyré's specialized studies on Galileo. E. W. Strong
replied with *Procedures and Metaphysics* (Berkeley, 1936). Most
historians would award the palm to Burtt and his followers, but
the question is by no means settled as the article by Hall in our
Readings indicates.

The Scientific Revolution has been better served by trans-
lators than almost any other period in the history of science.
From Copernicus through Newton, at least parts of the great treatises are available to the reader of English only. Special attention should be called to the editions of Newton's work which are
now coming from the Cambridge University Press. Newton's correspondence, his mathematical papers, and the *Principia* itself have
all recently been or are being edited with the highest standards
of scholarship. No one who contemplates a serious study of Newton's thought can do without these indispensable works. There is
not, unfortunately, a reliable guide for putting together all
these pieces. Frank Manuel has written a psychobiography of
Newton, *A Portrait of Newton* (Cambridge, Mass., 1968) which will
convince only those who are already converted to psychobiography.
The older biography by L. T. More is simply out of date and out
of touch with current scholarship.

VI. Suggestions for further reading: The Enlightenment

There is a vast literature on the Enlightenment but surprisingly little of it deals with science. Most is concentrated on
the *philosophes* who, though enamored of science, made few original

contributions to it. The best study of a *philosophe* which may
serve to paint the general intellectual background, as well as
introduce the reader to the relations between science and the
philosophes is Arthur Wilson's monumental biography, *Diderot* (New
York, 1972). Basil Willey's *The Eighteenth Century Background*
(New York, 1941) also provides some keen insights into the nature
of Enlightenment thought. Carl Boyer's *Concepts of the Calculus*
cited earlier deals adequately with the development of the calculus in its first, early vital period. René Dugas, *A History of
Mechanics* (New York, 1955) treats the 18th century in a fairly
complicated way. It is not for the beginner.
    The only modern treatment of the mathematical sciences in
the Enlightenment is the excellent work on Jean le Rond D'Alembert
by Thomas Hankins, *Jean D'Alembert: Science and the Enlightenment*
(Oxford, 1970). The tradition of experimental science that traces
itself back to Newton is dealt with in exhaustive and masterly
fashion by I. Bernard Cohen's *Franklin and Newton* (Philadelphia,
1956). The bibliography is superb. Paul F. Mottelay's *Bibliographical History of Electricity and Magnetism* (London, 1922) is
particularly rich for the 18th and early 19th centuries.
    The work of Henry Guerlac is fundamental for the history of
chemistry in the 18th century. His *Lavoisier: The Crucial Year*
(Ithaca, 1961) is a work distilled from a lifetime of careful scholarship on the chemical revolution. His many articles, scattered
throughout a number of scholarly publications, have revolutionized
the study of 18th century chemistry. These are now available in
book form: Henry Guerlac, *Essays and Papers in the History of
Modern Science* (Baltimore, 1977). Two works in the chemical
tradition that owe a great deal to Guerlac's pioneering efforts
are Robert Schofield's *Mechanism and Materialism* (Princeton, 1970)
and Arnold Thackray's *Atoms and Powers* (Cambridge, Mass., 1970).
    The literature in English on 18th century biology is skimpy.
A number of biographies or works on Carl Linné have appeared in
recent years, but none can be regarded as the definitive study.
There is some value to be found in Wilfred Blunt, *The Compleat
Naturalist; a Life of Linnaeus* (New York, 1971) and Alice Dickin-
son, *Carl Linnaeus; Pioneer of Modern Botany* (New York, 1967).
C. E. Raven, *John Ray, Naturalist, His Life and Works* (Cambridge,
1942) deals adequately with one of Linnaeus' predecessors. Arthur
O. Lovejoy, *The Great Chain of Being* (Cambridge, Mass., 1936)
and now in paperback provides a fascinating and influential
account of one of the basic biological concepts of the 18th century. For the rest, the reader will have to turn to such French
authors as Jacques Roger whose massive and authoritative *Les
sciences de la vie dans la pensée du xviiième siècle* (Paris, 1963)
treats almost every biological problem of interest in Enlightenment France. There is also a massive and detailed bibliography.

VII. Suggestions for further reading: The Nineteenth Century

    The best single work on the history of science (and of
thought, in general) in the 19th century remains the four volumes
composed by J. T. Merz. His *History of European Thought in the
Nineteenth Century* (4th unaltered edition, Edinburgh and London,

1923-1950) is a remarkable work. Drawing only upon published
sources, Merz produced a brilliant and coherent account of the
development of all the sciences in this great century of scientific achievement. The first two volumes deal with the "hard"
sciences and are a literal treasure-trove of bibliographical information. Merz's footnotes are required reading for anyone who
wishes to know both the primary and secondary sources of science
in the 19th century. Merz's work was written from a philosophical point of view. A work with a similar perspective is that by
M. Capek, *The Philosophical Impact of Contemporary Physics*
(Princeton, 1961). Capek also has read widely and his bibliography should be consulted. The literature on what we have called
Newtonian orthodoxy is not very large. The Schofield and Thackray
volumes referred to under the Enlightenment have many clear references to the definition of that orthodoxy. A symposium on the
work and impact of John Dalton has been edited by D. S. L. Cardwell, *John Dalton and the Progress of Science* (Manchester and New
York, 1968). The best biography of Dalton is that by Frank
Greenaway, *John Dalton and the Atom* (Ithaca, N.Y., 1966). Our
brief excursion into thermodynamics should be supplemented by
D. S. Cardwell, *From Watt to Clausius* (Ithaca, N.Y., 1971) which
not only lays bare the evolution of thermodynamic concepts, but
also clearly reveals their relations with an element that was to
assume ever greater importance as the 19th century progressed--
heavy industry. There is no respectable major modern work on the
Principle of the Conservation of Energy and the curious reader
must address him or herself to the original papers. These papers
are cited in the footnotes to the article that we have used by
T. S. Kuhn. These can be found in Marshall Clagett, ed., *Critical Problems in the History of Science* (Madison, Wis., 1959).
Close to the problem of the Conservation of Energy is Wilson
L. Scott, *The Conflict between Atomism and Conservation Theory
1644-1860* (London and New York, 1970). The origins of field
theory have been the subject of two books by L. Pearce Williams.
His *Michael Faraday, A Biography* (London and New York, 1965) has
been described as the definitive biography of this fundamentally
important interpreter of nature. The later *Origins of Field
Theory* (New York, 1967) was written for a popular audience and
tends to slide over some of the more difficult aspects of the
evolution of the concept of the electric and magnetic field.
Mary Hesse's *Forces and Fields* (London, 1961) is a brilliant
account of the ideas of force and field in the history of physics
but it is not for the mathematical novice. Similarly, Max Jammer
has dealt with the *Concepts of Force* (Cambridge, Mass., 1957) by
including some of its mathematical manifestations. We ought to
mention here his other works as well for they are all well worth
reading: *Concepts of Space* (Cambridge, Mass., 1954), *Concepts of
Mass* (Cambridge, Mass., 1961). There is one work that the reader
should be warned about for it has a high reputation, especially
among scientists, and it does not warrant it. This is E. T.
Whittaker's *History of the Theories of Aether and Electricity*, 2
vols. (London, 1951-53). Whittaker was a fine scientist and the
work bristles with proper scientific apparatus, but it is very
poor history. Its historical dimension is both false and naive

and the arguments that Whittaker develops, as well as his conclusions, are generally historically suspect. It should bear a large "Use with Caution" sign on the cover.

Stephen Brush of the University of Maryland has made the history of the kinetic theory his own by the publication of a number of volumes containing copies or translations of the original papers and unusually astute observations by Brush. The three volumes on Kinetic Theory are in paperback, published by the Pergamon Press of Oxford. There is no acceptable modern treatment of Clausius or of Maxwell in book form, although there is some growth in the monographic literature, particularly that concerning Maxwell.

The history of chemistry has received more attention than has that of physics. The fourth volume of J. R. Partington's work, mentioned earlier, should again be cited here for it offers the best bibliographical survey of chemistry in the 19th century available. Both primary and secondary sources are given lavishly and anyone interested in pursuing the history of modern chemistry should turn to the work for a firm bibliographical foundation. Aaron Ihde's *The Development of Modern Chemistry* (New York, 1964) is not so rich bibliographically, but it offers a more coherent account of the evolution of chemistry than does Partington. Trevore Levere's work on chemical affinity, *Affinity and Matter* (Oxford, 1971) provides many keen insights into this difficult aspect of chemical theory. W. G. Palmer's work on valence, *A History of the Concept of Valency to 1930* (Cambridge, 1965), also treats a fundamental chemical problem well. A more comprehensive treatment is offered by C. A. Russell, *The History of Valency* (Leicester, 1971). There is no history of stereochemistry or of physical chemistry beyond what is to be found in the general histories given above.

The history of biology and particularly the history of evolutionary theories has attracted a large number of writers, not all of whom are or were particularly well-equipped to handle their theme. We are fortunate in having a good bibliographical guide for the 19th century at the end of William Coleman's *Biology in the Nineteenth Century: Problems of Form, Function, and Transformation* (New York, 1971). We shall only single out a few titles for special mention here. The "Darwin problem" is one that requires some assistance if the lay reader is to achieve a balanced judgment. The problem is simple: biologists tend to write about Darwin from a uniquely biological (and historically narrow) viewpoint whereas historians have not always controlled the field of evolutionary biology as they should have. The pictures that each draws of Darwin, therefore, differ rather sharply. The contrast may be seen by comparing Sir Gavin de Beer's *Charles Darwin* (London, 1963) with Gertrude Himmelfarb's *Darwin and the Darwinian Revolution* (London, 1959). De Beer's biology is impeccable but he never succeeds in putting Darwin into a historical context; Himmelfarb is a superb historian but some of her biological ideas are highly suspect. Peter Vorzimmer's study, *Charles Darwin: The Years of Controversy* (Philadelphia, 1970) is important, as is H. Lewis McKinney's work on the co-enunciator of the principle of Natural Selection, Alfred Russell Wallace: *Wallace and Natural Selection* (New Haven and London, 1972).

VIII. Suggestions for further reading: Towards Modern Physics

There exists for quantum theory a massive bibliography com-
piled by T. S. Kuhn, J. Heilbron, P. Forman and L. Allen that is
essential for any serious student of the subject: *Sources for
History of Quantum Physics* (Philadelphia, 1967). The bibliography offered by Adolf Grünbaum in his masterly but difficult
Philosophical Problems of Space and Time (New York, 1963) is
equally valuable for the history of relativity theory. We await
Gerald Holton's work on Einstein impatiently. Readers should be
warned away from one popular history, George Gamow's *Thirty Years
that Shook Physics* (paperback): it is thoroughly untrustworthy as
history, although a charming memoir by one of the *enfants terri-
bles* who arrived on the scene of Quantum Mechanics when the QM
revolution had just been established. It is fitting and proper
to close by recommending that the reader go back to the original
source for one view of relativity theory. Albert Einstein and
Leopold Infeld wrote their *The Evolution of Physics* (New York,
1938) for the intelligent layman and it still remains the best
popular account of relativity available.

HENRY JOHN STEFFENS

L. PEARCE WILLIAMS

Volume III

Index